Contents

KU-672-512

Foreign &
Commonwealth
Office

Britain 1991

An official handbook

R.W. Jordan Esq
20 Rookery View,
Little Thurrock,
GRAYS,
Essex,
RM17 6AS

© Crown copyright 1991
First published 1991

ISBN 0 11 701550 4

HMSO publications are available from:

HMSO Publications Centre
(Mail and telephone orders only)
PO Box 276, London. SW8 5DT.
Telephone orders 071-873 9090
General enquiries 071-873 0011
(queuing system in operation for both numbers)

HMSO Bookshops
49 High Holborn, London. WC1V 6HB 071-873 0011 (counter service only)
258 Broad Street, Birmingham, B1 2HE 021 643 3757

Diagrams

Maps

Photographs

Acknowledgments for use of photographs appear on p 536.

Introduction

Britain 1991 is the forty-second handbook in the series. It is widely known as an established work of reference and is the mainstay of the reference facilities provided by British information services in many countries. It is sold by Her Majesty's Stationery Office throughout the world.

Britain 1991 describes many features in the life of the country, including the workings of the Government and other major institutions. It does not attempt an analytical approach to current events.

Care should be taken when studying British statistics to note whether they refer to England, to England and Wales (considered together for many administrative and other purposes), to Great Britain, which comprises England, Wales and Scotland, or to the United Kingdom (which is the same as Britain, that is, Great Britain and Northern Ireland) as a whole.

The factual and statistical information in *Britain 1991* is compiled with the co-operation of other government departments and agencies, and of many other organisations. Sources of more detailed and more topical information (including statistics) are mentioned in the text and a guide to official sources is given in Appendix 2.

The text, generally, is based on information available up to August/September 1990.

1 Land and People

Introduction

Britain comprises Great Britain (England, Wales and Scotland) and Northern Ireland, and is one of the 12 member states of the European Community. Its full name is the United Kingdom of Great Britain and Northern Ireland.

Physical Features

Britain constitutes the greater part of the British Isles, a geographical term for a group of islands lying off the north-west coast of mainland Europe. The largest of the islands is Great Britain (the mainlands of England, Wales and Scotland). The next largest comprises Northern Ireland and the Irish Republic. Off the southern coast of England is the Isle of Wight and off the extreme south west are the Isles of Scilly; off north Wales is Anglesey. Western Scotland is fringed by the large archipelago known as the Hebrides and to the north east of the Scottish mainland are Orkney and Shetland. All these have administrative ties with the mainland, but the Isle of Man in the Irish Sea and the Channel Islands between Great Britain and France are largely self-governing, and are not part of the United Kingdom.

With an area of some 242,400 sq km (93,600 sq miles), Britain is about the same size as New Zealand or Uganda, and half the size of France. It is just under 1,000 km (some 600 miles) from the south coast to the extreme north of Scotland and just under 500 km (some 300 miles) across in the widest part. The prime meridian of 0° passes through the old observatory at Greenwich in London.

The seas surrounding the British Isles are shallow, usually less than 90 m (300 ft), because the islands lie on the continental shelf. The shallow waters, warmed by the North Atlantic current, are important because they provide breeding grounds for fish.

The climate is generally mild and temperate. The prevailing winds are south-westerly and the weather from day to day is mainly influenced by depressions moving eastwards across the Atlantic. It is subject to frequent changes but to few extremes of temperature. It is rarely above 32°C (90°F) or below −10°C (14°F). Near sea-level in the west the mean annual temperature ranges from 8°C (46°F) in the Hebrides to 11°C (52°F) in the extreme south west of England; latitude for latitude, it is slightly lower in the east. The mean monthly temperature in the extreme north, at Lerwick (Shetland), ranges from 3°C (37°F) during the winter (December, January and February) to 11°C (52°F) during the summer (June, July and August); the corresponding figures for the Isle of Wight, in the extreme south, are 5°C (41°F) and 16°C (61°F). The average annual rainfall is more than 1,600 mm (over 60 inches) in the mountainous areas of the west and north but less than 800 mm (30 inches) over central and eastern parts. Rain is fairly well distributed throughout the year, but, on average, March to June are the driest months and September to January the wettest. The distribution of sunshine shows a general decrease from south to north, a decrease from the coast inland, and a decrease with altitude. During May, June and July (the months of longest daylight) the mean daily duration of sunshine varies from five hours in northern Scotland to eight hours in the Isle of Wight; during the months of shortest daylight (November, December and January) sunshine is at a minimum, with an average of an hour a day in northern Scotland and two hours a day on the south coast of England.

Historical Outline

The word 'Britain' derives from Greek and Latin names probably stemming from a Celtic original. Although in the prehistoric time-scale the Celts were relatively late arrivals in the British Isles (following cultures which had produced such notable monuments as the stone circles of Avebury and Stonehenge), it is only with them that Britain emerges into recorded history, and the term 'Celtic' is often used rather generally to distinguish the early inhabitants of the British Isles from the later Anglo-Saxon invaders.

Following expeditions by Julius Caesar in 55 and 54 BC, Britain was invaded by the Romans in AD 43 under the Emperor Claudius. An ordered civilisation was established under their rule for over 300 years, except in the territory north of Hadrian's Wall (the wall across northern England built on the orders of Hadrian, Roman Emperor from AD 117 to 138) and in some western areas. Christian missionaries arrived not only in Roman Britain but also in Scotland and Ireland.

England and Wales

The final Roman withdrawal in the fifth century, however, followed a period of increasing disorder during which the island began to be raided from northern Europe, mainly by peoples traditionally described as Angles (from Schleswig), Saxons and Jutes. It is from the Angles that the name 'England' derives. In the following two centuries the raids turned into settlement and a number of small kingdoms were established (with the Britons maintaining an independent existence in the areas now known as Wales and Cornwall). Among these kingdoms, more powerful ones emerged, claiming over-lordship over the whole country, first in the north (Northumbria), then in the midlands (Mercia) and finally in the south (Wessex). However, further raids and settlement by the Vikings from Scandinavia occurred, although in the tenth century the Wessex dynasty defeated the invading Danes and established a wide-ranging authority in England. A second wave of Danish invasions, however, led to the establishment of a Danish dynasty in England between 1017 and 1042, when the Wessex line was restored. The period between 1042 and 1066 saw the growing influence of the Normans, inhabitants of a duchy in northern France established by the Vikings and owing only nominal allegiance to the French king.

This culminated in the last successful invasion of England in 1066, following a disputed succession to the English throne. Duke William of Normandy enforced his claims by defeating the English at the Battle of Hastings in 1066. There was considerable settlement by Normans and others from France, French became the language of the nobility for the next three centuries and the legal and, to some extent, social structure was influenced by that prevailing across the Channel. Over the years the English monarchy began to establish its authority over increasingly wide areas of the British Isles.

Wales had remained a Celtic stronghold, although often within the English sphere of influence. Conflict among the various Welsh princes was frequent and unity was achieved only temporarily. However, with the death in battle in 1282 of Prince Llywelyn, Edward I launched a successful campaign to bring Wales under English rule. Wales was placed for the most part under the same laws as England and in 1301 Edward's heir was created Prince of Wales, a title which has subsequently been bestowed upon the eldest son of the Sovereign. Continued strong Welsh national feeling was indicated by the rising led by Owain Glyndŵr at the beginning of the fifteenth century, but a new dimension to the situation was provided by the accession to the English throne in 1485 of Henry VII of the Welsh House of Tudor. The Acts of Union of 1536 and 1542 united England and Wales administratively, politically and legally.

Scotland   Scotland was inhabited by the people known as Picts, but in the sixth century the Scots from Ireland or 'Scotia' settled in the area of Scotland now known as Argyll. Lothian was English in population, and Welsh Britons moved north from the invading English into Strathclyde. A united kingdom emerged in the ninth century while Scotland, like England, was endeavouring to defend itself against the Vikings. The establishment of a powerful monarchy in England, however, was to pose an intermittent but considerable threat to Scottish independence throughout the Middle Ages.

The eventual unification of the crowns reflected the fact that, as a result of the Reformation (see p 5), old national antagonisms had become less important than religious differences. Elizabeth I died in 1603 and, as she had no children, was succeeded by James VI of Scotland, who was the next in line to the throne. He ascended the English throne as James I of England. England, Wales and Scotland were henceforth known as Great Britain. Apart from the union of the monarchies, however, England and Scotland remained separate during the seventeenth century, except for an enforced unification by Oliver Cromwell early in the period of the Commonwealth (1649–60), after he had defeated royalist forces in Scotland. By the beginning of the following century political and economic arguments for a closer union were apparent in both countries. Eventually, in 1707, both sides agreed on the formation of a single parliament for Great Britain, although Scotland retained (and still has) its own system of law and church settlement. The Union was put under strain when Queen Anne died in 1714 and the Protestant George, Elector of Hanover (descended from a daughter of James I), succeeded to the British throne. Two unsuccessful 'Jacobite' rebellions, aiming to restore the Catholic Stuarts, took place in 1715 and 1745, drawing much support from Scotland.

Ireland   In Ireland, out of a patchwork of Celtic and pre-Celtic peoples similar to that in Britain, a number of kingdoms had emerged before the Christian era. Ireland, however, did not escape the incursions of the Vikings, who dominated the country during the tenth century.

In 1169 Henry II of England launched an invasion of Ireland, the overlordship of which he had been granted by the Pope, who was anxious to bring the Irish church into full obedience to Rome. Although a large part of the country came under the control of Anglo-Norman magnates, little direct authority was exercised from England during the Middle Ages.

The Tudor monarchs showed a much greater tendency to intervene in Ireland. Henry VIII's assumption of the title of King of Ireland in 1541 arose from his desire to apply the Reformation settlement and thereafter the religious issue was to produce far-reaching consequences. During the reign of Elizabeth I, a series of campaigns was waged against Irish insurgents. The main focus of the resistance was the northern province of Ulster and, with its collapse in 1607, Ulster became an area of settlement by immigrants from Scotland and England. Settlement by immigrants elsewhere in Ireland was on a lesser scale.

The English civil war of 1642 to 1652 led to further risings in Ireland, which were crushed by Cromwell. The restoration of the monarchy in 1660 was followed by the accession of the Roman Catholic James II to the throne in 1685, and there was more fighting after his deposition three years later in favour of his nephew and son-in-law, the Protestant William of Orange and his wife Mary.

During most of the eighteenth century there was an uneasy peace; towards its end various efforts were made by British governments to achieve stability. In 1782 the Irish Parliament (dating from medieval times) was given legislative independence; the only constitutional tie with Great Britain was the Crown. The Parliament represented, however, only the privileged Anglo-Irish minority, who had obtained possession of most of the agricultural land, and Catholics were excluded from it. Against the background of an abortive rebellion in 1798 and the prospect of intervention by France (with which Great Britain was at war almost continuously between 1793 and 1815) the Irish Parliament was induced to vote for union with what, from 1801, was to be the Parliament of the United Kingdom of Great Britain and Ireland.

The 'Irish question' continued as one of the major problems of British politics during the nineteenth century. In 1886 the Liberal Government introduced a Home Rule Bill which would have given an Irish Parliament authority over most internal matters while reserving to Britain control over external affairs. This led to a split in the Liberal Party and the failure of the Bill. It was not until 1914 that Home Rule was enacted by the Government of Ireland Act. Its implementation was, however, prevented by the threat of armed resistance on the part of the Protestant majority in Ulster and by the outbreak of the first world war.

Although a nationalist uprising in Dublin in 1916 was suppressed, a guerrilla force known as the Irish Republican Army (IRA) began operations against the British administration at the end of the first world war. In the face of the conflicting political aspirations of unionists and nationalists, the Government of Ireland Act 1920 provided for the establishment of two Home Rule parliaments, one in Dublin and the other in Belfast. The Act was implemented in 1921 in Northern Ireland, when six of the nine counties of the province of Ulster received their own Parliament and remained represented in, and subject to the supreme authority of, the British Parliament. In the South the IRA continued to fight for independence from the British administration. After the signature of a truce in June 1921 negotiations with southern Irish leaders led to the Anglo-Irish Treaty of December 1921, establishing the Irish Free State with dominion status. The Free State, a self-governing state outside the United Kingdom of Great Britain and Northern Ireland, became a republic in 1949.

Channel Islands and Isle of Man Although the Channel Islands and the Isle of Man are not part of the United Kingdom, they have a special relationship with it because of the antiquity of their connection with the Crown. The Channel Islands were part of the Duchy of Normandy in the tenth and eleventh centuries and have been dependent territories of the Crown since the Norman Conquest. The Isle of Man was under the nominal sovereignty of Norway until 1266, when it was ceded to Scotland, subsequently passing to the Earls of Derby for a period, but eventually coming under the direct administration of the Crown in 1765. Today the territories have their own legislative assemblies and systems of local administration and of law, and their own courts. The British Government is responsible for their defence, their international relations and, ultimately, their good government.

The position of the Channel Islands and the Isle of Man in the European Community is broadly that the islands remain outside the Community except for customs purposes and for certain aspects of the Common Agricultural Policy.

The Four Lands

In the following pages there are brief descriptions of a number of aspects of social, economic and political life for each of the four countries, England, Wales, Scotland and Northern Ireland, with some additional material on the political situation in Northern Ireland. Statistics on the four lands are contained in Table 1.1.

Table 1.1: General Statistics

	England	Wales	Scotland	Northern Ireland	United Kingdom
Population ('000, mid-1989 estimate)	47,689	2,873	5,091	1,583	57,236
Area (sq km)	130,439	20,766	77,080	14,147	242,432
Population density (persons per sq km)	366	138	66	112	236
Gross domestic product (£ per head, 1988)	6,958	5,709	6,387	5,173	6,795
Employees in employment ('000, June 1989)	19,290	980	1,959	515	22,745
Percentage of employees in:[a] (June 1989)					
agriculture, forestry and fishing	1·2	2·0	1·4	3·9	1·3
energy and water supply	2·0	3·1	2·9	1·5	2·1
manufacturing	23·2	24·8	21·3	20·2	23·0
construction	4·5	4·5	6·4	5·0	4·7
service industries	69·1	65·7	68·0	69·4	68·9
Unemployment rate (per cent, seasonally adjusted, June 1990)	6·2	7·8	9·3	15·1	6·3

[a]May not add up to 100 because of rounding.

ENGLAND

England is predominantly a lowland country, although there are upland regions in the north (the Pennine Chain, the Cumbrian mountains and the Yorkshire moorlands) and in the south west in Devon and Cornwall. The greatest concentrations of population are in the London and Thames estuary areas, the West Yorkshire and north-west industrial cities, the Midlands conurbation around Birmingham, the north-east conurbations on the rivers Tyne and Tees, and along the Channel coast.

The Church of England, which was separated from the Roman Catholic Church at the time of the Reformation, is the Established Church in England; the Sovereign must always be a member of the Church and appoints its two archbishops and 42 other diocesan bishops.

The English language is descended from the German tongue spoken by the Anglo-Saxons in the fifth and sixth centuries, subsequently being influenced by Latin and Norse vocabulary, and then transformed with the settlement by the Normans from France. English is spoken throughout

Britain

Shetland Islands

Orkney Islands

SCOTLAND

SCOTLAND

Hebrides

Western Isles

Outer

Inner Hebrides

Highland

Grampian

Tayside

Fife

Central

Edinburgh

Lothian

Strathclyde

Borders

Northumberland

Dumfries and
Galloway

Atlantic
Ocean

NORTHERN
IRELAND

Belfast

Tyne and Wear

Cumbria

Durham

Cleveland

North Yorkshire

North Sea

ENGLAND

Isle of Man

Lancashire

West
Yorkshire

Humberside

Irish Sea

Merseyside

1

South
Yorkshire

IRISH
REPUBLIC

Cheshire

Derbyshire

Lincolnshire

Clwyd

2

Gwynedd

Staffordshire

3

Leicester

Norfolk

WALES

Powys

4

Cambridge

Suffolk

Hereford and
Worcester

5

6

Dyfed

9

7

Gwent

Gloucestershire

Oxford

8

Essex

11

12

10

London

13

Cardiff

Avon

Berkshire

Kent

Wiltshire

Surrey

Somerset

Hampshire

West
Sussex

East
Sussex

Devon

Dorset

Isle of Wight

Strait of Dover

BELGIU

English Channel

Cornwall

FRANCE

Isles of Scilly

Channel Islands

0   50   100   150 km

0   50   100 miles

▬ ▬ ▬ International boundaries

▬ ▬ ▬ Country boundaries

· · · · · · County boundaries
(regional boundaries
in Scotland)

1. Greater Manchester
2. Nottinghamshire
3. Shropshire
4. West Midlands
5. Warwickshire
6. Northamptonshire
7. Bedfordshire
8. Hertfordshire
9. Buckinghamshire
10. Greater London
11. West Glamorgan
12. Mid Glamorgan
13. South Glamorgan

Britain and in many other countries. A study has suggested that it is used as an official language in over 60 countries, more than any other international language.

Government

England has no government minister or department exclusively responsible for its central administration of domestic affairs, in contrast to Wales, Scotland and Northern Ireland. Instead, responsibility is shared among a number of government departments, whose responsibilities in some cases also cover aspects of affairs in Wales and Scotland. There are 523 Members of Parliament for England in the House of Commons, and arrangements are made for the discussion of regional affairs. Of the two major political parties, the Conservatives find their support chiefly in suburban and rural areas and have a large majority of the parliamentary seats in the southern half of England and in East Anglia, while the Labour Party derives its main support from urban industrialised areas. In June 1990 England had 356 Conservative Members of Parliament, 156 Labour, 7 Liberal Democrat, 3 Social Democrat and the Speaker of the House of Commons.

Local government is administered through a two-tier system of counties subdivided into districts, except in London, where local government is the responsibility of 32 borough councils and the Corporation of the City of London; and in the metropolitan areas, where local government is carried out by the metropolitan district councils.

Eight 'standard' regions in England are defined, principally for statistical purposes: South East, East Anglia, South West, West Midlands, East Midlands, Yorkshire and Humberside, North West and North. Many government statistics are also available with the South East (much the most populous region) subdivided into Greater London and the Rest of the South East. These regions play no part in local government and frequently do not coincide with the regional units adopted by central government departments.

The legal system of England comprises on the one hand a historic body of conventions, known as 'common law' and 'equity', and on the other, parliamentary and European Community legislation. Common law stems from the work of the king's judges after the Norman Conquest of 1066, who sought to bring together into a single body of legal principles the various local customs of the Anglo-Saxons. Great reliance was placed on precedent, and the practice of reporting on cases began in the thirteenth century. Equity law derives from the practice of petitioning the King's Chancellor in cases not covered by common law. The English legal system is therefore distinct from many of those of Western Europe, which have codes deriving from Roman law.

The Economy

Up to the eighteenth century the English economy was mainly agrarian and the chief manufacture was woollen cloth. London, as the capital city and a major port and mercantile centre, and the textile areas (East Anglia, south-western England and West Yorkshire) were the most populous and prosperous regions. In the late eighteenth and nineteenth centuries, however, rapid growth took place in the Midlands, the north west, Yorkshire and the north east. Coalfields and iron ore deposits in these areas permitted Britain to become the first industrialised nation, basing its wealth on coalmining, on the manufacture of iron and steel, heavy machinery and textiles, on shipbuilding and on trade. East Anglia and the West Country, remote from areas of industrial development, were affected by agricultural depression and entered a period of relative decline.

In the twentieth century a second period of industrialisation, based on new sources of energy, new manufacturing industries and new forms of transport, has continued to change the broad pattern of regional and industrial development in England. In the 1920s and 1930s the northern industrial centres saw their traditional industries weakened owing to fluctuations in world trade and competition from other industrialising countries and, in some cases, from substitute products. London, its surrounding counties and the West Midlands generally benefited from the newer, more mobile, industries. These included chemicals (such as pharmaceuticals, dyes, plastics and artificial fibres), electrical and electronic engineering, vehicle manufacture, aircraft building, instrument engineering, aluminium and rubber manufacture and manufacture of a wide range of consumer goods, including processed food, drink and tobacco products as well as durables.

In the second half of the century economic trends and population growth have tended to favour smaller towns and rural areas, particularly those in parts of southern England and East Anglia. Employment in service industries accounts for an increasing share of total employment, expansion being particularly marked in financial and business services. New businesses in the service sector are being created at a rapid rate, and this growth is linked to a marked rise in self-employment. New forms of service activity have been developing; for example, the growth of computer services and information systems.

London is one of the world's leading centres of banking, insurance and other financial services. Decentralisation of some office services from the capital and improvements in road systems have led to an expansion in the service sector and high technology industries in the surrounding regions. There has been an increase in retailing activity, with the trend towards large shopping developments on the outskirts of towns, designed for shoppers with cars. London and the neighbouring counties account for half of central government services and a significant proportion of non-food wholesale distribution in England. After London and the South East (where 77 per cent of employees are engaged in the service sector), the South West has the next highest concentration of service industries.

East Anglia has been the fastest-growing English region in both population and employment since the 1960s. Although largely agricultural, high-technology industry has in recent years developed throughout the region. One significant example is the Cambridge Science Park, containing a number of science-based companies and research organisations with close collaborative links with the University. Food processing, diesel engines, electronics and instrument engineering are the strongest industries. Other particular growth points have been Peterborough and the east coast ports, which benefit from their relative proximity to the northern European Community countries and from recent improvements to the road and rail network.

Greater London and the industrial cities of the West Midlands, the North West, Yorkshire and Humberside and the North continue to represent the largest concentrations of manufacturing industry. London is an important area for products of all kinds, including food and drink (especially brewing), instrument engineering, electrical and electronic engineering, clothing, furniture and printing. Of importance in the surrounding south-eastern counties are pharmaceuticals, pumps, valves and compressors, and instrument engineering. Microelectronics and computer hardware and software are important (particularly along the 'M4 corridor' in Berkshire, in Hertfordshire, and around Chelmsford), as are motor vehicles, aerospace, building materials, timber, paper and plastics products. The North West has significant activity in food processing, chemicals, textile machinery, insulated wires and cables, computers, motor vehicles, aerospace, clothing and glass making. The world's largest flat glass maker, Pilkington, is based in St Helens. Lancashire is the centre of the cotton and allied textile industries.

The characteristic manufactures of the West Midlands are metals (steel tubes, iron castings and non-ferrous metals), machine tools, electrical engineering, motor vehicles, carpets, pottery (with about 70 per cent of Britain's ceramics industry located in Staffordshire) and rubber production. Of the other regions, Yorkshire and Humberside has important shares of cocoa, chocolate and confectionery production, iron and steel (particularly tool and special steel), machine tools, textile machinery, woollen and worsted goods (producing about two-thirds of Britain's wool textiles), carpets, clothing and glass containers. The North has general chemicals, iron and steel, process plant, marine engineering, and clothing; the East Midlands has steel tubes, iron castings, about two-thirds of Britain's hosiery and knitted goods industry, and footwear; and the South West has food and drink processing, aerospace, a range of engineering industries and paper products.

A number of industrial areas (in the North, the North West, Yorkshire and Humberside and the West Midlands) which suffered as a result of the decline in traditional manufacturing employment are benefiting from the Government's regional industrial policy. This aims to reduce regional disparities in employment opportunities by making investment incentives available in the areas of greatest need, especially those which have been dependent on declining industries. Policies to encourage enterprise have been intensified under the Enterprise Initiative, launched in 1988 and aimed particularly at small- and medium-sized businesses. Its objective is to increase competitiveness by improving management skills in key areas, thus expanding opportunities for wealth creation.

In agriculture, the number of mixed holdings has been falling, as part of a general tendency towards greater specialisation. Dairying is most common in the west of England; sheep and cattle are reared in the hilly and moorland areas of northern and south-western England; and arable farming, pig and poultry farming and horticulture are concentrated in the east and south. Horticulture is also important in the West Midlands. The principal fishing ports are on the east coast and in the South West.

England has plentiful energy resources in its coalfields and has access to offshore oil and gas reserves. About two-thirds of Britain's deep-mined coal is produced in the Yorkshire, Nottinghamshire, Leicestershire and Warwickshire coalfields. The world's first large-scale nuclear power station was established at Calder Hall in Cumbria in 1956, while substantial investment in reprocessing capacity is being undertaken nearby. Other nuclear power stations are on coastal sites, including several around the coasts of southern England. Important mineral deposits in England include aggregates for the construction industry (sand, gravel and crushed rock), industrial minerals (including clay, salt from the North West and china clay from Cornwall) and iron ore from the East Midlands and Humberside.

A motorway network has been constructed in England since the 1950s and comprises four long-distance arterial routes linking London and the cities of the Midlands, the North and North West and the South West, the London orbital route, and over 30 shorter motorways. In 1989 the Government announced that the motorway and trunk road programme was to be more than doubled to £12,000 million; a number of motorways are to be widened to accommodate the increasing levels of road traffic.

Considerable investment is in progress in the railways, both to improve inter-city services and to provide new rolling-stock for local services. In 1988 construction work started on a cross-Channel railway tunnel. This will link Britain directly with the European rail system and also take motorists across on a drive-on, drive-off vehicle shuttle service using specially designed shuttle trains. Services through the tunnel are planned to start in 1993.

The major airports are Heathrow (the busiest international airport in the world) and Gatwick, both serving London; and Manchester, Luton and Birmingham. A new passenger terminal is due to open in 1991 in connection with the first phase of the development of Stansted as London's third airport.

Tourism and the leisure industries have expanded considerably in recent years. Over half of expenditure by overseas visitors in Britain takes place in London, although areas outside London, encouraged by government policies to expand tourism in the regions, are becoming increasingly popular with overseas tourists. The South West is the most popular region for domestic tourism. Each region has its own particular attraction for tourists. For example, a number of areas, including Northumberland and Cumbria (whose peaks include Scafell, England's highest point, at 978 m, 3,210 ft), have hills and lakes which attract walkers, climbers and riders.

Cultural and Social Life

Among London's main cultural features are over 100 theatrical venues, including some 50 in the 'West End', together with fringe and suburban theatres; about a dozen major centres for music concerts, ballet and opera; four major art galleries; a dozen major museums (with over 80 smaller galleries and museums); and around 100 West End, local and independent cinemas. Much the same broad range of cultural interests is reflected in many other cities and towns.

There are many tourist attractions in England. Of those charging for admission, Madame Tussaud's (an exhibition in London of waxworks of famous people), Alton Towers (near Cheadle in Staffordshire) and the Tower of London received most visitors in 1988 (over 2 million each). Of those with free admission, Blackpool Pleasure Beach (6·5 million visitors), the British Museum in London and Albert Dock in Liverpool (over 4 million each) were the most popular.

Social clubs in most towns and cities attract well-known entertainers. In addition, many rural or outdoor recreations are strongly supported and there is active interest in numerous games and sports, many of which were devised in Britain.

The English love of gardens and landscapes is associated with a tradition of sightseeing visits to the many country houses, gardens and unspoilt rural and coastal areas. There are seven national parks, six forest parks, 34 designated 'areas of outstanding natural beauty', ten environmentally sensitive areas, almost 200 country parks approved by the Countryside Commission, over 6,000 conservation areas, 800 km (500 miles) of designated heritage coastline and about 2,000 historic buildings and over 3,000 gardens listed by the English Tourist Board. Newer developments include the opening of safari and wildlife parks and a growing number of 'theme' parks, all offering family activities and entertainments. Many regions and towns have associations with the great English writers and artists, such as William Shakespeare (Stratford-upon-Avon), William Wordsworth (the Lake District), Arnold Bennett (Stoke-on-Trent), the Brontë sisters (Yorkshire), Thomas Hardy (Dorset) and John Constable (Essex).

WALES

Wales is a country of hills and mountains with extensive tracts of high plateau and shorter stretches of mountain ranges deeply dissected by river valleys. The highest mountains are in Snowdonia in the north west; the highest peak is Snowdon (1,085 m, 3,560 ft). The lower-lying ground is largely confined to the relatively narrow coastal belt and the lower parts of the river valleys. The main areas of settlement are in the southern valleys and coastal areas, where two-thirds of the population live. The chief urban centres are Cardiff, Swansea, Newport and Wrexham. Wales is a principality; Prince Charles, the heir to the throne, was invested by the Queen with the title of Prince of Wales at Caernarfon Castle in 1969, when he was 20.

The country has its own Welsh language, spoken, according to the 1981 census, by 19 per cent of the population, chiefly in the rural north and west. The Welsh name of the country is Cymru. Measures adopted since the 1960s have helped to revive the use of the language, which is of Celtic origin. They include recognising the equal validity of Welsh with English in law courts, the encouragement of bilingual education in schools, and the extended use of Welsh for official purposes and in broadcasting. Welsh-language television programmes are transmitted in Wales by Sianel 4 Cymru (Channel 4 Wales). A Welsh Language Board was established in 1988 to advise on matters relating to the Welsh language.

There is no established church in Wales, the Anglican church having been disestablished in 1920 following decades of pressure from adherents of the Methodist and Baptist churches. Methodism in particular spread rapidly in Wales in the eighteenth century, assuming the nature of a popular movement among Welsh speakers and finding strong support later in industrial communities.

Government

The country returns 38 Members of Parliament and there are special arrangements for the discussion of Welsh affairs. For the last 60 years the industrial communities of Wales have tended to support the Labour Party in elections, ensuring a Labour majority in Wales. Wales has 25 Labour Members of Parliament, 7 Conservative, 3 Plaid Cymru (Welsh Nationalist) and 3 Liberal Democrat. Substantial administrative autonomy is centred on the Secretary of State for Wales, who is a member of the Cabinet and has wide-ranging responsibilities relating to the economy, welfare services and the provision of amenities. The headquarters of the administration is the Welsh Office in Cardiff, which also has an office in London. In 1979 proposals for the establishment of an elected Welsh assembly in Cardiff to take over policy-making and executive powers from central government were rejected in a referendum held in Wales. Local government is exercised through a system of elected authorities similar to that in England, and the legal system is identical with the English one.

The Economy

The south Wales coalfield was developed during the latter part of the industrial revolution in the middle of the nineteenth century. However, the economy was narrowly based, mainly on coal, iron, steel and tinplate, and contracted sharply during the 1920s and 1930s, resulting in severe employment problems and substantial emigration.

Notable features of the past three decades have been the continuing contraction of coalmining and iron and steel production (although Wales still accounts for about one-third of Britain's steel production), the advent of a more diverse range of manufacturing industries and the growth of service industries. Wales is developing as an important centre for electronics in Britain, and several new high-technology businesses in electronics and related industries have been established. Inward investment by overseas companies has been considerable, and there are over 280 overseas-owned or associated firms in Wales, employing about 55,000 people and accounting for around one in five jobs in the manufacturing sector. The financial and business services sector is expanding rapidly, as companies such as Rothschild's, the Trustee Savings Bank and the National Provident Institution have relocated major parts of their operation to Wales, providing support for industrial development. Government relocation has also bene-fited employment in Wales; for example, in late 1989 the Government's Property Services Agency decided to expand its Cardiff-based functions, creating 200 new jobs. The Welsh unemployment rate fell faster in 1989 than that of any other area of Britain.

South Wales remains the principal industrial area, but new industries and firms have been introduced in north-east Wales, around Wrexham and Deeside, and light industry has also been attracted to the towns in the rural areas in mid- and north Wales. A development corporation was set up in 1987 to stimulate the regeneration of the Cardiff Bay area, and in 1988 the Government announced a programme designed to improve economic, environmental and social conditions in the south Wales valleys. Regional aid in the valleys has covered projects involving 11,800 new jobs and private investment of about £300 million in the first three years of the programme. The Welsh Development Agency is investing about £76 million in factory building, and it is expected that a total of 960 hectares (2,400 acres) of derelict land in the valleys will be cleared. More than 1,000 companies based in Wales have made use of business reviews and consultants' advisory services under the Government's Enterprise Wales initiative, launched in 1988. An investment of £14 million in environmental improvement schemes was announced by the Government in August 1990.

Agriculture occupies about 80 per cent of the land area, the main activities being sheep and cattle rearing in the hill regions and dairy farming in the lowlands. Wales accounts for about 13 per cent of Forestry Commission area in Britain and over 20 per cent of Forestry Commission timber production.

Wales produces about 6 per cent of Britain's deep-mined coal and 10 per cent of opencast production, including all of its anthracite. The biggest pumped-storage power station in Europe is at Dinorwig, while there are nuclear power stations at Wylfa and Trawsfynydd.

Good communications exist in the south, with motorway links across the Severn Bridge to southern England and the Midlands, and high-speed rail services to a number of destinations in England. The A55, the main road along the north Wales coast, is being upgraded and a second crossing of the Severn is planned. Transatlantic flights to New York from Cardiff-Wales airport were introduced in 1989.

There has been expansion in the tourist and catering trades and in some areas of public administration. With its coastal resorts, and three national parks (Snowdonia, the Brecon Beacons and the Pembrokeshire Coast), as well as other areas of picturesque hill, lake and mountain country, Wales attracts many tourists, especially for outdoor holidays.

Cultural and Social Life

There is much literary, musical and dramatic activity in Wales and there is a National Library and National Museum. Welsh literature is one of the oldest in Europe. The country is well known for its choral singing and the Welsh National Opera has an international reputation. The special festivals of Wales, known as eisteddfodau, encourage Welsh literature and music. The largest is the Royal National Eisteddfod of Wales, held annually, entirely in Welsh, and consisting of competitions in music, singing, prose and poetry. The town of Llangollen has extended its eisteddfod to include artists from all over the world in the annual International Musical Eisteddfod. Famous modern Welsh artists have included the opera singers Sir Geraint Evans and Dame Gwyneth Jones. An active local press includes a number of Welsh language publications. Great interest is aroused by the annual rugby football competition in which sides from Wales, England, Scotland, Ireland and France take part.

Proposals under the Environmental Protection Bill would result in the creation of a new body, the Countryside Council for Wales. This would combine the functions of the Nature Conservancy Council and the Countryside Commission in Wales.

Health services are provided mainly under the National Health Service, administered by the Welsh Office, while personal social services and education (except at university level) are provided mainly through the local authorities. Educational provision is similar to that in England, except for the use of Welsh in some schools, particularly in the Welsh-speaking, largely rural, areas. The collegiate University of Wales, founded in 1893, comprises six member institutions.

SCOTLAND

Scotland may be divided broadly into three areas: the sparsely populated highlands and islands in the north, accounting for just over half the total area of the country; the central lowlands, containing three-quarters of the population and most of the industrial centres and cultivated farmland; and the southern uplands, containing a number of hill ranges, which border on England. The highest mountains are the Grampians in the central highlands, with Ben Nevis (1,343 m, 4,406 ft) the highest peak. The chief cities are the capital, Edinburgh; the main industrial centre, Glasgow; and the two regional centres, Aberdeen and Dundee.

The period from 1750 onwards has seen considerable and continuous emigration of Scots to England and overseas. However, the rate slowed markedly in the 1970s as the offshore oil and gas industries developed and there was inward migration to the north east of Scotland, although the outflow of people from Strathclyde has continued at a lower level. In the mid-nineteenth century, as Scotland industrialised rapidly, there was large-scale immigration from Ireland.

The period from 1750 until the beginning of the twentieth century was also one of stability and economic progress, and of achievements in many fields. Among famous Scots were David Hume, Robert Burns, Sir Walter Scott, Adam Smith, Robert Adam, James Watt, John MacAdam, Lord Kelvin, Alexander Graham Bell, James Clerk Maxwell and Marie Stopes.

The Church of Scotland, which became the established church in 1690, has complete freedom in all matters of doctrine, order and discipline. It is a Protestant church which is Presbyterian in form, being governed by a hierarchy of church courts, each of which includes lay people.

Government

There are special arrangements for the conduct of Scottish affairs within the British system of government and separate Acts of Parliament are passed for Scotland where appropriate. The 72 Scottish seats in the House of Commons are represented by 48 Labour Members of Parliament, 10 Conservative, 9 Liberal Democrat, 4 Scottish National and 1 Independent Labour. Since 1959 Scotland, like Wales, has had a majority of Labour Members of Parliament. Administrative tasks relating to a wide range of economic and social functions are the responsibility of the Secretary of State for Scotland, a member of the Cabinet, working through the Scottish Office, with its administrative headquarters in Edinburgh and an office in London. A proposal for an elected assembly for Scotland, on which a referendum was held in 1979, failed to gain the support of the required 40 per cent of the electorate to bring it into effect, even though a majority of those voting gave it their approval. Local government generally operates on a two-tier basis broadly similar to that in England and Wales but established by separate legislation. However, the three islands councils (for Orkney, Shetland and the Western Isles) are single-tier authorities.

The principles and procedures of the Scottish legal system (particularly in civil law) differ in many respects from those of England and Wales, stemming, in part, from the adoption of elements of other European legal systems, based on Roman law, during the sixteenth century.

The Economy   Scotland has experienced the same pressure on its traditional industries as the north of England and Wales. However, over the past decades its economy has been transformed, with a developing oil and gas industry, and investment by overseas companies making significant contributions to the growth of modern, technologically based industries. Under the Enterprise and New Towns (Scotland) Act 1990, the training, enterprise functions and environmental improvement activities administered by the Scottish Development Agency and the Training Agency will be brought together in a new agency known as Scottish Enterprise. Similarly, Highlands and Islands Enterprise will from April 1991 be formed by merging the functions of the Highlands and Islands Development Board and the Training Agency. Both bodies will be expected to contract with a network of employer-led local enterprise companies throughout Scotland, which will assess the needs of their local economies and promote appropriate economic development and environmental and training support to allow their localities to thrive.

The electronics sector has greatly contributed to the recent development of Scottish manufacturing industry, providing 13 per cent of its employment and 18 per cent of its output and investment. Between 1979 and 1989 Scottish electronics output more than quadrupled. The industry has particular strengths in communications and defence equipment, electronic data processing and control, and industrial instrumentation; the manufacture of electronic components accounts for much of the sector's activity. By mid-1988 about 230 plants were employing some 45,200 workers, one of the biggest concentrations of the electronics industry in Western Europe. Scotland accounts for more than half of Britain's output of integrated circuits and for over 10 per cent of European output. Many of the world's leading electronics companies manufacture in Scotland. The needs of large equipment and component makers are serviced by an extensive network of smaller companies supplying both components and support facilities.

Since the early 1970s the Scottish economy has also benefited from the growth of offshore-related industries following the discovery of oil and gas under the northern North Sea. Up to about 100,000 jobs are estimated to have arisen directly or indirectly as a result of North Sea activities.

Traditional industries, such as coal, steel and shipbuilding, have experienced a long-term decline in employment. Other traditional manufactures, such as high-quality tweeds and other textiles, and food and drink products, remain important. There are over 100 whisky distilleries in Scotland and the industry is a major export earner, with exports of almost £1,500 million in 1989.

Northern and north-east Scotland (particularly Aberdeen) have benefited most from offshore developments. However, Strathclyde, by far the most populous region, has experienced serious industrial decline and population loss, particularly in Glasgow. In the remainder of the central belt and in the five new towns (East Kilbride, Glenrothes, Livingston, Irvine and

Cumbernauld, which have benefited from inward investment and the growth of the electronics industry), trends have generally been more favourable. In Lothian the large concentration of financial and other service industries centred on Edinburgh has been a helpful influence. Problems of inner city dereliction and decay and peripheral housing estates in Scotland are being tackled with urban renewal projects designed to stimulate economic development and improve the local environment.

Scotland has about one-third of Britain's total agricultural land, but 71 per cent consists of hill grazing for cattle and sheep. About 11 per cent of the agricultural area is used for crops, and 58 per cent of this is under barley. Scotland accounts for nearly half of Britain's forest area and for over one-third of timber production; the bulk of new planting in Britain takes place in Scotland, most of it in the upland and mountain areas. Fishing remains an important activity; more than 75 per cent of total landings of fish in Britain are made at Scottish ports.

In Scotland nuclear and hydro-electric generation supply a higher proportion of energy than in any other part of Britain. Once Scotland's fifth nuclear power station—the 1,400 megawatt Advanced Gas-cooled Reactor at Torness (Lothian)—comes fully on stream, about 60 per cent of Scotland's electricity requirements will be met by nuclear power. Hydro-power and other renewables contribute about 15 per cent of Scottish electricity needs.

Communications, both domestic and international, have improved in many areas, particularly in the north and north east, owing to the stimulus of the offshore oil industry, of road- and bridge-building programmes and the improvement of ferry links to the Scottish islands. The offshore oil industry has also encouraged expansion in financial and business services, which have traditionally been strong in Scotland and are now one of the fastest-growing sectors of the Scottish economy. Tourism, which makes a significant contribution to the economy and to employment in Scotland as a whole, is estimated to generate, both directly and indirectly, nearly 132,000 jobs.

Cultural and Social Life

A vigorous cultural life in Scotland has as its highlight the annual Edinburgh International Festival, one of the world's leading cultural events. Notable performing arts bodies are the Scottish National Orchestra, Scottish Opera, Scottish Ballet, Scottish Chamber Orchestra, Scottish Baroque Ensemble and the BBC Scottish Symphony Orchestra. Scotland possesses excellent collections of the fine and applied arts, notably in the National Galleries of Scotland, the Royal Museums of Scotland and the City of Glasgow Museum and Art Galleries (including the Burrell collection, opened in 1983). The Government announced in 1989 that it would be funding the construction of a new Museum of Scotland, to be sited in Edinburgh. Glasgow was designated as European City of Culture for 1990.

Scots Gaelic is the indigenous language, with its own literary background. A language of ancient Celtic origin, it is spoken by some 80,000 people, mainly in the islands and north west of Scotland.

An active press includes six national daily morning newspapers, six local evening newspapers and four national Sunday newspapers. Television programmes are produced by BBC Scotland and by three independent companies, covering the highland, lowland and border regions. BBC Radio Scotland covers most of the population.

The educational tradition has been particularly strong in Scotland, helping many Scots to positions of eminence in the arts and sciences. There are eight universities, of which four (St Andrews, Glasgow, Aberdeen and Edinburgh) were established in the fifteenth and sixteenth centuries, while the other four have been established since 1964.

Over 57 per cent of Scotland's housing has been built since 1945, a higher proportion than in either England or Wales. The tenure pattern in Scotland is very different from that in the rest of Britain, with 42 per cent of housing rented from the public sector, compared with 25 per cent for Great Britain as a whole. As in the rest of Britain, there has been a noticeable growth in owner-occupied housing in recent years.

Scotland's cultural and historic associations, its varied scenic beauty, and the opportunities for sport and recreation are particular attractions. Golf originated in Scotland, and courses at St Andrews, Gleneagles, Turnberry, Muirfield, Troon and Prestwick are internationally renowned. Skiing is growing in importance, with centres at Aviemore, Glenshee, Glen Coe, Aonach Mhor and the Lecht, and further developments are planned. Under the Environmental Protection Bill, a separate Nature Conservancy Council would be created for Scotland; the existing council covers all of Great Britain.

NORTHERN IRELAND

Northern Ireland is at its nearest point only 21 km (13 miles) from Scotland. It has a 488-km (303-mile) border in the south and west with the Irish Republic. At its centre lies Lough Neagh, Britain's largest freshwater lake (381 sq km, 147 sq miles). Many of the principal towns lie in valleys leading from the Lough, including the capital, Belfast, which stands at the mouth of the river Lagan. The Mourne Mountains, rising sharply in the south east, include Slieve Donard, Northern Ireland's highest peak (852 m, 2,796 ft).

Just under two-thirds of Northern Ireland's population are descendants of Scots or English settlers who crossed to north-eastern Ireland mainly in the seventeenth century; most belong to the Protestant faith, and have a traditional loyalty to the maintenance of the union with Great Britain. The remainder, over a third, are Irish in origin and mainly Roman Catholic; many of them are nationalist in political opinion, favouring union with the Irish Republic.

Government
Background to Civil Disturbances

For 50 years from 1921 Northern Ireland had its own devolved Parliament in which the mainly Protestant Unionists consistently formed the majority and therefore constituted the Government after successive elections. Nationalists, who are predominantly Roman Catholic, resented this domination and their effective exclusion from political office. An active and articulate civil rights movement emerged during the late 1960s. Reforms were made but sectarian disturbances developed, which required the introduction of the Army in 1969 to support the police in keeping the peace. Subsequently, sectarian divisions were exploited by the actions of terrorists from both sides, but most notably by the Provisional Irish Republican Army, who claimed to be protecting the Roman Catholic minority.

From 1969 the Northern Ireland Government enacted reforms aimed at securing the minority's right to an effective voice in public bodies. A police authority representative of all sections of the community was created and commissioners became responsible for investigating complaints of mal-administration, including discrimination, against government departments and local authorities. A central housing executive became responsible for all public sector house-building and the allocation of houses according to need. Local government was restructured and electoral law, including the franchise and the arrangements for reviewing electoral boundaries, was reformed.

Direct Rule and Political Initiatives

Despite this reform programme, the inter-communal violence continued and the British Government concluded that the best hope of ending terrorism and achieving political progress would be for it to take over responsibility for law and order in Northern Ireland. The Northern Ireland Government felt unable to accept this and resigned; in 1972 direct rule began, with a United

Kingdom Cabinet minister becoming responsible for the functions previously exercised by the Northern Ireland Government.

Several attempts have been made to secure a stable and effective devolved government supported by both sides of the community. The most recent was the election in 1982 of a new 78-member Assembly charged with responsibility for making proposals to devolve powers on a basis which would command widespread acceptance throughout the community. It also performed scrutinising and consultative functions by commenting upon draft legislation and initiating reports on such matters as industry and education. Some members refused to take their seats on election. The unionist parties, who had a majority in the Assembly, decided not to fulfil the Assembly's statutory functions in March 1986 in protest at the Anglo-Irish Agreement (see below), and in June 1986 the Government dissolved the Assembly.

The Government's policy continues to be based on two fundamental principles. First, that there will be no change in Northern Ireland's constitutional status as part of the United Kingdom without the consent of a majority of people in Northern Ireland. A 'border poll' in 1973 showed that a clear majority wished to remain part of the United Kingdom, and in subsequent elections parties which support that position have continued to receive the majority of votes. Secondly, the Government continues to believe that a devolved form of administration would best meet Northern Ireland's needs, provided that it is acceptable to both parts of the community. To this end dialogue has been continuing since late 1989 between government and the local constitutional political parties to explore the extent of the common ground that now appears to exist between them. The Government hopes that this approach will be a prelude to discussions about arrangements for the transfer of powers and responsibilities to locally elected representatives.

Northern Ireland returns 17 members to the United Kingdom Parliament. In the last general election in 1987 the seats (and votes) were distributed as follows: Ulster Unionist 9 (37·8 per cent), Democratic Unionist 3 (11·7 per cent), Ulster Popular Unionist 1 (2·5 per cent), Social Democratic and Labour 3 (21·1 per cent), and Sinn Fein 1 (11·4 per cent); the last-mentioned member has not taken his seat. The Alliance Party received 10 per cent of the votes but no seats.

The Anglo-Irish Agreement

In November 1985 the United Kingdom and the Irish Republic concluded the Anglo-Irish Agreement, aimed at promoting peace and stability in Northern Ireland. The Agreement is binding in international law. It affirms that 'any change in the status of Northern Ireland would only come about with the consent of a majority of the people of Northern Ireland' but recognises that the majority wish is for no change in status. The Agreement says that, 'if in the future a majority of the people of Northern Ireland clearly wish for and formally consent to the establishment of a united Ireland', both governments 'will introduce and support in the respective Parliaments legislation to give effect to that wish'.

Under the Agreement an Intergovernmental Conference has been established to deal on a regular basis with political, security and legal matters and with the promotion of cross border co-operation. As specified in the Agreement, the Irish Government can use the machinery of the Conference to put forward its views on matters relating to Northern Ireland provided that these are not the responsibility of a devolved administration. The Conference, however, has no executive role or decision-making powers, as the Agreement makes clear: 'There is no derogation from the sovereignty of either the United Kingdom Government or the Irish Government, and each retains responsibility for the decisions and administration of government within its own jurisdiction.' A review of the Conference, carried out by both governments and completed in 1989, agreed that it had proved its value and that it would be developed further.

The Agreement was generally welcomed by the minority community, but there is considerable antipathy among Unionists. Their representatives maintain that the Agreement infringes the sovereignty of the British Government over Northern Ireland and that it is a step towards a united Ireland. The Government believes that this opposition is misguided, as sovereignty over Northern Ireland is not affected by the Agreement (see above). In its view, the Agreement offers benefits to both traditions in Northern Ireland without detracting from the rights of either.

Human Rights and Security Policy

The Government is committed to the protection of human rights in Northern Ireland. Britain is a signatory to the European Convention on Human Rights and allows individual petition. Legislation passed in 1973 outlaws discrimination by public bodies, including the Government, on the grounds of religious belief or political opinion. It also set up the independent Standing Advisory Commission on Human Rights, which advises the Government on the effectiveness of anti-discrimination legislation and on other human rights issues. In 1987 a central community relations unit was established within the Government to advise on all aspects of relations between the two traditions in Northern Ireland. Its main roles are to advise on the impact of government policies and programmes on community relations and to bring forward ideas on future action.

Discrimination in employment by public and private employers is also illegal and the Fair Employment Agency was established in 1976 to investigate complaints and enforce fair practices. The Fair Employment (Northern Ireland) Act 1989 outlawed indirect discrimination and replaced the Agency by a Fair Employment Commission responsible for investigating employment practices and issuing legally enforceable directions requiring an employer to take specific measures. The Act requires employers actively to promote and practise equality of opportunity and to submit annual returns on the religious composition of their workforces to the Commission. A new Fair Employment Tribunal adjudicates on complaints about religious or political discrimination and has the power to enforce the Commission's directions. New sanctions against employers in breach of their statutory obligations include the withholding of government grants and public sector contracts. A code of practice has been drawn up to provide advice to employers, trade unions, employment agencies and employees to help them comply with the Act.

While terrorism continues, certain emergency powers are in force. These include special powers of arrest in respect of certain serious crimes, non-jury courts to try those offences, and the proscription of organisations involved in terrorism. There has been much concern to reconcile these powers as far as possible with respect for individual liberties, and the powers are balanced by specific safeguards. The measures are temporary, need annual renewal by Parliament and are subject to annual independent review.

Most traditional rights, including freedom from persecution and freedom of speech, remain in force. However, in the belief that terrorists should not be allowed to draw support and sustenance from access to television and radio, the Government has banned the broadcasting of direct statements by representatives of proscribed organisations or their supporters.

The security forces are accountable to the law; if they break it, their members are liable to prosecution like any other members of the community. In addition, there is an independent police complaints commission to supervise police investigations into more serious complaints and, at its discretion, the investigation of others. Northern Ireland's legal system, and the safeguards it enshrines, are broadly similar to those in England and Wales.

The use of violence as a means of overcoming political differences has been condemned by the overwhelming majority of people living in Northern Ireland and, although terrorism continues, the overall level of violence is much lower than in the early 1970s. Since 1969 nearly 2,800 people have been killed as a result of the terrorist campaign. The police take the primary role in maintaining order; the Army's task is one of assisting the civil authorities, and the number of soldiers on service has been considerably reduced. Terrorists are brought to justice through the courts and are tried for criminal offences and not political beliefs.

The Economy   Population and industry are concentrated on the eastern seaboard, while the rest of Northern Ireland remains predominantly rural and reliant mainly upon agriculture for its livelihood. Since the end of the second world war two dominant trends have been apparent in the economy. First, employment in the traditionally important industries (shipbuilding, linen and agriculture) has declined. Secondly, there has been fast growth in the numbers seeking work, reflecting the relatively high rate of natural increase of the population, which is only partly offset by emigration from the province. These trends have combined to produce an unemployment rate in Northern Ireland persistently higher than in any other region in Britain. Between June 1987 and June 1990 the unemployment rate fell from 18 per cent to 13·6 per cent.

As with other developed economies, there has been a switch in emphasis from agriculture and manufacturing towards services. However, agriculture (predominantly livestock and livestock products) still accounts for 7 per cent of civil employment, over three times the proportion in Britain as a whole. Belfast has Britain's largest shipyard, and aerospace engineering is one of Northern Ireland's biggest manufacturing industries. Other industrial activities include the manufacture of textile machinery and a wide range of engineering products, tobacco and clothing. There has also been extensive development in vehicle components, oil-well equipment, electronics, tele-communications equipment, carpets, synthetic rubber, and food processing and packaging. The linen industry is currently enjoying a revival and farms are experimenting with growing flax.

Governments have offered more generous incentives than are available in the rest of the country to encourage new investment both from within Britain and from overseas. In 1989–90 the various industrial development agencies promoted almost 11,100 jobs in manufacturing, craft and tradeable services; total investment associated with these jobs was over £464·4 million. The establishment of enterprise zones in Belfast and Londonderry and the designation of Aldergrove airport as a freeport serve as additional incentives to investment.

In 1988 the Making Belfast Work initiative was launched to address the particular social, economic and environmental problems in the most disadvantaged areas of Belfast. For a five-year period which started in 1988-89, an additional £92·5 million has been allocated to create jobs and businesses, and to improve levels of skill, the physical environment, and health and living conditions. The Government is seeking to help local communities help themselves and to enlist the support of the private sector.

The modern diversification of the economy has helped to stimulate output, productivity and incomes, and has assisted in narrowing the gap between living standards in Northern Ireland and those in the rest of Britain. Manufacturing output increased by 8 per cent between 1983 and 1988 while output per employee hour rose by 7 per cent over this period. Gross domestic product per person rose from just under two-thirds of the British average in 1963 to some 76 per cent in 1988. Average earnings in 1989 were around 86 per cent of those in Great Britain.

The principle underlying Northern Ireland's financial relations with the rest of the country is that it has parity, both of taxation and services, with England, Scotland and Wales. To maintain social services at the level of those in Great Britain, to meet the cost of security measures and to compensate for the natural disadvantages of geography and lack of resources, the British Government's subvention to Northern Ireland in 1989–90 was £1,711 million.

The Anglo-Irish Agreement expressed the intention of both signatories to promote the economic and social development of those areas which had suffered from the instability of recent years and to try to secure international support for this work. In 1986 the British and Irish Governments signed an agreement setting up the International Fund for Ireland and donations have been received from the United States, Canada, New Zealand and the European Community. The Fund will have committed over £133 million by the end of 1990 to projects covering business enterprise, tourism, agriculture and fisheries, urban development, training and exchanges overseas, industrial promotion, and science and technology. Two investment companies, one on each side of the border, provide venture capital to new businesses. Three-quarters of the Fund is being spent in Northern Ireland and the rest in the Irish Republic's border counties.

Cultural and Social Life

Northern Ireland's landscape and natural features, cultural traditions and festivals continue to offer special attractions; it received some 1 million visitors in 1989. For many North Americans the land from which their forebears emigrated (a number of United States presidents have been descended from Northern Ireland families) has a unique interest. The story of this contribution to American life, the history of Northern Ireland, and other aspects of its culture, including its dialects and strong literary tradition, are recorded in the Ulster-American Folk Park, the Ulster Museum and the Ulster Folk and Transport Museum.

The Government provides financial support for arts and cultural activities related to the Irish language. Over 20,000 secondary school pupils currently study Irish; full degree courses and research programmes are available at Northern Ireland's two universities.

The Arts Council of Northern Ireland is a major contributor to cultural life. The annual Belfast Festival at Queen's University is the second largest international festival in Britain. Among musicians who have achieved international distinction are the flautist James Galway, the soprano Heather Harper and the pianist Barry Douglas.

The National Health Service provides hospital and practitioner services. Health and personal social services correspond fairly closely to those in the rest of Britain, although the administrative framework is different.

Although publicly maintained schools are open to children of all religions, in practice Protestants and Roman Catholics are for the most part educated in separate schools. In recent years a small number of integrated schools have been established to provide education for Protestant and Catholic children together. These schools began as independent schools and qualified for public funding on the same basis as other non-state schools only when their long-term viability had been adequately demonstrated. Under the

Education Reform (NI) Order 1989, new integrated schools may receive public funding from their inception. Additional provisions enable existing schools to seek integrated status if a majority of the pupils' parents vote to do so in a secret ballot. Contrary to developments in the rest of Britain, emphasis on the comprehensive principle in secondary schools has been very small. Links between the two universities and industry are well developed.

Considerable progress has been made in improving housing and the urban environment, notably in Belfast. In the last ten years the housing stock in Northern Ireland has increased by about 12 per cent and owner-occupation from 51 per cent to more than 60 per cent. Major town centre developments are taking place in Belfast, Londonderry and other towns, providing greatly improved shopping facilities.

Local television and radio programmes are broadcast and there is a local press; national radio and television networks are also received, and the national press is sold widely. Sport has an important role in the community, and many world-class sportsmen and sportswomen have come from Northern Ireland, including Barry McGuigan and Dave McAuley (boxing), Dennis Taylor and Alex Higgins (snooker), Joey Dunlop (motor-cycling) and Avril Malley (judo).

The Social Framework

The way of life of the people of Britain has been changing rapidly in the second half of the twentieth century. As in many other countries, underlying causes include a lower birth rate, longer expectation of life, a higher divorce rate, widening educational opportunities, technological progress and a higher standard of living.

POPULATION

With 57 million people in 1989, Britain ranks sixteenth in the world in terms of population. This compares with 38·2 million in 1901, about 9 million at the end of the seventeenth century and some 2 million at the end of the eleventh century. Early figures are based on contemporary estimates, but from the beginning of the nineteenth century relatively plentiful and reliable information is available, mainly from the compulsory registration since 1837 of births, marriages and deaths, and the censuses. These have been taken regularly every ten years since 1801, except in 1941, when, because of war, there was no census; the next census will be in 1991. After 1974 the population fell slightly for about four years, for the first time (other than in war) since records began, reflecting a temporary decline in the birth rate. Since then a slow upward trend has been resumed. Projections suggest that population growth will continue at a low rate. Britain's total population is expected, on mid-1988 based projections, to be 57·5 million in 1991, 59·2 million in 2001 and 60 million in 2011.

Birth Rates

In 1989 there were 777,300 live births in Britain, 10,300 fewer than in 1988. Births outnumbered deaths (657,700) by 119,600. The total period fertility rate (an indication of the average family size) remains below 2·1, the level leading to the long-term replacement of the population, although it is projected to increase from 1·8 in 1989 to 2 for women born in or after 1980.

Several factors may have contributed to the relatively low birth rate in recent years (13·6 live births per 1,000 population in 1989). The trends towards later marriage and towards postponing births have led to an increase in the average age of women having children (27·3 years in 1989 compared with 26·7 in 1979). Another feature is the current preference for smaller families than in the past, which has led to a significant decline in the proportion of families with four or more children. In 1988, 21 per cent of households in Great Britain consisted of a married couple with one or two children only, compared with 5 per cent of households which consisted of a married couple with three or more children.

Contraception has become more widespread and effective, making it easier to plan families, and voluntary sterilisation of men and women has also become more common. Of all pregnancies in England and Wales in 1988, 41·4 per cent were conceived outside marriage and of these over one-third were terminated by legal abortion.

Mortality

At birth the expectation of life for a man is about 72 years and for a woman 78 years, compared with 49 years for men and 52 years for women in 1901. Life expectancy in the older age groups has increased relatively little.

The general death rate has remained about the same for the past 40 years, at about 12 per 1,000 population. However, there has been a considerable decline in mortality at most ages, particularly among children and young adults. The infant mortality rate (deaths of infants under one year old per 1,000 live births) was 8·4 in 1989; neonatal mortality (deaths of infants under four weeks old per 1,000 live births) was 4·7 in 1989; and maternal mortality is about 0·07 per 1,000 live births.

The causes of the decline in mortality include better nutrition, rising standards of living, the advance of medical science, the growth of medical facilities, improved health measures, better working conditions, education in personal hygiene and the smaller size of families. Deaths resulting from infectious diseases (notably tuberculosis) have virtually disappeared. As in other countries the spread of AIDS (Acquired Immune Deficiency Syndrome) is causing concern; by the end of August 1990, 3,688 cases of AIDS had been reported, of which 1,975 had resulted in the patient's death. Deaths caused by circulatory diseases (including heart attacks and strokes) now account for nearly half of all deaths; mortality from heart disease in Britain remains high compared with that of other developed countries. The next largest cause of death is cancer (responsible for nearly one-quarter of deaths). Cigarette smoking is the greatest preventable cause of illness and death in Britain, accounting for some 100,000 premature deaths a year, but there has been a significant decline in the incidence of smoking, with 33 per cent of adult males and 30 per cent of adult females smoking cigarettes in 1988, as against 52 and 41 per cent respectively in 1972. In recent years there have been major initiatives to reduce drug abuse in Britain. For example, locally based drug prevention teams were announced in October 1989, to be set up in the areas most at risk from drug misuse.

Marriage and Divorce

In 1988 there were 394,000 marriages in Britain, of which 36 per cent were remarriages (of one or both parties), compared with about 20 per cent in 1971 and 14 per cent in 1961. Some 33 per cent of all marriages in 1988 were remarriages where one or both parties had been divorced. Of the population aged 16 or over in England and Wales in 1988, 59 per cent were married, 26 per cent single, 9 per cent widowed and 6 per cent divorced. The trend of the 1960s towards earlier marriage was reversed at the beginning of the 1970s, since when there has been a slow increase in the average age for first marriages, which in England and Wales is now 26 for men and 24 for women.

In 1988 about 13 decrees of divorce were made absolute for every 1,000 married couples in England and Wales, compared with two per 1,000 in 1961. The rates are lower in Scotland and Northern Ireland. In 1988 about

153,000 divorces were granted in England and Wales; the proportion granted to wives was about 71 per cent. The average age of people at the time of divorce in England and Wales is now about 38 for men and 35 for women.

Another feature, common to many other Western European countries, has been a considerable increase in cohabitation. Over one-quarter of women in Great Britain marrying during the period 1980 to 1984, where the marriage was the first for both parties, had lived with their husbands before marriage (compared with 7 per cent for those married in the early 1970s) and about 21 per cent of non-married women aged 18 to 49 were cohabiting during 1988. Cohabitation occurs more frequently for separated or divorced women than for single women. There is some evidence of a growing number of stable non-married relationships in that half of all births outside marriage (which now account for 26 per cent of live births in Britain compared with 6 per cent in 1961) are registered by both parents giving a single address as the usual place of residence.

Age and Sex Structure

Although the total population has remained relatively stable in the last decade, there has been a noticeable change in the age structure, particularly a decline in the proportion of young people under 16 and an increase in the proportion of elderly people, especially those aged 85 and over. The estimated age distribution of the British population in mid-1988 was roughly as follows: under 16 years, about 20 per cent; 16–64, 64 per cent; and 65 and over, 16 per cent. Some 18 per cent of the population were over the normal retirement ages (65 for men and 60 for women), compared with 15 per cent in 1961.

In mid-1989 there were an estimated 29·3 million females and 27·9 million males in Britain, representing a ratio of over 105 females to every 100 males. There are about 5 per cent more male than female births every year. Because of the higher mortality of men at all ages, however, there is a turning point, at about 50 years of age, beyond which the number of women exceeds the number of men. This imbalance increases with age so that there are many more women among the elderly.

Distribution of Population

The population density is about 236 inhabitants per sq km, which is well above the European Community average of 143 per sq km. England is the most densely populated, with 366 people per sq km (Greater London having a density of 4,288 people per sq km), and Scotland the least densely populated, with 66 people per sq km, while Wales and Northern Ireland have 138 and 112 people per sq km respectively.

Table 1.2 gives figures for some of Britain's largest, mainly urban, administrative districts. About half of the population lives in a belt across England, with south Lancashire and West Yorkshire at one end, the London area at the other, and the industrialised Midlands at its centre. Other areas with large populations are: the central lowlands of Scotland; north-east England from north of the river Tyne down to the river Tees; south-east Wales; the Bristol area; and the English Channel coast from Poole, in Dorset, eastwards.

Since the nineteenth century there has been a general trend, especially in London, for people to move away from the congested urban centres into the suburbs. There has also been a geographical redistribution of the population from Scotland and the northern regions of England to the South East, East Anglia, the South West and the East Midlands. Another feature has been an increase in the rate of retirement migration, the main recipient areas (where in some towns the elderly can form over one-third of the population) being the south coast of England and East Anglia.

Table 1.2: Size and Population of the Main Urban Areas, Mid-1989

	Area		Population
	sq km	sq miles	(thousands)
Greater London	1,580	609·7	6,756·4
Birmingham	264	102·0	992·5
Leeds	562	217·0	711·7
Glasgow	198	76·3	695·6
Sheffield	368	141·9	526·6
Bradford	370	142·9	467·7
Liverpool	113	43·6	465·9
Manchester	116	44·9	443·6
Edinburgh	261	100·6	433·2
Bristol	110	42·3	372·6
Coventry	97	37·3	304·1
Belfast	140	54·0	295·6
Cardiff	120	46·3	284·9

Migration

From 1983 to 1987 the earlier trend of net population loss from Britain due to migration had reversed, but in 1988 there was again a net loss of 21,000. Between 1984 and 1988 some 998,000 people left Britain to live abroad and about 1·1 million came from overseas to live in Britain, so that net immigration increased the population by about 114,000.[1] Of the 237,000 departing residents in 1988, 26 per cent left for Australia, Canada or New Zealand, 15 per cent for other Commonwealth countries, 25 per cent for other European Community countries, 13 per cent for the United States and 6 per cent for the Middle East. Of the 216,000 new residents, 17 per cent came from Australia, Canada or New Zealand, 19 per cent from other Commonwealth countries, 24 per cent from other European Community countries, 11 per cent from the United States and 8 per cent from the Middle East. The number of migrants from the European Community countries more than doubled between 1974–78 and 1984–88, while those going to these countries increased by only 50 per cent. There was also a 50 per cent increase both in the number of residents from the United States moving to Britain and in those moving from Britain to the United States over the same period. In 1988 about 41 per cent of those coming into Britain, and about 60 per cent of those going abroad, were British citizens.

Nationality

Nationality legislation is embodied in the British Nationality Act 1981, which came into force on 1 January 1983. Under this Act, citizenship of the United Kingdom and Colonies was replaced by three citizenships: British citizenship for people closely connected with Britain, the Channel Islands, and the Isle of Man; British Dependent Territories citizenship for people connected with the dependencies; and British Overseas citizenship for those citizens of the United Kingdom and Colonies who did not acquire either of the other citizenships. Almost all citizens of the United Kingdom and Colonies who had the right of abode in Britain when the Act came into force acquired British citizenship.

---

[1] International migration statistics used here exclude movements to and from the Irish Republic.

British citizenship is acquired automatically at birth by a child born in Britain if his or her father or mother is a British citizen or is settled in Britain. A child adopted in Britain by a British citizen is a British citizen. A child born abroad to a British citizen born, adopted, naturalised or registered in Britain is a British citizen by descent. The Act safeguards the citizenship of a child born abroad to a British citizen in Crown service, certain related services, or in service under a European Community institution.

British citizenship may also be acquired by registration of certain children born in Britain who do not automatically acquire such citizenship at birth or who have been born abroad to a parent who is a citizen by descent; by British Dependent Territories citizens, British Overseas citizens, British subjects under the Act (three very limited categories) and British protected persons after five years' residence in Britain (except for people from Gibraltar, who may be registered without residence); and by naturalisation for Commonwealth citizens, citizens of the Irish Republic, and foreign nationals. The British Nationality (Falkland Islands) Act 1983 conferred British citizenship (with effect from 1 January 1983) on those Falkland Islanders who did not acquire it under the 1981 Act. For naturalisation, which is at the Home Secretary's discretion, five years' residence, good character and sufficient knowledge of English, Welsh or Scottish Gaelic are required, except for the spouse of a British citizen, who needs only three years' residence and no language qualification.

Special arrangements covering the status of British Dependent Territories citizens connected with Hong Kong when the territory returns to the People's Republic of China in 1997 are made by the Hong Kong (British Nationality) Order 1986. Under this, such citizens are entitled, before 1997, to acquire a status known as British National (Overseas) and to hold a passport in that status.

In 1988, 65,000 people acquired citizenship by naturalisation or registration in Britain.

Immigration

Immigration into Britain is controlled by the Immigration Act 1971 (as amended by the British Nationality Act 1981 and the Immigration Act 1988) and the Immigration Rules made in accordance with the Act. British citizens under the British Nationality Act 1981 and those Commonwealth citizens who had the right of abode before 1 January 1983 (when the 1981 Act came into force) have the right of abode and are not subject to immigration control. Those who do not have this right require permission to enter and remain in Britain, which is given in accordance with the Rules. These Rules, which are subject to the scrutiny of Parliament, set out the requirements to be met by those seeking entry, whether in a temporary capacity, for example, as students or visitors, or with the intention of taking employment or setting up in business or for settlement as the dependants of a person already settled in Britain. All nationals from certain countries require prior entry clearance before they can enter Britain. Other nationals subject to immigration control require entry clearance when coming to settle in Britain and in certain other circumstances. Visas and other entry clearances are normally obtained from the nearest British diplomatic post in a person's home country.

In accordance with Britain's obligations under the Treaty of Rome, European Community nationals do not require entry clearances, nor are they subject to restrictions on their freedom to take or seek work. Britain similarly respects its obligations under the United Nations Convention and Protocol relating to the Status of Refugees. These include granting refugees the right of access to courts and the right to work, to education, to public relief and to freedom of religion.

In 1989, 49,100 people were accepted for settlement, about the same as in 1988. A quarter of these were from the South Asian sub-continent. Wives and children accounted for nearly half the total acceptances.

THE ECONOMIC AND SOCIAL PATTERN

This section deals (to some extent in broad and informal terms) with social developments affecting many sections of the population.

The majority of people (some 97 per cent) live in private households (in families or on their own). The remainder include residents in hotels, servicemen and people in educational or other institutions. In 1987 just under four-fifths of people living in private households lived in a unit headed by a married couple.

Among many changes in household and family structure is the continuing fall in the average size of households in Great Britain from over four people in 1911 to 3·09 in 1961 and 2·48 in 1988. The fall reflects a greater proportion of people living on their own (11 per cent) or in one-parent families, the increasing number of elderly people (more of whom are living alone) and the preferences of parents for smaller families. The trend towards smaller households (26 per cent of households consist of one person) is expected to continue and the number of one-person households is forecast to increase substantially in the next few years.

Housing, Transport and the Environment

A growing proportion of households, over 64 per cent, own or are buying their own homes. Owner-occupation is higher among married couples than for single, divorced or widowed household heads. The number of owner-occupied dwellings rose from over 4 million in 1951 to over 15 million in 1989. Four British households out of five live in houses rather than flats.

Recent housing developments have been concentrated in suburban areas. Many families now live in houses grouped in small terraces, or semi-detached or detached, usually of two storeys with gardens, and providing two main ground-floor living rooms, a kitchen, from two to four bedrooms, a bathroom and one or two lavatories. In inner urban areas slum clearance and redevelopment were major features of post-1945 public housing programmes. While high-rise flats were popular in the 1960s and 1970s, the emphasis in new building is now on low-rise, high-density designs, often incorporating gardens or patios. Many older buildings are being restored and converted to provide modern homes, with the help of a variety of government schemes and measures.

Housing standards are continually improving; some 98 per cent of households in Great Britain have exclusive use of a bath or shower and a similar proportion sole use of an inside lavatory (high percentages by international standards), while 76 per cent have central heating.

An important influence on the planning of housing and services has been the growth of car ownership; in 1988, 66 per cent of households had the use of at least one car or van, including 18 per cent with the use of two or more. Greater access to motorised transport and the construction of a network of modern trunk roads and motorways have resulted in a considerable increase in personal mobility and changed leisure patterns. Most detached or semi-detached houses in new suburban estates have garages, and out-of-town shopping centres, often including large supermarkets and do-it-yourself stores, are usually planned with the motorist in mind.

The growth in car ownership has brought very great benefits but also a number of problems, notably, in many towns and cities, increased congestion, noise and air pollution arising from motor vehicle emissions. Cars, taxis and motor cycles accounted for more than four-fifths of all passenger transport in Great Britain in 1988, compared with about half in

1961. Many public transport services have been reduced or withdrawn, especially in rural areas. However, greater competition in express coach services has resulted in more long-distance and commuter coach services, while local bus services have been deregulated, the main effect being the introduction of minibuses in many areas. Since 1986 the amount of lead measured in the air has fallen by half, following a reduction in the maximum permitted lead content in petrol in Britain. Unleaded petrol is now widely available and increasingly used by motorists, due partly to the lower level of excise duty on unleaded petrol.

Over the past 30 years there has been a steady reduction of the main atmospheric and freshwater pollutants that were of concern in the past, producing dramatic improvements in, for example, the quality of the air in cities and the condition of major rivers. Various forms of pollution from traffic and industrial processes remain a problem in some areas, however. A phased programme to reduce further sulphur dioxide and nitrogen oxide emissions from large combustion plants is being introduced, and Britain is taking action to protect and enhance the quality of the North Sea by reducing inputs of dangerous substances into rivers, estuaries and coastal waters, and ceasing the dumping of industrial waste. The Government is playing a full part in efforts by the international community to protect the global environment. In September 1990 it set out its environmental strategy for the future in a White Paper entitled *This Common Inheritance*.

There is a high degree of concern for the environment, as shown by the growth in the number of organisations (especially voluntary societies) concerned with conservation. Voluntary membership of environmental organisations has risen sharply. Between 1971 and 1990, for example, membership of the Royal Society for the Protection of Birds rose from 98,000 to 656,000, and that of the National Trust from 278,000 to over 1·8 million.

Living Standards

Marked improvements in the standard of living have taken place during the twentieth century. According to a United Nations report on human development published in 1990, Britain ranked tenth out of 130 nations on an index based on social indicators such as life span, literacy and basic purchasing power of people rather than on national wealth alone. Britain has also performed well economically. Although gross domestic product (GDP) per head fell in the early 1980s, Britain then experienced an economic recovery and had eight successive years of sustained growth at an annual average rate of over 3 per cent. Growth since 1980 has been among the highest in the European Community. The rate of growth slowed in 1989, to about 2 per cent, but was still spread through most sectors of the economy.

Long-term trends in the pattern of expenditure show a substantial rise in expenditure on housing, televisions, video recorders, telephones, electrical and some other durable goods, motor vehicles and a range of services. The diagram on p 28 shows the growth in availability of some key durables. Some 39 per cent of households in Great Britain have a microwave oven.

The general level of nutrition remains high. Over the last 25 years there have been substantial rises in the consumption of poultry, instant coffee and processed vegetables and fruit, while home consumption per person of mutton and lamb, beef and veal, bread, potatoes, eggs, milk, butter, sugar, tea and some other foods has fallen. However, another feature has been an increase in the number of meals eaten away from home, either at work or in restaurants, and a growth in the consumption of food from 'take-away' and 'fast-food' shops. In addition, the proportion of convenience foods eaten has

Availability of Certain Durable Goods

Per cent of households with goods

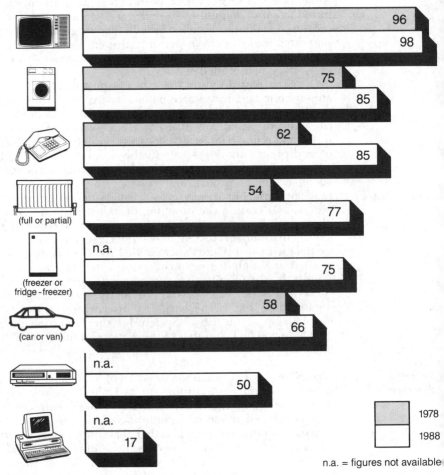

(full or partial)

(freezer or fridge - freezer)

(car or van)

96
98
75
85
62
85
54
77
n.a.
75
58
66
n.a.
50
n.a.
17

1978
1988

n.a. = figures not available

Source: *Family Expenditure Survey*

grown as women increasingly work outside the home and have less time to prepare meals, and as the variety of prepared foods and 'cook-chill' meals has risen in line with the growth in ownership of refrigerators and freezers. There is some evidence of consumption of food being influenced by health factors; for example, people are drinking more skimmed milk at the expense of whole milk and eating more wholemeal instead of white bread. Between 1961 and 1987 the consumption of brown and wholemeal bread increased over 2·5 times and the consumption of butter fell by two-thirds during the same period. The Government is encouraging the widest availability of wholesome food, while giving high priority to consumer safety.

The Food Safety Act 1990 replaces the existing food legislation in England and Wales and in Scotland with a single statute covering all of Great Britain. This will strengthen the enforcement of existing law, give powers for immediate closure of food premises when the public health is at risk, extend controls throughout the food chain, enable detailed legislation to be introduced to keep pace with new technology and increase the penalties for food safety offences.

There was little change in alcohol consumption between 1978 and 1987. Beer, with lager (now estimated to account for over half of beer sales), remains much the most popular alcoholic drink. A high proportion of beer is drunk in public houses ('pubs'), which are a traditional social centre for many people, and in clubs. Following the relaxation of restrictions on opening hours of public houses under the Licensing Act 1988, there are signs that they are becoming more popular with families: more meals are being served and the consumption of non-alcoholic drinks is increasing. Consumption of light (table) wine has increased considerably in recent years, although there has been little change in the consumption of higher strength wines such as sherry and port. The pattern of spirits consumption has also been changing, with a decline in the consumption of whisky and gin, and higher consumption of some other spirits. Partly to discourage drinking and driving, sales of non-alcoholic and low-alcohol drinks are being increasingly promoted, helped by a favourable excise duty structure.

Employment has been increasing since 1983, representing the longest period of continuous employment growth for nearly 30 years. However, the pattern of employment has altered considerably, with a long-term increase in the numbers employed in service industries. Another feature has been an increase in the number of self-employed, now accounting for 11 per cent of the workforce. The educational standards of adults have risen, with 12 per cent of men and 9 per cent of women aged 25–29 in Great Britain holding a degree or equivalent qualification in 1988, compared with 9 per cent and 3 per cent respectively of those aged 50–59. The average size of classes has fallen in recent years, both in primary and secondary schools.

Earnings from employment are the main source of income for most people; in 1988 wages and salaries accounted for 62 per cent of household income. The distribution of pre-tax income has remained relatively stable over a long period, the lower 50 per cent of income earners accounting for some 22 to 24 per cent of pre-tax income since 1949. The combined effect of the tax system and the receipt of benefits is to redistribute incomes on a more equal basis.

Wealth is less evenly distributed, with the richest 1 per cent of the population aged 18 or over owning 18 per cent of marketable wealth in 1987, and the richest 10 per cent having 50 per cent. The inclusion of 'non-marketable' rights in occupational and state pension schemes reduces these shares substantially, to 11 and 35 per cent respectively. Since the mid-1970s there has been little change in the distribution of marketable wealth or in that of marketable wealth plus occupational and state pension rights. The proportion of net wealth held in shares declined up to 1984, but has since increased somewhat. The Government's privatisation programme has had a major effect on the pattern of share ownership, with 24 per cent of the adult population in Great Britain owning shares, as against 7 per cent in 1979.

Women Considerable changes have occurred in the twentieth century in the economic and domestic lives of women, due, in part, to the removal of almost all sex discrimination in political and legal rights. At the heart of women's changed role has been the rise in the number of women, particularly married women, at work. With later marriages and the availability of effective methods of contraception there has been a decline in family size. Women as a result are involved in child-bearing for a shorter time and this, together with a variety of other factors which have made housework less burdensome, has made it possible even for women with young children to combine raising a family with employment. The growth of part-time work, job-sharing and flexible working hours, as well as training and retraining schemes, allows women to take advantage of more employment opportunities.

Women comprise about two-fifths of the workforce and the proportion of married women who work outside the home has grown to over one-half of those between the ages of 16 and 60. Married women are most likely to be in full-time employment if they are aged 16 to 29 with no children. By the mid-1990s the numbers of young people entering the workforce will have declined substantially and it is expected that the shortfall will be met to a considerable extent by recruiting more married women. There is still a significant difference between women's and men's earnings but the equal pay legislation which came into force at the end of 1975 has narrowed the gap. Women's average hourly earnings, exclusive of overtime (for full-time employees), increased from just over a half of those of men in 1970, to about three-quarters in 1989. Women's wages remain relatively low partly because women tend to work in lowly paid sectors of the economy, and because they work fewer hours than men. A major reform in the taxation of women came into effect in April 1990; since that date, their earnings have been taxed separately rather than being treated as part of their husbands' income for tax purposes.

Equal
Opportunities

The Sex Discrimination Acts 1975 and 1986 make discrimination between men and women unlawful in employment, education, training and the provision of housing, goods, facilities and services. Discriminatory advertisements which breach the Act are also unlawful. In most cases, complaints of discrimination are dealt with by industrial tribunals since they concern employment; others may be taken before county courts in England and Wales or the sheriff court in Scotland. Under the Equal Pay Act 1970, as amended in 1984, women in Great Britain are entitled to equal pay with men when doing work that is the same or broadly similar, or work which is of equal value. There is similar legislation on sex discrimination and equal pay in Northern Ireland.

The Equal Opportunities Commission, set up in 1975 (1976 in Northern Ireland under separate legislation), has powers to enforce the Sex Discrimination Acts and the Equal Pay Act. Its statutory duties are to work towards eliminating discrimination and to promote equality of opportunity. The Commission advises people of their rights under the Acts and may give financial or other assistance to help individuals to conduct a case before a court or tribunal. It also has power to conduct investigations and to issue notices requiring discriminatory practices to stop. In addition, it keeps legislation under review and may submit proposals for amending it to the ministers concerned.

Ethnic and
National
Minorities

For centuries people have been coming from many parts of the world to settle in Britain. Some came to avoid political or religious persecution, others to find a better way of life or an escape from poverty.

The Irish have long made homes in Britain. Many Jewish refugees started a new life in Britain towards the end of the nineteenth century and in the 1930s, and after 1945 large numbers of other European refugees settled in Britain. The large communities from the West Indies and the South Asian sub-continent date principally from the 1950s and 1960s. There are also sizeable groups from the United States and Canada, as well as Australians,

Chinese and various European communities such as Greek and Turkish Cypriots, Italians and Spaniards. More recently people from Latin America, Indo-China and Sri Lanka have sought refuge in Britain.

In 1986–88, according to the results of a sample survey, the non-white population of Great Britain numbered about 2·6 million (some 4·7 per cent of the total population), of whom about 45 per cent were born in Britain. Just over one-half of the ethnic minority population is of Indian, Pakistani or Bangladeshi origin; about one-fifth is of West Indian ethnic origin; and one in nine is of mixed ethnic origin. The proportion of men of working age in Great Britain who were economically active was higher among the white population and the West Indian/Guyanese group than among those from other ethnic groups. Among women the variation was greater: 73 per cent of those from the West Indian/Guyanese ethnic group were economically active, compared with 69 per cent in the white group, 57 per cent in the Indian group and 20 per cent in the Pakistani/Bangladeshi group (due, among other factors, to the larger proportion of children among this group).

Although members of the non-white population are concentrated in the inner cities, where there are problems of deprivation and racial discrimination, progress has undoubtedly been made over the last 20 years in several areas of life. Many individuals have achieved distinction in their careers and in public life, and the proportion of ethnic minority workers in professional and managerial jobs has increased. There are at present three black Members of Parliament and one Asian Member of Parliament and the number of ethnic minority councillors in local government is growing. Increasingly, black and Asian people are achieving distinction in law, medicine and teaching, while black sportsmen and women play a prominent role in athletics, boxing, football and cricket, and black performers have made a considerable impact in pop music and jazz. The growth of commercial enterprise has been significant, particularly among Asians, and there are numerous examples of self-help in ethnic minority communities.

The principal means of combating disadvantage is through the economic, environmental, educational and health programmes of central government and local authorities, as well as through special programmes which channel extra resources into projects to benefit ethnic minorities specifically. The latter provide, for example, specialist teachers for those groups of children who need English language tuition, business support services and measures to revive local economies and improve the environment in inner city areas. Cultural and recreational schemes are funded, including community and social centres for different ethnic minorities, and the health and personal social services make special provision for certain groups. In 1989 the Government announced plans to increase support for the local enterprise agencies established in 1985 to encourage the growth of black businesses in inner city areas. It also intends to enlarge and redirect its practical help to increase equal opportunities for members of ethnic minority groups through training; this would include, among other measures, greater provision for unemployed people who need training in English as a second language.

The welfare of ethnic minorities and good relations between minorities and the local community are promoted by race equality councils and other voluntary bodies. In recognition of the tensions that can arise between the police and ethnic minorities, consultation between the police and the community has been made a statutory requirement, liaison work is undertaken in schools and police training in race relations has received particular attention. Campaigns are run by the police to encourage the recruitment of officers from the ethnic minority communities and racially discriminatory behaviour by officers has been made an offence under the police discipline code.

Race Relations Act

Policies for promoting equality of opportunity in a multiracial society in which all citizens receive equal respect are pursued against a background of legislation against discrimination. The Race Relations Act 1976 makes discrimination unlawful on grounds of colour, race, nationality or ethnic or national origin in the provision of goods, facilities and services, in employment, training and related matters, in education, in housing and in advertising. It strengthened legislation passed in 1968 which, in turn, widened the scope of the first race relations legislation, enacted in 1965. It also strengthened the criminal law on incitement to racial hatred, which was further reinforced by the Public Order Act 1986.

The 1976 Act brought the law against racial discrimination into line with that against sex discrimination and gave complainants direct access to civil courts and, in the case of employment complaints, to industrial tribunals.

Commission for Racial Equality

The Commission for Racial Equality was established by the Race Relations Act 1976. It has power to investigate unlawful discriminatory practices and to issue non-discrimination notices, requiring such practices to cease. It has an important educational role and has issued codes of practice in employment and education and, in 1989, a draft code of practice on rented housing. It is also the principal source of advice for the general public about the Race Relations Act and has discretion to assist individuals with their complaints. In 1989 the Commission received over 1,300 requests for assistance and completed over 100 litigation cases. It can also undertake or fund research.

The Commission supports the work of over 80 race equality councils, which are autonomous voluntary bodies set up in most areas with a significant ethnic minority population to promote equality of opportunity and good relations at the local level. It makes grants towards the salaries of the race equality officers employed by the councils, most of whom also receive funds from their local authorities, and gives grants to ethnic minority self-help groups and to other projects run by or for the benefit of the minority communities.

Leisure Trends

Most people have considerably more free time, more ways in which to spend it and higher real incomes than previous generations. Agreed hours of full-time work are usually from 35 to 40 hours a week, although many people actually work somewhat longer because of voluntary overtime.

The most common leisure activities are home based, or social, such as visiting or entertaining relatives or friends. Television viewing is by far the most popular leisure pastime, and nearly all households have a television set, with 91 per cent in 1988 having a colour set. Some 51 per cent of households have two or more television sets and average viewing time for the population aged four and over is 25 hours a week. The proportion of households with a video recorder rose from 24 per cent in 1984 to 53 per cent in 1988. Moreover, the availability of new channels is spreading through cable and satellite television. Other popular pursuits include: listening to music, reading, do-it-yourself home improvements, gardening and going out for a meal or for a drink. About half the households in Britain have a pet, the most common being dogs and cats, of which there are thought to be roughly 7 million each in Britain.

Many people give up free time to work for voluntary organisations, of which there are over 250,000 in England and Wales. It is estimated that about one-quarter of the population is involved in some way in voluntary work in Britain, and there are now several major charitable fund-raising drives.

Sports and other pastimes have grown in popularity, reflected by increasing membership of the main organisations concerned with outdoor activities, although for some sports, such as greyhound racing, the number of spectators has been declining. Walking and swimming are the two most popular sporting activities, being almost equally undertaken by men and women. Snooker/billiards/pool and darts are the next most popular sports among men. Keep-fit, yoga, squash and cycling are among the sports where participation has been increasing in recent years.

Holidays

Holiday entitlements have increased for most employees. By the end of 1989, the average holiday entitlement among all employees was four weeks, although a significant proportion (22 per cent) have at least 24 days' leave. In 1989, 59 per cent of the adult population took at least one long holiday of four or more nights away from home. The number of long holidays taken by British residents was 52·5 million in 1989 (compared with 43·8 million in 1977), of which 31·5 million were taken in Britain. The most popular destinations for summer holidays are the West Country, Scotland and Wales. In addition, some 10 million shorter holidays were taken in Britain in 1989. British residents also took 21 million holidays overseas in 1989, of which 56 per cent involved 'package' arrangements. The most popular destinations were Spain, France and Greece, and 79 per cent of all holidays abroad in 1989 were taken in Europe. An increasing number of people take more than one holiday each year; the proportion of adults taking two or more holidays a year increased from 15 per cent in 1971 to 22 per cent in 1989.

2 Government

The British constitution, unlike that of most other countries, is not contained in any single document. Formed partly by statute, partly by common law and partly by convention, it can be altered by Act of Parliament, or by general agreement to create, vary or abolish a convention. The constitution thus adapts readily to changing political conditions and ideas.

The organs of government are clearly distinguishable, although their functions often intermingle and overlap. The legislature, Parliament, is the supreme authority. The executive consists of: (1) the Government—Cabinet and other ministers who are responsible for initiating and directing national policy; (2) government departments, which are responsible for national administration; (3) local authorities, which administer and manage many local services; and (4) public corporations responsible for operating particular nationalised industries or, for example, a social or cultural service, subject to ministerial control in varying degrees. The judiciary determines common law and interprets statutes, and is independent of both legislature and executive.

The Monarchy

The British people look to the Queen not only as their head of State, but also as the symbol of their nation's unity. The monarchy is the most ancient secular institution in Britain. During the last thousand years its continuity has only once been broken (by the establishment of a republic which lasted from 1649 to 1660) and, despite interruptions in the direct line of succession, the hereditary principle upon which it was founded has always been preserved. The royal title in Britain is: 'Elizabeth the Second, by the Grace of God of the United Kingdom of Great Britain and Northern Ireland and of Her other Realms and Territories Queen, Head of the Commonwealth, Defender of the Faith'. The form of the royal title is varied for those other member states of the Commonwealth of which the Queen is head of State,[1] to suit the particular circumstances of each. Other member states are republics or have their own monarchies.

The seat of the monarchy is in Great Britain. In the Channel Islands and the Isle of Man the Queen is represented by a Lieutenant-Governor. In the other member nations of the Commonwealth of which the Queen is head of State, her representative is the Governor-General, appointed by her on the

---

[1]The other Commonwealth countries of which the Queen is head of State are: Antigua and Barbuda, Australia, Bahamas, Barbados, Belize, Canada, Grenada, Jamaica, Mauritius, New Zealand, Papua New Guinea, Saint Christopher and Nevis, Saint Lucia, Saint Vincent and the Grenadines, Solomon Islands and Tuvalu.

The Royal Family

From the reign of Queen Victoria to August 1990

QUEEN VICTORIA 1819–1901
m. Prince Albert of Saxe-Coburg and Gotha (Prince Consort)

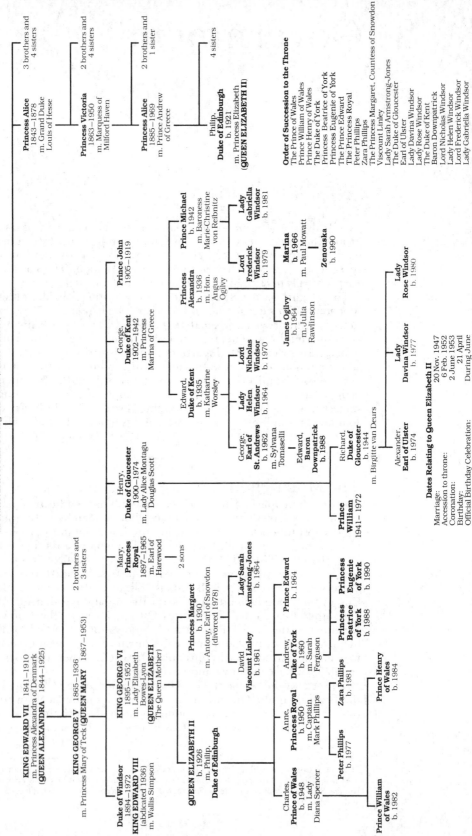

Order of Succession to the Throne
The Prince of Wales
Prince William of Wales
Prince Henry of Wales
The Duke of York
Princess Beatrice of York
Princess Eugenie of York
The Prince Edward
The Princess Royal
Peter Phillips
Zara Phillips
The Princess Margaret, Countess of Snowdon
Viscount Linley
Lady Sarah Armstrong-Jones
Earl of Ulster
The Duke of Gloucester
Lady Davina Windsor
Lady Rose Windsor
The Duke of Kent
Baron Downpatrick
Lord Nicholas Windsor
Lady Helen Windsor
Lord Frederick Windsor
Lord Gabriella Windsor

Dates Relating to Queen Elizabeth II

Marriage:	20 Nov. 1947
Accession to throne:	6 Feb. 1952
Coronation:	2 June 1953
Birthday:	21 April
Official Birthday Celebration:	During June

advice of the ministers of the country concerned and completely independent of the British Government.

In the British dependencies the Queen is usually represented by
governors, who are responsible to the British Government for the good
government of the countries concerned.

Succession,
Accession and
Coronation

The title to the Crown derives partly from statute and partly from common
law rules of descent. Lineal Protestant descendants of a granddaughter of
James I of England and VI of Scotland (Princess Sophia, the Electress of
Hanover) are alone eligible to succeed, and although succession is not bound
to continue in its present line, it can be altered only by common consent of
the Commonwealth nations, of which the Queen is Sovereign.

The sons of the Sovereign have precedence over the daughters in
succeeding to the throne. When a daughter succeeds, she becomes Queen
Regnant, and the powers of the Crown are vested in her as though she were
a king. While the consort of a king takes her husband's rank and style, the
constitution does not give any special rank or privileges to the husband of a
Queen Regnant, although in practice he fills an important role in the life of
the nation, as does the Duke of Edinburgh.

The Sovereign succeeds to the throne as soon as his or her predecessor dies
and there is no interregnum. He or she is at once proclaimed at an Accession
Council, to which all members of the Privy Council are summoned. The Lords
Spiritual and Temporal (see p 40), the Lord Mayor and Aldermen and other
leading citizens of the City of London are also invited.

The Sovereign's coronation follows the accession after a convenient
interval. It is a ceremony which has remained essentially the same for over a
thousand years, even if details have often been modified to conform to the
customs of the time. It takes place at Westminster Abbey in London in the
presence of representatives of the Houses of Parliament and of all the great
public interests of Britain, of the Prime Ministers and leading members of
the other Commonwealth nations, and of representatives of other countries.

Acts of
Government

The Queen personifies the State. In law, she is head of the executive, an
integral part of the legislature, head of the judiciary, the commander-in-
chief of all armed forces of the Crown and the 'supreme governor' of the
established Church of England. As a result of a long process of evolution,
during which the monarchy's absolute power has been progressively
reduced, the Queen acts on the advice of her ministers. Britain is governed
by Her Majesty's Government in the name of the Queen.

Within this framework, and in spite of a trend during the past hundred
years towards assigning powers directly to ministers, there are still important
acts of government which require the participation of the Queen. These
include summoning, proroguing (discontinuing until the next session
without dissolution) and dissolving Parliament; and giving Royal Assent to
Bills passed by Parliament. The Queen is also involved in appointing many
important office holders, including government ministers, judges, officers in
the armed forces, governors, diplomats, bishops and some other senior
clergy of the Church of England; conferring peerages, knighthoods and
other honours;[2] and remitting all or part of the penalty imposed on a person
convicted of a crime. An important function is appointing the Prime
Minister and by convention the Queen invites the leader of the political party

---

[2]Although most honours are conferred by the Queen on the advice of the Prime Minister, a few are
conferred on her personal selection—the Order of the Garter, the Order of the Thistle, the Order of
Merit and the Royal Victorian Order.

which commands a majority in the House of Commons to form a government. In international affairs the Queen, as head of State, has the power to declare war and make peace, to recognise foreign states and governments, to conclude treaties and to annex or cede territory.

With rare exceptions (as when appointing the Prime Minister), those acts involving the use of 'royal prerogative' powers are nowadays performed by government ministers who are responsible to Parliament and can be questioned about a particular policy. It is not necessary to have Parliament's authority to exercise these powers, although Parliament has the power to restrict or abolish a prerogative right.

Ministerial responsibility in no way detracts from the importance of the Queen's role in the smooth working of government. She holds meetings of the Privy Council, gives audiences to her ministers and other officials in Britain and overseas, receives accounts of Cabinet decisions, reads dispatches and signs numerous state papers. She must be informed and consulted on every aspect of national life, and she must show complete impartiality.

Such is the significance attached to these royal functions that provision has been made to appoint a regent to perform them should the Queen be totally incapacitated. The regent would be the Queen's eldest son, the Prince of Wales, then those in succession to the throne who are of age. In the event of the Queen's partial incapacity or absence abroad, there is provision to appoint Counsellors of State (the Duke of Edinburgh, the four adults next in line of succession, and the Queen Mother) to whom the Queen may delegate certain royal functions. However, Counsellors of State may not, for instance, dissolve Parliament (except on the Queen's express instructions), nor create peers.

Ceremonial and Royal Visits

Ceremonial has always been associated with British kings and queens, and, in spite of the change in the outlook of both the Sovereign and the people, many traditional customs and ceremonies are retained. Royal marriages and royal funerals are marked by public ceremony, and the Sovereign's birthday is officially celebrated in June by Trooping the Colour on Horse Guards Parade. State banquets take place when a foreign monarch or head of State visits Britain; investitures are held at Buckingham Palace and the Palace of Holyroodhouse in Scotland to bestow honours; and royal processions add significance to such occasions as a state opening of Parliament. Each year the Queen and other members of the royal family visit many parts of Britain. Their presence at scientific, artistic, industrial and charitable events of national and local importance attracts nationwide interest and publicity. The Queen pays state visits to foreign governments, accompanied by the Duke of Edinburgh. She also undertakes lengthy tours in the other countries of the Commonwealth. Other members of the royal family pay official visits overseas, occasionally representing the Queen, and often in connection with an organisation or a cause with which they are associated.

Royal Income and Expenditure

The expenditure incurred by the Queen in carrying out her public duties is financed from the Civil List and from public departments (which meet the cost of, for example, the royal yacht and the Queen's Flight). All such expenditure is approved by Parliament. About three-quarters of the Queen's Civil List provision is required to meet the cost of the staff who deal, among other things, with state papers and correspondence, the organisation of state occasions, visits and other public engagements undertaken by the Queen in Britain and overseas. The Queen's private expenditure as Sovereign is met from the Privy Purse, which is financed mainly from the revenue of the

Duchy of Lancaster;[3] her personal expenditure as a private individual is met from her own personal resources.

Under the Civil List Acts, other members of the royal family also receive parliamentary annual allowances to enable them to carry out their public duties. The Prince of Wales, however, receives no such allowance, since as Duke of Cornwall he is entitled to the net revenue of the estate of the Duchy of Cornwall. (He voluntarily surrenders a quarter of this revenue to the Exchequer.) The Queen pays into the Exchequer a sum equivalent to that provided by Parliament for certain members of the royal family. Civil List payments in 1990 amounted to £6·3 million. From January 1991 these payments will be fixed at £7·9 million a year for ten years.

Parliament

Parliament is the supreme legislative authority. Its three elements, the Queen, the House of Lords and the elected House of Commons, are outwardly separate and are constituted on different principles. They meet together only on occasions of symbolic significance such as the state opening of Parliament, when the Commons are summoned by the Queen to the House of Lords. When Parliament legislates, however, the agreement of each of its component parts is normally required.

Parliament can legislate for Britain as a whole, for any of the constituent parts of the country separately, or for any combination of them. It can also legislate for the Channel Islands and the Isle of Man, which are Crown dependencies and not part of Britain, having subordinate legislatures which make laws on island affairs.[4]

As there are no legal restraints imposed by a written constitution, Parliament is able to legislate as it pleases. It can make, abolish or change any law; and can destroy established conventions or turn a convention into law. It can also prolong its own life beyond the normal period without consulting the electorate.

In practice, however, Parliament does not assert its supremacy in this way. Its members bear in mind the common law and have tended to act in accordance with precedent and tradition. The validity of an Act of Parliament which has been duly passed, promulgated and published cannot be disputed in the law courts, but no Parliament would be likely to pass an Act which it knew would receive no public support. The House of Commons is directly responsible to the electorate, and in this century the House of Lords has recognised the priority of the elected chamber. The system of party government helps to ensure that Parliament legislates with its responsibility to the electorate in mind.

As a member of the European Community, Britain recognises the various types of Community legislation and wider policies, and sends 81 elected members to the European Parliament.

The Functions of Parliament   The main functions of Parliament are (1) to pass laws, (2) to provide, by voting taxation, the means of carrying on the work of government, (3) to

---

[3]The Duchy of Lancaster is an inheritance which, since 1399, has always been enjoyed by the reigning Sovereign; it is kept quite apart from his or her other possessions and is separately administered by the Chancellor of the Duchy.

[4]The legislatures of the Channel Islands (the States of Jersey and the States of Guernsey) and the Isle of Man (the Tynwald Court) consist of the Queen, the Privy Council and the local assemblies. It is the duty of the Home Secretary, as the Privy Council member primarily concerned with island affairs, to scrutinise each legislative measure before it is submitted to the Queen in Council.

scrutinise government policy and administration, including proposals for expenditure, and (4) to debate the major political issues of the day. In discharging these functions Parliament helps to bring the relevant facts and issues before the electorate. By custom, Parliament is also informed before the ratification of all important international treaties and agreements. The making of treaties is, however, a royal prerogative exercised on the advice of the Government and is not subject to parliamentary approval.

The Meeting of Parliament

A Parliament has a maximum duration of five years, but is often dissolved and a general election held before the end of this term. The maximum life has been prolonged by legislation in rare circumstances such as the two world wars. Dissolution and writs for a general election are ordered by the Queen on the advice of the Prime Minister.

The life of a Parliament is divided into sessions. Each usually lasts for one year—beginning and ending most often in October or November. It is interspersed with 'adjournments' at night, at weekends, at Christmas, Easter and the late (English) Spring Bank Holiday, and during a long summer recess starting in late July or early August. The average number of 'sitting' days in a session is about 170 in the House of Commons and about 160 in the House of Lords. At the start of each session the Queen's speech to Parliament outlines the Government's broad policies and proposed legislative programme. Each session is ended by prorogation. Parliament then 'stands prorogued' for about a week until the new session opens. Prorogation terminates nearly all parliamentary business: in particular, Bills which have not been enacted by the end of the session are lost.

The House of Lords

The House of Lords consists of the Lords Spiritual and the Lords Temporal. The Lords Spiritual are the Archbishops of Canterbury and York, the Bishops of London, Durham and Winchester, and the 21 next most senior diocesan bishops of the Church of England. The Lords Temporal consist of (1) all hereditary peers and peeresses of England, Scotland, Great Britain and the United Kingdom, (2) life peers created to assist the House in its judicial duties (Lords of Appeal or 'law lords'),[5] and (3) all other life peers. Hereditary peerages carry a right to sit in the House (subject to certain disqualifications), provided the holder establishes his or her claim and is aged 21 years or over. However, anyone succeeding to a peerage may, within 12 months of succession, disclaim that peerage for his or her lifetime. Disclaimants lose their right to sit in the House but gain the right to vote and to offer themselves as candidates at parliamentary elections.

Peerages, both hereditary and life, are conferred by the Sovereign on the advice of the Prime Minister. They are usually granted in recognition of service in politics or other walks of life or because one of the political parties wishes to have the recipient in the House of Lords. The House provides a place in Parliament for men and women whose advice is useful, but who do not wish to be involved in party politics.

In mid-1990 there were 1,189 members of the House of Lords, including the two archbishops and 24 bishops. The Lords Temporal consisted of 764 hereditary peers who had succeeded to their titles, 20 hereditary peers who have had their titles conferred on them (including the Prince of Wales), and 379 life peers, of whom 19 were 'law lords'. Of the total, 88 peers were not in

---

[5]The House of Lords is the final court of appeal for civil cases in Britain and for criminal cases in England, Wales and Northern Ireland.

receipt of a writ of summons and some 142 peers were on leave of absence from the House.[6] Irish peerages do not entitle their holders to membership of the House of Lords, but some peers of Ireland are entitled to sit in the House of Lords as holders of an English, Scottish, Great Britain or United Kingdom peerage.

Not all peers with a right to sit in the House of Lords attend the sittings. Peers who attend the House (the average daily attendance is some 320) receive no salary for their parliamentary work, but can recover expenses incurred in attending the House (for which there are maximum daily rates) and certain travelling expenses.

The House is presided over by the Lord Chancellor, who takes his place on the woolsack[7] as ex-officio Speaker of the House. In his absence his place may be taken by a deputy speaker, a deputy chairman or, if neither is present, by a speaker chosen by the Lords present. The first of the deputy speakers is the Chairman of Committees, who is appointed at the beginning of each session and takes the chair in all committees, unless the House decides otherwise. The Chairman and the Principal Deputy Chairman of Committees are Lords, but receive salaries as officers of the House.

The permanent officers of the House include the Clerk of the Parliaments, who is responsible for the records of proceedings and for the promulgation of Acts of Parliament. He is the accounting officer for money voted to the House, and is in charge of the administrative staff of the House, known as the Parliament Office. The Gentleman Usher of the Black Rod, who is also Serjeant-at-Arms in attendance upon the Lord Chancellor, is responsible for security, accommodation and services in the House of Lords' part of the Palace of Westminster. The Yeoman Usher is Deputy Serjeant-at-Arms and assists Black Rod in his duties.

The House of Commons

The House of Commons is elected by universal adult suffrage and consists of 650 Members of Parliament (MPs). At present there are 43 women, one Asian and three black MPs. Of the 650 seats, 523 are for England, 38 for Wales, 72 for Scotland, and 17 for Northern Ireland.

General elections are held after a Parliament has been dissolved and a new one summoned by the Queen. When an MP dies or resigns[8] or is given a peerage, a by-election takes place. Members are paid an annual salary of £26,701 (from January 1990) and an office costs allowance of up to £24,903. There are also a number of other allowances, including travel allowances, a supplement for London members and, for provincial members, subsistence allowances and allowances for second homes. (For ministers' salaries, see p 53.)

The chief officer of the House of Commons is the Speaker, elected by MPs to preside over the House. Other officers are the Chairman of Ways and Means and two deputy chairmen, who act as Deputy Speakers, elected by the House on the nomination of the Government but drawn from the Opposition as well as the government party. They, like the Speaker, neither

---

[6]Some hereditary peers do not establish their claim to succeed and so do not receive a writ of summons entitling them to sit in the House. Lords may apply for leave of absence for the duration, or for the remainder, of a Parliament.

[7]The woolsack is a seat in the form of a large cushion stuffed with wool from several Commonwealth countries; it is a tradition dating from the medieval period, when wool was the chief source of the country's wealth.

[8]An MP who wishes to resign from the House can only do so by using the technical device of applying for an office under the Crown (Crown Steward or Bailiff of the Chiltern Hundreds, or Steward of the Manor of Northstead), ancient offices which disqualify the holder from membership of the House but which carry no salary and have no responsibilities.

speak nor vote other than in their official capacity. Overall responsibility for the staffing, budget and administration of the House rests with the House of Commons Commission, a statutory body chaired by the Speaker.

Permanent officers (who are not MPs) include the Clerk of the House of Commons, who is the principal adviser to the Speaker on its privileges and procedures. His department has responsibilities relating to the conduct of the business of the House and its many committees. The Clerk is also accounting officer for the House. The Serjeant-at-Arms, who waits upon the Speaker, carries out certain orders of the House, is the official housekeeper of the Commons' part of the building, and is responsible for its security. Other officers serve the House in the Library, the Department of the Official Report (*Hansard*), the Administration Department and the Refreshment Department.

Parliamentary Electoral System

For electoral purposes Britain is divided into constituencies, each of which returns one member to the House of Commons. To ensure equitable representation four permanent Parliamentary Boundary Commissions, one each for England, Wales, Scotland and Northern Ireland, make periodic reviews of constituencies and recommend any adjustment of seats that may seem necessary in the light of population movements or other changes.

Elections are by secret ballot. British citizens, together with citizens of other Commonwealth countries and citizens of the Irish Republic resident in Britain, may vote provided they are aged 18 or over, registered in the annual register of electors for the constituency and not subject to any disqualification. People not entitled to vote include members of the House of Lords, patients detained under mental health legislation, sentenced prisoners and people convicted within the previous five years of corrupt or illegal election practices. Service voters (members of the armed forces and their spouses, Crown servants and staff of the British Council employed overseas, together with their wives or husbands if accompanying them) may be registered for an address in a constituency where they would live but for their service. The Representation of the People Act 1989 extended the right to vote for British citizens living abroad by increasing from 5 to 20 years the period during which they may apply to be registered to vote.

Each elector may cast one vote, normally in person at a polling station. Anyone who is entitled to an absent vote may vote by post or by proxy, but their postal ballot papers cannot be sent to addresses outside Britain. Service voters, overseas electors, electors who are physically incapacitated or unable to vote in person because of the nature of their work may vote by post (unless they are abroad at the time of the election) or by proxy for an indefinite period. Under the 1989 Act, any elector whose circumstances on polling day are such that he or she cannot reasonably be expected to vote in person at his or her allotted polling station—for example, an elector away on holiday—may apply for an absent vote.

Voting is not compulsory; 74·6 per cent of a total electorate of 43·6 million people voted in the general election in June 1987. The simple majority system of voting is used. A candidate is elected if he or she has a majority of votes over the next candidate (although not necessarily an absolute majority over all other candidates).

British citizens and citizens of other Commonwealth countries, together with citizens of the Irish Republic, may stand and be elected as MPs provided they are aged 21 or over and are not subject to any disqualification. Those disqualified include undischarged bankrupts; people sentenced to more than one year's imprisonment; clergy of the Church of England, Church of Scotland, Church of Ireland and Roman Catholic Church; peers; and holders of certain offices listed in the House of Commons Disqualification Act 1975. The latter include holders of judicial office, civil servants, some local government officers, members of the regular armed forces, or the police service, some members of public corporations and government commissions, and also British members of the legislature of any country or territory outside the Commonwealth. A candidate's nomination for election must be signed by two electors as proposer and seconder, and by eight other electors registered in the constituency. He or she does not require any party backing. A candidate must also deposit £500, which is forfeited if his or her votes do not exceed 5 per cent of those validly cast.

The maximum sum a candidate may spend on a general election campaign is £3,648 plus 3·1 pence for each elector in a borough constituency or 4·1 pence for each elector in a county constituency. A candidate may post an election address to each elector in the constituency, free of charge. All election expenses, apart from the candidate's personal expenses, are subject to the statutory limit. A review of candidates' election expenses is in progress.

The Political Party System

The party system, existing in one form or another since the eighteenth century, is an essential element in the working of the constitution.

The present system relies heavily upon the existence of organised political parties, each laying policies before the electorate for approval. The parties are not registered or formally recognised in law, but in practice most candidates in elections, and almost all winning candidates, belong to one of the main parties.

For the last 150 years a predominantly two-party system has operated, and since 1945 either the Conservative Party, which can trace its origins to the eighteenth century, or the Labour Party, which emerged in the last decade of the nineteenth century, has held power. A new party—the Social and Liberal Democrats (now known as the Liberal Democrats)—was formed in 1988 when members of the Liberal Party (which could trace its origins to the eighteenth century) merged with members of the Social Democratic Party, which was itself formed in 1981. Other parties include two nationalist parties, Plaid Cymru (founded in Wales in 1925) and the Scottish National Party (founded in 1934). In Northern Ireland there are a number of parties; the largest of those represented in the House of Commons is the Ulster Unionist Party, which was formed in the early part of this century, and the Democratic Unionist Party, founded in 1971 by a group which broke away from the Ulster Unionists.

Since 1945 seven general elections have been won by the Conservative Party and six by the Labour Party, and the great majority of members of the House of Commons have represented either one or other of these two parties. The percentages of votes cast for the main political parties in the last general election of June 1987 and the resulting distribution of seats in the House of Commons are given in Table 2.1.

The party which wins most seats (although not necessarily the most votes) at a general election, or which has the support of a majority of members in the House of Commons, usually forms the Government. By tradition, the leader of the majority party is asked by the Sovereign to form a government, and about 100 of its members in the House of Commons and the House of Lords receive ministerial appointments (including appointment to the Cabinet—see p 53) on the advice of the Prime Minister. The largest minority party becomes the official Opposition, with its own leader and 'shadow cabinet'.

Leaders of the Government and Opposition sit on the front benches of the Commons with their supporters (the backbenchers) sitting behind them.

Table 2.1: Percentages of Votes Cast, and Members Elected, in the 1987 General Election

Party	% of votes cast	Party	Members elected
Conservative	42·3	Conservative	375
Labour	30·8	Labour	229
Liberal–Social		Liberal	17
Democratic Alliance[a]	22·6	Social Democratic	5
Others	4·3	Scottish National	3
		Plaid Cymru	
		(Welsh Nationalist)	3
		Ulster Unionist	
		(Northern Ireland)	9
		Democratic Unionist	
		(Northern Ireland)	3
		Social Democratic and	
		Labour (Northern Ireland)	3
		Ulster Popular Unionist	
		(Northern Ireland)	1
		Sinn Fein (Northern Ireland)[b]	1
		Speaker[c]	1
		Total	650

[a] The former Liberal and Social Democratic Parties (see p 43) entered into an electoral alliance in 1981 and contested the general elections of 1983 and 1987 with a joint programme.
[b] The member of Sinn Fein (the political wing of the Provisional IRA) has not taken his seat.
[c] The Speaker's candidacy was as 'Mr Speaker seeking re-election'. (He was, before his election as Speaker, a Conservative MP.)

Note: On 1 September 1990 the state of the parties (excluding the Speaker and his three deputies) was as follows: Conservative 371, Labour 224, Liberal Democrats 19, Social Democratic 3, Scottish National 4, Plaid Cymru (Welsh Nationalist) 3, Ulster Unionist 9, Democratic Unionist 3, Social Democratic and Labour 3, Ulster Popular Unionist 1; Labour—Independent 1; Sinn Fein 1; there were 4 vacancies.

Similar arrangements for the parties also apply to the House of Lords; however, Lords who do not wish to be associated with any political party may sit on the 'cross-benches'. The effectiveness of the party system in Parliament rests largely on the relationship between the Government and the opposition parties. Depending on the relative voting strengths of the parties in the House of Commons, the Opposition might seek to overthrow the Government by securing its defeat on a 'matter of confidence'. In general, however, its aims are to contribute to the formulation of policy and legislation by constructive criticism; to oppose government proposals it considers objectionable; to secure concessions on government Bills; and to present its own policies in such a way as to enhance its chances of electoral success.

The detailed arrangements of government business are settled, under the direction of the Prime Minister and the Leaders of the two Houses, by the Government Chief Whips in consultation with the Opposition Chief Whips. The Chief Whips together constitute the 'usual channels' often referred to when the question of finding time for debating some particular issue is discussed. The Leaders of the two Houses are primarily responsible for the direction of business and for providing facilities for the Houses to debate matters about which they are concerned.

Outside Parliament, party control is exercised by the national and local organisations. Inside, it is exercised by the Chief Whips and their assistants (chosen within the party), whose duties include keeping members informed of forthcoming parliamentary business, maintaining the party's voting strength by ensuring members attend important debates, and conveying to the party leadership the opinions of backbench members. The importance a party attaches to a vote on a particular issue is indicated to the MPs by the underlining (once, twice or three times) on the notice sent to them each week by the Whips; failure to comply with a 'three-line whip' (the most important) is usually seen as rebellion against the party's policy. Party discipline tends to be less strong in the Lords than in the Commons, since Lords have less hope of high office and no need of party support in elections.

The Government Chief Whip in the Commons is Parliamentary Secretary to the Treasury. Of the other Government Whips, three are officers of the Royal Household (one of these is Deputy Chief Whip), five hold titular posts as Lords Commissioners of the Treasury and five are Assistant Whips. Salaries are also paid to the Opposition Chief Whips in both Houses and to two of the Opposition Assistant Whips in the Commons. The Government Whips in the Lords hold offices in the Royal Household and act as government spokesmen.

Annual assistance from public funds helps opposition parties carry out their parliamentary work at Westminster. It is limited to parties which had at least two members elected at the previous general election or one member elected and a minimum of 150,000 votes cast. The amount is £2,550 for every seat won, plus £5·10 for every 200 votes.

Parliamentary Procedure

Parliamentary procedure is based on custom and precedent. The system of debate is much the same in the two Houses: the subject starts off as a proposal or 'motion' by a member. When a motion has been moved, the Speaker proposes the question for debate. At the end of each debate the question may be agreed to without voting, or decided by a simple majority vote. The main difference between the two Houses is that the Speaker of the Lords has no authority to check debate or cut it short. Such matters are decided by the general feeling of the House. In the Commons the Speaker has full authority to enforce the rules and orders of the House. The Speaker of the Commons must guard against abuse of procedure or infringement of minority rights. The Speaker has discretion to allow or disallow a motion to end discussion so that a matter may be put to the vote. He has powers to put a stop to irrelevance and repetition in debate, and to save time in other ways. In cases of grave disorder the Speaker can adjourn or suspend the sitting. The Speaker may order members who have offended against the rules of behaviour of the House to leave or be suspended for a period of days.

The Speaker supervises voting in the Commons and announces the final result. In a tied vote the Speaker gives a casting vote, without expressing an opinion on the merits of the question. The voting procedure in the House of Lords is similar to that in the Commons, except that the Speaker or chairman has an ordinary vote.

The Commons has a public register of MPs' financial interests. Members with a financial interest in a matter before the House must declare it when taking part in a debate. To act as a disqualification from voting the interest must be direct, immediate and personal. In other proceedings of the House or in dealings with other members, ministers or civil servants, MPs must also disclose any relevant financial interest or benefit. There is no register of financial interests in the Lords, but Lords speaking in a debate in which they have a direct interest are expected to declare it.

Proceedings of both Houses are normally public. The minutes and speeches (*Hansard*) are published daily. The records of the Lords from 1497 and of the Commons from 1547, together with the parliamentary and political papers of certain past members of both Houses, are available to the public through the House of Lords Record Office. The proceedings of both Houses of Parliament may be broadcast on television and radio, either live or more usually in recorded or edited form.

Legislative Proceedings

The law undergoes constant reform in the courts as established principles are interpreted, clarified or reapplied to meet new circumstances. Substantial changes are the responsibility of Parliament and the Government through the normal legislative process.

A draft law takes the form of a parliamentary Bill. Most Bills are public Bills involving measures relating to public policy. Private Bills deal with matters of individual, corporate or local interest. Hybrid Bills are public Bills which may affect private rights. The passage of private Bills and hybrid Bills through Parliament is governed by a special procedure which allows those affected to make representations. Public Bills can be introduced, in either House, by a government minister or by an ordinary member. Most public Bills that become law are sponsored by the Government.

Before a government Bill is finally drafted, there is normally considerable consultation with professional bodies, voluntary organisations and other agencies interested in the subject matter. These include major interest and pressure groups which aim to promote a specific cause. Proposals for legislative changes are sometimes set out in government 'White Papers', which may be debated in Parliament before a Bill is introduced. From time to time consultative documents, sometimes called 'Green Papers', set out for public discussion government proposals which are still taking shape.

Bills must be passed by both Houses. As a rule government Bills likely to raise political controversy go through the Commons before being discussed in the Lords, while those of a technical but non-political nature often pass through the Lords first. A Bill with a mainly financial purpose is nearly always introduced in the Commons, and a Bill involving taxation must be based on resolutions agreed by that House, often after debate, before it can be introduced. If the main object of a Bill is to create a public charge, the Commons can proceed with it only if it is introduced by a minister or, if brought from the Lords, taken up by a minister. This arrangement gives the Government considerable control over financial legislation.

Private Members' Bills

At the beginning of each session private members of the Commons ballot for precedence in introducing a Bill on one of the Fridays specially allocated; the first 20 are successful. After the ballot a private member may also present a Bill after question time (see p 49), or seek to introduce a Bill under the 'ten minute rule', which allows two speeches, one in favour of and one against the measure, after which the House decides whether to allow the Bill to be brought in. Private members' Bills do not often proceed very far, but a few become law each session. If one secures a second reading, the Government usually introduces any necessary money resolution. Private members' Bills may be introduced in the House of Lords at any time, but the time that can be given to them in the Commons is limited.

Passage of Public Bills

The process of passing a public Bill is similar in both Houses. The Bill receives a formal first reading on introduction, is printed, and after a while (between one day and several weeks, depending on the nature of the Bill) it is given a second reading after a debate on its general principles and merits. In the Commons a non-controversial Bill may be referred to a second reading committee for its second reading debate. After a second reading in the Commons, a Bill is usually referred for detailed examination to a standing committee (see p 48). If the House so decides, the Bill may be referred to the

whole House sitting in committee. The committee stage is followed by the
report stage, during which further amendments may be considered. At the
third reading a Bill is reviewed in its final form and may again be debated.
The House may vote to limit the time devoted to examining a Bill by passing
a government timetable motion, commonly referred to as a 'guillotine'. After
the third reading a Commons Bill is sent to the Lords. After the second
reading in the Lords, a Bill is considered by a committee of the whole House
unless the House takes the rare decision to refer it to a Public Bill
Committee. It is then considered on report and read a third time; at all these
stages amendments may be made. A Bill which starts in the Lords and is
passed by that House is then sent to the Commons for all the stages there.
Amendments made by the second House generally must be agreed by the
first, or a compromise reached, before a Bill can become law.

Most government Bills introduced and passed in the Lords pass through
the Commons without difficulty. However, if a Lords Bill were unacceptable
to the Commons it would generally not become law. The Lords, on the other
hand, do not in general prevent a Bill insisted upon by the Commons from
finally becoming law, though they will often amend and return it for further
consideration by the Commons. In practice, the Lords pass Bills authorising
taxation or national expenditure without amendment. Under the Parliament
Acts 1911 and 1949, a Bill that deals only with taxation or expenditure must
become law within one month of being sent to the Lords, whether or not
they agree to it, unless the Commons directs otherwise. If no agreement is
reached between the two Houses on a non-financial Commons Bill the Lords
can delay the Bill for a period amounting (in practice) to at least 13 months.
At the end of this time the Bill may be submitted to the Queen for Royal
Assent, provided it has been passed a second time by the Commons. The
Parliament Acts make one important exception: a Bill to lengthen the life
of a Parliament would require the full assent of both Houses in the normal
way.

The limits to the power of the Lords, contained in the Parliament Acts, are
based on the belief that the principal legislative function of the non-elected
House nowadays is to act as a chamber of revision, complementing but not
rivalling the elected House.

When a Bill has passed through all its parliamentary stages, it is sent to the
Queen for Royal Assent, after which it is part of the law of the land and
known as an Act of Parliament. The Royal Assent has not been refused since
1707.

Private Bills

Private Bills are promoted by people or organisations outside Parliament
(often local authorities) to give them special powers not granted by the
general law. They go through substantially the same procedure as public
Bills, but most of the work is done in committee, where procedures follow a
semi-judicial pattern: the promoter must prove the need for the powers or
privileges sought and the objections of opposing interests are heard. Both
sides may be legally represented.

*Delegated
Legislation*

In order to relieve pressure on parliamentary time, much legislation gives
ministers and other authorities the power to regulate administrative details
by making 'delegated legislation'. To minimise the risk that powers thus
conferred on the executive might supersede or weaken parliamentary
government, they are normally delegated to authorities directly responsible
to Parliament. Moreover, the Acts of Parliament by which particular powers
are delegated often provide for some measure of parliamentary control over

legislation made in exercise of these powers, by reserving to Parliament the right to affirm or annul it. Certain Acts also require direct consultation with organisations affected before rules and orders can be made.

A joint committee of both Houses reports on the technical propriety of these 'statutory instruments'. In order to save time on the floor of the House, the Commons also uses standing committees to consider the merits of instruments, with any decisions reserved to the House.

Parliamentary Committees

Committees of the Whole House

Either House may resolve itself into a committee of the whole House to consider Bills in detail after their second reading. This permits unrestricted discussion, since the rule that a Member or Lord may speak only once on each issue does not apply in committee.

Standing Committees

House of Commons standing committees include those which examine public Bills at the committee stage and, in certain cases, at the second reading stage; two Scottish standing committees; and the Scottish and Welsh Grand Committees. Ordinary standing committees have no distinctive names, being referred to simply as Standing Committee A, B, C, and so on; and the membership is separately appointed to consider each specific Bill. Each committee has between 16 and 50 members, with a party balance reflecting as far as possible that in the House as a whole. The Scottish Grand Committee, which comprises all 72 Scottish members (and may be convened in Edinburgh), considers the principles of Scottish Bills referred to it at second reading stage, and Scottish estimates and other matters concerning Scotland only which may be referred to it. The Welsh Grand Committee, with all 38 Welsh members and up to five others, considers Bills referred to it at second reading stage, and matters concerning Wales only. There is also provision for a Northern Ireland committee to debate matters relating specifically to Northern Ireland. The Lords' equivalent to a standing committee, a Public Bill Committee, is rarely used.

Select Committees

Unlike standing committees, which proceed by way of formal debate, select committees are appointed, normally for the duration of a Parliament, to examine subjects by taking written and oral evidence. After private deliberation they present a report of their conclusions and recommendations. Select committees may be appointed to help Parliament with the control of the executive by examining aspects of public policy and administration. They also undertake responsibilities in connection with the internal operations and procedures of Parliament. In the former category come the 13 committees established by the House of Commons to examine the expenditure, administration and policy of the main government departments and related bodies. The Foreign Affairs Committee, for example, 'shadows' the work of the Foreign and Commonwealth Office. The committees are constituted on a party basis, in approximate proportion to party strength in the House.

Other regular Commons committees include those on European Legislation, Public Accounts, Members' Interests, the Parliamentary Commissioner for Administration, and House of Commons Services. The Committee of Selection and the Standing Orders Committee have duties relating to private Bills, and the Committee of Selection also chooses members to serve on standing and select committees. A Liaison Committee considers general matters relating to select committees. On rare occasions a parliamentary Bill is examined by a specially appointed select committee, a procedure additional to the usual legislative process: this occurs, for example, every few years for the Armed Forces Bill.

In their scrutiny of government policies, the committees question ministers, senior civil servants and interested bodies and individuals. Through hearings and published reports, they bring before Parliament and the public a body of fact and informed opinion on many important issues, and build up considerable expertise in their subjects of inquiry.

In the House of Lords, besides the Appeal and Appellate Committees, in which the bulk of the House's judicial work is transacted, there are two major select committees, with several sub-committees, on the European Communities and on Science and Technology. There are also select committees on House of Lords' Offices, Hybrid Instruments, Leave of Absence and Lords' Expenses, Personal Bills, Private Bill Standing Orders, Privileges, Procedure, Selection and Broadcasting.

Joint Committees Joint committees, with a membership drawn from both Houses, are appointed in each session to deal with Consolidation Bills and delegated legislation. The two Houses may also agree to set up joint select committees on other subjects.

Party Committees In addition to the official committees of the two Houses there are several unofficial party organisations or committees. The Conservative and Unionist Members' Committee (the 1922 Committee) consists of the backbench membership of the party in the House of Commons. When the Conservative Party is in office, ministers attend its meetings by invitation and not by right. When the party is in opposition, the whole membership of the party may attend meetings and the leader appoints a consultative committee, which acts as the party's 'shadow cabinet'.

The Parliamentary Labour Party is a corporate body comprising all members of the party in both Houses. When the Labour Party is in office a parliamentary committee, half of whose members are elected and half of whom are government representatives, acts as a channel of communication between the Government and its backbenchers in both Houses. When the party is in opposition the Parliamentary Labour Party is organised under the direction of an elected parliamentary committee, which acts as the 'shadow cabinet'.

Other Forms of Parliamentary Control The effectiveness of parliamentary control of the Government is a subject of continuing discussion, both inside and outside Parliament. In addition to the system of close scrutiny by select committees, the House of Commons offers a number of opportunities for a searching examination of government policy by both the Opposition and the Government's own backbenchers.

These include:

1. Question time, when for an hour on Monday, Tuesday, Wednesday and Thursday, ministers answer MPs' questions. The Prime Minister's question time takes place on Tuesday and Thursday. Parliamentary questions are one means of eliciting information about the Government's intentions. They are also a way of airing, and possibly securing redress of, grievances brought to MPs' notice by constituents. MPs may also put questions to ministers for written answers, which are published in *Hansard*, the official report.

2. The right of MPs to use motions for the adjournment of the House to open discussions on constituency cases or matters of public concern. There is a half-hour adjournment period at the end of the business of the day, while immediately before the adjournment for each recess (Christmas, Easter, spring and summer) a full day is spent discussing

matters raised by private members. Moreover, an MP wishing to discuss a 'specific and important matter that should have urgent consideration' may, at the end of question time, ask leave to move the adjournment of the House. If the Speaker accepts the terms of the motion, the MP asks the House for leave for the motion to be put forward. Leave can be given unanimously, or it can be given if 40 or more MPs support the motion or if fewer than 40 but more than ten support it and the House (on a vote) is in favour. Once leave has been given, the matter is debated for three hours, usually on the next day.

3. The 20 Opposition days each session, when the Opposition can choose subjects for debate. Of these days, 17 are at the disposal of the Leader of the Opposition and 3 at the disposal of the second largest opposition party.

4. Debates on the occasion of the passage, three times a year, of Consolidated Fund or Appropriation Bills, when members can exercise their traditional right of 'raising grievances' on matters for which any minister is responsible. This takes place after voting the necessary supplies (money) for the Government.

5. Debates on three days in each session on details of proposed government expenditure recommended for consideration by the Liaison Committee (see p 49).

Procedural opportunities for criticism of the Government also arise during the debate on the Queen's speech at the beginning of each session, during debates or motions of censure for which the Government gives up part of its own time, and during debates on the Government's legislative proposals.

Opportunities for criticism and examination of government policy are provided in the House of Lords at daily question time, during debates on general motions, in 'unstarred' questions (which can be debated) at the end of the day's business and during debates on specific legislative proposals.

The main responsibilities of Parliament, and more particularly of the House of Commons, in managing the revenue of the State and payments for the public service, are to authorise the taxes and duties to be levied and the various objects of expenditure and the sum to be spent on each. It also has to satisfy itself that the sums granted are spent only for the purposes which Parliament intended. No payment out of the central government's public funds can be made and no taxation, charges or loans authorised, except by Act of Parliament. However, interim payments can be made, within limits, from the Contingencies Fund. The Finance Act is the most important of the annual statutes which authorise the raising of revenue. The legislation is based on the Chancellor of the Exchequer's Budget statement, which is normally made annually in March or April and which includes a review of the public finances of the previous year, and proposals for meeting the estimated expenditure of the coming year. Scrutiny of public expenditure is carried out by House of Commons select committees (see p 48).

To keep the two Houses informed of European Community developments, and to enable them to scrutinise and debate Community policies and proposals, there is a select committee in each House (see p 48). Ministers also make regular statements about Community business.

Control is exercised finally by the ability of the House of Commons to force the Government to resign by passing a resolution of 'no confidence', or by rejecting a proposal for legislation which the Government considers so vital to its policy that it has made it a 'matter of confidence' or, finally, by refusing to vote the money required for the public service.

Parliamentary
Commissioner for
Administration

The Parliamentary Commissioner for Administration (the 'Parliamentary Ombudsman') investigates, independently, complaints of maladministration when asked to do so by MPs on behalf of members of the public. Powers of investigation extend to administrative actions by central government departments and certain executive and non-departmental bodies but not to policy decisions (which can be questioned in Parliament) nor to matters affecting relations with other countries. Complaints by British citizens arising from dealings with British diplomatic posts overseas are open to investigation in some circumstances. The Commissioner has access to departmental papers and reports the findings to the MP who presented the complaint. The Commissioner is required to report annually to Parliament. In addition, he or she publishes details of selected investigations at quarterly intervals and may submit other reports where necessary. A Commons select committee has responsibility for overseeing the Commissioner's work.

Parliamentary
Privilege

Each House of Parliament has certain rights and immunities to protect it from obstruction in carrying out its duties. The rights apply collectively to each House and individually to each member.

For the Commons the Speaker formally claims from the Queen 'their ancient and undoubted rights and privileges' at the beginning of each Parliament. These include freedom of speech; freedom from arrest in civil actions; exemption from serving on juries, or being compelled to attend court as witnesses; and the right of access to the Crown, which is a collective privilege of the House. Further privileges include the rights of the House to control its own proceedings (so that it is able, for instance, to exclude 'strangers'[9] if it wishes); to pronounce upon legal disqualifications for membership and to declare a seat vacant on such grounds; and to punish for breach of its privileges and for contempt.

The privileges of the House of Lords are broadly similar to those of the House of Commons.

The Privy Council

Until the eighteenth century, the Sovereign in Council, or Privy Council, was the chief source of executive power in the State. As the system of Cabinet government developed, however, the Privy Council became less prominent. Many powers were transferred to the Cabinet as an inner committee of the Council, and much of its work was handed over to newly created government departments, some of which were originally committees of the Privy Council.

Nowadays the main function of the Privy Council is to advise the Queen to approve Orders in Council (those made under prerogative powers, such as Orders approving the grant of royal charters of incorporation; and those made under statutory powers). Members of the Privy Council attending meetings at which Orders are made do not thereby become personally responsible for the policy upon which the Orders are based. This responsibility rests with the minister answerable for the subject matter of the Order in question, whether or not he or she was present at the meeting.

The Privy Council also advises the Crown on the issue of royal proclamations, some of the most important of which relate to prerogative acts (such as summoning or dissolving Parliament). The Council's own statutory responsibilities, which are independent of the powers of the Sovereign in Council, include powers of supervision over the registering bodies for the medical and allied professions.

---

[9] All those who are not members or officials of either House.

Apart from Cabinet ministers, who must be Privy Counsellors and are sworn in on first assuming office, membership of the Council (retained for life except for very occasional removals) is accorded by the Sovereign on the recommendation of the Prime Minister to eminent people in Britain and independent monarchical countries of the Commonwealth. There are about 400 Privy Counsellors. A full Council is summoned only on the death of the Sovereign or when the Sovereign announces his or her intention to marry.

Committees of the Privy Council

There are a number of advisory Privy Council committees, whose meetings differ from those of the Privy Council itself in that the Sovereign cannot constitutionally be present. These may be prerogative committees, such as those dealing with legislative matters submitted by the legislatures of the Channel Islands and the Isle of Man and with applications for charters of incorporation. They may also be provided for by statute, as are those for the universities of Oxford and Cambridge and the Scottish universities.

The Judicial Committee of the Privy Council is the final court of appeal for the courts of British dependencies, courts of independent members of the Commonwealth which have not discontinued the appeal, courts of the Channel Islands and the Isle of Man, and certain other courts, some professional and disciplinary committees and ecclesiastical sources.

Administrative work is carried out in the Privy Council Office under the Lord President of the Council, a Cabinet minister.

Her Majesty's Government

Her Majesty's Government is the body of ministers responsible for the administration of national affairs. The Prime Minister is appointed by the Queen, and all other ministers are appointed by the Queen on the recommendation of the Prime Minister. The majority of ministers are members of the Commons, although the Government is also fully represented by ministers in the Lords. The Lord Chancellor is always a member of the House of Lords.

Composition

The composition of governments can vary both in the number of ministers and in the titles of some offices. New ministerial offices may be created, others may be abolished, and functions may be transferred from one minister to another.

Prime Minister

The Prime Minister is also, by tradition, First Lord of the Treasury and Minister for the Civil Service. The head of the Government became known as the Prime Minister during the eighteenth century. The Prime Minister's unique position of authority derives from majority support in the House of Commons and from the power to choose ministers and to obtain their resignation or dismissal individually. By modern convention, the Prime Minister always sits in the House of Commons.

The Prime Minister informs the Queen at regular meetings of the general business of the Government, presides over the Cabinet, and is responsible for the allocation of functions among ministers.

The Prime Minister's other responsibilities include recommending to the Queen a number of appointments. These include: Church of England archbishops, bishops and deans and some 200 other clergy in Crown 'livings'; high judicial offices, such as the Lord Chief Justice; Privy Counsellors, Lord-Lieutenants and certain civil appointments, such as Lord High Commissioner to the General Assembly of the Church of Scotland, Poet Laureate, Constable of the Tower, and some university posts; and appointments to various public boards and institutions, such as the British Broadcasting Corporation (BBC), as well as various royal and statutory commissions. Recommendations are likewise made for the award of many civil honours and distinctions and of Civil List pensions (to people who have achieved eminence in science and the arts and are in some financial need). The Prime Minister also selects the trustees of certain national museums and institutions.

The Prime Minister's Office at 10 Downing Street (the official residence in central London) has a staff of civil servants who attend to the day-to-day discharge of the Prime Minister's numerous responsibilities. The Prime Minister may also appoint special advisers to the Office from time to time to assist in the formation of policies.

Departmental Ministers

Ministers in charge of government departments, who are usually in the Cabinet, are known as 'Secretary of State' or 'Minister', or may have a special title, as in the case of the Chancellor of the Exchequer.

Non-Departmental Ministers

The holders of various traditional offices, namely the Lord President of the Council, the Chancellor of the Duchy of Lancaster, the Lord Privy Seal, the Paymaster General and, from time to time, Ministers without Portfolio, may have few or no departmental duties and are thus available to perform any special duties the Prime Minister may wish to give them.

Lord Chancellor and Law Officers

The Lord Chancellor holds a special position, being a minister with departmental functions and also head of the judiciary. The four Law Officers of the Crown are: for England and Wales, the Attorney General and the Solicitor General; and for Scotland, the Lord Advocate and the Solicitor General for Scotland.

Ministers of State

Ministers of State usually work with ministers in charge of departments with responsibility for specific functions, and are sometimes given titles which reflect these particular functions. More than one may work in a department. A Minister of State may be given a seat in the Cabinet and be paid accordingly.

Junior Ministers

Junior ministers (generally Parliamentary Under-Secretaries of State or, where the senior minister is not a Secretary of State, simply Parliamentary Secretaries) share in parliamentary and departmental duties. They may also be given responsibility, directly under the departmental minister, for specific aspects of the department's work. The Parliamentary Secretary to the Treasury and other Lords Commissioners of the Treasury are in a different category as Government Whips (see p 45).

Ministerial Salaries

The salaries of ministers in the House of Commons range from £38,961 a year for junior ministers to £55,221 for Cabinet ministers. In the House of Lords salaries range from £33,241 for junior ministers to £44,591 for Cabinet ministers. The Prime Minister receives £66,851 and the Lord Chancellor £91,500.[10]

Ministers in the Commons, including the Prime Minister, receive a parliamentary salary of £20,101 a year (which is included in the above figures) in recognition of their constituency responsibilities and are entitled to claim the other allowances which are paid to all MPs (see p 41).[11]

---

[10] These figures show the salaries to which the holders are entitled; however, the Prime Minister has decided to draw no more than the salary payable to a Cabinet minister in the House of Commons.

[11] The Leader of the Opposition in the Commons receives a salary of £32,200 for the post, as well as the parliamentary salary of £20,101; the Leader of the Opposition in the Lords also receives a salary.

The Cabinet

The Cabinet is composed of about 20 ministers (the number can vary) chosen by the Prime Minister and may include departmental and non-departmental ministers.

The functions of the Cabinet are: the initiation and final determination of policies, the supreme control of government and the co-ordination of government departments. The exercise of these functions is vitally affected by the fact that the Cabinet is a group of party representatives, depending upon majority support in the House of Commons.

Cabinet Meetings

The Cabinet meets in private and its proceedings are confidential. Its members are bound by their oath as Privy Counsellors not to disclose information about its proceedings, although after Cabinet papers have been in existence for 30 years they may be made available for inspection in the Public Record Office at Kew, Surrey.

Normally the Cabinet meets for a few hours once or twice a week during parliamentary sittings, and rather less often when Parliament is not sitting. To keep the workload of the Cabinet within manageable limits, a great deal of work is carried on through the committee system, which involves the referring of issues either to a standing Cabinet committee or to an ad hoc committee composed of the ministers primarily concerned. The committee then considers the matter in detail and either disposes of it or reports upon it to the Cabinet with recommendations for action. The present Cabinet has four standing committees: a defence and overseas policy committee and an economic strategy committee, both chaired by the Prime Minister; and a home and social affairs committee and a legislation committee, both chaired by the Lord President of the Council. Sub-committees of the standing committees may be established. Membership and terms of reference of all Cabinet committees are confidential. Diaries published by several former ministers have given the public insight into Cabinet procedures in recent times.

Non-Cabinet ministers may be invited to attend meetings on matters affecting their departments, and may be members of Cabinet committees. Where appropriate, the Secretary of the Cabinet and other senior officials of the Cabinet Office also attend meetings of the Cabinet and its committees.

The Cabinet Office

The Cabinet Office, headed by the Secretary of the Cabinet, under the direction of the Prime Minister, comprises the Cabinet Secretariat, the Office of the Minister for the Civil Service and the Historical Section.

The Cabinet Secretariat serves ministers collectively in the conduct of Cabinet business and operates as an instrument in the co-ordination of policy at the highest level.

The Office of the Minister for the Civil Service is responsible for Civil Service central recruitment, senior and public appointments, policies on training, promotion and staff development, equal opportunities, occupational health and the non-financial aspects of personnel management.

The Historical Section of the Cabinet Office is in the process of completing the official histories of the second world war, and is responsible for preparing official histories of certain peacetime events.

Ministerial Responsibility

'Ministerial responsibility' refers both to the collective responsibility which ministers share for government policy and actions and to ministers' individual responsibility to Parliament for their departments' work.

The doctrine of collective responsibility means that the Cabinet acts unanimously even when Cabinet ministers do not all agree on a subject. The policy of departmental ministers must be consistent with the policy of the Government as a whole. Once the Government's policy on a matter has been decided, each minister is expected to support it or, if unable to, to resign. On rare occasions, ministers have been allowed free votes in Parliament on government policies involving important issues of principle.

The individual responsibility of a minister for the work of his or her department means that, as political head of that department, he or she is answerable for all its acts and omissions. He or she must bear the consequences of any defect of administration, any injustice to an individual or any aspect of policy which may be criticised in Parliament, whether personally responsible or not. Since most ministers are members of the House of Commons, they must answer questions and defend themselves against criticism in person. Departmental ministers in the House of Lords are represented in the Commons by someone qualified to speak on their behalf, usually a junior minister.

Departmental ministers normally decide all matters within their responsibility, although on important political matters they usually consult their colleagues collectively, either through the Cabinet or through a Cabinet committee. A decision by a departmental minister binds the Government as a whole.

The final responsibility of ministers is to Parliament. The knowledge that any departmental action may be reported to and examined in Parliament discourages the taking of arbitrary and ill-considered decisions.

On assuming office ministers must resign directorships in private and public companies, and must order their affairs so that there is no conflict between public duties and private interests.

Government Departments

Government departments are the main instruments for giving effect to government policy when Parliament has passed the necessary legislation, and for advising ministers. They may, and often do, work with and through local authorities, statutory boards, and government-sponsored organisations operating under various degrees of government control.

A change of government does not necessarily affect the number or general functions of government departments, although a radical change in policy may be accompanied by some organisational change.

The work of some departments (for instance, the Ministry of Defence) covers Britain as a whole. Other departments (such as the Department of Employment) cover England, Wales and Scotland, but not Northern Ireland. Others, such as the Department of the Environment, are mainly concerned with affairs in England. Some departments, such as the Department of Trade and Industry, maintain a regional organisation, and some which have direct contact with the public throughout the country (for example, the Department of Employment) also have local offices.

A department is usually headed by a minister. Certain departments in which questions of policy do not normally arise are headed by a permanent official, and a minister with other duties is responsible for them to Parliament. For instance, ministers in the Treasury are responsible for the Central Office of Information, Her Majesty's Stationery Office, HM Customs and Excise, the Inland Revenue and a number of other departments, including the Central Statistical Office, the Royal Mint, and the National Investment and Loans Office. Departments generally receive their funds directly out of money provided by Parliament and are staffed by members of the Civil Service.

Non-Departmental Public Bodies

A number of bodies with a role in the process of government are neither government departments nor part of a department (in April 1989 the figure was 1,555). Known as non-departmental public bodies, but often popularly described as 'quangos' ('quasi-autonomous non-governmental organisations', although there is no precise definition of the term), they are of three kinds: executive bodies, advisory bodies and tribunals.

Executive Bodies

Executive bodies normally employ staff and have their own budget. They consist of public bodies which carry out, among other duties, executive, administrative, regulatory or commercial functions. They operate typically within broad policy guidelines set by departmental ministers but are in varying degrees independent of government in carrying out their day-to-day responsibilities. Examples include the Arts Council of Great Britain, the British Council, the Commonwealth Development Corporation and the Commission for Racial Equality.

Tribunals

Tribunals are a specialised group of judicial bodies which are akin to courts of law. They are normally set up under statutory powers which also govern their constitution, functions and procedure. Tribunals often consist of laypeople, but they are generally chaired by someone who is legally qualified. They tend to be less expensive, and less formal, than courts of law. Independently of the executive, tribunals decide the rights and obligations of private citizens towards one another or towards a government department or other public authority. Important examples are industrial tribunals, rent tribunals and social security appeal tribunals. Tribunals usually consist of an uneven number of people so that a majority decision can be reached. Members are normally appointed by the minister concerned with the subject. Tribunals and advisory bodies do not normally employ staff or spend money themselves, but their expenses are paid by the government departments concerned.

Advisory Bodies

Many government departments are assisted by advisory councils or committees which undertake research and collect information, mainly to give ministers access to informed opinion before they come to a decision involving a legislative or executive act. In some cases a minister must consult a standing committee, but usually advisory bodies are appointed at the discretion of the minister.

The membership of the advisory councils and committees varies according to the nature of the work involved, and will usually include representatives of varying interests and professions.

In addition to the standing advisory bodies, there are committees set up by the Government to examine and make recommendations on specific matters. For certain important inquiries Royal Commissions, whose members are chosen for their wide experience and diverse knowledge, may be appointed. Royal Commissions examine written and oral evidence from government departments, interested organisations and individuals, and submit recommendations. The Government may accept the recommendations in whole or in part, or may decide to take no further action or to delay action. Inquiries may also be undertaken by departmental committees.

Government Information Services

Each of the main government departments has its own information division or directorate, public relations branch or news department. These are normally staffed by professional information officers responsible for communicating their department's policies and activities to the news media and the public (sometimes using publicity services provided by the Central Office of Information—see p 58) and for advising their departments on the public's reaction to them. As press adviser to the Prime Minister, the Prime Minister's Press Secretary and other staff in the Prime Minister's Press Office have direct and constant contact with the parliamentary press through regular meetings with the Lobby correspondents. The Lobby correspondents are a group of political correspondents who have the special privilege of access to the Lobby of the House of Commons where they can talk privately to government ministers and other members of the House. The Prime Minister's Press Office forms the accepted channel through which information about parliamentary business is conveyed to the media.

Distribution of Functions

An outline of the principal functions of the main government departments is given below. Departments are arranged in alphabetical order, except for the Scottish and Northern Ireland departments, which are grouped at the end of the section, and the Cabinet Office, described on p 54. Further information on the work of some departments is given in later chapters under the relevant subject headings.

DEPARTMENT	*Main areas of responsibility*
	The work of many of the departments listed on pp 57-60 covers Britain as a whole. Where this is not the case, the following abbreviations are used: (GB) for functions covering England, Wales and Scotland; (E, W & NI) for those covering England, Wales and Northern Ireland; (E & W) for those covering England and Wales; and (E) for those concerned with England only.
Ministry of Agriculture, Fisheries and Food	Policies for agriculture, horticulture, fisheries and food; responsibilities for related environmental and rural issues (E); food policies.
Office of Arts and Libraries	General promotion of arts (GB); library and information services (E with advice to W and NI); national museums (E); public libraries and local museums (E); British Library; national heritage.
Crown Prosecution Service	An independent department specialising in the prosecution of criminal offences; headed by the Director of Public Prosecutions, who is supervised by the Attorney General (E & W).
HM Customs and Excise	Collecting and accounting for revenues of Customs and Excise, including value added tax; agency functions including controlling certain imports and exports and compiling trade statistics.
Ministry of Defence	Defence policy and control and administration of the armed services.
Department of Education and Science	Policies for education (E); the Government's relations with universities (GB); fostering civil science in Britain and internationally.

DEPARTMENT	*Main areas of responsibility*
The Office of Electricity Regulation (OFFER)	Promotion of competition in the generation and supply of electricity; ensuring that all reasonable demands for electricity are satisfied; protection of consumer interests (GB).
Department of Employment	The Employment Service, employment policy and legislation; training policy and legislation; health and safety at work; industrial relations, wages councils, equal opportunities; small firms and tourism; statistics on labour and industrial matters (GB); the Careers Service (E); international representation on employment matters.
Department of Energy	Policies for all forms of energy, including its efficient use and the development of new sources; the Government's relations with the energy industries.
Department of the Environment	Policies for planning and regional development, local government, new towns, housing, construction, inner city matters, environmental protection, water, the countryside, sport and recreation, conservation, historic buildings and ancient monuments (E); and Property Services Agency (GB).
ECGD (Export Credits Guarantee Department)	Provision of insurance for exporters against the risk of not being paid for goods and services, and access to bank finance for exports; insurance cover for new investment overseas.
Foreign and Commonwealth Office	Conduct of Britain's overseas relations.
Office of Gas Supply	Monitoring of British Gas as the sole public gas supplier, ensuring compliance with its statutory obligations, and granting authorisations to other suppliers of gas through pipes; development of competition in the industrial market.
Department of Health	National Health Service, personal social services provided by local authorities, and certain aspects of public health, including hygiene (E).
Home Office	Administration of justice; criminal law; treatment of offenders, including probation; the prison service; the police; crime prevention; fire and civil defence services; licensing laws; scrutiny of local authority by-laws; control of firearms and dangerous drugs; electoral matters (E & W). Gaming and lotteries (GB). Regulation of broadcasting; passports, immigration and nationality; race relations and sex discrimination. Responsibilities relating to the Channel Islands and the Isle of Man.
Central Office of Information	An executive agency providing publicity material and other information services on behalf of government departments and a number of publicly funded organisations.
Board of Inland Revenue	Administration of direct taxes; collection of National Insurance contributions. Valuation of land and buildings (GB).

DEPARTMENT	Main areas of responsibility
The Law Officers' Departments	Provision of advice to the Government on English law and representation of the Crown in appropriate domestic and international cases, both civil and criminal, by the Law Officers of the Crown for England and Wales—the Attorney General and the Solicitor General (E & W). The Attorney General, who is also Attorney General for Northern Ireland, superintends the Treasury Solicitor's Department, the Crown Prosecution Service (E & W), the Serious Fraud Office (E, W & NI) and the Director of Public Prosecutions for Northern Ireland (NI).
The Lord Chancellor's Department	Administration of the Supreme Court (Court of Appeal, High Court, Crown Court) and the county courts (E & W), together with certain other courts and tribunals, and all work relating to judicial and quasi-judicial appointments. Responsibility for civil and criminal legal aid. Promotion of general reforms in the civil law. (The Home Office has important responsibilities for the criminal law.)
Ordnance Survey	Official surveying and mapping, including geodetic surveys and associated scientific work, and topographic surveys covering Great Britain and some overseas countries.
Overseas Development Administration	Administration of financial aid to, and technical co-operation in, developing countries.
Parliamentary Counsel	Drafting of government Bills (except those relating exclusively to Scotland); advising departments on parliamentary procedure (E, W & NI).
Paymaster General's Office	Provision of banking services for government departments other than the Boards of Inland Revenue and Customs and Excise, and the payment of public service pensions.
Office of Population Censuses and Surveys	Administration of the Marriage Acts and local registration of births, marriages and deaths; population estimates and projections; compilation of health statistics; censuses (E & W). Surveys for other government departments (GB).
HM Procurator General and Treasury Solicitor's Department	Provision of a common legal service for a large number of government departments. Duties include instructing Parliamentary Counsel on Bills and drafting subordinate legislation; providing litigation and conveyancing services; and giving general advice on the interpretation and application of the law (E & W).
Serious Fraud Office	Investigating and prosecuting serious or complex fraud under the supervision of the Attorney General (E, W & NI).
Department of Social Security	The social security system (GB). Three new executive agencies are to cover the main aspects of the Department's work: an Information Technology Services Agency; a Benefits Agency; and a Contributions Unit.
HMSO (Her Majesty's Stationery Office)	An executive agency providing stationery, printing and related services to Parliament, government departments and other public bodies; and publishing and selling government documents.

DEPARTMENT	Main areas of responsibility
Central Statistical Office	Preparing and interpreting key economic statistics needed for government policies; collecting and publishing business statistics; publishing annual statistical digests.
Office of Telecommunications (OFTEL)	Monitoring of British Telecom, Mercury, and other telecommunications operators; enforcing competition legislation and representing telecommunications users' interests.
Department of Trade and Industry	Industrial and commercial policy, promotion of enterprise and competition, information about new methods and opportunities, investor and consumer protection. Specific responsibilities include industrial innovation policy; regional industrial policy and inward investment promotion; management development and business/education links; international trade policy; commercial relations and export promotion; competition policy; company law; insolvency; radio regulation; patents and copyright protection (GB).
Department of Transport	Land, sea and air transport; sponsorship of the nationalised London Transport and British Rail; domestic and international civil aviation; international transport agreements; shipping and the ports industry; marine pollution; oversight of road transport (GB); motorways and trunk roads; road safety; and oversight of local authority transport (E).
HM Treasury	Broad economic strategy with particular responsibilities for public finance and expenditure, including control of staffing and pay in the Civil Service.
Office of Water Services	Monitoring the activities of companies appointed as water and sewerage undertakers (E & W).
Welsh Office	Many aspects of Welsh affairs, including health and personal social services; education, except for terms and conditions of service, student awards and the University of Wales; the Welsh language and culture; agriculture and fisheries; forestry; local government; housing; water and sewerage; environmental protection; sport; land use, including town and country planning; countryside and nature conservation; new towns, ancient monuments and historic buildings; roads; tourism; a range of matters affecting the careers service and the training activities of the Department of Employment in Wales; selective financial assistance to industry; the Urban Programme in Wales; the operation of the European Regional Development Fund in Wales and other European Community matters; non-departmental public bodies; civil emergencies; all financial aspects of these matters including Welsh revenue support grant; and oversight responsibilities for economic affairs and regional planning in Wales.
SCOTLAND	Scotland has its own system of law and wide administrative autonomy. The Secretary of State for Scotland, a Cabinet minister, has responsibility in Scotland (with some exceptions) for formulating and carrying out policy relating to agriculture and fisheries, education, law and order, environmental protection and conservation of the countryside, land-use planning, local government, housing, roads and certain aspects of transport services, social work and health.

The Secretary of State also has a major role in the planning and development of the Scottish economy, and important functions relating to industrial development, with responsibility for financial assistance to industry. He is also responsible for the Scottish Development Agency, the Highlands and Islands Development Board and new town development corporations, together with the training activities of the Department of Employment in Scotland[12] and for the Scottish Tourist Board and the careers service. The Secretary of State plays a full part in determining energy policy, particularly in relation to responsibility for the electricity supply industry in Scotland. He is also responsible for government interest in a range of other functions from fire services to sport and for overseeing many non-departmental public bodies.

The Secretary of State has overall responsibility for legal services in Scotland and is advised by the two Scottish Law Officers, the Lord Advocate and the Solicitor General for Scotland (see below).

The distinctive features and the different conditions and needs of Scotland and its people are reflected in separate Scottish legislation on many domestic matters or else in special provisions applying to Scotland alone, inserted in Acts which otherwise apply to Britain generally.

The Secretary of State discharges his responsibilities principally through the Scottish Office's five departments, supported by Central Services (see p 62) and through four smaller departments: the Department of the Registers of Scotland (now an executive agency), the Scottish Record Office, the General Register Office for Scotland and the Scottish Courts Administration.

British government departments with significant Scottish responsibilities have offices in Scotland with delegated powers and work closely with the Scottish Office. The British headquarters of several government departments are located in Scotland.

An outline of the main functions of the Scottish departments is given below.

DEPARTMENT	*Functions*
Department of Agriculture and Fisheries for Scotland	Promotion of the agricultural and fishing industries.
Scottish Development Department	Environment, including environmental protection and conservation of the countryside; land use planning; water supplies and sewerage; ancient monuments and historic buildings; general policy relating to local government; housing; building control; roads and certain transport functions.
Scottish Education Department	Education (excluding universities); student awards; libraries; museums and galleries; sport and recreation; the arts; social work services.

---

[12] From April 1991, the Scottish Development Agency will be reconstituted as Scottish Enterprise and the Highlands and Islands Development Board reconstituted as Highlands and Islands Enterprise.

DEPARTMENT	*Functions*
Scottish Home and Health Department	Central administration of law and order (including police service, criminal justice, legal aid and penal institutions); the National Health Service; fire, home defence and civil emergency services.
Industry Department for Scotland	Industrial and regional economic development matters; energy; tourism; urban regeneration; new towns.
Central Services	Services to the five Scottish departments. These include the Office of the Solicitor to the Secretary of State, the Scottish Information Office, Finance Divisions and Local Government Finance.
Lord Advocate's Department and Crown Office	Provision of legal advice to the Government on issues affecting Scotland and the principal representation of the Crown for litigation in Scotland by the Law Officers of the Crown for Scotland (the Lord Advocate and the Solicitor General for Scotland); control of all prosecution in Scotland.
Scottish Courts Administration	Organisation, administration and staffing of the Supreme and Sheriff courts and court offices; jurisdiction and procedure of civil courts; enforcement of judgments; and programme of Scottish Law Commission.
Other Administrative Departments	General Register Office for Scotland; Scottish Record Office; Department of the Registers of Scotland.

NORTHERN IRELAND

Between 1921 and 1972 Northern Ireland had its own Parliament and Government, subordinate to the Parliament at Westminster. However, in 1972, following the resignation of the Northern Ireland Government, the British Government assumed direct responsibility for its functions. Attempts have been made by successive governments to find a means of restoring devolved government to Northern Ireland on a basis that would command widespread acceptance throughout the community. The most recent attempt failed in June 1986, when the Northern Ireland Assembly, elected in 1982, was dissolved after it ceased to discharge its responsibility for making proposals for the resumption of devolved government and of monitoring the work of the Northern Ireland departments. The Government expressed the hope that a new Assembly would be established which would contribute to the better government and administration of Northern Ireland. To this end discussions have been continuing since late 1989 between the Government and the local constitutional political parties as a means of exploring the extent of the common ground which now appears to exist between them. This approach is viewed by the Government as a necessary prelude to discussions about arrangements for the transfer of powers and responsibilities to locally elected representatives in Northern Ireland.

The Secretary of State for Northern Ireland is the Cabinet minister responsible for Northern Ireland. Through the Northern Ireland Office he has direct responsibility for constitutional developments, law and order, security, and electoral matters. The work of the Northern Ireland departments, whose functions are listed below, is also subject to the direction and control of the Secretary of State.

DEPARTMENT	*Functions*
Department of Agriculture for Northern Ireland	Development of agricultural, forestry and fishing industries; administration of agricultural grant schemes; advisory service to farmers; agricultural research, education and training.
Department of Economic Development for Northern Ireland	Development of industry and commerce, as well as administration of government policy in relation to tourism, energy and minerals; administration of an employment service and labour training schemes and assistance to industrial development, through the Industrial Development Board for Northern Ireland.
Department of Education for Northern Ireland	Control of the five education and library boards and education as a whole, youth services, sport and recreation, cultural activities and community services and facilities, including the improvement of community relations.
Department of the Environment for Northern Ireland	Housing; planning; construction and maintenance of roads; transport and traffic management, and motor taxation; water and sewerage; environmental protection; ordnance survey; collection of rates; harbours; historic monuments and buildings; maintenance of public records; and certain controls over local government.
Department of Finance and Personnel	Control of public expenditure; liaison with HM Treasury and the Northern Ireland Office on financial matters, economic and social planning and research; Ulster Savings; charities; Valuation and Lands Service; policies for equal opportunities and personnel management; and general management and control of the Northern Ireland Civil Service.
Department of Health and Social Services for Northern Ireland	Health and personal social services; social security; social legislation; and the Office of the Registrar-General.

The Civil Service

The Civil Service is concerned with the conduct of the whole range of government activities as they affect the community, ranging from policy formulation to carrying out the day-to-day duties of public administration.

Civil servants are servants of the Crown. For all practical purposes the Crown in this context means and is represented by the Government of the day. There are special cases in which certain functions are conferred by law upon particular members or groups of members of the public service; but in general the executive powers of the Crown are exercised by and on the advice of Her Majesty's Ministers, who are in turn answerable to Parliament. The Civil Service as such has no constitutional responsibility separate from the duly constituted Government of the day. The duty of the individual civil servant is first and foremost to the Minister of the Crown who is in charge of the Department concerned. A change of minister, for whatever reason, does not involve a change of staff. Ministers sometimes appoint special advisers from outside the Civil Service. The advisers are normally paid from public funds, but their appointments come to an end when the Government's term of office finishes, or when the Minister to whom the special adviser is appointed leaves the Government or moves to another appointment.

The number of civil servants has fallen from 732,000 in April 1979 to 562,000 in April 1990, reflecting the Government's policy of controlling the cost and size of the Civil Service and of improving its efficiency. About half of all civil servants were engaged in the provision of public services, such as paying sickness benefits and pensions, collecting taxes and contributions, running employment services, staffing prisons, and providing services to industry and agriculture. Around a quarter were employed in the Ministry of Defence. The rest were divided between: central administrative and policy duties; support services, such as accommodation, printing and information; and largely financially self-supporting services, for instance, those provided by the Department for National Savings and the Royal Mint. The total includes about 67,000 'industrial' civil servants, mainly manual workers in government industrial establishments. Four-fifths of civil servants work outside London.

The Government is committed to achieving equality of opportunity for all its staff. In support of this commitment, the Civil Service is actively pursuing policies to increase employment and career opportunities for women, ethnic minorities and people with disabilities. The number of black and Asian people now employed in the Civil Service is proportionate to their representation in Britain's population as a whole.

Within the Civil Service, reforms of all aspects of the management of government departments are being implemented to ensure improved management performance, in particular through the greater accountability of individual managers based on clear objectives and responsibilities. These reforms include performance-related pay schemes, and other means to encourage and reward improved performance.

Executive Agencies: Next Steps Initiative

The Next Steps Initiative, launched in 1988, has been concerned with improving management in the Civil Service and the efficiency and quality of services provided to the public and to customers within government. This has involved setting up, to the greatest extent practicable, separate units or agencies to perform the executive functions of government. Agencies remain part of the Civil Service but under the terms of a framework document they enjoy greater delegation on financial, pay and personnel matters. Agencies are headed by chief executives who are personally responsible for the performance of the agency and for meeting the financial and quality of service targets which it is set. By July 1990 a total of more than 30 agencies had been set up covering around 70,000 staff. It is expected that this programme will have been applied to at least half the Civil Service by 1991.

Savings in public expenditure are also being sought by subjecting services in government departments to competitive tendering and by contracting out such services whenever commensurate with sound management and good value for money. By April 1989 savings of around £50 million net a year had been achieved.

Central Management and Structure

Responsibility for central co-ordination and management of the Civil Service is divided between the Treasury and the Cabinet Office (Office of the Minister for the Civil Service). In addition to its other functions, the Treasury is responsible for the structure of the Civil Service and the classification of posts. It is also responsible for recruitment policy and for controlling staffing, pay, pensions and allowances. The Office of the Minister for the Civil Service, which is part of the Cabinet Office and under the control of the Prime Minister, as Minister for the Civil Service, is responsible for the organisation, non-financial aspects of personnel management and overall efficiency of the Service. The function of official Head of the Home Civil Service is combined with that of Secretary to the Cabinet.

At the senior levels of the service, where management forms a major component of most jobs, there are service-wide common grading arrangements. These unified grades 1 to 7 are known as the Open Structure and cover grades from Permanent Secretary level to Principal level. Within the unified grades each post is filled by the person best equipped in terms of skills, ability and experience regardless of the occupational group to which he or she previously belonged.

Below this the structure of the non-industrial Civil Service is based on a system of occupational groups and classes, which are the basic groupings of staff for the purposes of personnel management. These include the Administration, Economist, Information Officer, Lawyer, Librarian, Professional and Technical (which includes architects, surveyors, and electrical and mechanical engineers), Secretarial, Science and Statistician Groups. These groups account for 66 per cent of non-industrial staff. Work requiring specialist skill is always done by qualified individuals.

Personnel management policies encourage the deployment of staff so that talent can be used to the best advantage, and higher posts are open to people of outstanding ability, whatever their specialist background or original method of entry into the Service. This ensures that people with the necessary qualities can gain suitably wide experience to fit them for posts at the highest levels. The exchange of staff between the Civil Service and industry is also encouraged.

The Diplomatic Service

The Diplomatic Service, a separate service of some 6,650 or so people, provides the majority of the staff for the Foreign and Commonwealth Office and at British diplomatic missions and consular posts abroad. Its functions include advising on policy, negotiating with overseas governments and conducting business in international organisations; promoting British exports and trade generally, administering aid, presenting British ideas, policies and objectives to the people of overseas countries; administering the remaining dependent territories; and protecting British interests abroad and British nationals overseas.

The Service has its own grade structure, linked for salary purposes with that of the Home Civil Service. Conditions of work are in many ways comparable, while taking into account the special demands of the Service, particularly of postings overseas. Members of the Home Civil Service and the armed forces, and individuals from the private sector, may also serve in the Foreign and Commonwealth Office and at overseas posts on loan or attachment.

Recruitment and Training

Recruitment of staff to the middle and higher levels of the Home Civil Service and the Diplomatic Service is the responsibility of the Civil Service Commission. In conjunction with departments, it ensures staff are selected solely on merit through fair and open competition. The selection of junior staff, such as those engaged in clerical and manual work, is made by the departments.

For the Administration Group, the central part of the Home and Diplomatic Civil Services, entry is at three levels relating broadly to the academic achievements of: a first or second class honours degree; GCE Advanced level; and GCSE grades A, B or C. The selection procedure for the highest of these levels (the Administration Trainee entry) comprises qualifying tests, followed by tests and interviews at the Civil Service Selection Board and an interview by the Final Selection Board. For the next level (the Executive Officer entry) selection involves a qualifying test followed by an interview. For the lower clerical level (the Administrative Officer/Assistant entry) selection is normally by interview of those holding the prescribed educational qualifications.

Entry to the Professional and Technology Group usually requires appropriate qualifications, and selection is by interview, taking account of past record. Graduates are offered a structured training programme leading to membership of the appropriate professional institution. Entry to the Science Group is at three levels: to the Scientific Officer level for graduates and those with Higher National Diplomas and Higher National Certificates; and to the Assistant Scientific Officer level for those with GCSEs or GCE Advanced level.

Many government departments and agencies employ training officers and tutors to help identify staff training needs and organise training by the most effective method (for example, formal courses or self-instruction). The Civil Service College provides a wide range of training courses in both management and specialist skills. Use is also made of external institutions.

Civil servants under the age of 18 may continue their general education by attending courses, usually for one day a week ('day release' schemes). All staff may be entitled to financial assistance to continue their education, though mainly in their own time. There are also opportunities for civil servants to obtain fellowships for research and study in areas of interest to themselves and to their departments and agencies.

Promotion and Terms of Service

Departments are responsible for promotion up to and including Grade 4. Normally promotion is from grade to grade, but there can be accelerated promotion for staff who show exceptional promise. Promotion or appointment to Grades 1 and 2 and all transfers between departments at these levels are approved by the Prime Minister, who is advised by the Head of the Home Civil Service. Promotions and appointments to Grade 3 are approved by the Cabinet Office.

Terms and conditions of employment for civil servants are generally subject to consultation between management and staff and their representatives.

Political and Private Activities

Civil servants are required to discharge loyally the duties assigned to them by the Government of the day of whatever political persuasion. It is essential that ministers and the public should have confidence that the personal views of civil servants do not influence the discharge of their official duties, given the role of the Civil Service in serving successive governments of different political complexions. The aim of the rules which govern political activities by civil servants is to allow them the greatest possible freedom to participate in public affairs consistent with their rights and duties as citizens without infringing these fundamental principles. The rules are therefore concerned with political activities liable to give public expression to political views rather than with privately held beliefs and opinions.

The Civil Service is divided into three groups for the purposes of deciding the extent to which individuals may take part in political activities. Those in the 'politically free' group, consisting of industrial staff and non-office grades, are free to engage in any political activity, including adoption as a candidate for the British or the European Parliament (although they would have to resign from the Service if elected). Those in the 'politically restricted' group, which comprises staff in Grade 7 and above as well as Administration Trainees, are debarred from national political activities but may apply for permission to take part in local political activities. The 'intermediate' group, which comprises all other civil servants, may apply for permission to take part in national or local political activity, apart from candidature for the British or the European Parliament.

Where required, permission is granted to the maximum extent consistent with the reputation of the Civil Service for political impartiality and the avoidance of any conflict with official duties. A code of discretion requires moderation and the avoidance of embarrassment to ministers.

Generally, there are no restrictions on the private activities of civil servants, provided that these do not bring discredit on the Civil Service, and that there is no possibility of conflict with official duties. For instance, a civil servant must comply with any departmental instruction on the need to seek authority before taking part in any outside activity which involves the use of official experience, or before accepting a directorship in any company holding a contract with his or her department.

Security

As a general rule the political views of civil servants are not a matter of official concern. However, no one whose loyalty is in doubt may be employed on work vital to the security of the State. For this reason certain posts are not open to those who are known to be members of communist or fascist organisations or of subversive groups, or associated with them in such a way as to raise legitimate doubts about their reliability, or to anyone whose reliability may be in doubt for any other reason.

Each department is responsible for its own internal security, advised as necessary by the Security Service. The Security Commission may investigate and report on breaches of security in the public service and advise on changes in security procedure, if requested to do so by the Prime Minister after consultation with the Leader of the Opposition.

Local Government

A wide range of public services is provided by democratically elected local authorities throughout Britain. The gradual expansion of local services, particularly in the period between the late 1940s and mid-1970s, led to a steady rise in local government expenditure and in its support from central funds. In recent years central government has sought to check this growth as part of a general policy of reducing public expenditure. A number of measures have been introduced, aimed at increasing the accountability of local government. These include the holding back of central government grant from authorities spending above government targets, and the establishment in England and Wales of the independent Audit Commission to audit accounts and ensure economical use of resources. The Government has legislated to promote greater competition in the provision of some local authority services. In Scotland there is an independent Commission for Local Authority Accounts and similar action has been taken to control local authority expenditure. Moreover, since staff costs form such a significant part of public expenditure, local authorities have been urged to reduce staff levels. Local authorities in England, Wales and Scotland are required to publish quarterly staffing levels for particular services.

The specific powers and duties of local authorities are conferred on them by Parliament, or by measures made under its authority. The actual administration, and the exercise of discretion within statutory limits, are the responsibility of the local authority. In the case of certain services, however, ministers have powers to secure a measure of national uniformity in the standard of a service provided, to safeguard public health, or to protect the rights of individual citizens. For some services the minister concerned has wide powers of supervision; for others there are strictly limited powers.

The main links between local authorities and central government are: in England, the Department of the Environment, although other departments (for example, the Department of Education and Science, and the Home Office) are concerned with various local government functions; in Scotland, the Scottish Office; in Wales, the Welsh Office; and in Northern Ireland, the Department of the Environment for Northern Ireland.

Principal Types of Local Authority England and Wales (outside Greater London) are divided into 53 counties, within which there are 369 districts. All the districts and 47 of the counties—the 'non-metropolitan' counties—have independent, locally elected councils with separate functions. County authorities provide the large-scale local government services, while the district authorities are responsible for the more local ones (see p 70).

In Greater London—an area of about 1,580 sq km (610 sq miles) and a population of some 6·8 million—the local government authorities are the councils of 32 London boroughs and the Corporation of the City of London, while in the six metropolitan counties there are 36 district councils.

Until 1986 Greater London and the metropolitan counties had their own councils, but these were abolished by the Local Government Act 1985, which was designed to create a more effective, economical and accountable system by removing a tier of local government. As a result, many of the functions previously carried out by the Greater London Council and the metropolitan county councils were transferred to the London borough and metropolitan district councils. However, a number of services require a statutory authority over areas wider than the boroughs and districts. These are waste regulation and disposal in certain areas; the police and fire services, including civil defence, and public transport in all metropolitan counties; and the fire service, including civil defence, in London. All are run by joint authorities composed of elected councillors nominated by the borough or district councils. In April 1990 responsibility for education in inner London was transferred from the Inner London Education Authority (ILEA) to individual inner London borough councils. The Local Government Act 1985 established seven residuary bodies to carry out the remaining tasks of the Greater London Council and the metropolitan county councils that were not assigned to successor authorities at that time. The Act also placed a duty on the residuary bodies to wind themselves up by March 1991.

Within rural districts in England, parish councils or meetings are focuses for local opinion as bodies with limited powers of local interest. In Wales community councils have similar functions.

On the mainland of Scotland local government is on a two-tier basis: nine regions are divided into 53 districts, each area having its own elected council. There are three virtually all-purpose authorities for Orkney, Shetland and the Western Isles. Provision is also made for local community councils, although these are not local authorities.

The areas and electoral arrangements of local authorities are kept under review by the Local Government Boundary Commissions for England, Wales and Scotland.

In Northern Ireland 26 district councils are responsible for local environmental and certain other services. Statutory bodies, such as the Northern Ireland Housing Executive and area boards, are responsible to central government departments for administering major services such as housing, education and libraries, and health and personal social services. Regional services such as roads, water and sewerage, and planning, are the responsibility of central government, through the Department of the Environment for Northern Ireland.

Election of Councils

Local authority councils consist of a number of elected unpaid councillors presided over by a chairman. Councillors can claim a flat-rate attendance allowance or a financial loss allowance for performing council business. They are also entitled to travelling and subsistence allowances. Parish and community councillors cannot claim expenses for duties.

In England, Wales and Northern Ireland each council annually elects a chairman and vice-chairman. Some districts have the ceremonial title of borough, or city, both granted by royal authority (in Northern Ireland, by the Secretary of State). In boroughs and cities the chairman is normally known as the Mayor. In the City of London and certain other large cities, he or she is known as the Lord Mayor. In Scotland the chairman of the district council of each of the four cities is called the Lord Provost. No specific title is laid down for the chairmen of other councils, but some are known as conveners, while others continue to use the old title of 'provost'.

Councillors are elected for four years. All county councils, London borough councils, and about two-thirds of non-metropolitan district councils are elected in their entirety every four years. In the remaining districts (including all metropolitan districts) one-third of the councillors are elected in each of the three years between county council elections.

In Scotland local elections are held every two years, alternately for districts and for regions and islands authorities, so that all types of authority are elected for four years at a time.

Anyone is entitled to vote at a local government election in Great Britain provided he or she is aged 18 years or over, is a British citizen, other Commonwealth citizen, or a citizen of the Irish Republic, is not subject to any legal incapacity and is on the electoral register. To qualify for registration a person must be resident in the council area on the qualifying date. In Northern Ireland there are slightly different requirements.

A candidate for election as councillor normally stands as a representative of one of the national political parties, or of some local interest, or as an independent. Candidates must be British citizens, other Commonwealth citizens or citizens of the Irish Republic, and aged 21 or over. They must also be registered as local electors in the area of the local authority to which they seek election; or have lived in or occupied (as owner or tenant) land or other premises in that area during the whole of the 12 months preceding the day on which they are nominated as candidates or, in that 12 months, have had their principal or only place of work there. No one may be elected to a council of which he or she is an employee, and there are some other disqualifications. Under the Elected Authorities (Northern Ireland) Act 1989, all candidates for district council elections are required to make a declaration against terrorism.

Local authority areas are generally divided into electoral areas for local council elections. Administrative counties in England and Wales are divided into electoral divisions, each returning one councillor. Districts in England, Wales and Northern Ireland are divided into 'wards', returning one councillor or more. In Scotland the electoral areas in the regions and islands areas are called electoral divisions, each returning a single member; the districts are divided into wards, similarly returning a single member. For parish or community council elections in England and Wales, each parish or community, or ward of a parish or community, forms an electoral area which returns one member or more.

The procedure for local government voting in Great Britain is similar to that for parliamentary elections. In Northern Ireland local government elections are held on the basis of proportional representation, and electoral wards are grouped into district electoral areas.

Functions and Services

Some functions of local authorities are primarily duties, others purely permissive.

Functions in England and Wales are divided between county and district councils. County councils are responsible for matters requiring planning and administration over wide areas or requiring the support of substantial resources. District councils administer more local functions.

English county councils are responsible for strategic planning, transport planning, highways, traffic regulation, education, consumer protection, refuse disposal, police, the fire service, libraries and the personal social services. District councils are responsible, for instance, for environmental health, housing, decisions on most planning applications, and refuse collection. They may also provide off-street car parks subject to the consent of the county council. Powers to carry out functions—such as the provision of museums, art galleries and parks—are available at both levels; arrangements depend on local agreement.

In the metropolitan counties the district councils are responsible for all services apart from the police, the fire service and public transport and, in some areas, waste regulation and disposal. In Greater London the boroughs and the City Corporation are responsible for similar functions but London's metropolitan police force is directly responsible to the Home Secretary. Responsibility for public transport lies with London Transport.

In Wales the division of functions between county and district councils is much the same as that between county and district councils in non-metropolitan areas of England.

Local authorities in England and Wales may arrange for any of their functions to be carried out on their behalf by another local authority, other than functions relating to education, police, the personal social services and national parks.

In Scotland the regional and district authorities discharge local government functions in a way broadly similar to that of authorities in England and Wales. Orkney, Shetland and the Western Isles, because of their isolation from the mainland, have single, virtually all-purpose authorities.

In Northern Ireland local environmental and certain other services, such as leisure and the arts, are administered by the district councils. Responsibility for planning, roads, water supply and sewerage services is exercised in each district through a divisional office of the Department of the Environment for Northern Ireland. Area boards, responsible to central departments, administer education, public libraries and the health and personal services locally. The Northern Ireland Housing Executive, responsible to the Department of the Environment, administers housing.

Internal Organisation of Local Authorities

Local authorities have considerable freedom to make arrangements for carrying out their duties. They may co-operate or share among themselves the discharge of their functions. Most use a committee system, whereby policy and principle are decided in full council, while the detailed administration of the various services is the responsibility of committees composed of selected members of the council and, where the authority chooses, 'persons of experience'. A council may delegate to a committee or

Parliamentary Democracy

The television control room of the House of Commons Broadcasting Unit, which makes television pictures available to approved broadcasters for use in news and current affairs programmes. After an eight-month trial period, the House of Commons voted in 1990 to allow its proceedings to be televised permanently.

Voting in Britain is not compulsory. At the last general election, in 1987, 74·6 per cent of the electorate turned out to vote.

Waterfronts

South Tenby harbour
and town, Wales.

Belfast docks,
Northern Ireland.

The Watershed,
St Augustine's Reach,
Bristol.

The Broomielaw,
Glasgow, Scotland.

Commonwealth Institute

In the Commonwealth Institute's Bhownagree Gallery Studio, Nigerian artist Ademola Akintola shows his work to local schoolchildren. The Institute is the centre of Commonwealth education and culture in Britain.

Schoolchildren and professional performers take part in the annual Trinidad Carnival at the Institute.

officer any function except in connection with raising loans, levying non-domestic rates, the community charge (see p 72) or making financial demands on other local authorities liable to contribute; these are legally reserved to the council as a whole. Some councils have policy advisory or co-ordinating committees which originate policy for implementation by the full council. The powers and duties of local authority committees (which may be advisory or executive) are usually laid down in formal standing orders. Parish and community councils in England and Wales are often able to do their work in full session, although they appoint committees from time to time as necessary.

The Local Government and Housing Act 1989 is designed to strengthen the democratic functioning of local authorities. This includes requiring council committees to reflect the political composition of the council, generally removing voting powers from co-opted members of decision-making committees and prohibiting the most senior officers from being members of other local authorities or undertaking public political activity. Some provisions of this Act have not been introduced in Northern Ireland.

Public Access The public (including the press) are admitted to council, committee and sub-committee meetings, and have a right of access to agendas, reports and minutes of meetings and certain background papers. Local authorities may exclude the public from meetings and withhold these papers only in limited circumstances specified by legislation.

Officers and Employees Over 2 million people are employed by local authorities in Great Britain. These include administrative, professional and technical staff, teachers, firefighters, those engaged on law and order services, and manual workers. Nearly half of all local government workers are employed in the education service.

Although a few appointments must be made by all the authorities responsible for the functions concerned, councils are individually responsible within national policy requirements for determining the size, composition and deployment of their workforces. In Northern Ireland each council must by law appoint a clerk of the council as its chief officer.

As a general rule, employees are of three kinds: heads of departments or chief officers; administrative, professional, clerical and technical staff; and manual workers. Senior staff appointments are usually made on the recommendation of the committee or committees involved. Most junior appointments are made by heads of departments, who are also responsible for engaging manual workers. Pay and conditions of service are generally a matter for each council, although there are scales recommended by national negotiating machinery set up by the local authorities themselves.

Authorities differ in the degree to which they employ their own permanent staff to carry out certain functions or use private firms under contract. The Government's policy of promoting value for money is encouraging the use of private firms where there are resultant economies. The Local Government Act 1988 requires authorities either to contract out or to expose to competition the following services: refuse collection, street cleaning, school and general catering, vehicle maintenance, ground maintenance and building cleaning, sport and leisure management. The current cost of this is estimated to be between £3,000 million and £5,000 million a year.

Local Authority Finance In 1989–90 expenditure by local authorities in Britain amounted to £51,200 million, one-quarter of general government expenditure. Current expenditure amounted to nearly £42,000 million, and capital expenditure, net of capital receipts, was £4,200 million and debt interest £5,100 million.

A new system of local authority finance was introduced in England and Wales in April 1990 and in Scotland in April 1989. The main features of the new arrangements are designed to strengthen local democratic accountability. First, domestic rates (local property taxes) have been replaced by a community charge set by each authority and payable by each resident adult. Secondly, there is a grant system compensating for differences in local authorities' needs and ability to raise revenue. Thirdly, in England and Wales a uniform business rate (uniform in the sense that a single poundage applies throughout England and throughout Wales) has been set, the proceeds of which are distributed to authorities in proportion to the number of people paying the community charge. In Scotland the business rate is not at present uniform.

Current Expenditure

In 1989–90 education accounted for 44 per cent of current expenditure. Most of the remainder was spent on roads and transport; housing and other environmental services; law, order and protective services; personal social services and social security.

Local authority current expenditure in Great Britain is financed from the community charge, the proceeds of the business rate pool and revenue support grant from central government. Revenue support grant is distributed so as to compensate for differences in the assessed cost for each authority of providing a standard level of services. The grant is distributed in such a way that local authorities with differing needs and local resources (that is, income from the community charge and the business rate) should be able to levy the community charge at a standard rate and provide a standard level of service. The community charge for standard spending is set at a different level in England and Wales. Specific grant is also paid to meet some of the costs of providing services such as the police and, in inner cities, the Urban Programme.

In Northern Ireland district councils receive central government grants. These comprise specific grants, which assist with the financing of certain functions (for example, the acquisition of open space) and certain capital projects (for example, leisure centres), and a general grant, which is paid by the Department of the Environment for Northern Ireland. The general grant compensates councils for loss of rate income arising from statutory derating of premises, and also contains a resources element which brings the rating resources of poorer councils up to a standard level determined by the Department.

Capital Expenditure

Local government capital expenditure is financed primarily by borrowing and from capital receipts from the disposal of land and buildings. These sources are supplemented mainly by capital grants and contributions from central government. Every year each local authority receives from central government credit approvals covering the main blocks of service for which it is responsible. Credit approvals are expressed as an amount of money and authorise the local authority to incur credit, including borrowing, on capital expenditure up to the amount specified. Also, part of the capital receipts generated by the authority can be used to finance capital expenditure; the remainder is set aside as provision to repay debt. In addition, local authorities can use revenue contributions to finance capital expenditure. Authorities have almost complete discretion to spend according to local priorities.

Northern Ireland

In Northern Ireland, occupiers of land and property pay rates to meet part of the cost of local services. Each occupier's payment is calculated annually by the rating authority by multiplying the rateable value of a property (broadly equivalent to its annual rental value) by the rate poundage—an amount per pound of rateable value fixed by the authority according to its projected financial needs. Rateable values are reassessed periodically, the last occasion having been in 1973. Industrial premises are fully derated, as are commercial premises in enterprise zones. Certain other properties, such as freight transport and recreational premises, are partially derated.

Loans

Local authorities are allowed to borrow money long term to finance new capital expenditure and also to refinance loans raised for capital finance, thus enabling flexible debt management. Authorities are not allowed to borrow long term to finance revenue expenditure but they may borrow money short term in anticipation of revenues. In Northern Ireland long-term borrowing by district councils is subject to central approval. In Scotland central approval is given to capital expenditure, not to loans.

Most long-term borrowing by authorities is from the Public Works Loan Board (or, in Northern Ireland, the Consolidated Fund). The Board draws its funds from the Government's National Loans Fund and thus allows authorities to enjoy interest rates lower than any institution except the Government. Authorities may also borrow from the capital market using means specified in legislation. All loan charges are secured against the revenues of the authority and represent a first charge on those revenues.

Control of Finance

Local councils normally have a finance committee to keep their financial policy under constant review. They must have their annual accounts audited by independent auditors appointed by the Audit Commission in England and Wales, or by the Commission for Local Authority Accounts in Scotland. In Northern Ireland this role is exercised by a local government audit section appointed by the Department of the Environment for Northern Ireland.

Local Government Complaints System

A complaints system for local government in England and Wales involves independent statutory Commissions for Local Administration comprising local commissioners (local government Ombudsmen). The English Commission has three local commissioners and the Welsh, one. In Scotland the statute provides for a single commissioner. All commissioners are responsible in their particular area for investigating citizens' allegations of injustice resulting from maladministration by local authorities.

In Northern Ireland a Commissioner for Complaints deals with complaints alleging injustices suffered as a result of maladministration by district councils and certain other public bodies.

Fire Services

Every part of Britain is covered by a local authority fire service, which is subject to some general oversight by central government. In Great Britain, the cost is shared between local authorities and central government, the latter contributing through the revenue support grant. In Northern Ireland, the fire service is financed wholly from central government funds.

Each of the 64 fire authorities must by law make provision for fire-fighting, and maintain a brigade of sufficient strength to meet all normal requirements. (In some parts of Scotland combined authorities provide fire cover.) Other authorities also maintain fire brigades, for instance, the Army and Royal Air Force Departments of the Ministry of Defence; the Civil

Aviation Authority at airports; and some large industrial and commercial concerns. These work in co-operation with the local authority fire services.

The Home Secretary and the Secretary of State for Scotland have central responsibility in England and Wales and in Scotland respectively. Central government is concerned mainly with ensuring the operational efficiency of brigades. Ministers have statutory powers to prescribe standards and general requirements on administrative and operational matters of service-wide significance. These include appointments and promotions, the provision of a central training institution, pensions and disciplinary matters. Their approval is also required for reductions in the fire-fighting establishments of fire brigades. Each minister is advised by a Central Fire Brigades Advisory Council, comprising the respective home departments, local authorities, fire service representative organisations and certain specialist advisers. In the home departments inspectorates of fire services advise on operational and technical matters. Most fire brigades include part-time personnel who provide fire cover in less densely populated areas in return for a retaining fee and call-out and attendance fees. Fire authorities also employ people for duties in controls, communications, and mobilising and staff duties. There are about 37,000 full-time and 14,000 part-time operational members of fire brigades in Britain.

The standardisation of some equipment is encouraged to assist compatibility when a fire is attended by more than one brigade. The principal types of fire-fighting appliances bought by fire authorities are based upon specifications approved by the Secretaries of State and issued in the form of advice by the Central Fire Brigades Advisory Councils. The specifications aim to describe the minimum standards required while allowing some freedom of design.

Each fire authority must appoint a Chief Fire Officer (Firemaster in Scotland) who exercises day-to-day control from brigade headquarters. Divisional officers in charge of the geographical areas into which most brigade regions are divided are responsible for mobilising forces. Constant communication is maintained between divisional and brigade headquarters. If additional resources are required to deal with an incident, neighbouring divisions, or a neighbouring fire brigade, are asked to provide assistance.

Fire Prevention

Fire authorities are concerned with fire precautions in most buildings used by the public and have major responsibility for enforcing legislation concerning fire precautions. They must also make efficient arrangements for giving advice on fire prevention, restricting the spread of fires, and means of escape. Courses in fire prevention are held at the Fire Service College for fire brigade officers. In addition to their enforcement and advisory duties, brigades are also involved in education and publicity to promote fire safety, particularly in the home. The Home Office and the Scottish Home and Health Department also promote fire safety in the home. Central government is advised on prevention by the Joint Fire Prevention Committee of the Central Fire Brigades Advisory Councils, representing the fire service and central and local authorities.

Research

Research into health hazards to fire-fighters, fire prevention, fire-brigade organisation and fire-fighting equipment is conducted by the Home Office with the help of the fire services through the Joint Committee on Fire Research of the Central Fire Brigades Advisory Councils. Individual research projects are undertaken by the Home Office Scientific Research and Development Branch or, under contract to the Home Office, by other government agencies, notably the Fire Research Station, or by private consultants. The Fire Research Station, part of the Building Research Establishment of the Department of the Environment, is the principal organisation studying and investigating the technical aspects of fire.

Special Services Fire authorities have discretion to use their brigades and equipment in a variety of non-fire emergencies. These are known as 'special services' and include rail, road and aircraft accidents, collapse of buildings, flooding of premises, leakage of harmful gas or liquids and the rescue of people or animals from dangerous situations. Fire authorities are entitled to levy a charge for such services.

Fire Losses The direct cost of damage to buildings and goods destroyed by fires in Britain in 1989 amounted to an estimated £792·4 million. (Consequential losses from the interruption of business are not included in this total.) Most fires involving heavy losses occur when the premises are unattended, and fires are more likely to start in storage areas than in production departments. Industries which suffer most severely include engineering and electrical firms; textiles; food, drink and tobacco warehousing; chemical and allied industries; paper, printing and publishing firms; and retailing.

Fire Casualties Over 900 people, particularly the elderly and young children, die in fires every year (most of them at home) and about a further 13,300 suffer injury. Among the chief causes of fatal fires are ignition of upholstery, bedding and clothing by smokers' materials and by heaters. Government regulations on the use of new, safer foam material in the upholstery of domestic furniture have been introduced.

3 Overseas Relations

Since 1945 Britain has progressively, and largely peacefully, dismantled its Empire. Yet it retains global interests, including continuing responsibilities for 14 dependent territories, and for 6 million British citizens who live overseas. Britain imports over one-third of its food and over one-half of its raw material requirements. Exports account for over a quarter of gross national product (GNP). London is a major world financial centre and Britain's overseas investments are the second largest in the world, fast catching up with Japan's.

Britain's overseas relations have been shaped by its history as a major trading and maritime power. The maintenance of peace and promotion of global stability and prosperity remain primary objectives of Britain's overseas policy today.

Britain regards multilateral co-operation as a key element in safeguarding its security and economic interests. As well as maintaining diplomatic relations with 165 countries, it is a member of some 120 international organisations, including the United Nations (see p 97), the North Atlantic Treaty Organisation (see p 92), and the European Community (see p 78).

Britain has close links with many developing countries, notably within the Commonwealth, which evolved out of the former British Empire and which links 50 independent countries in a representative cross-section of the international community. Commonwealth members have a language in common and close professional, academic and commercial ties. In all, Britain provides development assistance to over 120 independent countries as well as to its dependencies.

Britain also has strong links with the United States, including a common language and similar political and cultural traditions.

Administration The general conduct of overseas relations is the responsibility of the Secretary of State for Foreign and Commonwealth Affairs, supported by four Ministers of State, acting through the Foreign and Commonwealth Office (FCO) and over 200 British diplomatic posts overseas. The latter comprise embassies and high commissions in about 130 countries,[1] together with subordinate consulates-general and consulates, and missions at ten international organisations. These posts, like the FCO, are staffed by members of the Diplomatic Service and locally engaged people. Excluding supporting administrative and communications services, 30 per cent of front-line diplomatic staff and senior locally engaged staff are involved in commercial work such as export promotion and the protection of British commercial interests, 24 per cent in consular/entry clearance services, 18 per cent in political and economic work, 9 per cent in information and 8 per cent in other work.

---

[1] A few embassies are accredited to more than one country.

Other departments concerned with overseas relations include the Ministry of Defence, the Department of Trade and Industry, the Treasury and the Overseas Development Administration (ODA, which forms part of the FCO).

Where overseas policy involves matters within the responsibility of other departments, the FCO formulates policy in consultation with the departments concerned. The department with the predominant functional interest, even though it may be primarily domestic, takes the lead, particularly in policy concerning the European Community and international monetary matters. In the case of policy towards the Community, the FCO exercises its co-ordinating role through the machinery of the Cabinet Office.

Other bodies include the British Overseas Trade Board and the ECGD (Export Credits Guarantee Department), which provide export services for industry. Crown Agents helps to arrange purchases from British aid funds and appointments under technical co-operation programmes; it also provides mainly purchasing and management services to overseas governments and institutions.

The British Council

The British Council, an independent non-political organisation, promotes Britain abroad and is the principal agent for British cultural relations overseas. Represented in 90 countries, it provides a wide-ranging network of contacts between government departments, universities, colleges, and professional, business and arts organisations in Britain and around the world.

The Council has five main activities: it helps people to study, train or make professional contacts in Britain and enables British specialists to teach, advise or establish joint projects abroad; teaches English and promotes its use; provides library and information services; promotes British education, science and technology; and makes British arts and literature more widely known.

It employs qualified staff to teach English in its language centres, to run its libraries and to manage its own businesses. It also matches the needs and demands of countries overseas with the skills and services available from various organisations in Britain. Wherever possible, the Council uses its own operations to stimulate activity and expenditure by others.

The Council's expenditure in 1990–91 is estimated at £348 million. As well as providing its own programmes funded by government grant through the FCO (£99 million) and Council earnings (£80 million), it also manages training and education programmes on behalf of the ODA (£148 million) and the FCO (£21 million). Business sponsorship—almost £4 million in 1989–90—is making an increasing contribution to the Council's work.

In 1989–90 the Council brought 35,000 overseas students, trainees and professional visitors to Britain, and taught English to 66,000 students in its teaching centres overseas. The Council's 116 overseas libraries had a total membership of 428,000; issued 8 million books, periodicals, films and tapes; and handled 800,000 enquiries for information about Britain. In addition to their film and video stocks, many libraries have software demonstration equipment and on-line access to British databases. The Council also supported over 1,000 events in the visual arts, film and television, drama, dance and music, ranging from the classical to the contemporary.

Membership of the European Community

Britain is fully committed to active membership of the European Community, which is at the core of its European and wider foreign policy.

The Community's objectives, as set out in the Treaty of Rome and confirmed in the Single European Act of 1986, are to lay the foundations for a closer union between the peoples of Europe on the basis of a common internal market, the gradual approximation of member states' economic policies and a framework of common law. The Community has abolished internal tariffs and some other trade barriers, established a common external customs tariff and made provision for freer movement of labour, capital and services. Member states have agreed to establish a genuinely free internal market by the end of 1992. The Community also negotiates on behalf of its member states in international trade negotiations. Overseas countries having special links with the Community are accorded preferential treatment in aid and the development of trade. The Community accounts for about a fifth of world trade, and half of Britain's trade is with the other 11 member states.

The European Community

Community Institutions
Council of Ministers

Major policy decisions are taken by the Council of Ministers, on which member states are represented by foreign or other ministers as appropriate to the subject under discussion. The Presidency of the Council changes at six-monthly intervals; Britain will assume it for the fourth time from July to December 1992. Most Council decisions are taken on the basis of a proposal made by the European Commission; some may be decided by majority or qualified majority, with votes weighted according to each country's size, as set out in the Community treaties. In other cases the Council proceeds on the basis of unanimity. The Single European Act provides for improved decision-taking through more use of qualified majority voting, particularly on internal market measures.

Heads of Government meet twice a year as the European Council, which takes important decisions and discusses Community policies and world affairs generally.

European Commission

The European Commission puts forward policy proposals, executes decisions taken by the Council of Ministers and ensures that Community rules are correctly observed. It is composed of 17 Commissioners (two from Britain), nominated by member governments and appointed by common agreement, and is pledged to act independently of national or sectional interests.

European Parliament

The European Parliament, directly elected by the people in member states at five-yearly intervals, has 518 members, 81 of whom come from Britain. Members sit in groups according to party affiliation and not nationality. The most recent election took place in June 1989.

The Parliament is consulted on a wide range of issues before the Council takes final decisions. The Commission can be removed from office as a whole by a two-thirds majority of all members of the Parliament in a vote of censure. The Parliament adopts the Community's annual budget in agreement with the Council. Members may also put questions to the Council of Ministers and the Commission.

The Parliament's legislative powers were increased by the 1986 Single European Act. On certain categories of proposed legislation (notably that related to the single European market, free movement of workers and working conditions) the Parliament may give an opinion not just on a Commission proposal but also—in a second reading—on the position taken by the Council of Ministers on the proposal. The aim is to enable the Parliament to propose amendments at a second stage before the Council adopts the proposal as Community law. The Commission reconsiders its proposal in the light of the Parliament's amendments and the Council then reaches a final decision. If the Parliament rejects the Council's position, unanimity is required for the Council to act on a second reading. If the Parliament proposes amendments, the Council votes by qualified majority where the Commission has endorsed them and unanimously where the Commission has not done so. The Single European Act imposes a strict timetable on the consultation procedures in order to quicken decision-making.

New applications for membership of the Community must receive the assent of an absolute majority of the Parliament, as must the conclusion of agreements with third countries establishing an association involving reciprocal agreements.

Court of Justice

The Court of Justice, consisting of 13 judges, interprets and adjudicates on the meaning of the treaties and on any measures taken by the Council of Ministers and the Commission. It also hears complaints and appeals brought by or against Community institutions, member states or individuals and gives preliminary rulings on cases referred by courts in the member states. It represents the final authority on all aspects of Community law. The Single European Act provided for a Court of First Instance to relieve the Court of Justice of a substantial part of its workload and to enable the handing down of rulings to be speeded up. The new Court, which became operational in September 1989, has 12 members. Its jurisdiction covers disputes between officials of the Community and their employers, certain actions against Community institutions in relation to Community competition rules and some cases under the 1951 European Coal and Steel Community Treaty.

Court of Auditors The Court of Auditors examines all Community revenue and expenditure to see that it has been legally received and spent, and to ensure sound financial management.

Policy
Implementation Community policies are implemented by regulations, which are legally binding and directly applicable in all member countries, and directives, which are binding on the member states to which they are addressed but allow national authorities to decide on means of implementation. Decisions are binding on those to whom they are addressed (for example, member states, firms or individuals), while recommendations and opinions have no binding force. The Council of Ministers can also indicate a general policy direction through resolutions.

Political
Co-operation Member states have also set up machinery under which they consult each other and co-ordinate their positions on foreign policy matters of general interest. Known as political co-operation, these consultations include regular meetings of foreign ministers, monthly meetings of senior officials, and contacts at working level among those concerned with particular issues.

Finance The Community is financed by a system of levies on agricultural imports, customs duties and contributions from member states based on value added tax (VAT) levied on a harmonised base and on gross national product (GNP). These are known as 'own resources'. Because of an imbalance between Community policies a problem arose in the late 1970s over the excessive level of Britain's net contribution to the budget in relation to Britain's share of Community GNP.

Because Britain received considerably less from the Community budget than it contributed, it made a net contribution to the Community substantially in excess of that justified by its share of GNP. In June 1984, it was agreed that Britain should receive an annual abatement, deducted from its contribution, equal to two-thirds of the gap between its share of VAT contributions and its share of expenditure in the previous year.

In 1988 there was a further reform of the Community's finances which retained Britain's abatement, increased the ceiling on Community revenue from 1·4 per cent of the harmonised VAT base to 1·2 per cent of Community GNP, introduced new controls on Community spending, and imposed legally binding constraints on agricultural spending, including measures to cut back surplus stocks and discourage over-production.

Internal
Policies
The Single
Market In Britain's view, completion of a single, unified internal Community market by removing the remaining major barriers to the free movement of goods, services and capital is the most effective means of improving European competitiveness in world markets, so generating wealth and prosperity for its citizens. The Single European Act commits member states to establish a genuine single market by the end of 1992, and two-thirds of the programme is now agreed. It covers, for example, the liberalisation of capital movements, the mutual recognition of professional qualifications and the opening up of public procurement markets. Britain's current priorities include the simplification and eventual lifting of customs and other frontier restrictions on the free movement of goods, the removal of technical barriers to trade and the freeing of markets in services, especially financial services, insurance and transport.

Since 1988 the Government has sought to bring home to British businesses the importance of 1992 and to encourage companies to plan ahead to meet the challenges and opportunities it presents. The

Government believes that the Community, in completing the single market, should not erect trade barriers against other countries and should abide by its international trading obligations, particularly under the General Agreement on Tariffs and Trade.

Transport

Britain believes that a system of deregulated transport is an essential part of the single market. It therefore supported the 1988 regulation under which all quota restrictions on the movement of road haulage between member states will be removed by the beginning of 1993. It has also welcomed recent moves to increase competition in civil aviation and will press for further liberalising steps in all transport sectors. Britain's links with other member states will be improved with the completion of the Channel Tunnel, scheduled for 1993.

Monetary Policy

The European Monetary System was established in 1979 to promote monetary stability in Europe. It consists of an exchange rate mechanism (ERM), the European Currency Unit (ECU) and enlarged short- and medium-term credit facilities. The ECU is based on a 'basket' of the Community currencies, the value of which is recalculated daily.

Britain participated in the system from the outset, although not in the ERM, and deposited 20 per cent of its gold and dollar currency reserves with the European Monetary Co-operation Fund in exchange for ECUs. At the beginning of October 1990 Britain announced that it would become a member of the ERM.

In 1989 the European Council approved the first stage of a plan for Economic and Monetary Union (EMU) drawn up by a committee of governors of central banks. This stage, implementation of which began in July 1990, includes the strengthening of economic and monetary policy co-ordination, the completion of the single market, the strengthening of competition policy and all member states joining the ERM on equal terms. Britain is fully committed to stage one but has some reservations about full monetary union.

An Inter-Governmental Conference will take place in December 1990 in order to consider Treaty changes regarding EMU. As part of the preparation for this conference, Britain has suggested the creation of a European Monetary Fund (EMF) to manage the ERM, to co-ordinate exchange rate intervention with external currencies and to promote use of the ECU. Britain believes that the Fund could encourage more use of the ECU by issuing ECU bank notes for general circulation alongside member states' currencies, backed by EMF holdings of various Community currencies.

Research and Development

The British Government supports Community collaboration in longer term, precompetitive research and development to maximise economies of scale, improve Europe's technological base and assist companies in exploiting the single market. The Community's industrial research and development programmes are designed to promote the competitiveness of European industry in world markets. The new Framework Programme agreed for 1990–94 has a budget of £4,200 million and includes more work on information and communications technologies, the management of natural resources and strengthening the science and technology base of European industry.

The £1,000 million ESPRIT II programme supports research and development in microelectronics, information processing and application of information technology in such areas as computer integrated manufacturing. The £360 million RACE programme aims to help establish a strong Community manufacturing industry in broadband communications and to accelerate the emergence of a competitive market for tele-communications equipment and services by working towards European common standards. The £325 million BRITE/EURAM programme supports industrial precompetitive research covering advanced materials, design methodologies, manufacturing processes and aeronautics.

Other important Community programmes cover research into the environment, biotechnology, agriculture, health and energy. Under the new Framework Programme there is also a scheme providing funds for the exchange of researchers.

EUREKA is an initiative established in 1985 by the member states of the Community, the six members of the European Free Trade Association, Turkey and the Commission, to encourage projects in high technology products, processes and services. The initiative complements Community programmes and is concerned with the commercial exploitation of research and development and with removing barriers to commercial success.

Structural Funds   The Community's Structural Funds, administered by the Commission, support investment in industry and agriculture in the Community's less developed regions. There are three Funds—the European Regional Development Fund, the European Social Fund and the Guidance Section of the European Agricultural Guidance and Guarantee Fund. Infrastructure projects and productive investments are financed by the Regional Development Fund. The Social Fund supports training and employment measures for the long-term unemployed and young people. The Agricultural Guidance Fund supports agricultural restructuring and some rural development measures.

There are five priority objectives—promotion of economic development in poorer regions, converting regions seriously affected by industrial decline, combating long-term unemployment, facilitating the occupational integration of young people and, as part of the reform of the Common Agricultural Policy, promoting development in rural areas. The Funds' allocations are increasing from £5,000 million in 1987 to £9,000 million in 1993, at 1988 prices.

In 1988 Britain was allocated some £390 million from the Regional Development Fund and £405 million from the Social Fund.

Other Community programmes aim to assist the development of new economic activities in regions affected by the restructuring of the steel and coal industries.

In 1989 Britain received 14·2 per cent of lending within the Community by the European Investment Bank. The Bank was set up in 1958 to provide finance on a non-profit-making basis for investment to develop the Community's less favoured regions, modernise industry and help projects of common interest to two or more member states.

Employment and   Britain believes that the Community has an important role to play in tackling
Social Affairs   unemployment. In 1986 an action programme for employment growth was agreed based on proposals put forward by Britain, the Irish Republic and Italy. Britain believes that deregulation and competition within the internal market will create jobs, especially in small businesses.

In 1987 a programme was adopted, to run from 1988 to 1992, aimed at ensuring that all young people who wish to can receive one or more years' vocational training after leaving school. In 1988 the Social Affairs Council approved the second phase of the Community in Education and Training for Technology programme, allocating 200 million ECUs (about £130 million) over a five-year period beginning in 1990. Much of the aid which Britain receives from the Community's Social Fund (see p 83) goes towards training and retraining programmes for the young or unemployed.

In 1990 the Commission began bringing forward a series of proposals ranging widely over the fields of employment, and health and safety at work.

The Environment   Environmental pollution does not respect national boundaries and international co-operation is often necessary to deal with it. The Community has been active in this area for some 15 years and its role has been given explicit legal recognition in the Single European Act. Community environment policy is concerned with such issues as water and air pollution, the disposal of wastes, noise and the protection of wild birds. A regulation establishing the European Environment Agency was adopted by the Community in May 1990; this will bring together environmental information from existing bodies for the use of member states and the Commission.

In 1988 Britain and its Community partners agreed to reduce emissions of sulphur dioxide and nitrogen oxide from existing large combustion plants (such as power stations, refineries and other industrial plants) and to set stringent emission standards for new plants. Sulphur dioxide emissions are to be reduced by 60 per cent from 1980 levels by 2003, and nitrogen oxide emissions by 30 per cent of 1980 levels by 1998.

Britain is also concerned about pollution from vehicle exhausts, and, following a British initiative, the Council of Ministers adopted a directive in 1985 providing for the introduction of unleaded petrol throughout the Community not later than 1989. The market share of unleaded petrol in Britain is now over 30 per cent. Between 1987 and 1989, Britain and its Community partners agreed a set of directives on car exhaust emissions which are being implemented between 1989 and 1992. Emissions of nitrogen oxide, carbon monoxide and hydrocarbons will be reduced by about 60 per cent from each new car. All new cars will need catalytic converters to meet these standards.

In 1987 the Community signed the Montreal Protocol to the Vienna Convention for Protection of the Ozone Layer. In June 1990 an international conference in London, attended by nearly 60 developed and developing countries, agreed to phase out chlorofluorocarbons (CFCs) by 2000, with immediate cuts of 50 per cent (compared with 1986 levels) by 1995 and 85 per cent by 1997. It also agreed to phase out halons by 2000, except for agreed essential uses, with an immediate cut of 50 per cent by 1995. Controls on other ozone-depleting chemicals—carbon tetrachloride and methyl chloroform—were also agreed; the use of the former will be phased out completely by 2000 and the latter by 2005. Britain believes that CFCs should be banned by 1997 and is pressing the Community to ensure that member states do this.

At the Third North Sea Conference in March 1990, Britain, six other Community member states, Norway and Sweden agreed to phase out and destroy all remaining identifiable uses of polychlorinate biphenyls (PCBs) by 1999, to end incineration at sea by 1991 and to protect wildlife such as dolphins and porpoises. The Community has banned the import of harp and hooded seal pup skins and products. In June 1989 Britain banned imports of ivory from the African elephant, as did Community in August 1989.

Agriculture   The Common Agricultural Policy (CAP) is designed to secure food supply and to stabilise markets. Until recently, however, it had resulted in overproduction and unwanted food surpluses, which placed an increasing burden on the Community budget. To combat this, measures were taken to reform the CAP. In 1988 the British Government persuaded its partners to agree a guideline limit on overall agricultural spending and measures under which automatic cuts are made in the guaranteed price for a commodity if agreed production levels are exceeded. To complement these arrangements and to discourage overproduction, member states also agreed non-price measures, such as set-aside schemes, to take some agricultural land out of production. Food surpluses have been reduced as a result of these measures; butter stocks have been cut by 92 per cent from their highest levels and beef stocks by 85 per cent. Similarly, cereal surpluses are down by 38 per cent and there are virtually no milk product surpluses.

Fisheries

Britain has a particular interest in the control of Community fishing, since a sizeable proportion of the total catch taken in the area bounded by member states' 200-mile limits is in British waters. It therefore took an active role in negotiations on an agreement reached in 1983 on a new Community fisheries policy. This covers access to coastal waters, conservation of fish stocks, the allocation of catch quotas among member states within each year's total allowable catch, enforcement of these rules, and financial aid to promote the adaptation and development of the Community's fishing fleet.

Political Co-operation

The aim of European political co-operation on foreign policy issues is to maximise the influence of the Twelve in international affairs. As the result of a British initiative, the Single European Act places the basic commitments on a treaty basis.

East–West Relations

Britain considers that the 12 member states should ensure that a coherent Western European voice is heard in the management of East–West relations. The Twelve have welcomed the establishment of democracy in the German Democratic Republic, Hungary, Czechoslovakia and other countries in Central and Eastern Europe and are committed to assisting them in the change from centrally planned economies to market economies. Member states consider that the process of the Conference on Security and Co-operation in Europe (CSCE) has made a significant contribution to overcoming divisions between East and West, and are determined to play a full part at the CSCE Summit meeting proposed for late 1990. The Twelve are committed to a secure and stable balance of forces in Europe at lower levels.

The Middle East

In 1980 the European Council's Venice Declaration stated that a lasting solution to the Arab–Israeli dispute required the mutual acceptance of two basic principles—the right of all countries in the area, including Israel, to secure existence within guaranteed borders and the right of the Palestinian people to self-determination. The Twelve support the proposal for an international peace conference on the Middle East. They welcomed the Palestine National Council's recognition of the state of Israel and renunciation of terrorism in 1988. Member states have repeatedly called on Israel to withdraw from territory occupied in 1967 and meanwhile to administer its occupation in accordance with international law and human rights standards. The Community has a development programme for the occupied territories and has adopted measures to allow direct exports of agricultural and industrial products from them to the Community market.

The Twelve have also consistently emphasised the importance of the complete withdrawal of foreign forces from Lebanon, except for those whose presence is requested by the Lebanese Government, and of the obligation on all parties to co-operate with the UN Interim Force in Lebanon.

In response to Iraq's invasion of Kuwait in August 1990, the Twelve condemned the Iraqi action and urged Iraq to comply with UN Security Council resolution 660, calling for a withdrawal of its troops. The Community also agreed to implement another Security Council resolution (No 661) calling for trade sanctions against Iraq. Community regulations provide for a total ban by member states on the import or export of all goods originating in or coming from Iraq or Kuwait.

Central America

The Twelve have consistently supported the regional peace process in Central America embodied in the August 1987 agreement signed by Costa Rica, El Salvador, Guatemala, Honduras and Nicaragua. It provided for the implementation of a series of measures to establish peace and democracy in Central America. The Twelve also welcomed the progress made at subsequent meetings in 1989 and 1990. The holding of free and fair elections in Nicaragua in February 1990 with an extensive international observer presence, including the United Nations, was particularly welcome. The Twelve have also supported UN involvement in a security verification force established in late 1989 and in an international support and verification group whose task is to co-ordinate and monitor the de-mobilisation of the Contra guerrillas in Nicaragua.

The Community has a co-operation agreement with the five Central American countries and Panama, providing for closer economic and aid links with the region. It holds annual meetings at ministerial level with these six countries and with Colombia, Mexico and Venezuela as 'co-operating nations' to discuss these and other regional issues.

South Africa

The Twelve have repeatedly called for a peaceful end to the system of apartheid. They apply a policy which combines a programme of assistance to victims of apartheid and restrictive measures to encourage the South African Government to create a genuine national dialogue on the country's future. The major changes announced by South Africa in February 1990 included many of the specific demands that the Twelve have made, notably the release of Mr Nelson Mandela and other political prisoners and the lifting of the ban on the African National Congress and other organisations. Several meetings have taken place between representatives of the South African Government and the African National Congress. The Twelve have greatly welcomed these moves and have affirmed their willingness to consider a gradual relaxation of pressure on the South African Government when there is further clear evidence of the process of change continuing. The Community sent a fact-finding mission to South Africa in April 1990 which had contact with a range of South African opinion.

There is a voluntary code of conduct for EC companies with subsidiaries in South Africa which aims to improve conditions for black employees and to remove racial segregation at work.

The Twelve supported the implementation of the United Nations plan for the independence of Namibia which began in April 1989 and welcomed the achievement of this independence in March 1990. Member states made their own contributions to the work of the United Nations Transition Assistance Group, which supervised the independence process.

Terrorism and Crime

Because of the threat posed by international and other terrorism, member states have sought to act jointly against it. They have agreed not to export arms or other military equipment to countries clearly implicated in supporting terrorist activity and to take steps to prevent such material being diverted for terrorist purposes. In 1986, for instance, they agreed measures against both Libya and Syria following evidence of their involvement in terrorist activity. It is European Community policy that there should be no concessions made under duress to terrorists or their sponsors; that there should be solidarity between member states in their efforts to prevent terrorism and to bring the guilty to justice; and that terrorist attacks against any member state should be met with a concerted response. Counter-terrorist measures agreed include the establishment of a secure communications link between police forces and arrangements for regular assessments and analyses of terrorist threats to member states.

Regular meetings of ministers responsible for criminal justice take place to discuss common measures directed at terrorists and other criminals. The Government believes that with the introduction of the single market in 1992 some frontier controls will need to be retained to ensure that such people do not enjoy unlimited freedom to move from one member state to others.

Measures Against Drug Trafficking   The Community attaches great importance to co-operation against drug trafficking and discussions on law enforcement, international co-operation, assistance to developing countries, education and health take place regularly. A committee to combat drugs co-ordinates the Community's anti-drugs work and the international aspects are dealt with by a political co-operation working group. The Community believes that the problem requires a comprehensive strategy, tackling both demand and supply. Member states fully support the work of the United Nations in combating drug abuse and participate in regular meetings of the Council of Europe's Pompidou Group which is also concerned with anti-drugs measures. In June 1990 member states decided to set up a Community drugs intelligence unit.

Trade   Under the Treaty of Rome, the European Commission negotiates on behalf of the Community in major international trade negotiations. The Community seeks to preserve the world open trading system on which member states depend for future growth and jobs and to defend the interests of its members against protectionist measures. One of the Community's priorities is the successful conclusion of the Uruguay Round of trade negotiations launched in 1986 under the auspices of the General Agreement on Tariffs and Trade (GATT) and due to be completed in December 1990. The negotiations seek to strengthen GATT rules and disciplines; to liberalise trade in services and investment; to improve protection of intellectual property; to negotiate multilateral tariff reductions; and to establish a fair and market-oriented system for agricultural trade. The Community has agreed to increase its co-operation with the European Free Trade Association and reduce trade barriers.

The Community has association and co-operation agreements with all countries with a Mediterranean coastline (except Albania and Libya) and with Jordan; these give preferential access to Community markets. Non-preferential co-operation agreements have also been made with individual countries in South Asia and Latin America as well as with the People's Republic of China, the Association of South East Asian Nations, the Andean Pact and the Central American states. Trade relations with the developing countries of Africa, the Caribbean and the Pacific are governed by the Lo-mé Conventions (see p 88). Trade or trade and economic co-operation agreements are in place with Hungary, Czechoslovakia, Poland and the Soviet Union and the Community has established official relations with the

Council for Mutual Economic Assistance (Comecon). It has signed a trade and economic co-operation agreement with the Gulf Co-operation Council.

The Community's Generalised System of Preferences grants tariff-free access to the Community market for most industrial goods from developing countries and varying degrees of preferential access for their agricultural produce (mainly processed) and textiles. The scheme concentrates benefits on the poorer producers and countries. Certain categories of exports from the more competitive producers are excluded.

Aid

The fourth Lomé Convention, which governs aid, trade and co-operation between the Community and 68 developing countries in Africa, the Caribbean and the Pacific (ACP), was signed in December 1989. It will come into force following ratification, probably in late 1990 or early 1991. It runs for ten years with provision for review after five years; there will be two European Development Funds, each lasting five years. The Convention provides for aid totalling over £7,700 million for the first five years and up to £850 million in loans from the European Investment Bank over the same period. It also covers industrial and agricultural co-operation, a scheme designed to help stabilise the commodity export earnings of the ACP countries and assistance for ACP mineral producers whose production and income suffer from temporary disruptions beyond their control. In addition, it offers duty-free access to the Community for ACP exports of all industrial and most agricultural goods, including special arrangements for sugar, bananas, rum and beef. All British dependent territories (with the exception of Bermuda, Gibraltar and Hong Kong), together with the overseas territories of other Community members, are formally associated with the Community under provisions parallel to those of the Lomé Convention and with similar aid and trade benefits.

In 1987 the Council of Ministers approved a Community programme worth around £70 million to aid highly indebted low-income countries in sub-Saharan Africa undertaking significant structural adjustment efforts.

Britain played a leading part in the Community's adoption of an aid programme for developing countries in Asia and Latin America not covered by the Lomé Convention or having any other special relationship with the Community. This has grown steadily since 1976 and was worth some £226 million in 1988. Priority is given to rural development and agricultural production in the poorest countries, most of which are in Asia.

Co-operation and association agreements with individual countries and regional groupings also include provision for development aid. In 1987, for instance, new five-year financial protocols were agreed with most of the Community's Mediterranean partners. These provide for £430 million of Community aid and £706 million in loans from the European Investment Bank.

The Community's food aid programme is designed to be an effective instrument of development policy rather than a short-term expedient for the disposal of food surpluses. In 1989 it spent some £394 million on food aid, of which Britain's share was £77 million, much of which went to Africa.

The Commonwealth

The Commonwealth is a voluntary association of 50 independent states with a combined population of some 1,300 million, nearly a quarter of the world total. Commonwealth members include some of the richest and poorest nations of the world community and also some of the largest and smallest. Their peoples are drawn from practically all the world's main races, from all continents and from many faiths. Britain participates fully in all Commonwealth activities and values it as a means of increasing international understanding, stability and peace, and contributing to more balanced global economic development.

The members are Antigua and Barbuda, Australia, Bahamas, Bangladesh, Barbados, Belize, Botswana, Britain, Brunei, Canada, Cyprus, Dominica, The Gambia, Ghana, Grenada, Guyana, India, Jamaica, Kenya, Kiribati, Lesotho, Malawi, Malaysia, Maldives, Malta, Mauritius, Namibia, Nauru, New Zealand, Nigeria, Pakistan, Papua New Guinea, Saint Kitts and Nevis, Saint Lucia, Saint Vincent and the Grenadines, Seychelles, Sierra Leone, Singapore, Solomon Islands, Sri Lanka, Swaziland, Tanzania, Tonga, Trinidad and Tobago, Tuvalu, Uganda, Vanuatu, Western Samoa, Zambia and Zimbabwe. Nauru and Tuvalu are special members, entitled to take part in all Commonwealth meetings and activities, with the exception of Commonwealth heads of Government meetings. The Queen is recognised as head of the Commonwealth; she is also head of State in 17 of these countries.

The origin of the Commonwealth lies in the gradual granting of self-government to the older-established British colonies (later known as the Dominions) in Australia, Canada, New Zealand and South Africa,[2] where European settlement had occurred on a large scale. Their fully independent status in relation to Britain was legally formulated in the Statute of Westminster of 1931. The modern Commonwealth, comprising republics and national monarchies as well as monarchies under the Queen, became possible when it was agreed in 1949 that India, on becoming a republic, could continue to be a member. Since then, almost all of Britain's former dependent territories have attained their independence and have voluntarily joined the Commonwealth.[3]

Consultation

Consultation between Commonwealth member states takes place through diplomatic representatives known as high commissioners, meetings of heads of Government, specialised conferences of other ministers and officials, expert groups, and discussions at international conferences and the United Nations. Trade and cultural exhibitions and conferences of professional and unofficial medical, cultural, educational and economic organisations are other ways in which frequent contacts are made.

Heads of Government usually meet every two years. Proceedings are held in private, facilitating a frank and informal exchange of views. No votes are taken, decisions being reached by consensus. These meetings allow prime ministers and presidents to discuss international issues and decide on collective initiatives. Common views on matters of major international concern are formulated and reflected in the communiqués issued at the end of the meetings. Occasionally, separate declarations are made on particular issues. The 1989 meeting, for instance, issued a declaration expressing deep concern at the threat posed by serious deterioration of the environment and agreed a set of measures to arrest this. Another statement reaffirmed the central importance of a negotiated settlement in South Africa.

A summit of seven Commonwealth leaders, meeting in London in 1986, agreed on the need for measures against South Africa. Britain, while believing that mandatory economic sanctions would not succeed in promoting peaceful change, agreed to accept voluntary bans on new investment in, and the promotion of tourism to, South Africa, as well as to implement European Community decisions to ban the import of iron and steel. Following the release of Mr Nelson Mandela and other action taken

[2]South Africa ceased to be a member of the Commonwealth in 1961.
[3]Fiji's membership lapsed in 1987.

by the South African Government, Britain lifted these voluntary bans in February 1990 and decided not to discourage artists, scientists and academics from visiting South Africa. The Government believes that the changes taking place in South Africa vindicate a policy of contact rather than isolation.

With many small states among its members the Commonwealth has expressed concern about their security and development. At Nassau in 1985 Commonwealth leaders called for action to reduce the vulnerability of small states without affecting their independent and sovereign status. British policy is to co-operate with other member states in order to increase the security of small nations by encouraging regional co-operation and by providing economic aid and technical assistance.

The Commonwealth Secretariat

The Commonwealth Secretariat promotes consultation, disseminates information on matters of common concern, and organises meetings and conferences, including those of heads of Government and of ministers. It co-ordinates many Commonwealth activities related to international economic, social and political affairs, including education, food production and rural development, the role of women in development, human rights, youth programmes, management development, science and technology, law and health. The Secretariat also administers the Commonwealth Fund for Technical Co-operation.

Because of its neutral position the Secretariat has been able to make its good offices available in cases of dispute, and has carried out, on request, special assignments requiring demonstrable impartiality. The Secretary General is appointed by Commonwealth heads of Government.

Technical Co-operation

Britain contributes almost a third of the income of the Commonwealth Fund for Technical Co-operation, established within the Secretariat to provide technical assistance for economic and social development in Commonwealth developing countries. The Fund's experts undertake advisory assignments or fill specific posts and use consultancy firms to make studies for governments. Its fellowships and training programme helps raise levels of technical, industrial, managerial and other skills, and makes wide use of training facilities within developing member countries for the benefit of other developing countries. It has a special programme to help countries develop their exports, another on food production and rural development and a technical assistance group to give advice in key areas. An industrial development unit investigates the feasibility of establishing new industries in developing countries and helps to prepare and initiate agreed projects.

Expenditure by Britain on bilateral technical co-operation with Commonwealth developing countries in 1989 was £199 million, the greater part being spent on financing staff for service with Commonwealth governments and in funding training places in Britain for people from Commonwealth countries. The British aid programme finances the study in Britain of students from other Commonwealth countries. Other assistance includes sending volunteers to serve overseas, consultancy services, the supply of training and research equipment, and the provision of advice by British scientific and technical institutions. (About two-thirds of Britain's gross bilateral aid goes to Commonwealth countries, including Britain's remaining dependencies—see p 100.)

Commonwealth Organisations

The Commonwealth Foundation, financed by member governments, promotes closer co-operation among professional and other non-governmental organisations within the Commonwealth. It has assisted over 30 Commonwealth professional associations, and has helped in the creation and growth of many national ones; it has also supported 16 multidisciplinary professional centres. It promotes understanding of the work carried out by non-governmental organisations and is encouraging the strengthening of information links through the establishment of liaison units in each Commonwealth country.

The Commonwealth Institute in London promotes the Commonwealth, its countries and its peoples to the British public. Funded mainly by the British Government, it has three main galleries of permanent exhibitions and a changing programme of temporary exhibitions, conferences and performances. Its education service runs an extensive programme of teaching about the Commonwealth in schools around Britain. A wide range of books and other media can be borrowed.

The Commonwealth Trust is a centre for study and discussion, its library in London housing one of the largest collections on the Commonwealth. The Trust has branches in many countries.

Many unofficial organisations, professional bodies and voluntary societies also provide machinery for co-operation. These organisations include the Commonwealth Parliamentary Association, which organises an annual conference of parliamentarians, the Commonwealth Press Union, the Association of Commonwealth Universities, the Commonwealth Games Federation and the English Speaking Union of the Commonwealth.

DEPENDENCIES   There are 14 remaining British dependent territories: Anguilla; Bermuda; British Antarctic Territory; British Indian Ocean Territory; British Virgin Islands; Cayman Islands; Falkland Islands; Gibraltar; Hong Kong; Montserrat; Pitcairn, Ducie, Henderson and Oeno; St Helena and St Helena Dependencies (Ascension and Tristan da Cunha); South Georgia and the South Sandwich Islands; and the Turks and Caicos Islands. They have a combined population of nearly 6 million, of whom 5·8 million live in Hong Kong. Few are rich in natural resources, and some are scattered groups of islands. There are no permanent inhabitants in the British Antarctic Territory, British Indian Ocean Territory, South Georgia or the South Sandwich Islands. Most dependencies have considerable self-government, with their own legislature and civil service. Britain is generally responsible, through a Governor, for defence, internal security and foreign affairs.

Britain's policy is to give independence to those dependencies that want it and where it is practicable to do so. In the case of the Falkland Islands, which are the subject of a territorial claim by Argentina, the inhabitants wish to retain the link with Britain. The Government is committed to the defence of the Islanders' right to live under a government of their own choosing. The Islanders' right of self-determination is set out in the 1985 Falkland Islands Constitution.

Argentina and Chile have made claims to territory which overlaps part of the British Antarctic Territory. Claims to territorial sovereignty in the Antarctic, however, are suspended by the provisions of the 1959 Antarctic Treaty.

Gibraltar is the subject of a territorial claim by Spain. Border restrictions imposed by Spain in the 1960s were lifted in 1985 when Britain and Spain reached agreement on the method for handling their differences over Gibraltar. Britain wishes to see the development of practical co-operation between Gibraltar and Spain to the benefit of both peoples and remains committed to honouring the wishes of the people of Gibraltar as to their future, as set out in the 1969 Gibraltar Constitution.

Hong Kong   In 1984 an agreement was signed between Britain and the People's Republic of China on the future of Hong Kong. Under the Sino-British Joint

Declaration, which was ratified by the two governments in 1985, Britain will continue to be responsible for the administration of Hong Kong until 30 June 1997. Hong Kong will then become a Special Administrative Region (SAR) of the People's Republic of China, but its capitalist system and lifestyle will remain unchanged for at least 50 years. With the exception of foreign affairs and defence, the Hong Kong SAR will enjoy a high degree of autonomy, including executive, legislative and independent judicial power. The Government and legislature of the Hong Kong SAR will be composed of Hong Kong people. The Basic Law, which stipulates China's basic policies towards Hong Kong, as set out in the Joint Declaration, was enacted by the National People's Congress on 4 April 1990.

In February 1990 the British Government announced that the Hong Kong Government would introduce 18 directly elected seats into the Legislative Council in 1991. The Basic Law sets out a path for progressively increasing this number to 30 seats or 50 per cent by 2003 and the possibility of full direct elections in 2007.

In April 1990 legislation to give British citizenship to 50,000 key people in Hong Kong and their dependants—without their having to leave the territory in order to qualify—was passed. The purpose of the British Nationality (Hong Kong) Act is to persuade these people to remain in Hong Kong so that the territory can remain stable and prosperous up to and beyond 1997.

The problem of Vietnamese boat people in Hong Kong is still a matter of concern to the Government, over 34,000 having arrived in 1989. Although the number of new arrivals dropped during 1990, there are still nearly 55,000 in the territory. The main problem is how to deal with those found not to be refugees under internationally agreed screening procedures. Although the number volunteering to return to Vietnam has increased, voluntary returns alone will not be sufficient to provide a comprehensive solution to the problem.

International Peace and Security

Britain protects its territorial integrity and political independence, as well as the interests of its dependencies and of its allies, through a national security policy. This combines the maintenance of effective defence with measures to reduce international tension and encourage dialogue with the Soviet Union and with countries in Eastern and Central Europe.

British defence policy is based on the North Atlantic Treaty Organisation (NATO),[5] the guarantee for member countries of their security and freedom. NATO has always pursued a strategy of deterrence at the lowest possible level of forces, involving North American forces stationed in Europe and an appropriate mix of nuclear and conventional weapons. Although these are still needed as a counterbalance to continued Soviet military power, NATO is increasing its political role in response to the changing security architecture of Europe and the Soviet Union. Progress is being made in negotiations on reductions in conventional forces in Europe (CFE); implementing and verifying an agreement will be a major task. NATO is examining the arrangements for a unified Germany in NATO, and is looking at the future pattern for nuclear and conventional arms control.

[5]NATO's 16 member countries are Belgium, Britain, Canada, Denmark, France, the Federal Republic of Germany, Greece, Iceland, Italy, Luxembourg, the Netherlands, Norway, Portugal, Spain, Turkey and the United States. France, Iceland (which has no military forces) and Spain do not participate in NATO's integrated military structure.

Britain's defence resources are concentrated on key NATO tasks. However, the Government's defence policy is also designed to promote British and more general Western interests outside the NATO area. In addition, Britain demonstrates its worldwide interests by periodic military deployments and exercises overseas; by supporting United Nations and other peacekeeping efforts; and by providing military assistance and training to a number of friendly countries.

East–West Relations

Britain seeks improvements in East–West relations based on a broader understanding and on the recognition that East and West have a common interest in peace and enhanced security at significantly lower levels. It has welcomed the recent replacement of Communist dictatorships by democratically elected governments in Eastern and Central Europe and recognises the importance of recent political and economic reforms in the Soviet Union.

The Government believes that all parties should avoid policies which risk provoking confrontation and should aim instead for mutual accommodation and co-operation while exercising restraint in the conduct of international relations both in Europe and in the rest of the world. This is recognised in the 1975 Helsinki Final Act of the Conference on Security and Co-operation in Europe, which states that European security has to be considered in the broader context of world security.

Britain is committed to increasing its official and unofficial contacts with the Soviet Union and the new governments in Eastern and Central Europe. The meetings between the Prime Minister and the Soviet President in 1987, 1989 and 1990, and the series of other ministerial visits between Britain and the Soviet Union and Eastern European countries have reinforced the continuing improvements in East–West relations. These include the 1987 Intermediate Nuclear Forces (INF) Treaty, greater co-operation on regional issues, including Southern Africa and the withdrawal of Soviet forces from Afghanistan, and the improved human rights provisions of the CSCE agreement in 1989.

German Unification

Britain has always favoured German unification on the basis of self-determination. On 12 September 1990, along with France, the United States, the Soviet Union and the two German states, it signed a treaty on the external aspects of the unification of Germany and Berlin, which took place on 3 October. The treaty ended four-power responsibilities relating to Germany as a whole and Berlin. Germany's definitive borders will be the external borders of the Federal Republic of Germany and the German Democratic Republic. Soviet forces in eastern Germany and Berlin will be withdrawn by the end of 1994. While these remain, British, French and United States forces will, upon German request, remain stationed in Berlin. A unified Germany will be free to choose its alliances.

Economic Assistance

Britain recognises the magnitude of the task now being undertaken by the Soviet Union and the new governments in Central and Eastern Europe in transforming their centrally planned economies into market-based ones. The Government is helping those countries committed to economic and political change through bilateral assistance and through international institutions such as the European Community and the Paris Club of major developed nations. In 1989 Britain established a 'Know How' fund for Hungary and Poland covering training in such areas as management and financial services, banking and accountancy, and commercial law. The fund also finances the provision of advice on the running of democratic institutions such as an independent judiciary, a free media and different political parties. In March 1990 the fund was extended to Czechoslovakia. Britain is also supporting debt-rescheduling schemes being negotiated by the International Monetary Fund with several Eastern European countries. In addition, it is participating in other multilateral assistance plans, including World Bank loans and European Community agreements liberalising trade, aimed at encouraging the development of market economies.

Conference on Security and Co-operation in Europe

Britain welcomes the recent and significant improvements in the implementation of the provisions of the 1975 Helsinki Final Act. The CSCE process has assisted in increasing stability in Europe and improved co-operation between the 35 European and North American signatory states. While not legally binding, the Final Act established a large number of important political commitments and a code of behaviour for a more normal and open relationship between both governments and peoples in East and West. In order to achieve these goals, the signatories of the Final Act made undertakings about security, respect for human rights, and co-operation in economic, humanitarian and other matters. Meetings to review the application of the Final Act took place in Belgrade (1977–78), Madrid (1980–83) and Vienna (1987–89). The Madrid Conference also set up in Stockholm in 1984 a Conference on Confidence- and Security-Building Measures and Disarmament in Europe, as well as other meetings on such issues as human rights, culture and human contacts.

As a result of initiatives by Britain and other Western countries aimed at improving the implementation of the Final Act, participating states agreed in Vienna in 1989 to undertake new commitments, in particular in human rights (for example, on freedom of religion) and human contacts (for example, on freedom of movement). Various meetings have taken place on information, the environment, economic co-operation and human rights. More are planned before 1992, including meetings on culture and human rights.

At the Stockholm conference in 1986, the participating states signed an agreement (the Stockholm Document) on confidence-building measures designed to bring about a greater degree of openness and predictability in military activities. The agreement provided for advance notification and observation of planned military manoeuvres above specified thresholds and detailed information on their purpose, size, composition and dates, as well as intrusive provisions for verification in the form of on-site challenge inspections. In Britain's view, implementation of the Stockholm Document has continued to work well. In 1989, 15 inspections took place and six NATO and two Warsaw Pact exercises were observed, as well as two by neutral or non-aligned countries.

Following a British initiative in 1986, informal talks between NATO and the Warsaw Pact led to an agreement in January 1989 to establish within the framework of the Vienna CSCE Conference new sets of negotiations, which opened in Vienna in March 1989. In the first, which involves all CSCE countries, Britain and its NATO allies are seeking to expand the compliance and verification provisions of the Stockholm Document.

The second set of talks involves the 23 members of NATO and the Warsaw Pact. The talks aim to establish a stable and secure balance of conventional ground forces at lower levels in the whole of Europe.

Arms Control and Disarmament

Together with its NATO allies, Britain is committed to the search for significant, balanced and verifiable measures of arms control and disarmament, leading to increased security at lower levels of forces, and has played a prominent part in multilateral disarmament negotiations. Britain participates in the Conference on Disarmament in Geneva and in the negotiations in Vienna on conventional armed forces in Europe and on confidence- and security-building measures. It also takes an active part in other disarmament deliberations under the auspices of the United Nations.

Following the INF Treaty, Britain wants further progress in arms control. The priorities, as set out by NATO, are substantial reductions in United States and Soviet strategic nuclear arsenals, a global ban on chemical weapons, and the elimination of conventional imbalances in Europe.

Nuclear Weapons Britain strongly supports the nuclear and space talks between the United States and the Soviet Union which began in Geneva in 1985. It fully shares the agreed objective of working out effective agreements aimed at preventing an arms race in space and terminating it on earth, at limiting and reducing nuclear arms and at strengthening strategic stability.

The Government has welcomed the 1987 treaty between the United States and the Soviet Union under which both countries are eliminating all their ground-launched intermediate-range nuclear missiles throughout the world over a three-year period. Under the treaty, which came into effect in June 1988 and is the first arms control agreement designed to eliminate a whole class of nuclear weapons, missiles capable of carrying some 1,700 Soviet and 400 US warheads are being destroyed. Britain also supports the efforts of the superpowers to work towards a treaty aimed at reducing strategic offensive arms. The Government looks forward to the prospect of negotiations on shorter-range nuclear forces shortly after a treaty limiting conventional forces in Europe has been signed.

Nuclear Deterrent Britain's strategic nuclear deterrent is the minimum necessary for credible deterrence and is very small in comparison with Soviet nuclear forces. It will continue to be a minimum force even after the replacement of the submarine-launched Polaris force with a modernised missile system known as Trident.

In Britain's view, the priority is for reductions in the arsenals of the two superpowers. Britain has, however, made it clear that, if the US and Soviet strategic arsenals were to be very substantially reduced, it would review the position and consider how best it could contribute to arms control in the light of the reduced threat. But reductions would have to go much further than those under discussion in Geneva before the Government could consider bringing the British independent nuclear deterrent into arms control negotiations.

Non-Proliferation Britain has played a leading part in strengthening the regime of non-proliferation of nuclear weapons. It is a party to the most widely supported arms control agreement, the 1968 Non-Proliferation Treaty, which is designed to stop the spread of nuclear weapons by providing an assurance through international safeguards that nuclear facilities of non-nuclear-weapon states will not be used for making such weapons. It also protects the right of all countries to use nuclear energy for peaceful purposes.

Britain was the first nuclear-weapon state to conclude a voluntary agreement with the International Atomic Energy Agency for the application of safeguards to some nuclear installations. It has also undertaken not to use nuclear weapons against non-nuclear-weapon states which are parties to the Treaty or to other internationally binding commitments not to manufacture or acquire nuclear explosive devices. This undertaking would not apply in the case of an attack on Britain, its dependent territories, its armed forces or its allies by such a state in association or alliance with a nuclear-weapon state.

Britain will continue to make every effort to strengthen and expand the Treaty.

Nuclear Tests

Since for the foreseeable future Britain's security will depend on deterrence based in part on the possession of nuclear weapons, there will be a continuing requirement to conduct underground nuclear tests to ensure that Britain's nuclear weapons remain effective and up to date. Britain hopes that the 1974 Threshold Test Ban Treaty and the 1976 Peaceful Nuclear Explosions Treaty, which were negotiated by the United States and the Soviet Union and set ceilings for individual and group nuclear tests, will be ratified by the two countries soon. Verification protocols regarding the two treaties were signed by both countries in 1990. A comprehensive test ban, however, remains a long term goal, and progress towards this is dependent on a step-by-step approach which takes account of technical advances on verification as well as progress elsewhere in arms control and the attitude of other states.

Nuclear-Weapon-Free Zones

The Government thinks that the establishment of nuclear-weapon-free zones in certain parts of the world could contribute to regional security, to non-proliferation and to disarmament in general, provided that nuclear weapons do not already feature in the security of the region involved and that the balance of security is maintained.

Chemical and Biological Weapons

Britain is working towards a comprehensive and effectively verifiable worldwide ban on chemical weapons, having destroyed its own chemical weapons in the late 1950s. The negotiations for such a treaty take place at the Conference on Disarmament in Geneva, where Britain plays a leading role. It has presented a number of substantive papers, particularly on the issues of verification and confidence building.

Pending achievement of a global ban, Britain and some other Western nations have imposed export controls on certain chemicals which may be used to produce chemical weapons in order to curb further proliferation of such weapons.

The Government has welcomed the recent bilateral progress between the United States and the Soviet Union, particularly their 1990 agreement on the destruction of their stocks of chemical weapons down to 20 per cent of the current US stockpile.

Biological weapons are already prohibited under a 1972 convention. A review conference in 1986 reaffirmed the value of the convention and adopted a number of voluntary confidence-building measures involving exchanges of information aimed at strengthening the authority of the convention. A further review conference is to be held in 1991.

Conventional Weapons

Conventional weapons are by far the largest component of national armouries. Since March 1989 Britain has been participating with its NATO allies in new negotiations with the Warsaw Pact on conventional arms reductions, which are being held within the CSCE framework and involve all 23 NATO and Warsaw Pact states in an area from the Atlantic to the Urals mountains.

NATO's proposals aim to set limits on the number of battle tanks, armoured combat vehicles, artillery, attack helicopters and combat aircraft at some 10 to 15 per cent below current NATO holdings. In some cases this would involve cuts of over 50 per cent in Warsaw Pact holdings. There would also be rules limiting the proportions of the total holdings which any one country could possess and a limit on forces stationed by states in other countries. There would also be strict verification and monitoring.

At the United Nations Britain submitted memoranda setting out its arms control priorities at Special Sessions of the General Assembly on disarmament in 1978, 1982 and 1988. Britain also contributes to the UN Disarmament Commission, a deliberative body considering issues such as naval armaments and the reduction of military budgets which are not on the agenda of the Conference on Disarmament.

Britain and the United Nations

Britain is fully committed to the principles of the United Nations and its Charter and believes that all member states should ensure that the organisation functions as effectively as possible to maintain peace, assist developing countries and protect human rights and freedoms.

Keeping the Peace

Britain believes that the United Nations, as the only forum in which almost the whole international community is represented, should seek to resolve disputes which threaten international peace and stability. As a permanent member of the Security Council, Britain plays an active part in the Council's work and has sought to develop and improve its role in the peaceful settlement of disputes. Britain has also encouraged financial and administrative reform aimed at rationalising the work of the Organisation.

Britain strongly supports the United Nations' peacekeeping role, is the major contributor to the UN Force in Cyprus and has provided logistic support to the UN Interim Force in Lebanon. In 1989-90 Britain contributed an Army signals unit to Namibia to provide communications for the United Nations Transition Assistance Group monitoring the implementation of the UN plan for independence.

Human Rights

Britain has consistently supported United Nations efforts to promote human rights throughout the world through the establishment of internationally accepted standards. The UN Charter says that the United Nations should achieve international co-operation in promoting and encouraging respect for human rights and fundamental freedoms for all without distinction as to race, sex, language or religion. Britain believes that this and the subsequent practice of the United Nations has established human rights as a legitimate matter for international concern and that the UN Charter imposes on member governments an obligation to co-operate with appropriate UN bodies in the pursuit of policies which promote human rights.

Fundamental human rights provisions are set out in the Universal Declaration of Human Rights proclaimed by the General Assembly in 1948, and in the two International Covenants (one on Economic, Social and Cultural Rights and the other on Civil and Political Rights) which impose legal obligations on those who ratify them and which came into force in 1976. Britain played a large part in their drafting and ratified the two Covenants in 1976. Britain is also a party to other international instruments, including conventions on the elimination of racial discrimination and of discrimination against women, prevention of genocide, the abolition of slavery, the status of refugees and stateless persons, the political rights of women, the rights of the child and consent to marriage. In 1988 Britain ratified the UN Convention against Torture, which was adopted with British support by the General Assembly in 1984.

Britain constantly urges states to adhere to those standards which have been agreed internationally as the basis of the protection of human rights. It has also supported the idea of appointing representatives of the UN

Commission on Human Rights to investigate human rights abuses.

Britain plays a leading part in the discussion of human rights in the various United Nations bodies. In 1987 it was re-elected to the UN Commission on Human Rights for a further three-year term. There are British experts on the UN Sub-Commission and the Committee on the Elimination of Racial Discrimination.

Economic and Social Affairs
The UN Charter states that 'the promotion of the economic and social advancement of all peoples' is one of the principal aims of the United Nations; an estimated 90 per cent of the organisation's resources and staff is devoted to this end. With growing concern over the problems of economic development in poor countries, the UN system has become the largest single source of technical assistance for developing countries. It also provides considerable emergency and relief aid, assistance for refugees and help in combating the problems associated with drug production, trafficking and abuse.

Britain is the sixth largest contributor to the UN's regular budget, and provided in 1990 some £23 million, nearly 5 per cent of the total. In addition, in 1989, it contributed some £7·9 million to the World Health Organisation, £5·6 million to the International Labour Organisation and £8·6 million to the Food and Agriculture Organisation.

Britain provides considerable contributions to the UN's voluntary funds, donating £26 million in 1989 for the UN Development Programme, £19·4 million for the UN High Commissioner for Refugees, £5·6 million for the UN Relief and Works Agency for Palestinian Refugees, £9·6 million for the UN Children's Fund, £5·5 million for the UN Population Fund, and about £0·5 million for the World Food Programme. It is also a major donor to the UN Fund for Drug Abuse Control.

Britain encourages the deployment of UN resources towards the poorest countries and the poorest communities in the developing world. It also seeks to promote the most efficient use of UN development funds and improvements in the co-ordination, control and effectiveness of the system, in order to avoid unnecessary duplication by the various agencies.

In 1985 Britain withdrew from the United Nations Educational, Scientific and Cultural Organisation (UNESCO). Although Britain supports the ideals and objectives contained in UNESCO's constitution, it had major doubts about the effectiveness with which the Organisation was pursuing them. After a detailed review of UNESCO activities, Britain announced in 1990 that the reforms carried out were not yet sufficient to merit rejoining the Organisation. Aid amounting to £6·4 million, representing funds saved from the withdrawal, was allocated to a number of educational, scientific and cultural programmes in developing countries in 1989-90.

Other International Organisations

Britain is a member of many other international organisations, including those concerned with the management of the world economy. It is a founder member of the International Monetary Fund, established in 1945 (along with the World Bank) to regulate the international financial system and to provide a source of credit for member countries facing balance-of-payments problems. It has welcomed the creation by the Fund of facilities to provide special assistance to developing countries experiencing financial or trading difficulties. The Government strongly supports the objectives of the current Uruguay Round of negotiations conducted under the auspices of the General Agreement on Tariffs and Trade (see p 87).

Britain is also a member of the Organisation for Economic Co-operation and Development (OECD), an instrument for intergovernmental co-operation among 24 industrialised countries. The basic objectives of the OECD are to promote the economic growth of its members, to help less developed countries within and outside its own membership and to encourage worldwide trade expansion.

Other organisations to which Britain belongs or extends support include the regional development banks in Africa, the Caribbean, Latin America and Asia and specialist technical, agricultural and medical institutions.

Britain is a founder member of the Council of Europe, which works for greater European unity and aims to improve the conditions of life. Membership is open to any European parliamentary democracy which accepts the rule of law and the protection of fundamental human rights and freedoms.The 23 member states co-operate on culture, education, sport, social questions, legal affairs, health, crime and drug prevention, youth affairs and the improvement of the environment. The Council was responsible for the adoption in 1950 of the European Convention on Human Rights, which Britain was the first to ratify in 1951. In 1986 Britain renewed its acceptance for a further five years of the optional articles of the Convention which recognise both the right of individual petition and the compulsory jurisdiction of the European Court of Human Rights.

Development Co-operation

The objective of Britain's aid programme is the promotion of sustainable economic and social progress and the alleviation of poverty in developing countries. In meeting this objective weight is given to political, commercial and humanitarian considerations. Account is also taken of the effectiveness with which British aid can be used.

Gross public expenditure on the aid programme was £1,787 million in 1989. About 80 per cent of Britain's bilateral aid is directed to the poorer countries of the world. The Overseas Development Administration (ODA), which is responsible for formulating and implementing Britain's aid policy, maintains rigorous procedures to ensure that aid is correctly targeted and efficiently administered.

To ensure the best use of aid resources, individual country aid programmes take account of the needs of the recipient country, its development priorities, the activities of other donors and what Britain can offer by way of expertise, goods and services. Individual projects are carefully appraised before approval, monitored during progress against quantifiable targets and assessed in a project completion report. The British aid programme seeks to provide essential economic infrastructure in areas such as communications and power supplies; to improve education, health services or housing; to raise incomes and improve agricultural and industrial productivity; and to provide support for countries pursuing economic reform programmes agreed with the International Monetary Fund and the World Bank.

Britain has taken a number of measures to assist the poorest and most heavily indebted countries pursuing policies of economic reform. In 1987 it proposed international action to cut interest rates to well below market levels, to convert aid loans into grants and to allow for more generous rescheduling of debt. These proposals, and subsequent variations by other countries, were welcomed at the 1988 Economic Summit at Toronto. Concessionary debt rescheduling has since been arranged for 16 of the poorest countries in Africa. Britain has cancelled the official aid debt of 22 of the poorest countries. In addition, Britain is the largest contributor to the interest subsidy account of the IMF Enhanced Structural Adjustment Facility, which was established in 1988 to lend up to £4,500 million to the poorest countries on highly concessional terms—that is, at interest rates of 0.5 per cent.

Britain's aid represents part of a wider Western effort to help developing countries. In 1989 total net official development assistance disbursed by the 18 countries belonging to the OECD's Development Assistance Committee amounted to $46,500 million. It is estimated that in 1989 Arab countries provided $1,200 million and centrally planned economies $4,300 million.

In addition to official aid, the British private sector provides investment, technology and management expertise, and assists the development of indigenous resources and skills in developing countries. In 1989 estimated investment by British companies in developing countries amounted to £2,600 million. Trade, too, is important, developing countries providing 12 per cent of British imports in 1989.

Official and Other Flows

In 1989 total official flows[6] of aid amounted to some £1,856 million net, of which £1,576 million represented official development assistance and £280 million other official flows.

Aid volume performance is commonly measured as a proportion of gross national product (GNP), particularly with reference to the three UN targets for resource transfers to developing countries. These targets state that net official development assistance to developing countries should equal 0·7 per cent of GNP, to the least developed countries 0·15 per cent of GNP and that combined private and official flows should equal 1 per cent of GNP. Britain accepts the first and second targets in principle but is not committed to a timetable for reaching them. Successive governments have made it clear that progress must depend on Britain's economic situation and upon other calls on its resources. In 1989 net official development assistance was 0·31 per cent of GNP, close to the overall 0·33 per cent for donor countries belonging to the OECD's Development Assistance Committee. Total net financial flows from Britain to developing countries amounted to £2,252 million, 0·45 per cent of GNP.

Bilateral Aid

The main emphasis of the British aid programme is on the Commonwealth, which includes among its members some of the world's poorest countries. In 1989, about £1,113 million of gross public expenditure on overseas aid was disbursed bilaterally. Some 75 per cent of that directly allocated to countries went to the Commonwealth and to Britain's remaining dependencies. Aid was disbursed regionally as follows: Africa £510 million, Asia £301 million, Latin America and the Caribbean £90 million, Pacific £31 million, the Middle East £14 million and Europe £5 million. (A further £162 million was not allocable by continent.)

Major recipients included Bangladesh, India, Kenya, Malawi, Zambia, Tanzania, Mozambique, Pakistan, Sudan and Ghana. In line with the policy of concentrating aid on the poorest countries, 69 per cent of total gross bilateral aid was provided to those with an average annual income per head in 1987 of less than $700.

---

[6] 'Total official flows' is an international reporting concept. Its main component—official development assistance—is defined as official flows for development purposes with a grant (concessional) element of 25 per cent or more. The main British reporting concept is 'public expenditure on overseas aid', which differs from total official flows by excluding certain British flows which benefit developing countries but are not considered developmental, and by recording some contributions to multilateral agencies at a different time. All concepts can be measured before (gross) or after (net) deducting capital repayments.

Financial Aid

Gross bilateral financial aid in 1989 totalled £645 million. Aid for individual projects totalled £382 million, the principal sectors supported being agriculture, fisheries and forestry (£80 million), manufacturing (£36 million), energy (£76 million), mining (£28 million), transport and communications (£83 million) and social and community services (£39 million).

Other financial aid totalled £257 million, of which £190 million was for programme aid, £26·1 million for debt relief, £19·4 million for disaster relief, £16·8 million for food aid and £5·1 million for budgetary aid.

About 75 per cent of the ODA's bilateral financial aid in 1988 was provided in grants. Since 1975 development aid to the poorest countries has been on grant terms. In 1984 these terms were extended to the majority of recipients of British financial aid, and simplified loan terms were introduced for those countries still not qualifying for grants. Britain has more than fulfilled the 1978 resolution of the United Nations Conference on Trade and Development on easing the terms of financial aid.

Most financial aid—58 per cent in 1989—is tied to the purchase of goods, equipment and services from Britain, although there may be a substantial element for local costs and foreign content in contracts financed from tied aid in appropriate cases. Commitments can be untied, if the recipient agrees, to the extent that goods can be purchased either from the poorest developing countries or from Britain.

Aid Projects

More resources are being committed to the sustainable development of forestry; the ODA is involved in 165 projects in 22 countries costing over £150 million. Since August 1989 ODA forestry experts have visited Brazil, Cameroon, India, Malaysia, Nepal, Nigeria, Tanzania and Zimbabwe, and in November another £100 million was committed by Britain over the next three years for forestry activities. Britain is co-operating with Brazil to solve environmental problems, including schemes to manage and conserve the Amazon rainforest.

Other British aid projects include a major water and sanitation scheme in Karachi and the building of a power station in south-west Pakistan. Similarly, the power station in Maputo, Mozambique, is being repaired with British aid. In September 1989 Britain and India signed a £35 million aid agreement to improve primary education in the state of Andhra Pradesh in southern India; over 4,000 new classrooms will be built and over 1,100 teachers' centres upgraded, mostly in remote rural areas.

Britain is also helping Sierra Leone, Cameroon and Zaire in schemes to repair and maintain road bridges, by providing engineers, light vehicles and small-scale plant equipment. British projects in countries in southern Africa include £29 million for the rehabilitation of the Limpopo railway linking Zimbabwe to Maputo in Mozambique. Direct British support is being given to over 200 community projects and to a private sector scheme designed to build new, low cost owner-occupied homes in South Africa, the benefits going to members of the black population. In March 1990 Britain announced that it would provide aid worth £10 million to newly independent Namibia.

The Aid and Trade Provision is designed to match the mixed credit practices of other donors by providing aid in combination with export credits to support sound investment projects offering commercial opportunities to British exporters. Expenditure under this provision amounted to £51 million in 1989. In 1985 the Government introduced a new soft-loan facility under the Provision in order to respond to the preferences of certain developing countries and to counter the practices of competitors. Increased funds are being made available to enable British companies to win business annually with the provision. As a matter of general policy, however, the Government would like to see a reduction in the use of tied-aid financing by all exporting nations in the interests of more open competition and freer trade.

The Commonwealth Development Corporation is empowered to invest in Commonwealth countries which have achieved independence since 1948, in the remaining British dependencies and, with ministerial approval, in other developing countries. Its aim is to assist in the development of these countries' economies. By the end of 1989, the Corporation had total commitments of £1,166 million. Of this total, £462·8 million was in Africa, £346·1 million in Asia, £224·5 million in the Caribbean and Latin America, and £126·2 million in the Pacific Islands. Some £380·8 million was invested in basic development, £555·8 million in primary production and processing, and £229·4 million in industry and commerce.

Disaster Relief and Food Aid

Britain responds to disasters throughout the world by providing food, medical equipment, blankets, shelters and clothing, power generators, boats, bridges and other vital supplies. In 1988 British emergency aid was sent to the Soviet Union to help deal with the consequences of the Armenian earthquake, to the Caribbean and Central America following hurricanes Gilbert and Joan, and to Bangladesh in the aftermath of a cyclone. In September 1989 Britain provided almost £5 million for emergency relief to the Caribbean islands devastated by Hurricane Hugo. In sub-Saharan and southern Africa, Britain continued its contribution to disaster relief and food aid to help combat drought and famine. In addition to its multilateral aid contributions to UN agencies and the European Community (see p 103), Britain gave £111 million in bilateral disaster relief between 1984 and 1989. Emergency aid to Ethiopia in 1989 was £18·5 million. Furthermore, bilateral and multilateral food aid by Britain amounted to £110 million over the same period.

Many African countries suffering from famine are also victims of locusts; in response Britain has pledged more than £7·5 million for locust and pest control in Africa since the beginning of 1987. Britain and three other countries are financing research on the biological control of locusts.

Britain also helps refugees and people displaced by famine, political upheaval, civil war and invasion. Since 1980, for instance, over £70 million has been contributed to assist Afghan refugees. Worldwide, some £35 million is provided annually through non-governmental bodies and UN agencies.

Technical Co-operation

Technical co-operation, the transfer of specialised knowledge and skills from country to country, complements financial aid since expertise is often essential to the success of a programme of financial aid or investment. Expenditure on it has increased in recent years and was £419 million, nearly 38 per cent of gross bilateral aid, in 1989. This included £78 million for the provision of expert personnel, including volunteers, £110·5 million for students and trainees in Britain and overseas, £49·8 million for education and training programmes, £62·5 million for consultancy services, £27·4 million for research and development, and £20·8 million for equipment and supplies.

At the end of 1989 there were 2,939 people financed by Britain (other than volunteers) working in developing countries, of whom 1,470 were engaged in education, 492 in agriculture and related areas, and 213 in health services. In addition, there were nearly 1,400 volunteers, mainly qualified people with some relevant work experience, working in developing countries, about half in education. Recruitment, training and placing overseas are undertaken by voluntary bodies. The four main agencies are the Catholic Institute for International Relations, International Voluntary Service, United Nations Association International Service and Voluntary Service Overseas. More than 80 per cent of their costs are met by the Government.

Britain receives large numbers of students and trainees from developing countries. Some 13,300 were financed in 1989 under a variety of award schemes.

The ODA's scientific organisation, the Natural Resources Institute, collaborates with developing countries on increasing the productivity of their renewable natural resources. The Government provides support for many other institutions, including overseas units/divisions of the Transport and Road Research Laboratory, the Building Research Establishment, the British Geological Survey, the Overseas Surveys Directorate of the Ordnance Survey, and of Hydraulics Research Ltd. These organisations provide specialist information, advice and experts for service overseas, and undertake field and laboratory research investigations.

Multilateral Aid Britain is a major subscriber to the World Bank group of institutions—the International Bank for Reconstruction and Development, the International Development Association (IDA), the International Finance Corporation and the Multilateral Investment Guarantee Agency.

The resources of the IDA, which provides interest-free loans to developing countries unable to service loans on conventional terms, are replenished at roughly three-year intervals. The British commitment to its Ninth Replenishment, covering the three years starting in 1991, is £619 million towards a total of US$15,000 million.

Britain contributes to the resources of the Asian Development Bank, the Inter-American Development Bank, the Caribbean Development Bank and the African Development Bank. Its contribution to the United Nations Development Programme for 1989 was £27 million, and it is the largest source of expertise and the second largest of fellowships and equipment provided under the Programme. There is also a major British contribution to other UN agencies and programmes, including the World Health Organisation's special programme for the prevention and control of AIDS.

Almost half of British multilateral aid is channelled through the European Community's aid programme. Under the fourth Lomé Convention, Britain's commitment to Community aid over the next five years is £1,300 million out of a total of £8,500 million.

Voluntary Agencies Voluntary agencies play an important and distinctive role in developing countries in such areas as agriculture, health and nutrition, education projects, and emergency relief operations.

There are more than 200 agencies, including church and missionary societies. Among the best known are Oxfam, Christian Aid, the Save the Children Fund, and the Catholic Fund for Overseas Development. The funds are raised largely through regular donations and collections, legacies and trading activities, and, particularly in response to specific emergencies, through appeals in the media. The Government co-operates with the agencies in various ways, especially in immediate post-disaster relief and rehabilitation operations and through its Joint Funding Scheme. Under this scheme it meets half the cost of selected development projects undertaken by the agencies and aimed at helping the poorest people. Such projects include community health, non-formal education, agricultural training, water supply and projects concerned with the preservation of the environment and sustainable use of natural resources such as tropical forests. The scheme's budget has increased from £3·7 million in 1984–85 to £20 million in 1990–91.

Voluntary agencies' work on behalf of refugees overseas also receives official support.

4 Defence

The primary objectives of Britain's defence policy are to ensure the country's security, to preserve peace with freedom, and to enable it to pursue its legitimate interests both within Britain and overseas. Britain's policy is based on membership of the North Atlantic Treaty Organisation (NATO), a defensive alliance whose collective strength provides each of its members[1] with far greater security than any could achieve alone. Britain welcomes the election of democratic governments in Eastern Europe and moves towards democracy in the Soviet Union. It believes that British security can be protected by the continuing maintenance of collective defence with its NATO allies. At the same time, Britain and its NATO allies have recognised the need to readjust their military structure and strategy to the new security position and have outlined ways in which this would be done.

By far the greatest part of the defence budget goes, directly or indirectly, towards carrying out Britain's main defence roles in NATO, to which the majority of its armed forces are committed. In recent years the structure and balance of these forces have been improved to increase their combat effectiveness. As a result of these improvements Britain also has the flexibility to respond quickly and effectively to challenges to its interests outside the NATO area.

Changes in Europe

Despite important political and military changes in the Soviet Union and Eastern Europe, the Soviet Union remains a military superpower. NATO, therefore, is still needed to provide continuing stability and security during a period of political uncertainty in Europe. Britain also believes that NATO provides the most effective forum for transatlantic political co-operation and consultation on security and arms control, for co-ordinating the implementation of arms control agreements and for establishing the basis for further negotiations.

NATO Policy

NATO is a political and military alliance of countries sharing a common commitment to peace, democracy and the rule of law. Its aims are to prevent war and maintain the security of its members at the lowest possible levels of forces.

NATO continues to maintain collective security, taking account of the military forces stationed in Europe, and to pursue a strategy that deters wars of all kinds. Its flexible response strategy requires the Alliance to have the ability to respond to any form of potential military aggression with effective and up-to-date forces—conventional, sub-strategic nuclear or strategic nuclear—at an appropriate level to prevent an attacker from predicting with certainty the precise character of NATO's response. In this way the strategy aims to convince an attacker that the risks run would far outweigh any possible gains.

---

[1]NATO'S 16 member countries are Belgium, Britain, Canada, Denmark, France, the Federal Republic of Germany, Greece, Iceland, Italy, Luxembourg, the Netherlands, Norway, Portugal, Spain, Turkey and the United States.

In a declaration in July 1990, the allies reaffirmed their commitment to defend the territory of all NATO members. However, they also recognised that, as Europe was changing militarily and politically, the Alliance had to alter its structure and strategy. This will include the deployment of smaller, highly mobile forces; a change in the size and tasks of the Alliance's nuclear deterrent forces, with a reduced role for short-range nuclear systems; and a modified military strategy, reflecting a reduced reliance on nuclear weapons.

Britain plays a full part in the Alliance's efforts to negotiate balanced and verifiable arms control agreements. NATO believes that the first priority is a treaty to reduce and limit conventional forces in Europe (CFE), along with the completion of a package of confidence- and security-building measures. This would be followed by new conventional arms control negotiations aimed at further measures to limit the offensive capability of conventional arms forces in Europe. Once the CFE agreement is signed, new negotiations between the Soviet Union and the United States should take place on the reduction of short-range nuclear forces.

Britain supports the Strategic Arms Reduction Treaty (START) negotiations between the United States and the Soviet Union. Britain also plays a key role in negotiations at the Conference on Disarmament in Geneva. The most important issue under discussion is a global ban on chemical weapons.

The NATO allies have acknowledged that Western interests outside the NATO area may be threatened and recognise the need, in the last resort, for those members with the means to do so to take action in consultation with their allies.

Britain's NATO Contribution

Britain's contribution to NATO is concentrated in areas where it can best help to maintain Alliance security, principally NATO's strategic nuclear deterrent and the defence of the Central Region of Europe, the Eastern Atlantic and English Channel, and the British 'home' base and its immediate approaches.

Britain's strategic forces, equipped with improved Polaris missiles (to be replaced by a Trident force in the mid-1990s), provide an independent and European centre of decision-making within the Alliance, thereby guarding against any misconception that Europe's defence is ultimately dependent on the US nuclear guarantee. Britain has also committed its other nuclear systems to NATO.

Virtually all of the Royal Navy is committed to the Alliance. Permanent contributions are made to NATO's two standing naval forces, in the Atlantic and the Channel, and to its Mediterranean force when activated. The British Army of the Rhine (BAOR) and Royal Air Force (RAF) Germany are stationed in the Federal Republic of Germany. Under the 1954 Brussels Treaty,[2] BAOR has three armoured divisions (with supporting artillery): two divisions consist of three armoured brigades each and the other of two armoured brigades and an infantry brigade. A reinforcing division comprising one regular and two Territorial Army brigades is located in Britain. Nearly all the RAF's combat and support aircraft are assigned to NATO. RAF Germany's 15 squadrons (two of helicopters) are equipped for strike/attack, reconnaissance, close support, air defence and air transport roles, while RAF Strike Command, based in Britain, provides forces for these and for the maritime patrol and anti-submarine warfare roles.

---

[2]In 1988 the seven original members—Belgium, Britain, France, the Federal Republic of Germany, Italy, Luxembourg and the Netherlands—were joined by Portugal and Spain.

Britain also contributes ships and commando units to a British–Dutch amphibious force, ground and air units for the Allied Command Europe Mobile Force, and several squadrons for NATO's Strategic Air Reserve.

Forces from all three Services are stationed at Gibraltar, which, positioned at the western entry to the Mediterranean, is an important base for NATO.

Options for Change

Because of the changed military situation in Europe, the Government is proposing changes in defence provision. The strategic deterrent and a sub-strategic nuclear force, provided by dual-capable aircraft, would be retained. The air defence of Britain would be undertaken by Tornado F3 squadrons, supplemented by Hawk aircraft. Home defence forces and the fleet of mine counter-measures vessels would remain at their current level.

Although Britain will continue to play a full part in the defence of Europe, the Government envisages that the British forces stationed in Germany could be half their existing strength. When reinforced from Britain, BAOR could comprise two divisions rather than four as at present. RAF Germany could be reduced from 15 to nine squadrons, and two of the four RAF bases in Germany closed. An amphibious force will be retained which should reinforce NATO's northern region; also retained is the ability to provide air support to defend that area. A strategic reserve division is to be established, bringing together amphibious, parachute, air-mobile and armoured formations, with roles also in Europe or in national defence.

The Government proposes that Britain's maritime contribution to NATO should continue to include three aircraft carriers, smaller forces of destroyers and frigates (reduced to about 40), submarines and Nimrod aircraft.

Implementing these changes would result in the strength of the armed forces being reduced by 18 per cent to around 60,000 in the Royal Navy and the Royal Marines; 120,000 in the Army; and 75,000 in the Royal Air Force. The number of civilians employed by the Ministry of Defence would be similarly reduced.

Europe and the Alliance

Britain's contribution to NATO is part of the wider effort which the European allies make for the defence of the West, including the protection of their common interests outside the NATO area. The European allies provide the majority of NATO forces, as well as military facilities for United States contributions, communications and transport.

Britain and its European allies play a full part in the Independent European Programme Group, which promotes arms co-operation among European allies, and in the Conference of National Armaments Directors, the forum for defence equipment collaboration across the Atlantic. They also work together in the Eurogroup to improve their contributions to the Alliance and to achieve better use of available resources. In addition, the Western European Union (WEU) provides further impetus towards European defence and security co-operation. The WEU helped to co-ordinate contributions by member countries in mine clearance operations in the Gulf during the Iran–Iraq war in the late 1980s; in 1987 it also published a statement setting out how members intended to contribute to NATO's future security and to provide a basis for the development of the WEU as a forum for Western Europe's defence effort in support of the Alliance. WEU members have agreed to co-ordinate their participation in the multinational force in the Gulf (see p 108).

Outside the NATO Area

Britain maintains and improves its ability to operate outside the NATO area to protect its interests without diminishing its commitment to the Alliance. It has an airborne brigade which can be deployed to trouble spots should the need arise. British garrisons are maintained in Belize, Brunei, Cyprus, the Falkland Islands and, until 1997, Hong Kong.

It also provides the largest national troop contingent to the United Nations Force in Cyprus as well as giving support for the United Nations Interim Force in Lebanon, and contributes a detachment to the Multinational Force and Observers in Sinai. Britain is contributing contingents to the multilateral force deployed in the Middle East to help in the defence of Saudi Arabia and other Gulf states against the threat of Iraqi aggression. Considerable effort is devoted to the provision of military assistance and training to about 30 countries outside the NATO area, and Britain deploys its forces on visits and exercises in important areas.

Northern Ireland

Within Britain, the armed forces support the Royal Ulster Constabulary (RUC) in the fight against terrorism in Northern Ireland. The Army provides ten major regular units and nine battalions of the Ulster Defence Regiment. The Royal Navy, which carries out patrols to prevent arms smuggling, and the RAF also make substantial contributions; the Royal Marines support Army and Navy operations.

THE ARMED FORCES
Personnel

At the beginning of 1990 the strength of the armed forces, all volunteers, was 306,000: 63,500 in the Royal Navy and the Royal Marines, 152,900 in the Army and 89,600 in the Royal Air Force. The Ministry of Defence employed about 142,000 civilians (based in Britain) at the same date.

The 16,700 female personnel in the nursing and women's services (3,500 in the Royal Navy, 6,700 in the Army and 6,500 in the Royal Air Force) serve alongside servicemen in Britain and overseas.

Engagements for non-commissioned ranks range from 3 to 22 years, with a wide choice of length and terms of service. Subject to a minimum period of service, entrants may leave at any time, at 18 months' notice (12 months for certain engagements). Discharge may also be granted on compassionate grounds, by purchase, or on grounds of conscience. Commissions, either by promotion from the ranks or by direct entry based on educational and other qualifications, are granted for short, medium and long terms. All three Services have schemes for school, university and college sponsorships.

Non-commissioned personnel receive basic training supplemented by specialist training throughout their careers. Study for educational qualifications is encouraged and Service trade and technical training, highly valued by industry, leads to nationally recognised qualifications for many Service personnel.

Commissioned ranks receive initial training at the Britannia Royal Naval College, Dartmouth; the Royal Military Academy, Sandhurst; or the Royal Air Force College, Cranwell. This is followed by specialist training, often including degree courses at university or Service establishments. Higher training for officers is provided by the Royal Naval College, Greenwich; the Army Staff College at Camberley, and the Royal Air Force Staff College at Bracknell. Selected senior officers and civilian officials from Britain attend the Joint Services Defence College, Greenwich, and the Royal College of Defence Studies, London, which is also attended by officers and officials from other countries. These provide the wider background necessary for those destined to fill higher appointments.

Operational training includes joint-Service and inter-allied exercises. Training is provided for the armed forces of allied, Commonwealth and other countries.

Reserve Forces

Trained reserve and auxiliary forces supplement the regular forces on mobilisation and are able immediately to take their places either as formed units or as individual reinforcements. They are also a link between the Services and the civil community. Some members of these forces become reservists following a period of regular service (regular reserve); others are volunteers who train in their spare time. Volunteer reserve forces include the Territorial Army, whose role is to reinforce the ground forces committed to NATO and to help maintain a secure home base in Britain. Set up in 1985, a Home Service Force, linked to the Territorial Army and with a planned strength of about 5,000, would on mobilisation assist in guarding important civilian and military installations. Other volunteer forces include the Royal Naval and Royal Marines Reserves, the Royal Naval Auxiliary Service, the Royal Auxiliary Air Force and the Royal Air Force Volunteer Reserve. All, except the Royal Naval Auxiliary Service, have been expanded substantially in recent years or are planned to increase in strength in the near future. The Ulster Defence Regiment (see p 108) is also a reserve force.

At the end of 1989 regular reserves totalled 240,500, and volunteer reserves and auxiliary forces 91,400. The strength of the cadet forces, which make a significant contribution to recruitment to the regular forces, was 137,000.

COMBAT FORCES
Strategic Nuclear Forces

The Royal Navy's Polaris force comprises four nuclear submarines, each of which can remain on underwater patrol for long periods and is capable of carrying 16 nuclear-armed Polaris missiles. The missile system, incorporating improvements designed to penetrate anti-ballistic missile defences, will maintain the force's effectiveness until it is replaced in the mid-1990s by four Trident nuclear submarines. They will extend Britain's nuclear deterrent into the twenty-first century.

The Trident programme, which will cost an estimated £9,380 million (at 1989–90 prices), is expected to account on average for less than 3 per cent of the defence budget (and less than 6 per cent of the equipment budget) during its procurement period. It is also estimated that almost 70 per cent of the money for the project will be spent in Britain. Three of the submarines designed to carry Trident missiles are under construction.

Royal Navy Combat Forces

Britain's naval forces, while capable of operating throughout the world when required, are concentrated in the Eastern Atlantic and in the Channel, where they constitute the majority of naval forces immediately available to NATO. Their primary role is anti-submarine warfare, which is crucial to deterrence in peacetime and maritime operations in war. The navy includes three Invincible-class anti-submarine warfare carriers, deploying Sea King anti-submarine and airborne early warning helicopters, Sea Harrier aircraft, and Sea Dart air defence missiles; 17 nuclear-powered attack submarines (with another one on order) equipped with torpedoes and anti-ship missiles; and nine diesel-electric-powered submarines, including the more powerful Upholder class, the first of which entered service during 1990.

The navy also has about 50 destroyers and frigates (including the first of the new Type 23 frigate) for air defence, anti-submarine and general purpose duties. Most of these have weapon-carrying helicopters, and armaments include surface-to-surface, air defence, and anti-ship missiles. There are two amphibious assault ships, supporting vessels and the Royal Marines. Other ships include 40 mine counter-measures vessels, and offshore patrol vessels for protecting fishing interests and oil and gas installations.

In coming years Britain's contribution to NATO's maritime defence will be based on an improved anti-submarine warfare force. This will be made up of nuclear-powered attack submarines and advanced diesel-electric conventional submarines, of which four have been ordered; the Type 23 frigate (a further nine have been ordered); and Nimrod maritime patrol aircraft, equipped with Searchwater radar and armed with Harpoon anti-ship missiles and Stingray anti-submarine torpedoes. In addition, the surface fleet has been strengthened by 14 multi-role Type 22 frigates—13 are already in service and the building of the last ship is being completed—and by the new Sandown class of minehunter, of which five have been ordered (the first joined the fleet in 1989).

New or improved weapons will include the Harpoon missile for the last four Type 22 and for the new Type 23 frigates, the Sea Eagle anti-ship missile, Goalkeeper rapid firing guns, and, for submarines, the Spearfish torpedo. The Sea Wolf and Sea Dart air defence missiles are also being developed or improved, while a lightweight version of the Sea Wolf is being developed. The Type 23 frigate, which will also be armed with the ship- or air-launched Stingray torpedo, will be able to carry a number of different helicopters, including the EH101 helicopter when that enters service in the mid-1990s. The navy's Sea Harriers are being updated.

Army Combat Forces

The three armoured divisions in BAOR are equipped with Chieftain or Challenger tanks. Seven of the 12 Chieftain regiments in BAOR will be replaced with Challenger; replacements for the remainder have yet to be determined. The mobility of the infantry is being improved with the continuing introduction of Warrior armoured personnel carriers, fitted with a 30-mm cannon. The SA80 rifle and the light anti-tank weapon, LAW80, have further augmented the infantry's firepower.

Major improvements to the Army's air defences are planned for the 1990s. These include the formation of a third air defence regiment equipped with the Starstreak missile, a new air defence command and control system, and continuing improvements to the Rapier system. In 1989 the increased emphasis being placed on mobile operations led to the conversion of a brigade to the air-mobile role, with more Lynx helicopters. Major improvements are being made to the Lynx helicopter and its anti-tank missiles. The multiple-launch rocket system, which fires a variety of munitions at long-range targets, is planned to enter service during the 1990s. Tactical nuclear support is provided by the Lance missile and dual-capable artillery. The need for sophisticated command, control and communications systems is being met by the PTARMIGAN secure communications, the WAVELL computerised battlefield information and the BATES artillery targeting systems, among others.

Royal Air Force

Tornado F3 and Phantom aircraft, together with Rapier and Bloodhound surface-to-air missiles and Oerlikon guns directed by Skyguard radar, provide Britain's air defence. They are assisted by Shackleton airborne early warning aircraft and the ground radars and command, control and communication systems of the United Kingdom Air Defence Ground Environment. In addition, a number of Hawk trainer aircraft have been equipped with air-to-air missiles and cannon for local air defence. The strike/attack fleet has been re-equipped with the Tornado GR1; a variant of this aircraft is replacing some Jaguars to provide reconnaissance. Close air support for ground troops is given by the Harrier GR3, which is being replaced by the Harrier GR5. Fourteen Harrier T 10 training aircraft have been ordered for delivery later in 1990.

Nimrod maritime aircraft form part of Britain's anti-submarine warfare force, and also undertake long-range surveillance operations against surface ships, as well as providing offshore surveillance and fishery protection.

Improved Buccaneers, armed with Sea Eagle and Martel missiles, are employed in an anti-ship role.

Victor, TriStar and VC10 aircraft are used as tankers for in-flight refuelling. Tactical transport is provided by VC10 and Hercules aircraft, while Chinook, Puma and Wessex helicopters provide tactical support to ground forces. Sea King and Wessex helicopters perform search and rescue duties around the British Isles. Weapons in service include Skyflash, Sparrow, Sidewinder, Martel and Sea Eagle missiles, and guided and cluster bombs.

Improvements to Britain's air defences include the introduction of the Tornado F3, which is replacing the Phantom FG1, and the modernisation of the radar and command, control and communications systems.

From the early 1990s the Shackleton airborne early warning aircraft will be replaced by Boeing E-3D aircraft. The ability of the Tornado GR1 to attack at night will be enhanced; the new Harrier GR5 is also being upgraded to a night-attack version, GR7. All strike/attack and offensive support aircraft will be fitted with advanced electronic warfare equipment to increase their ability to survive. The Tornado GR1, already equipped with the British JP233 airfield attack weapon, will have the ALARM anti-radiation missile. The European Fighter Aircraft, which is being developed by Britain, the Federal Republic of Germany, Italy and Spain, will replace the Phantom. Air-to-air refuelling capacity is being increased by converting more VC10 aircraft into tankers. The Chinook fleet is to be updated, to extend its life into the next century.

Finance and Management

The defence budget for 1990–91 is over £21,000 million. Britain remains one of the highest contributors to NATO, with over £350 per capita spent on defence in 1989; 4 per cent of gross domestic product was devoted to defence expenditure, a proportion only exceeded in NATO by the United States and Greece.

Increased competition in the letting of contracts has improved both quality and value for money. About 40 per cent of Britain's defence expenditure is devoted to the purchase of equipment.

Organisation and Management

Within the Ministry of Defence a military–civilian Defence Staff is responsible for defence policy and strategy, operational requirements and commitments. An Office of Management and Budget handles budgets and resources. Each Service Chief of Staff reports through the Chief of Defence Staff to the Secretary of State on matters related to the fighting effectiveness, management, efficiency and morale of his Service. The management of the three forces is exercised through executive committees of the Service Boards, which are chaired by their respective Chiefs of Staff and act in accordance with centrally determined policy objectives and budgets. The Procurement Executive deals with the purchase of equipment, including equipment collaboration with allies and friendly nations.

Under a new system of budgeting taking effect in April 1991, military and civilian managers will be allowed to make the most efficient use of their allocated resources. This new approach is designed to promote better value for money, and to provide clear direction for local managers.

Defence Procurement

Nearly £8,300 million will be spent on equipment in 1990-91, making the Ministry of Defence British industry's largest customer. Contracts are awarded by open international competition where possible, and strict guidelines ensure that companies are placed under the maximum incentive to perform efficiently.

Research and Development

Research is undertaken by the Ministry's research establishments and under contract in industry and the universities. Around £431 million is expected to be spent on defence research and £2,034 million on development in 1990-91.

Nearly all design and development of defence equipment is carried out by industry. The Ministry is seeking to involve industry in the research programme and to promote civil applications. As part of the Government's policy of improving the strength of Britain's science base, the Ministry, together with the research councils, makes joint grants to academic institutions in areas of research relevant to defence. In order to obtain better value for money, four of the Ministry's non-nuclear research and development establishments are being combined into the Defence Research Agency, due to start operation in 1991.

Alliance Co-operation

International co-operation has been a feature of armaments procurement for over 20 years, and Britain was one of its pioneers in programmes such as the British–French Jaguar aircraft and the Lynx, Puma and Gazelle helicopters; the FH70 towed howitzer developed jointly with the Federal Republic of Germany and Italy; and the successful Tornado aircraft developed and produced with the same two partners. Britain also worked with the United States on the Harrier GR5.

In order to make better use of limited resources, Britain is playing an active role in forums such as NATO, the Conference of National Armaments Directors, and the Independent European Programme Group. In the latter, the majority of member countries have followed Britain and France in publishing bulletins of contract opportunities which open up the European defence equipment market.

Major new programmes under way include the EH101 helicopter (with Italy), the new European Fighter Aircraft (with the Federal Republic of Germany, Italy and Spain), the multiple-launch rocket system (with France, the Federal Republic of Germany, Italy and the United States) and anti-tank guided weapons (with France and the Federal Republic of Germany).

Defence Sales

Sales of British defence equipment enable allies and friendly governments to take advantage of Britain's extensive research and development programmes to improve their own defence. The Defence Export Services Organisation of the Ministry of Defence provides a wide range of assistance to industry in promoting equipment and negotiating contracts with overseas customers. This includes collecting market information, demonstrating equipment, providing expert military advice, training and support, staging exhibitions and negotiating with overseas governments.

Britain is one of the West's top three defence exporters, and new contracts signed in 1989 amounted to some £2,000 million. Export orders for defence equipment maintain some 150,000 jobs.

All exports of defence goods are controlled under a 1989 order and subject to strict licensing in accordance with procedures operated by the Department of Trade and Industry.

Civil Defence

Civil defence arrangements are based on the extended and adapted use of the peacetime resources of government departments, local authorities, emergency services and nationalised industries, supplemented by the efforts of voluntary organisations and individual volunteers. Since 1983 civil defence regulations require local authorities to make and keep up to date plans for a range of essential functions in the event of war; to arrange training and exercises for civil defence staff and volunteers; and to provide suitable emergency centres for the direction of civil defence in wartime. Following legislation in 1986, local authorities may use their civil defence resources in responding to peacetime emergencies.

Expenditure on civil defence has been growing steadily and was about £120 million in 1989-90. This is being used to improve the quality and readiness of central and local government planning; increase training opportunities arranged by the Home Office on staff college lines at the Emergency Planning College, Easingwold; help local authorities to plan for better community involvement in civil defence; and improve the emergency system for decentralised government control and communications. Improvements are also being made in the communications, equipment and administrative facilities of the United Kingdom Warning and Monitoring Organisation. This includes the civilian Royal Observer Corps, which is organised to provide public warning of an attack, of the location and strength of nuclear explosions, and of the distribution and level of radioactive fall-out.

5 Justice and the Law

Although the United Kingdom is a unitary state, England and Wales, Scotland and Northern Ireland all have their own legal systems, with considerable differences in law, organisation and practice. However, a large volume of modern legislation applies throughout the United Kingdom. There is a common distinction between criminal law, concerned with wrongful acts harmful to the community, and civil law, concerned with individuals' rights, duties and obligations towards one another.

The main sources of law are government legislation, common law and European Community law. Common law, the ancient law of the land deduced from custom and interpreted in court cases by judges, has never been precisely defined or codified but forms the basis of the law except when superseded by legislation. European Community law is confined mainly to economic and social matters; in certain circumstances it takes precedence over domestic law. It is normally applied by the domestic courts, but the most authoritative rulings are given by the Community's Court of Justice.

Certain changes to United Kingdom law have been enacted as a result of rulings of the European Court of Human Rights. These arose where domestic law was in breach of the Council of Europe's Convention for the Protection of Human Rights and Fundamental Freedoms, to which the United Kingdom is a party.

Criminal Justice

The Government's strategy for dealing with crime is to prevent it, where possible; to detect suspects; to convict the guilty and acquit the innocent; to deal with those found guilty; and to provide more effective support for the victims of crime. It is also concerned to maintain public confidence in the criminal justice system and a proper balance between the rights of the citizen and the needs of the community as a whole.

With continuing concern in Britain, as in many other countries, over rising crime rates, public expenditure on the criminal justice system has increased from about £2,000 million in 1979–80 to an estimated £7,000 million in 1989–90, an increase in real terms of about 50 per cent. Extra spending has taken place on the police, the probation service and prison building. More than two-thirds of expenditure is initially incurred by local government authorities, with the help of central government grants, mainly on the police.

Crime Statistics Differences in the legal systems, police recording practices and statistical classifications in the countries of the United Kingdom make it impracticable to analyse in detail trends in crime for the country as a whole. Nevertheless, it is clear that, as in Western Europe generally, there has been a substantial increase in crime since the early 1950s. However, official statistics cover only crime recorded by the police and can be affected by changes in the proportion of crimes which are undiscovered or unreported.

Table 5.1: Notifiable Crimes Recorded by the Police in England and Wales 1989

Offence group	Crimes Recorded	Crimes Cleared up
Violence against the person	176,959	136,066
Sexual offences	29,733	22,215
Burglary	827,354	226,604
Robbery	33,163	8,772
Theft and handling stolen goods	2,012,760	630,522
Fraud and forgery	134,490	89,429
Criminal damage	630,084	111,581
Other	26,202	25,222
Total	3,870,745	1,250,411

Source: Home Office.

Table 5.1 shows the number of offences recorded by the police in England and Wales in 1989 and their clear up rates. There were 3·9 million crimes in 1989,[1] of which 32·3 per cent were cleared up. Violence against the person acccounted for only 4·6 per cent of recorded crimes. The Scottish police recorded 493,000 crimes, of which 33 per cent were cleared up.

Crime tends to be concentrated in inner cities and deprived areas; the risk of burglary can be as high as one in ten houses a year in inner city areas, compared with one in 100 in rural areas. Rising affluence has provided more opportunities for casual property crime. In 1957, for example, car crime was only 10 per cent of total crime but 30 years later this had risen to over 25 per cent.

Most crime is committed by young males; it is opportunist and is not planned by hardened professional criminals although these do exist. Only a small proportion of young male offenders go on to become serious repeat offenders.

Crime Prevention

The national crime prevention programme is overseen by the Ministerial Group on Crime Prevention. National publicity campaigns, such as the Crack Crime campaign launched in 1988, are a regular feature of the Government's programmes. The Home Office's Crime Prevention Unit helps local agencies to design and implement preventive measures and to assess the results. In Scotland national publicity is administered through the Crime Prevention Committee.

Other government departments are brought together with the Home Office in the Ministerial Group to deal with crime prevention strategies. The Department of the Environment's Priority Estates Project and Estate Action Programme are designed to encourage improvements in the design, layout and management of housing estates. The gas and electricity suppliers have speeded up their programme of replacing domestic prepayment meters by cashless or 'token' meters, so removing a prime target for burglaries.

Local crime prevention panels—each one assisted by the police crime prevention department—identify crime problems and try to tackle them through publicity, marking goods and equipment and fund raising to buy security devices. The panels have been closely involved in setting up some

[1] Excluding 'other criminal damage' valued at £20 and under.

74,000 neighbourhood watch schemes in England and Wales. There are some 1,100 watch schemes in Scotland.

In 1988 an independent national crime prevention organisation, Crime Concern, was launched to encourage local initiatives such as crime prevention panels and neighbourhood watch schemes, and to stimulate business participation in crime prevention. Crime Concern in Scotland was established in 1989.

In 1986 five local projects were set up with government support to see how crime and the fear of crime could be reduced through action by local government, private businesses, the police and voluntary agencies. As part of the Government's Safer Cities projects, this model is being adapted for use in 20 inner city areas in England and Wales. Each project is led by a local committee, drawn from local agencies and supported by a co-ordinator funded by the Home Office. Four projects are also being established in Scotland. The aim is to encourage local communities to devise their own crime prevention activities. Similar projects are being funded by the Government in Northern Ireland.

Strengthening the Law

A number of measures to strengthen the criminal justice system have been taken. The Drug Trafficking Offences Act 1986 and the Criminal Justice (Scotland) Act 1987 provide powers to trace, freeze and confiscate the proceeds of trafficking. Under the Acts a court can issue an order requiring the offender to pay an amount equal to the full value of the proceeds arising from the trafficking. The laundering of illegal money associated with trafficking is unlawful. Because of the international nature of the problem, the legislation also provides for restraint and confiscation orders made by courts to be enforced against assets held overseas, and vice versa. These arrangements apply to countries with which mutual enforcement agreements have been concluded.

Under the Criminal Justice Act 1988 a court may also make a confiscation order against the proceeds arising from offences such as robbery, fraud, blackmail and insider dealing in shares. A Serious Fraud Office with wide powers to investigate and prosecute serious or complex fraud in England, Wales and Northern Ireland was established in 1988 under the Criminal Justice Act 1987.

Legislation has been passed to increase controls on firearms and the carrying of knives. In 1988 the Firearms (Amendment) Act 1988 prohibited the private ownership of certain highly dangerous types of weapon such as high-powered self-loading rifles and burst-fire weapons. It also tightened police regulation of the possession, safekeeping and movement of shotguns. Similar legislation applies in Northern Ireland. Under the Criminal Justice Act 1988 it is unlawful to manufacture, sell or import certain weapons such as knuckledusters or, in England and Wales, to carry a knife in a public place without good reason.

The Public Order Act 1986 and similar legislation in Northern Ireland strengthened the law against incitement to racial hatred and created a new offence of possessing inflammatory material. It also introduced in England and Wales a new order for convicted football hooligans to prevent them attending certain matches and created a new offence of disorderly conduct to enable police to deal with hooligan behaviour. The Act gave the police powers to impose conditions on assemblies in public places.

Helping the Victim

The Government is taking steps to ensure that proper consideration is given to the needs of victims of crime. There are more than 350 victim support schemes in England and Wales, covering 94 per cent of the population, with over 6,000 trained volunteer visitors. They are co-ordinated by a national organisation, Victim Support, which receives a government grant. The Government also finances local schemes to meet either the costs of paid co-ordinators or running costs. In February 1990 the Government published its Victims Charter, setting out for the first time the rights and expectations of victims of crime. Victim support schemes are expanding in Northern Ireland.

The courts can also help victims by granting a compensation order against a convicted criminal which takes precedence over a fine. The Criminal Justice Act 1988 requires courts in England and Wales to consider compensation in every appropriate case and to give reasons if it is not awarded.

Victims of violent crime may apply for compensation under the Criminal Injuries Compensation Scheme administered by a Board. Compensation is based on common law damages and is a lump-sum payment. In 1989–90 some 38,600 cases were resolved by the Criminal Injuries Compensation Board and nearly £75 million was paid in compensation. The Criminal Justice Act 1988 provided for the Scheme to be established on a statutory basis. Because of the need to tackle the backlog of unresolved cases and to improve the Board's service to claimants, this provision has been postponed and steps are being taken to streamline procedures under the present scheme. The Scheme allows foreign nationals to claim compensation for violent criminal acts against them in Britain.

In Northern Ireland there is separate, statutory provision in certain circumstances for compensation to be made from public funds for criminal injuries, and for malicious damage to property, including the resulting loss of profits.

In February 1990 Britain ratified the European Convention on the Compensation of Victims of Violent Crimes, under which mutual arrangements for compensation apply to citizens of those countries in which the Convention is in force; at present these are Denmark, France, Luxembourg, the Netherlands and Sweden.

Measures to Combat Terrorism

Legislation provides the authorities with certain exceptional powers for dealing with and preventing terrorist activities, while taking account of the need to achieve a proper balance between the safety of the public and the rights of the individual. While acknowledging that the special powers make inroads into civil liberties, the Government believes that they should continue in force as long as a substantial terrorist threat remains. Nobody can be imprisoned for political beliefs; all prisoners, except those awaiting trial, have been found guilty in court of criminal offences. The legislation is reviewed annually by an independent person whose reports are presented to Parliament.

The Northern Ireland (Emergency Provisions) Acts 1978 and 1987 give the security forces in Northern Ireland special powers to search, question and arrest suspected terrorists. They allow the Secretary of State to proscribe terrorist organisations. Certain serious terrorist offences are tried by a judge sitting alone without a jury because of the possibility of jurors being intimidated by terrorist organisations. The maximum period for which the police can hold a suspected terrorist on their own authority has been reduced from 72 to 48 hours. Statements obtained by the use or threat of violence are inadmissible in court. Renewable each year, the Emergency Provisions Acts expire in 1992.

The Prevention of Terrorism (Temporary Provisions) Act 1989 applies throughout the United Kingdom and is renewable annually by Parliament. It provides for the exclusion from Great Britain, Northern Ireland or the United Kingdom of people connected with terrorism related to Northern Ireland affairs and for the proscription of terrorist organisations in Great Britain. It also gives the police powers to arrest people suspected of being involved in terrorism without warrant and hold them for 48 hours and, with the approval of the Secretary of State, for up to a further five days. This provision also applies to suspected international terrorists.

It is a criminal offence to handle, give or receive funds for use in the furtherance of, or in connection with, terrorism. Police are able to apply for a court order to freeze a suspect's assets once he or she has been charged and funds can be confiscated if a person is convicted. The Act also provides for reciprocal enforcement agreements with other countries.

The Criminal Jurisdiction Act 1975 makes it possible to try in Northern Ireland a person accused of certain offences committed in the Irish Republic. It also enables evidence to be obtained in Northern Ireland for the trial of offences in the Irish Republic. Reciprocal legislation is in force in the Irish Republic.

Britain attaches great importance to international action to combat terrorism and plays an active part in the work of various bodies. These include a group of European Community ministers, which facilitates the exchange of information and intelligence about terrorism affecting member countries. Britain believes that there should be no concessions to terrorist demands and that international co-operation is essential in tracking down and arresting terrorists, and impeding the movement of international terrorists from one country to another.

THE POLICE SERVICE

There are 43 police forces in England and Wales, eight in Scotland and one in Northern Ireland (the Royal Ulster Constabulary). Outside London the service is organised on a county basis (regional in Scotland) though some counties and regions have combined forces. The Metropolitan Police Force and the City of London force are responsible for policing London. At the end of 1989 police strength in Great Britain was nearly 140,000. The Royal Ulster Constabulary numbered 8,260.

Because of the need to strike a balance between providing the police with effective powers and protecting individual freedom against any abuse of those powers, the Police and Criminal Evidence Act 1984 was introduced to clarify police powers in England and Wales to stop, search, arrest and detain suspects and to search premises for evidence. Separate legislation applies in Scotland, while a number of major reforms are being implemented in Northern Ireland to bring it in line with the 1984 Act.

Officers in Great Britain do not normally carry firearms, although in an emergency firearms can be issued quickly on the authority of a senior officer. In Northern Ireland police officers are issued with firearms for personal protection and other firearms are available for duty purposes.

The Interception of Communications Act 1985 sets out the grounds on which the Government is empowered to authorise interception of postal and telephone services. For the police, these are the prevention and detection of serious crime, and, in some instances, the protection of national security. The other ground for interception is the safeguarding of the economic well-being of Britain. Interception outside the procedures established by the Act is a criminal offence.

**Police
Authorities
and Chief
Constables**

Police forces are maintained by police authorities. In England and Wales these are committees of local county councillors and magistrates, and in Scotland the regional and islands councils. The police authority for London's Metropolitan Police Force is the Home Secretary. In Northern Ireland the police authority is appointed by the Secretary of State.

The police authority's functions, some subject to ministerial approval, include appointing the chief constable, deputy chief constable and assistant chief constables; fixing the maximum permitted strength of the force; and providing buildings and equipment. In the Metropolitan Police area the commissioner of police and his immediate subordinates are appointed on the recommendation of the Home Secretary. The police authorities are financed by central and local government.

Chief constables are responsible for the direction and control of police forces, including the appointment, promotion and discipline of all ranks below assistant chief constable. They are generally answerable to the police authorities on matters of efficiency, and must submit an annual report.

**Central
Authorities**

The Home Secretary and the Secretaries of State for Scotland and Northern Ireland approve the appointment of chief, deputy and assistant chief constables; where necessary they can require a police authority to retire a chief constable in the interests of efficiency, call for a report from a chief constable on matters relating to local policing or institute a local inquiry. They can make regulations covering such matters as qualifications for appointment, promotion and retirement; discipline; hours of duty, leave, pay and allowances; and uniform. Some of these regulations are first negotiable within the Police Negotiating Board for the United Kingdom. The Board consists of an independent chairman and representatives of the police authorities, police staff associations and the home departments. Matters of a non-negotiable kind and general questions are discussed by the Police Advisory Boards.

All police forces (except the Metropolitan Police) are subject to statutory inspection by inspectors of constabulary reporting to the appropriate Secretary of State. Inspectors maintain close touch with the forces they inspect and have advisory functions. At the request of the Commissioner, the inspectorate also undertakes inspections of selected parts of the Metropolitan Police.

**Status and
Duties**
Police Discipline

A British police officer may be sued or prosecuted for any wrongful act committed in carrying out duties. Police discipline codes are designed to prevent any abuse of the considerable powers enjoyed by a police officer and to maintain public confidence in the impartiality of the service. Statutory procedures, including an independent element, govern the way in which complaints from the public against the police are handled. The independent Police Complaints Authority has powers to supervise the investigation of any serious complaint against a police officer in England and Wales. In Scotland complaints against police officers involving allegations of any form of criminal conduct are investigated by an independent procurator fiscal service.

The security forces in Northern Ireland are accountable to the law. If they break it, their members are liable to prosecution and, in some cases, this has led to conviction. The Northern Ireland Independent Commission for Police Complaints is required to supervise the investigation of a complaint regarding death or serious injury and has the power to supervise that of any other complaint if it so wishes. In certain circumstances, the Secretary of State may direct the Commission to supervise the investigation of matters that are not the subject of a formal complaint.

Police Work

Police work ranges from the protection of people and of property, street patrolling and traffic control to crime prevention, criminal investigation and arresting suspected offenders. In urban areas, particularly, police officers have to deal with social problems and may bring in other social agencies and expert help.

Community Relations

Because the police cannot do their job without public support, virtually all forces have community liaison departments designed to develop closer contact between the force and the community. The Police and Criminal Evidence Act 1984 requires arrangements to be made for obtaining the views of people about the policing of their area. Almost all areas have police/community consultative groups. Particular efforts are made to develop relations with young people, through greater contact with schools; the Education Act 1986 places a duty on governing bodies and head teachers to describe in their annual reports the steps they take to strengthen their schools' links with the community, including the police.

Emphasis is placed on improving relations with ethnic minorities. The Government believes that all police officers should receive a thorough training in community and race relations. The Home Office sponsors two national courses in these subjects for community liaison officers and police managers. There is also a national specialist support unit responsible for improving community and race relations training for the police. Discriminatory behaviour by police officers is an offence under the Police Discipline Code. The Home Office organises recruitment advertising campaigns in the press in order to encourage black and Asian recruits to the police. In April 1990 there were 1,339 ethnic minority police officers in England and Wales.

To release as many uniformed police officers as possible for operational duties, police authorities employ over 42,100 full-time civilians in England and Wales and over 2,670 in Scotland. Traffic wardens—of whom there are over 4,610 in England and Wales and over 500 in Scotland—carry out duties concerned with traffic and parking. Wardens are under the control of the chief constable.

Each force has an attachment of volunteer special constables who perform police duties in their spare time, without pay, acting mainly as auxiliaries to the regular force. In Northern Ireland there is a 4,600-strong part-time and full-time paid reserve.

Members of the police service may not belong to a trade union nor may they withdraw their labour in furtherance of a trade dispute. All ranks, however, have their own staff associations to represent their interests.

Co-ordination of Police Operations

Several common services are provided by central government and by arrangements between forces. In England and Wales the most important of these cover forensic science, telecommunications and the central and provincial criminal records available to all forces. In Scotland the main common services cover centralised police training, the Scottish Crime Squad and the Scottish Criminal Record Office.

Certain special services such as liaison with the International Criminal Police Organisation (Interpol) are provided for other British forces by the Metropolitan Police. The National Drugs Intelligence Unit assists police forces and the Customs service throughout Britain. The services of the Fraud Squad, which is run jointly by the Metropolitan Police and City of London Police to investigate company frauds, are available in England and Wales.

Regional crime squads, co-ordinated at national level, deal with serious crime such as drug trafficking and are used whenever operations cannot be dealt with by individual police forces alone. In 1988 the specialist drug wings of the regional crime squads arrested and charged over 700 people, including 45 major traffickers.

In all areas of police work the use of scientific aids is widespread. A national police computer helps to rationalise records and speed up the dissemination of information.

Police Powers

Under the Police and Criminal Evidence Act 1984 a police officer in England and Wales has a general power of stop and search if he or she has reasonable grounds for suspicion that a person is carrying stolen goods, offensive weapons or burglary implements. The officer must, however, state and record the grounds for taking this action. The Act also defines police powers to arrest and detain people for questioning but provides a number of safeguards. In addition, there is a statutory right for suspects to have legal advice on arrest. The Act contains provisions for the tape recording of police interviews.

Arrest

In England and Wales arrests may be made with or without a warrant issued by a magistrate. The 1984 Act provides a general conditional power to arrest a person reasonably suspected of an offence, but this power can only be used where it is not possible or appropriate to proceed by way of summons to appear in court.

The Act categorises certain offences as 'arrestable' or 'serious arrestable' and provides a full power of arrest without warrant in respect of them for the protection of the public.

Detention, Treatment and Questioning

A code of practice on detention, treatment and questioning is one of five codes which the Home Secretary has issued under the 1984 Act. Failure to comply with their provisions can render a police officer liable to disciplinary proceedings.

An arrested person has a statutory right to consult a solicitor and to ask the police to notify a named person likely to take an interest in his or her welfare about the arrest. Where a person has been arrested in connection with a serious arrestable offence, but has not yet been charged, the police may delay for up to 36 hours the exercise of these rights in the interests of the investigation if certain criteria are met.

The police must caution a suspect before any questions are put for the purpose of obtaining evidence. Questions relating to an offence may normally not be put to a person after he or she has been charged with that offence or informed that he or she may be prosecuted for it.

Under the Act a person can be detained for up to a maximum of 96 hours without charge. A person can only be detained beyond 36 hours if a warrant is obtained from a magistrates' court.

Reviews must be made of a person's detention at regular intervals—six hours after initial detention and thereafter every nine hours as a maximum—to check whether the criteria for detention are still satisfied. If they are not, the person must be released immediately.

The Act provides for the tape recording of interviews with suspected offenders at police stations. This has already been adopted in some police authority areas, and will become standard throughout England and Wales by 1991. A code of practice governing these tape recordings has been approved by Parliament.

The Government is encouraging the establishment of schemes in England

and Wales whereby lay visitors make random checks on the treatment of persons detained in police stations and the conditions in which they are held. Lay visitor schemes have been established in the majority of Greater London boroughs and more are being set up in other parts of the country. The schemes have helped improve relations between the police and the local community, particularly in inner city areas.

A person who thinks that the grounds for detention are unlawful[2] may apply to the High Court for a writ of habeas corpus against the person who detained him or her, requiring that person to appear before the court to justify the detention. Similar procedures apply in Northern Ireland.

Charging

Once there is sufficient evidence, the police have to decide whether or not to charge the person with the offence. As an alternative to charging immediately, they can, for example, decide to defer charging, to caution, or to take no further action and release the person with or without bail. Where an immediate charge is appropriate the person may continue to be held in custody, if there are grounds for believing that detention is necessary for his or her own protection or to prevent harm to people or property. This also applies if there is a risk that the person could fail to appear in court or could interfere with the administration of justice. When no such considerations apply, the person must be released on or without bail. Where someone is detained after charge, he or she must be brought before a magistrates' court quickly. This will usually be no later than the following day.

Under the Prosecution of Offences Act 1985 there are time limits on the period from arrest to the beginning of trial in England and Wales. These are in force in most English counties and throughout Wales and are to be phased in elsewhere in England by the end of 1990. The limits are 56 days from first appearance before magistrates to summary trial or 70 days to committal for trial in the Crown Court. The limit is 112 days from committal to taking of the plea in the case of the Crown Court. When a time limit expires the defendant is entitled to bail unless the court extends the limit; it can only do this if satisfied that there is a good and sufficient reason and that the prosecution has acted expeditiously.

Grant of Bail by the Court

It is a basic principle in Britain that accused people should not be remanded in custody except where strictly necessary. Under the Bail Act 1976, which applies to England and Wales, the court decides whether a defendant should be released on bail pending trial. Unconditional bail may only be withheld in certain specified circumstances, for instance, if the court has substantial grounds for believing that the accused person would abscond, commit an offence, interfere with witnesses, or otherwise obstruct the course of justice if released on bail. A court may also impose conditions before granting bail. If bail is refused, the defendant may apply to a High Court judge or to the Crown Court for bail, and application can be made to the Crown Court for conditions imposed by a magistrates' court to be varied. The majority of people remanded by magistrates are given bail.

In some cases a court may grant bail to a defendant on condition that he or she lives in an approved bail or probation/bail hostel. There are 22 bail hostels with nearly 380 places; the 82 probation/bail hostels have almost 1,700 places. An expansion programme is underway to provide 1,000 additional bail places in the period from 1988 to 1993. The probation service has developed bail information schemes which provide the Crown

---

[2]Detention is lawful in pursuance of criminal justice, for contempt of court or of either House of Parliament and when expressly authorised by Parliament. It is also sometimes lawful in the case of the mentally disordered.

Prosecution Service with verified information about a defendant. This assists the Service when it takes decisions on whether to oppose bail and enables the courts to take an informed decision on whether to grant bail. Planned provision should allow 100 courts to be served by April 1992.

Scotland

In Scotland the police may detain and question a suspected person for a period of up to six hours. Thereafter the person must either be released or charged. An arrest must be accompanied by a criminal charge. Once a person has been charged, only voluntary statements will normally be allowed in evidence at the trial. The court will reject statements unless satisfied that they have been fairly obtained. The tape recording of interviews with suspects is being implemented over a period of two years which began in 1988.

Anyone arrested must be brought before a court with the least possible delay (generally not later than the first day after being taken into custody), or—in less serious cases—liberated by the police, often on a written undertaking to attend court on a specified date.

Where an accusation of a more serious offence is to be made, the accused is brought before the sheriff in private to be committed, either for further examination or until liberated in due course of law. A judicial examination may take place. A maximum of eight days may elapse between committal for further examination and committal for trial. No evidence needs to be presented to the sheriff for such committal.

Anyone accused of a crime, except murder or treason, is entitled to apply for release on bail. Even in cases of murder or treason, bail may be granted at the discretion of the Lord Advocate or a quorum of the High Court. Money bail has been virtually abolished and the courts, or the Lord Advocate, may release an accused person if he or she accepts certain conditions.

There is a right of appeal to the High Court by the accused person against the refusal of bail, or by the prosecutor against the granting of bail, or by either party against the conditions imposed. The writ of habeas corpus does not apply in Scotland, but if a person charged with a more serious offence has been kept in custody pending trial, the trial must begin within 110 days of the date of full committal. The trial of a person charged with a summary offence and held in custody must begin within 40 days of the date of first appearance in court.

CRIMINAL COURTS
Prosecution

In England and Wales the initial decision to begin criminal proceedings normally lies with the police. Once the police have brought a criminal charge, the papers are passed to the Crown Prosecution Service, which decides whether to prosecute. In Scotland procurators fiscal decide whether to bring proceedings. In Northern Ireland there is a Director of Public Prosecutions. In England and Wales (and exceptionally in Scotland) a private person may institute criminal proceedings.

Instead of prosecuting, the police can issue a caution. In Scotland the procurator fiscal may make use of various alternatives to prosecution (see p 125).

England and Wales

The Crown Prosecution Service, headed by the Director of Public Prosecutions, prosecutes criminal offences in magistrates' courts and the Crown Court. The Service is divided into 31 areas, each of which is run by a locally-based Chief Crown Prosecutor appointed by the Director. The Service provides lawyers to prosecute cases in the magistrates' courts and briefs barristers to appear in the Crown Court. Although the decision to prosecute is generally delegated to the lawyers in the area offices, some cases are dealt with by the headquarters of the Service. These include cases of national importance, exceptional difficulty or great public concern and those which require that suggestions of local influence be avoided. Such cases might include terrorist offences, breaches of the Official Secrets Acts, large-scale conspiracies to import drugs and the prosecution of police officers.

Scotland   Discharging his duties through the Crown Office and Procurator Fiscal Service, the Lord Advocate is responsible for prosecutions in the High Court of Justiciary, sheriff courts and district courts. There is no general right of private prosecution; with a few minor exceptions crimes and offences may be prosecuted only by the Lord Advocate or his deputes or by the locally-based procurators fiscal holding a commission from the Lord Advocate. The permanent adviser to the Lord Advocate on prosecution matters is the Crown Agent, who is head of the procurator fiscal service and is assisted in the Crown Office by a staff of legally qualified civil servants, all of whom have had experience as depute procurators fiscal.

Prosecutions in the High Court are prepared by procurators fiscal and Crown Office officials and prosecuted by the Lord Advocate, the Solicitor General for Scotland (the Lord Advocate's ministerial deputy) and advocate deputes, who are collectively known as Crown Counsel. Crimes tried before the sheriff and district courts are prepared and prosecuted by procurators fiscal. The police and other law enforcement agencies investigate crimes and offences and report to the procurator fiscal, who decides whether to prosecute, subject to the directions of Crown Counsel.

When dealing with minor crime, the procurator fiscal increasingly makes use of alternatives to prosecution such as formal warnings and fixed penalties. The offender is not obliged to accept such an offer but if he or she does so the prosecution loses the right to prosecute.

Northern Ireland   The Director of Public Prosecutions for Northern Ireland, who is responsible to the Attorney General, prosecutes all offences tried on indictment, and may do so in summary cases of a serious nature. Other summary offences are prosecuted by the police.

Serious Fraud Office   The Serious Fraud Office investigates and prosecutes the most serious and complex cases of fraud in England, Wales and Northern Ireland. Investigations are conducted by teams of lawyers, accountants, police officers and other specialists, each headed by a case controller who decides whether to prosecute, although this decision may, if necessary, be taken by a more senior lawyer. If proceedings are instituted, the case controller and the case secretary prepare the case for trial and instruct counsel for the prosecution. The Office has computer-aided equipment for the presentation of evidence in a graphic form to make it more comprehensible to jurors.

In Scotland the Crown Office Fraud Unit investigates and prepares—in co-operation with the police and other agencies—cases of serious and complex fraud. It also deals with drug profit confiscation procedures and international criminal investigations.

Courts in England and Wales   Criminal offences may be grouped into three categories. Very serious offences such as murder, manslaughter, rape and robbery are tried only by the Crown Court presided over by a judge sitting with a jury. Summary offences—the least serious offences and the vast majority of criminal cases—are tried by unpaid lay magistrates sitting without a jury. A third category of offences (such as theft, burglary or malicious wounding) are known as 'either way' offences; they can be tried either by magistrates or by the Crown Court, depending on the circumstances of each case and the wishes of the defendant.

All those charged with offences triable only in the Crown Court must first appear before a magistrates' court, which decides whether or not to commit them to the Court for trial. Committal proceedings also apply to 'either way' offences which it has been determined will be tried in the Crown Court. The magistrates court may also commit a defendant tried summarily in an 'either way' case, and found guilty, to the Crown Court for sentence.

Magistrates must as a rule sit in open court, to which the public and the media are admitted. A court normally consists of three lay magistrates—known as justices of the peace—advised on points of law and procedure by a legally qualified clerk or a qualified assistant. Magistrates are appointed by the Lord Chancellor, except in Lancashire, Greater Manchester and Merseyside, where appointments are made by the Chancellor of the Duchy of Lancaster. There are nearly 28,000 lay magistrates.

There are 63 full-time, legally qualified stipendiary magistrates who may sit alone and usually preside in courts in urban areas where the workload is heavy.

Cases involving people under 17 are heard in juvenile courts. These are specially constituted magistrates' courts which either sit apart from other courts or are held at a different time. Only limited categories of people may be present and media reports must not identify any juvenile appearing either as a defendant (unless a judge directs otherwise) or a witness. Where a young person under 17 is charged jointly with someone of 17 or over, the case is heard in an ordinary magistrates' court or the Crown Court. If the young person is found guilty, the court may transfer the case to a juvenile court for sentence unless satisfied that it is undesirable to do so.

The Crown Court sits at about 90 centres and is presided over by High Court judges, full-time 'circuit judges' and part-time recorders. All contested trials take place before a jury. Magistrates sit with a circuit judge or recorder to deal with appeals and committals for sentence.

In cases of serious or complex fraud, full committal proceedings in magistrates' courts may be bypassed at the discretion of the prosecution. However, there is a special procedure under which the accused is able to apply to the Crown Court to be discharged on the ground that there is no case to answer.

Appeals

A person convicted by a magistrates' court may appeal to the Crown Court against the sentence imposed if he or she has pleaded guilty; or against the conviction or sentence imposed if he or she has pleaded not guilty. Where the appeal is on a point of procedure or of law, either the prosecutor or the defendant may appeal from the magistrates' court to the High Court (see above). Appeals from the Crown Court, either against conviction or against sentence, are made to the Court of Appeal (Criminal Division). The House of Lords is the final appeal court for all cases, from either the High Court or the Court of Appeal. Before a case can go to the Lords, the court hearing the previous appeal must certify that it involves a point of law of general public importance and either that court or the Lords must grant leave for the appeal to be heard. The ten Lords of Appeal in Ordinary are the judges who deal with Lords appeals.

The Attorney General may seek the opinion of the Court of Appeal on a point of law which has arisen in a case where a person tried on indictment is acquitted; the Court has power to refer the point to the House of Lords if necessary. The acquittal in the original case is not affected, nor is the identity of the acquitted person revealed without his or her consent.

Under the Criminal Justice Act 1988, the Attorney General may refer a case to the Court of Appeal if he considers that a sentence passed by the Crown Court is over-lenient. This only applies to a case triable exclusively in the Crown Court. If the Court of Appeal agrees, it may increase the sentence within the statutory maximum laid down by Parliament for the offence.

Scotland

The High Court of Justiciary, which sits in Edinburgh and other major towns and cities, tries the most serious crimes and has exclusive jurisdiction in cases involving murder, treason and rape. The sheriff court is concerned with less serious offences and the district court with minor offences. Criminal cases are heard either under solemn procedure, when the judge sits with a jury of 15 members, or under summary procedure, when the judge sits without a jury. All cases in the High Court and the more serious ones in sheriff courts are tried by a judge and jury. Summary procedure is used in the less serious cases in the sheriff courts, and in all cases in the district courts. District courts are the administrative responsibility of the district and the islands local government authorities; the judges are lay justices of the peace and the local authorities may appoint up to one-quarter of their elected members to be ex-officio justices. In Glasgow there are four stipendiary magistrates who are full-time salaried lawyers and have equivalent criminal jurisdiction to a sheriff sitting under summary procedure.

Children under 16 who have committed an offence are normally dealt with by children's hearings (see p 137).

All appeals are dealt with by the High Court. In both solemn and summary procedure, an appeal may be brought by the accused against conviction, or sentence, or both. The Court may authorise a retrial if it sets aside a conviction. There is no further appeal to the House of Lords. In summary proceedings the prosecutor may appeal on a point of law against acquittal or sentence. The Lord Advocate may seek the opinion of the High Court on a point of law which has arisen in a case where a person tried on indictment is acquitted. The acquittal in the original case is not affected.

Northern Ireland

Cases involving minor summary offences are heard by magistrates' courts presided over by a full-time, legally qualified resident magistrate. Young offenders under 17 and young people under 17 who need care, protection and control are dealt with by a juvenile court. They consist of the resident magistrate and two lay members (at least one of whom must be a woman) specially qualified to deal with juveniles. Appeals from magistrates' courts are heard by the county court; an appeal on a point of law alone can be heard by the Northern Ireland Court of Appeal.

The Crown Court deals with criminal trials on indictment. It is served by High Court and county court judges. Proceedings are heard before a single judge, and all contested cases, other than those involving offences specified under emergency legislation, take place before a jury. Appeals from the Crown Court against conviction or sentence are heard by the Northern Ireland Court of Appeal. Procedures for a further appeal to the House of Lords are similar to those in England and Wales.

Those accused of terrorist type offences are tried in non-jury courts to avoid the intimidation of jurors. The onus remains on the prosecution to prove guilt beyond reasonable doubt and the defendant has the right to be represented by a lawyer of his or her choice. The judge must set out in a written statement the reasons for convicting and there is an automatic right of appeal against sentence on points of fact as well as of law. In 1989 some 50 per cent of people tried in the non-jury court were found not guilty.

Trial

Criminal trials in Britain have two parties: the prosecution and the defence. Since the law presumes the innocence of an accused person until guilt has been proved, the prosecution is not granted any advantage over the defence. A defendant (in Scotland called an accused) has the right to employ a legal adviser and may be granted legal aid from public funds. If remanded in custody, the person may be visited by a legal adviser to ensure a properly prepared defence. In England, Wales and Northern Ireland the prosecution usually tells the defence about relevant documents which it is not proposed to put in evidence and discloses them if asked to do so. The prosecution should also inform the defence of witnesses whose evidence may help the accused and whom the prosecution does not propose to call. The defence or prosecution may suggest that the defendant's mental state renders him or her unfit to be tried. If the jury (or in Scotland, the judge) decides that this is so, the defendant is admitted to a specified hospital.

Criminal trials are normally in open court and rules of evidence, which are concerned with the proof of facts, are rigorously applied. If evidence is improperly admitted, a conviction can be quashed on appeal. During the trial the defendant has the right to hear and cross-examine witnesses for the prosecution, normally through a lawyer. He or she can call his or her own witnesses who, if they will not attend voluntarily, may be legally compelled to do so. The defendant can also address the court in person or through a lawyer, the defence having the right to the last speech at the trial before the judge sums up. The defendant cannot be questioned without consenting to be sworn as a witness in his or her own defence. When he or she does testify, cross-examination about character or other conduct may be made only in exceptional circumstances; generally the prosecution may not introduce such evidence.

In England, Wales and Northern Ireland the judge in complex fraud cases may order a preparatory open Crown Court hearing to be held at which he or she can hear and settle points of law and define the issues to be put to the jury. The law on evidence has been changed to make it possible for courts to have before them a wider range of written evidence in the form of business documents which could be relevant to a successful prosecution.

The Jury

In jury trials the judge decides questions of law, sums up the evidence for the jury and instructs it on the relevant law, and discharges the accused or passes sentence. In England, Wales and Northern Ireland the jury is responsible for deciding whether a defendant is 'guilty' or 'not guilty', the latter verdict resulting in acquittal. If the jury cannot reach a unanimous verdict, the judge may direct it to bring in a majority verdict provided that, in the normal jury of 12 people, there are not more than two dissenters.

In Scotland the jury's verdict may be 'guilty', 'not guilty' or 'not proven'; the accused is acquitted if one of the last two verdicts is given. The jury consists of 15 people and a verdict of 'guilty' can only be reached if at least eight members are in favour. As a general rule no one may be convicted without corroborated evidence.

If the jury acquits the defendant, the prosecution has no right of appeal and the defendant cannot be tried again for the same offence. The defendant, however, has a right of appeal to the appropriate court if found guilty.

A jury is independent of the judiciary. Any attempt to interfere with a jury once it is sworn in is punishable under the Contempt of Court Act 1981.

Potential jurors are empanelled in court before the start of the trial. The prosecution and the defence may challenge individual jurors on the panel, giving reasons for doing so.

People between the ages of 18 and 65 (70 in England and Wales) whose names appear on the electoral register, with certain exceptions, are liable for jury service and their names are chosen at random. Ineligible people include judges, priests, people who have within the previous ten years been members of the legal profession, the Lord Chancellor's Department or the police, prison and probation services, and certain sufferers from mental illness. Other disqualified people include those who have, within the previous ten years, served a sentence of imprisonment, youth custody or detention, or been subject to a community service order. Disqualification also applies to anyone who, within the previous five years, has been placed on probation. Anyone who has been sentenced to five or more years' imprisonment is disqualified for life.

Coroners' Courts

Coroners investigate violent and unnatural deaths or sudden deaths where the cause is unknown. If the death is sudden and the cause unknown, the coroner need not hold an inquest if, after a post-mortem examination has been made, he or she is satisfied that the death was due to natural causes. He or she must do so where there is reason to believe that the deceased died a violent or unnatural death or died in prison or in other specified circumstances. It is the duty of the coroner's court to establish how, when and where the deceased died. A coroner may sit alone or, in certain circumstances, with a jury.

In Scotland the local procurator fiscal inquires privately into all sudden and suspicious deaths and may report the findings to the Crown Office. In a minority of cases a fatal accident inquiry may be held before the sheriff. For certain categories, such as deaths resulting from industrial accidents and deaths in custody, a fatal accident inquiry is mandatory. In addition, the Lord Advocate has discretion to instruct an inquiry in the public interest in cases where the circumstances give rise to serious public concern.

TREATMENT OF OFFENDERS

The Government's aim is to ensure that convicted criminals are punished justly and suitably according to the seriousness of their offences. It believes that those who commit very serious crimes, particularly crimes of violence, should receive long custodial sentences, but that many other crimes can best be punished within the community through compensation and reparation.

Legislation sets the maximum penalties for offences, the sentence being entirely a matter for the courts, subject to these maxima. The Court of Appeal (see p 126) issues guidance to the lower courts on sentencing issues when points of principle have arisen on individual cases which are the subject of appeal.

The Government is proposing a new and more coherent statutory framework of guidance on the principles governing sentences.

Custody

The Government believes that custody should be used only for offenders convicted of serious criminal offences or where the public needs to be protected from a dangerous offender. The Court of Appeal has stated that sentencers in England and Wales should examine each case in which custody is necessary to ensure that the term imposed is as short as possible, consistent with the courts' duty to protect the interests of the public and to punish and deter the criminal. The Government is proposing to introduce legislation in England and Wales which would require a court, before giving a custodial sentence, to be satisfied that the offence was so serious as to merit custody. The court would also have to give reasons if it considered a custodial sentence to be necessary; this would not, however apply to the most serious offences such as murder, manslaughter, rape or robbery, which invariably involve a custodial sentence. Longer custodial sentences—within the statutory maxima—would be given to persistent violent and sexual offenders in order to protect the public.

A magistrates' court in England and Wales cannot impose a term of more than six months' imprisonment for each offence tried summarily, but may impose consecutive sentences subject to an overall maximum of 12 months' imprisonment. If an offence carries a higher maximum penalty, the court may commit the defendant for sentence at the Crown Court, which may impose—within the permitted statutory maximum—any other custodial penalty. In all three legal systems there is a mandatory sentence of life imprisonment for murder. This is also the maximum penalty for a number of serious offences such as robbery, rape, arson and manslaughter.

In trials on indictment in Scotland the High Court may impose a sentence of imprisonment for any term up to life, and the sheriff court any term up to three years. The latter may send any person to the High Court for sentence if the court considers its powers are insufficient. In summary cases, the sheriff may normally impose up to three months' imprisonment or six months' for some repeated offences. The district court can impose a maximum term of imprisonment of 60 days.

In Northern Ireland the position is generally the same as for England and Wales. A magistrates' court, however, cannot commit an offender for sentencing at the Crown Court if it has tried the case.

The Death Penalty

The death penalty has been repealed for almost all offences. It remains on the statute book for the offences of treason, piracy with violence and some other treasonable and mutinous offences. However, it has not been used for any of these offences since 1946.

Non-custodial Treatment

The Government believes that more offenders, particularly those convicted of property crimes and less serious cases of violence, should be punished in the community. In its view this should involve fines and compensation to the victim, probation, community service, a new combined order linking probation and community service, or a new curfew order to be used by itself or with other orders.

Fines

The most common sentence is a fine. In England and Wales nearly 81 per cent of offenders convicted by the courts in 1988 received a fine; this included those convicted of motoring offences. In Scotland in 1988, 78 per cent of the 177,000 people with a charge proved against them received a fine. There is no limit to the fine (unless set by statute) which may be imposed on indictment; on summary conviction the maximum limit, except in certain exceptional circumstances, is £2,000 in England, Wales and Northern Ireland, and in Scotland £2,000 in the sheriff court and £1,000 in the district court.

The Government is proposing reforms under which fines would be more closely related to ability to pay. The court's penalty would be given in units which would then be translated into monetary values according to the offender's means.

Probation

The main duties of the probation service are to supervise offenders in the community, both under direct court orders and after release from custody. It also provides offenders in custody with help and advice. In England and Wales some 42,000 offenders began probation supervision in 1988; the figure for Scotland was 3,000.

A probation order can only be made by a court with the consent of the offender, who may be sentenced for the original offence if he or she fails to comply with the order's requirements or commits another offence while on probation. Probation orders curtail the freedom of those on whom they are made. The order requires regular contact to be made with the probation officer. Special conditions can be attached to the order; these may require the offender to attend a day centre for up to 60 days. Although intended as a punishment, the time spent by offenders under supervision in the community offers an opportunity for constructive work to reduce the likelihood of reoffending. In England and Wales a probation order can be made only for offenders aged 17 years or more. In Scotland the minimum age is 8, though in practice offenders under 16 are rarely considered; in Northern Ireland the minimum age is 10 years.

The probation service provides and maintains day centres and hostels together with schemes designed to meet the needs of a broad range of offenders. In England and Wales it also administers supervision orders, the community service scheme and supervises those released from prison on parole. In addition, some probation officers work in custodial establishments.

Under government proposals for England and Wales the courts would be able to combine a probation order with a fine for a single offence and day centres would be renamed probation centres to which national standards, including a core curriculum, would be applied. A probation order would also become a sentence of the court; at present it is imposed 'instead of sentencing', reflecting the original intention that probation should be used mainly for first, or relatively trivial, offenders.

In England and Wales the cost of the probation service is shared between central and local government. It is administered locally by probation committees of magistrates and members co-opted from the local community. In Scotland probation services are integrated with local authority social work departments. In Northern Ireland the service is administered by a probation board, whose membership is representative of the community and which is funded by central government.

Community Service

Offenders aged 16 or over (17 in Northern Ireland) convicted of imprisonable offences may, with their consent, be given community service orders. The court may order between 40 and 240 hours' unpaid service to be completed within 12 months; for 16-year-olds the maximum in England and Wales is 120 hours. Examples of work done include decorating the houses of elderly or disabled people and building adventure playgrounds. The number of community service orders made in England and Wales in 1988 was about 35,000; the figure for Scotland was 3,300 and that for Northern Ireland 720. The Government is proposing to introduce a new court order which could combine community service and probation, as is the case in Scotland. The maximum term for the probation element would be the same as a probation order and the maximum period of community service would be 100 hours.

Curfew Order

Legislation is proposed for England and Wales under which the courts would be empowered to issue a curfew order confining people to their homes at certain times in a bid to reduce crimes such as public disorder. It could also be combined with probation, community service or the proposed order linking probation and community service.

Compensation and Reparation

The courts may order an offender to pay compensation for personal injury, loss or damage resulting from an offence. The Government favours the courts making full use of their compensation powers. Under the Criminal Justice Act 1988 courts in England and Wales are required to give reasons for not awarding compensation to a victim who has suffered loss, injury or damage.

Courts may order the confiscation of proceeds gained by a criminal from drug trafficking and other offences such as robbery, fraud, blackmail and insider dealing in shares. In certain circumstances courts may also order forfeiture of property involved in the commission of crime; this does not apply in Northern Ireland.

Other Measures   The court in England and Wales may discharge a person absolutely or conditionally if it believes that punishment should not be inflicted and a probation order is not appropriate. If he or she is conditionally discharged, the offender remains liable to punishment for the offence if convicted of another offence within a period specified by the court (not more than three years). The Crown Court may 'bind over' an offender by requiring him or her to keep the peace and/or be of good behaviour. If this requirement is not complied with, the offender may be brought before the court and dealt with for the original offence. Alternatively the 'binding over' may mean that a sum of money will be forfeit if conditions stated by the court are not met.

In Scotland the same effects of conditional discharge and binding over are achieved by a system of deferral of sentence until a future date. During this period the accused is required to be of good behaviour and to meet any other conditions stipulated by the court.

Police cautions are used particularly for young offenders; the caution is a form of warning and no court action is taken.

Prisons   The Government aims to provide a humane and efficient prison service. The average inmate population in 1989 was nearly 48,600 in England and Wales, 5,000 in Scotland and 1,800 in Northern Ireland.

Prisons to which offenders may be committed directly by a court are known as 'local prisons'. Other prisons, known as training prisons, receive prisoners on transfer from local prisons. Some training prisons are 'open', with no barriers to prevent escape. In England, Scotland and Wales sentenced prisoners are classified into groups for security purposes. There are separate prisons for women.

There are no open prisons in Northern Ireland, where the majority of offenders are serving sentences for terrorist offences.

People awaiting trial in local prisons or in remand centres are entitled to privileges not granted to convicted prisoners. Those under 21 awaiting trial are, where possible, separated from convicted prisoners.

The Government is seeking to foster greater private sector involvement in the prison system of England and Wales. The building of new prisons is monitored by a Board, which includes a strong private sector element. The Government is to seek legislative powers to enable competitive tenders to be invited from the private sector for the operation of remand centres and for the work of escorting prisoners to and from courts and safeguarding them at court.

Many of the prisons in Great Britain were built in the nineteenth century and require major repairs. In order to cut down on overcrowding and ensure that all prisoners are housed in decent conditions, a major programme of improvement is in progress which will reduce substantially the number of cells without access to night sanitation. Eight new prisons have been opened in England and Wales and one in Scotland since 1985, and 13 others are at various stages of design and construction. Three of these are due to be completed by March 1991 and the remainder will follow in the period between 1992 and 1994. By March 1994 over 7,000 places at new prisons will have been added in England and Wales, and about 3,000 new places at existing establishments. In Northern Ireland there is no overcrowding in the six prison establishments, five of which have been built since 1970.

Remission of Sentence

Most prisoners in Great Britain are eligible for remission of one-third of their sentence. Prisoners serving a sentence of 12 months or less in England and Wales are entitled to half remission. Release on remission is unconditional and does not involve any official supervision in the community. It may be forfeited for serious misconduct in prison.

Northern Ireland

In Northern Ireland prisoners serving a sentence of more than five days are eligible for remission of half their sentence. A prisoner serving a sentence of more than 12 months who is released from prison with remission is liable to be ordered to serve the remainder of this sentence if convicted of fresh imprisonable offences during this period.

Under the Prevention of Terrorism (Temporary Provisions) Act 1989 the rate of remission for those convicted of terrorist-type offences and serving sentences of five years or more has been reduced to one-third. Any released prisoners convicted of another such offence before the expiry of the original sentence must serve the remainder of that sentence before serving any term for the second offence. Both these provisions apply to offences committed on or after 16 March 1989.

Parole

In England and Wales prisoners serving determinate sentences of more than 12 months become eligible for consideration for conditional release on parole licence when they have served one-third of the sentence, or six months, whichever expires the later. In Scotland they only qualify after 12 months.

The first stage in England and Wales is consideration by a local review committee attached to each prison. This is followed by scrutiny by Home Office officials, who refer the more difficult and complex cases to the Parole Board, which makes recommendations for release on parole. Home Office ministers take the final decision on whether to accept the recommendation. Less serious cases are dealt with by the Home Office without reference to the Board. A similar procedure operates in Scotland, where there is a separate Parole Board.

About three-quarters of prisoners serving sentences of less than two years receive parole. However, for those serving sentences of over five years for violence, arson, sexual offences or drug trafficking parole is granted only in exceptional circumstances, or for a few months at the end of the sentence.

The parole licence remains in force until the date on which the prisoner would otherwise have been released from prison. It prescribes the conditions, including the maintenance of contact with a supervising officer, with which the offender must comply. Parole is not available in Northern Ireland, which has more generous remission terms.

Proposals for Reform

The Government intends to introduce legislation reforming the remission and parole systems in England and Wales. Remission would be abolished, as would parole, for prisoners serving under four years and, instead, they would spend 50 per cent of their sentence in custody and then be released. For the remainder there would be a selective system of parole based on clear and published criteria. All prisoners sentenced to a year or more would be supervised on release until three-quarters of their sentence had passed. If convicted of another offence punishable with imprisonment and committed before the end of the original sentence, a released prisoner would be liable to serve all or part of the original sentence outstanding at the time the fresh offence was committed.

Proposals for the reform of the parole and remission systems in Scotland are under consideration.

Life Sentence
Prisoners

The release of prisoners serving life sentences is at the discretion of the Home Secretary or in Scotland the Secretary of State for Scotland, subject to a favourable recommendation by the relevant parole board and after consultation with the judiciary. The Secretaries of State do not, however, have to accept such a recommendation for release, nor are they bound by the views of the judiciary. People serving life sentences for the murder of police and prison officers, terrorist murders, murder by firearms in the course of robbery and the sexual or sadistic murder of children are normally detained for at least 20 years. At the end of 1989 there were about 2,600 life sentence prisoners detained in prisons in England and Wales, of whom about 200 had been detained for 15 years or more. The equivalent figures in Scotland were 437 and 31 respectively. On release, life sentence prisoners remain on licence for the rest of their lives and are subject to recall should their behaviour suggest that they might again be a danger to the public.

In Northern Ireland the Secretary of State reviews life sentence cases on the recommendation of an internal review body in such a way as to reflect their gravity and to take account of Northern Ireland's special circumstances.

Repatriation

Sentenced prisoners who are nationals of countries which have ratified the Council of Europe Convention on the Transfer of Sentenced Persons or similar international arrangements may apply to be returned to their own country to serve the rest of their sentence there.

Independent
Oversight of the
Prison System

Each establishment has appointed to it a board of visitors (visiting committee in Scotland), who act as independent observers on behalf of the Secretary of State. They are unpaid volunteers drawn from the local community. In England and Wales two members of the board must be magistrates. Their principal duty is to satisfy themselves as to the state of the prison premises, the administration of the prison, and the treatment of prisoners. They have the right of access at any time to any part of the establishment, and to any inmate, and may interview an inmate in private. They are required to make an annual report to the Secretary of State about the state of the prison and its administration, and can bring any matter to his attention.

Prison Industries,
Physical
Education and
Education

Prison industries aim to give inmates work experience which will assist them when released and to secure a return which will reduce the cost of the prison system. The main industries are clothing and textile manufacture, engineering, woodwork, laundering, farming and horticulture. Most production caters for internal needs and for other public services. A few prisoners are employed outside prison, some in community service projects. Inmates are paid at pocket money rates for work done; in some prisons incentive payment schemes provide an opportunity for higher earnings on the basis of output and skill.

Education is financed by the prison service and staffed by local education authorities. Full-time education of 15 hours a week is compulsory for young offenders below school leaving age. For older offenders it is voluntary. Some prisoners study for public examinations, including those of the Open University. Within the resources available there is an adult education

Overseas Aid

A CARE Britain health worker teaches basic health education to a family in Bangladesh. CARE Britain receives funding from the Overseas Development Administration (ODA).

ODA-sponsored British experts run pesticide application courses for small farmers in Bolivia.

Defence

British forces contributed to the United Nations Transition Assistance Group, which monitored Namibia's transition to independence in 1990.

HMS *Sandown*, the Navy's first single-role minehunter, demonstrates its manoeuvrability.

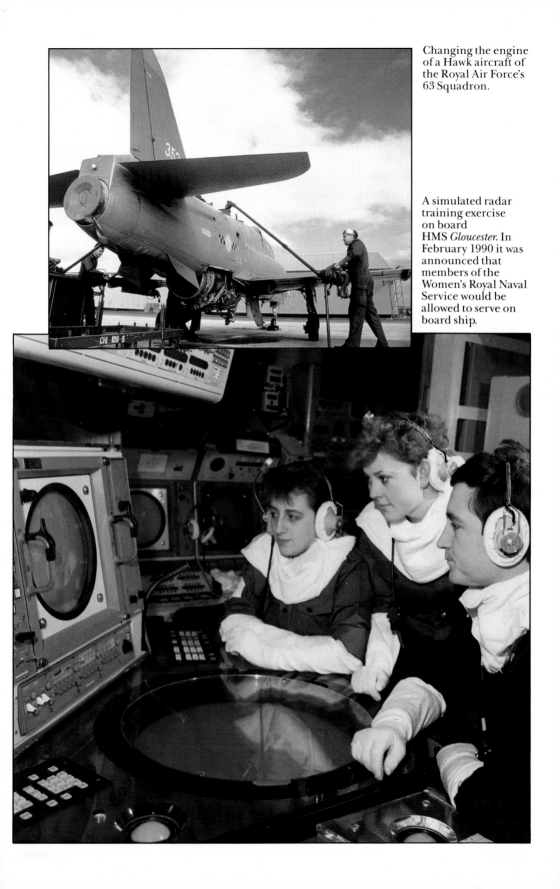

Changing the engine of a Hawk aircraft of the Royal Air Force's 63 Squadron.

A simulated radar training exercise on board HMS *Gloucester*. In February 1990 it was announced that members of the Women's Royal Naval Service would be allowed to serve on board ship.

Universities

Researchers at the Spacecraft Engineering Research Unit at the University of Surrey have pioneered low-cost access to space with their 'microsats'. In 1990 the unit launched two new satellites, one of which is being used to evaluate equipment for the European Space Agency.

Medical artist Richard Neave, of the University of Manchester's Department of Medical Illustration, reconstructs the likeness of a young girl killed in an earthquake on the island of Crete around 3700 years ago. His expertise is widely used by police forces in their forensic investigations.

curriculum. Library facilities provided through the local public library authority are available in all establishments. Voluntary vocational training courses are taught by prison and civilian instruction officers. Physical education is voluntary for adult offenders but compulsory for young offenders. Practically all prisons have physical education facilities, some of which are purpose built.

Education is offered on a voluntary basis to all prisoners and young offenders in Northern Ireland, the courses ranging from basic education to primary degrees and postgraduate research. At any one time around 55 per cent of the prison population are engaged in some form of education and training. A comprehensive library service, available in each establishment, is linked to a province-wide inter-library loan service.

Medical and Psychiatric Care

The prison medical service has a general responsibility for the physical and mental health of all those in custody. Each establishment has accommodation for sick people, and patients can also be transferred to National Health Service hospitals. Psychiatric care is available.

Privileges and Discipline

Prisoners may write and receive letters and be visited by relatives and friends, and those in some establishments may make telephone calls. Privileges include a personal radio, books, periodicals and newspapers, and the opportunity to make purchases from the canteen with money earned in prison. Depending on facilities prisoners may be granted the further privileges of dining and recreation in association, and watching television.

Breaches of discipline are dealt with by the prison governor, or by the boards of visitors, who have power to order forfeiture of remission.

Welfare

Prison officers deal with welfare matters and are supported in this by probation staff (in Scotland, social workers), who use their own professional skills to help individual prisoners understand more about the nature of their offending behaviour.

Religion and Spiritual Care

Anglican, Church of Scotland, Roman Catholic and Methodist chaplains share in a ministry to prisoners, providing opportunities for worship and spiritual counselling. They are supported by visiting ministers of other denominations and faiths as required. In a multi-faith and multicultural society particular attention is given to the needs of those of other major world faiths and ethnic minorities.

Preparation for Release

Many medium- and long-term prisoners in the later parts of their sentences may be granted home leave for periods of between two and five days. Its purpose is to to give the prisoner the opportunity to maintain links with family and friends, and, where leave is taken near the end of the sentence, to contact prospective employers and make firm plans for release.

The Pre-Release Employment Scheme provides an opportunity for selected long-term prisoners to spend their last six months before release in one of eight hostels, which are attached to prisons, to help them re-adapt to society. Hostellers work in the outside community and return to the hostel each evening. Frequent weekend leaves allow hostellers to renew ties with their families.

In Northern Ireland arrangements exist for prisoners serving fixed sentences to have short periods of leave near the end of their sentences and at Christmas. Life-sentence prisoners are given a nine-month pre-release programme which includes employment outside the prison.

Aftercare

The probation service (in Scotland, the local authority social work departments) provides professional social work support to offenders following their release. Most young offenders under the age of 22, adult offenders released on parole and those released on licence from a life sentence receive a period of compulsory supervision from the probation service. The National Association for the Care and Resettlement of Offenders (NACRO) and the Apex Trust (and their counterparts in Scotland) organise training—financed by the Government—for ex-offenders. Other government-aided assistance by voluntary bodies such as NACRO includes accommodation. The Northern Ireland Association for the Care and Resettlement of Offenders, also a voluntary group, is mainly concerned with assisting petty criminals and alcoholics towards rehabilitation and social awareness.

Young Offenders
England and Wales

In England and Wales criminal proceedings cannot be brought against children below the age of 10 years. Children between 10 and 17 charged with committing a criminal offence may be brought before a court, usually a juvenile court. A local authority may bring a child of any age under 17 to a juvenile court in a civil procedure known as care proceedings if, for example, it suspects that he or she is in moral danger or beyond parental control. Under both care and criminal proceedings a court may make a care order or a supervision order or, if the parents consent, an order requiring them to exercise proper care or control over the child. Before an order may be made in care proceedings or a care order made in criminal proceedings, it must be shown that the child is in need of care or control which he or she is unlikely to receive unless the order is made.

Under a care order, which is reviewed every six months and normally expires when the young person reaches 18 or 19, the local government social services authority becomes responsible for the child's accommodation. It may allow him or her to remain at home under supervision or place him or her with foster parents or in a voluntary or community home. For children too severely disturbed or disruptive to be treated in local authority homes, there are two special Youth Treatment Centres run by the Department of Health.

When implemented, the Children Act 1989 will reform both the grounds for, and effects of, care and supervision orders in care proceedings. Under the Act juvenile courts will no longer hear care proceedings and the care order in criminal proceedings will be abolished.

Under a supervision order (which may remain in force for not more than three years) a child normally lives at home under the supervision of a social worker or a probation officer. The court has power to require that the child complies with directions given by his or her supervisor or, in criminal proceedings, with requirements made by the court. The supervision order can be used to provide for a programme of constructive and remedial activities by means of a short residential course or, more usually, attendance at a day or evening centre.

In criminal proceedings, the courts may order payment of compensation, impose a fine or grant a conditional or absolute discharge. The Government believes that parents should be required to pay fines and compensation incurred by juvenile offenders. It is therefore proposing to tighten the law, under which courts would have to take into account parents' means as well as those of the juvenile when deciding the amount of a fine or compensation.

Offenders may be ordered to spend a total of up to 24 hours of their Saturday leisure time (up to three hours on any one occasion) at an attendance centre. The centres, which provide physical education and instruction in practical subjects, are for those found guilty of offences for which older people could be sent to prison. Offenders aged 16 may be ordered to perform up to 120 hours of community service.

Boys aged between 14 and 16, for whom a non-custodial sentence would not be appropriate, may be sent to a young offender institution; for those aged 14 the period is between three weeks and four months and for those aged 15 or 16 the maximum is 12 months. This sentence is also available for girls from the age of 15. In the case of a very serious crime, detention in a place approved by the Home Secretary may be ordered, and must be ordered in the case of homicide.

The custodial sentence for those aged between 17 and 20 years is also detention in a young offender's institution. The use of custody for this group, as with younger juvenile offenders, has dropped in recent years. From June 1985 to February 1990 the number detained as young offenders decreased from 10,104 to 6,238; of these the number of juveniles declined from 1,078 to 289. Detainees are eligible for parole and all are supervised on release. Alternative penalties include fines and compensation, attendance centre orders and community service (between 40 and 240 hours).

The Government is proposing major changes in arrangements for dealing with young offenders aged 16 and 17. In future both would appear in the juvenile court, which would be renamed the youth court. The maximum length of a community service order for 16-year-olds would be extended to 240 hours, thereby bringing this into line with the arrangements for 17-year-olds. In addition, both groups would be eligible for the proposed combined probation and community service order. The Government believes that custody could be abolished for 15-, 16- and 17-year-old girls and for 14-year-old boys, but that it should remain as an option for boys between 15 and 17. Custodial sentencing arrangements for 17-year-olds would be the same as those for 15- and 16-year-olds.

Scotland

In Scotland the age of criminal responsibility is eight years but prosecution of children under the age of 16 years in court is rare and normally takes place only where the offence is of a serious nature, or where a child is prosecuted together with an adult. Instead, children under 16 (or in certain circumstances those aged between 16 and 18 if subject to a supervision requirement) who have committed an offence or are considered to be in need of care and protection may be brought before a children's hearing consisting of three lay people drawn from a panel for each region or islands area. The hearing determines in an informal setting whether compulsory measures of care are required and, if so, the form they should take. An official 'reporter' decides whether a child should come before a hearing. If the grounds for referral are not accepted by the child or parents, or if the child is incapable of understanding the explanation of the grounds, the case goes to the sheriff for proof. If he finds the grounds established, the sheriff remits the case to the reporter to arrange a hearing. The sheriff also decides appeals against any decision of a children's hearing.

Custody is available to the courts for young people aged between 16 and 21; as in England and Wales they serve their sentence in a young offenders' institution. Remission of part of the sentence for good behaviour, release on parole and supervision on release are available.

Northern Ireland

Children between the ages of 10 and 13 and young persons between the ages of 14 and 16 who are charged with a criminal offence will normally be brought before a juvenile court. If found guilty of an offence punishable in the case of an adult by imprisonment, the court may order the child or young person to be placed in the care of a fit person, under supervision (if a child) or on probation. The offender may also be required to attend a day attendance centre, be sent to a training school or committed to custody in a remand home. Other options include a conditional or absolute discharge, a fine, costs, damages or payment of compensation. Parents or guardians may be required to ensure the person's good behaviour. If the court decides that care, protection or control are necessary, or if the child or young person has consistently failed to attend school, it may place the individual in a training school, commit him or her to the care of a fit person, order the parent or guardian to exercise proper care or guardianship, or make a supervision order.

Offenders aged between 17 and 21 who receive custodial sentences of less than three years serve them in a young offenders' centre.

Civil Justice

The Civil Law

The civil law of England, Wales and Northern Ireland covers business related to the family, property, contracts and torts (non-contractual wrongful acts suffered by one person at the hands of another). It also includes constitutional, administrative, industrial, maritime and ecclesiastical law. Scottish civil law has its own, often similar, branches.

CIVIL COURTS England and Wales

The limited civil jurisdiction of magistrates' courts extends to matrimonial proceedings for custody and maintenance orders, adoption orders, guardianship orders and family protection orders. The courts also have jurisdiction regarding public health and the recovery of community charge debts. Committees of magistrates license public houses, betting shops and clubs.

The jurisdiction of the 286 county courts covers actions founded upon contract and tort (with minor exceptions); trust and mortgage cases; and actions for the recovery of land. Other matters dealt with by them include landlord and tenant, adoption and divorce cases. Some cases are determined in those courts designated as divorce county courts, and outside London bankruptcies are dealt with in certain county courts. The courts also deal with complaints of race and sex discrimination. Where small claims are concerned, especially those involving consumers, there are special arbitration facilities and simplified procedures.

Each county court has one or more circuit judges assigned to it by the Lord Chancellor, and the regular sittings of the court are mostly taken by them. The judge normally sits alone, although, in exceptional cases, a trial may be with a jury.

The High Court is divided into the Chancery Division, the Queen's Bench Division and the Family Division. Its jurisdiction covers civil and some criminal cases, and it also deals with appeals. The Family Division is concerned with all jurisdiction affecting the family, including that relating to adoption and guardianship. The Chancery Division deals with the interpretation of wills and the administration of estates. Maritime and commercial law is the responsibility of admiralty and commercial courts of the Queen's Bench Division.

Each of the 80 or so judges of the High Court is attached to one division on appointment but may be transferred to any other division. In London the High Court sits at the Royal Courts of Justice; elsewhere sittings are held at 26 district registries at county court centres.

At present all cases above the upper financial limit of the county courts' jurisdiction—currently £5,000 in contract and tort—must start in the High

Court. The Courts and Legal Services Bill would enable the Lord Chancellor to abolish this county court limit and to reserve the High Court for specialist cases and for general cases of exceptional substance, complexity or importance. It is expected that in early 1991 an order made by the Lord Chancellor will require all but the most substantial personal injury cases to start in a county court. The Bill would also give the county courts wider powers to grant non-financial remedies such as injunctions.

New court rules have been introduced to help cut pre-trial delays.

Appeals

Appeals in matrimonial, adoption and guardianship proceedings heard by magistrates' courts go to a divisional court of the Family Division of the High Court. Appeals against decisions of the licensing committees of magistrates are heard by the Crown Court. Appeals from the High Court and county courts are heard in the Court of Appeal (Civil Division), consisting of the Master of the Rolls and 27 Lords Justices of Appeal, and may go on to the House of Lords, the final court of appeal in civil and criminal cases.

The judges in the House of Lords are the ten Lords of Appeal in Ordinary, who must have a quorum of three, but usually sit as a group of five. Lay peers do not attend the hearings of appeals, which normally take place in a committee room, but peers who hold or have held high judicial office may also sit. The president of the House in its judicial capacity is the Lord Chancellor.

Scotland

The main civil courts are the Court of Session and the sheriff court. The sheriff court deals with most civil litigation including all cases with a value of less than £1,500. Appeals may be made to the sheriff principal or directly to the Court of Session. This does not apply where the value of the case is under £1,500, when an appeal must first be made to the sheriff principal, who may sanction an appeal to the Court of Session on a point of law.

The Court of Session sits in Edinburgh, and in general has jurisdiction to deal with all kinds of action. It is divided into the Outer House, a court of first instance; and the Inner House, mainly an appeal court. Appeals to the Inner House may be made from the Outer House and from the sheriff court. From the Inner House an appeal may go to the House of Lords. The judges of the Court of Session are the same as those of the High Court of Justiciary.

The Scottish Land Court deals exclusively with matters concerning agriculture. Its chairman has the status and tenure of a judge of the Court of Session and its other members are lay specialists.

Northern Ireland

Minor civil cases in Northern Ireland are dealt with in county courts, though magistrates' courts also deal with certain limited classes of civil case. The superior civil law court is the High Court of Justice, from which an appeal may be made to the Court of Appeal. The House of Lords is the final civil appeal court.

Civil Proceedings

In England and Wales civil proceedings are instituted by the aggrieved person. Actions in the High Court are usually begun by a writ served on the defendant by the plaintiff, stating the nature of the claim. Before the case is set down for trial in the High Court, documents (pleadings) setting out the scope of the dispute are filed with the court; the pleadings are also served on the parties. County court proceedings are initiated by a summons served on the defendant by the court. In order to reduce delays, the High Court and the county courts have power to order pre-trial exchange of witness statements in certain cases. From early 1991, such exchange will be compulsory in most High Court and county court cases. Courts may impose penalties in costs on parties who unreasonably refuse to admit facts or disclose documents before trial.

A decree of divorce must be pronounced in open court, but a procedure for most undefended cases dispenses with the need to give evidence in court and permits written evidence to be considered by the registrar.

Civil proceedings, as a private matter, can usually be abandoned or ended by settlement between the parties at any time. Actions brought to court are usually tried without a jury, except in defamation, false imprisonment, or malicious prosecution cases, when either party may, except in certain special circumstances, insist on trial by jury; or a fraud case, when the defendant may claim this right. The jury decides questions of fact and awards damages to the injured party; majority verdicts may be accepted. Under the Courts and Legal Services Bill the Court of Appeal would be able to increase or reduce damages awarded by a jury if it considered them inadequate or excessive. At present this can only be done if the parties agree; otherwise the Court must order a retrial.

In civil cases heard by a magistrates' court, the court issues a summons to the defendant setting out details of the complaint and the date on which it will be heard. Parties and witnesses give their evidence at the court hearing. Domestic proceedings are normally heard by not more than three lay justices, including, where practicable, a woman; members of the public are not allowed to be present. The court may order provision for custody, access and supervision of children, as well as maintenance payments for spouses and children. The law is being changed to speed up civil proceedings in magistrates' courts by allowing written statements, expert opinions and hearsay evidence to be accepted in court without the presence of the witness unless the evidence is disputed and the disputing party requests the presence of the witness.

Judgments in civil cases are enforceable by the court. Most are for sums of money and may be enforced, in cases of default, by seizure of the debtor's goods or by a court order requiring an employer to make periodic payments to the court by deduction from the debtor's wages. Other judgments can take the form of an injunction restraining someone from performing an unlawful act. Refusal to obey a judgment may result in imprisonment for contempt of court. An arrest under an order of committal may be effected only on a warrant.

Normally the court orders the costs of an action to be paid by the party losing it, but, in the case of family law maintenance proceedings, a magistrates' court can order either party to pay the whole or part of the other's costs.

In Scotland proceedings in the Court of Session or ordinary actions in the sheriff court are initiated by serving the defender with a summons (an initial writ in the sheriff court). A defender who intends to contest the action must inform the court; if he or she does not appear, the court grants a decree in absence in favour of the pursuer.

In summary cases (involving small sums) in the sheriff court the statement of claim is incorporated in the summons. The procedure is designed to enable most actions to be carried through without the parties involved having to appear in court. Normally they (or their representatives) need appear only when an action is defended. A new small claims procedure was introduced in 1988.

Proceedings in Northern Ireland are similar to those in England and Wales. County court proceedings are begun by a civil bill served on the defendant; there are no pleadings in the county court. Judgments of civil courts and orders in respect of certain civil matters are enforceable through a procedure administered by the Enforcement of Judgments Office.

Restrictive Practices Court

The Restrictive Practices Court is a specialised United Kingdom court dealing with monopolies and restrictive trade practices. It comprises five judges and up to ten other people with expertise in industry, commerce or public life.

Administrative Tribunals

Administrative tribunals exercise judicial functions separate from the courts and tend to be more accessible, less formal and less expensive.

A number of important tribunals decide disputes between private citizens—for example, industrial tribunals have a major role in employment disputes. Some (such as those concerned with social security) resolve claims by private citizens against public authorities. A further group (including tax tribunals) decide disputed claims by public authorities against private citizens, while others decide such issues as the right to enter or visit the United Kingdom. Tribunal members are normally appointed by the minister concerned with the subject, but other authorities have the power of appointment in some cases. For example, the Lord Chancellor (and, in Scotland, the Lord President of the Court of Session) makes most appointments where a lawyer chairman or member is required.

In the case of many tribunals, a two-tier system operates, with an initial right of appeal to a lower tribunal and a final right of appeal, usually on a point of law, to a higher one. Appeals from some of the higher tribunals on a point of law only may be made to the High Court in England and Wales, to the Court of Session in Scotland, and to the Court of Appeal in Northern Ireland. There are a few exceptions including, for example, immigration appeals, where there is no right of appeal directly from the Immigration Appeals Tribunal to the courts.

The independent Council on Tribunals exercises general supervision over many tribunals, advising on draft legislation and rules of procedure, monitoring their activities and reporting on particular matters. A Scottish Committee of the Council exercises the same function in Scotland. The Council has a similar responsibility with regard to public inquiries.

Administration of the Law

GOVERNMENT RESPONSIBILITIES

Responsibility for the administration of justice rests with the Lord Chancellor, the Home Secretary and the Secretaries of State for Scotland and Northern Ireland. The Prime Minister recommends the highest judicial appointments to the Crown.

The judiciary is independent and its adjudications are not subject to ministerial direction or control.

England and Wales

The Lord Chancellor is the head of the judiciary. He is concerned with court procedure and is responsible for the administration of all courts other than magistrates' and coroners' courts, and for a number of administrative tribunals. He recommends all other judicial appointments to the Crown and appoints magistrates. He has general responsibility for the legal aid and advice schemes and for the administration of civil law reform.

The Home Secretary is concerned with the criminal law, the police service, prisons, and the probation and after-care service. He has general supervision over magistrates' courts, together with some specific responsibilities (such as approving the appointment of justices' clerks). He appoints a board of visitors to each prison establishment (see p 134). He is advised by the Parole

Board on the release of prisoners on licence. The Home Secretary is also responsible for advising the Queen on the exercise of the royal prerogative of mercy to pardon a person convicted of a crime or to remit all or part of a penalty imposed by a court.

The Attorney General and the Solicitor General are the Government's principal advisers on English law, and they represent the Crown in appropriate domestic and international cases. They are senior barristers, elected members of the House of Commons and hold ministerial posts. The Attorney General is also Attorney General for Northern Ireland. As well as exercising various civil law functions, the Attorney General has final responsibility for enforcing the criminal law. The Solicitor General is, in effect, the deputy of the Attorney General. As head of the Crown Prosecution Service, the Director of Public Prosecutions is subject to supervision by the Attorney General, as is the Director of the Serious Fraud Office.

Scotland

The Secretary of State for Scotland recommends the appointment of all judges other than the most senior ones, appoints the staff of the High Court of Justiciary and the Court of Session, and is responsible for the composition, staffing and organisation of the sheriff courts. District courts are staffed and administered by the district and islands local authorities. The Secretary of State is also responsible for the criminal law of Scotland, crime prevention, the police, the penal system and legal aid; he is advised on parole matters by the Parole Board for Scotland.

The Lord Advocate and the Solicitor General for Scotland are the chief legal advisers to the Government on Scottish questions and the principal representatives of the Crown for the purposes of litigation in Scotland. Both are government ministers. The Lord Advocate is closely concerned with questions of legal policy and administration and is responsible for the Scottish parliamentary draftsmen. He must exercise an independent discretion in carrying out his overall responsibility for the prosecution of crime.

Northern Ireland

The administration of all courts is the responsibility of the Lord Chancellor, while the Northern Ireland Office, under the Secretary of State, deals with the police and the penal system. The Lord Chancellor has general responsibility for the legal aid and advice scheme in Northern Ireland.

THE PERSONNEL OF THE LAW

The courts of the United Kingdom are the Queen's Courts, since the Crown is the historic source of all judicial power. The Queen, acting on the advice of ministers, is responsible for all appointments to the judiciary.

Judges

Judges are normally appointed from practising barristers, advocates (in Scotland), or solicitors (see below). Lay magistrates in England and Wales need no legal qualifications but are trained to give them sufficient knowledge of the law, including the rules of evidence, and of the nature and purpose of sentencing. The Scottish district court justices of the peace need no legal qualifications, but they too must take part in training. In Northern Ireland members of a lay panel who serve in juvenile courts undertake training courses; resident magistrates are drawn from practising solicitors or barristers.

The Legal Profession

The legal profession is divided into two branches: barristers (advocates in Scotland) and solicitors. Barristers are known collectively as the 'Bar', and collectively and individually as 'counsel'. Solicitors undertake legal business for individual and corporate clients, while barristers advise on legal problems submitted through solicitors and present cases in the higher courts. Certain functions are common to both, for example, presentation of cases in the lower courts. Although people are free to conduct their own cases, most people prefer to be legally represented in the more serious cases.

Bills before Parliament are designed to increase the provision of good quality legal services for clients in Great Britain by lifting restrictions on who can provide these services. Under the proposals solicitors would be able to acquire new rights of audience in the higher courts; building societies, banks and other financial organisations would be able to offer conveyancing services under a scheme providing important new safeguards to clients; and people in England and Wales wanting to take legal action would be able, like those in Scotland, to negotiate a form of 'no win, no fee' agreement with their legal advisers. The Bills also propose to strengthen the system of complaints against legal practitioners by creating Legal Services Ombudsmen able to investigate how the professional bodies handle these complaints. Similar proposals for Northern Ireland are being considered.

The professional organisations for barristers and advocates are the General Council of the Bar in England and Wales, the Faculty of Advocates in Scotland, and the General Council of the Bar of Northern Ireland and the Executive Council of the Inn of Court of Northern Ireland. For solicitors they are the Law Society of England and Wales, the Law Society of Scotland and the Law Society of Northern Ireland.

LEGAL AID

A person in need of legal advice or legal representation in court may qualify for help with the costs out of public funds, either free or with a contribution according to means under the 'Green Form' scheme. Civil legal aid schemes are administered by the Legal Aid Board, the Scottish Legal Aid Board and the Law Society of Northern Ireland.

Green Form Scheme

People whose income and savings are within certain limits are entitled to help from a solicitor on legal matters (with the exception of wills and conveyancing in England and Wales). Such help includes advice on the relevant law, writing letters on the client's behalf, and taking the opinion of a barrister or advocate. In England, Wales and Northern Ireland it may be extended to cover representation in civil proceedings in the magistrates' court, Mental Health Review Tribunal hearings and certain disciplinary proceedings before prisons' boards of visitors.

The scheme provides for initial work to be done up to a specified time limit of three hours for matrimonial work and two hours for other work.

Legal Aid in Civil Proceedings

Legal aid, which covers representation before the court, may be available for most civil proceedings to those who satisfy the financial eligibility conditions. An applicant for legal aid must also show not only that he or she has reasonable grounds for taking or defending proceedings but also that it is reasonable that he or she should receive legal aid. If legal aid is granted the case is conducted in the normal way, except that in England and Wales no money passes between the client and the solicitor; all payments are made through the Legal Aid Fund.

In certain limited circumstances the successful unassisted opponent of a legally aided party may recover his or her costs in the case from the Legal Aid Fund. Where the assisted person recovers or preserves money or property in the proceedings, the Legal Aid Fund may have a first charge on that money or property to recover money spent on the assisted person's behalf.

Legal Aid in Criminal Proceedings

In criminal proceedings in England and Wales a legal aid order may be made by the court concerned if it appears to be in the interests of justice and if a defendant qualifies for financial help. An order must be made (subject to means) when a person is committed for trial on a murder charge or where the prosecutor appeals or applies for leave to appeal from the Court of Appeal (Criminal Division) to the House of Lords. No person who is unrepresented can be given a custodial sentence for the first time unless given the opportunity to apply for legal aid.

The Legal Aid Board makes arrangements for duty solicitors to be present at magistrates' courts to provide initial advice and representation to unrepresented defendants, and also for them to be available, on a 24-hour basis, to give advice and assistance to suspects at police stations. The services of a duty solicitor are free.

In Scotland there is a duty solicitor scheme for accused people in custody in sheriff and district court cases. An 'interests of justice' and 'means' test applies only in summary cases, where decisions on applications for legal aid are taken by the Scottish Legal Aid Board. In Northern Ireland a voluntary duty solicitor scheme has been introduced at the principal magistrates' court in Belfast. Legal aid for criminal cases in Scotland and Northern Ireland is free.

Law Centres

In a number of urban areas law centres provide free legal advice and representation. Financed from various sources, often including local authorities, they usually employ full-time salaried lawyers and many have community workers. Much of their time is devoted to housing, employment, social security and immigration problems. Free advice is also available in Citizens Advice Bureaux, consumer and housing advice centres and in specialist advice centres run by various voluntary organisations.

LAW REFORM

In England and Wales the Law Commission is responsible for reviewing the law and making recommendations for its simplification and modernisation. A permanent body, the Commission reports to the Lord Chancellor and consists of a High Court judge and four other members who are required to be practising or academic lawyers. The Lord Chancellor also occasionally refers specific topics to the Law Reform Committee, nominating as members experts in the particular field of law involved. In criminal law matters the Home Secretary acts similarly with the Criminal Law Revision Committee. Any changes in the law are a matter for legislation.

Law reform in Scotland is the responsibility of the Scottish Law Commission, which reports to the Lord Advocate. Its constitution and functions are similar to those of the Law Commission for England and Wales.

In Northern Ireland the Law Reform Advisory Committee, which reports to the Secretary of State, reviews certain aspects of the civil law and makes recommendations for reform.

6 Social Welfare

The British social welfare system comprises the National Health Service (NHS), the personal social services and social security. The NHS provides a full range of medical services which are available to all residents, irrespective of means. Local authority personal social services and voluntary organisations provide help and advice to the most vulnerable members of the community. These include elderly, physically disabled, mentally ill and mentally handicapped people and children in need of care. The social security system is designed to secure a basic standard of living for people in financial need by providing income during periods of inability to earn (including periods of unemployment), help for families and assistance with costs arising from disablement.

Central government is directly responsible for the NHS, administered by a range of health authorities and boards throughout Britain acting as its agents, and for the social security system. Personal social services are administered by local authorities but central government is responsible for establishing national policies, issuing guidance and overseeing standards. Joint finance and planning between health and local authorities aims to prevent overlapping of services and to encourage the development of community services.

Planned spending on social welfare in 1990–91 is: health over £28,000 million and social security benefits nearly £55,600 million, while the standard spending assessment for personal social services is almost £4,400 million.

Spending on the health service has increased substantially in real terms since 1980, and is planned to grow further over the next two years. More patients are being treated than ever before. Spending on social security is rising because of increased numbers of beneficiaries, especially retirement pensioners, and the long-term sick and disabled. The value of retirement and most other long-term benefits has also increased in real terms since 1980. Major reforms to the social security system have been introduced under the Social Security Act 1986 to provide a clearer, simpler system more capable of meeting genuine need (see p 171). Spending on the personal social services is determined by local authorities. Central government has restricted the total expenditure of individual local authorities, but spending has risen substantially in real terms since the late 1970s, reflecting the priority given to this sector.

National Health Service and Community Care Act 1990   The National Health Service and Community Care Act 1990 provides for wide-ranging reform in management and patient care in the health and social care services. The provisions on reforming the NHS are based on proposals set out in a White Paper issued in 1989. These seek to offer patients better health care and a greater choice of services and to give greater satisfaction and rewards to those working in the service who respond to local needs. When implemented, the measures will enable the NHS to continue to be open to all, based on medical priority regardless of patients' income, and financed mainly out of general taxation.

The reforms in community care provision are based on a separate White Paper issued in November 1989. These will establish a new financial and managerial framework which will help to secure the delivery of good quality services in line with national objectives. They are intended to enable vulnerable groups in the community to live as normal a life as possible in their own homes, and to give them a greater say in how they live and how the services they need should be provided.

The reforms are designed to shape health and social care for the 1990s. The reforms in the NHS will be implemented in stages from April 1990 to April 1991; those for community care will take effect between April 1991 and April 1993. The reforms apply to England, Wales and Scotland; separate legislation is planned for Northern Ireland.

National Health Service

The NHS is based upon the principle that there should be a full range of publicly provided services designed to help the individual stay healthy. The services are intended to provide effective and appropriate treatment and care where necessary while making the best use of available resources. All taxpayers, employers and employees contribute to its cost so that those members of the community who do not require health care help to pay for those who do. Some forms of treatment, such as hospital care, are provided free; others (see pp 147 and 148) may be charged for.

Growth in real spending on the health service is being used to meet the needs of increasing numbers of elderly people, to take full advantage of advances in medical technology and to remedy shortfalls in areas such as renal services. It is also used to provide more appropriate types of care, often in the community rather than in hospital, for priority groups such as the elderly, the mentally ill and people with mental handicaps. Increased spending is, in addition, intended to combat the growing health problems arising from alcohol and drug misuse; and to remedy disparities in provision between the regions of Britain.

The Government emphasises the importance of preventive health services, and the responsibility of individuals for their own health. While great progress has been made in eliminating infectious diseases such as poliomyelitis and tuberculosis, there has been less success in controlling the major causes of early death and disability—heart disease, cancer and stroke. Most recently the threat of AIDS (Acquired Immune Deficiency Syndrome, see p 157) has proved a serious problem for public health services. Because of the close link between such diseases and individual life-styles or social habits, emphasis is placed on helping people to adopt healthier ways of living through education and other policies. A £3·8 million campaign was launched in 1987 to inform the public of the main risks of heart disease.

The Government stresses the need for a partnership between the public and private health sectors and for improving efficiency in order to secure the best value for money and the maximum patient care. In order to achieve more effective management of resources in the NHS, general managers drawn from inside and outside the health service have been appointed at regional, district and unit levels. Further measures have included improving the accountability of health authorities for the planning and management of their resources; increasing the proportion of total staff who provide direct patient care, such as doctors and nurses; and introducing a range of programmes to provide services at lower cost. Considerable savings have been generated through the policy of competitive tendering for hospital cleaning, catering and laundry services. Economies are also made in prescribing by restricting the use of expensive branded products in favour of cheaper but equally effective generic equivalents.

**ADMINIS-
TRATION**

The health ministers (the Secretary of State for Health in England and the Secretaries of State for Scotland, Wales and Northern Ireland) are res- ponsible for all aspects of the health services in their respective countries. The health departments (the Department of Health in England, the Scottish Home and Health Department, the Welsh Office and the Department of Health and Social Services in Northern Ireland) are responsible for national strategic planning.

District health authorities in England and Wales and health boards in Scotland are responsible for planning and operational control of all health services in their areas. England, because of its greater size and population, also has regional authorities responsible for regional planning, resource allocation, major capital building work and certain specialised hospital services. The authorities and boards co-operate closely with local authorities responsible for social work, environmental health, education and other services. Family health services authorities (health boards in Scotland) arrange for the provision of services by doctors, dentists, pharmacists and opticians. Community health councils represent local opinion on the health services provided. (In Scotland this function is exercised by local health councils.)

In Northern Ireland health and social services boards are responsible for all health and personal social services in their areas. The representation of public opinion on these services is provided for by district committees.

**Changes in
Local
Management**

Under the National Health Service and Community Care Act 1990 regional health authorities, district health authorities (health boards in Scotland) and family practitioner committees have been replaced by smaller bodies consisting of both executive and non-executive members. The new regional health authorities came into operation in July 1990, while the new district health authorities and the new family health services authorities (which have replaced the family practitioner committees) came into force in September 1990.

The Act will enable a wide variety of health service bodies to make contracts with one another for the provision of hospital and other services. Hospitals will be funded directly for the patients treated, making it easier for general practitioners to refer patients outside their area if treatment elsewhere is faster and better. Powers will exist for allocating resources where the urgent need for treatment does not allow NHS contracts to be arranged in advance.

Finance

Nearly 80 per cent of the cost of the health service in Great Britain is paid for through general taxation. The rest is met from the NHS contribution paid with the National Insurance contribution and from the charges towards the cost of certain items such as drugs prescribed by a family doctor, and dental treatment. Health authorities may raise funds from voluntary sources. Certain hospitals increase their revenue by taking private patients who pay the full cost of their accommodation and treatment.

The charges for medical prescriptions do not apply to the following: children under 16 years (or students under 19 and still in full-time education); expectant mothers and women who have had a baby in the last 12 months; women aged 60 and over and men aged 65 and over; patients

suffering from certain medical conditions; war and armed forces disablement pensioners (for treatment of their disability); people who are receiving income support or family credit (see p 175); and families with low
incomes. Around 75 per cent of prescription items are supplied free.

The Health and Medicines Act 1988 introduced charges for dental
examinations and a system of proportional charges for all types of dental
treatment. However, women who are pregnant or who have had a baby in
the last year, anyone under the age of 18 (or 19 if in full-time education), and
people receiving income support or family credit, do not have to pay. The
Act also introduced charges for sight tests, but these remain free to children,
those on low incomes, and certain other priority groups. Grants for the
repair and replacement of spectacles are made for certain disadvantaged
groups.

Family practitioners (doctors, dentists, opticians and pharmacists) are self-
employed and have contracts with the NHS. Family doctors (also known as
general practitioners or GPs) are paid by a system of fees and allowances
designed to reflect responsibilities, workload and practice expenses. Dentists
providing treatment in their own surgeries are paid on a prescribed scale of
fees. Pharmacists dispensing from their own premises are refunded the cost
of the items supplied, together with professional fees. Ophthalmic medical
practitioners and ophthalmic opticians taking part in the general ophthalmic
service receive approved fees for each sight test made.

The Health and Medicines Act 1988 clarifies the powers of health
authorities to act in a more commercial manner in selling facilities and
services for non-NHS use to the public and outside organisations, while
maintaining safeguards in relation to patient care.

Health Service Commissioners There are three Health Service Commissioner posts (for England, Scotland
and Wales) for dealing with complaints from members of the public about
the health service. All three posts are held by the Parliamentary Commissioner for Administration (Ombudsman), who reports annually to
ministers. The powers of the Health Service Commissioner cover the failure
of a health authority or family health services authority to carry out its
statutory duties, a failure in a service provided, or maladministration causing
injustice or hardship. It does not cover actions taken solely in the exercise of
clinical judgment or the actions of family practitioners, for which separate
complaints procedures exist. In Northern Ireland the Commissioner for
Complaints has a similar role.

PRIMARY HEALTH CARE Primary health care is offered by doctors, dentists, opticians and pharmacists
working within the NHS as independent practitioners, and by health visitors,
district nurses and midwives employed by the health authorities. A wide
range of other services is also available, including the school health service
and the chiropody service. The remedial professions of physiotherapy,
occupational therapy and speech therapy are making an increasingly
important contribution to primary care.

There have been substantial increases in primary health care staff in
recent years. For example, in England and Wales between 1978 and 1988,
the number of family doctors increased by 19 per cent (to 27,000) while the
average patient list size fell by 14 per cent (to 2,000).

Special funds have been earmarked by the Government for improving the
quality of primary health care in inner city areas. Efforts have also been
made to improve health services for black and ethnic minority groups. These
include new health projects in Britain's Chinese communities, and increased

central funding for health information material to be produced in many minority languages.

Family Practitioner Services

The family practitioner services are those given to patients by doctors, dentists, opticians and pharmacists of their own choice. Family doctors provide the first diagnosis in the case of illness and either prescribe a suitable course of treatment or refer a patient to the more specialised services and hospital consultants. Only ophthalmic medical practitioners and ophthalmic opticians may test sight; patients requiring treatment for a defect in sight or an eye disease are dealt with through the Hospital Eye Service. Spectacles are supplied by registered ophthalmic and dispensing opticians but unregistered opticians may also sell spectacles to adults under carefully prescribed conditions.

Group Practices and Health Centres

About four-fifths of family doctors in Britain work in partnerships or group practices, often as members of primary health-care teams, which also include health visitors and district nurses, and sometimes midwives, social workers and other professional staff. About a quarter of family doctors in Great Britain and over half in Northern Ireland work in modern and well-equipped health centres, where medical and nursing services are provided. Health centres may also have facilities for health education, family planning, speech therapy, chiropody, assessment of hearing, physiotherapy and remedial exercises. Dental, pharmaceutical and ophthalmic services, hospital outpatient and supporting social work services may also be provided.

Recent Developments

A new contract of service for general practitioners, which came into effect in April 1990, expands the range of services available to patients. It is intended to make the family doctor service more responsive to the needs of patients and to provide incentives for all doctors to reach the highest standards. The changes are designed to make it easier to see doctors at times convenient to patients; to encourage doctors to promote preventive medicine; and to make it easier for patients to change doctors. Doctors will receive supplements for patients living in deprived areas, for teaching students and carrying out their own night visits. More funds will be made available to improve facilities at doctors' practices.

Under the National Health Service and Community Care Act 1990, GP practices with at least 9,000 patients may apply for fund-holding status. This means that they will be responsible for their own NHS budget (the main elements of which would be the cost of drugs and of arranging mostly non-urgent hospital services). Practices without fund-holding status will be given annual amounts to cover their prescribing costs.

A new contract for dentists comes into force in October 1990. Under this, patients will be offered continuing care, and dentists will be encouraged to practise more preventive dentistry for children. There will be incentives for dentists to undertake further training.

Medical Audit

Medical audit systems intended to enable doctors to review the quality of their medical care are to be set up in all health authorities by April 1991. The Government has made £31 million available for the development of medical audit in 1990–91.

Health Visitors, District Nurses and Midwives

Health visitors are responsible for the preventive care and health education of families, particularly those with young children. They work closely with general practitioners, district nurses and other professions. District nurses give skilled nursing care to people at home or elsewhere outside hospital;

they also play an important role in health promotion and education. Although almost all babies are born in hospital, some antenatal care and most postnatal care is given in the community by midwives and general practitioners, who also care for women having their babies at home. Midwives are responsible for educating and supporting women and their families during the childbearing period.

HOSPITALS AND
SPECIALIST
SERVICES
A full range of hospital services is provided by district general hospitals. These include treatment and diagnostic facilities for in-patients, day-patients and outpatients; maternity departments; infectious disease units; psychiatric and geriatric facilities; rehabilitation facilities; convalescent homes and all forms of specialised treatment. There are also specialist hospitals or units for children, people suffering from mental illness or mental handicaps, and elderly people, and for the treatment of specific diseases. Examples of these include the world-famous Hospital for Sick Children, Great Ormond Street, and the Brompton Heart and Chest Hospital in London. Hospitals designated as teaching hospitals combine treatment facilities with training medical and other students, and research work.

Many of the hospitals in the NHS were built in the nineteenth century; some, such as St Bartholomew's and St Thomas' in London, trace their origins to much earlier charitable foundations. Much has been done to improve and extend existing buildings and many new hospitals have been or are being opened. Since 1979 in England 475 health building schemes, each costing £1 million or more, have been completed. Over 500 schemes, worth over £5,000 million in total, are at various stages of planning and construction. In Scotland 64 major health building schemes, providing over 7,300 beds, have been completed since 1979. A further 40 schemes are at various stages of development.

Recent policy in England and Wales has been to provide a balanced hospital service centred around a district general hospital, complemented as necessary by smaller, locally based hospitals and facilities.

The latest development in hospital planning in England is the nucleus hospital. This is designed to accommodate a full range of district general hospital facilities and is capable of being built in self-contained phases or as an extension to an existing hospital. By mid-1991, 61 nucleus hospitals had been completed and a further 24 were under construction. Those already open have proved economical to build and are providing high-quality and cost-effective services to patients. The world's first low-energy nucleus hospital, which is expected to use less than half the energy of a conventional nucleus hospital, is due to open on the Isle of Wight in late 1990. A similar hospital is being built in Northumberland.

In England NHS hospitals provide about 282,900 beds and have some 512,000 medical, dental, nursing and midwifery staff. The hospital service is now treating more patients a year than ever before: between 1978–79 and 1988–89 the number of in-patient cases treated rose by 23 per cent to over 6·6 million; the number of day case attendances by 81 per cent to 1·2 million; and outpatient attendances by 6 per cent to 36 million. Newer forms of treatment and diagnosis are being made more widely available. These include kidney dialysis, hip replacements, laser treatment for certain eye conditions, and body scanning.

In 1986 the Government launched a drive to reduce hospital waiting lists and times. By 1990 it had invested £109 million in a variety of projects, including mobile operating theatres and the purchase of equipment, to improve waiting times for patients.

Community services such as the psychiatric nursing service, day hospitals, and local authority day centres have expanded so that more patients remain in the community and others are sent home from hospital sooner.

Self-governing NHS Trusts

The National Health Service and Community Care Act 1990 sets out the procedure for enabling hospitals and other units to become independent of health authority control and establish themselves as self-governing NHS trusts. These will be run by boards of directors, and will be able to employ their own staff, conduct research and provide facilities for medical education and other forms of training. Self-governing NHS trusts will derive their income mainly through NHS contracts to provide services to health authorities and GP fund holders. Under the 1990 Act the trusts will be able to treat private patients.

Private Medical Treatment

The Government's policy is for the NHS and the independent sector to co-operate in meeting the nation's health needs. It believes that this will benefit the NHS by adding to the resources devoted to health care and offering flexibility to health authorities in the delivery of services. Some health authorities share expensive facilities and equipment with private hospitals, and NHS patients are sometimes treated (at public expense) in the private sector to reduce waiting lists.

The scale of private practice in relation to the NHS is, however, small. There are 78,500 beds in the independent health care sector, while approximately 3,000 beds in health service hospitals in England are authorised for private patients.

It is estimated that about three-quarters of those receiving acute treatment in private hospitals or NHS hospital pay-beds are covered by health insurance schemes which make provision for private health care in return for annual subscriptions. Over 3·2 million people subscribe to such schemes, half of them within group schemes, some arranged by firms on behalf of employees. Subscriptions often cover more than one person (for example, members of a family) and the total number of people covered by private medical insurance in Britain is estimated at nearly 6·8 million. The Government has introduced tax relief on private health insurance premiums paid by people aged 60 and over to encourage the increased use of private health facilities.

Many overseas patients come to Britain for treatment in private hospitals and clinics, and Harley Street in London is an internationally recognised centre for medical consultancy.

There is a growing interest in alternative therapies such as homoeopathy, osteopathy and acupuncture, which are mainly practised outside the NHS.

Organ Transplants

Over the past 25 years there have been significant developments in transplant surgery in Britain. The United Kingdom Transplant Service provides a centralised organ matching and distribution service. At the end of 1987 about 7,600 people were living with functioning kidney transplants and during 1989 over 1,700 kidney transplants were performed. A similar service exists for corneas, and in 1989 2,500 were transplanted.

Heart transplant operations have been conducted at Papworth Hospital in Cambridgeshire since 1979. There are other heart transplant centres at Harefield Hospital, West London, at the Freeman Hospital in Newcastle upon Tyne and at Wythenshawe Hospital, Manchester. Two further centres, in London and Sheffield, opened in April 1990. A programme of combined heart and lung transplants is in progress and in 1989 295 heart and 94 heart–lung transplants were performed. The world's first combined heart, lungs and liver transplant operation was carried out at Papworth in 1987.

Over 295 liver transplants were also performed in 1989. Pancreas transplants are also carried out.

A voluntary organ donor card system enables people to indicate their willingness to become organ donors in the event of their death. A publicity campaign to increase the number of card carriers was launched in 1988, when some 14 million donor cards were distributed to the public. The Human Organ Transplants Act 1989 bans commercial dealing in organs intended for transplant.

Blood Transfusion

The blood transfusion service in England and Wales collects over 2 million donations of blood and over 108,000 donations of plasma each year from voluntary unpaid donors; in Scotland the figures are over 298,000 and over 13,000 respectively. Regional transfusion centres recruit donors and organise donor sessions in towns and villages, factories and offices, and within the armed forces. Donors are normally aged between 18 and 65. The centres are also responsible for blood grouping and testing, maintaining blood banks, providing a consultancy service to hospitals, teaching in medical schools, and instructing doctors, nurses and technicians.

The Central Blood Laboratories Authority is responsible for the manufacture of blood products as well as for research. There is also increasing emphasis on the most effective use of blood and in particular its separation into components such as plasma for specific uses. A laboratory at Elstree, Hertfordshire, was opened in 1987 with the aim of meeting the needs for all blood products in England and Wales. Facilities in Scotland are being expanded to cope with rising demand.

Ambulance Services

The health authorities provide free transport by ambulance where necessary on medical grounds. The ambulance service performs accident and emergency work, dealing with sudden illness, and urgent maternity cases. It also carries out non-urgent work, providing transport for certain categories of people needing outpatient treatment at hospitals, clinics and day hospitals. In some areas voluntary organisations using their own vehicles or volunteers using their own cars help with non-urgent cases. In Scotland an air ambulance service is available in the islands and in the remoter parts of the mainland. Helicopter ambulances also serve several parts of England.

Rehabilitation

Rehabilitation begins at the onset of illness or of injury and continues throughout with the aim of helping people to adjust to changes in life-style and to live as normally as possible. Rehabilitation services are primarily intended for elderly, young, disabled, mentally ill and mentally handicapped people who need such help to resume life in the community. These services are offered in hospitals, centres in the community and in people's own homes through co-ordinated work by a range of professional workers. The staff may also work closely with the disablement resettlement service of the Department of Employment (the Department of Economic Development in Northern Ireland); the housing, education and social services departments of local authorities; and with the voluntary sector.

Medical services may provide free artificial limbs and eyes, hearing aids, surgical supports, wheelchairs, and other appliances. Following assessment, very severely physically handicapped patients may be provided with environmental control equipment which enables them to operate devices such as alarm bells, radio and television, telephones, and heating appliances. Nursing aids may be provided on loan for use in the home.

Local authorities may provide a range of facilities to help patients in the transition from hospital to their own homes, including the provision of aids, care from home helps, and professional help from occupational therapists and social workers. Voluntary organisations also provide help, complementing the work of the statutory agencies and widening the range of services.

Hospices

A number of hospices provide care for the terminally ill (including children) either directly in residential homes or through nursing and other assistance in the patient's own home. Control of symptoms and psychological support for patients and their families form the central features of the modern hospice movement, which started in Britain and is now worldwide. Some hospices are administered entirely by the NHS; the remainder, some of which receive support from public funds, are run by independent charities.

The Government intends to move towards providing a level of public funding for the hospice movement which matches voluntary donations. In 1990–91 public funding amounts to £20 million, an increase of 70 per cent compared with 1988–89. The Government is encouraging greater co-operation between the voluntary sector and health authorities in this field.

Parents and Children

Special preventive services are provided under the health service to safe-guard the health of expectant mothers and of mothers with young children. Services include free dental treatment, dried milk and vitamins; health education, which is available to parents before and after childbirth through talks, discussion groups and demonstrations; and vaccination and immunisation of children against certain infectious diseases (see p 159). Pregnant women receive antenatal care from their family doctor and hospital clinics, and women in paid employment have the right to visit the clinics during working hours. Some 99 per cent of women have their babies in hospital, returning home shortly afterwards to be attended by a midwife or health visitor and, where necessary, the family doctor. The Government attaches great importance to improving the quality of maternity services, and to making them more sensitive to the needs and wishes of mothers and their families. The perinatal mortality rate (the number of stillbirths and deaths in the first week of life) has fallen in England and Wales from 14·7 per 1,000 births in 1979 to 8·3 per 1,000 births in 1989.

A network of child health clinics run by district health authorities, and increasingly by general practices, enables doctors, dentists and health visitors to oversee the physical and mental health and development of pre-school children. Information on preventive services is given and welfare foods are distributed. The school health service offers health care and advice for schoolchildren, including medical and dental inspection and treatment where necessary.

Child guidance and child psychiatric services provide help and advice for children with psychological or emotional problems.

In recent years special efforts have been made to improve co-operation between the community-based child health services and local authority social services for children. This is particularly important in the prevention of child abuse and for the health and welfare of children in care.

Human Fertilisation and Embryology

The birth of the world's first 'test-tube baby' occurred in Britain in 1978, using the technique of *in vitro* fertilisation. This opened up new horizons for helping with problems of infertility and for the science of embryology. The social, ethical and legal implications were examined by a committee of inquiry under Baroness Warnock. Reporting in 1984, the committee concluded that certain specialised forms of infertility treatment, including artificial insemination by donor and *in vitro* fertilisation, were ethically acceptable, but recommended that surrogate motherhood (the practice whereby one woman bears a child for another) organised by agencies should be prohibited. Research on human embryos was considered acceptable, but only up to the fourteenth day after fertilisation. The committee concluded that a licensing authority should be established to regulate infertility services and research. Legislation to ban commercial surrogacy agencies, and advertising of or for surrogacy services, was passed in 1985.

Proposed
Legislation

The Human Fertilisation and Embryology Bill, now before Parliament, seeks to implement the main recommendations of the Warnock report, including the setting up of a licensing authority to regulate certain infertility treatments. Parliament was given a free vote on whether to ban human embryo research or to allow it under strict controls; it voted for the latter option. The Bill would also provide for the status of children born as a result of such treatments and would clarify the position on surrogacy where contracts were not legally enforceable. If implemented, these proposals would constitute one of the fullest and most wide-ranging pieces of legislation on assisted reproduction and embryo research in the world.

Family
Planning

Free family planning facilities are available from family doctors and from health authority family planning clinics, which also make services available to men.

Abortion

The Abortion Act 1967 allows the ending of pregnancy by a doctor if two doctors consider that its continuance would involve a greater risk to the life of the pregnant woman (or of injury to her physical or mental health or that of any existing children in the family) than if an abortion was carried out. An abortion may also be allowed if two doctors consider there is a substantial risk that if the child were born it would suffer from such physical or mental abnormalities as to be seriously handicapped.

Abortions are carried out in NHS hospitals or in private premises approved for the purpose by the Secretary of State. Over half of the legal abortions to women resident in England and Wales in 1989 were performed in private hospitals and clinics; in Scotland, 97 per cent of abortions take place in NHS hospitals.

The Act does not apply in Northern Ireland.

Drug Misuse

The growing misuse of dangerous drugs such as heroin and cocaine has emerged as a serious social and health problem, and the Government has made the fight against such misuse a major priority. Its strategy comprises action to reduce the supply of illicit drugs from abroad; provide more effective law enforcement by the police and customs services; and tighten controls on drugs produced and supplied in Britain. It also includes action to increase the deterrent effects of the law; to develop effective programmes to treat and rehabilitate misusers; and to discourage young people from experimenting with drugs. An interdepartmental ministerial group was established in 1984 to oversee the implementation of this strategy.

Research on various aspects of drug misuse is funded by several government departments. The Government is advised on a wide range of matters relating to drug misuse and connected social problems by the Advisory Council on the Misuse of Drugs.

Publicity
Campaigns

As part of its prevention policy, the Government began a major publicity campaign in 1985 to persuade young people not to take drugs, and to advise parents, teachers and other professional staff on how to recognise and combat the problem. Subsequent phases of the campaign have warned of the risks of transmitting HIV (human immunodeficiency virus), the virus which causes AIDS (see p 157), through the sharing of injecting equipment and of the dangers of heroin misuse. In February 1990 the Government launched a further £3·8 million campaign to promote awareness of the dangers of drug misuse among young people.

Treatment and Rehabilitation

Over £17·5 million was provided for local treatment and rehabilitation projects over a six-year period to 1989. Additional sums have been made available since 1986–87 through the health authorities in England for the further expansion of services for drug misusers. In 1990–91 over £15·5 million is allocated, including £9·5 million in response to the spread of HIV infection among drug misusers. Similar projects are in progress in Wales and in Scotland, where over £2 million is made available annually to health boards for the support of drug misuse services. A number of trial schemes are in progress, involving counselling and the exchange of clean for used syringes and needles.

Treatment for drug dependence is provided mainly on an outpatient basis. Many hospitals provide specialist treatment for drug misusers, mainly in psychiatric units, or have special drug treatment units. An increasing number of family doctors also treat drug misusers, but only certain specialist doctors are licensed to prescribe heroin, cocaine and dipipanone (Diconal). All doctors must notify the authorities of any patient they consider to be addicted to certain controlled drugs, and guidelines on good medical practice in the treatment of drug misuse have been issued to all doctors in Great Britain. The Home Secretary has statutory powers for dealing with doctors found to have prescribed irresponsibly.

Prevention

The Government has set up a drugs advisory service to advise district health authorities on the development of facilities in their areas. It continues to make funds available for local education authorities in England and Wales to appoint staff to promote and co-ordinate preventive work in their areas, especially for anti-drug misuse work in schools. The Government has also provided funding for the establishment of locally based drug prevention teams in nine selected areas in England and Wales, chiefly targeted at young people who may be at risk from drugs. Separate measures have been introduced in Scotland to discourage drug misuse through publicity campaigns and action in the education service and the community.

Other Sources of Provision

A number of non-statutory agencies work with and complement the health service provision. Advice and rehabilitation services including residential facilities, for example, are provided mainly by voluntary organisations. Support in the community is provided by the probation service and local social services departments.

Solvent Misuse

Action is also being taken by the Government to curb the problem of solvent misuse (the breathing in of vapour from glue, lighter fuel and other solvents) by young people. In 1985 legislation was passed in England and Wales making it an offence to supply such substances to children under 18 if the supplier knows or has reason to believe they are to be used to cause intoxication. (Such sales have been prosecuted successfully under common law in Scotland.) Information and guidance material have been distributed to retailers, parents, teachers and other professional workers to help them educate young people on the dangers of the habit and warn them against experimenting.

Smoking

Cigarette smoking is the greatest preventable cause of illness and death in Britain. It accounts for around 110,000 premature deaths and 30 million lost working days each year, and costs the NHS an estimated £500 million a year for the treatment of diseases caused by smoking (for example, heart disease, lung cancer and bronchitis). In addition, smoking by pregnant women can cause premature births and low birth weight in infants. Concerned at these harmful effects, the Government is following an active health education policy supported by voluntary agreements with the tobacco industry aimed at reducing the level of smoking.

Health Education

The Government aims to reduce adult smoking from the present level of 32 per cent and to reduce smoking by young people by one-third by 1994. A £2 million a year campaign directed at those aged 11 to 15 started in late 1989 and is planned to last until 1994. Education on the harmful effects of smoking is to be included in the National Curriculum for all pupils in publicly maintained schools in England and Wales. The Government also supports the work of the voluntary organisation Action on Smoking and Health (ASH), whose workplace services consultancy was introduced in 1989 to offer advice and help to employers in formulating smoking policies. The Government encourages the voluntary restriction of smoking in trains, buses, theatres and other public places. Health authorities have been asked to promote non-smoking as the normal practice in health service buildings and to give help and advice to people who want to give up smoking. The Government estimates that 'passive smoking', especially in the workplace and the home, may cause several hundred deaths through lung cancer every year.

Voluntary Agreements

Voluntary agreements between the Government and the tobacco industry regulate the advertising and promotion of tobacco products, changes in tobacco products and sports sponsorship by the industry. The agreement on tobacco advertising provides for the use of six different health warnings about the dangers of smoking and contains measures to protect groups at particular risk, such as children, young people and women in early childbearing years. Cigarette advertising is banned on television and radio by law. The voluntary agreement on sports sponsorship covers levels of spending, restrictions on sponsorship of events chiefly for spectators under 18 years and controls over the siting of advertising at televised events.

Legislative Measures

The Protection of Children (Tobacco) Act 1986 makes the sale of any type of tobacco product to children illegal. Regulations banning certain oral tobacco products known to cause oral cancer have been in force since March 1990. The Government proposes to replace some aspects of the voluntary system by legislation in 1992.

Alcohol Misuse

The far-reaching effects of alcohol misuse in terms of illness, family break-ups, inefficiency at work, loss of earnings, accidents and crime are widely acknowledged. The Government considers that the reduction of such misuse requires a range of action by central and local government, voluntary and community bodies, the health professions, business and trade unions.

The Government believes that emphasis should be placed on policies to prevent alcohol misuse and continues to seek better information about the causes of problem drinking. It also seeks to encourage healthier life-styles, and to provide earlier help for the problem drinker.

Treatment and rehabilitation include in-patient and outpatient services in general and psychiatric hospitals and specialised alcoholism treatment units.

Primary care teams (general practitioners, nurses and social workers) and voluntary organisations providing hostels, day centres and advisory services also play an important role.

There is close co-operation between statutory and voluntary organisations. The national voluntary agency, Alcohol Concern, which is in receipt of a government grant of £583,000 for 1990–91, plays a prominent role in the prevention of misuse, training for professional and voluntary workers, and improving the network of local voluntary agencies and their collaboration with statutory bodies. In March 1990 Alcohol Concern launched a workplace advisory service with initial government funding of £100,000 as part of a campaign to persuade companies that alcohol misuse is an industrial as well as a social problem. In 1990–91 Alcohol Concern is receiving additional funds to develop a network of services for all alcohol misusers. The Scottish Council on Alcohol undertakes similar work in Scotland. Research and surveys on various aspects of alcohol misuse are funded by several government departments.

In 1987 the Government established an interdepartmental group to develop strategy for combating the misuse of alcohol. Measures taken include legislative changes as well as steps to secure better health education and more effective action by local services and organisations. Legislation came into force in 1988 to strengthen the law banning the sale of alcohol to people under 18 years. At the same time, stricter controls on alcohol advertising were introduced. People appearing in advertisements must now be seen to be over 25 years of age; excessive drinking is not to be encouraged, shown or implied; and alcohol is not to be advertised alongside aggressive or anti-social behaviour. Independent television restricts the advertising of alcohol in programmes aimed at young people.

In 1989 the Government announced increased funding for the Health Education Authority's expanded alcohol education programme. This aims to reduce the harm caused by the misuse of alcohol by promoting sensible drinking as part of a healthy way of life. It also seeks to develop a climate of opinion which favours appropriate measures to prevent alcohol-related harm. Alcohol misuse co-ordinators have been appointed in each of the 14 regional health authorities with the aim of developing strategies to counter the misuse of alcohol.

AIDS

The number of cases of the disease AIDS reported in Britain has continued to rise: up to August 1990 there were 3,688 cases, of whom 1,975 (54 per cent) had died. Recent statistics show a steady increase in the number of AIDS cases among injecting drug users and people infected through heterosexual intercourse.

Government measures to limit the spread of AIDS have included measures to maintain the safety of blood and blood products through publicity aimed at blood donors, the screening of blood donations, the treatment of blood products for haemophiliacs, and the running of public education campaigns.

Public Education Campaigns

The first major public education campaign was launched in 1986. This involved national press, television, radio, cinema and poster advertising, a free national telephone advisory service and the delivery of leaflets to all households in Britain. Subsequent campaigns have been directed at the general population, students and young people, practising male homosexuals, people travelling overseas, and at drug misusers who risk contracting AIDS through injections of drugs by using shared needles and syringes. By the end of 1989 the Government had allocated £44 million for this work. Separate educational packages have also been prepared for particular groups of people, including prison staff and prisoners, school-children, and employers. It is thought that these campaigns have had considerable success in raising public awareness and knowledge about HIV-and AIDS-related issues.

Funding for Services

The Government continues to make additional funding available to health authorities and local authorities for treatment and advisory services, needle exchange schemes for drug misusers (see p 155) and training staff. In 1990-91 £128 million is being provided to health authorities and £9·8 million to local authorities towards the costs of providing HIV-related services. Government grants of £34 million have established the Macfarlane Trust to help haemophiliacs in Britain who have become infected with the AIDS virus as a result of treatment with infected blood products. In 1988 the Government announced two new steps to monitor the spread of HIV infection. These were anonymous and voluntary named screening tests for HIV; the surveys began in January 1990.

Research

In 1987 a £14·5 million research programme was launched with the aim of developing both a vaccine to prevent HIV infection and new anti-viral drugs to treat people already infected. A new drug, 'Retrovir' (zidovudine—AZT), which can prolong the life and improve the health of some AIDS sufferers, has been developed by a British pharmaceutical company.

Voluntary Agencies

A number of voluntary agencies receive financial support from the Government (some £1·8 million in 1990--91). Among them, the Terrence Higgins Trust, London Lighthouse and the Scottish AIDS Monitor promote knowledge about the disease and help people with AIDS. Both London Lighthouse and the Mildmay Mission Hospital provide hospice care and community support.

International Co-operation

Britain considers international co-operation to be of primary importance in the fight against AIDS and plays an active role in international efforts to combat its spread. Following a British initiative in 1986, the European Community decided to exchange information about the spread of the disease, and its prevention and treatment. It also agreed to consider what further co-operative measures should be taken by member states and the scope for further joint work in research. Britain has also co-sponsored resolutions on AIDS at the World Health Assembly, the United Nations Economic and Social Council and at the 1987, 1988 and 1989 United Nations General Assemblies.

The Government fully supports the work of the World Health Organ-isation (WHO) in leading and co-ordinating international action against the disease, and has so far committed nearly £7 million to WHO's Global Programme on AIDS, which is helping developing countries to set up nation-al AIDS control programmes. Britain has agreed to give nearly £7 million in support of national efforts in Africa and the Caribbean and is also giving about £3 million over six years to the International Planned Parenthood Federation for AIDS-related activities.

In 1988 Britain and WHO organised jointly the World Summit of Ministers of Health on Programmes for AIDS Prevention. This issued the London Declaration, stressing the need for governments to take urgent action against the global threat from AIDS, the central role of education and the need to protect human rights.

Infectious Diseases

District health authorities (health boards in Scotland) carry out programmes of immunisation against diphtheria, measles, rubella (for women of child-bearing age and girls only), poliomyelitis, tetanus, tuberculosis and whooping cough. A new combined vaccine against measles, mumps and rubella was introduced in 1988 to replace that for measles for children in the second year of life. A new programme for immunisation, which is designed to provide earlier protection for children, was introduced in 1990. Immunisation is voluntary, but parents are encouraged to protect their children. The proportion of children being vaccinated has been increasing since the end of 1978.

The Public Health Laboratory Service provides a network of bacteriological and virological laboratories throughout England and Wales which conduct research and assist in the diagnosis, prevention and control of communicable diseases. Its largest establishment is the Central Public Health Laboratory at Colindale, in north-west London, which includes the National Collection of Type Cultures, the Food Hygiene Laboratory, and laboratories specialising in the identification of infective micro-organisms. Two centres, one in England and one in Scotland, investigate and monitor human communicable diseases. Microbiological work in Scotland and Northern Ireland is carried out mainly in hospital laboratories.

Cancer Screening

The cervical screening programme aims to reduce deaths from cancer of the cervix by inviting women at risk to be screened regularly to identify and treat conditions that might otherwise develop into cancer. All district health authorities in England have had computerised call and recall systems since 1988, which enable all women aged between 20 and 64 to be invited regularly for cervical cancer screening. Similar arrangements apply in Wales, Scotland and Northern Ireland.

The Government is setting up a nation-wide breast cancer screening service for all women aged between 50 and 64. The service is now in force in most areas, and all eligible women in England and Wales should have their screening invitations by 1993 (and in Scotland by 1994).

Health Education

Health education aims to increase information, raise awareness and influence behaviour. Priority areas include heart disease, smoking, drugs and AIDS. In England health education is promoted by the Health Education Authority, a part of the National Health Service with the major executive responsibility for public education in Britain about AIDS (see p 157). In addition, in England the Authority's functions are to advise the Government on health education; plan and carry out programmes in co-operation with health authorities and other bodies; and sponsor research and evaluation. It also assists the provision of training, and provides a national centre of information and advice on health education. In Wales these functions are undertaken by the Welsh Health Promotion Authority. At present health education in Scotland is promoted by the Scottish Health Education Group, although there are plans to establish a new body. Health education support services in Northern Ireland are provided at present by a Health Promotion Unit; a statutory health promotion agency is to be established in October 1990.

Almost all health authorities have their own health education service, which works closely with health professionals, health visitors, community groups, local employers and others to determine the most suitable local programmes. Increased resources in the health service are being directed towards health education and preventive measures.

Healthier Eating

There has been growing public awareness in recent years of the importance of a healthy diet. In 1984 a report on diet and cardiovascular disease produced by the government Committee on Medical Aspects of Food Policy advised that a reduction of saturated fatty acids and fat in the diet could help to reduce the incidence or delay the onset of cardiovascular disease. To help people reduce their fat intake, the Government produced guidelines on the labelling of food to show nutrient content in a standard format. Nutritional labelling indicating the energy, fat, protein and carbohydrate content of food is being encouraged on a voluntary basis. Some supermarket chains have already introduced voluntary labelling schemes. Current work by the Committee includes a review of the relationship between diet and cardiovascular disease; matters relating to the nutrition of infants, children and the elderly; and revising the recommended daily amounts of energy and nutrients. In 1989 the Committee issued a report on the role of dietary sugars in human disease and on the diets of British schoolchildren. The Scottish Health Education Group (see above) has also produced a guide to healthier eating.

ENVIRON-MENTAL HEALTH

Environmental health officers employed by local authorities are responsible for the control of air pollution and noise, and food hygiene and safety. Their duties also cover the occupational health and safety aspects of a variety of premises, including offices and shops, the investigation of unfit housing, and in some instances refuse collection and home safety. Doctors who specialise in community medicine and are employed by the health authorities advise local authorities on the medical aspects of environmental health, infectious diseases and food poisoning. They may also co-operate with the authorities responsible for water supply and sewerage. Environmental health officers at ports and airports carry out duties concerned with shipping, inspection of imported foods and disease control. In Northern Ireland district councils are responsible for noise control; collection and disposal of refuse; clean air; and food composition, labelling and hygiene.

Safety of Food

It is illegal to sell food unfit for human consumption or to apply any treatment, process or additive to food which makes it injurious to health. Places where food or drink is prepared, handled, stored or sold must conform to certain hygiene standards. Environmental health officers may take for analysis or other examination samples of any food on sale or being distributed. Special regulations control the safety of particular foods such as milk, meat, ice-cream and shellfish.

The Food Safety Act 1990 contains measures to improve food safety in England, Wales and Scotland. These include tighter controls on unfit food, new enforcement measures, extended powers to cover new technical developments, the compulsory registration of commercial food premises, and greatly increased penalties for offenders. Separate legislation will be prepared for Northern Ireland.

In 1989 the Government established the Committee on Microbiological Food Safety, whose function is to examine the increasing incidence of food-borne illnesses, particularly from salmonella, listeria and campylobacter, and to recommend action where appropriate.

SAFETY OF MEDICINES

Under the Medicines Act 1968 the health and agriculture ministers are responsible for licensing the manufacture, marketing and import of medicines for human and veterinary use. The Medicines Commission advises the ministers on policy regarding such products. The Committees on Safety of Medicines, on Dental and Surgical Materials and on the Review of Medicines advise on the safety, quality and effectiveness of medicinal products. The Committee on Safety of Medicines also monitors adverse reactions to drugs. The Act also controls the advertising, labelling, packaging, distribution, sale and supply of medicinal products.

RESEARCH

In 1989–90 the health departments spent about £15·4 million on health research, in addition to expenditure by the Medical Research Council (the main government agency for the support of biomedical and clinical research). Priority areas include research into AIDS, primary health care, community care and child care, the NHS and personal social services workforce, public health and the NHS acute sector.

For England and Wales the Director of Research and Development at the Department of Health advises health ministers on the direction of centrally supported research, and, as a director of the NHS Management Executive, oversees research in the NHS. In Scotland the directly funded programme is administered by the Chief Scientist of the Scottish Home and Health Department.

The Department of Health is involved in international research and development, and takes part in the European Community's medical and public health research programme.

THE HEALTH PROFESSIONS
Doctors and Dentists

Only people on the medical or dentists' registers may practise as doctors or dentists in the NHS. University medical and dental schools are responsible for teaching; the NHS provides hospital facilities for training. Full registration as a doctor requires five or six years' training in a medical school and hospital, with a further year's experience in a hospital. For a dentist, four or more years' training at a dental school is required. The regulating body for the medical profession is the General Medical Council and for dentists, the General Dental Council. The main professional associations are the British Medical Association and the British Dental Association.

Nurses

The minimum period of training required to qualify for registration as a first level nurse in general, mental or mental handicapped nursing (and sick children's nursing in Scotland) is normally three years. Registration as a nurse at second level (enrolled nurse) takes two years (in Scotland 18 months). The Government is committed to a major reform of nurse education which is intended to place particular emphasis on health promotion as well as disease prevention. Midwifery training for registered general nurses takes 18 months, and for other student midwives in England three years. Health visitors are registered general nurses with midwifery or approved obstetric experience who have completed a one-year course in health visiting. District nurses are registered general nurses who have completed a six-month course followed by a period of supervised practice in district nursing.

The examining bodies for all nurses, midwives and health visitors are the National Boards for Nursing, Midwifery and Health Visiting established in England, Scotland, Wales and Northern Ireland. The United Kingdom Central Council for Nursing, Midwifery and Health Visiting is responsible for regulating and registering these professions.

Pharmacists

Pharmacists in general practice and in hospital must be registered with the Pharmaceutical Society of Great Britain or the Pharmaceutical Society of Northern Ireland. A three-year degree course approved by the Pharmaceutical Society followed by a year's approved training is necessary before registration. The majority of medicines can be supplied only by, or under the supervision of, a registered pharmacist.

Opticians

The General Optical Council regulates the professions of ophthalmic optician and dispensing optician. Only registered ophthalmic opticians (or registered ophthalmic medical practitioners) may test sight. Training of ophthalmic opticians takes four years, including a year of practical experience under supervision. Dispensing opticians take a two-year full-time course with a year's practical experience or a part-time day-release course while employed with an optician.

Other

State registration may also be obtained by chiropodists, dietitians, medical laboratory scientific officers, occupational therapists, orthoptists, physiotherapists and radiographers. The governing bodies are seven boards, corresponding to the professions, under the general supervision of the Council for Professions Supplementary to Medicine. Training lasts one to four years and only those who are state registered may be employed in the NHS and some other public services.

Dental therapists (who have taken a two-year training course) and dental hygienists (who have taken a training course of about a year) may carry out some simple dental work under the supervision of a registered dentist.

In mid-1990 a new group of NHS staff—health care assistants—began work in hospitals and the community. They are intended to support the work of more highly qualified staff.

ARRANGE-MENTS WITH OTHER COUNTRIES

The member states of the European Community have special health arrangements under which Community nationals resident in a member state are entitled to receive any treatment, either free or at a reduced cost, during visits to other Community countries. There are also arrangements to cover people who go to work or live in other Community countries. In addition, there are reciprocal arrangements with some other countries under which medical treatment is available to visitors if required immediately. Visitors are generally expected to pay if the purpose of their visit is to seek medical treatment. Visitors who are not covered by reciprocal arrangements are obliged to pay for any medical treatment they receive.

Personal Social Services

Responsibility for providing personal social services rests with the social services authorities (local authority social services departments in England and Wales, social work departments in Scotland, and health and social services boards in Northern Ireland). Their services are directed towards elderly people, children and young people, families, people with mental illness or with a physical or mental handicap, young offenders and other disadvantaged people and their carers. The major services include residential care, day care, services for those confined to their homes and various forms of social work. Close co-operation is maintained between local authority social services departments and health authorities (and other agencies).

Much of the care given to elderly and disabled people is provided in the community, by families, self-help groups and voluntary agencies. The statutory sector offers the skilled care needed in particular services.

The demand for personal social services is expected to rise over the next few years, owing to the increasing number of elderly people and the changing pattern of care for people suffering from mental illness or mental handicap, and for the long-term sick. (Britain expects to have 4·5 million people over 75 and 0·5 million over 90 by the year 2001.) The Government's policy, based on the 'Care in the Community' programme, is to transfer from hospital to care in the community patients who do not need hospital care. It believes that groups such as the elderly, the disabled, and mentally ill or handicapped people can lead more normal lives in the community, given suitable support and facilities.

Recent Developments

The National Health Service and Community Care Act 1990 sets out the Government's policy for the future organisation and management of community care services. The legislation, which will be introduced in stages from April 1991, gives local authorities the responsibility for assessing individual needs, planning care arrangements and implementing them within available resources. There will be a new system of funding for those seeking public support for residential and nursing home care. Local authorities will take responsibility for financial support of people in private and voluntary homes in addition to general social security entitlements. People living in residential care and nursing homes will retain their entitlement to receive help with their fees through the current scheme of special income support payments. The Government will transfer to local authorities the funds which it would otherwise have provided to finance care through social security payments to people in residential care and nursing homes. Wider powers will be given to the Social Services Inspectorate, which oversees the quality of management and care provided by social services departments. The Government believes that the new arrangements will provide more suitable services which are closer to individual needs and wishes, and offer better value for public money.

Elderly People

Services for elderly people are provided by statutory and voluntary bodies to help them to live at home whenever possible. (Only about 5 per cent of the elderly over 65 live in institutional accommodation.) These services may include advice and help given by social workers, domestic help, the provision of meals in the home, sitters-in, night attendants and laundry services as well as day centres, luncheon clubs and recreational facilities. Adaptations to the home can overcome difficulties in moving about, and a wide range of aids is available for people with difficulties affecting their hearing or eyesight. Alarm systems have been developed to help elderly people obtain help in an emergency. In some areas 'good neighbour' and visiting services are arranged by the local authority or a voluntary organisation.

Many local authorities provide free or subsidised travel to elderly people within their areas. Social services authorities also provide residential home care for the elderly and those in poor health, and register and inspect homes run by voluntary organisations or privately.

As part of their responsibility for public housing, local authorities provide homes designed for elderly people; some of these developments have resident wardens. Housing associations and private builders also build such accommodation.

Disabled People

Britain has an estimated 6 million adults with one or more disabilities, of whom around 400,000 (7 per cent) live in communal establishments. Local social services authorities provide a range of personal social services for disabled people to help with social rehabilitation and adjustment to disability. They are also required to establish the number of disabled people in their area and to publicise services, which may include advice on personal and social problems arising from disability, as well as occupational, educational, social and recreational facilities, either at day centres or elsewhere. They may also include adaptations to homes (such as ramps for wheelchairs, and ground-floor toilets); the delivery of cooked meals; and help in the home. In cases of special need, help may be given with installing a telephone or a television. Local authorities and voluntary organisations may provide severely disabled people with residential accommodation or temporary facilities to allow their carers relief from their duties. Specially designed housing may be available for those able to look after themselves.

Some authorities provide free or subsidised travel for disabled people on public transport, and they are encouraged to provide special means of access to public buildings. Special government regulations cover the provision of access for disabled people in the construction of new buildings.

The Independent Living Fund was set up in 1988 to provide financial help to very severely disabled people who need paid domestic support if they are to live in their own homes. The Fund, for which the Government provided over £20 million in 1990, will run for five years.

Results from the most comprehensive series of national surveys yet undertaken among people with disabilities in Great Britain were published between 1988 and 1989. The surveys covered adults and children both in private households and in communal establishments, with all types of disabilities, including those caused by mental illness and mental handicap. On the basis of this data the Government set out its proposals for reforming the structure of social security payments for disabled people in a White Paper published in January 1990. The measures would provide additional help to 850,000 disabled people.

People with Mental Handicaps

The Government's policy is to encourage the development at local level of a range of services for mentally handicapped people and their families through mutual co-operation between health and local authorities and voluntary and other organisations.

Services provided by social services authorities include short-term care, support for families in their own homes, provision for accommodation in ordinary housing and various types of day care. The main aims of the services are to ensure that as far as possible people with mental handicaps can lead full lives in their communities and that no one should be admitted to hospital unless it is necessary on health grounds.

Social services departments now provide most community services for mentally handicapped people. Specialised residential health provision, which may consist of small units in the community, is also provided for people with special needs, as is specialist health service support for those living elsewhere.

The transfer of mentally handicapped children in institutions to more ordinary living arrangements remains a priority.

Mentally Ill People

Arrangements made by social services authorities for providing preventive care and after care for mentally ill people in the community include day centres, social centres and residential care. Social workers help patients and their families with problems caused by mental illness. In some cases they can apply for a mentally disordered person to be compulsorily admitted to and detained in hospital. The rights of such patients were extended by legislation in 1983, and a Mental Health Act Commission was set up to provide better safeguards. Corresponding legislation was introduced for Scotland in 1984, and came into force in Northern Ireland in 1986.

In 1989 the Government announced a number of measures to improve the provision of services for mentally ill people. These include requiring district health authorities (health boards in Scotland) to plan individual health care programmes for all patients leaving hospital and a code of practice for compulsorily admitting and treating patients in hospital. Other measures include a review of public funding of voluntary organisations concerned with mental health and a new grant to local authorities to help meet the social care needs of patients. The National Health Service and Community Care Act 1990 contains a provision for implementing the last-mentioned proposal.

There are many voluntary organisations concerned with mental illness and mental handicap which play an important role in the provision of services for both of these groups of people.

Help to Families

The Government believes in the central importance of the family to the well-being of society and considers that stable adult relationships are needed to support and enhance family life. Social services authorities, through their own social workers and others, give help to families facing special problems. This includes services for children at risk of injury or neglect who need care away from their own families, and support for family carers who look after elderly and other family members in order to give them relief from their duties. They also help single parents, including unmarried mothers. There are now many refuges run by local authorities or voluntary organisations for women, often with young children, whose home conditions have become intolerable. The refuges provide short-term accommodation and support while attempts are made to relieve the women's problems. Many authorities also contribute to the cost of social work with families (such as marriage guidance) carried out by voluntary organisations.

In 1983 the Family Policy Studies Centre was established with public funds to review the impact of public policies on the family and to bring together research findings. The Self-help and Families Project provides funding for nine voluntary agencies to develop the ability of groups of families to help themselves.

The Government launched a three-year initiative in 1989 to increase voluntary sector provision in England for disadvantaged families with children under five. With funds of £2 million, it is enabling voluntary organisations to research and develop day care services, particularly for single parents and families living in temporary accommodation.

Child Care

Day care facilities for children under five are provided by local authorities, voluntary agencies and privately. In allocating places in their day nurseries and other facilities, local authorities give priority to children with special social or health needs. Local authorities also register childminders, private day nurseries and playgroups in their areas and provide support and advice services for them.

The authorities can offer advice and help to families in difficulties to promote the welfare of children. The aim is to act at an early stage to reduce the need to put children into care or bring them before a court.

Child Abuse

Cases of child abuse are the joint concern of many authorities, agencies and professions, and local review committees provide a forum for discussion and co-ordination and draw up policies and procedures for handling these cases. The Government established a central training initiative on child abuse in 1986. This consists of a variety of projects, including training for health visitors, school nurses, and local authority social services staff.

In England, Wales and Northern Ireland children under the age of 14 in child abuse cases are able to give evidence to courts through television links, thus sparing them from the need to give evidence in open court.

Children in Need   Authorities must take into care any child under the age of 17 who has no parent or guardian, who has been abandoned, or whose parents are unable to provide for him or her, if they are satisfied that such intervention is in the best interests of the child. The child remains in care until the age of 18 unless placed in the care of foster parents, other relations or friends. The local authority may find it necessary to assume the rights and duties of one or both parents. The parents must be notified and if they object the matter is decided in a court of law. When taking a decision concerning a child in care, the authorities have to give priority to the need to safeguard and promote the welfare of the child. Where children are in care, every effort is made to work with their families in order to enable the children to return home if appropriate.

Children in England and Wales may be brought before a juvenile court if they are neglected or ill-treated, exposed to moral danger, are beyond the control of parents, are not attending school or (if ten years or over) have committed an offence other than homicide. At the same time it must be shown that the children need care or control which they are unlikely to receive unless a care order or another order is made by the court. Local authorities are responsible for carrying out inquiries through social workers and consulting parents, schools and the police. Children may be committed to the care of a local authority under a care order if the court considers this appropriate. Alternatively, the court may order supervision by a social worker or a probation officer for up to three years.

Increasing use is being made of intermediate treatment, especially for young offenders. This is a community-based service which provides supervised activities, groupwork and individual advice; a short residential period may be included. A requirement to undergo intermediate treatment may be added to a supervision order by the court.

The Children Act 1989 contains a series of measures which reform the law on child care and family services in England and Wales. These are expected to come into force by October 1991. The legislation will help local authorities make better provision for children in need; strengthen the powers of the courts to protect children from abuse or neglect; and improve the balance between parents' and children's rights.

In Scotland children in trouble or in need may be brought before a children's hearing, which can impose a supervision requirement on a child if it thinks that compulsory measures are appropriate. Under these requirements most children are allowed to remain at home under the supervision of a social worker but some may live with foster parents or in a residential establishment while under supervision. Supervision requirements are reviewed at least once a year until ended by a children's hearing or by the Secretary of State. A review of child care legislation in Scotland is in progress.

In Northern Ireland the court may send children in need or in trouble to a training school, commit them to the care of a fit person (including a health and social services board), or make a supervision order. Children in trouble may be required to attend an attendance centre or may be detained in a remand home. There is no provision for intermediate treatment to be included as part of a supervision order in criminal cases. New child care legislation is being prepared in Northern Ireland. Where appropriate it will reflect the changes introduced in England and Wales and will make a distinction between the treatment of children in need of care and young offenders.

Fostering and   When appropriate, children in care are boarded out with foster parents, who
Community Homes receive payments to cover living costs. If a foster home is not considered

appropriate or cannot be found, the child may be placed in a children's home, voluntary home or other suitable residential accommodation. Community homes for children in care in England and Wales comprise local authority and some voluntary children's homes, and include community homes with education on the premises which provide long-term care, usually for more difficult children. In Scotland local authorities are responsible for placing children in their care in foster homes, in local authority or voluntary homes, or in residential schools. In Northern Ireland there are residential homes for children in the care of the health and social services boards; training schools and remand homes are administered separately. Regulations concerning registered voluntary homes and the boarding out of children in care are made by central government.

Adoption

Local authorities are required by law to provide an adoption service, either directly or by arrangement with a voluntary organisation. Agencies may offer adoptive parents an allowance if this would help to find a family for a child. Adoption is strictly regulated by law, and adoption societies must be approved by social services ministers. The Registrars-General keep confidential registers of adopted children. Adopted people may be given details of their original birth record on reaching the age of 18, and counselling is provided to help them understand the circumstances of their adoption. A review of adoption law is in progress.

Custodianship

A person who has cared for a child for some time (for example, a foster parent, step-parent or relative) may apply to a court for a custodianship order giving him or her legal custody of the child. This gives the custodian most of the rights and duties of a natural parent and enables him or her to make decisions about a child's day-to-day care and upbringing in the same way as a parent. Unlike an adoption order, a custodianship order may be revoked. The custodianship provisions do not extend to Northern Ireland.

Social Workers

The effective operation of the social services depends largely on professionally qualified social workers. Training courses in social work are provided by universities, polytechnics (in Scotland, central institutions) and colleges of further education. The length of courses depends on educational qualifications and experience and can extend from one to four years. The Central Council for Education and Training in Social Work is the statutory body responsible for social work training and offers advice to people considering entering the profession. The Council has proposed a range of improvements to the present system of qualifying training.

Professional social workers (including those working in the NHS) are mainly employed by the social services departments of local authorities. Others work in the probation service, the education welfare service, or in voluntary organisations.

Voluntary Social Services

There is a long tradition in Britain of voluntary service to the community, and the partnership between the voluntary and statutory sectors is encouraged by the Government. It has been estimated that about a third of all adults take part in some form of voluntary work during the course of a year. Local and health authorities plan and carry out their duties taking account of the work of voluntary organisations. Voluntary provision enables these authorities to continue the trend towards local community care rather than institutional care for the elderly, and for mentally ill and mentally handicapped people. Funding voluntary organisations also provides opportunities to try out new approaches to services which, if successful, can be included in mainstream statutory provision.

An Opportunities for Volunteering Scheme, together with an Unemployed Voluntary Action Fund in Scotland and a Community Volunteering Scheme in Northern Ireland, has assisted almost 3,000 local voluntary projects to enable unemployed volunteers to help disadvantaged groups in the community. Voluntary organisations also take part in several other government schemes, including the Employment Training programme and Youth Training.

Co-ordination of government interests in the voluntary sector throughout Britain is the responsibility of the Home Office Voluntary Services Unit.

Voluntary Organisations
Funding

Voluntary organisations receive income from several sources, including voluntary contributions, central and local government grants and earnings from commercial activities and investments. They also receive fees (from central and local government) as an increasing number of services are provided by the voluntary sector on a contractual basis. Some 500 bodies receive direct grants from government health and social services departments. In 1988–89 these amounted to over £38 million out of total central government funding of £344 million to voluntary organisations. A government report published in April 1990 provides the basis for improving arrangements to ensure that funds provided by Government to the voluntary sector are used efficiently and for good purposes. Tax changes in recent budgets have helped the voluntary movement secure more funds from industry and individuals. The Gift Aid scheme introduced in the 1990 Budget, for example, provides tax relief on gifts of between £600 and £5 million in any one year. Voluntary organisations benefit not only from direct donations from the private sector but also from gifts of goods, sponsorship, secondments and joint promotions.

Charities

Over 168,000 voluntary organisations are registered as charities, and in England and Wales the Charity Commission gives advice to trustees of charities, setting up schemes to modernise their purposes or improve their administration where necessary. The Commission also maintains a register of charities, gives consent to land transactions by charities and holds investments for them. Voluntary organisations may qualify for charitable status if they are established for purposes such as the relief of poverty, the advancement of education or religion or the promotion of certain other purposes of public benefit. These include good community relations, the prevention of racial discrimination, the protection of health and the promotion of equal opportunity. Legislation to strengthen the powers of the Charity Commissioners and improve the supervision of charities is proposed.

The Charities Aid Foundation, an independent body, is one of the main organisations that aid the flow of funds to charity from individuals, companies and grant-making trusts.

Co-ordinating Bodies

The National Council for Voluntary Organisations is the main co-ordinating body in England, providing central links between voluntary organisations, official bodies and the private sector. It works to extend the involvement of voluntary organisations with a broad range of social issues, to protect the interests and independence of voluntary agencies, and to provide them with advice, information and other services. Councils in Scotland, Wales and Northern Ireland perform similar functions. The National Association for Councils for Voluntary Service is another network providing resources, with over 200 local councils for voluntary service throughout England encouraging the development of local voluntary action, mainly in urban areas. The rural equivalent is Action with Rural Communities in England, representing 38 rural community councils.

Types of Voluntary Organisations

There are thousands of voluntary organisations concerned with health and social welfare, ranging from national bodies to small local groups. 'Self-help' groups have been the fastest expanding part of the voluntary sector over the last 20 or so years—examples include bodies which provide playgroups for pre-school children, or help their members to cope with a particular disability. Groups representing ethnic minorities and women's interests have also developed in recent years. Many organisations belong to larger associations or are represented on local or national co-ordinating councils or committees. Some are chiefly concerned with giving personal service, others with influencing public opinion and exchanging information. Some perform both functions. They may be staffed by both professional and voluntary workers.

Personal and Family Problems

Specialist voluntary organisations concerned with personal and family problems include family casework agencies like the Family Welfare Association, Family Service Units and the National Society for the Prevention of Cruelty to Children. They also include marriage guidance centres affiliated to Relate: National Marriage Guidance; Child Care (the National Council of Voluntary Child Care Organisations); the National Council for One Parent Families; Child Poverty Action Group and the Claimants' Union, which provide advice on social security benefits; and the Samaritans, which helps lonely, depressed and suicidal people.

Health and Disability

Voluntary service to both sick and disabled people is given by—among others—the British Red Cross Society, St John Ambulance, the Women's Royal Voluntary Service and the Leagues of Hospital Friends. Societies which help people with disabilities and difficulties include the Royal National Institute for the Blind, the Royal National Institute for the Deaf, the Royal Association for Disability and Rehabilitation, the Disabled Living Foundation, the Disablement Income Group, MIND (National Association for Mental Health), MENCAP (Royal Society for Mentally Handicapped Children and Adults), the Spastics Society, Alcoholics Anonymous, Age Concern, Help the Aged and their equivalents in Wales, Scotland and Northern Ireland.

Other Organisations

National organisations whose work is religious in inspiration include the Salvation Army, the Church Army, Toc H, the Board of Social Responsibility of the Church of Scotland, the Church of England Children's Society, the Church of England Council for Social Aid, the Young Men's Christian Association, the Young Women's Christian Association, the Catholic Marriage Advisory Council, the Jewish Welfare Board and the Church's Urban Fund.

Community service of many kinds is given by young people, often through organisations such as Community Service Volunteers, Scouts and Girl Guides, and the 'Time for God' scheme run by a group of churches.

A wide range of voluntary personal services is given by the Women's Royal Voluntary Service. These include bringing 'meals on wheels' to housebound invalids and old people, providing flats and residential clubs for the elderly, help with family problems, and assistance in hospitals during emergencies.

Over 1,300 Citizens Advice Bureaux help people who are in doubt about their rights or are not aware of the state or voluntary services available. Some areas have law centres and housing advisory centres.

The Volunteer Centre

The Volunteer Centre UK is a national voluntary organisation and centre for information and research on voluntary work. Its Scottish counterpart is Volunteer Development Scotland. There are many local volunteer bureaux, some part-time, which direct volunteers to opportunities in both the voluntary and statutory sectors.

Social Security

The general aim of the social security programme is to provide an efficient, responsive system of financial help for people who are elderly, sick, disabled, unemployed, widowed or bringing up children. Certain benefits provide an income for people who earn little or nothing because they are retired, unemployed or sick. Others provide income for widows; help with expenses arising from disablement; compensation for injury or disease caused at work or while in the armed forces; and help with the cost of bringing up children. There are also certain income-related benefits for people with inadequate incomes.

Social security benefits fall into two broad categories—contributory and non-contributory. Contributory benefits are paid from the National Insurance Fund, which consists of contributions from employed people and their employers, self-employed people and the Government. Non-contributory benefits are financed from general taxation revenue. Some non-contributory benefits are income-related (for example, income support) but others are not (for example, child benefit and mobility allowance), and the benefit is payable if the qualifying conditions are met. Appeals about claims for benefits are decided by independent tribunals.

Spending on social security has nearly doubled in real terms since 1970. Trends over the last five years have included a steady growth in the numbers of retirement pensioners and those receiving income-related benefits, and a steep rise in those getting disability benefits. There has also been a decline in the numbers of families receiving child benefit (due to a fall in the birth rate), and the numbers of widows and those receiving unemployment benefit.

Administration

The Department of Social Security administers most of the services in Great Britain; in Northern Ireland they are administered by the Department of Health and Social Services. Pensions and welfare services for war pensioners and their dependants are the responsibility of the Department of Social Security throughout Britain. The costs, including spending on administration, fall on central government. The housing benefit scheme is administered mainly by local authorities, which recover most of the cost from the Department of Social Security. Advice on social security is given to the Government by the Social Security Advisory Committee.

As part of a major government policy launched in 1988 to achieve better value for money and to improve services to the public, executive agencies set up within the Department of Social Security are to take responsibility for the major social security operations. An Information Technology Services

Agency, handling computing and telecommunications technology, was established in April 1990, while a Benefits Agency and a Contributions Unit are planned for April 1991.

As part of its plans to improve the management of the social security system and the quality of its service to the public, the Department of Social Security has begun the largest computerisation programme in Europe. This aims to link all of its local and central offices and the local offices of the unemployment benefit service into a single network.

Major Reforms   The Social Security Act 1986 implemented a wide-ranging reform of the social security system. Its main objectives are to make the system simpler, fairer and more effective in meeting genuine need in a way which encourages independence. The main reforms, introduced from 1988, include changes to the State Earnings-related Pension Scheme, which is additional to the basic state pension, and new arrangements to encourage personal and occupational pension schemes. The reforms include the introduction of new income-related benefits, entitlement to which is assessed using the same basic rules. These are: family credit; income support; and a restructured housing benefit scheme. The social fund in the form of loans or grants was introduced to help people on low incomes who have exceptional needs.

Advice about   The demand for advice about benefits is partly met by the Freeline Social
Benefits   Security Service, which handled over one million calls between April 1989 and March 1990. A complementary Advice Line service provides advice on social security for employers and the Ethnic Freeline Service provides information on social security matters in Urdu and Punjabi.

CONTRI-   Entitlement to National Insurance benefits such as retirement pension,
BUTIONS   sickness and invalidity benefit, unemployment benefit, maternity allowance and widow's benefit is dependent upon the payment of contributions. Industrial injuries benefits are non-contributory, but are also payable from the National Insurance Fund. There are four classes of contributions. Class 1 contributions are related to earnings and are paid by employees and employers. The contribution is lower if the employer operates a 'contracted-out' occupational pension scheme (see p 172). Self-employed people pay a flat rate Class 2 contribution and may have to pay a Class 4 contribution which is assessed as a percentage of profits or gains within certain limits; they are not eligible for unemployment and industrial injuries benefits. Voluntary Class 3 contributions are made by people wanting to safeguard rights to some benefits.

Employees who work after pensionable age (60 for women and 65 for men) do not pay contributions but the employer continues to be liable. People earning less than the lower earnings limit do not pay contributions; neither do their employers. Self-employed people with earnings below a set amount may apply for exemption; those over pensionable age do not pay contributions.

BENEFITS   For most benefits there are two contribution conditions. First, before benefit can be paid at all, a certain number of contributions have to be paid. Secondly, the full rate of benefit cannot be paid unless contributions have been made up to a specific level over a set period. Benefits are increased annually, the uprating being linked to increases in retail prices. The main benefits (payable weekly) are summarised below. The rates given are those effective from April 1990 until April 1991.

Retirement Pension

A state retirement pension is payable, on making a claim, to women at the age of 60 and men at the age of 65. The Sex Discrimination Act 1986 protects employees of different sexes in a particular occupation from being required to retire at different ages. This, however, has not affected the payment of state retirement pensions at different ages for men and women. The state pension scheme consists of a basic weekly pension of £46·90 for a single person and £75·10 for a married couple, together with an additional earnings-related pension. Pensioners may have unlimited earnings without affecting their pensions. Those who have put off their retirement during the five years after minimum pension age may earn extra pension. A non-contributory retirement pension of £28·20 is payable to people over the age of 80 who meet certain residence conditions, and who have not qualified for a contributory pension. People whose pensions do not give them enough to live on may be entitled to income support ranging from £11·80 to £17·05 for a single person and £17·95 to £24·25 for a couple.

Rights to basic pensions are safeguarded for mothers who are away from paid employment looking after children or for people giving up paid employment to care for severely disabled relatives. Women contributors receive the same basic pension as men with the same earnings, provided they have paid full-rate National Insurance contributions when working. From the year 2000 the earnings-related pension scheme will be based on a lifetime's revalued earnings instead of on the best 20 years. It will be calculated as 20 per cent rather than 25 per cent of earnings, to be phased in over ten years from 2000. The pensions of people retiring this century will be unaffected.

Occupational and Personal Pensions

Employers are free to 'contract out' their employees from the state scheme for the additional earnings-related pension and to provide their own occupational pension instead. However their pension must be at least as good as the state additional pension. The State remains responsible for the basic pension. There are at present around 50,000 occupational schemes, with over 10 million members—about half the working population.

As part of its reforms of the occupational pensions system, the Government has introduced measures to protect against inflation the pension rights of people who change jobs before pension age. The measures also give workers leaving a scheme the right to a fair transfer value; and require pension funds and other pension schemes to make available more information about their schemes.

The Social Security Act 1986 gives all employees the right to choose a personal pension rather than staying fully in the State Earnings-related Pension Scheme or in an employer's scheme. Such pensions qualify for contracting out of the State Earnings-related Pension Scheme and enable people to choose from a wide range of schemes available from banks, building societies and other financial institutions. Almost 3·7 million people have taken out personal pensions. The Social Security Act 1990 contains provisions which are designed to improve protection for occupational and personal pension schemes, including the appointment of a Pensions Ombudsman.

Mothers and Children

Under the statutory maternity pay scheme, women who leave employment to have a baby receive their maternity pay directly from their employer. To qualify, a woman must have worked for the same employer for at least six months up to and including the fifteenth week before the week her baby is due and have had average weekly earnings in the last eight weeks of that period which are not less than the lower earnings limit for National Insurance contributions. Statutory maternity pay is normally paid for 18 weeks. There are two rates: where a woman has been working for the same employer for at least two years, she is entitled to 90 per cent of her average weekly earnings for the first six weeks and to the lower rate of £39·25 for the remaining 12 weeks; where a woman has been employed for between six months and two years, she is entitled to payments for the full 18 weeks at the lower rate.

Women who are self-employed, have recently changed jobs or given up their job, and are therefore ineligible for maternity pay, may qualify for a weekly maternity allowance of £35·70, which is payable for 18 weeks. To qualify for this, a woman must have been employed or self-employed and paid standard rate National Insurance contributions for at least six months of the year ending 15 weeks before the baby is expected.

A payment of £100 from the social fund is available for each living child born or for a stillborn child if the pregnancy lasts for at least 28 weeks. It is also payable for an adopted baby if the mother or her partner are receiving income support or family credit.

Non-contributory child benefit of £7·25 is the main social security benefit for children. Tax free and normally paid to the mother, it is payable for children up to the age of 16 and for those up to 19 if they continue in full-time non-advanced education. In addition, one-parent benefit of £5·60 is payable to certain people bringing up one or more children on their own, whether as their parents or not. A non-contributory guardian's allowance of £9·65 for an orphaned child is payable to a person who is entitled to child benefit for that child. In certain circumstances it can be paid on the death of only one parent.

Widows

All women widowed receive a tax-free single payment of £1,000 following the death of their husbands, providing that their husbands had paid a minimum number of National Insurance contributions. Women whose husbands have died of an industrial injury or disease may also qualify, regardless of whether their husbands had paid National Insurance contributions. A widowed mother with a young family receives a widowed mother's allowance of £46·90 with a further £9·65 for each child. A widow's pension of £46·90 is payable to a widow who is 45 years or over when her husband dies or when her entitlement to widowed mother's allowance ends. Payment continues until the widow remarries or begins drawing retirement pension. Widows also benefit under the industrial injuries scheme.

A man whose wife dies when both are over pension age inherits his wife's pension rights just as a widow inherits her husband's rights.

Sick and Disabled People
Statutory Sick Pay and Sickness Benefit

There is a large variety of benefits for people unable to work because of sickness or disablement. Employers are responsible for paying statutory sick pay of between £39·25 and £52·50 with additions for a wife or other adult dependant for up to a maximum of 28 weeks to employees who satisfy the qualifying conditions. Employees who are not entitled to statutory sick pay can claim state sickness benefit of £35·70 instead, as can self-employed people.

Invalidity Pension and Allowance

An invalidity pension of £46·90 with additions of £28·20 for a husband or wife or other adult dependant and £9·65 for each child is payable when statutory sick pay or sickness benefit ends, if the beneficiary is still incapable of work. In the case of statutory sick pay the person must have satisfied the contribution condition for sickness benefit. An invalidity allowance of up to

£10 may be paid with the pension to people who become sick more than five years before minimum retirement age. An additional earnings-related pension may also be payable. (The Social Security Act 1990 will end entitlements to the additional pension element of invalidity benefit after the 1990–91 tax year.) If a person qualifies for both of these, he or she is paid an amount equal to the higher of the two.

Severe Disablement Allowance

A severe disablement allowance of £28·20 may be payable to people of working age who are unable to work and do not qualify for the National Insurance invalidity pension because they have not paid sufficient contributions.

Industrial Injuries Benefits

Various benefits are payable for disablement caused by an accident at work or a prescribed disease. Disablement benefit of up to £76·60 is usually paid after a qualifying period of 15 weeks if, as a result of an industrial accident or a prescribed disease, a person is physically or mentally disabled. During the qualifying period statutory sick pay or sickness benefit may be payable if the person is incapable of work. The degree of disablement is assessed by a medical authority and the amount paid depends on the extent of the disablement and how long it is expected to last. Disablement of 14 per cent or more attracts a weekly pension. Except for certain progressive respiratory diseases, disablement of less than 14 per cent does not attract basic benefit. In certain circumstances disablement benefits may be supplemented by a constant attendance allowance. An additional allowance may be payable in certain cases of exceptionally severe disablement.

Other Benefits

A non-contributory, tax-free attendance allowance of £37·55 or £25·05 may be payable to severely disabled people depending upon the amount of attention they require. There is no upper age limit. A non-contributory invalid care allowance of £28·20 may be payable to men and women aged between 16 and pension age who cannot take up paid employment because they are caring for a person receiving attendance allowance.

Physically disabled people unable or virtually unable to walk may be entitled to a tax-free mobility allowance of £26·25 to help with their transport costs. People aged between 5 and 66 may claim and payment can continue up to the age of 80.

An independent organisation called Motability helps disabled drivers and passengers wanting to use their mobility allowance to obtain a vehicle.

The Government has proposed that the attendance and mobility allowances should be replaced by a disability allowance for people disabled before the age of 65, and that a disability employment credit should be introduced to encourage those on disability benefits to take up employment.

Unemployment Benefit

Unemployment benefit of £37·35 for a single person or £60·40 for a couple is payable for up to a year in any one period of unemployment. Periods covered by unemployment or sickness benefit, maternity allowance or some training allowances which are eight weeks or less apart, are linked to form a single period of interruption of work. Everyone claiming unemployment benefit has to be available for work, but unemployed people wishing to do voluntary work in the community may do so in some cases without losing entitlement to benefit. The Social Security Act 1989 aims to ensure that people seeking unemployment benefit actively look for work and have good cause for rejecting any employment offered.

Income Support

Income support is payable to people who are not in work, or who work for less than 24 hours a week, and whose financial resources are below certain set levels. It consists of a personal allowance ranging from £21·90 for a single person or lone parent aged under 18 to £57·60 for a couple, at least one of whom is aged under 18, with additional sums for families, single parents, pensioners, and long-term sick and disabled people.

Housing Benefit

The housing benefit scheme offers help with the cost of rents to people with low incomes, using general assessment rules and benefit levels similar to those for the income support scheme. People whose net income is below certain specified levels receive housing benefit equivalent to 100 per cent of their rent.

Both income support and housing benefit schemes set a limit to the amount of capital a person may have and still remain entitled, and any income is taken into account after income tax and National Insurance contributions.

Community Charge Benefit

The community charge benefit is a rebate scheme which offers help with the cost of the community charge (a local tax) to those claiming income support and others with low incomes. Subject to rules similar to those governing the provision of income support and housing benefit (see above) people can receive rebates of up to 80 per cent of their community charge.

Family Credit

Family credit is payable to working families on modest incomes with children. The amount payable depends on a family's net income (excluding child benefits) and the number and ages of the children in the family. A maximum rate, consisting of an adult rate of £36·35 plus a rate for each child varying with age, is payable when the net income does not exceed £57·60 a week. The rate is then reduced by 70 pence for each pound by which net income exceeds this amount.

Social Fund

Discretionary payments, in the form of loans or grants, are available to people on low incomes who have special or emergency needs. There are three types: budgeting loans to help meet important occasional expenses, crisis loans for help in an emergency or a disaster, and community care grants to help people re-establish themselves or remain in the community and to ease exceptional pressure on families.

Payments are also made from the social fund to help with the costs of maternity or funerals or with heating during very cold weather. These payments are entitlements and are not subject to the same budgetary considerations as other social fund payments.

War Pensions and Related Services

Pensions are payable for disablement or death as a result of service in the armed forces or of certain injuries received in the merchant navy or civil defence during war-time, or to civilians injured by enemy action. The amount paid depends on the degree of disablement and rank held in service: the maximum disablement pension for a private soldier is £76·60. An allowance is also paid for dependants.

There are a number of extra allowances. The main ones are for unemployability, restricted mobility, the need for constant attendance, the provision of extra comforts, and as maintenance for a lowered standard of occupation. An age allowance of between £5·40 and £16·70 is payable to war pensioners aged 65 or over whose disablement is assessed at 40 per cent or more. Pensions are also paid to war widows and other dependants. (The pension for a private's widow is £60·95.)

The Department of Social Security maintains a welfare service for war pensioners, war widows and other dependants. It works closely with ex-Service organisations and other voluntary bodies which give financial aid and personal support to those disabled or bereaved as a result of war.

Taxation

Social security benefits, other than child, maternity, sickness, invalidity and disablement benefit, are regarded as taxable income. Various income tax reliefs and exemptions are allowed on account of age or a need to support dependants. The following benefits are not taxable: income support (except when paid to the unemployed and to people involved in industrial disputes), family credit, attendance allowance, mobility allowance, severe disablement allowance, industrial injuries disablement benefit, reduced earnings allowance, and war pensions.

Other Benefits

Other benefits for which unemployed people and those on low incomes may be eligible include exemption from health service charges (see p 147), grants towards the cost of spectacles, free school meals and free legal aid. Reduced charges are often made to the unemployed, for example, for adult education and exhibitions, and pensioners usually enjoy reduced transport fares.

Arrangements with Other Countries

As part of the European Community's efforts to promote the free movement of labour, regulations provide for equality of treatment and the protection of benefit rights for employed and self-employed people who move between member states. The regulations also cover retirement pensioners and other beneficiaries who have been employed, or self-employed, as well as dependants. Benefits covered include child benefit and those for sickness and maternity, unemployment, retirement, invalidity, accidents at work and occupational diseases.

Britain also has reciprocal social security agreements with a number of other countries. Their scope and the benefits they cover vary, but the majority cover most National Insurance benefits and family benefits.

7 Education

British education aims to develop fully the abilities of individuals, both young and old, for their own benefit and that of society as a whole. Compulsory schooling takes place between the ages of 4 or 5 and 16, although some provision is made for children under school age, and many pupils remain at school beyond the minimum leaving age. Post-school education, mainly at universities, polytechnics and colleges of further and higher education, is organised flexibly to provide a wide range of opportunities for academic and vocational education and continuing study throughout life.

Major Reforms　　During the last five years the education service has undergone the most far-reaching reform since the second world war (1939–45). Two major Acts of Parliament covering education mainly in England and Wales, and separate legislation for Scotland and for Northern Ireland, have been introduced in order to implement the principal aims of the Government's education policies. These are to raise standards at all levels of ability, increase parental choice, make further and higher education[1] more widely accessible and more responsive to the needs of the economy, and to achieve the best possible return from the resources invested in the education service.

In schools, the Government has aimed to improve school management, secure a broader and more balanced curriculum for all pupils so that they can develop the qualities and skills required for adult life and work in a technological age, reform the public examination system and improve the quality of teaching through better teacher selection, training and deployment. Schools are also encouraged to be more responsive to the needs of a multi-ethnic society. Measures are being taken to widen the choice of schools available and to ensure that schools respond effectively to the demands of parents and the broader community. Special attention is paid both to the provision of better pre-vocational education and training in schools and colleges for the 14- to 18-year-old age-group, and to the 40 per cent of lower-attaining pupils in the final years of compulsory education. An important objective has been to extend the knowledge and use of information technology in schools.

The Government's principal aims for the further education sector are to enable local education authorities and colleges to meet more fully the requirements of students and employers through the provision of a wide range of full- and part-time courses and to increase participation in further education and training, particularly among 16- to 19-year-olds. It is

---

[1]The terms 'higher education' and 'further education' are variously understood. However, under the Education Reform Act 1988, higher education is defined as higher courses in any institution—broadly, those of a standard higher than General Certificate of Education (GCE) Advanced (A) level or its equivalent—and further education as all other post-school courses.

committed to maintaining a high quality, cost-effective higher education system which helps to satisfy the nation's economic and social needs and at the same time offers the necessary opportunities for the advancement of knowledge and the pursuit of scholarship. Over the next 25 years the Government looks forward to a large increase in higher education in Britain, despite a forecast decline in the number of 18-year-olds by a third between 1985 and 1995. To help achieve this increase, it will seek to raise participation rates among 18-year-olds and to recruit more students from non-traditional groups, including ethnic minorities, by offering more flexible and varied courses.

Primary and Secondary Education

Measures to improve the quality and breadth of education and to extend parental choice and delegated decision-making in state-maintained schools in England and Wales are embodied in two recent Acts. The Education (No 2) Act 1986 contains provisions to reform the composition of school governing bodies (see p 183) and reallocate functions between school governors, local education authorities and head teachers; appraise the performance of teachers; and introduce more effective in-service training of teachers. The Education Reform Act 1988, covering both school and post-school education, provides for the establishment of a National Curriculum for children aged 5 to 16 in all state schools and for regular assessments of performance. From September 1990 secondary schools are required to admit pupils up to the limit of their available physical capacity if there is sufficient demand on behalf of children eligible for admission. This policy, known as 'more open enrolment', will further increase parental choice of schools. The 1988 Act gives all secondary as well as larger primary schools responsibility for managing the major part of their budgets, including staffing costs, as well as the opportunity to withdraw from local authority control (see pp 183 and 184). It also makes provision for the development of city technology colleges in disadvantaged urban areas (see p 179).

The School Boards (Scotland) Act 1988 requires Scottish education authorities to establish boards with the aim of increasing parental involvement in school management (see p 183). The Self-Governing Schools etc. (Scotland) Act 1989 contains provisions to enable parents to vote for local self-management of schools in place of control by education authorities. It also provides for the establishment of technology academies outside education authority control (with a similar role to that of city technology colleges—see p 179).

In Northern Ireland legislation which came into force in February 1990 makes provision for reforms broadly in line with those being implemented in England and Wales under the Education Reform Act 1988, and seeks to encourage further the development of integrated education (see pp 183 and 184).

Post-school Education

Under the Education Reform Act 1988, changes have also been introduced in the structure and funding of higher education to help institutions improve their management and planning, and become more flexible and more responsive to economic and social needs. The system of university funding has been reformed in England, Wales and Scotland: the University Grants Committee has been replaced by the Universities Funding Council, with executive powers to allocate finances to individual universities. Polytechnics and other major higher education colleges in England have been removed from local authority control, and incorporated as higher education corporations with boards of governors, half of whose members are drawn from industry, commerce and the professions. Their work is financed by the Polytechnics and Colleges Funding Council, with responsibilities parallel to those of the Universities Funding Council. Those further and higher education colleges remaining under local authority control are taking on greater responsibility for their annual budgets and including more employers on their governing bodies.

The Government intends to alter the balance of public funding for full-time undergraduate higher education from institutional grant paid through the funding bodies to tuition fees paid for individual students through the awards system (see p 193) from late 1990. This is intended to create a more direct link between institutional income and recruitment, encouraging institutions to increase their efficiency by making full use of capacity.

Legislation was introduced in both Scotland and Northern Ireland in 1989 to allow further education colleges to assume increased financial powers and managerial responsibilities so as to improve their efficiency and responsiveness to local demand.

Education–Business Links

The Government considers that co-operation between the education system and business is essential to help people of all ages acquire the skills necessary to maintain Britain's position as a leading industrial and trading nation at a time of rapid technological change and intense international economic competition. Many organisations already work to strengthen such links, and further contacts are being encouraged.

Much is being done under the Government's Technical and Vocational Education Initiative (TVEI—see p 187), to which £900 million has been allotted from 1987 to 1997. As a result of this and other initiatives, industrial and commercial matters are being allocated a more prominent place in school, college and university curricula and examinations. Businessmen and women are involved in curriculum development and enterprise activities for schoolchildren, and they have been enabled to take a bigger part in the management of schools, colleges and polytechnics by joining their governing bodies in greater numbers. The relevance of classroom activities to working life was central to the thinking behind the introduction of the General Certificate of Secondary Education and the Education Reform Act 1988.

In line with the concern to maintain British expertise in science, engineering and technology, a shift in provision is occurring in post-school education away from the arts and social sciences towards these subjects and towards directly vocational courses, while business and higher education institutions are being encouraged to collaborate more closely for their mutual benefit. The latter have been invited to provide enterprise training to students under the Government's Enterprise in Higher Education scheme, which is designed to ensure that students acquire the aptitudes and competence required by industry in the 1990s.

Under a government plan to promote further education, it is proposed that everyone up to the age of 19 should receive systematic education or training. A government review of the prospective needs for highly qualified staffing by industry, commerce and the public services was published in April 1990. This showed that the broad match between the supply of and demand for new graduates would be maintained over the next few years.

Secondary School Education

Under the Enterprise and Education Initiative, announced in 1988, the Government intends all pupils to have at least two weeks of suitable work experience before leaving school. It also aims to ensure that every year 10 per cent of teachers should be given the opportunity to gain some business experience; and that every trainee teacher should have an appreciation of the needs of employers.

City technology colleges, sponsored by industry and commerce, are being set up in urban areas in England and Wales to provide broadly based secondary education with a strong technological and business element. They are state-aided but independent of local education authorities. The colleges are managed by sponsors from universities and commerce, educational trusts, charities and other voluntary organisations. The first college opened in Solihull (West Midlands) in 1988, and by September 1990 seven were in operation.

In 1988 the Government launched the Compacts scheme as part of the Action for Cities programme (to regenerate inner city areas). Compacts are local agreements between employers, local education authorities and training providers in which young people, supported by their school or college, work to reach agreed targets, and employers undertake to provide further training or jobs for those attaining the targets. By August 1990, 38 Compacts were in operation, with over 300 schools participating, covering nearly 55,000 young people. The Government is providing more than £21 million over four years from 1990 to support Compacts.

The Government's local education and business partnerships initiative, announced in April 1990, is designed to foster the development of wide-ranging, formal partnerships between businesses and schools and other educational institutions at local level throughout Britain. It seeks to improve the coherence and co-ordination of government support and the integration of local and national education–business links programmes and activities.

Post-school Education

A network of employer-led Training and Enterprise Councils (TECs) is being built up by the Government in England and Wales. TECs are intended to make training and enterprise activities more relevant to the needs of employers and individuals locally. A total of 82 are expected to be established and, by June 1990, 15 had been set up. In Scotland, 22 local enterprise companies are being formed with a similar role to that of the TECs. In Northern Ireland a Training and Employment Agency was set up in April 1990 with responsibilities for a broad range of training and employment programmes and activities.

Some 11 TECs and local enterprise companies, working in close co-operation with local education authorities and other education interests, will run pilot schemes of Training Credits for young people to take effect from April 1991. The Training Credits schemes would offer an entitlement to train to approved standards for young people leaving full-time education.

Over 40 science parks have been set up by higher education institutions in conjunction with industrial scientists and technologists to promote the use of advanced technology, and more are planned. In addition, a network of regional technology centres has been established, bringing into contact colleges, polytechnics and universities within particular areas and linking them with local firms; the centres' incomes are derived from charges to companies which send their employees for training.

The Government's LINK scheme, announced in 1986, aims to encourage firms to work jointly with higher education institutes on government-funded research relevant to industrial needs. By July 1990, 22 LINK programmes had been approved, involving total government funding of some £151 million.

Administration

One of the distinctive features of the education service is the degree to which responsibility for provision is decentralised. Overall responsibility for all aspects of education in England, and for the Government's relations with and support for universities throughout Britain, rests with the Secretary of State for Education and Science. The Secretaries of State for Wales and for

Scotland have responsibility in their respective countries for non-university education, and are consulted about education in universities. The Secretary of State for Northern Ireland is responsible for both university and non-university education in the Province.

The government departments responsible for education are the Department of Education and Science in England, the Welsh Office, the Scottish Education Department, and the Department of Education for Northern Ireland. Their chief concerns are formulating education policies, allocating resources and influencing the other partners in the education service (the local education authorities, governing bodies of educational institutions, the teaching profession, the churches and voluntary organisations). The departments are also responsible for the supply and training of all teachers.

The provision of maintained, that is, publicly financed, school education and most post-school education outside universities has traditionally been the responsibility of local education authorities, which are funded by central government and (except in Northern Ireland) by local taxes. Their role, however, is being modified as a result of the Education Reform Act 1988 and other legislation (see pp 183 and 184). Until April 1990 education in inner London was the responsibility of a single body, the Inner London Education Authority (ILEA). However, with the aim of achieving a more cost-effective and responsive education service for the area, the ILEA has been abolished and its responsibilities transferred to individual inner London borough councils.

The local education authorities employ teachers and other staff, provide and maintain buildings, supply equipment and materials and, in England and Wales, award grants to students progressing to further and higher education. Universities are self-governing institutions receiving most of their income indirectly from central government grants. In Scotland the central institutions, which are roughly equivalent to the English polytechnics, and colleges of education, providing teacher training, are administered by independent governing bodies. In Northern Ireland colleges of education are controlled by the Department of Education and by a voluntary agency.

Finance

Estimated spending on education and science in Britain in 1989–90 was almost £25,000 million, more than 14 per cent of total public expenditure on services. About 70 per cent was incurred by local education authorities, which are directly responsible for the funding of most maintained schools and colleges of further education. The authorities make their own expenditure decisions according to local needs and circumstances, such as the number of school-age children.

Primary, Secondary and Further Education

In England and Wales education support grants and local education authority training grants enable the Government to support local education authority expenditure on educational activities of national priority. In 1990–91 the Government intends to provide grants of £209 million supporting total spending of £356 million. Most spending will be deployed on the implementation of the Education Reform Act, including activities related to the National Curriculum (nearly £100 million), local management of schools and colleges (£51 million), information technology in schools and colleges (£20 million), science and technology in primary schools (£8 million) and assessment (£20 million). The balance of the programme is aimed at improving the general efficiency and effectiveness of the education service.

The Government funds directly the recurring and capital costs both of grant-maintained schools which have opted to leave the local authority sector (see p 183) and of city technology colleges (see p 179) in England and Wales and comparable institutions in Scotland and Northern Ireland.

Higher Education Central government assistance for universities and other higher education institutions, together with grants and loans to students, accounts for some £4,500 million in 1990–91. The greater part of universities' income comes from public funds, largely as grant paid by the Government to the Universities Funding Council and to individual institutions such as the Open University, and as tuition fees paid for students through the awards system. The independent University of Buckingham receives no publicly funded grant, but some of its students have their fees paid from public funds through the awards system. In Northern Ireland grant is paid directly to the universities by central government following advice from the Universities Funding Council.

The Polytechnics and Colleges Funding Council, with funds from central government, was established under the Education Reform Act 1988 to finance higher courses in polytechnics and colleges of higher education in England that have become independent of local education authorities, as well as some higher education courses in establishments remaining under local authority control. Higher courses in Wales continue to be financed by local authorities. In Scotland all courses offered by the central institutions are funded by central government; advanced courses provided by local authority further education colleges are financed by the local authorities.

Many universities, polytechnics and other higher education institutions undertake training, research or consultancy for commercial firms, and the Government is encouraging them to secure a larger flow of funds from these sources. Further and higher education institutions are authorised to market inventions resulting from their research work and to sell goods and services arising as by-products of educational activities. A number of establishments have endowments or receive grants or gifts from foundations and from benefactors.

SCHOOLS Parents are required by law to see that their children receive efficient full-time education, at school or elsewhere, between the ages of 5 and 16 in Great Britain and 4 and 16 in Northern Ireland. Some 9 million children attend Britain's 35,000 schools (of which about 25,600 are primary or nursery and 4,900 secondary schools in the state sector). Most pupils receive free education financed from public funds, but a small proportion attend schools wholly independent of direct public financial support.

Boys and girls are taught together in most primary schools, and almost 90 per cent of pupils in maintained secondary schools in England and Wales and 61 per cent in Northern Ireland attend mixed schools. In Scotland nearly all secondary schools are mixed. Most independent schools for younger children are co-educational; the majority providing secondary education are single-sex, although the number of mixed schools is growing.

No fees are charged to parents of children at maintained schools, grant-maintained schools or city technology colleges, and books and equipment are free. In Northern Ireland at present a small proportion of grammar school pupils are fee-payers, but under legislation passed in 1989 Northern Ireland grammar schools will be required to discontinue the practice of admitting fee-paying pupils.

In England, Wales and Scotland parents have a statutory right to express a preference for a particular school for their children, and have an effective channel of appeal at local level (there are plans to extend this to Northern

Ireland). Schools are obliged to publish basic information about themselves and their public examination results.

Management
England and
Wales

Schools supported from public funds are of two main kinds in England and Wales: county schools and voluntary schools. County schools are provided and maintained by local education authorities wholly out of public funds. Voluntary schools, mostly established by religious denominations, are also wholly maintained from public funds but the governors of some types of voluntary school contribute to capital costs. Around one-third of the 23,300 maintained primary and secondary schools in England are voluntary schools, most of them Anglican or Roman Catholic.

Each publicly maintained school has a governing body which includes governors appointed by the local education authority and teacher and parent representatives. Under the Education (No 2) Act 1986, most maintained schools must have equal numbers of parent and local authority governors so that no single interest predominates. Governing bodies are responsible for the main policies of their schools and for the preparation of a statement of their schools' curricular aims and objectives. They also have final responsibility for school discipline and a large say in the appointment and dismissal of staff.

The role of governing bodies in England and Wales has been further enlarged by the Education Reform Act 1988. Since April 1990 local education authorities have delegated responsibility for the management of school budgets to all secondary schools and primary schools with more than 200 pupils. The Act also enables all English and Welsh secondary schools, as well as primary schools with over 300 pupils, to seek to withdraw from local authority control, following a ballot of parents, and to be directly financed by central government as grant-maintained non-fee-paying schools.

Scotland

In Scotland most of the schools supported from public funds are provided by education authorities and are known as public schools (in England this term is used for a type of independent school—see p 185). The School Boards (Scotland) Act 1988 requires education authorities to establish school boards to play a part in the administration and management of schools. The boards consist of elected parent and staff members as well as co-opted members and their aim is to provide an opportunity for greater parental involvement and to promote closer links between home, school and local community. The Self-Governing Schools etc. (Scotland) Act 1989 allows parents of children at public schools to opt for local self-management, following a ballot, and to receive funding directly from central government (see p 178).

Northern Ireland

In Northern Ireland there are three main categories of grant-aided school: controlled schools, owned and managed by the area education and library boards and having all their expenditure met from public funds; voluntary schools, mainly under Roman Catholic management and also maintained largely by public funds; and voluntary grammar schools, which may be under Roman Catholic or non-denominational management and receive grants from the Department of Education. All grant-aided schools include elected parents and teachers on their boards of governors. While all Northern Ireland schools must be open to pupils of all religions, most Catholic pupils attend Catholic schools and most Protestant children are enrolled at local authority schools. The policy of successive governments has been to encourage integrated education, providing for both Protestant and Roman Catholic pupils, where there is a local desire for it. A small number of integrated schools have been opened with assistance from charitable trusts and there are five integrated primary and two secondary schools grant-aided by the Department of Education.

The Education Reform (Northern Ireland) Order 1989 provides for the introduction of financial delegation in Northern Ireland, initially only to secondary schools; this includes the power to manage staff numbers. Primary and nursery school governors will have delegated responsibility for managing part of their budget. To assist those parents and schools with a commitment to the co-education of Protestant and Roman Catholic children, the legislation contains provision for grant-aided schools to opt for grant-maintained integrated status after a ballot of parents. Controlled grant-maintained integrated schools will be run by boards of governors under the supervision of local authorities and are to be directly financed by central government. New and independent schools can also apply for grant-maintained status. Integrated schools must be conducted in such a way as to be likely to attract reasonable numbers of both Protestant and Catholic children.

Nursery and Primary Schools

Although there is no statutory requirement to provide education for the under-fives, successive governments have enabled nursery education to expand. Just under half of three- and four-year-olds receive education in nursery schools or classes or in infants' classes in primary schools. In addition, many children attend pre-school playgroups, most of which are organised by parents and affiliated to the Pre-School Playgroups Association.

Compulsory education begins at five (four in Northern Ireland), when children go to infant schools or departments; at seven many go on to junior schools or departments. The usual age for transfer from primary to secondary schools is 11 in England, Wales and Northern Ireland, but some local authorities in England have established 'first' schools for pupils aged 5 to 8, 9 or 10 and 'middle' schools covering various age-ranges between 8 and 14. In Scotland primary schools take children from 5 to 12.

Secondary Schools

The publicly maintained system of education aims to give all children an education suited to their particular abilities. Almost nine-tenths of the maintained secondary school population in Great Britain attend comprehensive schools, which take pupils without reference to ability or aptitude and provide a wide range of secondary education for all or most of the children in a district. The schools can be organised in a number of ways. They include those that take the full secondary school age-range from 11 to 18; middle schools, whose pupils move on to senior comprehensive schools at 12, 13 or 14, leaving at 16 or 18; and schools with an age-range of 11 or 12 to 16, combined with a sixth-form or a tertiary college for pupils over 16. Tertiary colleges offer a full range of vocational courses for students over 16, as well as academic courses. Most other children receive secondary education in 'grammar' or 'secondary modern' schools, to which they are allocated after selection procedures at the age of 11. By August 1990, 48 schools had achieved grant-maintained status under the Education Reform Act's 'opting out' provisions (see p 178).

Scottish secondary education is almost completely non-selective; the majority of schools are six-year comprehensives. Because of local circumstances some comprehensive schools run courses lasting only four years or less; their pupils may transfer at the end of the second or fourth years to a six-year comprehensive. The Government, in partnership with private sponsors, intends to set up technology academies in Scotland with a role similar to that of the city technology colleges in England and Wales (see p 179).

In Northern Ireland secondary education is organised largely along selective lines, based on a system of testing, although in certain areas secondary schools are run on a non-selective basis.

Independent Schools

Independent schools are outside the publicly maintained sector, but they must register with the appropriate education department and are open to inspection. They can be required to remedy serious shortcomings in their accommodation or instruction, and to exclude anyone regarded as unsuitable to teach in or to be the owner of a school. About 7 per cent of British schoolchildren attend independent schools.

There are about 2,400 independent schools educating 600,000 pupils of all ages. They charge fees varying from around £250 a term for day pupils at nursery age to £2,900 a term for senior boarding pupils. Many offer bursaries to help pupils from less well-off families. Such pupils may also be helped by local education authorities—particularly if the authorities' own schools cannot meet the needs of individual children—or by the Government's Assisted Places Scheme, under which assistance is given according to parental income. Over 350 schools participate in the scheme. The Government also gives income-related help with fees to pupils at certain specialist music and ballet schools.

There is great variety of provision within the independent sector, ranging from small kindergarten to large day and boarding schools and from new and in some cases experimental schools to ancient foundations. The 600 boys', girls' and mixed preparatory schools are so called because they prepare children for the Common Entrance Examination to senior schools. The normal age-range is from seven-plus to 11, 12 or 13, but many of the schools now have pre-preparatory departments for younger children. A number of independent schools have been established by religious and ethnic minorities.

Independent schools for older pupils—from 11, 12 or 13 to 18 or 19—include about 550 which are sometimes referred to as 'public schools'. These are schools belonging to the Headmasters' Conference, the Governing Bodies Association, the Society of Headmasters and Headmistresses of Independent Schools, the Girls' Schools Association and the Governing Bodies of Girls' Schools Association. They should not be confused with the state-supported public schools in Scotland.

Special Educational Needs

Special educational needs comprise learning difficulties of all kinds, including mental and physical disabilities which hinder or prevent learning. Local education authorities are required, in the case of children whose learning difficulties are severe or complex, to assess the child's special educational needs and to provide a statement or record of these needs. Wherever possible, children with special educational needs are educated in ordinary schools, provided that the parents' wishes have been taken into account, and that this is compatible with meeting the needs of the child, with the provision of efficient education for the other children in the school, and with the efficient use of resources. In Scotland the choice of school is a matter for agreement between education authorities and parents.

There are nearly 1,900 special schools (both day and boarding), including those run by voluntary organisations. They cater for a wide variety of pupils with special educational needs (some 120,000) who cannot be educated at ordinary schools.

Teachers

Teachers in publicly maintained schools are appointed by local education authorities or school governing bodies. There are over 530,000 teachers in maintained and independent schools, and the average pupil–teacher ratio for all schools is 17 to 1. Teachers in maintained schools must hold qualifications approved by the appropriate education department (see p 197).

The Curriculum
England
and Wales

Under the Education (No 2) Act 1986, head teachers in England and Wales have been responsible for determining and organising the curriculum within their schools, taking into consideration the policy of their local education authority and that of their governing body. The Government favours widening educational opportunities as much as possible through a broad and balanced curriculum which is differentiated to meet the individual needs of pupils and is relevant to the requirements of the modern world.

Under the Education Reform Act 1988, the introduction of a National Curriculum in primary and secondary schools in England and Wales began in 1989 and is being phased in over several years. The National Curriculum, which the Government believes should occupy not less than 70 per cent of teaching time, consists of the core subjects of English, mathematics and science, as well as the other foundation subjects of history, geography, technology, music, art, physical education and (for secondary level pupils) a modern foreign language. Economic and industrial awareness are important cross-curricular themes in the National Curriculum.

In Wales the Welsh language constitutes a core subject in Welsh-speaking schools and a foundation subject elsewhere under the National Curriculum. In the primary sector 80 per cent of schools either use Welsh as a teaching medium or teach it as a second language, while nearly 90 per cent of secondary schools teach Welsh as a first or second language.

Attainment targets are being devised to establish what children should normally be expected to know, understand and be able to do at the ages of 7, 11, 14, and 16, enabling the progress of each child to be measured against national standards. Pupils' performance in relation to attainment targets will be assessed and reported on at the four key stages. Regulations have been introduced covering the manner and form in which assessments of individual pupils are to be made available to parents and others (see p 190).

Religious education, already compulsory under the Education Act 1944, is required for all pupils as part of the basic curriculum, although parents have a right to withdraw their children from religious education classes (see p 188). The content of religious education courses is determined locally.

Scotland

The content and management of the curriculum in Scotland are the responsibility of education authorities and individual head teachers, though guidance is provided by the Secretary of State for Scotland and the Scottish Consultative Council on the Curriculum. The Council has issued guidelines to secondary head teachers recommending that secondary level pupils should follow a broad and balanced curriculum consisting of English, mathematics, science, a modern European language, social studies, technological activities, art, music or drama, religious and moral education, and physical education. A major programme of curricular review and development is in progress for the 5-to-14 age-range. The Government is to issue new guidelines on all aspects of the curriculum. New guidelines are also to be published on assessment, and standardised tests in English and mathematics will be introduced for primary school pupils at stages 4 and 7 (normally at ages 8 and 12).

A flexible system of vocational courses for 16- to 18-year-olds based on modules or short units of study has been introduced in schools and colleges in disciplines ranging from business and administration to engineering and industrial production. Though designed primarily to improve the preparation of young people for working life, the courses are also intended to meet the needs of many adults entering training or returning to education. The courses lead to the award of a National Certificate.

A committee has been established to review courses and assessment arrangements in the final two years of secondary schooling. Provision is made for teaching in Gaelic in Gaelic-speaking areas.

Northern Ireland In Northern Ireland major programmes of curriculum review and development are in progress in both primary and secondary schools. The aim in the secondary sector is to improve the quality and relevance of education for all pupils in the 11-to-16 age-group by promoting, in particular, courses in science and technology, and the development of economic awareness and information technology across the curriculum.

A common curriculum is being introduced in all grant-aided schools, based on six broad areas of study: English, mathematics, science and technology, the environment and society, creative and expressive studies, and (for secondary and Irish-speaking primary schools) language studies. Religious education will be compulsory at all stages. Attainment targets, programmes of study and methods of assessment (at ages 8, 11, 14 and 16) will be specified for all compulsory subjects. In addition, the school curriculum will include six compulsory cross-curricular themes: 'education for mutual understanding', cultural heritage, health education, information technology, and (in secondary schools) economic awareness and careers education.

Ethnic Minority Over the last 20 years or so the education authorities have done much to
Children meet the special needs of ethnic minority children. English language teaching has received priority, but attention has been increasingly directed at the use of mother tongues, especially in the early years. Emphasis has been placed on the need for schools to take account of the ethnic and cultural backgrounds of pupils. Measures are being taken not only to improve the achievement of ethnic minority pupils but also to prepare all children, not just those of ethnic minority origin, for living in a multi-ethnic society.

Curriculum In England curriculum development is promoted by the National
Development Curriculum Council and in Wales by the Curriculum Council for Wales. At some 480 teachers' centres, teachers meet for curriculum development work, discussion and in-service training. In Scotland such development work is undertaken by the Scottish Consultative Council on the Curriculum and in Northern Ireland by the Northern Ireland Council for Educational Development (NICED). A Northern Ireland Curriculum Council, which will take over the functions of the NICED and keep all aspects of the curriculum under review, is being established.

Technical and Recognising the need to equip pupils of all abilities with the skills needed for
Vocational adult and working life, the Government launched the Technical and
Education Vocational Education Initiative (TVEI) in England and Wales in 1983 and in
Initiative Scotland in 1984. Originally a series of pilot projects, it was extended into a national scheme in 1987. The scheme is funded and administered by the Department of Employment working in close co-operation with local education authorities. The TVEI is intended to ensure that the education of 14- to 18-year-olds provides them with learning opportunities which will equip them for working life. This is implemented by ensuring that the school curriculum relates to the working environment, and by improving skills and

qualifications, particularly in science, technology and modern languages. The initiative aims to include all students aged 14 to 18 in maintained schools and colleges by mid-1993. An estimated 500,000 students in some 3,000 schools and colleges are participating in the TVEI.

In Northern Ireland the Vocational Education Programme was introduced in 1987 with the same broad objectives as the TVEI. The Programme will come to an end during 1990–91, but the key curricular areas of science, technology, information technology and economic awareness, which it has sought to encourage, will be covered fully under the new common curriculum.

Religious Education and Collective Worship in Schools

In England and Wales county and voluntary schools are required to provide religious education and a daily act of collective worship for all pupils except those withdrawn by their parents. Under the Education Reform Act 1988 due recognition must be given to the place of Christianity within religious education and collective worship in county schools. The Act allows daily collective worship to be organised at times other than the beginning of the day, and permits separate acts of worship for different groups of pupils. In county schools, and sometimes in voluntary schools, non-denominational religious education is given in accordance with a locally agreed syllabus which may include the comparative study of religions. Syllabuses have been revised in many areas to take account of the faiths of the local population. In all kinds of voluntary schools there is the opportunity for denominational religious education.

In Scotland education authorities are required to see that schools practise religious observance and give pupils religious instruction; parents may withdraw their children if they wish. Certain schools provide for Roman Catholic children but in all schools there are safeguards for the individual conscience.

In Northern Ireland, too, schools are obliged to offer religious education and collective worship, although parents have the right to withdraw their children from both. In controlled schools clergy have a right of access which may be used for denominational instruction and in voluntary schools collective worship and religious education are controlled by the management authorities. Provision has been made for religious education to have an agreed core syllabus which schools can expand according to their own needs and wishes.

Examinations
England, Wales and Northern Ireland

The principal examinations taken by secondary school pupils in England, Wales and Northern Ireland around the age of 16 are those leading to the General Certificate of Secondary Education (GCSE). This replaced the General Certificate of Education (GCE) Ordinary (O) level and the Certificate of Secondary Education (CSE) in 1988. GCSE courses were introduced in 1986 with a view to raising standards of performance. GCSE examinations are usually taken after five years of secondary education and have a seven-point scale of grades denoted by the letters A to G. Grades A to C have standards at least as high as GCE O level grades A to C and CSE grade 1, which were the normal qualifying grades for more advanced education or training. The Government intends the GCSE to be the principal means for assessing attainment at stage 4 of the National Curriculum.

The GCE Advanced (A) level is normally taken after a further two years of study. New examinations, Advanced Supplementary (AS) levels, were examined for the first time in 1989 and provide an opportunity for sixth-form pupils to study a wider range of subjects than before. Students specialising in the arts and humanities, for example, are able to continue to study mathematics and technological subjects at the new level. Requiring the same standard of work but with only half the content of A levels, AS levels are designed to occupy half the teaching and study time of an A level. A levels or a mixture of A and AS levels are the main standard for entrance to university and other higher education and to many forms of professional training.

The Certificate of Pre-Vocational Education, awarded for the first time in 1986, is intended for those at school or college who wish to continue in full-time education for a year after the age of 16 to prepare either for work or for vocational and other courses. In common with other Business & Technician Education Council (BTEC—see p 196) qualifications, it can serve as a stepping stone into higher education. The Certificate is devised by BTEC and the City and Guilds of London Institute (see p 196).

Scotland

The public examination system in Scotland is different from that in other parts of Britain. Scottish pupils take the Scottish Certificate of Education (SCE) at Standard grade and Ordinary grade at the end of their fourth year of secondary education (equivalent to the fifth year in England and Wales). Pupils in the fifth and sixth years sit the SCE Higher grade; passes at this grade are the basis for entry to university, colleges of education or professional training. For those who have completed their main studies at the Higher grade but wish to continue studies in particular subjects there is the Certificate of Sixth Year Studies (CSYS). The Standard grade courses and examinations, which are replacing the Ordinary grade, cater for the whole ability range. The Higher and CSYS examinations are being revised to ensure compatibility with the Standard grade, and are undergoing review.

Under the Government's plan for the reform of non-advanced further education in Scotland, the National Certificate was introduced in 1984–85 for students over 16 who had successfully completed a programme of vocational courses based on study units known as modules (see p 186). These modules are now being used in schools for pupils in the 14-to-18 age-range, and other short courses specifically for use in schools are being devised. A new system of Scottish Vocational Qualifications similar to that of the National Council for Vocational Qualifications (see p 196) is being introduced.

School Examinations and Assessment Councils

All GCSE and other qualifications offered to pupils of compulsory school age in maintained schools in England and Wales must be approved by the Government. Associated syllabuses and assessment procedures must comply with national guidelines and be approved by the School Examinations and Assessment Council. The aim is to secure a reasonably wide choice of qualifications and syllabuses which promote a broad, balanced curriculum and support the National Curriculum.

The Council keeps under review all aspects of examinations and assessment in England and Wales and carries out research and development. It co-operates with the National Curriculum Council (for England) and the Curriculum Council for Wales on work connected with the National Curriculum in schools.

The Northern Ireland School Examinations and Assessment Council was established in April 1990. It inherited the full range of duties of its predecessor, the Northern Ireland School Examinations Council, and its functions also include formal assessments associated with the statutory curriculum.

**Progress
Reports**

A system of school reporting of individual pupils' achievement was introduced in April 1990, under which parents in England and Wales will receive a yearly progress report on their child's National Curriculum achievements and results in public examinations. In Scotland the report card system is being reformed to give parents a clearer view of their children's progress. In Northern Ireland there is a commitment for all pupils to be issued with a record of their performance on leaving primary and secondary school.

**Educational
Standards**

Her Majesty's Inspectors report to the Government on the quality of education provided in all schools and in most further and higher education establishments outside the universities, and advise education authorities and schools as well as the Government. They also report on the youth service and education provision in hospitals, prisons and youth custody centres, and the armed services. Their reports on individual establishments are published. Local education authorities employ inspectors or advisers to guide them or maintained schools.

The Evaluation and Monitoring Unit, which is part of the School Examinations and Assessment Council (see p 189), is mainly concerned with the evaluation of the assessment arrangements for the National Curriculum. In England, Wales and Northern Ireland programmes of monitoring have been carried out in English language and mathematics at the ages of 11 and 15, in science at the ages of 11, 13 and 15, and in the first foreign language at the age of 13. A survey of performance at the age of 15 in design and technology was undertaken in 1988. In Scotland the Assessment of Achievement research programme has surveyed attainments of pupils in English and mathematics at ages 8, 12 and 14.

**Information
Technology**

Britain has developed a world lead in several aspects of the use of information technology (IT) in education. In 1987 the Government announced a major five-year strategy to integrate the use of IT throughout the school curriculum and extend its benefits as widely as possible to children of all ages, aptitudes and abilities. The main objectives of the first three years of the programme, which began in 1988, are to increase the number of microcomputers in schools; provide support for the appointment of advisory teachers trained in the applications of IT; and offer in-service training for teachers in the effective use of IT in their specialist subject areas. Government-supported expenditure in the first three years amounts to some £81 million.

The application of IT is featuring in programmes of study and attainment targets for core and foundation subjects of the National Curriculum. The Government is making available £410,000 to the National Educational Resources Information Service (an electronic database, see p 191) to place all National Curriculum programmes of study, attainment targets and statements of attainment on the database between 1989 and 1992. New computer software to help teach the National Curriculum is being financed by the Government at a cost of £750,000 from 1989–90 to 1992–93. The development programme, which is managed by the National Council for Educational Technology (see below), will provide software and related materials for the National Curriculum for such areas as handling data in mathematics lessons; supporting practical work in science; and creating design projects in design and technology.

The National Council for Educational Technology has been set up by the Government to evaluate the newest technologies in terms of their application to education. Financed by the Department of Education and Science, its objectives are to support, encourage, develop and apply the use of learning systems and new technologies, including microcomputers, electronic systems and other aspects of information technology, to all aspects of education and training. In this way, the Council provides an integrated professional service covering educational and information technology throughout Britain.

Educational Aids

Teachers and pupils use a range of aids to assist the processes of teaching and learning. The government-funded National Educational Resources Information Service enables schools to find out about a large range of teaching aids. Most schools have audio-visual equipment such as slide projectors and overhead projectors, and educational broadcasting is of major importance. Each year almost 500 hours of school radio and over 900 hours of television are transmitted nationally by the BBC and the independent broadcasting companies. Teachers' notes, pupils' pamphlets and computer software accompany many broadcast series. Virtually all primary and secondary schools now have microcomputers which are used for computer-assisted learning (see p 190).

Careers Education and Guidance

Increasing importance is being attached by schools and colleges to careers education to increase young people's awareness of further and higher education and careers opportunities, and generally help them to prepare for adult and working life. As a result, links between schools and the careers service are being strengthened. The work of the careers service at local level is supported by careers information material produced by the Government's Careers and Occupational Information Centre. The Government is sponsoring the development of a computer-assisted careers guidance system for students in universities, polytechnics and colleges, known as PROSPECT (HE).

Health and Welfare of Schoolchildren

Physical education, including organised games, is part of the curriculum of all maintained schools, and playing fields must be available for pupils over the age of eight. Most secondary schools have a gymnasium.

The government health departments are responsible for the medical inspection of schoolchildren and for advice on, and treatment of, specific medical and dental problems associated with children of school age. The Government believes that the education service has a role to play in preventing and dealing with juvenile drug misuse and in helping to prevent the spread of AIDS.

Local education authorities are free to decide what milk, meals or other refreshment to offer at their schools, and what charges to make. (In Northern Ireland school meals must be provided for primary school pupils.) Provision has to be made free of charge, however, for pupils from families receiving certain social security benefits. Under certain conditions the authorities must supply free school transport, and they have discretionary powers to help with the cost of travel to school.

Corporal punishment is prohibited by law in maintained schools in Britain.

POST-SCHOOL EDUCATION

About two-fifths of young people receive some form of post-school education, compared with a fifth in 1965, and 1 in 6 of all young people enter higher education. The number of degrees awarded by age-group is comparable with that of other developed countries, and the proportion of people in further and higher education also compares well, taking into account the large proportion of part-time students and the large group of students receiving professional training in firms rather than in educational institutions.

Post-school education is provided at universities, polytechnics, the Scottish central institutions and colleges of education, further and higher education colleges, adult education centres, colleges of technology, tertiary colleges, colleges of art and design, and agricultural and horticultural colleges. There are also many independent specialist establishments, such as secretarial and correspondence colleges, and colleges for teaching English as a foreign language. Several voluntary and public bodies offer cultural and general education, sometimes with assistance from local education authorities and central government, and many education and training schemes are run by public or private organisations, or firms.

The Government aims to improve awareness of the opportunities for further and higher education and training through the development of national information services, such as the Educational Counselling and Credit Transfer Information Service funded by the Department of Education and Science.

The Further Education Unit, with funding from the Department of Education and Science, is an advisory and development body for further education.

Higher Education

Higher education is provided by universities, polytechnics, the Scottish central institutions and colleges of education and institutions of further and higher education, some concerned wholly with teacher training. The Government considers that access to higher education courses should be available to all those who can benefit from them and who have the necessary intellectual competence, motivation and maturity. Although GCE A levels and their equivalents in Scotland have traditionally been the standard for entry to higher education courses, other qualifications and courses are now considered equally appropriate. These are AS levels, some BTEC qualifications (see p 196) and access/foundation courses (see p 196).

In 1988–89 there were over 1 million students in higher education, 29 per cent more than in 1979. The Government aims to secure further increases in participation, and the number of students in full-time higher education is expected to rise by some 10 per cent between 1988–89 and 1992–93. One of the Government's main aims in higher education is to bring about a change in the balance of provision in favour of scientific, technological and directly vocational courses.

In order to maintain British expertise in information technology and related fields, a number of government schemes have been introduced in the last eight years to expand higher education and research in electronics, engineering and computer science by making available extra student places, and additional staff and research fellowships in universities, polytechnics and Scottish central institutions. One such scheme, the Engineering and Technology Programme, announced in 1985, has provided around 5,000 student places in engineering, information technology and related scientific disciplines. In 1988 the Department of Employment brought in a Graduate Enterprise Programme offering 450 places on management training courses for recently qualified graduates intending to start their own businesses.

Further Education

Further education in England and Wales comprises all provision outside schools to people aged over 16 of a standard up to and including GCE A level (or equivalent). Courses are run by some 490 colleges of further education, many of which also offer higher education courses. The great majority of such colleges are controlled by local education authorities. In Scotland the new modular courses at the non-advanced level (see pp 186 and 189) can be taken in schools, further education colleges or as part of government training schemes.

Much of the provision outside the universities is broadly vocational. It extends from lower-level technical and commercial courses to advanced courses for those aiming at higher-level posts in commerce, industry and administration, or taking up a variety of professions (for example, town planning or estate management). However, most colleges provide non-vocational courses, including GCSE and GCE A level courses. The system is flexible and enables the student to acquire whatever qualifications his or her capabilities and time allow.

A large number of students on further education courses attend part time, either by day release or block release from employment or during the evenings. A particular feature of the further education system is its strong ties with commerce and industry: a major part of the further education sector is devoted to work-related studies. Co-operation with the business world is encouraged by the Government and its agencies, and employers are often involved in designing courses.

Further education colleges supply much of the education element in training programmes like Youth Training and Employment Training, both sponsored by the Training Agency. Youth Training offers two years' planned work experience and training to 16-year-old school-leavers and one year's to 17-year-old school-leavers. All young people on Youth Training will be offered training and vocational education leading to qualifications at or equivalent to a minimum of level two in the framework established by the National Council for Vocational Qualifications (see p 196). Employment Training provides a flexible training programme of up to 12 months especially for the longer-term unemployed.

The Education Reform Act 1988 requires every local education authority in England and Wales to prepare a scheme outlining procedures for planning further education provision, setting college budgets and delegating control over budgets to college governing bodies. They must also increase employer representation on governing bodies. Legislation was introduced in both Scotland and Northern Ireland in 1989 to institute financial delegation in further education colleges and to strengthen industrial and commercial representation on their governing bodies, at least half of whose members must represent employment interests.

Students

Around one million students took full-time courses in 1988–89, including sandwich courses (where substantial periods of full-time study alternate with periods of supervised experience on a relevant job), at universities[2] and major establishments of further and higher education in Britain. Of these about 330,000 were at universities, while another 310,000 were following higher courses at colleges of further and higher education, polytechnics and Scottish central institutions and other colleges. More than 400,000 were taking further education courses, the majority of which lead to recognised vocational or educational qualifications.

There were also nearly 4 million part-time students, some of whom are released by their employers for further education during working hours. Many of the remainder take part in adult education classes.

Over 90 per cent of full-time students on higher courses are helped by grants from public funds, which are mandatory for those students taking first degree and other comparable courses who qualify under national rules. Grants for other courses may be given at the discretion of a local education authority. Grants cover tuition fees and maintenance, but parents contribute to maintenance costs according to their income. They are awarded by

[2]Excluding the University of Buckingham.

local education authorities in England and Wales up to first degree level. Equivalent schemes are administered in Scotland by the Scottish Education Department, and in Northern Ireland mainly by the education and library boards. Grants for postgraduate study and research are offered by the education departments and by the research councils. Some scholarships are available from endowments and also from particular industries or companies.

Developments

Under the Education (Student Loans) Act 1990 and corresponding Northern Ireland legislation, all home students in full-time higher education below postgraduate level will be eligible, from late 1990, for an interest-free top-up maintenance loan initially averaging over £400 a year, in addition to a maintenance grant. The standard repayment period will initially be five years, with repayment beginning in the April following graduation for students earning more than 85 per cent of the average national wage.

This legislation is designed to share the cost of student maintenance more equitably between students, parents and the taxpayer, as well as to promote a stronger sense of self-reliance among students. It is intended that loans will eventually provide about half of a student's maintenance entitlement.

Universities

There are 47 universities in Britain, including the Open University, compared with 17 in 1945. They are governed by royal charters or in some cases by Act of Parliament, and enjoy complete academic freedom, appointing their own staff and deciding which students to admit, what and how to teach, and which degrees to award. The English universities are: Aston (Birmingham), Bath, Birmingham, Bradford, Bristol, Brunel (London), Cambridge, City (London), Durham, East Anglia (Norwich), Essex, Exeter, Hull, Keele, Kent at Canterbury, Lancaster, Leeds, Leicester, Liverpool, London, Loughborough, Manchester, University of Manchester Institute of Science and Technology, Newcastle upon Tyne, Nottingham, Oxford, Reading, Salford, Sheffield, Southampton, Surrey, Sussex, Warwick, York and the independent University of Buckingham. The Royal College of Art, the Cranfield Institute of Technology, the London Graduate School of Business Studies and the Manchester Business School also have university status. The federated University of Wales comprises six constituent institutions. The Scottish universities are: Aberdeen, Dundee, Edinburgh, Glasgow, Heriot-Watt (Edinburgh), St Andrews, Stirling and Strathclyde (Glasgow). In Northern Ireland there are the Queen's University of Belfast and the University of Ulster.

The universities of Oxford and Cambridge date from the twelfth and thirteenth centuries, and the Scottish universities of St Andrews, Glasgow, Aberdeen and Edinburgh from the fifteenth and sixteenth centuries. All the other universities in Britain were founded in the nineteenth and twentieth centuries.

Admission to universities is by examination or selection. Of the total number of full-time university students in 1988–89 (excluding those at the University of Buckingham), 58,000 were postgraduate. About half lived in colleges, halls of residence and other accommodation owned by universities. There are around 30,000 full-time university teachers paid wholly from university funds. The ratio of full-time staff to full-time students is about 1 to 11, one of the most favourable in the world.

Except at the Open University, first degree courses are mainly full time and usually last three or four years, though medical and veterinary courses normally require five or six years. Degree titles vary according to the practice of each university. In England, Wales and Northern Ireland the most common titles for a first degree are Bachelor of Arts (BA) or Bachelor of Science (BSc) and for a second degree Master of Arts (MA), Master of Science (MSc), and Doctor of Philosophy (PhD). In the older Scottish universities Master is used for a first degree in arts subjects. Uniformity of standards between universities is promoted by employing external examiners for all university examinations, and the general pattern of teaching is similar throughout Britain.

Research is an important feature of university work; many staff combine research with their teaching duties and about half of postgraduate students are engaged on research projects. The Government intends to pursue a policy of separate funding for teaching and research in the university sector. It is encouraging universities to co-operate closely with industry on research projects. In 1987 a new information technology institute, sponsored jointly by industry and the Cranfield Institute of Technology, was opened to link academic and commercial interests.

The Open University

The Open University is a non-residential university offering degree and other courses for adult students of all ages throughout Britain. In the main it uses a combination of specially produced printed texts, correspondence tuition, television and radio broadcasts, audio and video cassettes, and summer schools, together with a network of study centres for contact with part-time tutors and counsellors, and with fellow students. No formal academic qualifications are required to register for these courses, but the standards of the University's degrees are the same as those of other universities. Its first degree, for which courses began in 1971, is the BA (Open), a general degree awarded on a system of credits for each course completed. In 1990 there were 72,000 registered undergraduates, and in all 102,000 first degrees have been awarded since the University's inception.

The University also has a programme of higher degrees, BPhil, MPhil and PhD, available through research, and MA and MSc through taught courses. More than 2,800 students were registered on higher degree courses in 1990. A Master of Business Administration (MBA) degree course was introduced in 1989.

The fastest-growing aspect of the University's work is the Continuing Education Programme, which includes short courses of community education, in-service training for teachers, health and social welfare workers and other professional staff, and up-dating courses for managers, scientists and technologists. Some of these are presented as multi-media courses in the same way as the undergraduate programme, while others are in the form of self-contained study packs. In 1990 some 130,000 students were following these courses.

While students must normally be resident in Britain, undergraduate and Business School courses are also available to English-speakers in Belgium, Luxembourg and the Netherlands. The University has advised many other countries on setting up similar institutions. It is also making a substantial contribution to the new Commonwealth of Learning project, which brings together distance-teaching establishments and students throughout the Commonwealth.

Polytechnics and Other Institutions

A major contribution to post-school education in England and Wales is made by the 31 polytechnics, which have been established since 1967. They offer mainly higher education courses in a wide range of subjects, including those leading to first and higher degrees and certain graduate-equivalent qualifications. They also offer courses leading to the examinations of the chief professional bodies, and to qualifications such as those of the Business &

Technician Education Council (see below). One-year 'access' courses provide a foundation and an appropriate test before enrolment on a course of higher education for prospective students who lack the standard entry qualifications. Polytechnics have close links with commerce and industry, and many polytechnic students have jobs and attend on a part-time basis. Similar provision is made in Scotland in the 15 central institutions and a number of further education colleges, and in Northern Ireland by the University of Ulster.

Institutes and colleges of higher education, formed by the integration of teacher training with the rest of higher education, account for a significant proportion of higher education students, and other further education colleges run some, usually specialised, higher education courses.

Council for National Academic Awards

An increasing number of students on higher education courses in Great Britain outside the universities take courses leading to the qualifications of the Council for National Academic Awards (CNAA). The Council awards degrees and other academic qualifications comparable in standard with those granted by the universities. The courses range from science and technology to the arts, social studies, business studies and law, but the proportion of technology, business or other broadly vocational courses is much higher than in universities.

Since 1987 institutions running CNAA-approved courses have been able to apply to have delegated responsibility for approving and reviewing their own courses. By August 1990 a total of 40 institutions had been accredited by the CNAA for taught degree courses.

Vocational Qualifications

The National Council for Vocational Qualifications (NCVQ) was set up in 1986 to reform and rationalise the vocational qualifications system in England, Wales and Northern Ireland. The Council aims to make qualifications more relevant to the needs of employment by basing them on standards of competence set by industry. It is establishing a new framework of National Vocational Qualifications (NVQs) based on defined levels of achievement to which qualifications in all sectors can be assigned or accredited. By January 1990 nearly 200 qualifications drawn from 40 different employment sectors had been accredited. The aim is to have the framework for levels 1 to 4 (from the most basic level to the management supervisory level) fully operational by the end of 1992, and eventually it is expected to extend the framework to cover all occupational levels up to and including the professions.

The competence-based system is being extended in Scotland (which already has its own modular system) through a new system of Scottish Vocational Qualifications (SVQs) along the lines of NVQs. SVQs will be accredited by the Scottish Vocational Education Council (see below).

Other Examining Bodies

The Business & Technician Education Council (BTEC) plans and administers a unified national system of courses at all levels for students in industry, commerce and public administration in England, Wales and Northern Ireland. Courses leading to BTEC awards are available at polytechnics, colleges of further and higher education, and in some schools. The Scottish Vocational Education Council (SCOTVEC) is the principal examining and awarding body in the field of further education in Scotland. SCOTVEC is responsible for administering and developing the non-advanced SCOTVEC National Certificate and the advanced level Higher National Certificate and Higher National Diploma.

Qualifications in a wide range of occupational areas are offered by the City and Guilds of London Institute, and a variety of qualifications in commercial and office practice are awarded by the Royal Society of Arts.

Teacher Training
Courses and Qualifications

Almost all entrants to teaching in maintained and special schools in England and Wales complete a recognised course of initial teacher training. Such courses are offered by university departments of education as well as by many polytechnics and colleges. Non-graduates usually qualify by taking a four-year Bachelor of Education (BEd) honours degree. There are also specially designed two-year BEd courses—mostly in subjects where there is a shortage of teachers at the secondary level—for suitably qualified people. Graduates normally take a one-year Postgraduate Certificate of Education (PGCE), and two-year PGCE courses are available in the secondary shortage subjects for those whose first degree in an associated subject included at least one year's study of the subject they intend to teach.

Articled teacher courses, offering school-based teacher training for graduates, were introduced in September 1990. Trainees, who receive a bursary, take on a progressively greater teaching load, and formal training is provided both in initial teacher-training institutions and in school by college tutors and school teachers. In 1989 the Government introduced a licensed teacher scheme in England and Wales to assist entry into the profession for people who may not have formal teacher-training qualifications but who have relevant qualifications and experience. Participants generally have to complete a period of two years as a licensed teacher before achieving qualified teacher status. Support is also offered for local initiatives to encourage mature people to return to teaching. In addition, the Government has made it easier for teachers trained abroad to take up posts in English and Welsh schools.

In Scotland all teachers in education authority schools must be registered with the General Teaching Council for Scotland. It is government policy that all entrants to the teaching profession in Scotland should be graduates. New primary teachers qualify either through a four-year BEd course or a one-year postgraduate course of teacher training at a college of education. Teachers of academic subjects at secondary schools must hold a degree containing two passes in the subject which they wish to teach. In certain subjects, a relevant specialist diploma has been acceptable in place of a degree, but this provision is being phased out. Secondary teachers must undertake a one-year postgraduate training course. For music and technology, four-year BEd courses are also available, and for physical education all teachers take BEd courses.

In Northern Ireland teacher training is provided by the two universities and the two colleges of education. The principal courses are BEd Honours (four years), BA Honours (Education) and the one-year postgraduate Certificate of Education.

Measures to Improve Standards

The Government has taken steps to improve the quality of teaching by revising selection, training and placement procedures for new teachers, and by making available more in-service training opportunities. Management training courses for head teachers are also being provided. The Government believes that more systematic planning is required by schools and local education authorities to match in-service training to both the career needs of teachers and to the curricular needs of schools. A major new in-service training programme to improve the quality of teaching in schools and institutions of further education was introduced under the Education (No 2) Act 1986 (see p 178).

Measures to strengthen initial teacher training in England, Wales and

Northern Ireland have included the issuing of criteria which courses must meet and the establishment of the Council for the Accreditation of Teacher Education to review courses against the criteria. The Government intends to establish a national framework allowing teachers' employers in England and Wales to appraise the performance of teachers. Local education authorities, voluntary-aided schools and grant-maintained schools will be able to decide whether and how quickly to introduce appraisal.

In Scotland all courses have been revised following recommendations of working parties on teacher training. All new pre-service and major in-service courses provided by colleges of education must be approved by the Scottish Education Department and a validating body. Local education authorities are to be asked to implement national guidelines for the introduction of systematic schemes of staff development and appraisal for teachers. The Government has taken reserve powers requiring authorities to operate schemes prescribed by it in the event of a breakdown of voluntary agreements.

Adult and Continuing Education

The scope of adult and continuing education has widened in recent years. In addition to the development of the individual through cultural, physical and craft pursuits, it now covers basic education (for example, in literacy and numeracy); education for disadvantaged groups and those with special needs, such as ethnic minorities or disabled people; consumer education; health education; and pre-retirement education. Continuing education also includes training for those in employment to enable them to keep pace with technological change.

The Government has taken a number of initiatives to improve opportunities for both adult and continuing education. In 1982 it launched the Professional, Industrial and Commercial Updating Programme (PICKUP), designed to help colleges, polytechnics and universities to meet the need to up-date and broaden the skills of those in mid-career in industry, commerce and the professions. By 1992 the Government aims to have one in ten of Britain's workforce attending job skills updating courses every year under PICKUP.

The availability of open learning opportunities has been extended with the formation in 1987 of the Open College, an independent company set up with government support. The College brings together broadcasters, educationists and sponsors, and provides vocational education and training courses below degree level. Over 150,000 people have taken courses since 1987 and the College has delivered training for about 1,000 firms. Up to £12 million is being allocated by the Government for the College's commercial activities as well as £6 million for broadcasting. The Open College of the Arts, also launched in 1987, offers an art foundation course to those wishing to study at home.

Apart from provision for mature students at universities, courses are offered by the Open University, further education colleges, adult education centres, residential colleges, extra-mural departments of universities and other bodies such as voluntary organisations. Most of the provision is made by the local education authorities in a wide variety of establishments, including schools used for adult evening classes and 'community schools', which offer educational, social and cultural opportunities for the wider community. A majority of courses are part time. Local authorities also maintain or aid many of the short-term residential colleges or centres which run courses lasting between a weekend and a fortnight. Long-term residential colleges, grant-aided by central government departments, have courses of one or two years and aim to provide a liberal education for adults with few or no formal academic qualifications. Most students admitted are entitled to full maintenance grants.

University extra-mural departments and the Workers' Educational Association, the largest recognised voluntary educational body in Britain, offer extended part-time courses of liberal studies. They also run short courses for special (including vocational) interests. Various kinds of education and training are provided by many other organisations, for example, the National Federation of Women's Institutes, the Young Men's Christian Association and the Pre-Retirement Association.

The National Institute of Adult Continuing Education is a centre of information, research, development work and publication for adult and continuing education. It also acts as a channel of co-operation and consultation for the many interested organisations in England and Wales. The Institute administers with government funding the Unit for the Development of Adult Continuing Education, which undertakes research and development work. The Institute's counterpart in Scotland is the Scottish Institute of Adult and Continuing Education.

The Adult Literacy and Basic Skills Unit (ALBSU) is the central focus for adult literacy, numeracy and communications skills in England and Wales. A three-year literacy and numeracy initiative was launched in 1989 as a joint venture between the Government and the BBC. It involves the use of television and radio and specially printed material to improve the communications skills of an estimated 6 million adults. New nationally recognised qualifications in communication and numeracy are being developed, and a referral service is being created to put people in contact with 60 new open-learning centres and other local learning facilities.

In Scotland the Scottish Community Education Council advises the Government and promotes all community education matters, including adult literacy and basic education, and the youth service.

In Northern Ireland the Council for Continuing Education advises the Department of Education on adult and continuing education matters. The role of the Council is under review.

Teaching Methods

The general pattern of teaching and learning on full-time courses of higher education remains a mixture of lectures; prescribed or suggested reading; seminars and tutorials; essays, exercises and tests; and, where appropriate, practical work or work experience. Educational aids are widely used.

Radio and television programmes, both specifically educational and general, are important media for continuing education and are often linked to supplementary publications, courses and activities. The BBC, the independent television companies and Channel 4 present programmes which range from basic education and progressive vocational training to domestic, social and craft skills. The BBC also works with the Open University (see p 195), producing and broadcasting radio and television programmes that form part of the University's courses. Channel 4 has a similar relationship with the Open College.

EDUCATIONAL RESEARCH

Research into the theory and practice of education and the organisation of educational services is supported financially by central and local government, the Economic and Social Research Council, philanthropic organisations, universities and other higher education institutions, teachers' associations and certain independent bodies.

The major research institute outside the universities is the autonomous National Foundation for Educational Research in England and Wales. Its income is derived mainly from funds received from research projects and from corporate members, including local education authorities, teachers' organisations and universities; the Foundation also receives a small government grant. The Scottish Council for Research in Education and the Northern Ireland Council for Educational Research have similar functions.

EDUCATIONAL
LINKS
OVERSEAS

Schoolchildren, students, teachers and others concerned with education come to Britain from overseas to study, and British people work and train overseas. Many opportunities for such movement are the result of international co-operation at government level within the European Community and within the Commonwealth. Educational schemes, courses and professional contacts are organised in Britain by officially funded and voluntary organisations. The British aid programme encourages links between educational institutions in Britain and developing countries.

British membership of the European Community has created closer ties with other member countries. Member states must seek to incorporate a European perspective into their education systems. Both in schools and in the colleges and universities in Britain there has been an expansion of interest in European studies and languages, and exchanges of teachers, schoolchildren and students take place. The European Community's European Action Scheme for Mobility of University Students (ERASMUS), for instance, promotes the exchange of students and academic staff throughout the Community. In 1990–91, 168 further and higher education institutes in Britain are expected to take part in 828 exchange schemes. Britain has adhered to the Statute of the European Schools (nine of which have been established throughout the Community, including one at Culham, Oxfordshire) to provide education for children of people employed in Community institutions. The European Community Action Programme for Education and Training for Technology (COMETT) aims to foster co-operation between higher education establishments and companies throughout the Community. The UK Centre for European Education, with government financing, promotes a European dimension in education.

**Overseas
Students in
Britain**

Students come to Britain from all over the world to study. British universities, polytechnics and other further and higher education establishments have built up their reputation overseas by offering tuition of the highest standards, maintaining low student-to-staff ratios, and providing relevant courses and qualifications.

In the academic year 1988–89 there were about 49,000 overseas students at universities and 23,000 at polytechnics and other public sector establishments of further and higher education. In addition, many thousands of people from abroad were training for nursing, law, banking and accountancy, and service and other industries. Almost half of all overseas students were from the Commonwealth and Britain's dependencies. Many come to Britain for advanced training: one-third of students enrolled for full-time postgraduate study or research in Britain in 1988–89 came from overseas.

A number of British colleges of further education have entered into arrangements with British universities to provide 'bridging' courses for overseas students before they enter university.

Most overseas students pay their own fees and expenses or hold awards from their own governments. Those following courses of higher or further education pay fees which cover the full cost of their courses. Nationals of other member countries of the European Community generally pay the lower level of fees that applies to British students.

*Government
Scholarship
Schemes*

The Government continues, however, to make considerable provision for students and trainees from overseas under its overseas aid programme and other award and scholarship schemes. In 1989–90 more than 24,000 overseas students were supported (including some studying overseas) at a cost of some £127 million. Around three-quarters are from developing countries, most of them from the Commonwealth, studying under the Technical Co-operation and Training Programme, which is financed from the aid programme. Under the Overseas Development Administration Shared Scholarship Scheme, launched in 1986–87, 750 awards are available over five years, mainly at postgraduate level, for students from the developing countries of the Commonwealth, with costs being shared between the Government and the educational institutions.

The Foreign and Commonwealth Office Scholarships and Awards Scheme (FCOSAS), which operates in some 140 countries, is designed to bring to Britain present and future leaders, decision-makers and formers of opinion. A notable feature of the FCOSAS is the increasing number of awards jointly funded by the Foreign and Commonwealth Office in partnership with the private sector and academic institutions. The Department of Trade and Industry also finances a trade-related scholarship scheme in partnership with British industry. Outside the aid programme, the Overseas Research Students Awards Scheme, funded by the Department of Education and Science, provides assistance for overseas research students of high ability to attend British universities.

Other Schemes

Many public and private scholarships and fellowships are available to students from overseas (and to British students who want to study overseas). Among the best known, and open to men and women in all walks of life, are the British Council Scholarships, the Commonwealth Scholarship and Fellowship Plan, the Fulbright Scholarship Scheme, the Marshall Scholarships, the Rhodes Scholarships, the Churchill Scholarships and the Confederation of British Industry Scholarships. Most British universities and colleges offer scholarships for which graduates of any nationality are eligible.

English as a Foreign Language

The continuing increase in interest in English as a foreign language is reflected in the growth of the number of private language schools in Britain. Some 250 of the estimated 1,000 private schools are recognised by the British Council. The Council has expanded its own teaching of English overseas by opening centres and extending existing ones (53 in all by June 1990); it also runs a programme for teaching English related to specific jobs and skills. Other British language schools enable people to learn English in their own countries, while in Britain university language and linguistics departments are an important resource. The Government's aid programme supports the teaching of English in many developing countries by financing major projects in schools, universities and other institutions. Publications and other material relating to English language teaching have increased in number and are now a large component in many publishers' lists, constituting a major export.

BBC English, the English teaching arm of the BBC's World Service, offers a worldwide facility for the individual learner at home.

Educational Exchanges
The British Council

The promotion of cultural and educational relations with other countries is a major concern of the British Council, which plays an important part in the management of the aid programme to education. It recruits teachers for work overseas, organises short overseas visits by British experts, and encourages cultural exchange visits. It also runs schemes to foster academic interchange between universities and higher education institutions in Britain and other countries, and exchange schemes in other scientific, educational and cultural areas. Co-operation between universities in Britain and developing countries is promoted with funding from the Overseas Development Administration. It is brought about through recruiting staff for overseas universities, the secondment of staff from British universities, interdepartmental faculty links, local staff development, short-term teaching and advisory visits, and general consultancy services.

The Central Bureau for Educational Visits and Exchanges

The Central Bureau for Educational Visits and Exchanges acts as the national centre for information on all forms of educational visits and exchanges. It develops and administers exchange and interchange schemes, provides information and advice on opportunities for study and other activities abroad, and awards grants and bursaries.

Among the schemes for professional exchange which the Bureau administers are teacher exchange in Europe and the United States; short courses for teachers; and study visits for teaching staff and administrative staff and education specialists, as well as those in further and higher education. Vocational training programmes include the Language Assistants scheme and the Junior Language Assistants scheme, which provide teaching experience and the chance to put language skills into practice. Opportunities for young people include school and class links and the European Community Young Worker Exchange scheme, which enables 18- to 28-year-olds to gain work or professional experience in another Community country.

The Association of Commonwealth Universities

The Association of Commonwealth Universities promotes contact and co-operation between 343 member universities in 30 Commonwealth countries or regions. It assists student and staff mobility by administering various award schemes including, for Britain, the Commonwealth Scholarship and Fellowship Plan and the Overseas Development Administration Shared Scholarship Scheme, and by providing an academic appointments service. It publishes information about Commonwealth universities, courses and scholarships, and organises meetings in different parts of the world.

Other Organisations

The Commonwealth Education Liaison Committee supplements normal direct dealings on education between Commonwealth countries. The United Kingdom Council for Overseas Student Affairs is an independent body serving overseas students, and those concerned with student affairs.

The Youth Exchange Centre, managed by the British Council, provides advice, information, training and grants to British youth groups involved in international exchanges. The Centre is the national agency for the European Community-sponsored exchange scheme, Youth for Europe.

The Youth Service

The youth service forms part of the education system and is concerned with promoting the personal development and social education of young people by providing opportunities for them to participate in a broad range of leisure time and extra-curricular activities. Young people take part in the youth service on a voluntary basis. Extending the breadth of experiences open to young people and giving them opportunities to participate in the running of their organisations are seen as key elements in the provision.

The youth service is a partnership between central government, local authorities and voluntary youth organisations. At local level the youth service is provided by voluntary organisations and local education authorities. Government education departments formulate broad policy objectives and encourage their implementation through financial assistance and advice. Recognising the need to achieve better planning, management and co-ordination of the youth service in England, in 1988 the Government announced new arrangements for periodic consultations with the youth service. These take the form of national conferences attended by representatives of both the statutory and voluntary sectors of the youth service, at which major issues of common concern are discussed. The first was held in 1989.

In Scotland the youth service forms a part of adult education, which is integrated within community education. The Scottish Community Education Council has the role of promoting community education. The Youth Council for Northern Ireland, with executive and advisory powers, was set up in 1989.

Voluntary Youth Organisations

National voluntary youth organisations undertake the major share of youth activities through local groups which raise most of their day-to-day expenses by their own efforts. Many receive financial and other help from local education authorities, which also make available facilities in many areas. The voluntary organisations vary greatly in character and include the uniformed and church organisations. Many local authorities and voluntary youth organisations have responded to new needs in society by making provision, for example, for the young unemployed, young people from the ethnic minorities, young people in inner cities or rural areas and those in trouble or especially vulnerable. Young Enterprise is a national organisation which gives people aged 15 to 19 the chance to gain practical business experience by helping them form and run their own companies. Other areas of concern are homelessness and provision for handicapped young people.

Among the largest voluntary youth organisations are the Scout and Girl Guides Associations (with about 560,000 and 710,000 members), and the Young Men's Christian Association (1 million), all of which have worldwide affiliations, Youth Clubs UK (about 685,000), the National Association of Boys' Clubs (170,000), and clubs run by the churches. Organisations like the Outward Bound Trust provide opportunities for adventurous outdoor pursuits. The three pre-service organisations (the Sea Cadet Corps, Army Cadet Force and Air Training Corps), with a membership of some 75,000, undertake activities related to the work of the armed forces.

Many authorities have youth committees on which official and voluntary bodies are represented, and employ youth officers to co-ordinate youth work and to arrange in-service training. There are also youth councils, which are representative bodies of young people from local youth organisations.

Youth Service Bodies

At national level many voluntary organisations belong to the National Council for Voluntary Youth Services, a representative and consultative body which aims to develop the partnership between voluntary and statutory bodies in England. Similar councils exist in Wales, Scotland and Northern Ireland. The British Youth Council is a national forum for young people, youth organisations and youth councils, including the youth wings of the major political parties, and represents young people at an international level. The youth service in England and Wales can draw on information, advice, training and research services provided by the National Youth Bureau, which is funded primarily by central government.

From April 1991 government funding of the five national youth service bodies in England and Wales—the National Youth Bureau, the Council for Education and Training in Youth and Community Work, the National Council for Voluntary Youth Services, the National Association of Young People's Counselling and Advisory Services, and the British Youth Council—will be channelled through a single national youth agency. This will be responsible for working with both voluntary and local authority sectors to improve the quality, range and effectiveness of their work.

Youth Workers In England and Wales a basic two-year training course at certain universities and higher education colleges leads to the status of qualified youth and community worker; several undergraduate part-time and postgraduate courses are also available. In Scotland one-, two- and three-year courses are provided at colleges of education and in Northern Ireland courses are run by the University of Ulster.

Full-time youth workers are supported by some 500,000 part-time workers, both qualified and unqualified, many of them unpaid. Short courses and conferences are held on youth and community work. There are also in-service courses for serving youth workers and officers. Initial and in-service courses are validated by the Council for Education and Training in Youth and Community Work. Youth counselling is supported by the National Association of Young People's Counselling and Advisory Services.

Other Organisations Concerned with Young People A substantial sum of money is awarded by the many grant-giving foundations and trusts each year for activities involving young people. The Royal Jubilee Trusts were formed in 1978 from King George's Jubilee Trust (set up in 1935) and The Queen's Silver Jubilee Trust (set up in 1978). King George's Jubilee Trust, which has distributed nearly £7 million since 1935, supports work involving young people aged 8 to 25. The Queen's Silver Jubilee Trust, which has awarded over £11 million since 1978, supports young people up to the age of 25 involved in voluntary community service work. In addition, The Prince's Trust, which was set up in 1976 to help disadvantaged young people aged 14 to 25, has paid some £3 million to individuals and small ad hoc groups.

The Duke of Edinburgh's Award Scheme operates through local authorities, schools, youth organisations and industrial firms. It enables young people from Britain and other Commonwealth countries to take part, with voluntary help from adults, in a variety of challenging activities in four areas: community service, expeditions, the development of personal interests and social and practical skills, and physical recreation.

Voluntary Service by Young People Thousands of young people voluntarily undertake community service designed to help those in need, including elderly and disabled people, and many others work on environmental projects. Organisations providing opportunities for community service, such as Community Service Volunteers, International Voluntary Service and the British Trust for Conservation Volunteers, receive grants from the Government. Many schools also organise community service work as part of the curriculum, and voluntary work in the community is sponsored by a number of churches.

A new national scheme, 'Young Volunteers in the Community', was launched in April 1990. Operated jointly by The Prince's Trust and the Commission on Citizenship, the scheme is recruiting young people aged 16 to 24 to work on a variety of community projects for 12 to 18 weeks.

8 Planning, Urban Regeneration and Housing

Britain seeks to reconcile the conflicting demands for land from industry, commerce, housing, transport, agriculture and recreation, and to protect and enhance the environment by means of a comprehensive statutory system of land-use planning and development control. Most development requires 'planning permission', and applications are dealt with in the light of development plans (which set out land use strategies for each area on such matters as housing and industry) and of any other material considerations. However, many minor developments do not need a specific planning application. The Government's wish is to remove unnecessary planning controls as part of its policy to promote private enterprise. A comprehensive programme to revitalise the inner cities and other urban areas (such as peripheral housing estates) includes a number of initiatives designed to encourage enterprise, employment and educational opportunities, and to improve the quality of housing.

Planning

The system of land-use planning in Great Britain involves a centralised structure under the Secretaries of State for the Environment, Wales and Scotland; and compulsory planning duties for local authorities. The Department of the Environment brings together the major responsibilities in England for land-use planning, housing and construction, countryside policy and environmental protection. The Welsh Office and the Scottish Development Department have broadly equivalent responsibilities. The Department of the Environment provides national and regional guidance on planning matters, while strategic planning at the county level is the responsibility of the county councils. District councils are responsible for local plans and development control. In the metropolitan areas and London, the borough and district councils are preparing new unitary development plans for each administrative area. In Scotland planning functions are undertaken by regional and district councils, whose responsibilities are divided on a basis broadly similar to that in England and Wales. In the more rural regions and the islands, all planning responsibilities are carried out by the regional and islands councils respectively. In Northern Ireland the Department of the Environment for Northern Ireland is responsible for planning matters through six divisional planning offices, which work closely with the district councils.

The Government's aim is for the maximum use to be made of urban land for new development, having regard to the need to retain valuable amenity space within the urban environment and the need to ensure that the cumulative effects of development do not harm the character of established residential areas.

Development Plans

The present development plan system in England and Wales involves 'structure', 'local' and unitary development plans. Structure plans are prepared by county planning authorities and require ministerial approval. They set out broad policies for the development and other use of land. Local plans provide detailed guidance for development expected to start within about ten years; they are normally prepared by district planning authorities, although sometimes by county planning authorities, and must conform generally to the approved structure plan. Local plans are adopted by the planning authorities without being subject to ministerial approval, unless the Secretary of State intervenes. Unitary development plans will set out the strategic and detailed development control policies for each metropolitan district or borough. All plans are kept under review and may be altered from time to time. Planning authorities must take account of any strategic or regional guidance issued by the Secretary of State when formulating the plans.

In Scotland structure plans are prepared by regional or islands authorities and local plans by those districts with planning responsibilities, and by general planning and islands authorities. Regional and islands authorities may also produce a regional report outlining their priorities and policies. Under Northern Ireland's single-tier system, plans are prepared by the Department of the Environment for Northern Ireland.

In a White Paper published in 1989, the Government announced its intention to reform the planning system in the non-metropolitan areas of England and Wales by introducing mandatory district-wide local plans and streamlining procedures for adoption. The strategic role of the counties would continue under the new system but their planning policies would not be subject to the formal approval of the Secretary of State. They would be required to ensure that their statements were consistent with any regional guidance issued by the Secretary of State. The Government is considering arrangements for legislation. Pending legislation, it is encouraging county councils to review their structure plans, and also to form regional planning conferences to identify the strategic planning issues and prepare advice.

Public Participation

Members of the public and interested organisations are given an opportunity to express their views on the planning of their areas during the formative stages of the structure and local plans. Local planning authorities must ensure publicity for proposed inclusions in the plans; representations may be made about them to the authorities. There are also provisions for objecting to prepared plans. In the case of structure plans the Secretary of State normally holds an examination in public of matters on which he or she requires more information in order to reach a decision. In the case of local plans objectors have a right to be heard at a public local inquiry held by the planning authorities. There are similar provisions for participation in the preparation of unitary development plans.

Where specific proposals for development differ greatly from the intentions of a development plan, they must be publicised locally. Other schemes affecting a large number of people are usually advertised by the local planning authority, and applications seeking permission for certain types of development—for example, those affecting conservation areas—must also be advertised. In Scotland there is a system which requires the applicant to notify the proprietors of land and buildings adjoining the site of a proposed development at the same time as the application is submitted to the local planning authority. The applicant has a right of appeal to the Secretary of State if planning permission is refused or is granted subject to conditions.

Similar provision is made in Northern Ireland for public participation in the planning process and for the hearing of representations at public inquiries. For planning applications which do not give rise to public inquiries the applicant has a right of appeal to the independent Planning Appeals Commission.

Major Schemes   The Secretaries of State can direct that a planning application be referred to them for decision. This power is usually exercised only in respect of proposals of national or regional importance which give rise to substantial controversy—for example, proposals for a major new power station. The applicant and the local planning authority have the right to be heard by a person appointed by the Secretary of State and a public inquiry is normally held for this purpose. In the case of development schemes of exceptional importance the departments concerned have set up procedures to help the parties to resolve procedural matters beforehand and to streamline the inquiry procedures. Where highway development is proposed, the government minister concerned can hold such inquiries as he or she considers appropriate; these generally relate to the compulsory acquisition of land. In Northern Ireland, major planning applications are dealt with under the Planning (NI) Order 1972, which allows for a public inquiry in certain circumstances.

Regulations for implementing the European Community directive on Environmental Assessment came into force in 1988 (1989 in Northern Ireland). The regulations require that development consent shall not be given for projects which are likely to have significant effects upon the environment without first taking into consideration the environmental statement for the project plus representations from those consulted, including authorities with environmental responsibilities and the public. The developer must provide the environmental statement, which should describe the project and its likely significant effects and, where significant adverse effects are identified, propose measures to avoid, reduce or remedy those effects.

New Towns   The 32 new towns designated since 1946—21 in England, two in Wales, five in Scotland and four in Northern Ireland—have now largely achieved their aims of dispersal of industry and population from congested cities and the stimulation of regional economies. They have a total population of over 2 million; several have become regional centres for shopping and office accommodation. The new town development corporations' priorities now are to maximise private investment in housing and employment, and to achieve balanced communities able to generate their own growth.

With the completion of the new towns programme, the development corporations which administered the new towns are being dissolved. The remaining two corporations in England will be wound up by 1992 and dissolution of the five Scottish development corporations will begin in 1991. In Wales responsibility for Newtown rests with the Development Board for Rural Wales, while the corporation responsible for Cwmbran was dissolved in 1988.

Architectural Standards   High standards in new building are encouraged by the Government. The Department of the Environment, in collaboration with the independent Royal Institute of British Architects (RIBA) and the National House-Building Council, sponsors the biennial Housing Design Awards Scheme for

England and Northern Ireland, with categories for renovation as well as new building. Scotland and Wales have similar award schemes. The Government also encourages the use of architectural competitions, and has set an example in the award of some of its own contracts. Royal Fine Art Commissions for England and Wales and for Scotland advise government departments, planning authorities and other public bodies on questions of public amenity or artistic importance.

The RIBA, the principal professional body for architects, exercises control over standards in architectural education and encourages high architectural standards in the profession. The Royal Incorporation of Architects in Scotland is allied to it, as is the Royal Society of Ulster Architects.

The Government advises local planning authorities not to impose their architectural tastes on developers. The Government's view is that only exceptionally should local planning authorities control design details, if the sensitive character of the area or the particular building justifies it, and that the pursuit of the highest architectural standards should not be deflected by debate about style.

Urban Regeneration

Revitalising the run-down inner areas of towns and cities is a government priority. Much has been achieved already, but problems remain, including a lack of private investment in local economies, high unemployment, physical dereliction and decay. Inner city populations often have a high proportion of the disadvantaged and the elderly.

The 'Action for Cities' initiative, a comprehensive package of measures for urban revival, was launched in 1988. The economic recovery of inner city areas is being encouraged by the promotion of enterprise and new business. Job prospects are being improved, the environment is being enhanced and inner city areas are being made safer and more attractive places in which to live and work. The initiative involves government departments in a co-ordinated effort, the main contributing programmes being those of the Department of the Environment, the Department of Trade and Industry and the Department of Employment. However, other departments are also making important contributions, and a major aspect is effective co-operation between central and local government, private business and voluntary organisations. The Government is planning to spend more than £4,000 million in the inner cities in 1990–91 (some 20 per cent more than in 1989–90), spread across a range of programmes.

Urban problems in Scotland and Northern Ireland are being tackled by Partnerships in Scotland and Action Teams in Northern Ireland, as well as by many other government programmes (see pp 209–12).

Urban Programme

The Urban Programme was the first major public spending programme directed solely at the inner cities. It is a special allocation to selected local authorities in addition to their normal resources, concentrated on 57 target areas where the problems are greatest and the levels of deprivation most severe, in order to achieve a greater impact with available funds (see map, pp 210-11). The local authorities concerned receive grant at 75 per cent from central government in support of approved projects. The programme provides grant to some 10,000 projects at any one time and is directed at economic, social, environmental and housing problems. Priority is given to capital projects which strengthen and revive the local economy and foster enterprise, though projects which improve the physical and social environment remain important.

In 1989–90 the Urban Programme supported more than 500 new firms and helped to create or preserve 45,000 jobs. It improved over 2,000 buildings and around 1,700 hectares (4,250 acres) of unsightly land. It also supported environmental improvement schemes for over 78,000 council homes and about 60,000 inner city training places. The Government has initially allocated £258 million for spending on the Urban Programme in 1990–91, up £13 million on the previous year.

City Action Teams

Eight 'City Action Teams' have been established to co-ordinate the range of government programmes for tackling inner city problems. These teams bring together the regional officials of the Department of Employment, its Training Agency, the Department of the Environment and the Department of Trade and Industry to ensure that their main programmes are working together effectively. They act as a central contact point with government for businesses and community organisations. They have small special budgets for tackling local inner city problems which relate to unemployment, enterprise generation and environmental improvement.

Task Forces

'Task Forces', first set up in 1986 to intensify and bring together the efforts of government departments, local government, the private sector and the local community to regenerate inner cities, are small, locally based teams working in 16 inner city areas (see map, pp 210-11). Task Forces aim to help local people by increasing their chances of gaining employment and by building up local businesses. They also support schemes which improve the environment or reduce crime where these are linked directly to the creation of jobs. Since their inception they have committed some £49 million to over 1,700 projects. They are not permanent; an important part of their work is to build up local organisations to which they can hand over as they withdraw. Two new Task Forces were announced in February 1990, for Derby and the Wirral.

Urban Development Corporations

Urban Development Corporations have been set up by the Government in order to reverse large-scale urban decline. The first two were established in London Docklands and Merseyside in 1981. By the end of March 1990 the London Docklands Development Corporation had received over £760 million in government grant and secured private investment commitments of about £7,000 million. It has reclaimed over 300 hectares (741 acres) of derelict land for housing, commercial and recreational use. Over 13,000 homes have been completed and 30,000 jobs have been attracted to the area. The Merseyside Development Corporation has reclaimed 340 hectares (840 acres) of derelict land, and 270,000 sq m (2·9 million sq ft) of buildings have been refurbished in its area.

Five new corporations were set up in 1987: Trafford Park (Greater Manchester), Teesside, Tyne and Wear, Black Country (West Midlands) and Cardiff Bay. Four more—in Bristol, Leeds, central Manchester and Sheffield—were set up in 1988–89. Urban Development Corporations cover about 16,000 hectares (about 40,000 acres), and public expenditure on the programme will be £542 million in 1990–91.

City Grant

City Grant was introduced in 1988 to simplify the grants available for encouraging private sector developments in inner cities; it replaced the Urban Development Grant and the Urban Regeneration Grant. It is paid direct to the private sector for projects which contribute to the regeneration of an urban area. By the end of April 1990, 127 schemes had been approved, with £104 million of public money bringing in £505 million of private

Urban Policy Initiatives

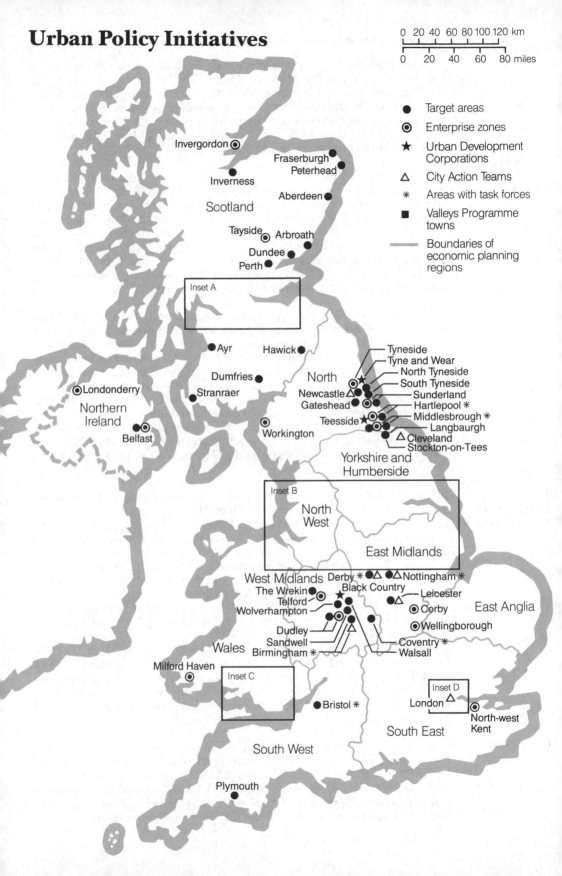

0 20 40 60 80 100 120 km	
0 20 40 60 80 miles	

● Target areas

◉ Enterprise zones

★ Urban Development Corporations

△ City Action Teams

∗ Areas with task forces

■ Valleys Programme towns

── Boundaries of economic planning regions

Invergordon

Fraserburgh
Peterhead

Inverness

Aberdeen

Scotland

Tayside Arbroath

Dundee

Perth

Inset A

Ayr Hawick

Dumfries

North

Londonderry

Stranraer

Northern Ireland

Workington

Belfast

Tyneside
Tyne and Wear
North Tyneside
South Tyneside
Newcastle Sunderland
Gateshead Hartlepool ∗
Middlesbrough ∗
Teesside Langbaurgh
Cleveland
Stockton-on-Tees

Yorkshire and Humberside

Inset B

North West

East Midlands

West Midlands Derby ∗ △ △ Nottingham ∗
The Wrekin Black Country Leicester
Telford East Anglia
Wolverhampton ◉ Corby
Dudley ◉ Wellingborough
Sandwell Coventry ∗
Birmingham ∗ Walsall
Wales

Milford Haven

Inset C

Bristol ∗

Inset D
London △ ◉
North-west Kent

South East

South West

Plymouth

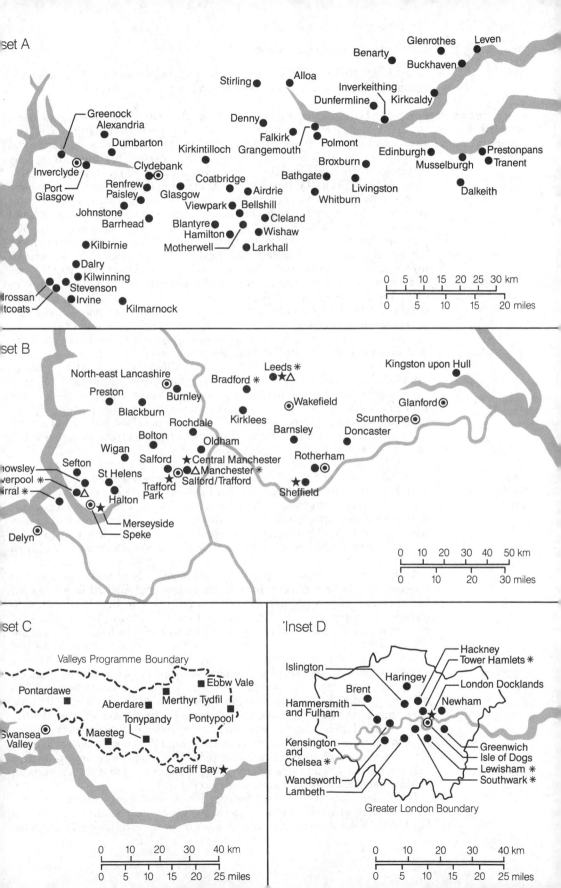

Inset A

Greenock
Alexandria
Dumbarton
Inverclyde
Clydebank
Kirkintilloch
Port Glasgow
Renfrew
Paisley
Glasgow
Coatbridge
Airdrie
Johnstone
Viewpark
Bellshill
Barrhead
Blantyre
Cleland
Hamilton
Wishaw
Motherwell
Larkhall
Kilbirnie
Dalry
Kilwinning
Stevenson
rossan
Irvine
tcoats
Kilmarnock

Stirling
Alloa
Denny
Falkirk
Grangemouth
Polmont
Bathgate
Whitburn
Benarty
Glenrothes
Leven
Buckhaven
Inverkeithing
Dunfermline
Kirkcaldy
Edinburgh
Prestonpans
Broxburn
Musselburgh
Tranent
Livingston
Dalkeith

| 0 | 5 | 10 | 15 | 20 | 25 | 30 km |

| 0 | 5 | 10 | 15 | 20 miles |

Inset B

North-east Lancashire
Preston
Burnley
Blackburn
Bolton
Rochdale
Oldham
Wigan
Salford
St Helens
Sefton
nowsley
Central Manchester
Manchester
Salford/Trafford
Halton
Trafford Park
Merseyside
Speke
verpool
rral
Delyn
Kirklees
Barnsley
Leeds
Bradford
Wakefield
Doncaster
Sheffield
Rotherham
Kingston upon Hull
Glanford
Scunthorpe

| 0 | 10 | 20 | 30 | 40 | 50 km |

| 0 | 10 | 20 | 30 miles |

Inset C

Valleys Programme Boundary

Pontardawe
Aberdare
Ebbw Vale
Merthyr Tydfil
Tonypandy
Pontypool
Maesteg
Swansea Valley
Cardiff Bay

| 0 | 10 | 20 | 30 | 40 km |

| 0 | 5 | 10 | 15 | 20 | 25 miles |

Inset D

Islington
Hackney
Tower Hamlets
Haringey
Brent
London Docklands
Hammersmith and Fulham
Newham
Kensington and Chelsea
Greenwich
Isle of Dogs
Lewisham
Southwark
Wandsworth
Lambeth

Greater London Boundary

| 0 | 10 | 20 | 30 | 40 km |

| 0 | 5 | 10 | 15 | 20 | 25 miles |

investment. Under these schemes, some 15,700 jobs and 3,100 homes were being provided and 188 hectares (470 acres) were being reclaimed.

Enterprise and Simplified Planning Zones

Since 1981 the Government has set up 27 'enterprise zones' (see map, pp 210-11); each zone runs for a period of ten years from designation. The aim of this experimental policy is to see how far industrial and commercial activity can be stimulated by the removal of certain tax burdens and by relaxing or speeding up the application of a number of administrative controls. Benefits in the zones include exemption from the uniform business rate (the local property tax payable by non-domestic property owners); 100 per cent allowances for corporation and income tax purposes for capital expenditure on industrial and commercial buildings; a much simplified planning system in which many forms of development are automatically permitted; and a reduction in government requests for statistical information. A recent study showed that, by December 1987, 97,600 jobs were established in enterprise zones. The Government has decided not to extend the scheme generally, although its view is that in exceptional circumstances the creation of a new zone might be the best way of tackling a particular local problem. The early zones are reaching the end of their life; research has been commissioned to identify the circumstances in which the benefits available in enterprise zones are most effective.

The Housing and Planning Act 1986 provided for the establishment of 'simplified planning zones', intended to stimulate regeneration by removing the uncertainty from the planning system. They use a simplified planning framework already in use in enterprise zones, under which advance planning permission is given for specified types of development within a zone without payment of a fee. A simplified planning zone scheme lasts for ten years.

Land Reclamation and Use

The 1988 Derelict Land Survey found that there was just under 40,500 hectares (100,000 acres) of derelict land in England, 11 per cent less than in 1982. Although much land had been reclaimed, substantial areas had become derelict during this period. Derelict land is often concentrated in places associated with nineteenth-century industrial development, but the continuing restructuring of particular industries has added significantly to this problem in certain areas.

In England government grants are available to local authorities and to other public bodies, to the private sector and to nationalised industries for the reclamation of such land in order to bring it into beneficial use or to improve its appearance. In 1990–91 the funding available for derelict land reclamation in England will be about £72 million, of which some £21 million will be spent on derelict land reclamation in the inner cities. Between 1 April 1979 and 31 March 1989 some 13,000 hectares (over 32,000 acres) of derelict land were reclaimed in England with the aid of some £523 million of grant. The 1990–91 programme should allow an additional 1,265 hectares (some 3,125 acres) to be reclaimed. In September 1989 the Government announced proposals to alter policy objectives so as to identify sites for development and environmental improvement; to encourage more local authorities to set up their own derelict land programmes; to give more financial incentives to voluntary groups to carry out more environmental restoration work; and to promote nature conservation and the creation of wildlife habitats on suitably reclaimed derelict sites.

In Scotland and Wales responsibility for derelict land reclamation rests with the respective development agencies, which may acquire and reclaim land, employ local authorities as their agents (in Scotland) or make grants to local authorities for the purpose (in Wales). In 1988 the pilot Scottish Vacant Land Survey identified 7,400 hectares (18,280 acres) of derelict land and a further 5,060 hectares (12,500 acres) of vacant urban land. Together with surveys in subsequent years, it will provide a basis for programming the treatment of derelict land and help to bring vacant urban land into use. In Northern Ireland grants may be paid to landowners who restore or improve derelict sites.

In Wales land use is also encouraged by the Land Authority for Wales, a statutory body with powers to make land available for development in circumstances where the private sector would find this difficult or impossible.

Registers of Unused and Under-used Land

In England the Government has instituted registers of unused and under-used land held by local authorities, nationalised industries and other public bodies. The Secretary of State for the Environment has powers to direct a public body to dispose of registered land. Directions in respect of 79 sites had been issued by the end of March 1989; a total area of 33,000 hectares (about 82,400 acres) was still listed on the registers. Under the 'public request to order disposal' scheme, the public is encouraged to request such directions. Owners, who have the primary responsibility for managing their own land, were asked in 1989 to draw up their own registers. These have been available to the public since October 1989. Registers are also published for certain areas of Wales.

Education, Training and Employment

The first of a network of 20 City Technology Colleges was opened near Birmingham in 1988; seven are currently in operation. Another seven have been approved by the Secretary of State for Education and Science to open in September 1991. Intended to raise educational standards, the colleges are funded jointly by the Government and industry.

A number of schools/industry 'Compacts' have been introduced in deprived urban areas since August 1988. Groups of employers work with schools to guarantee a job with training for all school-leavers aged 16 to 18 who meet agreed targets for motivation and achievement. By August 1990 there were 38 Compacts operational and another ten in development, with almost 55,000 young people, more than 5,000 employers and over 300 schools involved. Compacts will operate in all inner city target areas by the end of 1990.

Employment and training programmes, such as jobclubs to help the unemployed back into work, Youth Training for young people aged 16 and 17, and Employment Training, aimed particularly at adults unemployed for more than six months, are helping many people in the inner cities. In mid-1990, there were 500 inner city jobclubs, one-third of young people from the inner cities were participating in Youth Training and nearly 50 per cent of unemployed inner city residents had joined Employment Training. A total of 55,000 people were helped by jobclubs in 1988–89. Between March 1988 (when the Action for Cities initiative was launched) and February 1990, unemployment in the inner cities fell by one–third and long-term unemployment by 40 per cent.

Other Measures

Higher than average crime rates, and the fear of crime, are particular problems in the inner cities. Safer Cities projects bring together all sections of the local community to tackle crime-related problems. The starting point for a project is the preparation of a detailed local crime profile, which a Home Office project team can then use to draw up an action plan. Examples of help include improving street lighting and fitting good quality locks to houses on estates with a high burglary rate. A total of 16 Safer Cities projects are under way, supporting 220 local crime prevention initiatives with the help of grants worth £1·6 million. Four more projects will be established.

The Government encourages tourism as a force for the improvement of inner city areas, and several major projects which create a cultural and artistic focus for inner city regeneration have been undertaken: for example, the Tate Gallery of the North at the Albert Dock in Liverpool and the Design Museum in London's Docklands. In 1990 the 'Vision for Cities' initiative was launched to help businesses in the inner cities to focus on the investment opportunities which tourism brings.

There has been major investment in road schemes of benefit to inner city areas. One example, announced in February 1990, is the Bristol Spine Road, which will cost £55 million. This will be funded jointly by the Department of Transport and the Department of the Environment; however, developers who would benefit would also be expected to contribute.

The Government's priorities for inner city housing are to secure a wide range of good quality housing available for rent or purchase, and to improve conditions and opportunities for residents, particularly on local authority estates (see p 220).

Research

The Government commissions research aimed at improving policies for regenerating inner cities and returning derelict land to productive use; 16 new research projects are being launched in 1990–91. The programme has a budget of £725,000. Priority themes for research are to assess the impact of urban policy measures upon the urban economy, environment and community; to increase understanding of changing urban conditions; to distil and disseminate examples of good practice in urban regeneration projects; to find ways of strengthening the capacity and role of the private and voluntary sectors; and to study emerging policy issues.

Wales

Spending on the Urban Programme in Wales is expected to be £37·2 million in 1990–91, with priority being given to the ten most deprived urban areas. Urban Investment Grant was introduced in April 1989 to simplify the grants available to support private sector projects, replacing Urban Development Grant and Urban Regeneration Grant.

The Programme for the Valleys, launched in 1988, is the most extensive programme of economic and urban regeneration undertaken in Wales, and covers an area of some 2,200 sq km (860 sq miles) in the south Wales valleys (see map, p 211). It involves increased levels of factory building, land clearance and Urban Programme support, as well as action to stimulate private enterprise; improve health care and educational services; support private housing improvements; and strengthen tourism, the arts and voluntary organisations.

The Cardiff Bay Development Corporation was set up in 1987 to bring forward redevelopment in an area of south Cardiff which was once the commercial centre of the city. By the end of March 1990 the Corporation had received some £59 million in government grant. Government support for the Corporation in 1990–91 will be almost £32 million; it will receive some £100 million over three years. The Corporation's regeneration strategy includes proposals for the construction of a barrage across Cardiff harbour mouth, which would create a large freshwater lake and 12 km (7 miles) of waterside frontage. It is expected that over 30,000 new jobs will be created and that over £1,200 million of private investment will be attracted.

Scotland

The main principle behind the Government's 1988 White Paper on urban regeneration in Scotland is to encourage residents to take more responsibility for the improvement and the revitalisation of their own communities. The focus of this process is the establishment of four Partnerships in peripheral estates in Dundee, Edinburgh, Glasgow and Paisley. Led by the Scottish Office and involving various public bodies, the private sector and the local community, they aim to improve local housing; to increase employment prospects by providing access to training and education; and to tackle social and environmental problems on the estates. Other similar estates and inner city areas continue to receive substantial government support. The Government and its agencies will spend some £450 million in urban Scotland in 1990–91, including £69 million (compared with £44 million in 1988–89) on the Urban Programme in Scotland. The Scottish Development Agency operates a Local Enterprise Grants for Urban Projects scheme to encourage private sector investment in deprived areas. Much run-down housing has been restored by community-based housing associations and tenant ownership co-operatives. Scottish Homes (see p 219) promotes the continued growth of such bodies alongside home ownership initiatives.

Northern Ireland

In Belfast, a comprehensive development programme aims to revitalise the commercial areas of the inner city. In 1990–91 regeneration programmes have a combined allocation of over £28 million. Eight Action Teams have been established to tackle the problems of particularly deprived areas of the city. The 'Making Belfast Work' initiative, launched in 1988 to stimulate greater economic activity and improve the quality of the environment in the most disadvantaged areas, was extended in 1989 for a further three years, with an additional allocation of £15 million for 1989–90 and £45 million for the subsequent two years.

A £65 million development project for Londonderry was announced in late 1989. This will include a large investment from United States developers; an initiative launched in 1987 to foster investment links between Londonderry and Boston, Massachusetts, was instrumental in obtaining this.

Housing

The pattern of housing tenure has changed considerably in recent years, with a substantial increase in owner-occupation and a decline in the private rented sector. Between the end of 1971 and 1989, the proportion of owner-occupied dwellings in Great Britain rose from about 50 per cent to 65 per cent. The promotion of home ownership and more choice in the rented sector are central to government housing policy. New house construction is undertaken by both public and private sectors, but the majority of dwellings are now built by the private sector for sale to owner-occupiers. Housing associations are becoming the main providers of additional housing in the subsidised rented sector, while local authorities are being encouraged to see their housing role as more of an enabling one, working with housing associations and the private sector to increase the supply of low-cost housing for rent without necessarily providing the housing themselves. In order to stimulate the private rented sector, which has declined to less than 10 per cent of the total stock, the Housing Act 1988 deregulated rents on new private sector lettings.

Administration

The Secretary of State for the Environment in England and the Secretaries of State for Wales, Scotland and Northern Ireland are responsible for formulating housing policy and supervising the housing programme. Although the policies are broadly similar throughout Britain, provisions in

Northern Ireland and Scotland differ somewhat from those in England and Wales.

The construction or structural alteration of housing is subject to building regulations laid down by the Government. Nearly all house construction in the private sector has been regulated by an independent organisation, the National House-Building Council. The Council sets standards and enforces them by inspection and certification, and provides a ten-year guarantee against major structural defects. In 1989 the Housing Standards Co Ltd began operating a similar service.

Home Ownership

The proportion of people owning their own homes has risen from 29 per cent to 66 per cent in the last 40 years, and the number of owner-occupied dwellings in Great Britain amounted to some 15 million at the end of 1989, compared with 4 million in 1950. Most public sector tenants have the right to buy the homes they occupy at discounts which vary according to the length of their occupancy. Local authorities have been asked to encourage low-cost home ownership in a variety of ways, for example, by selling land to builders to construct homes for first-time buyers, or to individuals or groups to build their own homes in partnership with private builders. Changes in mobility have put pressure on rural housing in many areas. In 1989 the Department of the Environment announced that, where local planning authorities in England were satisfied that there was a need for low-cost housing in rural areas, sites which would not normally be released for housing development could exceptionally be released, provided arrangements were made to reserve the housing for local needs. In Scotland, Scottish Homes is developing a rural housing strategy. In Northern Ireland shared ownership has been developed by the Northern Ireland Co-ownership Housing Association.

Mortgage Loans

Most people buy their homes with a mortgage loan, with the property as security. Building societies are the largest source of such loans, although banks and other financial institutions also take a significant share of the mortgage market, while some companies also make loans for house purchase to their own employees.

The amount that lenders are prepared to advance to a would-be house purchaser is generally calculated as a multiple of his or her annual income, typically up to three times earnings, and the term of the loan is commonly 25 years. The two major forms of mortgage are 'repayment' and 'endowment' mortgages. In the former, the borrower repays principal and interest on the sum outstanding. In the latter, he or she pays only interest to the lender but also puts money into an endowment policy, which on maturity provides a lump sum to repay the principal. Owner-occupiers are entitled to tax relief on interest payments arising from their mortgage loans on up to £30,000 on their main home only.

Public Sector Housing

Most of the public housing in Great Britain is provided by 460 local housing authorities. The authorities are: in England and Wales, apart from London, the district councils; in London, the London borough councils and the Common Council of the City of London; and in Scotland, the district and islands councils. Public housing is also provided by the new town authorities, Scottish Homes (which has a stock of some 75,000 houses) and the Development Board for Rural Wales. The Northern Ireland Housing Executive is responsible for the provision and management of public housing in Northern Ireland. Public housing authorities own about 6 million houses and flats; the Northern Ireland Housing Executive owns over

170,000 homes. A number of local authorities have transferred their stock to housing associations, and others are considering doing so.

Local authorities meet the capital costs of new house construction and of modernisation of their existing stock by raising loans on the open market, by borrowing from the Public Works Loan Board (an independent statutory body set up to make loans to local authorities) or from the capital receipts from the sale of local authority houses and housing land. They receive revenue subsidies to meet part of the difference between their costs, including debt charges and maintenance, and the rents charged. The Northern Ireland Housing Executive is similarly financed.

Sheltered housing (usually accommodation with an alarm system and resident warden) is provided for those elderly people who need this degree of support. However, increasing emphasis is being placed on schemes to help elderly people to continue to live in their own homes and on schemes to adapt existing housing to meet the needs of physically handicapped people.

Local authorities have a statutory duty under the Housing Act 1985 to ensure that accommodation is provided for people who are unintentionally homeless and who have dependent children or who are vulnerable on such grounds as age or disability. In November 1989 the conclusions of a review of the homelessness legislation were announced. The legislation itself will remain unchanged but local authorities will be given improved guidance on how best to discharge their statutory duties towards homeless applicants. The Department of the Environment is working on an amended code of guidance which will aim for greater consistency between authorities in implementing the legislation. The worst problems of homelessness are concentrated in London and the South East. In order to make an immediate impact on this problem, an additional £250 million has been made available over two years. The primary aim is to move families out of bed-and-breakfast accommodation by bringing empty local authority dwellings back into use.

The Housing Act 1980 and subsequent legislation have established a charter for public sector tenants in England and Wales, giving them statutory rights which include security of tenure. With a few exceptions, public sector tenants of at least two years' standing are entitled to buy their house or flat at a discount which depends on the length of occupation. Similar provisions are made for Scotland and Northern Ireland under separate legislation. In October 1989 Scottish Homes introduced its trial Rents to Mortgages scheme, under which its tenants and those of the Scottish New Town Development Corporations may buy their own homes with payments more or less equivalent to previous rents. By the end of 1989, 1·6 million council, housing association and new town homes had been sold in Great Britain and 40,000 Housing Executive homes had been sold in Northern Ireland.

Under the Local Government and Housing Act 1989, which came into force in April 1990, councils in England and Wales have had their Housing Revenue Accounts (HRAs) 'ring-fenced'; funds in the HRA must now be kept separate and devoted to housing, while other funds cannot be used for this purpose. This will ensure that the money paid in rents by local authority tenants is used to run and improve the council stock. A new HRA subsidy has replaced the old housing subsidy, the rent rebate subsidy and the support given to housing through the rate support grant. It will total some £3,000 million a year to meet the excess of authorities' notional outgoings over their notional rent income.

The Housing Act 1988 and the Housing (Scotland) Act 1988 (see p 219) enable public sector tenants to change their landlord where they are not satisfied with the service provided by their local authority.

The Government is committed to making it easier for people who live in rented housing to move. Three existing mobility bodies have been merged to form a single organisation, HOMES, to provide a more effective service. The key aim is to provide mobility between the local authority and housing association sectors, coupled with the efficient use of the national housing stock.

Privately Rented Housing

There has been a steady decline in the number of rented dwellings available from private landlords, from over 50 per cent of the housing stock in 1951 to 7 per cent in Great Britain in 1989. Many landlords are individuals owning a small amount of property, but some rented housing is provided by large property companies.

The Government's policy is to increase the availability of privately rented accommodation and it is encouraging a greater variety of agencies to let such accommodation. This is being implemented through the Housing Act 1988 for England and Wales and the Housing (Scotland) Act 1988, which provide for the deregulation of new private sector lettings and, for council tenants, the right to choose a new landlord.

The Housing Acts created two forms of tenancy: the assured tenancy which gives the tenant long-term security in return for a freely negotiated market rent; and the assured shorthold tenancy (short assured tenancy in Scotland), which is for a fixed term, at a rent negotiated between landlord and tenant. Existing lettings were unaffected by this; they continue on the old basis. The Acts strengthen the law concerning harassment of tenants, which is a criminal offence, and provide for improved compensation for tenants driven out by harassment or illegally evicted. Tenants and most other residential occupiers may not be evicted without a court order. In Northern Ireland only certain pre-1956 properties subject to rent restriction come under statutory control. Rent levels are linked to those of the Northern Ireland Housing Executive, and both landlords and tenants may apply to a rent assessment committee for rent determination in cases where the current rent is considered to be inappropriate. Rent increases are permitted only for properties which meet a prescribed standard. The only assured tenancies in Northern Ireland are those on properties made available under a Business Expansion Scheme; lettings under the shorthold concept are available.

Housing Benefit

Government support is being focused on tenants rather than on property, through the housing benefit system. Depending on their personal circumstances, occupiers may qualify for housing benefit to help them pay their rent.

Housing Associations

Housing associations, which are non-profit-making, are now the main providers of additional low-cost housing for rent and for sale to those on low incomes and in the greatest housing need. The housing association sector is expanding rapidly; associations now own and manage over 500,000 homes and 46,700 hostel bed-spaces in England alone. Many associations specialise in providing accommodation to meet the special needs of the elderly, the disabled and the mentally disordered.

People in housing need with insufficient income to obtain a mortgage for outright purchase may be able to participate in a scheme in which a housing association buys the home and sells a share in it to them, allowing them to rent the remainder and to purchase it later if they wish. Housing associations can also purchase older properties to improve for sale. These activities are eligible for government grants.

In Great Britain housing schemes carried out by associations qualify for Housing Association Grant if the association concerned is one of about 2,800 registered with the Housing Corporation (in England), Scottish Homes or Housing for Wales. These three organisations are statutory bodies which supervise and pay grant to housing associations in their respective parts of Great Britain. Broadly similar assistance is available to associations in Northern Ireland. Housing for Wales and Scottish Homes were set up in 1989 to carry out the functions formerly undertaken in Wales and Scotland by the Housing Corporation, which now operates in England only. Scottish Homes incorporated both the Housing Corporation in Scotland and the Scottish Special Housing Association. It has a wide range of general functions and powers, both providing financial assistance to housing associations and directly owning and managing housing.

The Housing Act 1988 and the Housing (Scotland) Act 1988 established a new framework for the financing of housing associations. The grant system was changed to facilitate the maximum use of private sector finance and thereby increase the number of homes that associations can provide for a given level of government grant. The grant rates are still set, however, so that the associations can continue their traditional role of providing housing for people with lower incomes.

The Government plans to increase the resources distributed to housing associations through the Housing Corporation over the next three years, from £938 million in 1989–90 to £1,736 million in 1992–93. The Government also aims to increase the amount of private finance being used by housing associations, allowing more homes to be built with the available public resources than would otherwise be the case. Approved 1990–91 expenditure for Scottish Homes totals £357 million, of which £208 million will go to housing associations.

In England tenants' rights are protected under the Tenants' Guarantee, which is enforced by the statutory bodies and covers matters such as tenancy terms, principles for determining rent levels and the allocation of tenancies. Under the guarantee tenants receive contractual rights in addition to their basic statutory rights, and associations are required to set and maintain rents at levels within the reach of people in lower paid employment. In Scotland, similar non-statutory guidance, in the form of a model tenancy agreement, is being proposed jointly by Scottish Homes and the Scottish Federation of Housing Associations.

Improving Older Houses

In urban areas of Britain slum clearance and redevelopment used to be major features of housing policy, but there has been a trend in recent years towards the retention of existing communities, accompanied by the modernisation and conversion of sub-standard homes. Housing conditions have improved considerably, but problems remain in some areas where there are concentrations of dwellings lacking basic amenities or requiring substantial repairs; and there are still some pockets of unfit housing for which demolition is the best solution. The emphasis now is on area renewal, with an integrated approach to renewal and renovation.

In Scotland some groups of tenants are joining together to form community-based housing associations and tenant ownership co-operatives. Scottish Homes has been given a major role in tackling housing-related urban dereliction, in co-operation with local communities, the private sector, local authorities and other statutory agencies. It intends to use experience learned in urban settings in formulating the improvement element of its rural strategy.

Estate Action Programme

The Government's Estate Action Programme helps local authorities in England and Wales to find new ways of tackling the problems of run-down council estates. Central to the solutions being developed with local authorities are local housing management along the lines advocated by the Priority Estates Project (see below); joint ventures with private developers for refurbishing neglected and formerly difficult-to-let properties; new ways of running council estates such as estate management boards or tenant management co-operatives; and linking local employment and business enterprise initiatives with improving housing conditions on estates. Estate Action provides local authorities with additional resources to pay for the physical improvements which form part of an agreed package of measures. Each scheme is designed to meet the needs of the individual estate. During 1989–90, approval was given to 160 new schemes and continuing support was given to 213 schemes, involving expenditure of £90 million. Resources available for 1990–91 amount to £180 million.

Priority Estates Project

The Priority Estates Project (PEP) promotes locally based housing management, under which control of landlords' services is devolved to a local team with maximum involvement and consultation of residents. There are 11 projects on estates in England and Wales, and many more local authorities are now applying local management to their own estates.

Housing Action Trusts

The Housing Act 1988 provides for the establishment in England and Wales of Housing Action Trusts to focus resources on some of the most run-down areas of predominantly local authority housing. Tenants vote on whether a Housing Action Trust should be set up for their area. If the majority of tenants who vote support the proposal, the trust takes over responsibility for local authority housing in designated areas in order to renovate it, improve the environment, provide community facilities and stimulate local enterprise. When it has completed its work, the trust passes the housing on to other owners and managers, such as housing associations or tenants' co-operatives, or back to the local housing authority. All new landlords must be approved by the Housing Corporation.

Home Improvement Grants

About 1·6 million home improvement grants were paid in respect of privately owned dwellings in Great Britain between 1980 and 1988. Under the Local Government and Housing Act 1989, a single system of renovation grants was introduced in England and Wales in July 1990 to help private owners and some tenants with the costs of essential repair and improvement work. A mandatory grant enables dwellings to be brought up to a new and more effective fitness standard, with discretionary grant available for a wider range of works. Grants of up to 100 per cent may be available, subject to a test of the occupants' resources. Grants are also available in certain circumstances for the provision of facilities for the disabled and for the repair of houses in multiple occupation and of the common parts of blocks of flats. Minor works assistance is also available to help people in receipt of income-related benefits with small-scale jobs. In Scotland, Scottish Homes has the power to provide improvement and repair grants to complement the role of local authorities in private house renewal.

Housing Renewal Areas

'Housing renewal areas' were introduced for England and Wales in the Local Government and Housing Act 1989 with effect from April 1990. Renewal areas are intended to provide a sharper focus to area action, covering both renovation and selective redevelopment and taking account of a wider range of issues than just housing. Authorities are free to declare renewal areas without the specific consent of the Secretaries of State for the Environment and for Wales, provided they fulfil certain criteria. Authorities have additional powers to acquire land in renewal areas and to carry out improvement works for which additional government support is available.

In Scotland housing action area powers are available for the improvement of areas in which at least half the houses fail to meet a statutory tolerable standard. Since 1975, 1,780 housing action areas have been declared. Outside such areas in Scotland local authorities have powers to apply improvement orders to houses below the statutory tolerable standard or lacking certain basic amenities. Government financial aid is also given towards the costs incurred by local authorities in improving the environment of predominantly residential areas.

Northern Ireland has a large number of houses which are either unfit or in serious disrepair. Since 1977, 52 housing action areas have been declared, involving a continuous programme of rehabilitation, 'enveloping' (renovation of the external fabric of whole terraces that have deteriorated beyond routine repair) and associated environmental improvement schemes. In addition, the Northern Ireland Housing Executive undertakes a programme of improvement of its own stock.

9 Environmental Protection

For more than a century Britain has been evolving policies to protect the environment against pollution from industry and other sources. Legislation to control air and water pollution; to conserve wildlife, landscape, historic monuments and buildings; and to plan land use was introduced at an early stage. It has been revised regularly to meet changing circumstances. Recently, with increasing scientific understanding of the global implications of pollution caused by modern development, the Government has been considering how its own policies and actions can be further guided by the principle of 'sustainable development', called for in the report of the World Commission on Environment and Development in 1987.

Britain supports international co-operation on matters of environmental protection. The Government is making considerable investment in environmental research to gain a proper understanding of the science of environmental issues before taking action. Britain is active in the scientific assessment of climate change for the Intergovernmental Panel on Climate Change, which was set up jointly by the United Nations Environment Programme and the World Meteorological Organisation.

Increasingly, much of Britain's law on pollution control is being developed in co-operation with other member states of the European Community and organisations such as the Organisation for Economic Co-operation and Development and the United Nations and its agencies. The laws protecting the environment are being further strengthened by the Environmental Protection Bill, which would provide added safeguards for the natural environment. The Government published a White Paper on the environment in September 1990. The paper, entitled *This Common Inheritance*, points the way towards Britain's future policy on the environment.

The Department of the Environment is responsible for countryside policy and environmental protection in England; the Welsh Office, the Scottish Development Department and the Department of the Environment for Northern Ireland have broadly equivalent responsibilities. There is also a strong conservation movement in Britain. A wide range of voluntary organisations are actively involved in environmental conservation and protection.

Conservation

Historic Buildings, Ancient Monuments and Conservation Areas

Lists of buildings of special architectural or historical interest are compiled by the Secretary of State for the Environment and the Secretaries of State for Scotland and Wales. Some 435,000 buildings are listed in England, some 36,000 in Scotland and 13,000 in Wales. It is against the law to demolish, extend or alter the character of any listed building without special consent from the local planning authority or the appropriate Secretary of State.

Emergency 'building preservation notices' can be served by the local planning authority to protect buildings not yet listed. Ancient monuments are similarly protected through a system of scheduling. There are 13,000 scheduled ancient monuments in England, about 5,000 in Scotland and over 2,600 in Wales.

Maintaining royal parks (which are open to the public) and palaces is the responsibility of the Secretaries of State for the Environment and Scotland. English Heritage (the Historic Buildings and Monuments Commission for England) is charged with protecting and conserving England's architectural and archaeological heritage. It manages some 400 ancient monuments on behalf of the Secretary of State for the Environment and gives grants for the repair of ancient monuments, historic buildings and buildings in conservation areas in England. In Scotland and Wales similar functions are performed by Historic Buildings and Monuments, Scotland, which cares for over 330 monuments; and by Cadw: Welsh Historic Monuments, which manages 125, with advice from an ancient monuments board and a historic buildings council for each country. Local authorities can make grants and loans for any building of architectural or historic interest.

The National Heritage Memorial Fund provides assistance towards the cost of acquiring, maintaining or preserving land, buildings, works of art and other items of outstanding interest which are also of importance to the national heritage. In 1989–90 the Fund assisted in the preservation of 69 heritage items.

Local planning authorities have designated for special protection about 6,300 'conservation areas' of particular architectural or historic interest in England; there are 362 in Wales and some 540 in Scotland. Grants and loans are available from the appropriate historic buildings and monuments body for works which make a significant contribution towards the preservation or improvement of such an area.

The Department of the Environment for Northern Ireland has 165 historic monuments in its care, and some 1,000 monuments are scheduled for protection. It is also responsible for designating conservation areas; there are about 7,500 listed buildings and 26 conservation areas. It may also provide grants and loans to help with the repair and maintenance of listed buildings and to preserve or enhance conservation areas. It is advised by a Historic Buildings Council and a Historic Monuments Council.

The Government also supports the work of the voluntary sector in the protection of Britain's heritage. The Department of the Environment made grants totalling £341,000 to 16 such organisations in 1989–90. Among the voluntary organisations which campaign for the preservation of buildings are the Society for the Protection of Ancient Buildings, the Ancient Monuments Society; the Georgian Group; the Architectural Heritage Society of Scotland; the Ulster Architectural Heritage Society; the Victorian Society; and the Council for British Archaeology. An independent charity, the National Trust (for Places of Historic Interest or Natural Beauty) owns and protects about 300 properties open to the public, in addition to nearly 228,000 hectares (564,000 acres) of land. Scotland has its own National Trust.

The Civic Trust, with associate trusts in Wales and north-east England, makes annual awards for development and restoration work which enhances its surroundings. It undertakes urban regeneration projects and acts as an 'umbrella' organisation for 1,000 local amenity societies. The Scottish Civic Trust fulfils a parallel role in Scotland. The Architectural Heritage Fund provides short-term loan capital to help preservation trusts preserve and rehabilitate old buildings.

Tree Preservation and Planting

Local planning authorities have powers to protect trees and woodlands in the interests of amenity by means of tree preservation orders. It is in general an offence to fell, damage or destroy a protected tree and the courts can impose substantial fines. Where protected trees are felled in contravention of an order or are removed because they are dying, dead or dangerous, a replacement tree is required.

The Government encourages a wide range of amenity and commercial tree planting through a system of grants. In October 1987 an estimated 15 million trees in the south and east of England were destroyed by hurricane-force winds. To help replace amenity trees the Government has allocated over £15 million in the period to 1992–93, most of which is being distributed through Task Force Trees, a special unit of the Countryside Commission. Further losses, estimated at 4 million trees, were caused by storms early in 1990, and a new package of aid for replacement planting was announced in March 1990.

Green Belts

'Green Belts' are areas where it is intended that land should be left open and free from inappropriate building development, and where people can seek recreation. They have been established around some major cities, including London, Merseyside, Greater Manchester and the West Midlands. They are intended to restrict the sprawl of large built-up areas, to prevent neighbouring towns merging, to preserve the special character of historic towns and to assist in urban regeneration. Some 1·5 million hectares (3·8 million acres) are designated as Green Belt in England, equivalent to 12 per cent of the land area. The Government attaches great importance to the protection of Green Belts and expects local planning authorities to do likewise when considering applications for planning permission.

The Coast

Local planning authorities along the coastline are responsible for planning land use at the coast; they also attempt to safeguard and enhance the coast's natural attractions and preserve areas of scientific interest. The protection of the coastline against erosion is administered centrally by the Ministry of Agriculture, Fisheries and Food, the Welsh Office and the Scottish Office. Certain stretches of undeveloped coast of particular scenic beauty in England and Wales are treated as heritage coast; jointly with local authorities, the Countryside Commission has defined 41 coasts, protecting 1,400 km (870 miles).

The National Trust, with its Enterprise Neptune campaign, raises funds for the nation to acquire stretches of coastline of great natural beauty and recreational value. More than £13 million has been raised so far and the Trust now protects 826 km (514 miles) of coastline in England, Wales and Northern Ireland, and is working to acquire a further 630 km (390 miles) considered at risk. The National Trust for Scotland owns large parts of the Scottish coastline and protects others through conservation agreements.

Exceptionally, economic arguments may outweigh other interests. Coastal planning guidelines drawn up by the Scottish Development Department aim to ensure that oil-related activities and other major developments are sited to make the best use of existing labour and infrastructure and to minimise the effect on remote and unspoilt coastlines. Provision has also been made for funds to be set aside for restoration of sites once there is no further need of them.

Countryside Commission and Countryside Commission for Scotland

Countryside Commissions (for England and Wales, and for Scotland) are responsible for conserving and enhancing the natural beauty and amenity of the countryside. They encourage the provision and improvement of facilities for open-air recreation. These arrangements would be altered by the Environmental Protection Bill (see p 230). Activities include the provision by local authorities (sometimes in association with other bodies) and private individuals of country parks and picnic sites often within easy reach of towns, the provision or improvement of recreational paths and the encouragement of amenity tree-planting schemes. The Countryside Commission recognises 235 country parks and 267 picnic sites in England and Wales. In Scotland 35 country parks are recognised and a large number of local authority and private sector schemes for the provision of a variety of countryside facilities have been approved for grant aid. The Commissions undertake research projects and experimental schemes, working in consultation with local authorities and bodies such as the Nature Conservancy Council (see p 227) and the Sports Councils. The Commissions give financial assistance to public, private and voluntary bodies, and individuals carrying out countryside recreation and amenity projects and landscape conservation projects. Total funding for the Commissions in 1990–91 is over £25 million for England and Wales and over £6 million for Scotland.

National Parks, Areas of Outstanding Natural Beauty and National Scenic Areas

The Countryside Commission (for England and Wales) is empowered to designate, for confirmation by the Secretaries of State for the Environment and for Wales, national parks and 'areas of outstanding natural beauty' (AONBs) and to define heritage coasts in conjunction with local authorities. It can also make proposals for the creation of long-distance footpaths and bridleways.

Ten National Parks cover 13,600 sq km (5,250 sq miles) of England and Wales, 9 per cent of total land area. Their first aim is to provide protection for the outstanding countryside they contain; their second aim is to provide opportunities for access and outdoor recreation. The parks are 'national' in the sense that they are of value to the nation as a whole. However, they are not nationally owned and most of the land remains in private hands. Special national park authorities have been set up, funded by central and local government. These act as the development control authority for their areas, negotiate public access and land management agreements, encourage farmers to manage their land in the traditional way, plant trees, set up information centres, look after footpaths and employ rangers. In 1989, a further special authority was set up to look after the Norfolk and Suffolk Broads, even though technically this area does not have national park status.

Some 38 AONBs have been designated, covering around 19,300 sq km (7,450 sq miles) of England and Wales, equivalent to 13 per cent of total land area. They comprise parts of the countryside which lack extensive areas of open country suitable for recreation and hence national park status, but have an important landscape quality. There are no special administrative arrangements for AONBs, but local authorities are encouraged to give them attention in their planning and countryside conservation work.

In Northern Ireland the Council for Nature Conservation and the Countryside advises the Department of the Environment for Northern Ireland on the preservation of amenities and the designation of areas of outstanding natural beauty. Nine such areas have been designated, covering 282,000 hectares (698,000 acres), and seven areas are being managed as country parks and one as a regional park.

In Scotland there are no national parks as such, but there are three regional parks and 40 'national scenic areas', covering more than 1 million hectares (2·5 million acres), or 13 per cent of the country, where certain kinds of development are subject to consultation with the Countryside Commission for Scotland, and in the event of a disagreement, with the Secretary of State for Scotland. More than 98 per cent of the land in Scotland is designated countryside within which the Commission may provide grants for a wide range of countryside projects.

There are 11 forest parks in Great Britain, covering some 244,000 hectares (603,000 acres) and administered by the Forestry Commission. There are nine in Northern Ireland, where they are administered by the Forest Service of the Department of Agriculture.

Many voluntary organisations are concerned to preserve the amenities of the countryside. These include the Councils for the Protection of Rural England and of Rural Wales, the Association for the Protection of Rural Scotland and the Ulster Society for the Preservation of the Countryside.

Public Rights of Way and Open Country

County councils in England and Wales are responsible for keeping public rights of way signposted and free from obstruction. Public paths are maintained by local authorities, which also supervise landowners' duties to repair stiles and gates. In Scotland, planning authorities are responsible for asserting and protecting rights of way. Local authorities in Great Britain can create paths, close paths no longer needed for public use and divert paths to meet the needs of either the public or landowners. In England and Wales there are some 225,000 km (140,000 miles) of rights of way. There are ten approved national trails in England and Wales, covering some 2,800 km (1,740 miles), and three approved long-distance routes in Scotland, covering some 580 km (360 miles).

There is no automatic right of public access to open country, although many landowners allow it more or less freely. Local planning authorities can secure access by means of agreements with landowners. If agreements cannot be reached, authorities may acquire land or make orders for public access. Similar powers cover Scotland and Northern Ireland; in Northern Ireland the primary responsibility lies with district councils.

Common land, much of which is open to the public, totals an estimated 600,000 hectares (1·5 million acres) in England and Wales (there is no common land in Scotland or Northern Ireland). This land is usually privately owned, but people other than the owner may have various rights over it, for example, as pasture land. Commons are protected by law and cannot be built on or enclosed without consent of the Secretaries of State for the Environment or Wales.

Nature Conservation

The official body responsible for nature conservation in Great Britain is the Nature Conservancy Council (NCC). It has the functions of establishing, maintaining and managing nature reserves; advising the Government, providing general information and advice, giving grants and supporting research. Under the Environmental Protection Bill, the NCC would be split into three bodies, one each for England, Wales and Scotland. From 1 April 1991 the Welsh body, to be known as the Countryside Council for Wales, would be formed by merging the functions of the NCC and Countryside Commission in Wales. The Scottish successor body would merge with the Countryside Commission for Scotland from April 1992 to form a new agency, to be known as Scottish Natural Heritage. There would be a joint committee comprising representatives from the three bodies and from Northern Ireland, together with eminent scientists, to advise ministers on matters of national and international importance to nature conservation.

There are 234 national nature reserves covering some 166,000 hectares (410,000 acres). The first statutory marine reserve, the island of Lundy, off the Devon coast, was designated in 1986 on the advice of the NCC, and more are proposed. Some 5,000 sites of special scientific interest (SSSIs) have been notified for their plants, animals or geological or physiographical features.

The Forestry Commission has 344 SSSIs on its land—covering 70,000 hectares (173,000 acres)—on which nature conservation is a primary objective. Local authorities have declared about 150 local nature reserves. County nature conservation trusts and the Royal Society for the Protection of Birds play an important part in protecting wildlife, having established between them some 1,800 reserves. The county trusts are affiliated to a parent organisation, the Royal Society for Nature Conservation. The Royal Society for the Protection of Birds is the largest voluntary wildlife conservation body in Europe.

In Northern Ireland the Council for Nature Conservation and the Countryside advises the Department of the Environment for Northern Ireland on nature conservation matters, including the establishment and management of land and marine nature reserves and the declaration of areas of special scientific interest. Some 45 national nature reserves have been established and 24 areas of special scientific interest declared.

Wildlife in Britain is protected largely by the Wildlife and Countryside Act 1981. This extended the list of protected species, restricted the introduction into the countryside of animals not normally found in the wild, and afforded greater protection for SSSIs and other important habitats. The Act also makes provision for reviews of the list of protected species to be conducted by the NCC every five years and submitted to the Secretary of State for the Environment. The first review, submitted in 1986, led to 69 species of animal and 31 species of plant being added to the list. In Northern Ireland two Orders, which came into force in 1985, have brought legislation into line with the rest of Britain on species and habitat protection.

Britain plays a full part in international action to conserve wildlife. Conservation measures promoted by the Government have included a ban (in conjunction with other European Community countries) on the import of whale products and harp and hooded seal pup skins, and stricter controls for the protection of wild birds. In conjunction with the other countries of the North Sea Conference (see p 232), Britain agreed in March 1990 to take action to protect and conserve dolphins and porpoises. In view of the serious decline in the African elephant population, the Government supported the transfer of the African elephant to Appendix I of the Convention on International Trade in Endangered Species of Wild Fauna and Flora, which resulted in a ban on commercial trade in ivory. The Government, however, exempted Hong Kong from the ban for six months to allow traders properly to dispose of existing legally acquired stocks and to enable ivory carvers to find alternative employment. This exemption expired in July 1990.

Environmental Improvement Schemes   The Government assists local voluntary organisations to promote projects such as creating parks, footpaths and other areas of greenery in cities, conserving the industrial heritage and the natural environment, and recycling waste. The Department of the Environment makes grants through the Urban Programme and the Special Grants Programme to support projects with either direct or indirect environmental gains. Spending from the former on such projects exceeded £3 million in 1989–90; grants from the latter totalled almost £1·1 million. In addition to advising on the Government's programme of Environmentally Sensitive Areas, a voluntary scheme under which farmers are offered payments for agreeing to farm along environmentally beneficial lines, the Countryside Commission, acting on behalf of the Department of the Environment, provides incentives for farmers in the Ministry of Agriculture, Fisheries and Food set-aside scheme, under which farmers are compensated for agreeing to take land out of production. The Scottish Development Department made £208,000 available in 1989–90 to environmental organisations under its Special Grants (Environmental) Programme. The Secretary of State for Scotland has set up the Central Scotland Woodlands Company, which aims to improve the environment in the Scottish central belt through careful tree planting.

The Groundwork Foundation, a partnership of public bodies, the private sector, voluntary organisations and individuals, aims to tackle environmental problems arising from dereliction and vandalism and to increase public awareness of the opportunities to change and improve local environments.

World Heritage Sites

Britain is fully represented in the World Heritage List, which was established under the World Heritage Convention to identify and secure lasting protection for those parts of the world heritage of outstanding universal value. So far 13 sites in Britain have been listed: Canterbury Cathedral, together with St Augustine's Abbey and St Martin's Church; Durham Cathedral and Castle; Studley Royal Gardens and Fountains Abbey, both in North Yorkshire; Ironbridge Gorge, with its iron bridge and museum of industrial archaeology, in Shropshire; the prehistoric stone circles of Stonehenge and Avebury in Wiltshire; Blenheim Palace in Oxfordshire; the City of Bath; Hadrian's Wall; the Tower of London and the Palace of Westminster with Westminster Abbey and St Margaret's in London; the islands of St Kilda in Scotland, with their historical and archaeological records of life in a primitive community; the castles and town walls of King Edward I in Gwynedd in Wales; and the Giant's Causeway and Causeway Coast, formed of columnar basalt, a lava which has cooled into hexagonal pillars, in Northern Ireland.

Control of Pollution

The Control of Pollution Act 1974 is being supplemented by the Environmental Protection Bill. The 1974 Act, which applies to Great Britain, sets out a wide range of powers and duties for local authorities, including control over waste, air pollution and noise. It also contains important provisions on the release of information to the public on environmental conditions. It introduced a new system for the comprehensive planning of waste disposal operations so as to ensure that disposal is carried out to satisfactory standards. Similar legislation applies in Northern Ireland. These provisions are being developed and tightened by the Environmental Protection Bill, which would introduce important new powers for the control of pollution.

Administration

Executive responsibility for pollution control is divided between local authorities and central government agencies. Local authorities are responsible for matters such as collection and disposal of domestic wastes; control of air pollution from domestic and many industrial premises; and noise abatement measures. Under the Water Act 1989 a new body, the National Rivers Authority (NRA), has taken over responsibility for the control of water pollution in England and Wales; in Scotland, the river purification authorities have statutory responsibility for water pollution control. Her Majesty's Inspectorate of Pollution has an important role in the control of air pollution from some industrial processes, and of radioactive and hazardous waste. Under the Environmental Protection Bill, this would be expanded through the mechanism of 'integrated pollution control' (see p 230).

An independent standing Royal Commission on Environmental Pollution advises the Government on national and international matters concerning the pollution of the environment, on the adequacy of research and on the future possibilities of danger to the environment. So far it has produced 13 reports.

Central government makes policy, exercises general budgetary control, promotes legislation and advises pollution control authorities on policy implementation. The Secretary of State for the Environment has general responsibility for co-ordinating the work of the Government on environmental protection and is assisted by a Central Directorate of Environmental Protection within the Department. In Scotland, Wales and Northern Ireland the respective Secretaries of State are responsible for pollution control co-ordination within their countries. They are assisted by the Scottish Development Department, the Environment and Local Government Division of the Welsh Office and the Environmental Protection Division of the Department of the Environment for Northern Ireland respectively.

Pollution Inspectorates

Her Majesty's Inspectorate of Pollution (HMIP) was formed in 1987 by the amalgamation of the former Industrial Air Pollution Inspectorate of the Health and Safety Executive, the Radiochemical Inspectorate and the Hazardous Waste Inspectorate, together with a new Water Pollution Inspectorate, into a single unified inspectorate for England and Wales. Under the Environmental Protection Bill, a system of 'integrated pollution control' (IPC) would be set up under the supervision of HMIP for the control of certain categories of industrial pollution. The most harmful processes would be specified for IPC, requiring consent from the Inspectorate. Less harmful air pollution would be controlled under a system of local authority air pollution control. In granting a consent for discharges under IPC, the Inspectorate would require the use of the best available techniques not entailing excessive cost to prevent or minimise polluting emissions and to ensure that all substances released were made harmless.

Her Majesty's Industrial Pollution Inspectorate is the Scottish equivalent of HMIP, and would administer IPC jointly with the river purification authorities. In Northern Ireland broadly similar controls are exercised by the Environmental Protection Division of the Department of the Environment for Northern Ireland, and the implications of introducing a system of IPC are being considered.

The Land

Under the Control of Pollution Act 1974, waste disposal authorities are responsible for regulating the disposal of controlled wastes. The Act requires them to draw up and revise periodically a waste disposal plan. It also establishes a licensing system for waste disposal sites, treatment plants and storage facilities receiving controlled wastes. It provides for a more intensive control system for certain especially hazardous or difficult wastes. HMIP and the Hazardous Waste Inspectorate for Scotland advise local authorities on how to improve their control of waste management and on how to work towards environmentally acceptable standards for dealing with hazardous wastes.

Under the Environmental Protection Bill, several new measures would strengthen existing curbs on waste disposal. Responsibility for waste would rest with the person who produces it and everyone who handles it through to final disposal or reclamation. Only fit and proper persons would be licensed to run disposal sites, and operators would have to care for their sites after closure until all risks of gas or pollution were eliminated. Local authorities' waste disposal operations would be set up as competitive 'arm's length' companies so as to separate them from the authorities' other job of policing

Architecture

The white walls and grey slate domes of the new Courts of Justice, Truro, in south-west England, blend into the surrounding residential areas. The foyer, with its dramatic horizontal mouldings and angular pillars, makes maximum use of natural lighting.

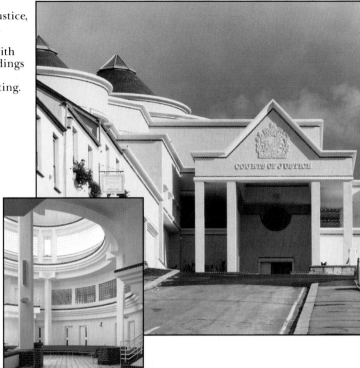

Derelict land at Bute East Dock, Cardiff, was cleared for the site of South Glamorgan County Hall, completed in 1988. Two shallow lagoons with fountains provide a focal point at the dock edge.

Parks and Gardens

The restored Palm House,
Kew Gardens, Surrey.

Rowallane Gardens,
County Down,
Northern Ireland.

Margam, near Port Talbot,
West Glamorgan, Wales.

Edzell Castle, Angus, Scotland.

Protecting the Environment

The Pennine way is a popular
route for walkers, but the
thousands of visitors have caused
severe footpath erosion round
the High Force waterfall,
threatening surrounding vegetation.
Conservation workers are
strengthening the path by laying
a sheet of 'geotextile' fabric
between two layers of crushed rock.

A complex space instrument known
as ISAMS, developed and built by
British Aerospace, Oxford and
Reading Universities and the
Rutherford Appleton Laboratory,
will be launched in 1991.
By scanning the atmosphere it will
be able to provide important data
on climatic change and the
depletion of the ozone layer.

standards. Waste regulation authorities would be made both more locally accountable and more closely supervised by HMIP. In Scotland, the responsibility for collection, disposal and regulation will remain with the district and islands councils, whose waste management function will be examined by the Scottish Hazardous Waste Inspectorate. The Government would also take powers to control international shipments of waste.

It is a criminal offence to leave litter in any public place in the open air or to dump rubbish except in designated places. The maximum penalty for this, currently set at £400, would be increased under the Environmental Protection Bill to £1,000. The Bill would also introduce new powers for the issue of litter abatement orders and new duties on local authorities to keep their public land as free of litter as practicable.

To help counteract the problem of litter, financial support is given to the Tidy Britain Group (£3 million in 1989–90), which provides a comprehensive litter abatement programme in collaboration with local authorities. The Group secures sponsorship from industry to undertake litter abatement promotions and programmes such as its recently announced Neighbourhood Litter Watch scheme; 1990 was designated as Tidy Britain Year.

Recycling and Materials Reclamation

The Government encourages the reclamation and recycling of waste materials wherever this is practicable; its target is for half of all recyclable household waste to be re-used by 2000. Local authorities reclaim about 20,000 tonnes of waste paper and about 30,000 tonnes of metals each year. There are over 4,000 'bottle banks' in Britain, where the public can deposit used glass containers for recycling. There are also similar 'can banks' and 'paper banks' to collect these materials for recycling. Voluntary organisations also arrange collections of waste material. Under the Environmental Protection Bill, local authorities would have a duty to make plans for the recycling of waste.

Water Pollution

There has been a general improvement in water quality in Britain since the 1950s. A comprehensive survey in 1985 classified 90 per cent of river length in England and Wales as of good or fair quality, that is, capable of supporting game or coarse fish populations, suitable for drinking water abstraction and of moderate to high amenity value. Surveys of river quality in Scotland and Northern Ireland in 1985 showed that 99 per cent of Scotland's rivers were unpolluted or of fairly good quality, and that 96 per cent were of good or fair quality in Northern Ireland. These standards compare favourably with those in other European Community countries, where a study has shown that on average only 75 per cent of rivers are of a comparable standard.

Over the past 30 years, progress has been made in cleaning up the major estuaries of the east coast of England and Scotland—the Thames, Humber, Tees, Tyne and Forth—which had become heavily polluted through industrial and sewage discharges. The appearance and amenity value of these estuaries have been improved and they now support varied populations of fish and other wildlife. A 25-year scheme supported by the Government and the European Community aims to reduce river pollution and improve water quality throughout the Mersey river basin and estuary. Other major schemes in progress include programmes to improve water quality in the Clyde in Scotland and the Lagan in Northern Ireland.

Among the main causes of poor river quality are discharges from substandard sewage treatment works and pollution from agriculture. The water and sewerage companies have capital expenditure programmes designed to bring substandard sewage treatment works into compliance with their discharge consents by 1992. A number of measures are being introduced to combat farm pollution of rivers and streams.

There are comprehensive controls over effluent discharges to rivers, estuaries, coastal waters and underground waters. Information about discharge consents granted and effluent and water quality is publicly available on registers maintained by the NRA, by the river purification authorities in Scotland and by the Environmental Protection Division of the Department of the Environment for Northern Ireland. More than 95 per cent of the population in Britain live in properties connected to a sewer, and sewage treatment works serve over four-fifths of the population.

Under the Water Act 1989, the utility functions of water supply, sewerage and sewage treatment in England and Wales were separated from responsibility for protecting the water environment, which was transferred to the NRA. The Environmental Protection Bill would introduce the system of IPC for the most harmful discharges (see p 230).

In Scotland, where the system of public ownership of water supplies continues, the Government is implementing an adapted form of IPC. In Northern Ireland water pollution control is the responsibility of the Environmental Protection Division of the Department of the Environment for Northern Ireland.

The Government is committed to the implementation of a number of European Community directives for the protection and improvement of water quality, for example, on the quality of surface water for abstraction for drinking water, the quality needed to support freshwater fisheries and the quality of water for bathing areas (see p 233).

The Marine Environment

Britain is a leading participant in the series of North Sea Conferences. This international forum of the countries bordering the North Sea provides the prime focus for the development of Britain's policies on the marine environment. The Third North Sea Conference met in March 1990 in The Hague, and the measures agreed will be applied by Britain to all its coastal waters, not just the North Sea.

Prevention of marine pollution from ships is based largely on international conventions drawn up under the auspices of the International Maritime Organisation, a United Nations agency with headquarters in London, and implemented for British ships by domestic legislation. The Merchant Shipping (Prevention of Oil Pollution) Regulations 1983 and 1988 and the Prevention of Oil Pollution Act 1986 require ships to be fitted with specific pollution control equipment. They make it an offence for ships of any nationality to discharge oil, oily mixtures or ships' garbage into British territorial waters. It is also an offence for British-registered ships to make similar discharges anywhere into the sea, except in accordance with the regulations. Enforcement of these regulations is undertaken by the Department of Transport. Powers to control dumping at sea would be further strengthened by the Environmental Protection Bill.

Offshore oil operators must ensure that oil does not escape into the sea and are required to have contingency plans for dealing with oil spilled accidentally. Discharges containing oil are controlled under the Prevention of Oil Pollution Act 1971. It was agreed at the Third North Sea Conference progressively to eliminate discharges of oil-based drilling cuttings from offshore platforms.

The Department of Transport's Marine Pollution Control Unit is responsible for dealing with pollution at sea when oil (or other dangerous substances) from a shipping casualty threatens major coastal pollution or is likely to harm important fisheries or concentrations of sea birds. The Unit maintains a national contingency plan and dispersant spraying, cargo transfer, mechanical recovery and beach-cleaning resources. It also has two remote sensing aircraft capable of detecting possible illegal discharges and of quantifying oil pollution.

The Food and Environment Protection Act 1985 tightened the controls over dumping at sea. Under the Act a licence has to be obtained for the permanent deposit of any substance or article into the sea and tidal waters below the high water mark. Dumping at sea is permitted where no harm to the marine environment can be shown and where there are no practicable alternatives on land. Nevertheless, a timetable for ending the dumping of industrial waste at sea was announced by the Government in March 1990. The Government's intention is that no industrial waste should be dumped at sea beyond 1993. Britain has already stopped the dumping at sea of more than half the industrial wastes which were licensed in 1987. No more waste will be licensed for incineration at sea after the end of 1990.

Progress in reducing the amount of other toxic substances released into the sea was reported in the Action Plan submitted to the North Sea Conference. The Government's target is a reduction of the order of 50 per cent by 1995, and of 70 per cent in the most dangerous substances such as cadmium, mercury, dioxins and lead. Substantial reductions have already been achieved. For example, the discharge of mercury into Britain's coastal waters fell by 26 per cent between 1985 and 1988, and the discharge of cadmium fell by 18 per cent.

The Government has announced investment of around £1,500 million to provide increased sewage treatment, while a £1,400-million programme is intended to improve the quality of Britain's bathing waters. The Government has announced that marine dumping of sewage sludge will be terminated completely by the end of 1998.

In the 1989 tests of bathing water quality, it was found that 76 per cent of identified bathing waters (304 out of 401) in England and Wales met the mandatory coliform bacteria standards of the European Community Bathing Water directive. This compared with 66 per cent of the then identified beaches in 1988 and 55 per cent in 1987. In Scotland, 16 of the 23 bathing waters—70 per cent—met the coliform standard in 1989, compared with 52 per cent in 1988. In Northern Ireland all 16 of the identified bathing waters met the directive. The Government expects over 95 per cent of bathing waters to meet the directive's standards by the mid-1990s and to achieve full compliance within ten years.

Air Pollution   Responsibility for clean air rests primarily with local authorities. Under the Clean Air Acts 1956 and 1968 they may declare 'smoke control areas' within which the emission of smoke from chimneys is an offence. About two-thirds of the premises in conurbations are covered by smoke control orders — over 6,000 are in force. Emissions from most industrial premises are also subject to the control of local authorities under the Clean Air Acts and the Public Health Acts. The emission of dark smoke from any trade or industrial premises or from the chimney of any building is in general prohibited, and new furnaces must be capable as far as is practicable of smokeless operation. Under the Environmental Protection Bill, local authorities would receive streamlined powers to abate statutory nuisances (which include smoke, dust and smells). Atmospheric discharges from the most polluting processes would be subject to the IPC regime. Less harmful discharges would come under the local authority air pollution control regime. Similar legislation and controls to the present ones apply in Northern Ireland.

Considerable progress has been made towards the achievement of cleaner air and a better environment in the last 30 years or so. Total emissions of smoke in the air have fallen by over 85 per cent since 1960. The domestic smoke control programme has been particularly important in achieving this result. London no longer has the dense smoke-laden 'smogs' of the 1950s and in central London winter sunshine has increased by about 50 per cent since 1958. Similar improvement has been achieved in other cities, including Glasgow and Sheffield.

In 1989 the Government announced the establishment of an air pollution monitoring system to make information available on levels of air pollution in urban areas. A daily summary will be published whenever the World Health Organisation guidelines for carbon monoxide, nitrogen dioxide and sulphur dioxide are breached.

Sulphur Dioxide and Nitrogen Oxide Emissions and Acid Rain

National sulphur dioxide emissions have fallen by about 40 per cent since 1970. In 1988 agreement was reached on the European Community directive on the control of emissions from large combustion plants. Britain accepted a phased programme of reductions in sulphur dioxide emissions from existing large combustion plants of 20 per cent of 1980 levels by 1993, 40 per cent by 1998 and 60 per cent by 2003, and agreed to reduce nitrogen oxide emissions by 15 per cent by 1993 and 30 per cent by 1998. The Government is now implementing this directive. Flue gas desulphurisation equipment is being fitted to Drax power station in North Yorkshire. In 1988 Britain signed the Nitrogen Oxide Protocol to the United Nations/Economic Commission for Europe Convention on Long-Range Transboundary Air Pollution, making a commitment to reduce overall nitrogen oxide emissions to their 1987 levels by 1994.

The damaging effect of acid depositions from combustion processes on rivers, lakes and soils has been shown by scientific research. Britain is spending £10 million a year on an extensive research programme into the causes and effects of acid rain, and the likely results of possible abatement technologies. It is also participating in international research programmes and monitoring schemes. A five-year surface water acidification research programme, run under the aegis of the Royal Society and the Norwegian and Swedish academies of science, was concluded in 1990. It yielded valuable information on the links between sulphur emissions and acidification. Following the decreases in emissions of sulphur dioxide over the past 20 years, research has found the first signs of a decrease in acidification in some lochs in south-west Scotland.

Vehicle Emissions

There are around 24 million vehicles on Britain's roads, contributing substantially to Britain's total emissions of carbon dioxide, carbon monoxide, hydrocarbons and oxides of nitrogen. Since 1970 a series of increasingly stringent regulations on petrol, and later diesel, cars and light vans has been implemented by the Government to bring carbon monoxide emissions from each new car down by 50 per cent and hydrocarbon and nitrogen oxide emissions by over 30 per cent. The European Community has agreed strict new standards for these vehicles, which will reduce all emissions from new cars by a further 80 per cent and in effect require new petrol-engined cars to be fitted with fully-controlled catalytic converters. The Community is committed to looking into possible controls on carbon dioxide emissions from cars. Britain is also pressing the Community to introduce by the mid-1990s emission standards for heavy goods vehicles as close as possible to the United States 1994 limits—the strictest being implemented anywhere in the world.

The amount of lead in the air in Britain has halved since the permitted lead content in petrol was reduced in 1986 from 0·4 to 0·15 grammes a litre. Britain had previously taken a leading role in negotiating a European Community directive which required unleaded petrol to be available throughout the Community by October 1989. Over 95 per cent of petrol stations in Britain now stock the new fuel. From 1 October 1990 new cars in Britain will have to be able to run on unleaded petrol. A substantial tax differential has been created in favour of unleaded fuel, and demand for it has risen rapidly. By April 1990 unleaded petrol accounted for over 32 per cent of petrol sales in England.

Chlorofluoro-carbons and the Ozone Layer

The Government is committed to the elimination as soon as practicable of chlorofluorocarbons (CFCs)—synthetic gases widely used in aerosols, in the manufacture of foams, as solvents and in refrigeration—that damage the ozone layer. The British Antarctic Survey first published observations of unusual depletions in the ozone layer in 1985, and in the same year the Department of the Environment and the Meteorological Office set up the Stratospheric Ozone Review Group to review understanding of stratospheric ozone and to recommend areas for further study. Since then much scientific evidence has been gathered which clearly implicates CFCs in ozone depletions. The Government is involved in research into ways of reducing the use of CFCs, for example, in 1989 inviting proposals for research into new technology aimed at reducing CFC emissions and promoting their cost-effective recovery from waste goods such as refrigerators and foam.

Britain is closely involved in international measures to prevent further damage to the ozone layer of the atmosphere by CFCs. In 1987 Britain signed the Montreal Protocol to the Vienna Convention on the Protection of the Ozone Layer, which restricted use and production of CFCs. Britain hosted an international conference on the ozone layer in London in March 1989 (together with the United Nations Environment Programme), and also the second meeting of the parties to the Montreal Protocol, which took place in June 1990. This latter meeting agreed to phase out CFCs by the year 2000, and set intermediate targets of a 50 per cent reduction by 1995 and an 85 per cent reduction by 1997. It was further agreed that an additional meeting should be held in 1992 with the objective of accelerating the reduction schedule. Controls were agreed on other ozone-depleting substances, including halons, carbon tetrachloride and methyl chloroform. The Government also announced in June 1990 that Britain would contribute at least $9 million to help developing countries tackle the threat of ozone depletion; this sum will be increased to $15 million if other countries such as India and the People's Republic of China join the Protocol.

Climate Change

CFCs and other gases, such as carbon dioxide, contribute to the 'greenhouse effect'. A growing concentration of these gases is expected to lead to a gradual increase in global average temperatures, which could lead to a rise in sea levels as a result of thermal expansion of sea water and melting of land ice. Britain led the first working group of the Intergovernmental Panel on Climate Change (IPCC), which carried out an assessment of the available scientific evidence on climate change and published its report in August 1990. Britain is contributing £750,000 to the work of the IPCC.

The Government is giving priority to the improvement of understanding of the science of climate change. The research councils allocated some £29 million in 1989–90 towards research into all aspects of global climate change. In April 1990 the Department of the Environment and the Meteorological

Office opened the Hadley Centre for Climate Prediction and Research, building on the climate modelling programme of the Meteorological Office. It will develop and refine mathematical models of the climate to reduce uncertainties in predictions of global climate change and to provide predictions of timescales and of regional changes. The cost of the combined programme will be about £10 million in 1990–91.

British measures to combat global warming include reductions in CFC emissions (see p 235), building regulations to promote the energy efficiency of new houses and the non-fossil fuel obligation in the Electricity Act 1989, which requires that a large proportion of Britain's electricity be generated in ways that will not promote global warming. The White Paper reaffirmed Britain's willingness to return carbon dioxide emissions to 1990 levels by 2005, provided other countries take similar action.

Noise

The Control of Pollution Act 1974 (and similar legislation in Northern Ireland) requires local authorities to inspect their areas for noise nuisance and gives them the power to serve a noise abatement notice on a person responsible for it. It also enables them to designate 'noise abatement zones' within which registered levels of noise from certain premises may not be increased without their permission. The Act contains specific provisions to control noise from construction and demolition sites and the use of loudspeakers in the streets. It also contains provisions enabling individuals to take action through the courts against noise amounting to a nuisance. The present noise abatement procedures are being used as the model on which the streamlined procedures in the Environmental Protection Bill for the abatement of other statutory nuisances would be based. In 1989 the Government announced a review of noise legislation to be completed in 1990. Government spending on environmental noise research is expected to be about £600,000 in 1990–91.

Transport is a major source of noise pollution, and control measures are aimed at reducing noise at source, through requirements limiting the noise that aircraft and motor vehicles may make, and at protecting people from its effects. The Road Vehicles (Construction and Use) Regulations 1986 set out the permissible noise levels for various classes of new vehicle. More stringent limits are being introduced for new vehicles between October 1988 and April 1991.

Under the Land Compensation Act 1973 and similar legislation in Scotland, compensation is payable for loss in property values caused by physical factors, including noise from new or improved public works such as roads and airports. Regulations under the Acts also enable highway authorities to carry out or make grants for insulation of homes subject to specified levels of increased noise caused by new or improved roads. Noise insulation may also be provided where construction work for new roads may seriously affect nearby homes.

Noise emission levels of almost all aircraft on the United Kingdom Register are regulated in accordance with standards agreed by the International Civil Aviation Organisation. Since 1986 all subsonic jets on the United Kingdom Register have had to comply with these standards, and this requirement was extended to overseas-registered aircraft in 1988. Various operational restrictions have been introduced to reduce noise disturbance further at Heathrow, Gatwick and Stansted, where the Secretary of State for Transport has assumed responsibility for noise abatement. These measures include restrictions on the type and number of aircraft operating at night, the routing of departing aircraft on noise preferential routes, and quiet take-off and landing procedures. The population affected by aircraft noise at

Heathrow fell from nearly 1·5 million in 1978 to less than 340,000 in 1988, even though the number of air transport movements increased by about a quarter.

Radioactivity

Radiation from industrial and other processes represents only a small fraction of that to which the population is exposed; most is naturally occurring. Nevertheless, that fraction is subject to stringent control because of possible effects on health. Under the Radioactive Substances Act 1960 most users of radioactive materials other than those subject to licence under the Nuclear Installations Act 1965 must be registered by the appropriate department, and authorisation is also required for the disposal of radioactive waste. The Health and Safety Executive, through its Nuclear Installations Inspectorate, is the authority responsible for the granting of nuclear site licences for commercial nuclear installations. No installation may be constructed or operated without a licence granted by the Executive.

The National Radiological Protection Board (NRPB), established under the Radiological Protection Act 1970, provides an authoritative point of reference on radiological protection. Following the accident at the Chernobyl nuclear power station in the Soviet Union in 1986, the Government has set up a national radiation monitoring network (RIMNET). Ultimately, more than 80 stations throughout Britain will continuously monitor radiation in order to improve emergency arrangements in the event of a nuclear accident overseas. In 1987 the Government announced measures to deal with the problem of naturally occurring radon gas in houses, including a free survey by the NRPB for householders living in radon-affected areas. In 1990 it accepted the NRPB's advice, made following further scientific research into the danger to health posed by radon, that the level above which action should be taken to reduce exposure to radon in homes should be reduced from 400 becquerels to 200 becquerels per cubic metre.

Radioactive Waste Disposal

Radioactive wastes vary widely in nature and level of activity, and the practices followed reflect this. Some wastes are dispersed safely in the environment. UK Nirex Ltd is responsible for developing and operating a disposal facility for solid wastes with a low or intermediate level of activity and is seeking to identify a suitable location for a deep dual-purpose facility. The Department of the Environment is also sponsoring research, in collaboration with other countries, into disposal of high-level wastes, but these will first be stored in vitrified form for at least 50 years. The Department's 1990–91 budget for research into radioactive substances totals £10 million.

Genetically Modified Organisms

Under the Environmental Protection Bill, there would be stronger controls over genetically-modified organisms (GMOs). Anyone who intends to import, acquire, keep or release GMOs would first have to carry out an environmental risk assessment. The Secretary of State for the Environment would have powers to prevent the import, acquisition, keeping or release of GMOs where this would involve a significant risk of damage to the environment, and inspectors would have the power to destroy or render harmless organisms which were likely to cause damage to the environment. A unified system of administrative control for GMOs would be developed in parallel with these provisions; this would involve the Department of the Environment, the Health and Safety Executive and other interested departments.

Environmental Research

Research into environmental protection is co-ordinated by the Department of the Environment. It has been estimated that total spending on research into global issues approaches £150 million a year, while £16 million is spent on renewable energy research. Government spending on research into marine protection is about £50 million, with a large additional effort by industry. The Department of the Environment expects to spend £37 million in 1990–91 on research into subjects including climate change, toxic chemicals, GMOs, waste disposal, and water quality and health. Other departments have substantial programmes, notably the Ministry of Agriculture, Fisheries and Food, the Department of Energy and other official bodies such as the NRA, the NCC and the Meteorological Office.

Basic and strategic environmental research is sponsored by the Department of Education and Science through the research councils for agriculture and food, medicine, economic and social sciences, science and engineering, and the natural environment. A key participant is the Natural Environment Research Council (NERC), which had a budget of about £120 million for 1989–90. It was established in 1965 to undertake and support research in the environmental sciences and to support specialised postgraduate training. The Council is responsible for the British Geological Survey, the British Antarctic Survey and 12 other research bodies. Its programmes encompass the marine, earth, terrestrial, freshwater, polar and atmospheric sciences. The NERC stresses international collaborative work on global environmental issues such as climate change (see p 235). It is, for example, helping to develop global atmospheric climate models, strengthening atmospheric research in the Arctic and participating in the World Ocean Circulation Experiment, which aims to assess the role of the ocean in modifying the earth's climate. Other work includes the North Sea Project, involving the development of a numerical model of water quality for the North Sea.

10 Religion

Everyone in Britain has the right to religious freedom (in teaching, worship and observance) without interference from the community or the State. Churches and religious societies may own property, run schools, and promote their beliefs in speech and writing. There is no religious bar to the holding of public office, although ministers of the Church of England and the Church of Scotland cannot become Members of Parliament.

Britain has a long tradition of religious tolerance, and the past 30 years have seen the acceptance of a wide variety of religious beliefs and traditions brought in by large numbers of immigrants of different nationalities. There are now large and growing communities of Muslims, Hindus and Sikhs, and arrangements are made at places of work to allow the members of non-Christian religions to follow their religious observances.

Freedom of conscience in religious matters in Britain was achieved gradually from the seventeenth century onwards. The laws discriminating against minority religious groups were gradually administered less harshly and then finally repealed. Heresy ceased to be a legal offence with the passing of the Ecclesiastical Jurisdiction Act 1677, and the Toleration Act 1688 granted freedom of worship to Protestant minority groups. In 1828 the repeal of the Test and Corporation Acts gave nonconformists full political rights, making it possible for them to be appointed to public office. Roman Catholics gained political rights under the Roman Catholic Relief Act 1829, and the Jewish Relief Act 1858 enabled Jews to become Members of Parliament. In addition, the religious tests imposed on prospective students and academic staff of the universities of Oxford, Cambridge and Durham were successively abolished by Acts of 1854, 1856 and 1871. Similar restrictions on the staff of Scottish universities were formally removed in 1932.

There are two established churches in Britain, that is, churches legally recognised as official churches of the State: in England the (Anglican) Church of England, and in Scotland the (Presbyterian) Church of Scotland. Clergy of the established churches work in services run by the State, such as the armed forces, national hospitals and prisons, and are paid a salary for such services by the State. Clergy of other religious groups are also appointed. Voluntary schools provided by religious denominations may be wholly or partly maintained from public funds.

The churches' involvement in broader social issues and the practical help they give to groups of many kinds—from young people to the bereaved and homeless—were highlighted in the Church of England report *Faith in the City: A Call for Action by Church and Nation*, published in 1985. This made recommendations for improving conditions in the inner cities and other socially deprived areas and led to the establishment in 1988 of the Church of England's Church Urban Fund, which aims to raise money for the Church's work in inner city and other priority areas. By May 1990 it had raised more than £15 million and given grants to more than 220 inner city projects. A second report, *Living Faith in the City*, was published in January 1990.

There is no standard information about the number of members of religious groups since questions are not normally asked about religious beliefs in censuses or for other official purposes. Each church adopts its own way of counting its members, and membership figures are therefore approximate.

There has been a fall in recent years in both the number of full-time ministers and the number of adults recorded as members of the larger Christian churches. At the same time there has been significant growth in a range of independent and Pentecostal churches, and in new religious movements. However, the churches today share a desire to work together and the ecumenical movement is well supported.

Religious education in publicly maintained schools is already required by law in England, Wales and Scotland, and under the Education Reform Act 1988 forms part of the basic curriculum for all pupils in England and Wales. The Act requires due recognition to be given to the place of Christianity in teaching at county schools, but the subject also covers other faiths. Schools also have to provide a daily act of collective worship. The Education (Scotland) Act 1980 imposes similar requirements in Scotland. Members of non-Christian religions may have a separate assembly if there are enough of them to justify it. Where schools have pupils of different religious faiths, a multi-faith assembly may be held. Parents may withdraw their children from both religious education and collective worship if they wish.

The Broadcasting Bill, which is before Parliament, would allow Christian and other religious groups to compete for licences to have their own radio stations. They would also be able to seek licences for cable and satellite television channels. The Bill would also require those running television stations on the new Channel 3 service (which is to replace the Independent Television network) to show religious programmes at peak times.

The Church of England

The Church of England, founded by St Augustine in AD 597, became the established church of the land in the Reformation in the sixteenth century. Its form of worship was set out in the Book of Common Prayer, dating from 1549. The Church of England's relationship with the State is one of mutual obligation—privileges accorded to the Church balanced by certain duties it must fulfil. The Sovereign must always be a member of the Church, and promise to uphold it. Church of England archbishops, bishops and deans are appointed by the Sovereign on the advice of the Prime Minister, and all clergy swear their allegiance to the Crown. The Church can regulate its own worship. The two archbishops (of Canterbury and York), the bishops of London, Durham and Winchester, and 21 other bishops (according to their seniority as diocesan bishops) sit in the House of Lords. Clergy of the Church (together with those of the Church of Scotland, the Church of Ireland and the Roman Catholic Church) are not allowed to sit in the House of Commons.

The Church has two provinces: Canterbury, comprising 30 dioceses (including the Diocese of Europe), and York, which has 14 dioceses. The Archbishop of Canterbury is 'Primate of All England', and the Archbishop of York 'Primate of England'. The dioceses are divided into 13,250 parishes. In 1987 it was estimated that, in the two provinces (excluding the Diocese of Europe), some 230,000 people were baptised into the Church; of these 187,000 were under one year old (29 per cent of live births). In the same year there were 65,850 confirmations. Attendances at services on a normal Sunday are around 1·2 million. Many people who rarely, if ever, attend services (amounting to perhaps half the population), still regard themselves as belonging to the Church of England.

The central governing body, the General Synod, has both spiritual authority and legislative and administrative powers; bishops, clergy and lay members are involved in decisions. Lay members are involved in church government in the parishes as churchwardens and through parochial church councils. The Synod is the centre of an administrative system dealing with such matters as missionary work, inter-church relations, social questions, and recruitment and training for the ministry (including theological colleges). It also covers church work in Britain and overseas, the care of church buildings, church schools (which are maintained from public funds), colleges of education, and centres for training women in pastoral work. At present, only men may join the priesthood, but in 1987 the General Synod voted to proceed with legislation to enable women to become priests; final decisions on the matter, however, are not expected to be taken for some years. The Deacons (Ordination of Women) Measure 1986 has made it possible for women to become deacons.

Church finance is administered locally, with contributions to a central fund running central services, including capital spending on theological colleges and grants for training candidates for ordination. The State makes no direct contribution to church expenses. The Church's investment income is mainly managed by the Church Commissioners, the body largely responsible for clergy incomes and pensions.

The Anglican Communion

The Anglican Communion comprises 28 autonomous provinces in Britain and overseas and three regional councils overseas with a local membership of about 70 million. In the British Isles there are four provinces: the Church of England (established), the Church in Wales, the Scottish Episcopal Church in Scotland, and the Church of Ireland.

Every ten years the Lambeth Conference meets for consultation between all Anglican bishops. The last Conference was held in Canterbury in 1988. Presided over by the Archbishop of Canterbury, the Conference has no executive authority, but enjoys great prestige. Its findings on doctrine, discipline, relations with other churches, and attitudes to political and social questions are widely studied. The Anglican Consultative Council (an assembly of laypeople and clergy as well as of bishops) meets every two or three years and is intended to allow consultations within the Anglican Communion and to serve as a means of joint action. The Council met in Wales in 1990.

The Church of Scotland

The Church of Scotland has a presbyterian form of government, that is, government by elders, all (including ministers) of equal rank. It became the national church following the Scottish Reformation and legislation of the Scottish Parliament, consolidated in the Treaty of Union 1707 and the Church of Scotland Act 1921, the latter confirming its complete freedom in all spiritual matters. It appoints its own office bearers and its decisions on questions of doctrine, worship, government and discipline are not subject to any civil authority.

Both men and women may join the ministry and each of 1,360 churches is governed locally by the Kirk Session, consisting of the minister and the elected elders of the Church. Above the Kirk Session is the Court of the Presbytery, then the Court of the Synod, and finally the General Assembly, consisting of elected ministers and elders. This meets annually under the presidency of an elected moderator, who serves for one year. The Sovereign is represented at the General Assembly by the Lord High Commissioner. The adult communicant membership of the Church of Scotland is over 800,000.

The Free Churches

The term 'Free Churches' is often used to describe those Protestant churches in Britain which, unlike the Church of England and the Church of Scotland, are not established as official churches of the State. In the course of history they have developed their own forms of belief, church order and worship. All the major Free Churches—Methodist, Baptist, United Reformed and Salvation Army—allow both men and women to become ministers.

The Methodist Church, the largest of the Free Churches with just over 430,000 adult full members and a community of more than 1·3 million, originated in the eighteenth century following the evangelical revival under John Wesley. The present church is based on a 1932 union of most of the separate Methodist Churches. The Methodist Church in Ireland has over 14,000 members in Northern Ireland.

The Baptists are mainly organised in groups of churches, most of which belong to the Baptist Union of Great Britain (formed in 1812), with a membership of about 165,000. There are also separate Baptist Unions for Scotland, Wales and Ireland, and other Baptist Churches.

The United Reformed Church, with some 124,000 members, was formed in 1972, when the Congregational Church in England and Wales (the oldest Protestant minority in Britain) and the Presbyterian Church of England merged. This was the first union of two different churches in Britain since the Reformation in the sixteenth century.

Among the other Free Churches are the Presbyterian Church in Ireland: the Presbyterian (or Calvinistic Methodist) Church of Wales; and a number of independent Scottish Presbyterian churches.

Other Protestant Churches include the Unitarians, Free Christians, and the Pentecostalists, who are increasing in number. The two main bodies operating in Britain are the Assemblies of God and the Elim Pentecostal Church, many of whose members are of West Indian origin. There is also a growing number of black-led churches.

The Religious Society of Friends (Quakers), with about 18,000 adult members in Britain and 450 places of worship, came into being in the middle of the seventeenth century under the leadership of George Fox. Silent worship is central to its life as a religious organisation.

The Salvation Army, founded in Britain in 1865, has since spread to 90 other countries. Within Britain there are 65,000 members and nearly 1,000 centres of worship. The Salvation Army is well known for its Christian evangelism and practical care. This is expressed through the work of some 130 social service centres, ranging from hostels for the homeless to homes for those in need, and through its prison chaplaincy service.

A recent development in Christian worship has been the house church movement, which began in the early 1970s and now has an estimated membership of 120,000. (Attendance is greater than membership.) Members hold services and prayer meetings in private houses, and take turns to act as chairman. House churches receive money from their members to enable them to support their leaders and carry out missionary and social work.

There are also a number of other religious organisations in Britain which were founded in the United States in the last century. These include the Jehovah's Witnesses, the Church of Jesus Christ of the Latter-Day Saints (the Mormon Church), the Christian Scientists and the Spiritualists.

The Roman Catholic Church

The formal structure of the Roman Catholic Church in England and Wales, which had ceased to exist after the Reformation in the sixteenth century, was restored in 1850. The Scottish Church's formal structure ceased to exist in the early seventeenth century and was restored in 1878. However, throughout this period Catholicism never disappeared entirely. There are now seven Roman Catholic provinces in Great Britain, each under an archbishop; 30 dioceses, each under a bishop (22 in England and Wales, eight in Scotland); and over 3,000 parishes. In Northern Ireland there are six dioceses, some with territory partly in the Irish Republic. About one British citizen in ten normally claims to be a Roman Catholic. Only men may become priests. In 1982 Pope John Paul II paid a pastoral visit to Britain, the first by a reigning pope.

The Roman Catholic Church attaches great importance to the education of its children and requires its members to try to bring up their children in the Catholic faith. A number of Catholic schools are staffed by members of religious orders (to the extent of one teacher in 21). These orders also undertake other social work such as nursing, child care, and running homes for old people. The majority of Catholic schools are maintained out of public funds and new schools may be established with government grants.

Jewry

Jews first settled in England at the time of the Norman Conquest in the latter half of the eleventh century, but the present community in Britain dates from 1656, having been founded by those of Spanish and Portuguese origin (known as Sephardim). Later and more numerous settlers came from Germany and Eastern Europe; they are known as Ashkenazim. The present community, numbering about 350,000, is the second largest in Europe.

The community is divided into two main groups. Some 75 per cent of the majority Ashkenazi Jews are Orthodox and most acknowledge the authority of the Chief Rabbi. The Sephardi Orthodox element follow their own spiritual head (the Haham). The Reform movement, which was founded in 1840, and the Liberal and Progressive movement, which followed in 1901, account for most of the remaining 25 per cent.

Jewish congregations in Britain number about 300. About one in three Jewish children attend Jewish schools (some of them supported by public funds). There are a number of charitable and welfare agencies caring for elderly and handicapped people.

The officially recognised representative body is the Board of Deputies of British Jews.

The Muslim Community

The most recent estimates suggest that Britain's Muslim population is around one million. The largest number originate from Pakistan and Bangladesh, while sizeable groups have come from India, Cyprus, the Arab world, Malaysia and parts of Africa. There is also a growing community of British-born Muslims, mainly the children of immigrant parents, but including an increasing number of converts to Islam. There are some 300 mosques and numerous prayer centres throughout Britain. Mosques are not only places of worship; they are also cultural and social centres offering instruction in the Muslim way of life and facilities for social and welfare activities. The first was established at Woking in Surrey in 1890, and they now range from converted houses in the inner areas of many industrial towns to the Central Mosque in London and its associated Islamic Cultural Centre, which is one of the most important Muslim institutions in the Western world. The Central Mosque has the largest congregation in Britain, and during festivals it may number over 60,000. There are also important mosques and cultural centres in Liverpool, Manchester, Leicester, Edinburgh and Glasgow.

Many of the mosques belong to various Muslim organisations and both the Sunni and the Shia traditions within Islam are represented among the

Muslim community in Britain. Members of some of the major Sufi traditions have also developed branches in British cities.

Other Religious Communities

Christian communities of foreign origin, including the Orthodox, Lutheran and Reformed Churches of various European countries, together with the Armenian Church, have established their own centres of worship, particularly in London.

There is a large Sikh community in Britain, comprising approximately 500,000, the members of which originate mainly from India. The largest groups of Sikhs are in Greater London, Manchester, Birmingham, Nottingham and Wolverhampton. Sikh temples or gurdwaras cater for the religious, educational, social, and cultural needs of their community. The oldest central gurdwara in London was established in 1908 and the largest one is in Southall, Middlesex. There are over 170 gurdwaras in Britain.

The Hindu community in Britain comprises around 300,000 members and also originates largely from India. The largest groups of Hindus are to be found in Leicester, north and north-west London, Birmingham and Bradford. The first Hindu temple or mandir was opened in Leicester in 1969; there are now over 150 mandirs in Britain.

In Britain there are also about 130 Buddhist groups and some 55 centres, with at least 13 monasteries and a number of temples. All the main schools of Buddhism are represented. The Buddhist Society, with its headquarters in London, publicises the principles of Buddhism and encourages their study and practice; it does not belong to any particular school of Buddhism.

New Religious Movements

A large number of new religious movements or cults, largely established since the second world war (1939–45) and often with overseas origins, are active in Britain. In response to public concern about the activities of some of these cults the Government has since 1987 provided funding for the Information Network Focus on Religious Movements (INFORM), which is also supported by the main churches. The aims of INFORM are to conduct research into new religious movements and to provide objective information about them.

Co-operation among the Churches

A new organisation, the Council of Churches for Britain and Ireland, was established in September 1990. This replaced the former British Council of Churches and took over its role as the main overall body for the Christian churches in Britain. The Council co-ordinates the work of the churches grouped in separate national ecumenical bodies for England, Scotland, Wales, and Ireland. For the first time, the new Council includes the Roman Catholic and many black-led churches as full members.

The Free Church Federal Council includes most of the Free Churches of England and Wales. It promotes unity and joint action among the Free Churches and is a channel for communication with central and local government. It also has black-led churches as full members.

Inter-church discussions about the issues involved in the search for unity now take place through international as well as national bodies. The Roman Catholic and Orthodox Churches are represented on some of these as well as the Anglican and some of the Free Churches.

The Anglican and the main Free Churches are also members of the World Council of Churches. This links together some 300 churches in over 100 countries for co-operation and the study of common problems. The Council of Christians and Jews works for better understanding among members of the two religions and deals with problems in the social field.

The Sharing of Church Buildings Act 1969 enables agreements to be made by two or more churches for sharing church buildings.

11 National Economy

From 1981 the British economy has grown at an annual average rate of over 3 per cent. Investment, export volume, the number of jobs and productivity have all risen substantially. However, after falling sharply in the early 1980s, the rate of inflation has risen since early 1988. The figure for 1989 was just under 8 per cent; by August 1990 it was 10·6 per cent at an annual rate. Unemployment amounted to about 1·7 million in August 1990, having exceeded 3 million in 1985 and 1986.

The current account of the balance of payments has been in deficit since 1986, following six successive years of surplus.

ECONOMIC
BACKGROUND

Britain has an open economy, in which international trade is a vital part of economic performance. In 1989 exports of goods and services accounted for about one-quarter of its gross domestic product (GDP)—a comparatively high share among the major economies. The proportion has increased over the last two decades, from about 20 per cent in the early 1960s. Similar rises have occurred in most other developed countries, reflecting the growing importance of international trade in an increasingly interdependent world economy.

The economy is primarily—and increasingly—based on private enterprise, and government policy is aimed at encouraging and expanding the private sector, which accounts for about three-quarters of GDP and over two-thirds of total employment.

While manufacturing, the traditional engine of economic growth in Britain, continues to play a vital role, recent decades have generally seen a faster growth in the services sector (although manufacturing has grown faster since 1987), in response to rising living standards. An adjustment to the relative size of the manufacturing sector has also resulted from the growth of North Sea oil output. Services account for three-fifths of GDP and for two-thirds of employment, compared with about half of both GDP and employment in 1950. Manufacturing accounts for about a quarter of each compared with over a third in 1950.

Around 2 per cent of Britain's workforce is engaged in agriculture—a lower proportion than in any other major industrialised country. However, because of a high level of productivity, Britain is able to produce nearly two-thirds of its own food.

With the exploitation of oil and natural gas from the Continental Shelf under the North Sea, the country is self-sufficient in energy in net terms and expects to remain so for some years. Together, the extraction of oil and gas accounted for some 2 per cent of GDP in 1989. Coal—traditionally the most important source of energy—still meets over a third of Britain's energy needs.

One of the largest exporters of visible goods, Britain accounts for about 5 per cent of the world total. It is among the major exporters of aerospace products, electrical equipment, most types of machinery, chemicals and oil.

It is also one of the world's largest importers of agricultural products, raw materials and semi-manufactures.

In about half the years since the end of the second world war in 1945, a deficit on Britain's visible trade has been offset by a surplus on transactions in invisibles. The significant contribution made by invisibles to the current account is partly a reflection of Britain's position as a major financial centre. However, the surplus on invisibles declined sharply in 1989, mainly because of a fall in net investment income and an increase in net transfers to European Community institutions The banks, insurance underwriters and brokers, and other financial institutions of the City of London provide worldwide financial services, and the City contains one of the most comprehensive and advanced capital markets in the world.

Values for some of the main economic indicators in selected years since 1979 are shown in Table 11.1.

Table 11.1: Economic Indicators

	1979	1984	1989
Gross domestic product (average estimate)[a]	330,600	343,945	411,076
Exports[a]	88,924	96,786	118,570
Imports[a]	83,814	96,655	137,859
Consumers' expenditure[a]	195,664	210,472	271,707
Gross domestic fixed capital formation[a]	56,450	58,034	81,048
Percentage increase in retail prices index	13·4	5·0	7·8
Workforce in employment (000s)	25,393	24,235	26,329
Percentage of workforce unemployed	4·9	11·6	6·3

Sources: *United Kingdom National Accounts 1990 Edition*; *Economic Trends Annual Supplement, 1990 Edition*; *Employment Gazette.*
[a] £ million at 1985 market prices.

Economic Growth

The marked rise in living standards in recent years has been accompanied by the emergence of new industries and the renewal and improvement of much of the country's infrastructure. Growth was relatively steady until the early 1970s although low in comparison with the performance in most other industrialised countries. It averaged 2 to 3 per cent annually in the years leading up to 1973, but then fell to a still lower level—about 1 per cent a year from then until the recession of the early 1980s. Since then, however, the average rate of growth has been over 3 per cent a year. Since 1980 Britain has had the highest average rate of growth of the major European Community countries apart from Spain.

Inflation and Competitiveness

From the late 1960s until about 1980 Britain had generally high annual rates of inflation. Huge rises in the price of oil in 1973–74 and 1979, and substantial increases in the money supply and public spending were followed by upsurges in inflation; retail prices rose by 24 per cent in 1975 and by 18 per cent in 1980. Earnings also grew rapidly; in 1980 the rate of increase was 21 per cent. Inflation started to fall in the early 1980s but picked up towards the end of the 1980s; the annual rate was 10·6 per cent by August 1990. In the year to July 1990 earnings rose at an underlying rate of some 10 per cent.

Industrial Production

In the decade to 1973 output of the manufacturing industries grew at a faster rate than the economy as a whole. After the oil price rises of 1973–74, however, and with increasing competition from overseas—from both developed and newly industrialising countries—manufacturing output fell sharply; in 1975 it was 8 per cent lower than two years previously. It then increased from this trough but, following another oil price rise and stagnation in the world economy, fell back by over 14 per cent between 1979 and 1981. It has since grown steadily to pass its 1973–74 peak. Manufacturing output grew especially sharply between 1986 and 1988—by 13 per cent. The rate of increase slowed in 1989 to a little under 5 per cent.

By 1985 output of the production industries as a whole (manufacturing, energy and water) had risen above its earlier peak of 1979; by 1989 it was over 11 per cent higher than in 1979. In 1986 energy output was about twice the level of ten years earlier but, with oil output having passed its peak level of the mid-1980s, then fell by 14 per cent by 1989.

Investment

Fixed investment grew by just over 5 per cent a year during the 1960s but changed comparatively little between 1970 and 1983. Since 1983 it has increased by about 7 per cent a year on average. Sharply rising company profits have been a contributory factor. Over the decade 1979–89 there was an increase in the private sector's share of fixed investment from 71 per cent to 86 per cent (due in part to privatisation). Over the same period there was a rise in the share of investment undertaken by the services sector and a fall in that carried out by manufacturing. An improvement in the quality of investment has contributed to the rise in the net real rate of return on capital employed in non-North Sea industrial and commercial companies. In 1988 this was some 10 per cent, the highest since the late 1960s.

Employment and Productivity

Britain's workforce in employment amounts to over 27 million, having increased by 3·6 million in the seven years to March 1990. Over half the jobs created over the period were full-time. Since June 1979 self-employment has risen by over 70 per cent to reach 3·3 million. The number of women seeking work has also risen. As the workforce has expanded, unemployment has not fallen as quickly as employment has risen. As in other industrialised countries, there has been concern about the level of unemployment. However, with the economy growing rapidly, unemployment fell by 1·6 million between July 1986 and August 1990, when it amounted to some 1·7 million, equal to 5·8 per cent of the workforce. The figure is well below the average for the European Community. Since April 1990, with the rate of economic activity slowing, unemployment has been rising.

The shedding of surplus labour in the early 1980s and renewed growth have led to gains in productivity. Between 1980 and 1989 output per head rose by 23 per cent in the economy as a whole and by 57 per cent in manufacturing alone.

As a result of demographic changes, the population of working age will grow more slowly during the 1990s than in recent years, with a fall in the number of young people. The increase in Great Britain between 1988 and 2001 is projected at 0·6 million, compared with a rise of 2·4 million in the previous 13 years. Accordingly, there will be a need for increased flexibility among those in work and for employers to tap new sources of recruitment. The Government has launched a new training framework, involving a greater role for employers; over 80 local, employer-led Training and Enterprise Councils are being created in England and Wales, as are similar bodies in Scotland.

Overseas Sector

Britain's overseas trade performance fluctuated during the 1970s. In general, imports of food, energy, raw materials and manufactured goods were greater than visible exports, around 80 per cent of which were manufactured goods. This deficit on visible trade was wholly or partly offset by a surplus on invisibles, which cover earnings from services, together with interest, profits and dividends, and transfers.

In the years 1980 to 1982 Britain ran surpluses on visible trade. Since then, however, imports—especially of manufactures—have tended to rise more sharply than exports (although the trend was reversed in 1989) and the deficit on visible trade has reappeared. After a long period of deterioration in the balance of trade in manufactures there was a deficit in 1983, which has continued in subsequent years. Substantial net earnings on invisible transactions, however, kept the current account in surplus up to 1985.

Membership of the European Community (throughout which a single market is to be established by the end of 1992) has had a major impact on Britain's pattern of trade, increasing the proportion with other member countries. Between 1972 and 1989 the proportion of Britain's exports of goods going to other members of the Community rose from 34 to 50 per cent. Imports followed a similar trend. Trade with Japan and with the newly industrialised countries, including Singapore, Korea, Taiwan and Malaysia, has risen substantially.

The invisibles account has had to adapt to new conditions, in particular the abolition of exchange controls in 1979 and the growth in world markets of insurance, banking, tourism, construction, consultancy and other services. In 1989 exports of services were valued at around one-third of exports of goods.

The substantial cumulative surplus on current account in the first half of the 1980s contributed to a corresponding increase in Britain's net external assets. These are estimated to have risen from £12,000 million at the end of 1979 to some £113,000 million at the end of 1989—third in size to those of Japan and the Federal Republic of Germany. These assets enable recent current account deficits to be readily financed. Following the abolition of exchange controls, investment outflows increased sharply. Portfolio investment has been high since the mid-1980s, partly a reflection of investment by banks as they moved into lending in readily marketable forms (such as floating rate notes) and away from traditional loans. In 1987 there was net portfolio disinvestment by British residents but by 1988 net portfolio investment had been resumed and it grew substantially in 1989. Net direct investment is at a consistently high level.

Oil

The development of North Sea oil and gas production has had a significant effect on the economy; in 1989 Britain was the world's eighth largest oil producer. The benefits to the balance of payments began to appear in the second half of the 1970s and in 1980 Britain had its first surplus on oil trade. In 1974 oil accounted for some 4 per cent of Britain's visible exports and 19 per cent of visible imports. In 1989 the proportions were 6 per cent and 4 per cent respectively (the export proportion having been as high as 21 per cent in the mid-1980s). The oil surplus reached its peak in 1985, at £8,100 million. With the fall in oil prices (see p 246) the surplus has fallen and amounted to some £1,500 million in 1989. Exports, mainly to other European Community countries, are equivalent to about half of domestic production. They are partly offset in balance-of-payments terms by imports of other grades of crude oil from the Middle East and elsewhere.

North Sea oil helped to alleviate the fall in real national income which Britain, along with other industrialised countries, suffered following the oil price rises of the 1970s. It has helped to ease the task of controlling public sector borrowing, contributing to the Government's counter-inflation strategy. Even as production—which reached a peak in the mid-1980s—runs down, the stock of external assets that has been built up, largely during the period of oil surpluses, provides a steady flow of income.

ECONOMIC STRATEGY

British governments traditionally sought to influence the rate of growth and the level of employment by macroeconomic policy measures (for example, by variations in government expenditure, taxes or controls on consumer credit). Increases in wages and prices have had an adverse effect on competitiveness, profitability and business confidence. This has been associated with increases in unemployment. At various times governments attempted to control pay rises and (less frequently) price rises by voluntary or statutory controls, but such policies were largely unsuccessful.

The Government's economic objectives may be summarised as the establishment of conditions that stimulate enterprise and encourage the creation of wealth. Macroeconomic (monetary and fiscal) policies are directed mainly at bringing down the rate of inflation and ultimately achieving price stability. They are set in the context of a medium-term financial strategy, which is reviewed each year in the Budget. Microeconomic policies are aimed at improving the working of markets by encouraging enterprise, efficiency and flexibility, and so improving the supply side performance of the economy (see p 250). Together these policies are aimed at improving the division of the increase in money GDP between output growth and inflation, and helping to create jobs.

Monetary Policy

The central aim of monetary policy, which the Government sees as lying at the heart of macroeconomic policy, is the creation of conditions that will exert steady downward pressure on the rate of growth of money GDP, so bringing down the rate of inflation. Interest rates are the essential instrument of monetary policy and they are set so as to bring such conditions about. Narrow money as measured by M0[1] has had a stable relationship with money GDP over a number of years and has proved a reliable indicator of monetary conditions. A target range of 1 to 5 per cent has been set for M0 growth in 1990–91. Changes in broad money, or liquidity, have become increasingly difficult to interpret; far-reaching changes in financial practices have meant that there is no simple relationship between the growth in broad money and in money GDP. Consequently, no explicit target range is set for broad money, though the assessment of monetary conditions continues to take broad money into account.

The Exchange Rate

The exchange rate plays a central role both in domestic monetary decisions and in international policy co-operation. The Government regards the exchange rate as an important indicator of monetary conditions and as part of the transmission mechanism through which monetary policy affects inflation. The Government does not allow increases in domestic costs to be accommodated either by monetary expansion or by exchange rate depreciation. The major industrialised countries share an interest in establishing more stable exchange rates.

Britain is a member of the European Monetary System, including the exchange rate mechanism (ERM). Under the ERM the central exchange rate for the pound is 2·95 Deutsche Marks, with a permitted fluctuation of 6 per cent in either direction.

---

[1] M0 is notes and coin in circulation with the public and banks' holdings of cash and their operational balances at the Bank of England.

Fiscal Policy

Monetary policy has been complemented by a firm fiscal policy whose aim has been a progressive reduction in public borrowing as a proportion of GDP by seeking to limit the share of GDP taken up by public expenditure. General government expenditure, excluding privatisation proceeds (which count as negative expenditure), fell as a proportion of GDP from nearly 47 per cent in 1982–83 to 39 per cent in 1989–90. In the early years of the financial strategy the public sector borrowing requirement amounted to around 5 per cent of GDP, but by 1989–90 this had been turned into a public sector debt repayment of some 1·25 per cent of GDP—a third successive annual surplus. The Government's aim is to maintain a balanced budget in the medium term.

Supply Side Policies

While designing macroeconomic policy with the intent of reducing inflation, the Government has sought to improve the supply response, and thus the efficiency, of the economy through microeconomic policies. Action has been taken to expose more of the economy to market forces. Direct controls (for example, on pay, prices, foreign exchange, dividend payments and commercial credit) have been abolished and competition in domestic markets strengthened. In addition, labour market reforms have been introduced, measures taken to encourage saving and share ownership, and a substantial amount of activity transferred from the public to the private sector by privatisation and contracting work out. Finally, efforts have been made to improve value for money in the public sector, largely by transferring many of the executive functions of government to new executive agencies, and regulatory burdens on business reduced.

In the labour market the Government has sought to improve work incentives by reducing personal income tax rates and raising tax thresholds. It has also, through the tax system, encouraged the extension of share ownership among employees. A scheme of income tax relief has been introduced to encourage the spread of profit-related pay. The Government has also taken steps to achieve a better-balanced legal framework for industrial relations and has expanded training opportunities. Obstacles to the mobility of labour have been reduced. For example, the rights of those leaving occupational pension schemes early have been improved and new arrangements for personal pensions introduced, both of which will reduce the pension disadvantage of changing jobs. The Government has enacted legislation to limit the scope of wages councils. It has stressed the link between pay and jobs and has repeatedly pointed out that wages must rise more slowly if adverse effects on employment are to be avoided.

To improve the working of capital markets, the Government has abolished controls on foreign exchange transactions, dividends, hire purchase and bank lending. Competition among financial institutions is being encouraged within a new statutory framework of investor protection. The Government has also taken steps to reduce the distorting effects of the tax system on investment and savings decisions by, among other things, reforming corporation tax (the burden of which has been eased) and the system of capital allowances. Planning restrictions on industrial investment have been eased, while government support to industry has become more selective and, where appropriate, more closely related to job creation. Particular efforts have been made to improve the flow of investment funds to small firms, to assist innovation in industry and to attract industry to the inner cities.

Economic Management

HM Treasury has prime responsibility for the formulation and conduct of economic policy, which also involves the Departments of Trade and

Industry, Employment, Energy, the Environment and Transport, and the Ministry of Agriculture, Fisheries and Food.

Other bodies are concerned with specific aspects of economic policy. These include the Bank of England (the central bank), the National Economic Development Council (in which the Government meets representatives of management, trade unions and other interests), the Office of Fair Trading and the Monopolies and Mergers Commission.

On matters of major public policy such as the broad economic strategy, and on the economic problems it faces, the Government makes known its purposes and keeps in touch with developments throughout the economy by means of informal and continuous links with the chief industrial, financial, labour and other interests. Final responsibility for the broad lines of economic policy rests with the Cabinet.

NATIONAL INCOME AND EXPENDITURE

The value of all goods and services produced in the economy is measured by GDP. This can be expressed either in terms of market prices (the prices people pay for the goods and services they buy) or at factor cost (the cost of the goods and services before adding taxes and subtracting subsidies). It can also be expressed in current prices or in constant prices (that is, removing the effects of inflation in order to measure the underlying growth in the economy). In 1989 GDP at current factor cost totalled £439,000 million.

Gross domestic product is conventionally estimated in three different ways as the sum total of expenditure, income or output. Each method yields the same total in principle, but in practice there are slight differences. The output measure is usually considered the most reliable measure of short-term movements. In 1989 the index of the average estimate of GDP at constant factor cost was 115·7 (1985 = 100), compared with 92·6 in 1979, an increase of some 25 per cent.

Table 11.2 gives figures for the average estimate of GDP, at both current market prices and current factor cost, and also shows how two other main aggregates used in the national accounts, gross national product and national income, are derived.

Table 11.2: Gross Domestic Product, Gross National Product and National Income

£ million

	1979	1989
Total final expenditure	252,857	654,849
less imports of goods and services	−54,346	−142,527
Gross domestic product at market prices[a]	198,262	513,242
plus net property income from abroad	1,205	4,582
Gross national product at market prices[a]	199,467	517,824
less factor cost adjustment (taxes less subsidies)	−25,027	−74,468
Gross domestic product at factor cost[a]	173,235	438,774
Net property income from abroad	1,205	4,582
Gross national product at factor cost[a]	174,440	443,356
less capital consumption	−22,827	−56,186
National income (net national product at factor cost)[a]	151,613	387,170

Source: *United Kingdom National Accounts 1990 Edition.*
[a] Average estimate.

Table 11.3 shows the categories of total final expenditure in 1989. Consumers' expenditure accounted for just over 50 per cent of total final expenditure, and exports and goods for nearly 19 per cent.

Table 11.3: Total Final Expenditure in 1989 at Market Prices

	£ million	per cent
Consumers' expenditure	328,453	50·2
General government final consumption	99,426	15·2
Gross domestic fixed capital formation	100,472	15·3
Value of physical increase in stocks and work in progress	3,102	0·5
Total domestic expenditure	531,453	81·2
Exports of goods and services	123,396	18·8
Total final expenditure	654,849	100·0

Source: *United Kingdom National Accounts 1990 Edition.*

Personal Incomes and Expenditure

Personal disposable income (that is, personal incomes after deductions—mainly taxation and social security contributions) rose rapidly and fairly steadily from £136,000 million in 1979 to £352,000 million in 1989, 5·3 per cent higher in real terms than in 1988. Consumers' expenditure amounted to 74·4 per cent of pre-tax personal income in 1989, compared with 70·4 per cent in 1979.

Table 11.4 shows the pattern of consumers' expenditure in 1989. Housing, food, alcoholic drink, clothing and footwear, and fuel and power together accounted for 42 per cent of the total. Consumers' expenditure increased by 3·9 per cent in real terms between 1988 and 1989. The changes in the pattern between 1979 and 1989 in Britain were paralleled in other industrialised countries, with declining proportions spent on food, tobacco, clothing and footwear, and fuel and power. Over the longer term, as incomes rise, people tend to spend increasing proportions on services.

Table 11.4: Consumers' Expenditure in 1979 and 1989

	1979	1989	
	per cent	per cent	£ million
Food (household expenditure)	17·5	11·9	39,181
Alcoholic drink	7·2	6·0	19,818
Tobacco	3·5	2·5	8,196
Clothing and footwear	7·6	5·9	19,511
Housing	13·1	15·1	49,618
Fuel and power	4·4	3·5	11,335
Household goods and services	7·5	6·6	21,529
Transport and communications	16·7	17·4	57,066
Recreation, entertainment and education	9·2	9·1	29,781
Other goods and services	12·4	17·8	58,470
Other items[a]	0·9	4·2	13,948
Total	100·0	100·0	328,453

Source: *United Kingdom National Accounts 1990 Edition.*
[a] Household expenditure overseas plus final expenditure by private non-profit-making bodies plus national accounts statistical adjustment minus expenditure by foreign tourists in Britain.

Saving as a percentage of personal disposable income has varied over the last decade and in 1989 was 6·7 per cent, down from 13·1 per cent in 1980. The recent reduction in the saving ratio partly reflects an adjustment to declining rates of inflation: during periods of rapidly rising prices people need to increase their rate of saving to maintain the real value of assets fixed in money terms. The 1990 Budget contained a number of measures designed to encourage saving over the long term.

Sources of Income The proportion of total personal income accounted for by income from employment was 64 per cent in 1989; average gross weekly earnings in April 1989 in Great Britain were £264 for full-time male workers and £178 for full-time female workers. The three other main sources of personal income were self-employment (12 per cent), income from rent, dividends and interest (10 per cent) and current grants from general government (13 per cent).

Current Government Expenditure Final consumption by central government and local authorities amounted to £99,000 million in 1989; it rose by 11 per cent in real terms over the period 1979 to 1989. The main cause of this was the growth over the period in the social services, health, and law and order.

In addition to their expenditure on goods and services, public authorities transfer large sums to other sectors, mainly the personal sector, by way of National Insurance and other social security benefits, grants, and interest and subsidies. Central government also makes grants to local authorities to finance about half of their current expenditure.

Gross Domestic Product by Industry Table 11.5 shows GDP by industry in 1979 and 1989. Over a period of time agriculture and manufacturing have come to account for smaller proportions of national income, while services have grown relatively; services now account for 64 per cent of GDP.

Table 11.5: Gross Domestic Product by Industry[a]

	1979		1989	
	£ million	per cent	£ million	per cent
Agriculture, forestry and fishing	3,690	2·1	6,561	1·5
Energy and water supply	13,864	8·1	22,619	5·2
Manufacturing	48,835	28·4	97,380	22·2
Construction	10,637	6·2	30,274	6·9
Distribution, hotels and catering; repairs	22,855	13·3	62,133	14·2
Transport and communications	13,210	7·7	30,074	6·9
Banking, finance, insurance, business services and leasing	20,001	11·6	86,628	19·8
Ownership of dwellings	10,306	6·0	25,482	5·8
Public administration, defence and social security	11,439	6·7	29,571	6·8
Education and health services	14,146	8·2	42,547	9·7
Other services	9,227	5·4	29,715	6·8
Total	178,210	103·8	462,984	105·8
Adjustment for financial services	−6,494	−3·8	−25,242	−5·8
Gross domestic product at factor cost (income-based)	171,716	100·0	437,742	100·0

Source: *United Kingdom National Accounts 1990 Edition.*
[a]Before provision for depreciation but after deducting stock appreciation.
Differences between totals and the sums of their component parts are due to rounding.

12 Framework of Industry and Commerce

Introduction

Among the most prominent trends in industrial activity in Britain since the mid-1970s have been the growth of the offshore oil and gas industries and their related products and services; the rapid development of electronic and microelectronic technologies and their application to a wide range of other sectors; a steady increase in the share of output and employment accounted for by private sector enterprises as privatisation has progressed; and a continuous rise in the service industries' share of total employment. Industrial output has risen steadily since the recession of 1980–81, which, as in other market economies, was largely brought about by a rise in world oil prices.

This chapter outlines some of the general features of industrial and commercial performance and organisation, and goes on to describe government policies and legislation, the functioning of markets and research and innovation.

Performance

OUTPUT, EMPLOYMENT AND PRODUCTIVITY

In early 1990 total output was some 30 per cent higher than at its trough in 1981. It was only during 1985, however, that output in the production industries regained the level of mid-1979, which had been the high point of a period of growth since 1976. A marked increase in productivity has been a major feature of recovery. Gains in productivity since the early 1980s,

Table 12.1: Gross Domestic Product[a] by Industry in 1989

Standard Industrial Classification Revised 1985		£ million	% of total[b]	% Employment[b]
0	Agriculture, forestry and fishing	6,561	1·5	1·3
1	Energy and water supply	22,619	5·2	2·1
2—4	Manufacturing	97,380	22·5	23·1
5	Construction	30,274	6·9	4·7
6—9	Services	306,150	69·9	68·9
	Adjustment for financial services	−25,242	−5·8	—
Gross domestic product at factor cost (income-based)		437,742	100·0	100·0

Sources: *United Kingdom National Accounts 1990 Edition* and *Employment Gazette*.
[a]Before depreciation but after providing for stock appreciation.
[b]The difference between the totals and the sums of their component parts are due to rounding.

however, have meant that this increased output was produced with fewer workers. Consequently, employment, though increasing, is still lower than in 1981. Table 12.1 shows gross domestic product (GDP) by sector and the percentage of total GDP and of total employment in each sector in 1989. Output per head in Britain has in the past been lower than in some other major industrialised countries but it rose sharply from 1981. In recent years the growth has been among the highest in the major industrialised nations, although the rate of increase slowed by the late 1980s. The index of output per head for the economy as a whole was 107·1 (1985=100) in 1989. The productivity of the manufacturing sector improved more rapidly than in other major industrialised countries and in 1989 the index stood at 120·0. The metals manufacturing sector achieved sustained gains in productivity during the 1980s against a background of declining employment, such that output per head was 69 per cent greater in 1989 than in 1985. Employment in most sectors of the economy rose between 1988 and 1989. Table 12·2 shows output and employment indices for these years.

Table 12.2: Output and Employment (Indices: 1985 = 100)

	Output		Employment[a]	
	Index 1988	Index 1989	Index 1988	Index 1989
Agriculture, forestry and fishing	96·6	97·9	91·6	87·2
Production industries	109·7	110·2	95·9	95·8
of which: Energy and water supply	99·3	89·8	79·6	82·5
Manufacturing	114·3	119·2	97·4	97·6
Construction	120·7	125·7	102·4	104·2
Services	115·4	119·3	107·9	111·3
of which: Distribution, repairs, hotels and catering	119·4	122·5	103·3	107·2
Transport and communications	119·6	125·7	99·8	102·4
Financial and business services	134·0	144·0	119·9	129·6
Other services	114·0	119·0	107·1	108·9
Whole economy	108·1	113·1	104·0	106·2

Sources: *United Kingdom National Accounts 1990 Edition* and *Employment Gazette.*
[a]Excluding self-employment.

Investment

Investment in the manufacturing, construction, distribution, transport, communications, and financial services industries and in 'other services' grew by 6·9 per cent in real terms in 1989. Investment in major sectors of the economy in 1989 (at 1985 prices) is shown in Table 12.3. The figures for manufacturing industry do not include expenditure on leased assets since these are attributed to the service industries on the basis of ownership. Manufacturing industry is, however, a major user of leased assets. The practice of leasing grew from the early 1970s, but the trend was distorted in the mid-1980s following changes in the tax treatment of capital investment. Leasing rose sharply in 1985 but then declined, recovering to stand at 27·5 per cent more than its 1985 level in 1988.

Table 12.3: Gross Domestic Fixed Capital Formation (Investment) by Sector

	£ million 1989 (at 1985 prices)	Index 1989 (1985 = 100)
Agriculture, forestry and fishing	1,067	108·2
Oil and gas extraction	2,100	74·5
Other energy and water supply	4,310	109·8
Manufacturing	10,787	123·4
Construction and services	44,552	153·3
Dwellings	14,042	118·5
Transfer costs of land and buildings	2,590	87·1
National accounts statistical adjustment	1,600	—
Whole economy	81,048	134·3

Source: *United Kingdom National Accounts 1990 Edition.*

Profitability

The quality of investment undertaken has shown a marked improvement in recent years, contributing to a net real rate of return on capital employed by all non-North Sea industrial and commercial companies of some 10 per cent in 1988 (the most recent year for which data are available)—the highest since 1969.

Inward Investment

Britain is recognised as an attractive location for inward direct investment. This reflects its membership of the European Community and proximity to other European markets, stable labour relations and comparatively low rates of corporate and personal taxation. Direct investment from overseas is encouraged, overseas-owned firms generally being offered the same facilities and incentives as British-owned ones.

The Invest in Britain Bureau of the Department of Trade and Industry (DTI) provides foreign companies with advice and assistance on all aspects of locating and relocating businesses in Britain, and on expanding existing facilities. It reported 283 new inward investment projects in 1989. The promotion of England as a location for inward investment projects is handled by the English unit of the DTI. Similar advice and assistance is also available in Scotland through Locate in Scotland; in Wales through Welsh Development International, the investment arm of the Welsh Development Agency; and in Northern Ireland through the Industrial Development Board, Northern Ireland.

At the end of 1989 total United States investment in Britain was valued at $58,800 million, representing 41 per cent of United States investment in the European Community. Britain has for many years been the leading country for United States manufacturing investment in Europe. Since 1951 Britain has attracted around 38 per cent of Japanese investment in what is now the European Community. The value of Japanese investment in Britain is $10,554 million.

Organisation and Ownership

The forms of industrial and commercial organisation and the patterns of ownership and control are varied. The main categories of organisation are: unincorporated businesses (sole traders and partnerships), of which there are more than 1 million; incorporated companies; and public sector enterprises, which are owned by the Government (see pp 258-9). Incorporation means that companies are entered on an official register of companies (see p 274). At the end of 1989 there were over 1·2 million companies on the register, although about 14 per cent of these were in liquidation or in the process of removal. About 11,000 of these companies were public limited companies. Although not numerous, co-operative enterprises increased in number from about 900 in 1979 to about 1,500 in 1989.

In some sectors a small number of large companies and their subsidiaries are responsible for a large proportion of total production, notably in the vehicle, aerospace and transport equipment industries. However, it is rare for only a few shareholders to have a controlling interest, since shares in these companies are usually distributed among many holders or held by insurance companies or pension funds representing a cross-section of the community.

Private enterprises generate about three-quarters of total domestic income. They account for the greater part of activity in the agricultural, manufacturing, construction, distributive, financial and miscellaneous service sectors. Public ownership has become less significant with privatisation (see p 263). The private sector accounted for 79 per cent of total domestic expenditure in 1989, general government for 20 per cent and public corporations for 1 per cent.

About 230 British-registered company groups and independent companies reporting during 1988 each had an annual turnover of more than £500 million. The annual turnover of British Petroleum (BP) makes it the sixth largest company in the world and the second largest in Europe. The British element of Royal Dutch/Shell is the third largest in Europe by turnover and five other British firms are among the top 25 European companies.

Nationalised Industries

The electricity supply industry in Great Britain is being privatised, which will leave as the major nationalised industries British Coal, British Rail, the Post Office and London Transport. In total the industries account for less than 4 per cent of GDP and employ about 2·5 per cent of all those in employment.

The managing boards and staffs of the nationalised industries are not civil servants. However, the boards are responsible to ministers, who appoint the chairmen and members. Ministers are responsible for agreeing with the industries their general strategies and have the power to give general directions as to how the industry should be run, but are not involved in day-to-day management. The Government's policy is to encourage the nationalised industries to behave as far as possible as commercial enterprises. This is carried out through the financial framework, set by the Government, within which the industries are expected to operate. The main elements of the framework are: clear government objectives for the industries; regular corporate plans and performance reviews; agreed principles relating to investment appraisal and pricing; financial targets and performance aims; external financing limits; and systematic monitoring.

To ensure that nationalised industry investment earns an adequate economic return, there is a 'required rate of return' which investment programmes are expected to achieve. The current rate is 8 per cent in real terms before tax. Financial targets are set for individual nationalised industries to give them a framework similar to those of private sector companies, which need to earn profits. The financial target is usually supported by a series of performance aims, covering costs and, where appropriate, standards of service. Performance aims are considered particularly important for industries with some monopoly power, where financial targets would not automatically impose pressures for operating efficiency. External financing limits, which control the amount of finance (grants and borrowing) that a nationalised industry can raise in any financial year, are an important operating control. They are set in the light of a nationalised industry's financial target and its expected performance and investment requirements. The proportion of investment financed from internally generated funds has risen in recent years.

External scrutiny of nationalised industry efficiency is conducted by the Monopolies and Mergers Commission (see p 270), which carries out a number of investigations each year at the instigation of ministers. Where appropriate, investigations may also be undertaken by management consultants. Nationalised industry matters are also considered by parliamentary committees such as the Treasury and Civil Service Committee and the Public Accounts Committee.

Industrial Associations

There are several types of voluntary association representing private enterprises and covering, with varying degrees of completeness, most of British industry. The central body representing British business and industry is the Confederation of British Industry (CBI). The CBI directly represents about 250,000 parent and subsidiary companies, as well as the members of some 150 trade associations and employers' organisations and the majority of public sector enterprises. For its members, the CBI provides a lobby, a forum and a service. It represents their views nationally to the Government and the public as well as internationally. CBI representatives sit on such bodies as the National Economic Development Council and the Health and Safety Commission. The CBI provides a forum where members can exchange views and experiences and discuss ways of tackling common problems. It offers information and advice on subjects which members may be unable to cover themselves, in particular, on overseas markets, health and safety, company law, environmental issues and employment affairs.

The decentralised body representing business and industry is the Association of British Chambers of commerce, which represents over 75,000 businesses in 97 chambers. Chambers of commerce provide a forum for business, representing their views and interests to the Government both at national and local levels. Chambers promote local economic development, for example, through regeneration projects, tourism, inward investment promotion and business services, including overseas trade missions, exhibitions and training conferences.

Trade associations consist of companies producing or selling a particular product or group of products. They exist to provide common services, regulate trading practices and represent their members to government departments. Employers' organisations are usually concerned with the negotiation of wages and conditions of work in a particular industrial sector, although sometimes one institution may combine this function with that of a trade association. At the end of 1989 there were 281 employers' organisations.

Other voluntary associations include industrial development associations for particular regions or areas and the Scottish Council (Development and Industry) in Scotland.

Industrial Financing

Over half of companies' funds for investment and other purposes are internally generated. Banks provide the chief external source of finance, but companies increasingly turned to equity finance from the mid-1980s. The main forms of short-term finance available in the private sector are bank overdrafts, trade credit and factoring (making cash available to a company in exchange for debts owing to it). Types of medium- and long-term finance include bank loans, the mortgaging of property and the issue of shares and other securities to the public through The International Stock Exchange. The leasing of equipment may also be regarded as a form of finance. Other sources of finance for industry include the Government, the European Community and specialist financial institutions.

The 1980s were particularly notable for the growth of schemes involving venture capital (equity funds made available by financial institutions in support of innovative or other new and growing business ventures). Investment by the 124 full members of the British Venture Capital Association, the umbrella organisation for all significant sources of venture capital in Britain, reached £1,650 million in 1989, representing an 18 per cent increase compared with funds invested in 1988. The industry has invested some £5,000 million since 1984 and currently commands an investment pool of more than £6,000 million. There has also been a rise in the number of 'buy-outs', in which the staff or management of a company raise the finance to purchase it, and 'buy-ins', in which the staff or management of one firm purchase another. In the period from 1979 to 1989 there were nearly 3,000, with a total value of more than £20,300 million.

Management Development and Industrial Training

Management education is provided by many polytechnics and colleges of higher and further education. Some regional management centres have been established in England and Wales by associations of these colleges, and there are several similar organisations in Scotland. Universities make an important contribution, especially through the full-time postgraduate programmes at business schools such as those of London, Manchester, Durham, Warwick and Strathclyde universities. Training courses for managers are offered by several independent colleges, including the Management College (Henley-on-Thames), Ashridge College (Berkhamsted) and the Cranfield School of Management (Bedford). Open and distance learning opportunities are becoming more widely available. The British Institute of Management, which aims to encourage excellence in management, has a particular interest in management training. There are a number of other professional bodies concerned with standards and training in specialised branches of management.

The Open University, which provides degree courses using distance learning techniques, notably television broadcasts, has set up the Open University Business School, which offers part-time courses leading to a diploma in management, of which more than 200 have been awarded. The School has been used by over 3,000 companies and organisations since it opened in 1983. Managers continue to work while studying, which is of particular use to those small companies which cannot afford to release staff on a full-time basis.

The Management Charter Initiative, an employer-led initiative to promote management development, was launched in 1987. Over 500 member organisations now subscribe to a code of best practice and support the Initiative's aims of developing a competence-based structure of management qualifications and providing a forum for all those involved in management development.

Government Management Initiatives

The DTI is working with other government departments and with industry to improve management education and development and to spread awareness about best management practices. It strongly supports the Management Charter Initiative (see above). The consultancy support offered by the DTI to businesses with fewer than 500 employees is designed to help businesses improve their management performance. Another programme, 'Managing into the 90s', is designed to encourage managers to evaluate the role of design and quality, manufacturing management, and purchasing and supply, within an overall business strategy leading to improved competitiveness.

The DTI has also encouraged the growth of links between industry and higher education in recent years, primarily through collaborative research. One of the most successful ways has been the Teaching Company Scheme, under which young graduates undertake key projects in companies under the joint supervision of academic and company staff.

Engineering Council

The Engineering Council was established under Royal Charter in 1981. Its objectives are to promote the science and practice of engineering and to advance education in engineering. The Council maintains a register of 300,000 chartered engineers, incorporated engineers and engineering technicians. In co-operation with the various professional institutions and other organisations concerned with training in engineering, it has set standards for education, training and experience, and accredited courses by which people qualify for registration. The Council is advised by some 300 industrial affiliates, which are employers of engineers, on industrial requirements for engineers and technicians.

Government Policies and Legislation

The DTI has the main responsibility for the Government's relations with industry and commerce. Specific responsibilities include technology and research, overseas trade and export promotion, competition policy and consumer affairs, company legislation and the Patent Office. Through the Invest in Britain Bureau, it provides advice and assistance to foreign companies on locating in Britain.

Other departments whose responsibilities have a bearing on industrial and commercial activity include HM Treasury, the Department of Employment, the Departments of Energy, Transport and the Environment, and the Ministry of Agriculture, Fisheries and Food. The Scottish, Welsh and Northern Ireland Offices are responsible for the range of industrial policies in their areas.

The results of a review of policies and organisation of the DTI were published in 1988. They confirmed the Government's belief that economic decisions are best taken by those competing in the market place, and that the responsibility of government is to create the right climate for markets to work better, and to encourage enterprise.

The Enterprise Initiative

The Enterprise Initiative, announced at the same time, brings together a wide range of the services that the DTI provides for industry and commerce. Central to the Enterprise Initiative are the six consultancy initiatives, which encourage small and medium-sized businesses to use outside consultancy services as a regular part of their management strategy. These offer consultancy support in design, marketing, manufacturing systems, quality, business planning, and financial and information systems. In Scotland and Wales these initiatives are operated by the respective Development Agencies. Assistance is available to businesses with fewer than 500 employees. In the Assisted Areas (see p 266) and Urban Programme Areas, two-thirds of the costs of a project are met; elsewhere the rate is 50 per cent. Some £66 million is being provided in 1990–91 to support the consultancy initiatives.

The emphasis of the Department's work has therefore been increasingly on the promotion of open markets through competition policy, privatisation, deregulation and international trade negotiations. Positive attitudes to enterprise are being encouraged through improved links between business and education. Smaller firms, in particular, are being helped to gain access to the specialised skills and information essential to successful enterprise in a competitive market. There is special emphasis on promoting enterprise in the less prosperous regions.

These changes, designed to meet the needs of an expanding economy, are being reflected in the pattern of DTI spending and in that of its organisation. Within a smaller total, expenditure on innovation has increased substantially. There has been a shift from near-market support for individual companies towards collaborative research. In April 1990 the DTI was reorganised to bring business into more direct contact with officials dealing with particular policies. Expertise on such subjects as the single European market, technology, international trade policy, the environment, deregulation and standards is now concentrated in divisions and branches which have responsibility for a single, related set of activities. Where the DTI has specific responsibilities and most contact with a particular market sector—for example, aerospace, shipbuilding, vehicles and steel—task forces deal directly with businesses. A Market Intelligence Unit carries out assessments of sectors' performance and maintains a basic core of information about individual markets on behalf of the rest of the Department.

Single European Market The Government is firmly committed to the objective of completing the single European market by the target date of the end of 1992. This will provide major benefits for business and consumers and improve European competitiveness in world markets. The DTI's 'Europe—Open for Business' campaign is designed to bring home to business the importance of 1992 and the need to prepare for the single market.

Small Firms The contribution of small businesses to the British economy is now well established. Small firms bring competition and innovation, and are an important source of new jobs and products. They employ 36 per cent of the private sector workforce and are producing 21 per cent of British turnover.

The Government's policies of achieving steady growth and of setting lower levels of public expenditure and personal taxation have helped to create conditions in which people are willing to invest and start businesses. New businesses were set up at a net rate of almost 1,700 a week in 1989, compared with just over 300 a week in 1980. The stock of businesses, most of which are small, increased by 29 per cent in the 1980s.

The Government recognises that creating a suitable economic environment is not enough by itself. It therefore runs a number of schemes which provide either direct assistance or advice and guidance on a wide range of business problems affecting small firms. In addition to DTI schemes such as the consultancy initiatives, the Department of Employment (in England) runs schemes aimed at small firms; there are corresponding schemes in Wales, Scotland and Northern Ireland. These include the Small Firms Service, which provides information, advice and counselling to prospective and established small businesses, and the Loan Guarantee Scheme, under which the Government guarantees repayment of 70 per cent of medium-term loans made by financial institutions (rising to 85 per cent of loans in inner city Task Force areas).

The Business Expansion Scheme improves the flow of equity finance to small firms by offering tax incentives to individuals who invest in qualifying unquoted companies, and the Enterprise Allowance Scheme enables unemployed people to claim an allowance while establishing a new business. In addition, the Government has introduced a range of tax concessions as well as training for people setting up their own businesses, and has encouraged the development of new advisory services and of new sources of venture capital within the private sector.

Deregulation

The Government seeks to create a framework in which enterprise can flourish by removing barriers to market entry and constraints on business growth. It therefore wishes to minimise the requirements imposed on businesses by central (and local) government which divert resources from mainstream commercial activities.

All proposed requirements, whether of British or European Community origin, are examined for their impact on business. The costs to business are taken into account in deciding whether and how they should be imposed. Existing controls are also reviewed to identify any which may be unnecessary or outdated. One important mechanism is the annual rolling programme of deregulation reviews to which departments contribute. The deregulation initiative is co-ordinated by the DTI's Deregulation Unit, working with regulatory departments' own units. Other government departments with regulatory responsibilities have their own deregulation units.

Privatisation

The Government believes that the best way to improve the performance of the nationalised industries in the long term is to expose them to market forces, through privatisation and the promotion of competition. Privatisation has also provided a major opportunity for the Government to pursue its policy of widening share ownership, encouraging both employees and the general public to take a direct stake in British industry. Employees in privatised companies are normally given a preferential right to buy shares in the new companies. Between 1979 and 1989 the Government privatised 29 major businesses (including the flotation of the ten water and sewerage companies of England and Wales following enabling legislation in 1989), with net proceeds of some £24,500 million. This has led to a substantial increase in the proportion of the adult population who are shareholders to 24 per cent in 1990, compared with 7 per cent in 1979.

Major businesses which have been privatised include British Gas, British Telecom, British Steel, British Aerospace, Cable and Wireless, British Airways, Royal Ordnance, the Rover Group, Britoil, Rolls-Royce, BAA (formerly the British Airports Authority) and most of British Shipbuilders. Many other state enterprises have also been sold and about 800,000 jobs have been transferred to the private sector. The electricity supply industry in Great Britain will be privatised by mid-1991. To stimulate efficiency, the Government has relaxed the statutory monopolies of a number of nationalised industries.

Government Finance

In 1989-90 the DTI spent £1,373 million on regional and all other forms of industrial support. Following the 1988 review of policy (see p 261), it is expected that marked changes in support will occur in the next few years. Spending on consultancy services by small and medium-sized businesses will increase, with a shift away from automatic and near-market support for individual companies towards consultancy services, technology transfer and collaborative research. Combined with the initiatives on business and education, management development and the encouragement of enterprise in less prosperous areas of Britain, these changes imply an increase in spending over that planned before the policy review.

Taxation

The rates of corporate taxation have been progressively reduced. In the case of business plant and machinery there is an annual allowance against profits for tax purposes of 25 per cent (on a reducing balance basis), beginning in the year in which expenditure occurs. There is an allowance for investment in industrial building of 4 per cent a year. Special arrangements exist for short-life (often high-technology) assets. There are 100 per cent allowances for capital expenditure on scientific research, and, in designated Enterprise Zones, for expenditure on construction.

Training

A well-trained workforce is essential for economic growth, and recent technological advances have created a need for an even greater quantity, range and quality of technical and vocational training, both for young people and for adults. The main responsibility for training rests with employers and individuals. The Business & Technician Education Council (BTEC), a privately funded body, deals with the education and training of technicians and their equivalents in the professions and commerce. It designs syllabuses and validates courses offered at colleges of further education and elsewhere in England and Wales; its Scottish counterpart is the Scottish Vocational Education Council.

The first Training and Enterprise Councils have been set up. The Government envisages a network of about 80 such councils in England and Wales. They will seek to evaluate local labour markets with the help of managers and directors of businesses, aiming to create training opportunities suited to local needs. In Scotland, a network of 22 local enterprise companies with a range of functions is being established to work with Scottish Enterprise and Highlands and Islands Enterprise (see p 268).

Employment Training, a programme operating since September 1988, combines a number of other programmes. It is administered by the Training Agency within the Department of Employment. Another programme is Youth Training, which offers a course of planned work experience integrated with off-the-job training for 16- and 17-year-old school-leavers. The Government encourages employers and others to give adult training a high priority and to secure an adequate supply of people with up-to-date skills.

Business and Education

The pilot network of City Technology Colleges, which was announced by the Department of Education and Science in 1986, provides a broadly based secondary education with a strong technological content, and involves employers in the management of the colleges. A similar initiative is planned in Scotland.

The Enterprise and Education Initiative has three main aims: that every young person should have two or more weeks of work experience before leaving school; that each year 10 per cent of teachers should have the opportunity to gain some experience in businesses; and that every trainee teacher should have the opportunity to gain an appreciation of the needs of employers and of the importance of links between schools and employers.

DESIGN, QUALITY, STANDARDS AND AWARDS
Design

Good design is seen as an important factor for improving commercial success. The DTI encourages industry and commerce to pay more attention to good design and to integrate it with other management functions. It organises conferences to underline the importance of design and has encouraged design education at all levels, including business education.

The DTI's main agent for design promotion is the Design Council. The Council has responsibility for the design element of the 'Managing into the 90s' programme. It also offers advice and assistance on design matters through its offices in London, Cardiff, Wolverhampton, Manchester, Belfast and Glasgow. Its activities include giving advice on design problems; the organising of conferences and seminars; providing help for design education; training courses; and the production of a range of publications and videos. The DTI's consultancy initiative on design, operated by the Design Council, offers firms employing up to 500 people 5 to 15 days of subsidised consultancy. The Council provides annual awards for consumer and contract goods, engineering products and components, computer software, medical equipment, and motor vehicles and accessories. The Chartered Society of Designers is the professional body representing the interests of designers and the Design Business Association is the trade association for design consultants.

Quality and Standards

An important aim of government policy is to enhance the quality of British goods and services by encouraging an integrated approach by industry and commerce to quality at all stages of design, production, marketing and delivery to customers.

Through its support for consultancy projects the Government is helping small and medium-sized firms to learn about and apply quality-management techniques based on a national standard which meets international requirements. To increase customer confidence, companies are being encouraged to obtain certification to this standard. This National Accreditation Council for Certification Bodies was set up to assess and officially approve the competence and performance of organisations undertaking such certification. Companies certified by accredited bodies are permitted to use the national quality mark.

The British Standards Institution (BSI), a voluntary body, is responsible for setting national standards. It works with industry and government to produce standards which are of the required quality, relevant to the needs of the market, internationally respected, and suitable for public purchasing and regulatory purposes. With government support, the BSI has become increasingly involved in European and international standards-making; the common standards will contribute to the aim of creating a single internal market in the European Community by 1992. About 30 per cent of the 10,535 British Standards are now identical with international standards. Resource, a joint venture between the BSI and the Government, has been launched to promote collaboration with overseas countries in standards, quality assurance, metrology and testing.

Measurement Standards

The National Physical Laboratory (NPL) provides most of the measurement standards and associated calibration facilities necessary to ensure that measurements in Britain are made on a common basis and to the required accuracy. It maintains links with other national standards laboratories to ensure international compatibility in standards and measurement essential for overseas trade and technological co-operation. The NPL's National Measurement Accreditation Service (NAMAS) provides a focal point for the voluntary accreditation of calibration and testing facilities in Britain. It forms a link between the national standards maintained by the NPL and accredited measurement laboratories. NAMAS-accredited laboratories offer calibration of scientific instruments and provide official certificates in many areas, primarily the physical, chemical and engineering fields. Related NPL functions are research in scientific and technological areas of national importance, such as engineering materials and information technology.

Standards associated with analytical measurement are the responsibility of the Laboratory of the Government Chemist (LGC). International agreement is based on the provision of appropriate standards and the utilisation of approved methods of analysis. These standards and approved methods also form the basis for NAMAS accreditation of laboratories carrying out analytical measurement. In addition, the LGC undertakes research on the development of special materials and chemical sensors, and provides an analytical and advisory service for revenue protection, human and animal health, the environment and consumer safety.

The National Weights and Measures Laboratory is responsible for administering the Weights and Measures Act 1985, which is largely concerned with standards and measuring equipment for use in trade. The Government has accepted most of the recommendations of the committee appointed to review the metrological control of weighing and measuring equipment for commercial use, including the introduction of a self-verification scheme. Similar arrangements are likely to feature in new European Community directives on measuring instruments, which will replace national legislation by 1992, ensuring free circulation of approved equipment within the Community.

Industrial Awards

Recognition of outstanding industrial performance is conferred annually by the Queen's Awards for Export and Technology. The Queen's Awards are granted on the recommendation of the Prime Minister's Advisory Committee, which includes senior representatives from industry, commerce, the trade unions and government departments. All firms incorporated in Britain are eligible to apply, regardless of size and their products or services. Other awards include the Export Awards for Smaller Manufacturers (for firms employing fewer than 200 people) and the MacRobert Award, the major award for engineering in Britain made by the Fellowship of Engineering for successful technological innovation.

REGIONAL INDUSTRIAL DEVELOPMENT

Regional industrial policy operates within a general economic framework designed to encourage enterprise and economic growth in all areas of Britain. In some areas, however, specific additional help is needed, which is provided under the Regional Initiative. Help is focused on the Assisted Areas—Development Areas and Intermediate Areas (see map).

The principal instruments are regional selective assistance, available throughout the Assisted Areas for investment projects undertaken by firms provided they meet certain criteria; and Regional Enterprise Grants, available in Development Areas to support investment and innovation in firms with fewer than 25 employees. The English Industrial Estates Corporation provides industrial and commercial premises in certain parts of the Assisted Areas in England where private sector provision is deficient.

Regional industrial policy is the DTI's responsibility, with similar policies administered in Scotland by the Scottish Office and in Wales by the Welsh Office.

Northern Ireland

The Industrial Development Board, formed in 1982, offers a wide range of incentives for manufacturing and service industry projects which create jobs. Such projects may be eligible for interest relief grants, favourable rental terms for factories, and grants to assist with setting-up costs and research and development costs. The Board can also provide equity and loan capital for new and expanding businesses, assist the development of new high-technology products and processes, and promote joint ventures with overseas companies. The incentives available to manufacturing industry include training grants, exemption from rates (local property taxes) for manufacturing premises, 30 per cent grants for approved energy conservation projects, grants to attract and retain good management, and an advisory service on quality and production methods. A similar range of

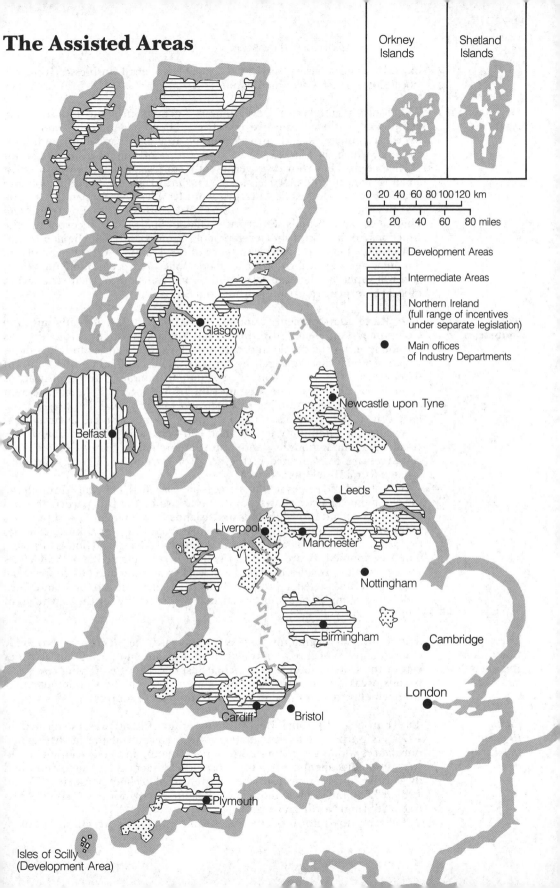

The Assisted Areas

Orkney Islands

Shetland Islands

0 20 40 60 80 100 120 km

0 20 40 60 80 miles

Development Areas

Intermediate Areas

Northern Ireland (full range of incentives under separate legislation)

● Main offices of Industry Departments

Glasgow

Newcastle upon Tyne

Belfast

Leeds

Liverpool

Manchester

Nottingham

Birmingham

Cambridge

Cardiff

Bristol

London

Plymouth

Isles of Scilly (Development Area)

incentives and advisory services is available to small businesses from the Local Enterprise Development Unit.

Development Agencies

The Scottish and Welsh Development Agencies promote industrial development in their respective countries. They encourage investment by overseas companies and provide equity and loan capital for industrial projects, which they are expected to do with a maximum of private sector participation. They provide government factories, and have powers to assist small firms, promote new technology and undertake land reclamation and urban renewal. Under the Enterprise and New Towns (Scotland) Act 1990 two new bodies will be created from April 1991: Scottish Enterprise and Highlands and Islands Enterprise. These bodies will incorporate the functions of the Scottish Development Agency and the Highlands and Islands Development Board with those of the Training Agency in Scotland. The new agencies will co-ordinate major policy and programme initiatives, and will supervise the economic and training functions of the new network of local enterprise companies throughout Scotland.

Rural Industries

The Rural Development Commission is responsible for advising the Government on issues affecting rural England and for promoting its economic and social development. It provides small factories and workshops which are built and managed by English Estates, and administers a grant scheme for the conversion of redundant buildings to industrial or commercial premises. The Commission provides technical, management and financial advice, training facilities and loans to small businesses from local offices. The Commission also supports voluntary bodies in rural areas to encourage community activity and self-help, and provides finance for small-scale rural housing and transport schemes. The Commission's resources are concentrated in the areas of greatest need, which are designated Rural Development Areas.

In Scotland and Wales similar services are provided, generally through the development agencies, but separate bodies cater for two particular rural areas. In Scotland the Highlands and Islands Development Board provides loans and grants for viable projects in manufacturing, agriculture, fisheries and services, makes available training grants and advice, and builds factories. The Development Board for Rural Wales (usually referred to as 'Mid-Wales Development') provides factories, key worker housing and advice for small businesses. It has a general responsibility to promote the economic and social well-being of mid-Wales and a particular responsibility for the new town of Newtown, Powys.

European Community Regional Policy and Aid

The European Community seeks to increase the degree of economic cohesion and to ensure a more balanced distribution of economic activities within the Community. The principal responsibility for helping less prosperous areas remains with national authorities, but the Community may complement schemes through aid from a number of sources.

European Regional Development Fund

The European Regional Development Fund (ERDF) was established in 1975. Its purpose is to contribute to the correction of the main regional imbalances within the Community by participating in the development and structural adjustment of regions whose development is lagging behind and by assisting areas seriously affected by industrial decline. Between 1975 and 1989, £3,650 million was allocated to Britain, mainly for the Assisted Areas (see p 268) and Northern Ireland.

Following the reform of the European Community Structural Funds in

1988, the ERDF, the European Social Fund and the Guidance Section of the European Agricultural Guidance and Guarantee Fund had their total funding allocation doubled for the period 1987–93, effective from 1989. The total budget for the three funds in 1993 will be £10,300 million at 1988 prices.

The emphasis of the ERDF is on 'Objective 1' regions, mostly in southern Europe, but including Northern Ireland. Up to 80 per cent of the ERDF may go to these regions. In 1989 the Commission announced that the allocation for Northern Ireland was to be £550 million at 1989 prices over the period 1989–93. In 1989 the European Commission confirmed its 'Objective 2' (Industrial Areas) list, which included most British and some other areas which gained some eligibility for the first time. Britain's allocation is £1,100 million between 1989 and 1991.

European Investment Bank
The European Investment Bank (EIB) is a self-governing institution set up by the Treaty of Rome with member states of the European Community subscribing to its capital. The Bank's aims are to help to stimulate development in less-favoured regions, to modernise or convert industries, to help to create new activities and to offset structural difficulties affecting certain sectors. The EIB also serves projects of common interest to several member states or the Community as a whole. It has lent nearly £8,000 million since 1973 for projects in Britain, mostly for public works, infrastructure works, and manufacturing projects in the Assisted Areas.

European Coal and Steel Community
The European Coal and Steel Community (ECSC) provides loans and grants to encourage rational distribution of production and a high level of productivity in the coal and steel industries while safeguarding employment and avoiding unfair competition. Areas eligible for aid are coal industry projects, conversion schemes, construction of housing for workers, allowances for redeployed workers, and research, including research of a social or medical nature.

Functioning and Regulation of Markets

While preferring to let markets operate with as little regulatory machinery as possible, the Government recognises that action may be needed to ensure that markets remain open and fair. Therefore the stimulation of competition and the control of practices which are restrictive or anti-competitive are important features of government policy. Responsibilities are exercised by the DTI; by the Office of Fair Trading, a government agency headed by a Director General; and by the Monopolies and Mergers Commission.

Related policies concern consumer and investor protection, the conduct of companies and their officers, insolvency, and the openness of markets for foreign trade and investment. This section concentrates on policies covering domestic markets.

Within the public sector the Government has taken a number of steps to increase the exposure of trading organisations to competition, notably through privatisation (see p 263). Within the DTI the work of the Enterprise and Deregulation Unit is specifically concerned with reducing regulations which inhibit competition, innovation or consumer choice (see p 263). The competition policy division is primarily responsible for competition issues.

COMPETITION POLICY
Competition policy is supported by machinery for scrutinising and regulating monopolies, mergers, anti-competitive practices and restrictive trade practices, and by powers to regulate any structural changes or anti-

competitive practice found to operate against the public interest. The Fair Trading Act 1973 deals with monopolies and mergers; the Restrictive Trade Practices Act 1976 deals with restrictive agreements; the Resale Prices Act 1976 deals with resale price maintenance; the Competition Act 1980 deals with anti-competitive practices; and provisions contained in the Financial Services Act 1986 deal with competition policy considerations relevant to the financial services sector. In 1989 the Government published a White Paper on restrictive trade practices (see p 272).

The Government is taking steps to increase competition in professional services by tackling unjustifiable restrictive practices, including restrictions on fee scales and on advertising. The opticians' monopoly on the dispensing of spectacles and the solicitors' monopoly on conveyancing have been ended. Certain professional groups (for example, accountants, solicitors, veterinary surgeons, stockbrokers, doctors, dentists and surveyors) have eased the restrictions on advertising by their members. Building societies are now allowed to offer a greater range of services, thus bringing more competition into financial services and estate agency. The Courts and Legal Services Bill provides for ending the separation of professional practice between barristers and solicitors with the intention of increasing competition.

Monopolies and Mergers

The Secretary of State for Trade and Industry and the Director General of Fair Trading can refer monopolies for investigation by the Monopolies and Mergers Commission, an independent body. Its members are drawn from a variety of backgrounds, including lawyers, economists, industrialists and trade unionists. The legislation defines a monopoly as a situation where at least a quarter of a particular kind of product or service is supplied by a single person or a group of connected companies or by two or more people acting in a way which prevents, restricts, or distorts competition. The market definition of a monopoly can relate to all of Britain or part of it. If the Commission finds that a monopoly situation has effects which operate against the public interest, the Secretary of State for Trade and Industry has powers to take action by order to remedy or prevent the harm which the Commission considers may exist. Alternatively the Director General may be asked to negotiate undertakings to remedy the adverse effects identified by the Commission.

The Government believes that the market is, in most cases, the best judge of the advantages and disadvantages of mergers. Accordingly, its policy provides for the great majority of mergers which do not pose a threat to competition to be decided by the market. However, it recognises the need to intervene where mergers could lead to a significant reduction in competition or otherwise raise matters of public concern; this is provided for by the Fair Trading Act 1973.

Such a merger is defined as occurring when two or more enterprises are brought under common ownership or control and, as a result, the newly created enterprise supplies at least 25 per cent of any product or services, or an existing 25 per cent market share is increased, or the total value of gross assets to be taken over would exceed £30 million. A merger situation or proposed merger situation may be referred to the Commission by the Secretary of State after he has considered advice from the Director General. If the Commission finds that a merger or proposed merger may be expected to operate against the public interest, the Secretary of State can prevent it or impose conditions on it either by asking the Director General to obtain suitable undertakings from the companies involved to remedy the adverse effects identified, or by making a statutory order. If the merger has already taken place, the Secretary of State can take similar action to undo it. The Fair Trading Act 1973 contains special provisions for newspaper mergers.

The conclusions of the Government's review of mergers policy, published in 1988, reaffirmed that merger reference decisions would continue to be made primarily, though not exclusively, on competition grounds. In evaluating the competitive situation, account would be taken of the extent of competition in the domestic market from overseas sources and of the competitive position of British firms in overseas markets.

The Companies Act 1989 (see p 274) introduced a number of changes aimed at improving merger control procedures: a voluntary procedure for pre-notification of proposed mergers which would, for the majority of cases, permit a prompt clearance; provision for the acceptance of statutory undertakings by the parties concerned so as to obviate the need for a full investigation by the Monopolies and Mergers Commission in certain cases; and the temporary prohibition on dealing in one another's shares by the parties to a merger referred to the Commission.

The Competition Act 1980 gives the Secretary of State powers to refer to the Commission any questions concerning the efficiency and costs of the service provided by, or the possible abuse of a monopoly situation by, certain bodies in the public sector. The results of inquiries are reported to Parliament.

Financial Services   The Financial Services Act 1986 offers greater protection to investors by establishing a new regulatory framework for the industry. The Act was modified by the provisions of the Companies Act 1989, which empower the Securities and Investments Board (SIB) to set out general principles governing the conduct of investment business.

Under the Financial Services Act 1986, the Director General of Fair Trading is required to consider the implications for competition of rules, regulations, guidance and other arrangements and practices of the regulatory bodies, investment exchanges and clearing houses. The Director General is also required to report to the Secretary of State for Trade and Industry where a significant or potentially significant effect on competition has been identified. If the Secretary of State agrees with this view and does not consider that the provisions are necessary for the protection of investors, the Secretary of State may refuse or revoke recognition of the organisation or require it to make alterations to its provisions.

European Community   The objective of the European Community's competition policy is to ensure that there is free and fair competition in trade between member states and that state barriers to trade which the Treaty of Rome seeks to dismantle are not replaced by private barriers which fragment the common market. The competition rules are set out in articles of the Treaty of Rome which are directly applicable to member states and in regulations made under the articles. In most areas of economic activity their enforcement is primarily the responsibility of the European Commission, which has powers to investigate and terminate alleged infringements and to impose fines.

The Treaty prohibits agreements or concerted practices which may affect trade between member states and have as their object, or effect, the prevention, restriction or distortion of competition within the common market. Agreements meeting specified criteria may be exempted from this prohibition and, subject to particular conditions and safeguards, certain categories of agreement are exempted completely. The latter include certain agreements in exclusive distribution and exclusive purchasing, franchising, patent licensing, 'know-how' licensing, co-operative research and development, specialisation, motor vehicle distribution and servicing, and air services within the European Community. The Treaty also prohibits any abuse of a dominant position within the common market or a substantial part of it to the extent that it affects trade between member states.

In 1989 a regulation for the control of mergers at European level was agreed by the European Community and came into force in September 1990. This provides for the European Commission to control mergers having a Community dimension defined in terms of aggregate turnover, turnover of the undertakings within the Community and turnover within different member states. Qualifying mergers must be notified and will be prohibited if the European Commission determines that they create or strengthen a dominant position as a result of which effective competition would be significantly impeded.

Anti-competitive Practices

Subject to limited exemptions, the Director General of Fair Trading can investigate any business practice (whether in the public or private sectors) which may restrict, distort or prevent competition in the production, supply or acquisition of goods or services in Britain. If the Director General concludes that a practice is anti-competitive, an undertaking may be sought from the business responsible for the practice or, in default of such an undertaking, the matter may be referred to the Monopolies and Mergers Commission to establish whether it operates against the public interest. On an adverse finding by the Commission, the Secretary of State has powers to take remedial action.

Restrictive Trade Practices

Under the Restrictive Trade Practices Act 1976, certain kinds of commercial agreements that contain restrictions have to be notified to the Director General of Fair Trading for registration. Broadly, an agreement is registrable if it is between two or more people who are involved in the production or supply of goods or the supply of services in Britain and who accept some limitation on their freedom to make their own decisions about matters such as prices or conditions of sale. Failure to register an agreement within the required period means that the restrictions are void and unenforceable and the parties may be liable to legal proceedings.

Once an agreement has been registered, the Director General is under a general duty to refer it to the Restrictive Practices Court, and the Court must declare the restrictions contrary to the public interest unless the parties can satisfy the Court by reference to criteria laid down in the Act that this is not the case. Restrictions declared contrary to the public interest are void, and the Court can order the parties not to give effect to them or make any similar agreement. In practice, however, the great majority of agreements never reach the Court because, for example, the parties elect to give up the restrictions rather than go to court, or the Secretary of State accepts the Director General's advice that the restrictions are not significant enough to warrant reference to the Court.

In 1989 the Government published a White Paper which set out proposals to amend the existing legislation. These would prohibit agreements which had the effect of preventing, restricting or distorting competition unless an exemption had been granted because they had offsetting economic benefits. The present requirement to register agreements would be abolished. The Director General's powers of investigation would be strengthened. Financial penalties for violation of the prohibition would be proposed by a new tribunal and the scope for private actions extended. Few of the existing exemptions from the Restrictive Trade Practices Act—for example, those for many professional services—would automatically be carried over into the new legislation.

Consumer Protection

The Government believes that consumers are best protected by open and competitive markets offering the widest range of choice in goods and services, backed by adequate information. In addition to laws designed to benefit customers by encouraging effective competition, there are laws designed to ensure that consumers are adequately protected.

The Director General of Fair Trading has a number of duties and powers under existing legislation (including the Fair Trading Act 1973) which provide machinery for the continuous review of consumer affairs. It also allows for action to deal with trading practices which unfairly affect consumers' interests, for action against persistent offenders under existing law, and for the negotiation of self-regulatory codes of practice to raise trading standards. The Director General is responsible for the operation of legislation which regulates consumer credit and hire business and estate agency work. The Director General also has responsibilities under legislation controlling misleading advertisements.

The Food Safety Act 1990 revises and streamlines the large body of food law in Great Britain. It contains new measures to enhance food safety and protect the consumer, including tougher penalties and better enforcement powers. The Medicines Act 1968 provides for the control of medicinal products and certain other substances and articles through a system of licences and certificates. A range of legislation governs the sale and supply of goods and services, among which are the Sale of Goods Act 1979 and the Trade Descriptions Act 1968. The marking and accuracy of quantities are regulated by the Weights and Measures Act 1985. The Consumer Credit Act 1974 provides comprehensive protection for consumers who enter into credit or hire transactions. The Consumer Protection Act 1987 implements a harmonised European Community regime of civil law covering product liability and establishes a general criminal offence of supplying unsafe consumer goods.

The European Community's consumer programme covers a number of important activities, such as health and safety, protection of the consumer's economic interests, promotion of consumer education and strengthening the representation of consumers. The views of British consumer organisations are represented in Europe by the Consumers in the European Community Group (UK).

Consumer Advice and Information

Advice and information on consumer matters is provided to the general public at local level by Citizens Advice Bureaux and the trading standards or consumer protection departments of local authorities, and in some areas by specialist Consumer Advice Centres.

The independent, non-statutory National Consumer Council (and the associated councils for Scotland and Wales), which receives government finance, ensures that the consumer's view is made known to those in government, industry and elsewhere whose decisions affect the consumer's interest. In Northern Ireland the General Consumer Council for Northern Ireland has wide-ranging responsibilities in consumer protection and consumer affairs in general.

Consumer councils for the energy, rail and other nationalised industries and the privatised gas industry investigate questions of concern to the consumer, while some trade associations in industry and commerce have established codes of practice. In addition, several private organisations work to further consumer interests. The largest is the Consumers' Association, funded by the subscriptions of its membership of over one million. The Association conducts an extensive programme of comparative testing of goods and investigation of services; its views and test reports are published in its monthly magazines and other publications. The Association also provides a legal advice service for an additional subscription. Local consumer groups, many belonging to a national federation, also promote consumers' interests and provide information and advice.

Company Law   The formation and conduct of companies are mainly regulated by the Companies Acts 1985 and 1989. 'Incorporation' involves registering with the Registrar of Companies in Cardiff, Edinburgh or Belfast, depending on whether a company's registered office is in England or Wales, Scotland or Northern Ireland. The Acts also deal with capital structure, the rights and duties of directors and members, and the preparation and filing of accounts. Most corporate businesses are 'limited liability' companies. Each company is a legal entity distinct from its members, who are not as such liable for its debts. The liability of members of a limited company is limited to contributing an amount related to their shareholding. In unincorporated businesses, such as sole proprietorships or partnerships, by contrast, individuals are personally liable for any business debts (except where a member of a partnership is a limited liability company).

Companies may be either public or private. A company must satisfy three conditions before it can be a public limited company (plc): it must be limited by shares and have a share capital; it must state in its memorandum of association that it is to be a public limited company; and it must meet specified minimum capital requirements. All other registered companies are, by definition, private companies and, as such, prohibited from offering their shares to the public.

The Companies Act 1989 builds on the Companies Act 1985, itself a consolidation of the Companies Acts 1948–83. The Companies Acts are designed to meet the need for proper regulation in the business environment, securing open markets to meet the needs of enterprise and creating greater safeguards for those wishing to invest in companies or do business with them. They implement European Community directives dealing with company and group accounts and their auditing. They also permit the implementation of changes in policy aimed at reducing unnecessary burdens on business, strengthen existing rules for the disclosure of interest in shares, and refine and strengthen powers to investigate companies.

There are, in addition, the Business Names Act 1985, which regulates the names under which people may carry on business in Great Britain; and the Company Securities (Insider Dealing) Act 1985, which restates the law on insider dealing. Powers to appoint inspectors to investigate possible insider dealing were introduced in the Financial Services Act 1986.

The Insolvency Act 1985 affects both corporate and individual insolvency proceedings. It introduced for England, Wales and Scotland a licensing procedure to ensure the professional competence, integrity and independence of people who act as trustees of bankrupt individuals, or as liquidators, receivers or administrators of insolvent companies. Substantially changing the Companies Act 1985, the Act amended and supplemented the legislation relating to the winding-up of limited companies and the appointment of receivers in England, Wales and Scotland. Subsequently these parts were consolidated with the Insolvency Act 1985 into the Insolvency Act 1986 and the Company Directors Disqualification Act 1986.

To improve the investigation and prosecution of fraud, a Serious Fraud

Office has been set up to collaborate with police work on fraud cases; restrictions on the use of documentary evidence in court cases have been relaxed; and court procedures have been streamlined.

Industrial and Intellectual Property

There is a substantial body of legislation designed to secure the rights of the originators of inventions, new industrial designs and trade marks. These matters are administered by the Patent Office, which includes the Design Registry and the Trade Marks Registry. The Patent Office is a division of the DTI. Protection is also available under the European Patent Convention and the Patent Co-operation Treaty, and benefits may be claimed in other countries by virtue of the International Convention for the Protection of Industrial Property.

The Government is concerned to encourage innovation by providing a more adequate legal and administrative system for the protection of the ownership of ideas by means of patents, registered designs, trade marks and copyright. Measures taken in recent years include a sharp increase in penalties for making and trading in pirate sound and film recordings (including video); the extension of copyright protection to owners of computer software; the widening of the law on trade marks to embrace services; and the introduction of powers for customs authorities to prevent the entry of counterfeit goods. Further fundamental changes were introduced in the Copyright, Designs and Patents Act 1988. It included provisions to combat the unauthorised reproduction of copyright material, introduce a new form of protection for designs, establish a framework of civil law for the protection of performers, and make the arrangements for litigation regarding patents cheaper and simpler.

In September 1990 the Government published a White Paper which proposed changes designed to modernise and simplify existing trade marks law, and to make trade mark registration and protection easier.

Research and Innovation

Britain was a pioneer in both computing and telecommunications and remains among the leading nations in the production of micro- and mini-computers as well as in the provision of computing services and systems.

British firms are also in the forefront of technical innovation in the aerospace industry, especially in the application of electronics. In the pharmaceuticals sector, the three best-selling drugs in the world in 1987 were discovered and produced in British laboratories. In medical technology British companies and hospitals have been among the leaders in applying techniques such as magnetic resonance imaging and laser surgery.

Biotechnology has gained a new impetus from research achievements in genetic engineering and cell fusion. The DTI and other government bodies are encouraging the exploitation of new developments. A Biotechnology Unit at the Laboratory of the Government Chemist is the focus for government co-operation with industry.

Research Policy

Priorities in science and technology policy are decided by ministers collectively under the leadership of the Prime Minister. Ministers are assisted by the Advisory Council on Science and Technology (ACOST), which was set up in 1987 and maintains a secretariat in the Cabinet Office. In general, the Government's view is that research and development with obvious commercial application should be the responsibility of industry. The Government funds basic and strategic research to provide the foundations for future exploitation. It favours a selective approach to funding based primarily on the scientific quality of research, but it is for industry to identify important areas and decide what should be exploited.

Research and Development Expenditure

Industrial expenditure on research and development in 1988 was £6,861 million, of which £1,133 million came from government sources, £830 million from overseas and £4,898 million from other sources (mostly from private sector companies themselves). The main areas of expenditure were electronics (£2,064 million), chemicals (£1,574 million), aerospace (£814 million), motor vehicles (£468 million) and mechanical engineering (£301 million).

Research and Technology Initiative

Following the DTI's review of its policies in 1988, it has concentrated on encouraging collaborative research projects, both in Britain and internationally, and on assisting the transfer of technology, especially between the academic world and industry. In consequence it has ended most of its schemes of support to single companies, although it is continuing to provide encouragement for small high-technology companies through the Small Firms Merit Award for Research and Technology (SMART) competition, and for very small companies in the Development Areas (see map, p 267). The policy is focused on situations in which research is necessary before commercial applications can be developed or in which the benefits of research are likely to be widespread.

Collaborative Research

In order to maximise the strengths of industries and researchers, the DTI encourages British companies to participate in technological collaboration with other firms and research communities. There are four main ways in which collaborative research is encouraged and supported:

1. The LINK programme encourages companies to undertake joint research with higher education institutions and research councils. The research is pre-competitive but industrially relevant.

2. Eureka is a scheme to encourage European co-operation in the development and production of high-technology products with global sales potential, and has the support of 19 European governments and the European Commission. British companies and research institutions are full participants in 81 of the 297 projects announced and have expressed an interest in others.

3. National collaborative research programmes promote longer-term industrially led projects between British companies in advanced technologies. The role of the DTI is to help establish the collaborative links both among firms and between firms and the research community at the pre-competitive stage. The DTI is currently running collaborative programmes in advanced robotics, computer-aided engineering, gallium arsenide (a semi-conductor material with the potential to provide very fast microelectronic operations), and high temperature superconductivity (electrical conduction with zero resistance).

4. General industrial collaborative projects have a variety of roles. Support is given to research and technology organisations serving the research and development needs of industries in which small and medium-sized firms often predominate. Some projects encourage the adoption of technology originating in the science base, particularly in the Government's research establishments. Others are collaborative projects involving only industrial participants in joint research for companies with similar interests.

Within the context of these policies the Government has considered the next stage in a national collaborative research programme in information technology. The Government has continued with its support for ESPRIT (European Strategic Programme of Research into Information Technology), and under ESPRIT II (1988–92) there will be a British contribution through the Community budget of some £200 million. A new programme of support by the Community for information technology will entail a further contribution by Britain of some £180 million.

The Government also recognises that some resources should be devoted to national programmes complementary to ESPRIT. The largest of these is the Information Advanced Technology Programme, which is funded jointly by the DTI and the Science and Engineering Research Council, which are providing £34 million and approximately £27 million respectively in the period 1988-92. British companies are also encouraged to participate in European Community research and development programmes.

Technology Transfer

The DTI aims to encourage technology transfer, particularly in three areas: links between industry and educational institutions, research councils and government research establishments; the access of small firms to sources of technology, especially in those localities where technology transfer networks are least developed; and the diffusion of new technologies likely to have pervasive applications but in novel and unfamiliar ways, often requiring changes in other aspects of existing products and processes.

The range of the DTI's programmes includes: the establishment of regional technology centres; programmes to promote and facilitate widespread adoption of modern manufacturing techniques and technologies and of information technology; and access to technical information from overseas.

DTI Research Establishments

The Department's research establishments are the National Physical Laboratory (see p 265), the National Engineering Laboratory (research and development in mechanical engineering, including manufacturing systems and robotics, materials applications, thermodynamics and fluid power systems), the Warren Spring Laboratory (environmental process engineering) and the Laboratory of the Government Chemist (see p 265).

Following a review of the structure of the four establishments, it was announced in 1988 that they should concentrate on research required by the Government rather than on industrially relevant research and development. In the case of the National Engineering Laboratory, where roughly three-quarters of the work is for the benefit of industry, the Government's view is that ownership should eventually be transferred to the private sector. The Warren Spring Laboratory and the Laboratory of the Government Chemist have become executive agencies within the public sector in order to increase their flexibility and responsibility. The other laboratories are also to become executive agencies.

British Technology Group

British Technology Group (BTG) promotes the development of new technology into commercial products, particularly where the technology originates from public sector sources, such as universities, polytechnics, research councils and government research establishments. It offers to take responsibility for protecting and licensing inventions from these sources, provides funds for development, seeks licensees and negotiates licence agreements with industry.

As part of its technology transfer role, BTG also provides finance to British industry to encourage innovation, most commonly through equity or project finance. Project finance offers companies up to 50 per cent of their development costs. BTG also helps companies with licensing exploitation of their developed inventions overseas. BTG approaches transactions on a commercial basis and expects to recover its investment by means of a percentage levy on sales of the resulting product or process. In cases where a particular technology requires the setting up of a new company, BTG can perform a catalytic role in launching start-up companies.

BTG also has a role in assisting technology transfer between companies. It assesses the patent position and commercial potential of companies' proprietary technology and licenses this technology to other companies worldwide. BTG currently has a portfolio of over 7,000 British patents and patent applications worldwide and some 500 licence agreements with more than 100 industrial firms in Britain and overseas. It has 600 development projects at universities and other public sector institutions, and projects with industrial companies. Its licensing activities provide most of its income, which in 1989–90 was just over £25 million.

Some of the major technical achievements which it has exploited or supported are cephalosporin antibiotics, pyrethin analogues, cancellous bone pins, cholesterol assays, dental silicate cement and magnetic resonance imaging.

13 Manufacturing Industry

Introduction

Manufacturing accounted for 22 per cent of gross domestic product (GDP) in 1989 and for about one-fifth of the workforce in employment. Around 80 per cent of visible exports consisted of manufactured or semi-manufactured goods. Almost all manufacturing is carried out by private businesses, the Government having returned manufacturing enterprises in state ownership to the private sector in the 1980s.

Structure

Table 13.1 shows the number of businesses in manufacturing in 1988. Of those employing over 1,000 people, some 24 per cent were engaged in all kinds of engineering, 23 per cent in motor vehicle and other transport equipment manufacturing and just over 16 per cent in the food, drink and tobacco industries. The ten largest manufacturing concerns (by £ million turnover in the latest financial year) are Imperial Chemical Industries (11,699), BAT Industries (11,358), Hanson Trust (7,396), Unilever (7,364), Grand Metropolitan (6,029), Ford Motor Company (5,936), British Aerospace (5,639), General Electric Company (5,553), British Steel (4,906) and Allied Lyons (4,504).

Table 13.1: Manufacturing—Size of Businesses by Turnover and Employment

Annual turnover (£'000)	Number of businesses[a] 1988–89	Employment size	Number of businesses[a] 1988–89	Employment[b]
23–50[c]	36,100	1–9	103,573	295,290
51–100	26,524	10–19	13,864	197,613
101–250	32,346	20–49	15,464	476,404
251–500	19,305	50–99	6,234	429,637
501–1,000	13,754	100–199	3,631	501,469
1,001–5,000	16,069	200–499	2,456	751,287
over 5,000	6,343	500–999	806	555,810
		1,000 and over	577	1,664,852
Total	150,441	Total	146,605	4,872,362

Source: *Size Analysis of United Kingdom Businesses 1990. Business Monitor PA 1003.*
[a]Defined as legal units, which includes companies, public corporations, partnerships, sole proprietors, general government and non-profit-making bodies.
[b]Employment figures are mainly derived from Central Statistical Office inquiries and from value added tax (VAT) sources and relate generally to 1988.
[c]The number of businesses analysed by turnover excludes 19,578 units with turnover up to £22,100, the threshold for filing compulsory VAT returns during the 12 months ended spring 1989.

Growth

Manufacturing output, output per head and profitability have all risen from the low point of the recession of 1980-81. In 1989 output was 27·2 per cent higher than in 1983 (see Table 13.2). Output per head increased by about 20 per cent between 1985 and 1989—a better record than that of the other major industrialised economies. Net manufacturing profitability, in terms of the rate of return on capital employed, rose steadily in the 1980s. The index of output finally exceeded its 1979 level in 1987 and reached 119·3 in 1989 (1985=100). Part of the improvement in productivity reflects the shedding of labour in the early 1980s which firms undertook in response to the recession. Manufacturing employment in Great Britain fell from 7·1 million in 1979 to 5·8 million in 1982; in 1989 it was 5·1 million. Productivity rose until the late 1980s and has since stabilised.

Table 13.2: Indices of Manufacturing Output (1985 = 100)

	Share of output 1985 (weight per 1,000)	1983	1988	1989
Metal manufacturing	38	94·2	122·0	125·0
Other minerals and mineral products	50	97·1	117·4	119·8
Chemicals and man-made fibres	104	90·9	113·6	118·9
Other metal goods	53	96·5	111·7	112·6
Mechanical engineering	124	94·3	105·6	110·3
Electrical and instrument engineering	142	84·4	117·7	126·7
Motor vehicles and parts	55	95·2	119·7	125·2
Aerospace and other transport equipment	53	104·0	110·3	131·8
Food, drink and tobacco	131	99·5	105·6	106·0
Textiles	31	93·4	102·2	97·5
Clothing, footwear and leather	37	91·9	102·4	100·2
Paper, printing and publishing	102	93·4	125·0	131·8
Other manufacturing	80	93·8	128·1	132·5
Total	1,000	93·8	114·3	119·3

Source: Central Statistical Office.

The recovery since 1981 has been most notable in chemicals and electrical and instrument engineering, both in terms of output and productivity. Productivity has also grown sharply in metal manufacturing (see Table 13.3), where there has been extensive reorganisation and modernisation.

Investment in manufacturing tends to be cyclical and 1983 saw the beginning of an upturn following a decline after 1979. In terms of constant (1985) prices, fixed investment exceeded its 1979 level to reach £10,271 million in 1988 and rose a further 5 per cent in 1989. Total fixed capital expenditure in manufacturing (excluding leased assets) at current prices was

£12,426 million in 1989, comprising £10,223 million in plant and machinery, £1,595 million in new building work and £608 million in vehicles. Investment by sector is shown in Table 13.3. In addition, assets worth a further £1,620 million were leased to manufacturers by the financial community.

The underlying level of exports of manufactured goods has risen in volume terms. On the basis of overseas trade statistics, the index stood at 131·9 in 1989 (1985=100). This represented a considerable recovery from 1981. Manufacturing exports rose to nearly £75,500 million in 1989, on an industry basis, compared with £40,000 million in 1983 and £34,800 million in 1980, at current prices. Manufacturing exports accounted for 30 per cent of total sales in 1989.

Among the leading exports in 1989 were motor vehicles and other transport equipment (£14,622 million), chemicals and man-made fibres (£13,088 million), electrical and electronic engineering products (£12,638 million), mechanical engineering and metal goods (£11,920 million), aerospace products (£7,114 million), and metal manufacturing and mineral products (£6,632 million).

Import volumes rose strongly in the 1980s, with the index reaching 151·3 in 1989 (1985=100). Imports were valued at £92,300 million in 1989. Manufacturing imports accounted for about 37 per cent of home demand in 1989.

High-technology Industries

The high-technology manufacturing industries in Britain divide into the broad categories of electrical, electronic and instrument engineering, chemicals and aerospace. The definition is arrived at primarily by selecting industries with the highest levels of research and development spending in relation to their gross output. In some cases assessments of the ratio of scientific and technical staff to other staff are also counted.

Most of the electrical and electronic industries—office machinery, electronic data-processing equipment, basic electrical equipment, telecommunications equipment, electric instruments and control systems, radio and electronic capital goods, and components—are included. Within instrument engineering, precision equipment for measuring and checking, and medical, optical, photographic and filming equipment are included. In chemicals the definition covers specialised organics, plastics materials, synthetic resins, synthetic rubbers and pharmaceuticals. Aerospace production as a whole is defined as high-technology. The high-technology industries have shown strong growth in recent years, with levels of output, productivity and exports well above the average for manufacturing.

Take-up of Advanced Technology

Microelectronics are increasingly used in production processes in Britain. Of 20,400 engineering sites surveyed in 1989, 60 per cent used computers for some aspect of manufacturing management. Some 48 per cent of 12,300 design sites used mechanical design, while 25 per cent of 14,900 sites with machine tools used Computer Aided Design (CAD). About 95,000 computers were installed in the engineering sector in 1989, valued at £2,200 million, and firms reported that new expenditure on computer equipment was planned to reach £1,100 million during 1990. Many British concerns are also making use of advanced materials, such as carbon fibre composites in the aerospace industry, new types of plastics in the automotive sector and high-fibre, cholesterol-free protein in food production.

In the traditional branches of heavy industry, re-equipment and rationalisation have led to significant improvements in productivity in recent years. For example, British Steel's modernisation of its facilities at Port Talbot in south Wales and elsewhere helped the company to raise labour productivity levels above those of its main international competitors. The widespread adoption of Advanced Manufacturing Techniques (AMT) has enabled the motor vehicle industry to become more efficient. This sector spent almost twice as much on research and development in 1988 as in 1983, as did the chemicals industry.

The Government provides financial assistance to companies and research organisations seeking to develop and improve the technologies needed by industry. It has, for example, made available resources to encourage and assist companies to take advantage of the emerging technologies of multi-vendor computer communications.

The Sectors of Manufacturing

The relative sizes of the various branches of manufacturing are shown in the first columns of Tables 13.2 and 13.3. Table 13.3 also shows employment, productivity and investment levels in each sector. A more detailed description of the main branches is given in the sections that follow. The statistics in Tables 13.4–13.12 are supplied by the Department of Trade and Industry and the Central Statistical Office. Sales figures given are for the sale of the principal products of each industry, so that they exclude, for example, any non-electrical goods produced by firms classified as part of the electronics industry. Where reference is made in the text to the total sales of an industry, the total includes principal products, merchanted goods, the sale of waste products, services and work done. For this reason, total sales figures are generally higher than those given for principal products. In all cases, the figures given are for the most recent year available.

Mineral and Metal Products
Iron and Steel Products

Britain is the world's tenth largest steel-producing nation. British producers delivered 16·9 million tonnes of finished steel in 1989, of which 65 per cent was sold on the home market and the remainder exported. Britain's steel industry has operated a balance of payments surplus continuously since 1983. The major areas of steel production are Wales, Scotland and northern England, and substantial primary production of steel takes place in the Midlands.

British Steel plc is the fourth largest steel company in the Western world and accounts for some 76 per cent of crude steel production in Britain. British Steel's output is based on flat products, plate, heavy sections, tubes and stainless items. Its products are used principally in the packaging, construction, automotive, engineering, transport, metal goods and energy industries for many different applications.

Some 40 other steel-producing firms, represented by the British Independent Steel Producers' Association, are engaged in the manufacture of engineering and other special steels, wire rod and wire products, reinforcements for use in the construction industry, and other more specialised goods. They are responsible for about 40 per cent by value of total British steel deliveries.

The industry has achieved significant advances in operational and cost efficiency over the past decade as a result of extensive rationalisation, investment in modern plant and continuous improvement of operating performance. At the same time, product ranges have been extended and product quality enhanced.

Table 13.3: Output, Employment, Productivity and Investment in Manufacturing

	Net output (£ million) 1988	Employment[a] June 1989 ('000)	Index of employment 1989 (1985=100)	Index of output per head 1989 (1985=100)	Gross domestic fixed capital formation (£ million) 1989
Metal manufacturing	3,694	} 346	74.0	168.6	3,799
Other minerals and mineral products	5,122		89.0	134.5	
Chemicals and man-made fibres	9,932	322	95.6	124.4	
Other metal goods	4,866	336	104.3	108.0	
Mechanical engineering	10,235	790	106.1	103.9	
Electrical and instrument engineering	12,830	735	95.6	132.6	4,098
Motor vehicles and parts	5,089	268	99.2	126.2	
Aerospace and other transport equipment	4,729	219	80.9	162.9	
Food, drink and tobacco	10,913	553	97.9	108.3	
Textiles	2,765	} 529	93.7	104.0	4,529
Clothing, footwear and leather	3,055		101.6	98.6	
Paper, printing and publishing	9,725	492	104.2	126.5	
Other manufacturing	8,241	540	116.7	113.6	
Total	91,196	5,129	99.3	120.1	12,426

Source: Central Statistical Office and *Employment Gazette*.
[a]Employees in employment in Great Britain.

Table 13.4: Mineral and Metal Products

	Sales[a] (£ million) 1988	Exports (£ million) 1989	Imports (£ million) 1989
Metal manufacturing	7,929	5,255	6,426
of which: iron and steel products	5,659	2,790	2,649
non-ferrous metals	2,270	2,465	3,777
Non-metallic mineral products	7,453	1,377	1,587
of which: glass and glassware	1,302	358	638
ceramic and heat-resistant goods	1,395	496	364

[a]Sales and trade figures are not suitable for purposes of comparison, since they are given for different years.

Non-ferrous Metals

Output of non-ferrous metals and their alloys in 1989 included primary aluminium, of which nearly 526,000 tonnes were delivered, and secondary aluminium, of which 107,000 tonnes were delivered. Some 102,500 tonnes of copper and copper alloy semi-manufactures were exported. Primary metal production relies mainly on imported ores, concentrates and partially refined metal. Secondary and recycled metal plays an important part in raw material supply.

Britain is a major producer of specialised alloys for high-technology requirements in the aerospace, electronic, petrochemical, and nuclear and other fuel industries. Titanium and titanium alloys are produced and used in aircraft production, power generation and North Sea oil production. Nickel alloys are produced, notably for use in aero-engines operating in high temperature environments.

Nearly half of the industry is situated in the Midlands and Wales. In recent years considerable progress has been made in the development of 'superplastic' alloys, which are more ductile and elastic than conventional alloys. Aluminium lithium is a relatively new alloy which has been developed by British Alcan Aluminium and is used in aircraft. It is lighter, stronger and stiffer than normal aluminium.

Ceramics

The ceramics industry comprises manufacturers of a wide range of clay products, including domestic pottery, sanitaryware and tiles, and clay pipes used in the building trade. Total sales of ceramic goods in 1989 were £1,207 million. The domestic pottery industry is an important element within the group. It includes the manufacture of china, earthenware and stoneware, and accounts for over 30 per cent of the industry's output. Production of tableware is concentrated in Stoke-on-Trent. Britain is the world's leading manufacturer of fine bone china, much of which is exported.

Research is being conducted into ceramics for use in housebuilding and diesel and jet engines. Important industrial ceramics invented in Britain include silicon carbides developed by the United Kingdom Atomic Energy Authority and sialons developed at the University of Newcastle upon Tyne.

Other Mineral Products

Glass-reinforced cement composites for the construction industry were invented in Britain in the early 1970s and are manufactured under licence in over 40 countries.

British companies manufactured 5,800 types of bottle and jar in 1989, forming a large part of the glass industry. They are major suppliers to the food, drink and pharmaceutical industries. Another major sector is devoted to the manufacture of flat glass in its various forms, chiefly by the float glass process developed in Britain by Pilkington Brothers and licensed to glassmakers throughout the world. Pilkington has also developed an energy-saving window glass which reflects room heat without impairing visibility. Sales of flat glass principal products amounted to £751 million in 1989. Britain is the world's biggest exporter of china clay (kaolin). In 1989 some 3·1 million tonnes, valued at £211 million, were sold overseas. The main company involved is English China Clays.

Chemicals and Man-made Fibres

Britain's chemicals industry is the third largest in Western Europe and the fifth largest in the Western world. Nearly half of its production of principal products is exported, and in 1989 it had a trade surplus of more than £2,100 million. One company, Imperial Chemical Industries (ICI), accounts for a substantial part of the industry's production and is the fourth largest chemicals company in the world. Traditionally Britain has been a major producer of basic industrial chemicals, such as inorganic and basic organic chemicals, plastics and fertilisers. Sales of the principal fertiliser products reached £635 million in 1989. Although these sectors still make up about 38 per cent of the industry's output, the most rapid growth in recent years has been in the production of speciality and 'problem-solving' chemicals, especially pharmaceuticals, pesticides and cosmetics. The value of chemicals produced increased by 4·4 per cent between 1988 and 1989.

Table 13.5: Chemicals and Man-made Fibres

	Sales[a] (£ million) 1988	Exports (£ million) 1989	Imports (£ million) 1989
Chemicals and man-made fibres	25,423	13,088	10,969
of which: basic industrial chemicals	10,230	6,299	6,322
specialised industrial products	4,359	2,078	1,292
pharmaceuticals	4,779	2,142	1,134
soap and toilet preparations	2,531	663	426

[a]See Table 13.4, footnote a.

Chemicals

Sales of the principal products of organic chemicals amounted to £4,000 million in 1989 and those of miscellaneous chemicals for industrial use were in excess of £2,800 million; the surplus on overseas trade in the latter sector was nearly £460 million.

Notable recent British discoveries and developments in agricultural chemicals include pyrethroid insecticides, ICI's diquat and paraquat herbicides, systemic fungicides and aphicides, genetically engineered microbial pesticides and methods of encouraging natural parasites to attack common pests in horticulture. A substantial proportion of world research and development in agrochemicals is conducted in Britain.

Exports of cosmetics, toiletries and perfumery in 1989 were £480 million, compared with imports of £317 million. The home market amounted to about £1,500 million.

A high proportion of inorganic chemicals production consists of relatively simple bulk chemicals, such as sulphuric acid and metallic and non-metallic oxides, serving as basic materials for industry. The most important products sold in the organic chemicals range (by weight) are ethylene (1·5 million tonnes produced in 1989), benzene (626,700 tonnes) and propylene (440,500 tonnes).

Plastics

About one-third of semi-manufactured plastics production is exported. Expansion in recent years has mainly been in thermoplastic materials, of which the most important are polyethylene, polyvinyl chloride, polystyrene and polypropylene. Total sales of plastics packaging products, valued at just over £2,000 million in 1989, were largely accounted for by the home market. Output rose by nearly 45 per cent between 1985 and 1989. A new group of plastics materials reinforced with carbon fibres is also in commercial production. They have up to three times the strength but are only 20 per cent of the weight of steel, and are being increasingly used in aircraft and vehicle manufacture. ICI has produced the world's first biodegradable thermoplastic, Biopol, which has so far been used as a slow release agent for drugs and herbicides, as well as for making bottles and films that can be disposed of without polluting the environment. Synthetic rubbers in large-scale production include butadiene-based neoprene for tyres, high-styrene for shoe soles and flooring, and oil-resistant nitrile rubbers.

With the development of multi-layer technology, plastics are fast replacing traditional packaging materials such as paper, tin and glass.

Specialised products in the paint industry include new ranges of synthetic resins and pigments, powder coatings, non-drip and quick-drying paints and paints needing only one top coat. Two significant recent innovations have been solid emulsion paint and a temporary water-based finish, which can be removed easily by chemical treatment, for vehicle bodies and road markings. ICI is the world's largest paint manufacturer. Sales of the principal paint and varnish products were nearly £1,600 million in 1989.

Pharmaceuticals

The pharmaceutical industry in Britain includes some of the world's largest multi-national research-intensive manufacturers, as well as middle-sized and smaller specialist companies, with a total gross output in 1989 of around £6,000 million. Pharmaceutical exports were valued at £2,142 million; the industry's trade surplus of £955 million was the second largest of all manufacturing sectors. Employing over 70,000 people directly, it supports employment for 250,000 others in related activities.

The pharmaceutical industry invested more than £800 million in research and development in 1989. This sum amounts to more than 10 per cent of all manufacturing industry's research and development in Britain, representing about 8 per cent of total world expenditure on medicines research. Progress in pharmaceutical research has helped to reduce dramatically the impact of former scourges such as polio, tuberculosis, diphtheria and measles. Other diseases have proved harder to conquer, but British pharmaceutical laboratories continue to search for innovative medicines to treat the whole range of illness and disability.

British firms make 11 of the world's 50 best-selling medicines. Glaxo's ulcer treatment Zantac and ICI's beta-blocker Tenormin, for the treatment of high blood pressure, are respectively the first and fifth best-selling medicines in the world. The United States subsidiary of Britain's Wellcome Foundation developed Retrovir (also called Zidovudine), the first treatment for HIV infection to gain government approval, as well as Zovirax, the first routine treatment for the herpes group of viruses. Other recent major developments pioneered in Britain are semi-synthetic penicillins and cephalosporins, both powerful antibiotics, and new treatments for asthma, arthritis and coronary heart disease.

In biotechnology, Britain has made major advances in the development of human insulin, genetically-engineered vaccines and the production of antibiotics by fermentation. The British company Celltech was the first licensed by the United States Food and Drug Authority for the large-scale production of monoclonal antibodies, proteins which can seek out a particular substance. They are used to diagnose diseases, identify different blood types and can be used in the treatment of a range of conditions, including cancer.

Britain leads in the development of molecular graphics, which contribute to the rational design of new and improved medicines through a computer-aided technique for analysing the structures of complicated organic molecules on a visual display unit.

Fibres

The main types of man-made fibre are still those first de-veloped—regenerated cellulosic fibres such as viscose and the major syn-thetic fibres such as nylon polyamide, polyester and acrylics. Extensive research continues to produce a wide variety of innovative products with characteristics designed to meet market needs, such as anti-static and flame-retardant fibres. More specialist products include the aramids (with very high thermal stability and strength), elastanes (giving very high stretch and recovery), melded fabrics (produced without the need for knitting or weaving), and carbon fibres (originally developed for the aerospace industry but now finding applications in other areas, such as the motor vehicle and sports goods industries).

Metal Goods and Mechanical Engineering

Since much of the production of this industry is of capital equipment, it suffered particularly during the recession which began in 1979. However, from 1984 there was a recovery in the industry. Exports of mechanical engineering machinery amounted to about 14 per cent of all visible exports in 1989.

Of particular importance are fabricated steel products, total sales of which reached £2,500 million in 1989. Output includes pressure vessels, heat exchangers and storage tanks for chemical and oil-refining (process) plant, steam-raising boilers (including those of high capacity for power stations), nuclear reactors, water and sewage treatment plant, and fabricated steelwork for bridges, buildings and industrial installations. Sales of boilers and process plant fabrications in 1989 were nearly £2,000 million.

Britain is among the Western world's largest producers of tractors, which make up over three-quarters of the country's total output of agricultural equipment. Sales of the principal products of the tractor industry were more than £1,200 million in 1989, of which about £780 million was accounted for by overseas sales. Recent technical innovations include computer-controlled tractors, a highly efficient pesticide sprayer and combined mower/conditioners that significantly reduce the drying time for grass. Much of the new machinery is designed for use in a variety of conditions to meet the needs of overseas farmers. The Royal International Agricultural Exhibition, held annually near Coventry, has a specialised tropical machinery centre, where demonstrations of such machinery are given.

Almost all of Britain's machine tools are purchased by the engineering, vehicles and metal goods industries. The most commonly used metal-cutting machine tools are milling, grinding and turning machines. The manufacture of computerised, numerically-controlled machine tools and the adoption of flexible manufacturing systems have become increasingly important. Total

Table 13.6: Mechanical Engineering and Metal Goods

	Sales[a] (£ million) 1988	Exports (£ million) 1989	Imports (£ million) 1989
Mechanical engineering	23,425	10,285	10,264
of which: industrial plant and steelwork	3,285	507	499
agricultural machinery and tractors	1,523	973	676
machine tools	2,002	814	1,035
machinery for process industries and non-metallic materials working	2,911	2,164	2,547
mining, construction and mechanical handling equipment	3,977	1,861	1,692
Other metal goods	11,012	1,635	2,277

[a]See Table 13.4, footnote a.

sales of metal-working machine tools doubled between 1984 and 1989, when they reached about £1,400 million, and exports rose by two-thirds over the same period.

In 1989, most sales of textile machinery were to export markets. Recent British innovations include computerised colour matching and weave simulation, friction spinning, high-speed computer-controlled knitting machines and electronic jacquard attachments for weaving looms.

Overseas sales of mining machinery and tunnelling equipment are substantial, while exports of construction equipment amounted to £1,086 million in 1989 (almost three-quarters of output). J. C. Bamford Ltd is the world's first and second largest manufacturer of backhoe loaders and telescopic handlers respectively. It exports over 60 per cent of its output. The British mining equipment industry is very strong, especially in the production of coal-cutting and road-heading (shearing) equipment, hydraulic roof supports, conveying equipment, flameproof transformers, switchgear, and subsurface transport equipment and control systems. The main products of the mechanical handling equipment industry are cranes and transporters, lifting devices, escalators, conveyors, powered industrial trucks and air bridges. Electronically controlled and automatic handling systems are also produced. Britain is an important producer of other machinery such as industrial engines, pumps, valves and compressors, and pneumatic and hydraulic equipment.

Despite an overall decline in the castings industry, some foundries have been investing in new melting, moulding and quality control equipment. Cosworth Engineering, for example, has developed a high-quality aluminium casting process and uses it to produce cylinder heads in quantity for Mercedes-Benz and Ford cars.

Electrical, Electronic and Instrument Engineering

Output by this group of industries has grown steadily since 1982. Sales of the principal products of basic electrical equipment amounted to about £3,000 million in 1989. Total sales of electronic data-processing equipment rose by 82 per cent between 1985 and 1989, reaching more than £7,400 million.

Computers   The computer sector, which has grown strongly over the past five years, produces an extensive range of computer systems, central processors and peripheral equipment. They range from large computers for large-scale data-processing and scientific work to mini- and microcomputers for use in control and automation systems and for home, educational and office use. Britain is one of the top three markets in Western Europe for data-processing equipment; expenditure on data-processing as a proportion of GDP is the highest in Western Europe. Reflecting the importance of Britain as a market, many of the leading overseas manufacturers of data-processing equipment—for example, IBM, Unisys, Compaq and Seiko—have established manufacturing plants in Britain. Other companies have concentrated on developing new products for specialised markets. For example, the transputer, produced by Inmos, is effectively a computer on a single chip, which can be combined with hundreds of others in parallel to form a machine as powerful as existing 'supercomputers' but at less than a quarter of their price. British firms and research organisations, with government support, are also heavily involved in the development and application of the new family of 'three-five' semiconductor materials, such as gallium arsenide, which are already used in a number of microwave devices, and which will ultimately enable much faster computers to be produced.

Table 13.7: Electrical, Electronic and Instrument Engineering

	Sales[a] (£ million) 1988	Exports (£ million) 1989	Imports (£ million) 1989
Data-processing equipment	5,229	5,356	6,714
Basic electrical equipment	2,692	1,505	1,510
Communications equipment	1,970	467	712
Electrical instruments and control systems	1,588	n.a	n.a.
Radio and electronic capital goods	3,189	1,639	1,482
Electronic components	2,816	2,455	3,565
Consumer electrical and electronic goods	2,024	1,216	2,615
Instrument engineering	2,953	n.a	n.a

[a]See Table 13.4, footnote a.
n.a. = not available.

Communications Equipment   The main communications products are switching and transmission equipment, telephones and terminals for telex, facsimile and teletext. British Telecom (BT) is the main customer for network equipment and carries out research and development work in co-operation with suppliers. Mercury Communications is licensed to compete with BT in the provision of network services, while the market for terminals and telephones has been fully liberalised. Innovative work is being particularly stimulated by the expansion of cable television and the growth in value added network services. There has been rapid expansion in the market for cellular telephones since 1984.

One important part of the industry produces transmission equipment and cables for telecommunications and information networks and other purposes. Its products include submarine and high-specification data-carrying cables. BT, supported by a technically advanced cable industry, has led the way in the development of optical fibre communications systems. BT has also paved the way for simpler and cheaper optical cables by laying the first non-repeatered cable, over 100 km (62 miles) long, and developing the first all-optical repeater. Well over half of the world's undersea communications cables (of all types) have been made and laid by another British company, STC Submarine Systems, which, with its United States and French partners, completed the laying of the first transatlantic optical fibre cable, TAT 8, in 1988. Britain also has a world lead in the transmission of computerised data along telephone lines for reproduction on television screens. Sales of telegraph and telephone apparatus and equipment by British firms more than doubled between 1979 and 1989.

Another expanding sector of the industry is that covering the manufacture of radio communications equipment, radar, radio and sonar navigational aids for ships and aircraft, thermal imaging systems, alarms and signalling equipment, public broadcasting equipment and other capital goods. Radar was invented in Britain and British firms are still in the forefront of technical advances. Racal Avionics' X-band radar can distinguish different types of aircraft flying at very low altitude and is in use at airports in several countries. Cable and Wireless has the submarine cable-laying robot 'CIRRUS', which can work at depths of up to 1 km (3,280 ft) controlled entirely by a computer on its mother ship.

A range of electrical and electronic measurement and test equipment is made in Britain, as well as analytical instruments. Production of process control equipment is a large and expanding area, along with the manufacture of numerical control and indication equipment for use in machine tools. British companies are among the leaders in several types of advanced electronic medical equipment. Pioneering work has been undertaken in magnetic resonance imaging (MRI), a technique in which the patient is placed in a strong magnetic field and scanned with radiofrequency energy. The resulting information is processed by computer to construct images of internal organs and tissues. MRI enables large areas of the body to be examined internally without recourse to surgery or potentially harmful radiation. Developments in laser technology since the 1960s helped British doctors in 1986 to invent new techniques for destroying cancers in their early stages and for unblocking arteries.

British companies also produce other advanced electronic medical equipment, including ultrasound scanners, electromyography systems and patient monitoring systems for intensive and coronary care and other uses.

The comprehensive indigenous electronics components industry is supplemented by subsidiaries of a number of large overseas companies. The manufacture of integrated circuits is an area of particularly rapid change. Britain has strength in the manufacture of advanced components over a wide range of products and application areas.

Electrical Engineering and Appliances

The electrical engineering industry manufactures a wide variety of products for the electricity supply sector, ranging from power plant, cable transformers and switchgear to lighting, plugs and sockets and other installation equipment. It makes extensive use of advanced technologies in its products and processes.

The domestic electrical appliance sector is dominated by a few large firms. The major electronic consumer goods produced are radio and television sets, and high-fidelity audio and video equipment. In the audio field British manufacturers have a reputation for high-quality goods but are less strong in the mass market.

The instrument engineering industry produces measuring, photographic, cinematographic and reprographic equipment; watches, clocks and other timing devices; and medical and surgical instruments and appliances. Its precision instrument and medical branches both earn significant and growing export surpluses, but the sector as a whole is contracting.

Motor Vehicles and Other Transport Equipment (excluding Aerospace)

Total sales of motor vehicles, engines and parts were just over £21,610 million in 1989. Car output is dominated by five groups, accounting for 99 per cent of the total. They are Rover (in which the Government had a majority shareholding prior to the sale of the company to British Aerospace in 1988), Ford (which acquired Jaguar in 1989), Vauxhall, Peugeot-Talbot and Nissan. The remainder is in the hands of smaller, specialist producers such as Lotus and Rolls-Royce, whose cars are renowned for their quality and durability. The West Midlands and the South East account for the major proportion of total employment in the motor industry.

The industry has faced increased competition from imports, particularly from continental Europe and Japan. However, British manufacturers are responding by forming collaborative ventures. Rover's 800, 200 and 400 ranges were designed and developed in collaboration with Honda. Recent inward investment projects by Nissan, Honda and Toyota, locating vehicle—and in some cases engine—plants in Britain, financed by overseas firms, will lead to increased production and employment in the sector in the mid-1990s.

Table 13.8: Motor Vehicles and Other Transport Equipment

	Sales[a] (£ million) 1988	Exports (£ million) 1989	Imports (£ million) 1989
Motor vehicles (including bodies, trailers, caravans and engines)	12,137	3,922	9,787
Motor vehicle parts	4,888	2,831	3,700
Other transport equipment	7,908	7,556	4,554
of which: shipbuilding and repairing	868	313	186

[a]See Table 13.4, footnote a.

Major component manufacturers include GKN, which developed a viscous control unit improving vehicle traction and stability; Lucas, which pioneered direct fuel injection for small automotive diesel engines; T&N, which has recently launched more efficient pistons for engines; and BBA Automotive Components, with its new automatic clutch and throttle system.

Total sales by British manufacturers of motor cycles, pedal cycles and miscellaneous vehicles were £252 million in 1989. The largest pedal cycle manufacturer is Raleigh, which was taken over by the specially created Derby International Corporation in 1987.

Shipbuilding and Marine Engineering

Britain has a long tradition of shipbuilding and remains active in the construction, conversion and repair of merchant vessels, warships and offshore structures.

The largest sector is the building of warships, including both nuclear-powered and diesel-electric submarines, frigates, glass-reinforced plastics vessels, fast patrol craft and specialist naval auxiliaries. As well as meeting all the needs of the Royal Navy, the warship yards build and convert ships for overseas governments.

British yards build some of the most sophisticated and technologically complex merchant vessels in the world, including ferries and offshore support and research vessels, as well as more traditional ships and craft of all kinds for the leisure market. In 1989 British merchant shipbuilders completed orders for the construction of all kinds of vessels with a total value of £674 million. The shipbuilding industry is supplemented by ship-repairers, including the Royal Dockyards, which the Government leased to commercial management in 1987. Repairers also modernise and convert all types of vessels and floating structures. The British marine equipment industry offers a complete range of products from engines to sophisticated navigational systems.

More than two decades of oil exploitation in the North Sea have generated a major offshore industry, now mature, in Britain. Shipbuilders and fabricators build fixed platforms and semi-submersible units for drilling, production and emergency/maintenance support, drill ships, jack-up rigs, modules and offshore loading systems. Several thousand manufacturing and service industry firms supply a wide range of goods and services, including consultancy, design, project management, and research and development, to the offshore industry. In conjunction with the Offshore Supplies Office of the Department of Energy, the Department of Trade and Industry has a responsibility for promoting Britain's offshore interests overseas and maintains a central co-ordination unit to assist this activity.

Aerospace

Britain's aerospace industry is the third largest in the world, behind those of the United States and the Soviet Union. In 1989 it had a turnover of more than £11,400 million. Exports, according to the Society of British Aerospace Companies, totalled £7,890 million and contributed £3,220 million in net terms to the balance of payments. Over the past decade, the industry has doubled its productivity, doubled its turnover and trebled its exports in real terms.

As the largest British exporter of manufactured goods, British Aerospace (BAe) manufactures an extensive range of aerospace, space and electronic products. It has developed its own family of civil aircraft, with seating capacities ranging from 5 to 122 seats, which includes the 146 family of regional airliners (one of the world's quietest jetliners), the ATP (advanced turboprop) airliner, the 125 (the world's best-selling middle-sized business jet) and the Jetstream 31 and 41 commuterliners. BAe owns a 20 per cent share of the European consortium Airbus Industrie, which has sold over 1,400 airliners. BAe supplies the wings of the whole family of Airbus Industrie airliners.

The military production of BAe includes the V-STOL Harrier, the Hawk trainer and the Tornado combat aircraft in collaboration with German and Italian manufacturers. BAe also produces the Harrier II and Goshawk (a development of the Hawk for the United States Navy) jointly with the United States firm McDonnell Douglas. As a partner of Eurofighter, BAe has a 33 per cent share of the production of the European Fighter Aircraft (EFA), which is being produced in collaboration with German, Italian and Spanish manufacturers. BAe is a major producer of air-, sea- and ground-launched guided weapons, including the Rapier air defence system and naval Seawolf system.

Short Brothers of Belfast produces a range of aerospace products, including the Shorts 330 and 360 commuter airliners and the military freighter version of the 330 known as the Sherpa. It also produces the Tucano, a turboprop basic military trainer which is in use with the Royal Air Force. The company, which was privatised in 1989 by its sale to the Canadian

Table 13.9: Aerospace

	Sales[a] (£ million) 1988	Exports (£ million) 1989	Imports (£ million) 1989
Aircraft and associated equipment	4,883	2,144	994
Aero-engines and parts		2,685	1,810
Total, including products not specified above	8,466	7,114	3,997

[a] See Table 13.4, footnote a.

firm Bombardier, also produces guided missiles and a wide range of airframe components, some of them in composites, for other aerospace manufacturers overseas, such as the wings for the Dutch Fokker 100 twin-jet airliners.

In addition to its production of aerospace equipment, Westland manufactures a range of helicopters, notably the Sea King and Lynx military helicopters and the civilian W30. In collaboration with Agusta of Italy, Westland is developing the multi-role EH101 three-engine helicopter, which will be delivered to the Royal Navy and the Italian Navy by the mid-1990s. The company is a leading manufacturer of composite helicopter blades.

Rolls-Royce is one of the three major manufacturers of aero-engines in the Western world, with a turnover in 1989 of some £2,360 million and an order book at the end of 1989 of £4,500 million. The company's civil engine group produces engines for airliners and executive and corporate jets. Its RB211-535 engines have been selected by 75 per cent of the airlines using Boeing 757 airliners. The RB211-524G and H engines, which were launched in 1986 with orders from Cathay Pacific and British Airways to power their Boeing 747-400 airliners, entered service in 1989. The company's new Tay turbofan engines are in service with the Gulfstream IV and Fokker 100 airliners, and are also available as replacement engines for older aircraft. Rolls-Royce is a partner in the five-nation International Aero Engine consortium which produces the V2500 aero-engine, now in service on the new Airbus Industrie A320 airliner.

The military engine group of Rolls-Royce produces a wide range of engines for military aircraft and helicopters. These include the Turbo-Union RB199 for the Panavia Tornado; the Pegasus series of vectored thrust engines for the Harrier, the Adour and the Spey jets; and the RTM 322 and MTR390 helicopter engines. Rolls-Royce is a partner in Eurojet, a consortium from four countries formed to develop the EJ200 for the Eurofighter's EFA. In addition, the company produces gas turbines for power generation and for oil and gas pumping, gas turbine power for 25 of the world's navies, and propulsion systems for the Royal Navy's nuclear-powered submarines.

Aviation equipment manufacturers provide a wide range of systems essential to engines and aircraft, including engine and flight controls, electrical generation, mechanical and hydraulic power systems, cabin furnishings, flight-deck control and information displays. British firms have made important advances in the development of ejector seats, fire-fighting equipment and flight simulators, and are playing a major role in the development of both fly-by-wire and fly-by-light technology, where control surfaces are moved by means of automatic electronic signalling and fibre optics respectively, rather than by mechanical means. They provide radar and air traffic control equipment and ground power supplies to airports and airlines throughout the world.

Satellite Equipment

Over 400 companies in Britain are involved in space activities. The British industry's major strength is in the manufacture of satellites. British Aerospace (Space Systems) is Europe's largest—and the world's third largest—producer of communications satellites. It has been the prime contractor for all such spacecraft launched by the European Space Agency (ESA), as well as for scientific probes such as the Giotto satellite. BAe has developed and built 18 space pallets (payload and instrument carriers) for the United States Space Shuttle and has over 20 orders for the SPELDA lightweight payload bay structure for the ESA's Ariane 4 rocket launcher, which enables Ariane to launch two or more spacecraft independently during the same mission. British Aerospace (Space Systems) was the prime contractor for the Olympus 1 satellite, the world's most powerful communications satellite, launched in June 1989.

Marconi Space Systems (a subsidiary of GEC) has acted as principal contractor on many telecommunications satellite payloads, including those for the ESA's Olympus satellite (Inmarsat). BAe is prime contractor for the second generation of Inmarsat satellites. GEC Ferranti Defence Systems produce the inertial guidance system for the European Ariane launcher and Pilkington Space Technology is the world's leading producer of solar cell coverglasses for satellites.

The trade association for the industry is the Society of British Aerospace Companies, which organises a major international air show at Farnborough, Hampshire, every two years (the most recent was in September 1990).

Food, Drink and Tobacco

Britain has a large and sophisticated food processing industry, which has accounted for a growing proportion of total domestic food supply in recent decades. The industry's interests are advanced by Food From Britain, a body with a wide remit to improve the marketing of British food and agricultural produce both domestically and overseas.

Convenience foods (particularly frozen foods, annual sales of which now exceed £3,000 million), yoghurts and instant snacks have formed the fastest-growing sector of the food market in recent years. The market in health and slimming foods is also growing.

Production of milk was some 14,473 million litres in 1989, of which nearly half was for sale as liquid milk. Eight out of ten households in Britain receive milk through a doorstep delivery system employing about 35,000 people driving electric vehicles. Domestic milk consumption per head (2 litres—3·5 pints—per week in 1989) is among the highest in the world. Consumption of skimmed milk is rising as some people seek to reduce the fat content in their diet.

The main milk products are butter (134,000 tonnes produced in 1989), cheese (285,000 tonnes), condensed milk (201,000 tonnes) and dried whole and skimmed milk (234,000 tonnes). The dairy industry accounted for 74 per cent of new butter supplies to the British market in 1989, 67 per cent of new cheese supplies and nearly all of other milk products. Butter exports in 1989 were 72,000 tonnes and cheese exports 37,000 tonnes, compared with 62,000 tonnes and 15,000 tonnes respectively in 1979. The other main exports are skimmed and whole milk powder (80,000 and 75,000 tonnes respectively in 1989).

About 80 per cent of bread is manufactured in large mechanised bakeries, most of which use a British process (the 'Chorleywood' process). This process or similar procedures are used in many other countries. After years of decline, overall consumption of bread stabilised in the 1980s. There has been increased demand for wholemeal varieties at the expense of the standard sliced white loaf, though recently this has slackened with the introduction of soft-grained white bread. Biscuit exports were valued at £105 million in 1989.

Table 13.10: Food, Drink and Tobacco

	Sales[a] (£ million) 1988	Exports (£ million) 1989	Imports (£ million) 1989
Food manufacturing	33,852	2,995	7,371
of which: meat products	4,254	717	1,892
milk and milk products	3,840	472	703
flour-based products	4,532	196	143
sugar and confectionery	2,028	95	487
cocoa and chocolate			
goods	3,279	338	387
animal feedstuffs	4,084	198	141
Drinks[b]	6,081	1,895	1,502
of which: brewing and malting	1,981	130	180
distilling and			
compounding	1,944	1,668	237
soft drinks	1,857	59	372
Tobacco[b]	1,962	512	107

[a]See Table 13.4, footnote a.
[b]Sales figures exclude duty paid.

Of prime importance among the alcoholic drinks produced in Britain is Scotch whisky. There are 114 distilleries in Scotland and the well-known brands of blended Scotch whisky are made from the products of a number of different distilleries. Guinness plc, owners of the United Distillers plc and of Arthur Bell and Sons, accounts for 40 per cent of Scotch whisky output and 25 per cent of the British market. Some 85 per cent of all Scotch whisky produced is exported. The value of whisky exports was £1,470 million in 1989, the United States taking nearly a fifth by volume.

In the brewing and malting industry there are six major brewery groups whose products are sold nationally. Demand for traditional cask-conditioned ales grew substantially in the 1970s but has now stabilised. The main raw materials used are malt, sugar, other cereals and hops. British malt, which is made almost entirely from home-grown barley, is used by brewers throughout the world. Lager has increased steadily in popularity since the late 1960s and accounts for nearly 50 per cent of beer sales. In 1989 sales of beer in Britain exceeded £10,800 million, over 2·5 per cent of GDP.

The soft drinks industry has expanded markedly in the last decade. There are some very large companies among about 20 producing brands which are marketed on a national scale. Sales of the principal soft drink products reached £2,258 million in 1989, an increase of 41 per cent compared with the figure for 1985.

The British tobacco industry manufactures 99 per cent of cigarettes and tobacco goods sold in Britain. Almost all of domestic output is provided by three major manufacturers (Imperial Tobacco, Gallaher and Carreras Rothmans). The industry specialises in the production of high-quality cigarettes made from flue-cured tobacco and achieves significant exports, with the participation of BAT Industries: countries in Europe, the Middle East and Africa are important markets. Britain's most important sources of raw tobacco are Brazil, the United States, Zimbabwe, India and Canada.

Textiles, Footwear, Clothing and Leather

Textiles, footwear, clothing and leather make a substantial contribution to the British economy in terms of employment, exports and turnover. Together, they employ 521,000 people, equal to 2·4 per cent of total employment and just over 10 per cent of manufacturing employment. For textiles, there is a high degree of regional concentration. Particularly important areas are the North West (mainly cotton), West Yorkshire (mainly wool), the East Midlands (lace and knitwear), Scotland and Northern Ireland. Most of the clothing industry is widely scattered throughout the country and does not represent a large proportion of employment in any region, although there are significant concentrations in the inner city areas of cities such as Manchester, Leicester, Leeds and London. The industries' main products are yarn, woven and knitted fabrics, apparel, industrial and household textiles, and carpets based mainly on wool, cotton and man-made fibres.

Table 13.11: Textiles, Footwear, Clothing and Leather

	Sales[a] (£ million) 1988	Exports (£ million) 1989	Imports (£ million) 1989
Textile industry	6,545	2,315	4,302
of which: woollen and worsted			
industry	1,469	635	437
cotton and silk industry	1,096	546	1,836
hosiery and other			
knitwear	1,860	553	1,111
carpets, rugs and matting	1,134	206	456
Footwear	1,174	222	961
Clothing, hats and gloves	4,279	943	2,515
Made-up textiles	984	130	242
Leather and leather goods	838	374	553

[a]See Table 13.4, footnote a.

The textile industry has around 4,900 firms, comprising a few large multi-process companies, including two of the largest in the world—Coats Viyella and Courtaulds Textiles—and a large number of small and medium-sized firms. Increased investment in new machinery and enhanced attention to design, training and marketing have helped the industry to raise its competitiveness.

The Multi-Fibre Arrangement of the General Agreement on Tariffs and Trade allows a measure of restraint on imports of textiles and clothing from low-cost countries into the European Community.

Britain's wool textile industry is one of the largest in the world. In the last few years the industry's export earnings have been consistently high. There are two main branches, woollens and worsted. An increasing amount of man-made fibre is blended with wool. West Yorkshire is the main producing area, but Scotland and the west of England are also famous as specialised producers of high-quality yarn and cloth. Large quantities of raw wool are scoured and cleaned in Britain in preparation for spinning. British mills also process the bulk of rare fibres such as cashmere and mohair. Sales of the principal products of the woollen and worsted industry amounted to £1,380 million in 1989, exports accounting for £635 million of this total, to give a trade surplus of nearly £200 million.

Low-cost competition has cut progressively into British markets for cotton. Production includes yarn and fabrics of cotton, spun man-made fibres and mixtures of these. The linen industry is centred in Northern Ireland.

About half the value of carpet and rug output is made up of tufted carpets, in the production of which the pile, usually with a high man-made fibre content, is inserted into a pre-woven backing. Woven carpets, mainly Axminster, account for most of the remainder of sales. There is a higher wool content in woven types, although in these, too, more use is being made of man-made fibres. The high quality and variety of design make Britain one of the world's leading producers of woven carpets. Industrial textiles account for an increasing proportion of the industry's output, covering products such as conveyor belting and geotextiles used in civil engineering projects. Many of these are non-woven, made of fibres assembled using advanced techniques.

Jute products are manufactured in the Dundee area. Jute yarn and man-made polypropylene yarn are used in the manufacture of carpets, cordage and ropes, and woven into fabrics for a wide range of applications in the packaging, upholstery, building and motor vehicle industries.

The clothing industry is labour intensive, with about 11,000 companies accounting for 5·6 per cent of total manufacturing employment. While a wide range of clothing is imported from the rest of Europe and Asia, British industry supplies two-thirds of domestic demand. Exports have risen since the mid-1970s and the British fashion designer industry became prominent during the 1980s. The hosiery and knitwear industry comprises about 1,600 companies, mainly in the East Midlands and Scotland, of which most are of small to medium size. The footwear manufacturing industry is made up predominantly of small companies. Imports have risen to high levels in recent years, accounting for about 70 per cent of total sales in 1989.

Other Manufacturing

The wooden furniture industry is very diverse, comprising some 6,200 companies which supply the domestic, contract and institutional markets. Domestic production of wood for industrial use has been steadily increasing and deliveries in 1989 amounted to just over 6 million cubic metres (212 million cubic feet). There were 112 paper and board mills employing 33,000 people in 1989, operated by 21 companies. Among the largest British groups are Wiggins Teape, St Regis and Davidsons. Overseas paper and board groups with manufacturing investments in Britain include Georgia Pacific, Kimberly Clark, Consolidated Bathurst, the Scott Corporation and United Paper Mills of Finland. Total sales of pulp, paper and board manufactures exceeded £2,100 million in 1989.

There has been a substantial growth in newsprint production in Britain. British newsprint producers now supply about 28 per cent of British demand.

There has been a significant trend towards waste-based packaging grades in order to reduce the industry's reliance on imported woodpulp supplies. The use of recycled waste paper is increasing and research is helping to extend it. Waste paper provides about half of the industry's fibre needs. Domestically produced wood pulp represents only a small percentage of raw material supplies.

Total sales and receipts of general British publishers and printers doubled between 1984 and 1989. Mergers have led to the formation of large groups in newspaper, magazine and book publishing, the largest being the Maxwell

Communications Corporation. However, general printing, engraving, bookbinding and a large part of publishing still include many small firms. With the increasing use of new technology, such as computer typesetting, fragmentation of the industry into small specialised units took place in the 1980s. The book-publishing industry is a major exporter, selling one-third of production in overseas markets. Security printers (of, for example, banknotes and postage stamps) are important exporters, the major company being De La Rue. Total employment in the paper, printing and publishing industries in 1989 was 484,000. About half of employment in the printing and publishing industry, and more than half of its output, is concentrated in firms based in the South East.

Table 13.12: Other Manufacturing

	Sales[a] (£ million) 1988	Exports (£ million) 1989	Imports (£ million) 1989
Timber and wooden furniture	7,509	443	3,247
Paper and paper products	8,850	1,314	4,908
Printing and publishing	11,947	1,047	873
Processing of rubber and plastics	10,102	2,266	3,118
Toys and sports goods	573	362	783

[a]See Table 13.4, footnote a.

Rubber tyres and tubes sold by British manufacturers in 1989 were valued at £1,075 million, about half of which went overseas. The most important other rubber goods are vehicle components and accessories, conveyor belting, cables, hoses, latex foam products, and footwear, gloves and clothing. Tyre manufacturers include subsidiaries of United States and other overseas companies. The industry's consumption of rubber includes natural, synthetic and recycled rubber.

There are some 530 manufacturers of a wide range of toys and games and 425 manufacturers of sports equipment. British fishing tackle and golf and tennis equipment are established in export markets. Jewellery, gold and silverware and the refining of precious metals are industries with a strong craft tradition.

14 Construction and Service Industries

Introduction

In 1989 services contributed around 64 per cent of gross domestic product, compared with 45 per cent in 1960, and accounted for 69 per cent of employees in employment, compared with 48 per cent in 1960. Overseas trade in services, particularly financial services, has also grown, and in 1989 overseas earnings from services amounted to about 40 per cent of the value of exports of manufactures.

Between 1978 and 1980 total service employment in Britain rose by 500,000; it then fell for two years, but recovered again to grow from about 13·1 million in 1982 to 15·7 million in 1989, a net increase of 2·6 million jobs, compared with a net decline of some 837,000 in production industries. Much of this was accounted for by growth in part-time (principally female) employment. Since the late 1970s employment has grown more rapidly in the private sector than in the public sector, partly reflecting the Government's policy of restricting employment in public sector services. The fastest-growing sectors in the 1970s, measured by employment, were leisure and personal services, financial services, distribution, and hotels and catering. In the 1980s financial services, which are discussed in other chapters, continued to grow strongly.

Among the reasons for the growth in services is the tendency to spend a greater proportion of income on personal, financial and leisure services as real incomes rise. While consumers have to some extent exchanged services such as public transport, laundries and cinemas for goods such as cars, washing-machines and television sets, this has generated demand for fresh services in the distribution, maintenance and repair of these goods. Increased consumer expenditure on the running costs of cars is a significant factor in the rise in consumer expenditure on services. Demand for British air travel, hotel and catering services has resulted from the increase in real incomes in other countries. By the same token, the substantial rise in real disposable incomes in Britain has resulted in more holidays being taken by Britons both within Britain and overseas.

Other factors include a greater readiness to use an increasingly wide variety of banking services and the spread of home ownership, which has increased demand for legal and estate agency services. Demographic changes, such as the increasing proportion of elderly people in the population, help to explain the growth of medical services.

Changes in technology have also played a part in the growth of services. Examples range from the computer services industry to the provision of cash and credit by means of cards, and the growth of information systems such as viewdata and teletext.

A notable trend is the growth in franchising, an operation in which a company owning the rights to a particular form of trading licenses them to franchisees, usually by means of an initial payment with continuing royalties.

Cleaning services, film processing, print shops, hairdressing and cosmetics, fitness centres, courier delivery, car rental, engine tuning and servicing, and fast food retailing have been among the major areas where franchising has developed. It is estimated that franchising's share of total retail sales is presently about 10 per cent, a figure which is likely to increase in the 1990s.

Construction

The construction industry, excluding materials, accounts for 6·5 per cent of gross domestic product. The industry experienced growth during 1989, with the total value of output in Great Britain reaching £46,120 million, of which new work accounted for £27,330 million (59 per cent) and repairs and maintenance the remainder. In housing, new work was valued at £8,080 million and repairs and maintenance at £10,200 million. About 1 million people are employed in the industry, accounting for 4·7 per cent of the employed labour force. There are also more than 500,000 self-employed.

Efficiency and productivity are benefiting from new computerised techniques such as the use of electronic load safety measures for cranes, distance measuring equipment, computerised stock ordering and job costing, and computer-aided design. Increasingly, major contractors are managing projects (particularly higher value ones) and using subcontractors to do the actual work.

Government promotion of the construction market is the responsibility of the Department of the Environment. Building regulations prescribe minimum standards of construction in England and Wales. Made by the Secretary of State for the Environment and administered and enforced by local authorities, the regulations apply to new building, the installation or replacement of fittings, and alterations and extensions to existing buildings. There are broadly similar controls under separate legislation in Scotland and Northern Ireland. As an alternative to local authority building control and in order to simplify procedures, an optional system of private certification of compliance with building regulations is provided for in the Housing and Building Control Act 1984 and was introduced in 1985. The British Board of Agrément, sponsored by the Department, assesses and issues reports and certificates relating to products and systems for use in the construction industry. The Government is concerned to see quality assurance extended to the construction process as well as to the materials used.

Structure

Construction work is carried out both by private contractors and by public authorities which employ their own labour. In 1989 over 90 per cent of the work was done by private firms. Although there were over 100,000 firms employing two or more people, 95 per cent of them employed fewer than 25. Some large firms are vertically integrated, owning quarries and workshops, mechanised plant and standard builders' equipment; some undertake responsibility for projects from initial design to finished building. All but the smallest projects are generally carried out under professional direction, either by architects or, in the case of the more complicated civil engineering projects, by consulting engineers. The latter, acting on behalf of a client, may advise on the feasibility of projects, draw up plans and supervise the construction work.

In Britain the financial control of projects and some of the work normally associated with architects is carried out by surveyors of various disciplines. Financial aspects and control of project costs are undertaken by quantity surveyors and construction surveyors. The inspection and maintenance of buildings are carried out by building surveyors. In addition, town planning and municipal surveyors deal with local planning issues. There are also independent estates and valuation surveyors who deal with the management of privately owned property.

On 1 April 1990, the Property Services Agency, previously responsible for all construction projects undertaken directly by the Government, including work for the armed forces in Britain and overseas, was restructured into two separate organisations. These are Property Holdings and PSA Services. Property Holdings performs the government landlord functions for its Common User Estate, as well as other long-term government activities. PSA Services comprises four operating divisions. PSA Projects offers management and design services for major projects. PSA Building Management provides a range of services in maintenance and estates surveying and the management and design of locally designed projects. PSA Specialist Services offers a range of specialist professional services in relation both to specific commissions and to other supervisory support services. PSA International provides a range of services overseas almost exclusively in support of the Ministry of Defence and is the marketing arm of PSA Services overseas.

Housing

During 1989 a total of 163,000 dwellings were started in Great Britain. Starts in the public sector were 23,000 and those for private owners 140,000. Some 166,000 dwellings were completed, 22,000 in the public sector and 144,000 in the private sector.

Major Construction Projects

Among important construction projects in hand or recently completed in Britain are the new British Library, the extensive development in London's former docklands (including the Limehouse link road), the M25 motorway widening scheme, the Dartford Bridge, the A55 Conwy Tunnel, the Glasgow Concert Hall and the Channel Tunnel.

Consultancy

In 1989 members of the Association of Consulting Engineers won contracts to become involved in new overseas commissions for construction projects worth nearly £7,800 million. British companies provided consulting engineering services in 1989 for many projects around the world. At the beginning of 1990 the total value of overseas projects in which members of the Association were involved amounted to more than £34,000 million. The most important sources of new work by value were the Far East (including Hong Kong, the People's Republic of China, Japan and the Republic of Korea), the rest of Asia, Australasia and the Middle East. Among the biggest projects were the Greater Cairo Wastewater Scheme, valued at some £1,000 million; the Great Man-made River Project in Libya, costed at £2,300 million; and a feasibility study for the Madrid–Barcelona high-speed railway in Spain, valued at £6,600 million.

Commercial structural work and the construction of thermal power stations accounted for 59 per cent of the value of all projects. British consulting engineers, process engineers and chartered surveyors had estimated net earnings of £425 million in 1989 from overseas commissions.

Contracting

Overseas construction contracts awarded to British companies in 1989 included a £550 million residential and commercial complex in Saudi Arabia; a link for the transmission of power between the north and south islands of New Zealand, valued at £200 million; and a conference and exhibition centre in Singapore, costed at £500 million.

The export interests of the various sectors of the British construction industry are promoted by the Export Group for the Constructional Industries, the Association of Consulting Engineers, the British Consultants

Bureau (whose members include architects, surveyors and management consultants), the Building Materials Export Group, the Federation of Manufacturers of Construction Equipment and Cranes, and the British Water Industries Group.

Research and Advisory Services

The Government's national research and advisory body on construction and building is the Building Research Establishment, which is part of the Department of the Environment. It has four laboratories, including a fire research station, and is the site of a building energy management systems centre. Research is also carried out by the major construction and materials firms, universities, colleges of technology and research associations, which also provide advisory services.

The Building Centre Group consists of four building centres throughout Britain, most of which provide exhibition and information services on materials, products, techniques and building services.

Service Industries

DISTRIBUTION

There were 4·5 million people engaged in the distributive and allied trades in Great Britain in early 1990, together with a large number of owners of businesses. There were 932,000 people in wholesaling, some 2·2 million in retailing, just under 1·1 million in hotels and catering, and 215,000 in the repair of vehicles and consumer goods. The distributive and allied trades accounted for about 14 per cent of national income in 1989.

WHOLESALE TRADES

According to the most recently published Census of Production, there were 115,000 businesses, with a turnover valued at over £187,000 million (see Table 14.1), engaged in wholesaling and dealing in Great Britain in 1987. This represented a growth in stock of businesses of 26 per cent and of turnover at current prices of 77 per cent since 1980. The most important sectors within the wholesaling industry by proportion of total turnover were food and drink (20 per cent), industrial materials and petroleum products

Table 14·1: Wholesale Trade in Great Britain 1987[a]

	Number of businesses	Turnover[b] (£ million)
Food and drink	16,764	36,987
Petroleum products	1,008	22,392
Clothing, furs, textiles and footware	10,020	8,521
Coal and oil merchants	3,683	2,277
Builders' merchants	4,527	7,488
Agricultural supplies and livestock dealing	3,205	7,920
Industrial materials	5,891	22,714
Scrap and waste products	4,084	2,151
Industrial and agricultural machinery	8,415	12,257
Operational leasing	3,027	3,068
Other goods	54,354	61,310
Total wholesaling and dealing	114,978	187,085

Source: *Business Monitor SDA26. Wholesaling, 1987.*
[a] Figures cover businesses registered for value added tax with an annual turnover of £142,000 or more and are grossed up to include those not surveyed.
[b] Excludes value added tax.

(12 per cent each) and a general category of sales in which is included chemists' sundries, electrical goods, and paper and board products (33 per cent). This last category of goods achieved the greatest growth of any wholesale sector between 1980 and 1987, rising from about 24 per cent to 33 per cent of total turnover. The largest drop in market share was experienced by the wholesale petroleum products sector, which fell from 20 per cent of the total to about 12 per cent during the same period, while the share of food and drink sales was stable.

The co-operative movement in Britain, represented by the Co-operative Union, has its own wholesale organisation, the Co-operative Wholesale Society (CWS), with 237 outlets, to serve the needs of retail societies; its turnover was £2,559 million in 1988–89. Retail societies are encouraged to buy from the CWS, which is the principal supplier to the 85 retail co-operative societies, and it is also a major retailer in Scotland, Northern Ireland and south-east England. Co-operative Retail Services (CRS), with about 497 outlets, is the largest group within the co-operative movement and accounts for about one-fifth of its annual turnover. The CWS, the CRS and the Co-operative Union are all based in Manchester. The Institute of Grocery Distribution estimates that there were more than 3,700 co-operative outlets of all kinds in 1988, of which nearly half sold food and drink.

In the food and drink trade almost all large retailers now carry out the functions of the wholesaler by having their own buying and central distribution operations. Elsewhere in the trade voluntary groups have been formed by wholesalers with small independent retailers, in which the retailers are encouraged by discounts and other incentives to buy as much as possible from the wholesaler. This has helped to preserve many smaller retail outlets for the wholesaler, including the traditional 'corner shops' and village stores, of value to the local community, and has given small retailers the advantages of bulk buying and co-ordinated distribution.

London's wholesale markets play a significant part in the distribution of foodstuffs. New Covent Garden is the main market for fruit and vegetables, Smithfield for meat and Billingsgate for fish.

RETAIL TRADES   Of the 25 largest retailers in Western Europe by sales reported in either financial or calendar years embracing 1987 to 1989, ten were British firms. Turnover of the retail trades has been growing slowly in real terms in recent years. The Census of Production 1987 found about 241,000 retail businesses, with 345,000 outlets, in Great Britain (see Table 14.2). While employment in the retail trades fell by about 100,000 people between 1980 and 1987, and the numbers of retail businesses and outlets fell by 6 per cent, total retail turnover increased from £59,800 million to £105,000 million, a rise attributable in large measure to the increase in retail prices. In recent years, the large multiple retailers (those with ten or more outlets) have grown in size, decreasing their store numbers but increasing outlet size and diversifying their product ranges. Decline has been particularly evident among small independent businesses and retail co-operative societies. Shops selling durable household goods have experienced the fastest growth in turnover in recent years, while hire and repair businesses and food retailers have recorded the slowest growth.

The largest multiple retailers in the grocery market are Sainsbury, Tesco, Safeway, Asda and Gateway. In 1989–90 Sainsbury had some 358 stores and the company's sales amounted to nearly £6,211 million. Tesco had about 379 outlets and sales were valued at over £5,402 million. Retail co-operative societies are voluntary organisations controlled by their members, membership being open to anyone paying a small deposit on a minimum

Table 14.2: Retail Trade in Great Britain 1987[a]

	Number of businesses	Number of outlets	Number of people engaged ('000s)	Turnover[b] (£ million)
Single-outlet retailers	213,378	213,378	786	29,522
Small multiple retailers	26,613	69,384	306	12,180
Large multiple retailers (ten or more retail outlets)	862	62,706	1,228	62,925
Food retailers	73,681	98,016	806	37,146
Drink, confectionery and tobacco retailers	47,296	59,810	272	10,538
Clothing, footwear and leather goods retailers	31,162	58,380	293	10,255
Household goods retailers	42,760	60,406	307	17,353
Other non-food retailers	38,973	52,473	233	8,983
Mixed retail businesses	4,937	11,363	375	19,060
Hire and repair businesses	2,045	5,020	32	1,293
Total retail trade	240,853	345,467	2,319	104,627

Source: *Business Monitor SDA 25. Retailing, 1987.*
[a]Figures cover businesses registered for value added tax; it is estimated that the total number of retail businesses too small to register for value added tax is about 30,000, but these businesses account for no more than 0·5 per cent of total retail turnover.
[b]Includes value added tax.
Note: Differences between totals and the sums of their component parts are due to rounding.

share. Retail co-operatives and the Co-operative Wholesale Society (see p 303) are members of the Co-operative Union, as are a number of other co-operative bodies such as the Co-operative Bank.

The leading mixed retail businesses are Marks and Spencer (with sales of £5,600 million in 1989–90), Boots, Kingfisher, Storehouse, W. H. Smith, Argos, Littlewoods, Savacentre and John Menzies.

About 20 million people regularly purchase goods through mail order catalogues. In 1989 sales by general mail order totalled some £3,700 million, representing 3 per cent of all retail sales and 4·7 per cent of non-food retail sales. The volume of mail order sales increased rapidly in the 1970s but fell back in the period 1980–84. Leading items sold by the general mail order catalogue companies include clothing, footwear, furniture, household textiles, televisions, radios and electrical goods. The leading mail order catalogue businesses are Great Universal Stores, Littlewoods, Grattan/Next, Freemans, Empire and J. D. Williams.

Trends

One of the most significant trends in retailing in recent years has been the increase in the proportion of turnover accounted for by large multiple retailers; the nine largest have nearly 71 per cent of retail turnover. Other developments include an increase in very large self-service stores selling a wide variety of products, diversification by food multiples into selling a wider range of goods, the creation of specially designed shopping precincts, the growth of shops selling computers, software and video-cassettes, and an increasing emphasis on price competition.

Large Shopping Centres

Britain has a wide range of complementary shopping facilities inside and outside town and city centres. There continues to be a demand for the services provided by small, specialised shops, but the trend is towards larger shops in order to increase efficiency and the range of goods available. The main multiple grocery companies have been steadily increasing the size of their stores both in towns and cities and on suburban and out-of-town sites. Also, retailers of goods such as do-it-yourself products, furniture and electrical appliances have for some years found it advantageous to develop retail warehouses outside town and city centres, particularly to attract shoppers with cars. More recently, there has been a trend towards the grouping of retail warehouses into retail warehouse parks.

Proposals have also been made recently for a number of regional out-of-town shopping centres, sometimes as part of retail and leisure complexes, on sites which offer good access to large numbers of customers with cars and ample space for car parking, and which benefit from low acquisition and operating costs. One of the few such centres built to date is the Metro Centre at Gateshead, Tyne and Wear, which includes over 93,000 sq m (1 million sq ft) of floorspace. The Meadowhall shopping centre in Sheffield opened in September 1990, and the Lakeside centre at Thurrock in Essex is due to open shortly.

Britain also has a wide variety of purpose-built shopping centres in towns and cities, and there is increasing interest in the modernisation and redevelopment of these and other town centre facilities in order to improve their attractiveness and their ability to compete efficiently.

All new retail development requires planning permission from the local planning authority. These authorities must consult the Department of the Environment and equivalent departments in Scotland and Northern Ireland before granting permission for developments of 23,325 sq m (250,000 sq ft) or more. The Government's policy is to encourage the provision of a wide range of shopping facilities to the public, while ensuring that the cumulative effects of major new retail development do not undermine the viability and vitality of existing town centres.

Diversification

Many of the large multiple groups have diversified over the last few years to offer a much bigger range of goods and services than previously. This has been especially noticeable for the large food retailers, which often sell non-food products such as beer, wines and spirits, clothing and household appliances, as well as packaged groceries. Another trend is that many superstores and large supermarkets offer fresh as well as packaged food, often with special counters or areas for fresh meat, fish, vegetables and bread baked on the premises. Some large retailers have in recent years begun to provide financial and estate agency services.

Promotions

Retailers are placing greater emphasis both on price competition and quality as a means of promoting sales. With the growth of payments by credit card, certain of the large retailers have issued their own credit cards for regular customers in an attempt to increase sales, particularly of high-value goods.

Use of Technology

Laser-scanning electronic check-outs are already having a major impact on retailing in Britain. Substantial savings are expected from improved stock control and a reduction of individual price marking in stores. Key Markets introduced the first operational laser-scanning electronic check-out in Britain at Spalding (Lincolnshire) in 1979. Computerised shopping services are being introduced in the home which enable people to order goods from retailers. Some large multiple retailers are using electronic order and invoice systems in dealing with their suppliers, following a legal change permitting tax invoices in forms other than paper. Small independent retailers are also using electronic ordering, pricing and delivery systems. High-speed labelling techniques are being adopted, including the use of electronic printers which can overprint labels, the use of pressure-sensitive glues and printing in foil instead of ink.

'EFTPOS' (electronic funds transfer at point of sale) is a system which enables shoppers to pay for goods using a debit or credit card to transfer funds electronically via terminals in retail premises. Several major EFTPOS schemes are well established, with altogether more than 60,000 terminals, a number that is growing quickly. In many cases the terminals are integrated with the retailers' in-house computer systems.

Vehicle and Petrol Retailing

In 1989 there were 450,000 people employed in Britain in the retail distribution of motor vehicles and parts, in petrol stations and in the repair and recovery of vehicles. The retail motor trade consists of firms selling vehicles, which had about 8,085 franchised new car outlets in 1989 (the largest of which was Ford, with 1,700); those selling car parts and accessories; those providing car hire; fitting centres for replacement tyres and automotive parts; and driving schools.

In spite of the continuing increase in the number of road vehicles, the number of petrol stations is declining, and at the end of 1989 there were under 20,000, representing a drop of 18 per cent since 1982. However, during the same period the average outlet increased its physical turnover of petrol by more than 50 per cent. One-third of all outlets were owned by oil companies, a figure which remained broadly constant throughout the 1980s. The companies with the largest number of outlets retailing petrol in 1989 were Shell (2,832), Esso (2,564) and BP/National (2,047). There were about 15,000 outlets selling diesel fuel. Unleaded petrol continued to become more widely available in 1989 and is now sold at more than 90 per cent of outlets. Its sales now account for about 30 per cent of the petrol retailing market. Between 1982 and 1989 the proportion of self-service petrol stations rose from about 30 per cent of the total to 55 per cent.

Hotels and Catering

The hotel and catering trades employed 1·1 million people in Great Britain in 1989: 284,000 people were employed in hotels and other residential establishments; 280,000 in public houses and bars; 272,000 in restaurants, cafés and snack bars; 142,000 in clubs; and 127,000 in canteens. A large number of self-employed people are also engaged in hotels and catering. There were about 54,000 hotels in Great Britain in 1988–89, with a turnover of £4,050 million in 1988. Many licensed hotels as well as most of the numerous guest houses are small, with fewer than 20 rooms. Of the major hotel business groups, the biggest is Trusthouse Forte plc, which runs 800 hotels, including some 290 in Britain, and has catering and leisure interests. Among the largest firms running holiday centres (including holiday camps with full board, self-catering centres and caravan parks) are Butlins, Warner Holidays and Pontins, with 40, 29 and 21 centres respectively.

Many restaurants, snack bars, cafés, fish and chip shops and other establishments sell take-away food. Britain has a very wide range of restaurants, of which a substantial number specialise in Chinese, Italian, Indian and Greek foods. 'Fast-food' catering, in which establishments sell hot food such as hamburgers or chicken to be eaten either on the premises or elsewhere, is becoming increasingly significant.

Sales of beer from licensed premises were £9,850 million in 1988; those of spirits were £4,520 million; and those of wines were £4,151 million. There were about 87,700 public houses ('pubs', which mainly sell beer, wines, soft drinks and spirits for consumption on the premises) in Britain in 1988. Many public houses are owned by the large brewing companies, which either provide managers to run them or offer tenancy agreements; others, called free houses, are independently owned and managed. In 1989 the Government announced that it proposed to act in several areas to strengthen competition in the sale of beer and other drinks in public houses; 1990 saw the restructuring of many aspects of the brewing industry in response to this.

BUSINESS SERVICES

Business services include advertising, market research, management consultancy, exhibition and conference facilities, computing services and auction houses. Most of these sectors have grown rapidly in recent years.

Advertising

Advertising expenditure rose by 10·6 per cent in 1989 to £7,555 million. The press accounted for nearly 64 per cent of the total, television for 30 per cent, posters for nearly 4 per cent, and commercial radio and cinema for the rest. These proportions have remained roughly constant since 1983. By product category, the largest advertising expenditure is on food, retail and mail order services, financial services, motor cars and leisure equipment. Campaigns are planned mainly by advertising agencies, of which there are several hundred in Britain; in some cases they also provide marketing, consumer research and other services.

Computing Services

The computing services industry comprises software houses, whose services include the writing of bespoke (application specific) software; production of packaged software for more general applications; consultancy; facilities management; computer bureau services, which process customers' data; and systems houses, which provide complete computer systems (hardware and software). It also includes companies providing information technology education and training, third party maintenance, contingency planning, and recruitment and contract staff.

The industry is one of the fastest growing sectors of the British economy. The turnover of companies in the Computing Services Association totalled over £3,000 million in 1989. Members of the Association provide employment for over 60,000 people, representing about 75 per cent of the computing services industry in Britain. The industry has traditionally been strong in professional services and bespoke software, and has been especially active in the provision of systems in the financial services sector. New developments include the adoption of advanced software engineering techniques, the design of systems kernels, systems integration and facilities management.

Management Consultancy

There are about 11,800 management consultants in Britain, of whom 3,600 are practising members of the Institute of Management Consultants. Among the largest management consultancy companies are the 33 members of the Management Consultancies Association, whose turnover amounted to £650 million in 1989. Revenue earned within Britain comprised £575 million, an increase of 37 per cent on the previous year, while overseas revenue amounted to £75 million. The Association reports a growing demand for services supporting the application of information technology, particularly microprocessing, to all aspects of business. The Association's members account for some 65 per cent of Britain's fee-paying management consultancy market.

Market Research

The 31 members of the Association of Market Survey Organisations (AMSO) accounted for about 75 per cent of total turnover by market research companies in 1989. The turnover of AMSO members increased to £239 million in 1989 from £205 million in 1988. The largest company, the AGB group, had a turnover of £45 million. Research on behalf of business-to-business services and industrial goods by AMSO members accounted for 60 per cent of revenue, while research for all consumer goods accounted for the remaining 40 per cent.

Exhibition and Conference Centres

Britain is one of the world's three leading countries for international conferences (the others being the United States and France). With the steady increase in new and renovated facilities, some 80 towns and cities are well equipped to hold conferences and exhibitions. Among the most modern purpose-built conference and exhibition centres are the International Conference Centre and the National Exhibition Centre at Birmingham, the Wembley Conference Centre, the Queen Elizabeth II Conference Centre and the Barbican Centre for Arts and Conferences in London, the Brighton Centre in East Sussex, the Harrogate Centre in North Yorkshire, the Bournemouth International Centre in Dorset, St David's Hall in Cardiff, the Scottish Exhibition and Conference Centre in Glasgow, the G-MEX Centre in Manchester, the Royal Centre in Nottingham, the English Riviera Centre in Torquay and the Aberdeen Exhibition and Conference Centre. Other large exhibition facilities are the Earls Court, Olympia, Alexandra Palace, London Arena (Docklands) and Wembley Arena sites in London. New centres are being constructed in Birmingham, Glasgow and Cardiff.

Auction Houses

Britain's chief auction houses are active in the international auction markets for works of art, trading on the acknowledged expertise of British valuers and dealers. The two largest houses, Sotheby's and Christie's, are established worldwide and their turnovers have expanded rapidly in recent years. Sotheby's handled sales valued at £1,820 million in 1989, while Christie's handled sales valued at £1,329 million, increases compared with 1988 of nearly 80 per cent and 70 per cent respectively.

MISCELLA-NEOUS SERVICES

Some 13,400 businesses provided film, theatre, literary, musical, broadcasting and related services in Great Britain in 1988. There are many self-employed people in these fields. About 500,000 people work in arts-related activities in Britain. Scientists, engineers and technicians engaged in industrial research and development and their support staff number 183,000. There were 13,800 businesses connected with sport, recreation, gambling and betting, at least 10,500 hairdressing and beauty parlours and some 8,900 dry cleaners. Other services include sanitation, photographic studios, religious organisations, tourist offices, learned societies, employers and trade union organisations, and firms providing funeral services and managing cemeteries and crematoria.

Films and Television

Recent years have seen further development of the independent programme production sector, and of specialised film and television services. The British Broadcasting Corporation and the commercial television stations have agreed to meet a government target whereby 25 per cent of original programmes will be made by independent producers by 1993. New technical developments include origination on professional standard video as opposed to film, and an increasing use of computer-generated graphics and picture manipulation in both production and post-production work. Production of films for cinema (an activity particularly cyclical in nature) declined in the mid-1980s.

    The Department of Trade and Industry conducts an annual inquiry into the value of overseas transactions relating to the production and exhibition of cinema and television material. For many years the inquiry has shown a surplus of receipts over expenditure. In 1989 receipts by film and television companies were £457 million, while expenditure was £380 million. Film companies' receipts totalled £263 million and television companies' receipts £194 million. A total of 101 film companies and 21 television broadcasting companies reported overseas transactions in the 1989 inquiry.

TOURISM AND TRAVEL

Tourism is one of Britain's most important industries and is a major and growing source of employment. It is estimated that about 1·5 million jobs in Britain were supported by tourism spending in 1989. The British Tourist Authority forecasts that around 200,000 new jobs will be created in the period 1988–93.

In 1989 overseas residents made 17·2 million visits to Britain—an increase since 1988 of 9 per cent; they spent £6,850 million, compared with £6,200 million in the previous year. British residents made 31·1 million trips abroad, an increase of 8 per cent compared with 1988, and spent £9,380 million, giving a deficit on the travel account of £2,530 million. Over 84 per cent of these visits were to Western Europe. About 62 per cent of overseas visitors to Britain came from Western Europe and 20 per cent from North America.

A total of 2,971 travel agencies, with about 8,000 offices (over 90 per cent of the total), belong to the Association of British Travel Agents (ABTA). In general, travel agents are small businesses but many ABTA members have more than one office. There are a few large firms—for example, Lunn Poly, with some 500 branches, and Thomas Cook, with about 365. Computerised information and booking systems are used extensively in travel agencies. There are also 700 tour operator members of ABTA; some 344 companies are both retail agents and tour operators. ABTA operates financial protection schemes to safeguard its members' customers, maintains codes of conduct drawn up with the Office of Fair Trading, and offers a free conciliation service to help to resolve complaints against members and an independent arbitration scheme for tour operators' customers.

Tourist Authorities

Official support for the promotion of tourism to and within Britain is provided by the British Tourist Authority (BTA) and the tourist boards for England, Scotland, Wales and Northern Ireland. The boards have been asked by the Government to encourage tourism in regions where unemployment is high and where there is potential for development. Following a review of both tourism promotion and the development of tourism in England in 1988, the Government determined that the existing organisation needed to be simplified and that, while government financial support should be continued, it needed to be more sharply focused. The BTA has been asked to improve cost-effectiveness and to extend partnerships with the industry, to devolve greater authority to its overseas markets and to transfer some of its operations to the private sector. The English Tourist Board (ETB) has been asked to devolve many of its activities and to allocate more of its funding to regional tourist boards, thus allowing them scope to increase their marketing activities and their encouragement of local tourism. The centralised operations of both the BTA and the ETB are to be scaled down.

At the same time, a new strategy for the development of tourism in Northern Ireland was announced, which concentrates on the stimulation of demand through different marketing, the co-ordinated development of the industry through improved access, accommodation and amenities, and the identification of tourism attractions in Northern Ireland as centres of international excellence.

Throughout Britain over 16,000 hotels and other serviced ac commodation are inspected and Crown classified by the tourist boards. Th classifications 'Listed' and one to five crowns indicate the range of facilitie and services provided. Those with higher quality standards are distinguishe by the terms 'Approved', 'Commended' or 'Highly Commended' along side their classification. A similar arrangement applies to self-caterin accommodation. The quality standard of holiday caravans, chalets an camping parks is indicated by a 'Q' symbol and one to five ticks. Informatio on tourist facilities and accommodation is available from official touris information centres throughout Britain (most of which are administered b local government) and on videotext information services in Britain an overseas.

15 Energy and Natural Resources

Energy and non-fuel minerals make an important contribution to the British economy. The approximate value of minerals produced in 1988 was £15,293 million (representing about 3·8 per cent of gross domestic product), of which crude oil accounted for 45 per cent, coal 28 per cent and natural gas 13 per cent.

All minerals in Great Britain are privately owned, with the exception of gold, silver, oil and natural gas (which are owned by the Crown), and coal and some minerals associated with coal. In Northern Ireland gold and silver are owned by the Crown, while rights to petroleum and other minerals are vested in the Government. On the United Kingdom Continental Shelf the right to exploit all minerals except coal is vested in the Crown. The exclusive right to extract coal, or license others to do so, both on land in Great Britain and under the sea, is vested in the British Coal Corporation. Normally, ownership of minerals belongs to the owner of the land surface but in some areas, particularly those with a long history of mining, these rights have become separated. Mining and quarrying, apart from coalmining, are usually carried out by privately owned companies.

Water resources are normally sufficient for domestic and industrial requirements; supplies are obtained from surface sources such as mountain lakes and from underground sources by such means as wells and boreholes.

Energy

Britain has the largest energy resources of any country in the European Community and is a major world producer of oil, natural gas and coal. The other main primary sources are nuclear power and some water power; secondary sources are electricity, coke and very small quantities of town gas. Since 1980 Britain has been self-sufficient in energy in net terms as a result of offshore oil production, and self-sufficiency should be maintained for a number of years. There are large reserves of coal, which is expected to continue to supply a significant proportion of the country's energy needs. Nuclear power provided nearly 21 per cent of electricity available from the British public supply system in 1989.

Private sector companies carry out offshore oil and gas production and oil refining, while a publicly owned body is at present responsible for most coal production. The electricity supply industry in Great Britain, apart from nuclear power, is to be privatised, as is the electricity supply industry in Northern Ireland. The Secretary of State for Energy is responsible for these industries in Great Britain, except for electricity in Scotland, which is under the Secretary of State for Scotland. The Secretary of State for Northern Ireland is responsible for all energy matters there.

Energy Policy   Energy policy is designed to ensure the secure, adequate and economic provision of energy to meet Britain's requirements. The Government, while encouraging the exploitation of Britain's diversity of energy sources, seeks to ensure that all economic forms of energy are produced, supplied and used as efficiently as possible, having regard also to the international application of the technologies involved. The Government stresses the importance of the continued profitable development of Britain's oil and gas resources, the development of a competitive coal industry, the safe and economic development of nuclear power, and the most cost-effective use of energy through the adoption of energy efficiency measures. It also funds an extensive research and development programme into renewable sources of energy.

Privatisation has already had a considerable impact in the energy field, with the transfer of British Gas, Britoil and Enterprise Oil, and the planned transfer of the electricity supply industry, to the private sector. The Government wishes to privatise the coal industry during the next Parliament. It considers that these industries will thus improve their competitiveness and efficiency, free of government pressures, and attract new investment to provide cheaper and cleaner energy.

Britain is actively engaged in international collaboration on energy questions, notably through its membership of the European Community and of the International Energy Agency (a body with 21 member countries attached to the Organisation for Economic Co-operation and Development).

ENERGY CONSUMPTION   Inland primary energy consumption amounted to 340·2 million tonnes of coal equivalent in 1989 (see Table 15.1), about the same as in 1988. Energy consumption by final users in 1989 amounted to 59,078 million therms[1] on a 'heat supplied' basis, of which transport consumed 32 per cent, industrial users 28 per cent, domestic users about 27 per cent, and commerce, agriculture and public services 13 per cent.

Table 15.1: Inland Energy Consumption (in terms of primary sources)

million tonnes coal equivalent

	1979	1984	1987	1988	1989
Oil	139·0	135·2	109·3	116·1	118·2
Coal	129·6	79·0	116·2	112·0	108·1
Natural gas	71·1	76·5	85·9	81·5	80·5
Nuclear energy	13·8	19·5	19·8	22·9	25·9
Hydro-electric power	2·2	2·1	2·1	2·4	2·3
Net imports of electricity	—	—	4·7	5·2	5·2
Total	355·7	312·2	338·1	340·1	340·2

Source: Department of Energy.
Note: Differences between totals and the sums of their component parts are due to rounding.

ENERGY EFFICIENCY   The Government encourages the improvement of energy efficiency through the work of the Energy Efficiency Office (EEO). Since its establishment in 1983 the EEO has promoted efficiency in various ways, and significant energy savings are being achieved every year. The Government believes that

[1] 1 therm = 105,506 kilojoules.

energy efficiency can make a significant contribution to alleviating the problems of climate change, which could threaten sustainable development.

The EEO, with a budget of £26 million in 1990–91, is now concentrating on key areas of energy use and offers advice backed by technical support. In particular, it promotes the work of its regional energy efficiency officers and provides a best practice programme which gives industrial and commercial consumers advice on energy efficiency and on how it can be implemented.

The Home Energy Efficiency Scheme provides advice and grants to low-income households for insulation measures, such as loft, tank and pipe insulation, draughtproofing and hot-water tank insulation. Householders are eligible if they receive income support, housing benefit, family credit or community charge benefit.

The Government promotes investment in combined heat and power (CHP)—the co-generation of electricity and heat—within the best practice programme. Some 500 CHP plants, both in industry and buildings, are in operation. They contribute about 3 per cent of electricity demand in Britain.

OIL AND GAS

Britain's energy position is strengthened by substantial oil and gas reserves offshore in the United Kingdom Continental Shelf (UKCS). The total area covered by production licences is 98,893 sq km (38,183 sq miles) out of a total designated area of about 651,650 sq km (251,600 sq miles), over which Britain has exercised its rights to explore and exploit the seabed and subsoil. The Government has granted exploration and production licences as a result of 11 offshore licensing rounds since 1964. In 1990 it launched the twelfth round and the first separate round of offshore licensing for frontier areas. Expenditure on offshore and onshore exploration and development amounted to some £2,650 million in 1989. By the end of 1989, 4,004 wells had been or were being drilled in the UKCS: 1,832 development wells, 1,364 exploration wells and 808 appraisal wells.

Offshore Supplies

Britain's offshore supplies industry is the second largest in the world and has headed considerable technological advance. The Offshore Supplies Office (OSO) of the Department of Energy is responsible for promoting a fair commercial opportunity for British suppliers in the UKCS and throughout the world. It is estimated that British suppliers are winning orders worth between £2,000 million and £3,000 million a year worldwide.

The OSO provides the secretariat for the Offshore Industry Advisory Board. The Board is the principal source of high-level co-ordinated advice on the development of strategy for Britain's offshore supplies industry. It is assisted by four sub-committees: the Offshore Industry Liaison Committee reviews UKCS activity; the International Collaboration Advisory Group promotes mutually beneficial collaboration with other countries; the Offshore Industry Exports Advisory Group considers export strategy; and the Offshore Energy Technology Board (OETB) determines priorities for research and development.

OIL

Before the 1970s Britain was almost wholly dependent for its oil supplies on imports, the only indigenous supplies coming from a small number of land-based oilfields. However, the first notable offshore discovery of oil in the UKCS was made in 1969 and the first oil was brought ashore in 1975. Output of crude oil from the UKCS in 1989 averaged 1·18 million barrels (252,050 tonnes) a day, making Britain the world's eighth largest producer.

North Sea Fields

There were 44 offshore fields producing crude oil at the end of 1989, and the Secretary of State for Energy approved 13 new offshore development projects during the year.

The largest producing fields are Brent and Forties. Production from most large fields is controlled from production platforms of either steel or concrete which have been built to withstand severe weather, including gusts of wind of up to 260 km/h (160 mph) and waves of 30 m (100 ft).

Primary oil production, including condensates and petroleum gases, amounted to about 91·8 million tonnes in 1989 (see Table 15.2). Output is forecast to decline slowly, but Britain should remain self-sufficient in oil well into the 1990s and a significant producer into the twenty-first century. The Government's oil policy is intended to encourage exploration and development with the objective of maximising economic oil production for the foreseeable future. Remaining recoverable reserves of UKCS oil in the proven plus probable categories amount to between 510 and 1,200 million tonnes, while the total remaining reserves of the UKCS could be as high as 5,160 million tonnes. The Petroleum Act 1987 empowers the Secretary of State to require those responsible to submit to him for approval programmes setting out measures to be taken in connection with the abandonment of offshore installations and pipelines.

Table 15.2: Oil Statistics

million tonnes

	1979	1984	1987	1988	1989
Oil production[a]					
land	0·1	0·3	0·6	0·8	0·7
offshore	77·7	125·6	122·8	113·7	91·0
Refinery output	90·6	73·2	74·7	79·8	81·4
Deliveries of petroleum products for inland consumption	84·6	81·4	67·7	72·3	73·0
Exports (including re-exports)					
crude petroleum	38·8	75·9	80·6	70·5	49·2
refined petroleum products and process oils	14·4	16·4	18·7	18·9	20·1
Imports:					
crude petroleum	57·9	25·0	33·1	32·8	36·3
refined petroleum products and process oils	16·0	28·5	20·8	21·4	21·7

Sources: Department of Energy and HM Customs and Excise.
[a] Crude oil plus condensates and petroleum gases derived at onshore treatment plants.

Structure of the Oil Industry

About 250 companies, including several large oil companies, operate in Britain or engage in work in the UKCS. The two leading British oil companies are British Petroleum (BP) and Shell Transport and Trading, which are the two largest industrial companies in Britain in terms of turnover. Exploration and development of the UKCS are carried out by the private sector. The Government now takes all royalty from UKCS oil in cash and has terminated its rights under participation agreements with the oil companies.

Oil

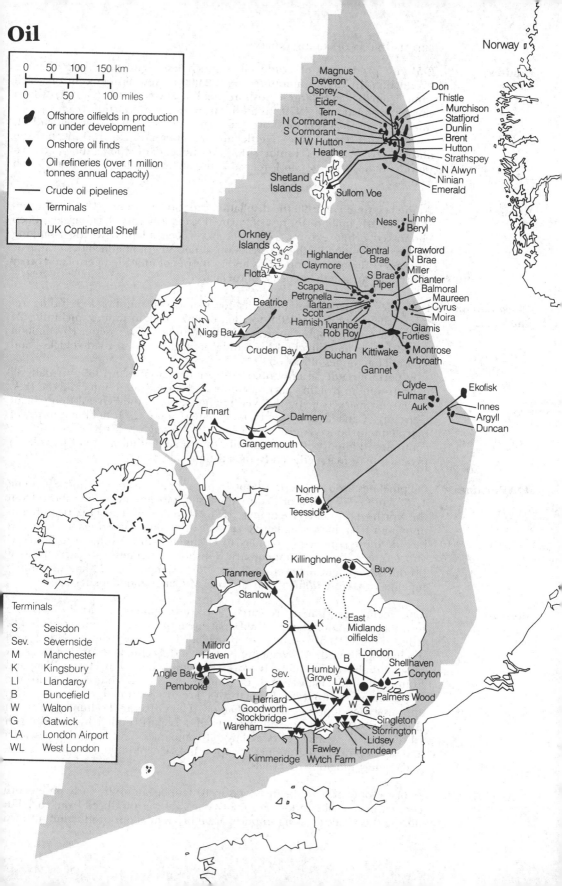

Scale bars:
0 50 100 150 km
0 50 100 miles

Legend:
- Offshore oilfields in production or under development
- ▼ Onshore oil finds
- Oil refineries (over 1 million tonnes annual capacity)
- Crude oil pipelines
- ▲ Terminals
- UK Continental Shelf

Norway

Magnus
Deveron
Osprey
Eider
Tern
N Cormorant
S Cormorant
N W Hutton
Heather

Don
Thistle
Murchison
Statfjord
Dunlin
Brent
Hutton
Strathspey
N Alwyn
Ninian
Emerald

Shetland Islands
Sullom Voe

Orkney Islands

Ness
Linnhe
Beryl

Highlander
Claymore
Flotta
Scapa
Petronella
Tartan
Scott
Hamish
Ivanhoe
Rob Roy
Buchan

Central Brae
S Brae
Piper

Crawford
N Brae
Miller
Chanter
Balmoral
Maureen
Cyrus
Moira

Beatrice

Nigg Bay ▲
Cruden Bay ▲

Glamis
Forties
Kittiwake
Gannet

Montrose
Arbroath

Finnart ▲

Dalmeny
Grangemouth ▲

Clyde
Fulmar
Auk

Ekofisk
Innes
Argyll
Duncan

North Tees
Teesside ▲

Killingholme
Buoy

Tranmere ▲
Stanlow

M

East Midlands oilfields

S
K

London
B
Shellhaven
Coryton

Milford Haven
Angle Bay
Pembroke

LI

Sev.

Humbly Grove
LA
WL
Palmers Wood

Herriard
Goodworth
Stockbridge
Wareham

Singleton
Storrington
Lidsey
Horndean

W
G

Kimmeridge
Fawley
Wytch Farm

Terminals

S	Seisdon
Sev.	Severnside
M	Manchester
K	Kingsbury
LI	Llandarcy
B	Buncefield
W	Walton
G	Gatwick
LA	London Airport
WL	West London

Land-based Fields

Onshore production of crude oil is much less significant than offshore production. In 1989 it amounted to 722,000 tonnes, 66 per cent of which came from Britain's largest onshore field at Wytch Farm (Dorset), which started production in 1979. In addition to minor production from various mining licensees, other onshore fields include Humbly Grove, Horndean and Herriard (Hampshire), Nettleham and Stampton North (Lincolnshire) and Crosby Warren (Humberside). At the end of 1989, 268 landward petroleum licences were in force, covering an area of 46,000 sq km (17,800 sq miles).

Refineries

At the beginning of 1990 the distillation capacity of Britain's 13 oil refineries stood at 91 million tonnes a year. Excess capacity has largely been eliminated, while existing refineries have been adapted to the changing pattern of demand by the construction of new upgrading facilities ('catalytic crackers'), which are leading to a higher output of unleaded petrol and other lighter products at the expense of fuel oil.

Consumption and Trade

Deliveries of petroleum products for inland consumption (excluding refinery consumption) in 1989 totalled over 73 million tonnes, including 24 million tonnes of motor spirit, 8·5 million tonnes of kerosene, 18·4 million tonnes of gas and diesel oil (including derv fuel used in road vehicles) and 11·1 million tonnes of fuel oil.

Exports of crude oil amounted to 49·2 million tonnes in 1989. Virtually all exports went to Britain's partners in the European Community and the IEA, the largest markets being the Netherlands, France, the Federal Republic of Germany, Canada and the United States. Some 20·1 million tonnes of petroleum products were also exported. Though self-sufficient, Britain continues to import other crude oils, to enable the full range of petroleum products to be made efficiently and economically.

Oil Pipelines

Oil pipelines brought ashore about 75 per cent of offshore oil in 1989. Some 1,733 km (1,077 miles) of major submarine pipeline bring oil ashore from the North Sea oilfields (see map, p 315). Major crude oil onshore pipelines in operation from harbours, land terminals or offshore moorings to refineries include those connecting Finnart to Grangemouth, Tranmere to Stanlow, and Cruden Bay to Grangemouth. Onshore pipelines also carry refined products to major marketing areas; for example, a 423-km (263-mile) pipeline runs from Milford Haven to the Midlands and Manchester.

Research

The main government research and development effort in offshore technology is undertaken by the Department of Energy through the OETB. Advice on offshore safety is provided by the Offshore Safety and Technology Board. A Petroleum Science and Technology Institute was set up in Edinburgh in 1989. It works in conjunction with Heriot-Watt and Edinburgh universities, and is funded by 35 oil companies and the Department of Energy. Its activities are concentrated on exploration, appraisal, development and production. The Offshore Technology Park in Aberdeen comprises several projects and is part-funded by the Scottish Development Agency. The leading oil companies have extensive research and development programmes in support of oil exploration and production, and on new and improved fuels.

GAS

Public supply of manufactured gas in Britain began in the early nineteenth century in central London. For many years gas was produced from coal, but during the 1960s growing imports of oil brought about production of town gas from oil-based feedstocks. Following the first commercial natural gas discovery in the UKCS in 1965 and the start of offshore gas production in 1967, supplies of offshore natural gas grew rapidly and by 1977 natural gas had replaced town gas in the public supply system in Great Britain. Some £12,000 million has been spent on developing natural gas resources on the UKCS and over 720,000 million cubic metres have been produced.

Structure

Under the Gas Act 1986, the gas industry in Great Britain, in state ownership since 1949, was privatised and the assets of the British Gas Corporation transferred to the new company, British Gas plc. The Act also established the Office of Gas Supply, to monitor British Gas's activities as a public gas supplier, and the Gas Consumers Council, to look after the interests of consumers.

British Gas has about 2·5 million shareholders. In 1989–90 the turnover of British Gas and its subsidiary companies amounted to £7,983 million, of which gas supply accounted for £6,909 million. Current cost operating profit was £1,095 million. British Gas has over 79,000 employees.

Production

Total production of natural gas from the 28 fields in the UKCS in 1989 amounted to 44,745 million cubic metres. This includes gas used for drilling, production and pumping operations. Gas produced and used on North Sea production platforms and at terminals accounted for 3,139 million cubic metres, leaving 41,606 million for general supply. Supplies of UKCS gas to British Gas (41,000 million cubic metres in 1989) were slightly lower than in 1988 and accounted for 79·8 per cent of its total natural gas supplies, the remainder coming from Norway. UKCS production comes mainly from eight major gasfields: Leman, Frigg (UK), Indefatigable, North Alwyn, Viking, Hewett, West Sole and Victor. In addition, gas from the South Morecambe field in the Irish Sea and from the twin North Sean and South Sean fields is used to augment supplies to meet peak demand in winter. In 1989 two new gas developments were approved, Welland North and Welland South, and one incremental project, Audrey phase 2.

Remaining recoverable gas reserves, including possible gas from existing discoveries and potential future discoveries, are estimated to be in the range of 890,000 million to 3·18 million million cubic metres. Indigenous offshore natural gas reserves are likely to meet most of the British demand well into the next century.

Transmission and Storage

The British Gas national and regional high-pressure pipeline system of some 17,600 km (11,100 miles) transports natural gas around Great Britain. It is supplied from four North Sea shore terminals, and from a terminal in Barrow-in-Furness (Cumbria). The high-pressure transmission system is inspected regularly.

Various methods of storage of natural gas to meet peak load conditions are used, including salt cavities and storage facilities for liquefied natural gas. British Gas has also developed the partially depleted Rough field as a major gas store. This, the first such use of an offshore field, involves the injection into the Rough reservoir in summer of gas drawn from the national transmission system for recovery at high rates during periods of peak winter demand.

Consumption

Sales of gas by the supply industry in Britain totalled 18,552 million therms in 1989–90. About 47 per cent of all gas sold by British Gas to its 17·7 million consumers is for industrial and commercial purposes, the remainder being for household use. Gas is used extensively in industries requiring the control

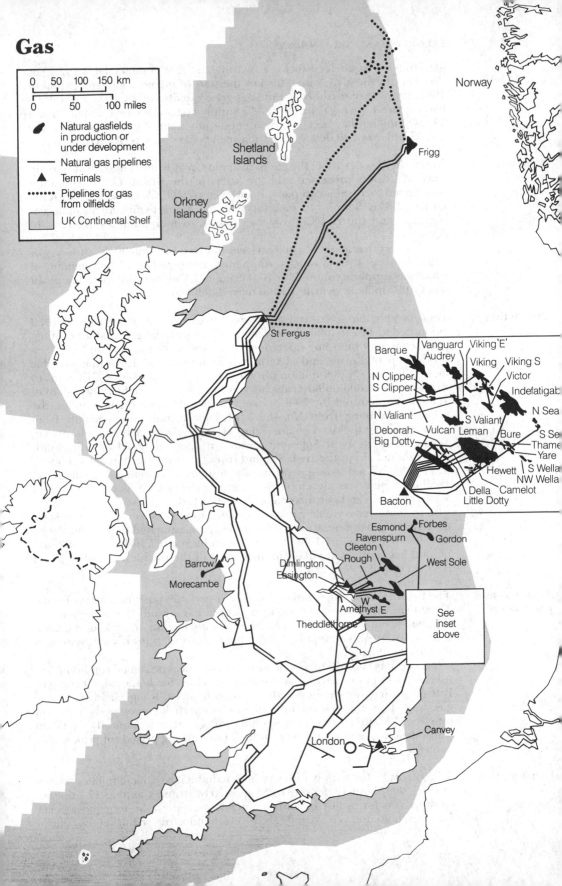

Gas

Scale:
0 50 100 150 km
0 50 100 miles

- ⬭ Natural gasfields in production or under development
- — Natural gas pipelines
- ▲ Terminals
- ⋯ Pipelines for gas from oilfields
- ▨ UK Continental Shelf

Norway

Shetland Islands

Orkney Islands

Frigg

St Fergus

Barrow

Morecambe

Inset (See inset above):

Barque
Vanguard
Audrey
Viking 'E'
Viking
Viking S
N Clipper
S Clipper
Victor
Indefatigab
N Sea
N Valiant
S Valiant
Deborah
Big Dotty
Vulcan
Leman
Bure
S Se
Thame
Yare
Hewett
S Wella
NW Wella
Della
Camelot
Little Dotty
Bacton

Esmond
Forbes
Ravenspurn
Gordon
Cleeton
Rough
West Sole
Dimlington
Easington
W
Amethyst E
Theddlethorpe

See inset above

Canvey
London

of temperatures to a fine degree of accuracy, such as the pottery industry, and in certain processes for making iron and steel products. In 1989–90, 5,743 million therms of gas were sold to industry in Britain, and 2,919 million therms to commercial and other non-domestic users. An increasingly large part of domestic demand is for gas for central heating. In 1989–90, 9,890 million therms were sold to domestic users.

Research

British Gas spends some £75 million a year on its research and development programme, principally carried out at five establishments throughout Britain. It has information exchange and research agreements with a number of overseas gas companies and carries out research in collaboration with universities and industry both in Britain and overseas. Its research programme covers engineering, design, materials technology and instrumentation, and electronics, related to all aspects of the gas business, from exploration and production, storage and transmission, and pipeline inspection to distribution and utilisation.

British Gas makes a wide range of technology, products, processes and services available worldwide.

COAL

Coalmining in Britain can be traced back to Roman times. It recommenced in the thirteenth century. It played a crucial part in the industrial revolution of the eighteenth and nineteenth centuries, and in its peak year, 1913, the industry produced 292 million tonnes of coal, exported 74·2 million tonnes and employed over a million workers. In 1947 the coalmines passed into public ownership by means of the Coal Industry Nationalisation Act 1946, which set up the National Coal Board, subsequently the British Coal Corporation. The Government has announced that it will introduce legislation to privatise the coal industry during the next Parliament. The Coal Industry Act 1990 provides for a major capital reconstruction of British Coal, and includes clauses enabling the Secretary of State for Energy to reduce or extinguish its accumulated group losses at the end of the 1989–90 financial year and to pay further grants in respect of redundancy and restructuring costs.

British Coal Corporation

British Coal has, with limited exceptions, exclusive rights over the extraction of coal in Great Britain. It is empowered to license private operators to work mines with an employee limit of 150 and opencast sites with a production limit of 250,000 tonnes so that underground and opencast deposits too small for British Coal to work can be usefully exploited. It also has powers to work other minerals, where discoveries are made in the course of searching for, or working, coal; and to engage in certain petrochemicals activities beneficial to the future of the coal industry. Retail sales are largely in private hands, although British Coal makes bulk sales to large industrial consumers and has signed three-year contracts to supply coal to the electricity generating companies in England and Wales.

Production

In 1989–90 total output of 96·8 million tonnes comprised 75·2 million tonnes of deep-mined coal, 18·3 million tonnes from opencast mines and 3·3 million tonnes from other sources (including licensed collieries and tip coal). At the end of March 1990 there were 73 British Coal collieries in operation. The main coal-bearing regions are shown on the map on p 320. Where mining operations have ceased, British Coal has accepted responsibility for the restoration of the surface area of collieries and of tips which close in the four years after 31 March 1990.

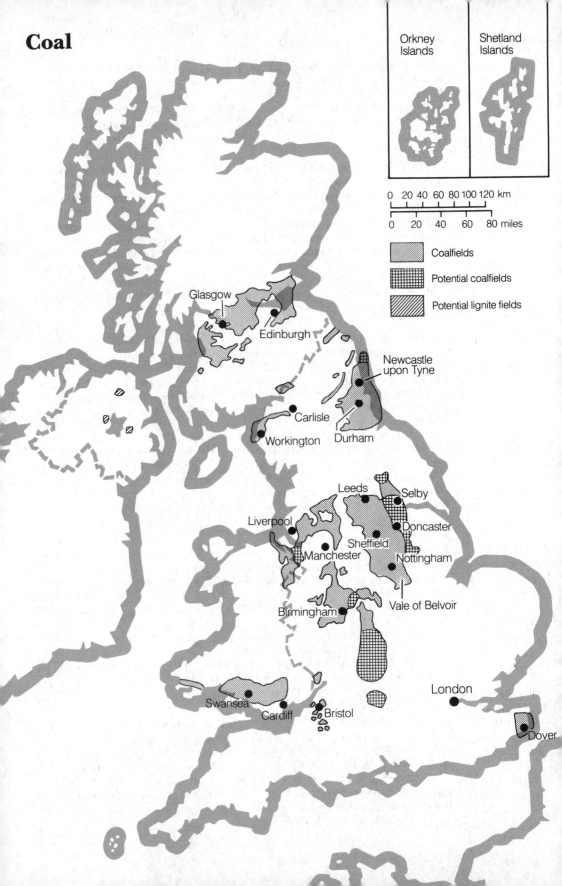

Coal

Orkney Islands
Shetland Islands

0 20 40 60 80 100 120 km
0 20 40 60 80 miles

Coalfields
Potential coalfields
Potential lignite fields

Glasgow
Edinburgh
Newcastle upon Tyne
Carlisle
Workington
Durham
Leeds
Selby
Liverpool
Doncaster
Manchester
Sheffield
Nottingham
Birmingham
Vale of Belvoir
Swansea
Cardiff
Bristol
London
Dover

Development

Britain's coal industry is one of the largest in Western Europe, and one of the world's most technologically advanced. British Coal has a substantial capital investment programme, which amounted to £505 million in 1989–90. Technical progress has been concentrated on equipment capable of obtaining higher output from fewer faces. By early 1990 some 50 to 60 per cent of all coal faces were equipped with heavy duty supports available in all seam sections. New designs of power loader and face conveyor are being brought in whenever they are cost-effective. Production at the new mining complex at Selby in North Yorkshire (one of the world's most advanced deep mines) is planned to build up to 10 million tonnes a year. Total estimated expenditure on the development of a new mine at Asfordby within the Vale of Belvoir (Leicestershire) is £471 million.

Significant reserves of lignite (brown coal) have been discovered in Northern Ireland in the clay basins around Lough Neagh and at Ballymoney. Companies under government licence are prospecting to determine their extent, possibly over 1,000 million tonnes.

Consumption

In 1989–90 inland consumption of coal was 108·9 million tonnes, of which 75 per cent was by power stations, 10 per cent by coke ovens and 4 per cent by domestic users. With a substantial proportion of coal being used by power stations for electricity generation, British Coal sales of coal to them totalled 77·7 million tonnes in 1989–90. Exports of coal in 1989–90 were 2·5 million tonnes, while imports amounted to 12·3 million tonnes.

Research

In 1989–90 British Coal spent £27·5 million on research. It has two main research establishments: Technical Department at Stanhope Bretby in Staffordshire, for work on mining methods and equipment, and developing systems for remote and automatic control; and the Coal Research Establishment at Stoke Orchard (near Cheltenham), concentrating on the utilisation of coal, including research and development on improved combustion and coal and ash handling techniques, together with new ways of making gaseous, liquid and smokeless fuels from coal. These developments aim to ensure the clean and efficient use of coal. The coal liquefaction plant at Point of Ayr (Clwyd), opened in 1990 and costing £40 million, converts 2·5 tonnes of coal a day into petrol, diesel and other transport fuels. The Government has offered 50 per cent of the cost (up to a total of £8 million) of a programme aimed at speeding the development of cleaner coal-fired electricity. This is part of a £27 million project to bring topping cycle technology, which offers a 20 per cent reduction in carbon dioxide emissions from coal-fired power stations, to the demonstration stage by the early 1990s.

ELECTRICITY

Under the Electricity Act 1947 the electricity supply industry in Great Britain was brought into public ownership in 1948, although two subsequent Acts (1954 and 1957) effected a measure of decentralisation. Electricity from the supply system is available to all premises in Britain except for some very remote households. The main transmission system (national grid) in Great Britain is one of the largest fully interconnected power networks in the Western world.

Restructuring and Privatisation

The Electricity Act 1989 provides for the restructuring and offer for sale of certain parts of the electricity supply industry in England and Wales and in Scotland. In the Government's view, privatisation would promote competition in generation and supply, which would be in the customer's interest, and would leave generating and supply companies free to manage their commercial opportunities without interference from government.

In England and Wales the Central Electricity Generating Board (CEGB), responsible for the operation and maintenance of power stations and owner of the national grid, has been split into four companies: PowerGen, owning 37 per cent of the CEGB's non-nuclear generating capacity; National Power, comprising 63 per cent of the CEGB's non-nuclear generating capacity; a publicly owned nuclear company, Nuclear Electric plc; and the National Grid Company, owned through a holding company by the 12 regional electricity companies. These are the successor companies to the area electricity boards and each has a statutory duty to offer terms for the supply of electricity. It is expected that the sale of the supply companies will take place in November 1990; those of National Power and PowerGen are planned to take place in February 1991.

The Electricity Council, the central co-ordinating body of the industry in England and Wales, has been replaced. Some of its service functions are carried on by the Electricity Association, jointly owned by the electricity companies of Great Britain. Regulation of the industry is in the care of the Office of Electricity Regulation, headed by the Director General of Electricity Supply, who is responsible for the promotion of competition and oversees the protection of consumer interests.

Restructuring in Scotland has created three companies. Two vertically integrated regional companies, Scottish Power plc, based on the SSEB (but without its nuclear capacity), and Scottish Hydro-Electric plc, based on the NSHEB, generate, transmit and distribute electricity. They also buy it from Scottish Nuclear Ltd, a government-owned company which operates the nuclear power stations at Hunterston (Strathclyde) and Torness (Lothian). Scottish Power and Scottish Hydro-Electric will be offered for sale in May or June 1991. The boundary separating their areas runs from Loch Long on the Firth of Clyde to Newburgh on the Firth of Tay (see map, p 323).

The Government has also announced its intention to privatise the electricity supply industry in Northern Ireland, where generation, transmission and distribution are at present carried out by Northern Ireland Electricity, a public corporation.

Consumption

Sales of electricity in 1989 amounted to 267,343 gigawatt hours (GWh). Domestic users took 35 per cent of the total, industry 36 per cent and commercial and other users the remainder. About one-fifth of domestic sales is for space heating, one-sixth for water heating and one-tenth for cooking. Electricity is used in industry mainly for motive power, melting, heating and lighting. It is supplied to some 25 million consumers, of whom 22 million are in England and Wales, 1·7 million are supplied by Scottish Power, 600,000 by Scottish Hydro-Electric and 599,000 are in Northern Ireland.

Generation

Generation by the public electricity supply industry in Britain amounted to 292,911 GWh in 1989. Conventional steam power stations provided over 75 per cent of the total, nuclear stations 23 per cent, and gas turbine, hydro-electric and diesel plant 2 per cent. Public supply power stations consumed 123·7 million tonnes of coal equivalent in 1989, of which coal accounted for 65 per cent and oil 7·6 per cent. The output capacity of the 167 generating stations of the electricity boards at the end of March 1989 totalled 66,996 megawatts (MW). An analysis of electricity generation by and output capacity of the public supply system is given in Table 15.3.

Generation of electricity outside the public supply system is relatively small (19,797 GWh in 1989). The major sources outside the fuel industries are the chemicals, engineering, paper, and iron and steel industries, and the nuclear power plants of the United Kingdom Atomic Energy Authority (UKAEA)

Electricity

Orkney Islands

Shetland Islands

	km
0 20 40 60 80 100 120 km	
0 20 40 60 80 miles	

■ Conventional power stations (1,000 MW and over)

● Nuclear power stations

○ Under construction

◆ Power-producing reactors of the UKAEA or BNFL

★ Hydro-electric power stations (over 45-MW capacity)

▲ Pumped storage schemes

Dounreay ◆

Fasnakyle ★

▲ Foyers

Peterhead ■

Errochty ★

Rannoch ★

Cruachan ▲

Clunie ★

Lochay ★

Sloy ★

erated by
ottish Power

Longannet ■

Torness ●

Inverkip ■

Cockenzie ■

Hunterston B ● ● Hunterston A

Chapelcross ◆

Blyth B ■

Hartlepool ●

Calder Hall ◆

Heysham I ● ● Heysham II

Ferrybridge C ■ Drax ■

Eggborough ■

Wylfa ●

Fiddler's Ferry ■

Cottam ■ ■ West Burton

▲ Dinorwig

▲ Ffestiniog

● Trawsfynydd

Ratcliffe-on-Soar ■

Rheidol ★

Sizewell A ●
Sizewell B ○

Tilbury

W. Thurrock ■ ● Bradwell

Pembroke ■

Aberthaw B ■

● Oldbury

Didcot ■

Littlebrook ■ ■ Grain

Kingsnorth

Hinkley Pt. A ● ● Hinkley Pt. B

Fawley ■

Dungeness B ● ●
Dungeness A

Winfrith ◆

Table 15.3: Generation by and Capacity of Public Supply Power Stations

	Electricity generated (GWh)			Per cent	Output capacity[a]
	1979	1984	1989	1989	(MW)
Nuclear plant	34,604	49,498	66,740	23	6,973
Other steam plant	239,317	209,121	219,714	75	51,882
Gas turbines and oil engines	758	1,947	542	—	2,982
Pumped-storage plant	1,175	2,055	2,067	1	2,788
Other hydro-electric plant	3,628	3,368	3,845	1	1,293
Total	279,482	265,990	292,911	100	65,922[b]
Electricity supplied (net)[c]	259,836	246,367	271,729		

Source: Department of Energy.
[a] At 31 December 1988.
[b] This total includes 4 MW of wind power.
[c] Electricity generated less electricity used at power stations (including electricity used for pumping at pumped-storage stations).
Note: Differences between totals and the sums of their component parts are due to rounding.

and British Nuclear Fuels plc. In 1989 these nuclear plants supplied 4,994 GWh of electricity to the public supply system.

The Electricity Act 1989 allows independent generators to compete on equal terms with the major generators and have equal access to the grid transmission and local distribution systems.

The last large-scale power stations to be built were based on turbines of 500 MW and 660 MW. Station capacities have increased and there are 15 stations with a capacity of 2,000 MW or more each, including Kingsnorth (Kent), Europe's largest mixed-fuel station burning either coal or oil. The Drax coal-fired station (North Yorkshire), which has an output capacity of 4,000 MW, is the largest coal-fired station in Western Europe. The larger turbines have a higher thermal efficiency (the ratio of the net electrical energy output to the heat energy input) than earlier units, and their introduction, coupled with the closure of less efficient plant, has resulted in a gradual rise in overall thermal efficiency, leading to substantial savings in fuel consumption. Average thermal efficiency of conventional steam stations in England and Wales was 33·7 per cent in 1989–90. The Government is considering proposals for future generation capacity in Northern Ireland, from the mid-1990s, including a lignite-fired power station.

To control acid emissions the Government expects National Power and PowerGen each to fit some flue gas desulphurisation equipment to coal-fired power stations. The first of these operations, at Drax, is in progress. In addition, the Government has endorsed a ten-year programme to control nitrogen oxide emissions through the installation of low nitrogen oxide burners at the 12 largest power stations, at an estimated cost of £190 million.

The Government encourages the construction of combined cycle gas turbine (CCGT) power stations, which emit about half the amount of carbon dioxide of a coal-fired station. Five CCGT stations in England have been given planning permission.

The pumped-storage station at Dinorwig (Gwynedd), the largest of its type in Europe, has an average generated output of 1,728 MW. (In pumped-storage schemes electricity generated in off-peak periods is used to pump water to high-level reservoirs from which it descends to drive turbines, rapidly providing a large supply of electricity at peak periods or to meet sudden increases in demand.)

The National Grid Company, together with Electricité de France, runs a 2,000-MW cross-Channel cable link, which started operating in 1986, increasing the capacity for the transmission of electricity between the two countries. Transmission lines linking the Scottish and English grid systems enable cross-border trading. This interconnector is run jointly by the National Grid Company and the two Scottish regional companies. It has a nominal capacity of 850 MW, with an increase to 1,600 MW planned by 1993–94.

Nuclear Power   Britain has been developing nuclear power since 1956, when the world's first industrial-scale nuclear power station, at Calder Hall (Cumbria), began to supply electricity to the national grid. There are 16 nuclear power stations in operation: nine Magnox stations (with capacities ranging from 200 to 840 MW) and seven Advanced Gas-cooled Reactor stations (AGRs; ranging from 1,200 MW to 1,320 MW). Construction of a pressurised water reactor (PWR) of 1,182 MW at Sizewell (Suffolk) should be completed in 1994.

Nuclear Power   The Government wishes to preserve the strategic role of nuclear power,
and Privatisation   maintain diversity of supply, avoid too great a reliance on a single fuel and obtain the benefits of this environmentally clean source of energy. It has decided that all the nuclear power stations in Great Britain will remain in the public sector and will review the prospects for nuclear power as the PWR at Sizewell nears completion. The Magnox stations, AGRs and PWR in England and Wales are contained in a new company, Nuclear Electric plc, which will provide between 15 and 20 per cent of electricity in England and Wales in the mid-1990s. The two AGRs in Scotland supply 50 per cent of all the Scottish electricity requirement.

In England and Wales the regional electricity supply companies are statutorily obliged to buy a minimum amount of non-fossil-fuelled generating capacity, including nuclear. Since the price of nuclear electricity is likely to be somewhat higher than that of fossil-fuelled electricity, a levy may be raised on all sales from sources which could be environmentally damaging, including fossil fuels, so that the additional cost is shared by all electricity suppliers. Although the Electricity Act 1989 allows for a similar obligation there, the Government has no plans at present to introduce one in Scotland, which already has a high level of non-fossil-fuelled generating capacity.

British Nuclear   British Nuclear Fuels plc provides services covering the whole nuclear fuel
Fuels   cycle: uranium conversion, uranium enrichment (through its shareholding in Urenco Ltd), fuel element fabrication, transport and reprocessing of spent fuel, and the manufacture of specialised fuel element components. All of its shares are held by the Government. The company, with headquarters at Risley (Cheshire), conducts operations at four further sites: Springfields (Lancashire), where fuel is manufactured; Capenhurst (Cheshire), where uranium is enriched to provide fuel for nuclear reactors; Sellafield (Cumbria), where Calder Hall is located and where spent fuel is reprocessed; and Chapelcross (Dumfries and Galloway).

There is a large-scale investment programme in progress involving expenditure of some £5,500 million over the next ten years. The major part of this expenditure relates to the Sellafield site and comprises the refurbishment of facilities for treating spent fuel from Magnox power stations, the construction of a thermal oxide reprocessing plant (THORP) which will take spent fuel from British and overseas oxide reactors, and the construction of facilities to process and package radioactive waste. Treatment plants worth some £500 million are being built to further the company's objective of virtually eliminating the radioactivity levels of liquid discharges. The remainder of the programme involves the construction of further centrifuge enrichment plant at Capenhurst, and refurbishment and construction of new plant at Springfields.

Nuclear Research   The nuclear research and development funded by the Department of Energy is carried out by the UKAEA, which has been reorganised as nine semi-autonomous businesses operating as AEA Technology. Those specialising in key aspects of nuclear research and development are AEA Thermal Reactors, AEA Fast Reactors, AEA Fuel Services, AEA Decommissioning and Radwaste, and AEA Fusion. The work is carried out at six sites: Harwell and Culham (Oxfordshire), Risley, Winfrith (Dorset), Windscale (Cumbria) and Dounreay (Highland). In addition, safety research is carried out by AEA Safety and Reliability at Culcheth (Cheshire). AEA Technology operates as a trading fund, which allows it to function commercially, and its research and development work funded by the Department of Energy is on a customer-contractor basis. AEA Technology is a major international supplier of contract services with numerous customers, including the electricity generators, British Nuclear Fuels plc, other government departments, and industry.

Co-operation on nuclear energy between Britain and other countries takes place within a framework of intergovernmental agreements and membership of bodies such as the International Atomic Energy Agency and the Nuclear Energy Agency, as well as through direct links on research between AEA Technology and equivalent organisations overseas.

Britain takes part in the co-operative research programmes of the European Atomic Energy Community (Euratom), including one on establishing the feasibility of achieving controlled thermonuclear fusion. A major component of this programme is the Joint European Torus (JET) project at Culham, which started operating in 1983. In 1988 the UKAEA agreed with its French and German counterparts to set out the terms for European fast reactor research and development collaboration. Permission has been given for the building of a demonstration fast reactor reprocessing plant at Dounreay, the focus of fast reactor development in Britain.

Nuclear Safety   The Government and the nuclear industry give high priority to safety at nuclear installations and the industry has an excellent safety record. Britain has a rigorous system of nuclear safety regulation, enforced by the Health and Safety Executive's Nuclear Installations Inspectorate, which ensures that high standards of safety are incorporated into the design, construction, operation, maintenance and eventual decommissioning of all nuclear plant. While the safety of such plant in Britain is the ultimate responsibility of the nuclear operator, the Inspectorate has extensive powers and an operator must satisfy it before a licence is granted. Operators must protect their workers and the public by complying with the Health and Safety at Work etc. Act 1974, as well as with the conditions of their nuclear site licences under the Nuclear Installations Act 1965. The Inspectorate has the power to shut down a plant if it is believed to be unsafe and may also require improvements to an installation if it thinks the appropriate safety standards are not being met.

Discharges have to be kept within the limits and conditions set by

Industrial Technology

At the National Engineering Laboratory, East Kilbride, Scotland, engineers have designed and built a suite of wire rope testing machines, enabling them to assess accurately the performance of the large-diameter wire ropes used for anchoring structures in the offshore oil industry.

An engineer at Switched Reluctance Drives tests one of the company's 'intelligent' motors. Microchip technology has contributed to making the motors more efficient, adaptable and controllable than conventional ones.

Service Industries

Blackpool Pleasure Beach attracts over 6·5 million visitors a year.

Billingsgate, in London, is Britain's largest inland fish market. About four-fifths of the fish and fish products it handles comes from domestic sources.

The fine art auctioneers Sotheby's are established worldwide and handled sales valued at £1,820 million in 1989–90.

The Scottish Conference and Exhibition Centre, Glasgow, provides a venue for a wide variety of events, including large sporting or entertainment events with audiences of up to 10,000.

Exports

Established in 1976, the Body Shop produces and sells naturally-based skin and hair care preparations. Its overseas earnings have more than doubled in two years and in 1990 it won a Queen's Award for Export.

One of the most spectacular modern buildings in the City of London belongs to Lloyd's, an incorporated society of private insurers whose origins go back to the seventeenth century. It has built up a considerable worldwide market in insurance.

authorisations granted under the Radioactive Substances Act 1960. In England and Wales authorisations are granted jointly by the Secretary of State for the Environment and the Minister of Agriculture, Fisheries and Food, and in Scotland by the Secretary of State for Scotland. The terms of the authorisations ensure that those most exposed to discharges receive less than the maximum dose limit recommended by the International Commission on Radiological Protection. Within the limits, operators of nuclear facilities are required to keep discharges as low as reasonably achievable and failure to do so makes them liable to prosecution. Compliance with the legislation is overseen by Her Majesty's Inspectorate of Pollution in England and Wales, and by Her Majesty's Industrial Pollution Inspectorate in Scotland.

Britain plays a major part in international discussions on nuclear safety, and has a number of bilateral agreements and arrangements, with, for example, France, the Soviet Union and the United States, covering the exchange of information relating to all matters affecting nuclear safety. International conventions have been established on the early notification of a nuclear accident with possible transboundary effects, and on the mutual provision of assistance in the event of a nuclear accident or radiological emergency.

Emergency Plans The precautions taken in the design and construction of nuclear installations in Britain and the high safety standards in their operation and maintenance reduce the chance of accidents which might affect the public to an extremely low level. However, all operators are required to prepare emergency plans, including those for dealing with an accidental release of radioactivity, which are regularly tested in exercises under the supervision of the Nuclear Installations Inspectorate.

Research on Electricity A collective programme of research in England and Wales is the responsibility of the industry as a whole. Some of the work is already done in collaboration with Scottish Power, Scottish Hydro-Electric and Northern Ireland Electricity, which contribute towards its cost (£194 million in 1987–88). There is also collaboration between the supply industry and the plant manufacturers to co-ordinate research on plant and systems. The research establishments comprise the Central Electricity Research Laboratories at Leatherhead (Surrey; National Power), the Berkeley Nuclear Laboratories (Gloucestershire; Nuclear Electric) and the Marchwood Engineering Laboratories on Southampton Water (PowerGen). Research on distribution technology and electricity utilisation is at present undertaken at the Electricity Association Research Centre at Capenhurst and by the regional electricity companies.

RENEWABLE SOURCES OF ENERGY The Department of Energy is supporting research and development in the renewable energy technologies, to stimulate the full economic exploitation of alternative energy sources and encourage industry to develop internal and export markets. The present phase of its detailed research programme, published in 1988 and comprising over 250 projects with a financial commitment of £60 million, aims to promote the commercialisation of those renewable technologies which are economically attractive and to reduce the uncertainty in the economics and potential contribution of those which are promising but still uncertain. The Department is providing £20·3 million in funding for 1990–91 and work is concentrated on the most promising technologies.

Wind Power

Wind power constitutes one of the most promising renewable energy sources for electricity generation. Experimental wind farms, jointly funded by the Department of Energy and the electricity generating companies, and costing up to £30 million, are planned to be built between 1990 and 1992 at sites in England and Wales. Each wind farm will have an area of 3 to 4 sq km (1·2 to 1·5 sq miles) and will contain about 25 vertical- or horizontal-axis turbines, each 30 m (100 ft) high with 30-m diameter blades and with an output of 300 to 500 kW. They are expected to provide electricity for 15,000 people. At one of the sites, Capel Cynon (Dyfed), investigations are well advanced. The Department supports other major projects: two vertical-axis wind turbines, inaugurated in 1986 and 1990 at Carmarthen Bay (Dyfed); a 300-kW turbine also at Carmarthen Bay; a 3-MW, 60-m (200-ft) turbine, in collaboration with Scottish Hydro-Electric, on Orkney, inaugurated in 1987; a 1-MW, 55-m (180-ft) diameter turbine at Richborough (Kent), inaugurated in 1990; and two 300-kW turbines at the National Engineering Laboratory (East Kilbride), which are being commissioned in 1990. The Energy Research Group of the Science and Engineering Research Council is supporting a number of projects on the integration of wind and diesel electrical generation, which has particular relevance to small, isolated communities.

Geothermal Energy

Under its geothermal hot dry rock programme, the Department is investigating the economic possibilities of extracting heat from rocks at a depth of 2 to 6 km (1·25 to 4 miles). Research involving government expenditure of over £25 million since 1977 has been extended at a cost of £8·15 million over three years from 1988. The work is mainly carried out by the Camborne School of Mines in Cornwall, where a project is being conducted to establish the technology for creating a suitable deep underground heat exchange zone from which the heat could be withdrawn. A conceptual design study was started in 1989 and a review of hot dry rock research and development is being carried out in 1990.

Tidal Power

Tidal power is one of the most promising of the renewable technologies for large-scale electricity generation. Its exceptionally high tidal range makes the Severn estuary one of the best potential sites in the world, and the Department of Energy has funded, with the Severn Tidal Power Group and the electricity supply industry, a £4·2 million study into the viability of a Severn tidal barrage, of which a general report has been published. The Government has made a 50 per cent contribution to two phases of studies, costing £2 million, on an energy barrage on the Mersey estuary. The Government and the Mersey Barrage Company are jointly funding a third phase of studies.

Passive Solar Design

Passive solar design is considered the best way to utilise solar energy in Britain and has already proved cost-effective in both domestic and non-domestic buildings, using their form and fabric to admit, store and distribute solar energy for heating and improving daylight. The Department of Energy has increased expenditure on its research and development programme, which includes over 30 projects worth some £3·6 million and involves architects, schools of architecture and developers; while the Department of Trade and Industry has funded work on photovoltaic cells, which convert sunlight directly to electricity. A major project initiated in 1987, with European Community backing and including the British glass manufacturer Pilkington plc, was the establishment of a test centre at Strathclyde University to facilitate experiments on passive solar design and equipment.

Biofuels

Biofuels offer possibly the largest contribution from the renewable energy resources in the medium term. The main work of the Department's programme is on the combustion of wastes, anaerobic digestion (particularly as applied to the production and use of landfill gas) and energy forestry.

Wave Energy

The Department also has a research and development programme into wave energy, based on a project on the island of Islay. The small-scale shoreline device has been constructed by the Queen's University of Belfast, which is carrying out a complementary study to assess the potential for shoreline devices in Britain.

Non-fuel Minerals

Although much of Britain's requirements of industrial raw materials is met by imports, non-fuel minerals produced in Britain make an important contribution to the economy. Output of non-fuel minerals in 1988 totalled over 384 million tonnes, valued at £1,854 million. The total number of employees in the extraction industry was some 43,000 in 1988. The locations of some of the more important minerals produced in Britain are shown on the map on p 330.

Exploration

Exploration for and exploitation of indigenous metalliferous mineral resources to meet the needs of industry are being encouraged by the Government. The British Geological Survey is carrying out a long-term programme for the Department of Trade and Industry aimed at identifying areas with the potential for economic extraction of minerals.

Table 15.4: Production of Some of the Main Non-fuel Minerals

million tonnes

	1978	1983	1988
Sand and gravel	110·2	107·0	136·4
Silica sand	6·2	4·0	4·3
Igneous rock	35·3	36·9	52·0
Limestone and dolomite	88·8	94·0	125·7
Chalk	16·7[a]	12·4[a]	14·5[a]
Sandstone	13·4	14·7	18·9
Gypsum	3·2	2·9	n.a.
Salt including salt in brine	7·3	6·3	6·1
Common clay and shale	25·5[a]	22·4[a]	18·9[a]
China clay and ball clay	4·2	3·4	3·9
Fireclay	1·4[a]	0·7[a]	1·1
Iron ore	4·2	0·4	0·2
Potash	0·2	0·5	0·8
Fluorspar	0·2	0·1	0·1

Source: *United Kingdom Minerals Yearbook 1989.*
[a] Great Britain only.
n.a. = not available.

Production

The tonnage extracted of some of the main non-fuel minerals produced in Britain is given in Table 15.4. In terms of value, production of sand and gravel was estimated at £543 million in 1988, limestone and dolomite £498

Some Minerals Produced in Britain

Orkney Islands

Shetland Islands

talc
talc

0 20 40 60 80 100 120 km

0 20 40 60 80 miles

● Major metallic and industrial mineral workings

▲ Major mineral deposits (unworked)

silica sand

barytes, lead, zinc

▲ gold

barytes

gold

silica sand

silica sand

gold

salt

diatomite

fluorspar, lead

NORTHERN PENNINE OREFIELD

gypsum

hematite   barytes

salt   potash

silica sand

silica sand

salt

copper, zinc, lead, silver

silica sand

SOUTHERN PENNINE OREFIELD

salt

salt

fluorspar, barytes, lead

gypsum

gold

CHESHIRE SALTFIELD

gypsum   gypsum

silica sand

silica sand

fuller's earth

fuller's earth

silica sand

fuller's earth

celestite

fuller's earth

silica sand

gypsum

ball clay

ball clay   ball clay

china clay

china clay

china clay

tin, zinc

tungsten, tin

tin

million, clays £285 million, igneous rock £200 million, sandstone £68 million, potash £58 million, salt £39 million, chalk £38 million, gypsum and anhydrite £24 million, tin £14 million and fluorspar £10 million. Britain is a major world producer of several important industrial minerals, including china clay, ball clay, fuller's earth, celestite and gypsum; and produces significant amounts of limestone, dolomite, chalk, slate, fluorspar, potash, salt, silica sands, fireclay, common clay and shale, barytes and talc, mostly for home consumption. Small amounts of diatomite, calcspar, chert and flint, anhydrite and china stone are also produced. In 1988 the production of metal in non-ferrous ores totalled 10,800 tonnes, mainly tin and zinc from Cornwall. The Cornish mines, one of the very few sources of tin in the European Community, produced some 3,400 tonnes in 1988, satisfying about half of Britain's demand. Small amounts of copper and silver were produced in association with tin and zinc, and some lead and zinc with barytes and fluorspar. A little gold came from a mine in north Wales.

Production of sand and gravel, and crushed rock (from limestone, igneous rock and sandstone), as aggregates for use in construction constitutes two-thirds, by value, of Britain's output of non-fuel minerals. Britain is the world's second largest producer of marine-dredged sand and gravel (22 million tonnes in 1988).

Water

Britain's water supplies are obtained partly from surface sources such as mountain lakes, streams impounded in upland gathering grounds and river intakes, and partly from underground sources by means of wells, adits and boreholes. Water for public supply in England and Wales amounted to 16,896 megalitres (Ml) a day in 1988–89 and average daily supply per head was over 336 litres. About 99 per cent of the population in Great Britain and 96 per cent in Northern Ireland are connected to the public water supply system.

With the abolition of the rating system, on which charges for domestic water, sewerage and sewage disposal were largely based, the Government has said that it is for each water undertaking in England and Wales to decide how it wishes to charge, and has given them until the year 2000 to introduce new methods of charging. Water metering is one of the choices being considered. Since 1981 optional metering for domestic users has been available throughout England and Wales. Local trials of compulsory domestic metering in England started in 1989 and will last for about three years. Industrial users are charged for their water supply according to actual metered consumption.

England and Wales

In England and Wales the Secretaries of State for the Environment and for Wales, and the Director General of Water Services are responsible for the general oversight of the water industry and for enforcing the duties which the Water Act 1989 places upon the water and sewerage companies. The Minister of Agriculture, Fisheries and Food and the Secretary of State for Wales are responsible for policy relating to land drainage, flood protection, sea defence, and the protection and development of fisheries.

Water Service Companies

Under the Water Act 1989 the utility functions of the water authorities in England and Wales have been privatised. The ten water and sewerage companies, through their principal operating subsidiaries, the water service companies, are responsible for water supply, sewerage and sewage treatment.

It is the Government's view that freedom from government intervention in management and from public ownership constraints on financing will help to improve service standards and enable the new companies to attract investment. It is also envisaged that the companies will have scope for innovation and diversification into various commercial undertakings.

A system of economic regulation and guaranteed standards of service is overseen by the Director General of Water Services, and there is a new system of safeguarding and improving the quality of water supplies.

National Rivers Authority

The National Rivers Authority, an independent body, has regulatory and river management functions including pollution control and quality regulation of river, coastal and ground waters; management of water resources; land drainage; flood protection; fisheries; nature conservation and recreation.

Statutory Water Companies

The 29 statutory water companies operate as water undertakers in certain areas. Should they convert to plc status, they may also become sewerage undertakers by agreement with the relevant water service company or on sites where no service exists.

Supplies

Some 26,875 Ml a day were abstracted in England and Wales in 1987–88, of which public water supplies accounted for 17,250 Ml a day. The CEGB took some 4,600 Ml a day, primarily for cooling in connection with electricity generation, other industry about 3,700 Ml a day, and the remainder was used in agriculture and fish farming.

Scotland

In Scotland responsibility for public water supply, sewerage and sewage disposal rests with the nine regional and three islands councils. In addition, the Central Scotland Water Development Board is primarily responsible for developing large water sources and supplying water in bulk to its five constituent member authorities, the regional councils in central Scotland. Water is charged for according to type of consumer: those paying community water charges; non-domestic consumers paying by means of non-domestic water rates; and non-domestic consumers paying through metered charges. Charges and rates are decided by each authority.

Scotland has a relative abundance of unpolluted water from upland sources. An average of 2,204 Ml a day was supplied in Scotland in 1988–89. The Secretary of State for Scotland is responsible for the promotion of the conservation of water resources and the provision by water authorities of adequate water supplies, and has a duty to promote the cleanliness of rivers and other inland waters, and the tidal waters of Scotland. River purification authorities have a statutory responsibility for water pollution control.

Northern Ireland

The Department of the Environment for Northern Ireland is responsible for public water supply and sewerage throughout Northern Ireland. The Department is also responsible for the conservation and cleanliness of water resources and, with the Department of Agriculture for Northern Ireland, may prepare a water management programme with respect to water resources in any area. There is a domestic water charge which is contained in the regional rate, while agriculture, commerce and industry pay metered charges. There are abundant potential supplies of water for both domestic and industrial use. An average of 659 Ml of water a day was supplied in 1988–89.

Development Projects

The water industry in England and Wales is committed to a ten-year investment programme costing over £26,000 million. Thames Water is constructing an 80-km (50-mile) distribution system to meet the growing demand for water in London. This is due to be completed in 1996. Another example is North West Water, which has embarked on a major 25-year programme of investment to clean up the polluted rivers of the Mersey Basin.

Research

Several organisations and centres of expertise provide water research services to government, the National Rivers Authority, water companies and the Scottish river purification boards. The Water Research Centre has main laboratories at Medmenham (Buckinghamshire) and at Swindon (Wiltshire). Research undertaken covers environmental issues, treatment processes, mains and pipeline rehabilitation, and drinking water safety. Other organisations conducting research include Hydraulics Research Limited, universities, the Meteorological Office, the Ministry of Agriculture, Fisheries and Food, and several institutes of the Natural Environment Research Council.

16 Agriculture, Fisheries and Forestry

Agriculture

British agriculture is noted for its high level of efficiency and productivity. About 2·2 per cent of the working population are engaged in agriculture. Self-sufficiency in food and feed is estimated at 56 per cent of all food and feed, and at 75 per cent of indigenous-type food and feed. Food and beverages accounted for about 10 per cent of Britain's imports by value in 1989, compared with about a quarter in the 1960s. The agricultural contribution to gross domestic product was £6,025 million in 1989, about 1·4 per cent of the total. Britain is also a major exporter of agricultural produce and food products, agrochemicals and agricultural machinery.

The Government aims to foster an efficient and competitive agriculture industry through the provision and sponsorship of research, development and advisory services, the provision of financial support where appropriate, measures to control disease, pests and pollution, and improved marketing arrangements for food and food products. It also encourages the industry to adopt high standards on animal welfare. The Agriculture Act 1986 gives agriculture ministers a responsibility to achieve a balance between the interests of agriculture, the economic and social interests of rural areas, conservation and recreation. Schemes have been introduced to encourage the planting of new farm woodlands and the use of farmland for a variety of alternative projects. The European Community set-aside scheme encourages agricultural stabilisers by offering an alternative to surplus production and an opportunity for farmers affected by reductions in support to diversify.

Land Use

Some 77 per cent of the land area is used for agriculture, the rest being mountain, forest or put to urban and other uses. The area of agricultural land has been declining, although there has been a reduction in the net rate of loss in recent years. There are 12 million hectares (30 million acres) under crops and grass. Some 6 million hectares (over 15 million acres) are used for rough grazing; most of it is in hilly areas. Soils vary from the thin poor ones of highland Britain to the rich fertile soils of low-lying areas such as the fenlands of eastern England. The temperate climate and the relatively even distribution of rainfall over the year ensure a long growing season; streams rarely dry up and grassland normally remains green throughout the year.

Farming

In 1989 there were some 257,000 farm holdings in Britain, of which about 75 per cent in England, Scotland and Wales were wholly or mainly owner-occupied, while virtually all the farms in Northern Ireland are owner-occupied. The average area (including rough grazing) of full-time businesses is 107·3 hectares (265 acres). It is estimated that the 12 per cent of holdings in the largest size group accounted for 57 per cent of activity, while the smallest size of holding (45 per cent of farms) accounted for only 2·6 per cent of activity. In Wales and Northern Ireland output from smaller farms is more significant than in the rest of Britain.

The number of people engaged in agriculture in 1989 was about 573,000. Labour productivity has increased by 58 per cent since 1979. Total income from farming (that of farmers, partners, directors and their spouses) was £2,167 million in 1989, 11 per cent more than in 1988.

There are over 500,000 tractors and some 53,000 combine harvesters in use. A wide variety of other machines for harvesting and preserving grass are also employed. Horticultural crops such as blackcurrants and brussels sprouts are frequently harvested by machine, and milking machines are used on the vast majority of dairy farms. Most farms have a direct electricity supply, the remainder having their own generators.

Dairy herd monitoring, account analysis, budgeting and the monitoring of cash-flow and performance have all benefited in recent years from computer technology. Computer models of typical farms allow many varieties of crops and livestock to be considered, as well as demands for labour, land, capital and buildings.

PRODUCTION

Home production of the principal foods is shown as a percentage by weight of total supplies (that is, output plus imports minus exports) in Table 16.1.

Table 16.1: British Production as a Percentage of Total Supplies

Food product	1978–80 average	1989 (provisional)
Red carcase meat	86	93
Eggs	101	99
Milk for human consumption (as liquid)	100	100
Cheese	69	67
Butter	48	74
Sugar (as refined)	45	58
Wheat	78	122
Potatoes	n.a.	87

Source: Ministry of Agriculture, Fisheries and Food.
n.a. = not available.

Livestock

About three-fifths of full-time farms are devoted mainly to dairying or beef cattle and sheep. The majority of sheep and cattle are reared in the hill and moorland areas of Scotland, Wales, Northern Ireland and northern and south-western England. Beef fattening occurs partly in better grassland areas, as does dairying, and partly on arable farms. British livestock breeders have developed many of the cattle, sheep and pig breeds with worldwide reputations, for example, the Hereford and Aberdeen Angus beef breeds, the Jersey, Guernsey and Ayrshire dairy breeds, Large White pigs and a number of sheep breeds. Because of developments in artificial insemination and embryo transfer, Britain is able to export semen and embryos from high-quality donor animals.

Table 16·2 shows the number of livestock and output of livestock products.

Cattle and Sheep

Most dairy cattle in England and Wales and a significant proportion in Scotland and Northern Ireland are bred by artificial insemination. In 1989 the average size of dairy herds in Britain was 62, while the average yield of milk per dairy cow was 4,999 litres (1,100 gallons). Average household consumption of liquid (including low-fat) milk per head in 1989 was 2·0 litres (3·5 pints) per week.

Table 16.2: Livestock and Livestock Products

	1978–80 average	1987	1988	1989 (provisional)
Cattle and calves ('000 head)	13,561	12,158	11,872	12,016
Sheep and lambs ('000 head)	30,388	38,701	40,942	42,885
Pigs ('000 head)	7,802	7,942	7,980	7,717
Poultry ('000 head)[a]	128,537	128,628	130,809	120,198
Milk (million litres)	15,291	14,811	14,444	14,246
Eggs (million dozen)	1,171	1,025	1,041	943
Beef and veal ('000 tonnes)	1,078	1,118	947	967
Mutton and lamb ('000 tonnes)	257	311	343	383
Pork ('000 tonnes)	674	780	802	741
Bacon and ham ('000 tonnes)	213	197	197	193
Poultry meat ('000 tonnes)	n.a.	987	1,048	1,004

Source: Ministry of Agriculture, Fisheries and Food.
[a]Excluding ducks, geese and turkeys. Data for 1987-89 cannot be compared with data for earlier years owing to changes in coverage of poultry holdings.
n.a. = not available.

About two-thirds of home-fed beef production derives from the national dairy herd, in which the Friesian breed is predominant. The remainder is derived from suckler herds producing high-quality beef calves in the hills and uplands, where the traditional British beef breeds, such as Hereford and Aberdeen Angus, continue to be important. Imported breeds which have established themselves include the Charolais, Limousin, Simmental and Belgian Blue.

Britain has a long tradition of sheep production, with more than 40 breeds and many crosses between them. Research has provided vaccine and serum protection against nearly all the epidemic diseases. Although lamb production is the main source of income for sheep farmers, wool is also important.

Grass supplies 60 to 80 per cent of the feed for cattle and sheep. Grass production has been enhanced by the increased use of fertilisers, irrigation and methods of grazing control, and improved herbage conservation for winter feed. Rough grazings are used for extensively grazed sheep and cattle, producing young animals for fattening elsewhere.

Pigs and Poultry

Pig production occurs in most areas but is particularly important in eastern and northern England. There is an increasing concentration into specialist units and larger herds.

Output of poultry meat has continued to benefit from better husbandry and genetic improvements. Since 1979 British production has increased by just over a third and stayed at over 1 million tonnes in 1989. Production of broilers from holdings of over 100,000 birds accounts for over a half of total production. In 1989 British egg production fell by 100 million dozen, reflecting concern about salmonella. Over two-thirds of laying birds are in flocks of 20,000 or more. Britain remains broadly self-sufficient in poultry meat and eggs.

Animal Welfare

The welfare of farm animals is protected by regulations and it is an offence to cause unnecessary pain or distress to commercially reared livestock. For example, there are regulations requiring owners of intensive units to arrange for the daily inspection of their stock and the equipment on which it depends. There are advisory codes and recommendations for the welfare of all major species of farm animals and compliance is monitored by the State Veterinary Service. The Government has announced an animal welfare initiative, designed to get common standards throughout Europe.

The Farm Animal Welfare Council, an independent body set up by the Government, keeps under review the welfare of farm animals on agricultural land, at markets, in transit and at the place of slaughter, and advises on any legislative changes it considers necessary. The Government has adopted most of its recommendations for the protection of livestock at markets, including tighter controls on the marketing of calves.

Crops

The farms devoted primarily to arable crops are found mainly in eastern and central southern England and eastern Scotland. In Britain in 1989 cereals were grown on 3·9 million hectares (9·6 million acres). Production of cereals, at 22·4 million tonnes, was higher than in the previous two years. Between 40 and 50 per cent of available wheat supplies (allowing for imports and exports) are normally used for flour milling, and about 50 per cent for animal feed. About 30 per cent of barley supplies are used for malting and distilling, and the remainder for animal feed. After many years of growth, the recent decreases in the area and yield of oilseed rape continued in 1989.

Large-scale potato and vegetable production is undertaken in the fens (in Cambridgeshire and south Lincolnshire), the alluvial areas around the rivers

Table 16.3: Main Crops

	1978–80 average	1987	1988	1989 (provisional)
Wheat				
Area ('000 hectares)	1,357	1,994	1,886	2,104
Harvest ('000 tonnes)	7,419	11,940	11,750	13,843
Yield (tonnes per hectare)	5·46	5·99	6·23	6·58
Barley				
Area ('000 hectares)	2,343	1,830	1,878	1,657
Harvest ('000 tonnes)	9,933	9,225	8,773	7,960
Yield (tonnes per hectare)	4·25	5·04	4·67	4·80
Oats				
Area ('000 hectares)	155	99	120	120
Harvest ('000 tonnes)	615	452	540	550
Yield (tonnes per hectare)	3·97	4·59	4·50	4·60
Potatoes				
Area ('000 hectares)	208	179	181	176
Harvest ('000 tonnes)	6,908	6,713	6,899	6,269
Yield (tonnes per hectare)	33·20	37·60	38·10	35·70
Oilseed rape				
Area ('000 hectares)	77	388	347	323
Harvest ('000 tonnes)	213	1,353	1,040	953
Yield (tonnes per hectare)	2·78	3·49	3·00	2·95
Sugar beet				
Area ('000 hectares)	209	200	198	194
Harvest ('000 tonnes)	7,373	7,992	8,152	8,000
Yield (tonnes per hectare)	35·23	39·91	41·30	41·24

Sources: *Agriculture in the United Kingdom: 1989* and *Agricultural Census June 1989.*

Thames and Humber and the peaty lands in south Lancashire. Early potatoes are an important crop in south-west Wales, Kent and south-west England. High-grade seed potatoes are grown in Scotland and Northern Ireland.

Sugar from home-grown sugar beet provides over 50 per cent of requirements, most of the remainder being refined from raw cane sugar imported from developing countries under the Lomé Convention.

Table 16.3 gives figures on the area, harvest and yield of the main crops.

Horticulture
In 1989 the land utilised for horticulture was about 201,000 hectares (497,000 acres). Vegetables grown in the open (excluding potatoes) accounted for 71·7 per cent, orchards for 14·4 per cent, small fruit for 6·3 per cent and ornamentals (including hardy nursery stock and flowers grown in the open) for 7·7 per cent. More than one vegetable crop is, in some cases, taken from the same area of land in a year, so that the estimated area actually cropped in 1989 was 234,000 hectares (579,000 acres).

Field vegetables account for about 38 per cent of the value of horticultural output and are widely grown throughout the country. Most horticultural enterprises are increasing productivity with the help of improved planting material, new techniques and the widespread use of machinery. Some field vegetables, for example, are raised in blocks of compressed peat or loose-filled cells, a technique which reduces root damage and allows plants to establish themselves more reliably and evenly. There are government grants for replanting apple and pear trees.

Glasshouses are used for growing tomatoes, cucumbers, sweet peppers, lettuces, flowers, pot plants and nursery stock. Widespread use is made of automatic control of heating and ventilation, and semi-automatic control of watering. Energy-efficient glasshouses use thermal screens, while low-cost plastic tunnels extend the season for certain crops previously grown in the open. Government grants are available for replacing heated glass and heating systems.

Under the European Community's Common Agricultural Policy (see p 341), a wide range of horticultural produce is subject to common quality standards.

Organic Farming
The Government encourages organic farming along with other farming enterprises. The board of the United Kingdom Register of Organic Food Standards, an independent body set up with government support by Food From Britain in 1987, has drawn up national standards for organic food production. Support is also provided from the Government's research and development programme and, as appropriate, through national grant schemes and by advice from the agricultural advisory service.

Food Safety
The Food Safety Directorate was set up in 1989 within the Ministry of Agriculture, Fisheries and Food in order to focus ministry resources more effectively on maintaining the safety and quality of Britain's food supplies. Food safety responsibilities are separated from food production responsibilities within the Ministry. In addition, a consumer panel has been set up, to give consumers a direct means of conveying their views on food safety and consumer protection issues to the Government. The Food Safety Act 1990 revises and streamlines the existing body of food law in Great Britain so that food safety and consumer protection may be improved throughout the food chain. The Act combines basic rules with enabling powers, so that detailed regulations can adapt to technological change and innovation. It introduces more effective enforcing powers and greatly increased penalties for offenders.

EXPORTS

The Government is keen to encourage the growth of exports related to agriculture, and their volume increased in the ten years up to 1987, although in 1988 it fell. The volume of these exports rose strongly in 1989, when their value amounted to £6,273 million, the main markets being Western Europe, North America and the Middle East. Exports include speciality products such as fresh salmon, Scotch whisky, biscuits, jams and conserves, as well as beef and lamb carcases and cheese. Food From Britain is a national organisation which promotes the marketing of food and agricultural produce in the domestic and overseas markets. It receives support for its export activity from the British Food Export Council, while the British Agricultural Export Committee of the London Chamber of Commerce represents exporters of technology, expertise and equipment. The Agricultural Engineers' Association represents exporters of agricultural and horticultural machinery. In 1989 Britain exported £846 million of farm machinery and spares.

One of the world's largest agricultural events, the annual Royal International Agricultural Exhibition, held at Stoneleigh in Warwickshire, provides an opportunity for overseas visitors to see the latest techniques and improvements in British agriculture. Over 225,000 visitors attended in 1989, of whom some 20,000 were from overseas. Virtually every British agricultural machinery manufacturer is represented at the exhibition, which is also the most important pedigree livestock event in the country. Other major agricultural displays include the annual Royal Smithfield Show, held in London, which exhibits agricultural machinery, livestock and carcases; the Royal Highland Show; the Royal Welsh Show; and the Royal Ulster Agricultural Show. There are also important regional shows.

MARKETING

Agricultural products are marketed by private traders, producers' co-operatives and marketing boards. The latter are producers' organisations (each including a minority of independent members appointed by agriculture ministers) with certain statutory powers to regulate the marketing of milk, wool and potatoes. For the most part the boards buy from producers or control contracts between producers and first-hand buyers; the Potato Marketing Board, however, maintains only a broad control over marketing conditions, leaving producers free to deal individually with buyers. For home-grown cereals, meat and livestock, apples and pears, there are marketing organisations representing producer, distributor and independent interests.

Food From Britain is responsible for improving the marketing of food and agricultural products, both in the domestic market and abroad. Its quality assurance schemes for producers guarantee a variety of food products. Grants are sometimes available to improve the marketing and processing of agricultural products.

Co-operatives

A substantial amount of agricultural and horticultural produce is handled by marketing co-operatives, whose turnover is around £1,500 million a year. Since the late 1970s a number of central co-operative grain stores have been established, and new vegetable groups and fruit-marketing co-operatives have been formed to meet the demand from retailers for a continuous supply of fresh, quality produce. Food From Britain provides a range of advisory services for co-operatives and the Government may assist their development with grants.

ROLE OF THE GOVERNMENT

Four government departments have joint responsibility—the Ministry of Agriculture, Fisheries and Food; the Department of Agriculture and

Fisheries for Scotland; the Welsh Office; and the Department of Agriculture for Northern Ireland.

Common Agricultural Policy

The European Community's Common Agricultural Policy (CAP) accounts for about two-thirds of the Community's budget and aims to ensure stable agricultural markets and a fair standard of living for agricultural producers, and to guarantee regular supplies of food at reasonable prices. For many commodities minimum prices are set annually at which agencies of the member states will purchase products, and there are levies on imports to maintain internal support prices. Intervention stocks can be disposed of within the Community where this can be done without disrupting internal markets. Exports are facilitated by the provision of export refunds to bridge any gap between Community prices and world prices. In some cases, in particular in the beef and sheep sectors, there are also direct payments to producers.

The support prices, as well as rates of levy, export refunds and other aids, are set in European Currency Units and are converted into the currencies of the member states at fixed rates of exchange—'green rates'—which can be out of line with the market rate of exchange between each currency and the European Currency Unit. Monetary compensatory amounts, based on the percentage difference between the green and market rates of each currency, are applied to prevent distortions in trade. They operate as import subsidies and export levies for countries whose currencies' market rates are below the green rates, and as import levies and export subsidies for countries whose currencies' market rates are above the green rates.

Nearly all the Community's agricultural expenditure (£18,000 million in 1989) is channelled through the European Agricultural Guidance and Guarantee Fund. The Fund's guarantee section finances market support arrangements, while the guidance section provides funds for structural reform—for example, farm modernisation and investment—and payments to assist certain farmers to change to alternative enterprises.

Agricultural production under the CAP has increased considerably in recent years, partly in response to rapid technical progress and farming efficiency, but also reflecting the high level of price support under the CAP. As consumption has remained relatively stable, this has resulted in the emergence of surpluses.

Britain has consistently pressed for CAP reform, to bring supply and demand into better balance and to increase the role of market forces in agriculture. Considerable progress has been made. Average effective Community support levels have been reduced in real terms each year since 1984. The most notable step towards achieving these objectives was the package of reforms agreed by the European Council of Ministers in 1988. This introduced a legally binding limit on CAP market support expenditure and brought in or extended stabilisers for most CAP commodities. Stabilisers ensure that CAP support is automatically cut if production exceeds specified quantities. Significant price cuts of up to 20 per cent have already been made in a number of sectors. Further reforms, restricting intervention in the beef regime, were agreed in 1989.

Each of the price-fixing settlements in 1988, 1989 and 1990 consolidated this reform process, the cost being within the guidelines established by the Council, and the stabiliser mechanisms remained intact. The settlements also helped to improve the competitive position of British farmers. Green pound devaluations were agreed which represent a significant step in the process of meeting the Community's commitment to phasing out the differences between 'green' and market rates of exchange by the end of 1992.

Price Guarantees, Grants and Subsidies

Expenditure in Britain in 1989–90 on price guarantees, grants and subsidies and on CAP market regulations was estimated to be £257 million and £998 million respectively. About £1,359 million was reimbursed from the Community budget.

Potatoes and wool are not covered by the CAP; potato market support measures are operated through the Potato Marketing Board and the Department of Agriculture for Northern Ireland, and a price stabilisation fund for wool is administered by the British Wool Marketing Board. The Government intends to end the guarantee arrangements when parliamentary time permits.

Producers also receive support through certain capital and production grants, some based on Community decisions. Grants are available to assist farmers and horticulturists with or without improvement plans, and there is special financial help for hill and upland farmers in the form of headage payments on cattle and sheep (known as compensatory allowances). Community assistance may also be made to help to improve facilities for the marketing and processing of agricultural products, while launching aid is available to production and marketing groups in the horticultural sector.

Smallholdings and Crofts

Local authorities provide some 5,800 statutory smallholdings in England and 950 in Wales. They make loans of up to 75 per cent of required working capital to their tenants. Land settlement in Scotland has always been carried out by the Government, which, while now seeking to dispose of holdings to its sitting tenants, still owns and maintains about 116,600 hectares (228,150 acres) of land settlement estates, comprising some 1,525 crofts and holdings.

In the crofting areas of Scotland (in Strathclyde, Highland, Western Isles, Orkney and Shetland) much of the land is held by tenants known as 'crofters'. Crofting is administered by the Crofters Commission, and benefits from government grants for land improvements and some other agricultural work.

Tenancy Legislation

The agricultural holdings legislation protects the interests and rights of landlords and tenants, with provision for arbitration in the event of a dispute. Most agricultural tenants have the right to contest a notice to quit, which is then ineffective unless the landlord obtains consent to its operation from an independent body (in England and Wales, the Agricultural Land Tribunal and in Scotland, the Scottish Land Court). On termination of tenancy, the tenant is entitled to compensation in accordance with a special code. Practically all farms in Northern Ireland are owner-occupied, but, under a practice known as 'conacre', occupiers not wishing to farm all their land let it annually to others. About one-fifth of agricultural land is so let, and is used mainly for grazing.

Agriculture and Protection of the Countryside

Agriculture ministers have a general duty, under the Agriculture Act 1986, to seek to achieve a reasonable balance between the needs of an efficient and stable agriculture industry and other interests in the countryside, including the conservation of its natural beauty and amenity and the promotion of its enjoyment by the public. In addition, they are required to further conservation of the countryside in the administration of farm capital grant schemes both in national parks and in sites of special scientific interest designated by the Nature Conservancy Council.

The Government has introduced the Environmentally Sensitive Areas (ESAs) Scheme, under which 19 areas in Britain—ten in England, five in Scotland, two in Wales and two in Northern Ireland—have been designated.

They are notable for the quality of their landscape and the wealth of their flora and fauna, which make them vulnerable to change in farming practices. The areas are diverse in character and include low-lying wetland grazing marshes, chalk downs and upland tracts of heather—for example, the Broads in England; Breadalbane in Scotland; the Lleyn Peninsula in Wales; and Mourne and Slieve Croob in Northern Ireland. The scheme is voluntary and farmers in ESAs are offered agreements under which they receive payments (partly funded by the European Community) for farming along environmentally beneficial lines intended to conserve the special character of the area.

Government grant schemes to increase the opportunities open to farmers to develop new sources of income as an alternative to surplus production and to enhance environmental protection include the Farm Diversification Scheme, which encourages new business enterprises on farms. This scheme has attracted over 2,500 applications since it started in 1988. The Farm Woodland Scheme assists the planting of woodlands on productive agricultural land, with incentives for broadleaved trees and a planting limit of 36,000 hectares (88,960 acres) over three years. The Farm and Conservation Grant Scheme focuses assistance on measures to contain farm pollution and to improve conservation. The European Community set-aside scheme, introduced in Britain in 1988, offers annual payments to farmers to take at least 20 per cent of their arable land out of agricultural production for five years. Additional payments for managing set-aside land for the benefit of wildlife, landscape and the local community are available under the Countryside Premium Scheme (at present limited to eastern England). The Government has also designated ten nitrate sensitive areas in England, where payments will be made to farmers who voluntarily undertake to restrict their agricultural practices and thus prevent unacceptable levels of nitrate leaching from farmland into water sources.

Professional, Scientific and Technical Services	In England and Wales the Government's Agricultural Development and Advisory Service (ADAS) provides a wide range of professional, scientific, technical and veterinary services for agriculture and its ancillary industries. Most types of advice and servicing are on a fee-paying basis, although initial advice to farmers on conservation, rural diversification (including use of land for woodlands) and animal welfare is available free. Similar services are provided in Scotland by the Department of Agriculture and Fisheries, the Scottish Agricultural College and a section of the State Veterinary Service. In Northern Ireland these services are available from the Department of Agriculture's advisory and scientific services.

These organisations also advise the Government on the scientific, technical and business implications of policy proposals and assist in implementing policies concerning animal and plant health, disease and pest eradication, food hygiene, animal welfare, land drainage and other capital grant schemes, and safeguarding agricultural land in relation to other land uses.

ADAS carries out research and development work under commission from the Ministry of Agriculture, Fisheries and Food, and works under contract directly for others and for levy-funded bodies. These undertakings are carried out at the Central Science Laboratory and the Central Veterinary Laboratory; at a range of husbandry farms and horticulture stations across England and Wales; and through regional centres or on clients' premises. A diagnostic service for the practising veterinary surgeon is provided at 19 veterinary investigation centres.

CONTROL OF DISEASES AND PESTS

Farm Animals

Britain is free from many serious animal diseases. If they were to occur, diseases such as foot-and-mouth disease and classical swine fever would be combated by a slaughter policy applied to all animals infected or exposed to infection, and by control over animal movements during the outbreaks.

The Government has taken comprehensive measures to tackle the new cattle disease, bovine spongiform encephalopathy, and to ensure that consumers are protected from any remote risk. Acting on the best available scientific advice, it has banned the feeding of ruminant protein to ruminants; ordered the destruction of the milk and carcases of affected animals; banned from human use those offals from other cattle which might be harbouring the agent; and committed significant funding for research (see p 345). It has also established an expert committee to advise on matters relating to spongiform encephalopathies.

The Government has also introduced comprehensive measures to combat salmonella in eggs and poultry, including the compulsory monitoring of poultry flocks and the slaughter with compensation of salmonella-infected flocks.

Strict controls are exercised on the import of animals, birds, meat, and meat products so as to prevent the introduction of animal or avian diseases. Special measures apply to prevent the introduction of rabies, and dogs, cats and certain other mammals are subject to import licence and six months' quarantine. There are severe penalties for breaking the law. There have been no cases of rabies outside quarantine in Britain since 1970.

Professional advice and action on the control of animal disease and the welfare of farm livestock are the responsibility of the government veterinary services. They have laboratory facilities and investigation centres performing specialist research work and advising private practitioners responsible for treating animals on the farm.

Fish

The health of Britain's farmed and wild fish stocks is excellent. The fisheries departments operate statutory controls to prevent the introduction and spread of serious diseases of fish and shellfish. These controls include the licensing of live fish imports and deposits of shellfish on the seabed, and movement restrictions on sites where outbreaks of notifiable diseases have been confirmed.

Plants

The agriculture departments are responsible for limiting the spread of plant pests and diseases and for preventing the introduction of new ones. They also issue the health certificates required by other countries to accompany plant material exported from Britain. Certification schemes are operated to encourage the development of healthy and true-to-type planting stocks.

Pesticides

The supply and use of pesticides, and their maximum residue levels, are controlled under the Food and Environment Protection Act 1985 and the Control of Pesticides Regulations 1986 made under it. All pesticides supplied for use in Britain must have been approved under statutory arrangements for their safety, efficacy and, where appropriate, humaneness in use. The Government has instituted a review of those pesticides which were approved before 1981 and intends to speed the consideration of applications for new pesticides.

Veterinary Medicinal Products

The manufacture, sale and supply of veterinary medicinal products are prohibited except under licence. Licences are issued by the agriculture ministers, who are advised on safety, quality and efficacy by the Veterinary Products Committee, which comprises independent experts.

AGRICULTURAL AND FOOD RESEARCH The agriculture departments, the Agricultural and Food Research Council (AFRC) and private industry share responsibility for research, which is carried out in a network of research institutes, specialist laboratories and experimental farms, in the British Society for Horticultural Research, set up in 1990, and in university departments.

The total government-funded programme of research and development in agriculture and food amounts to some £220 million a year and aims to maintain an efficient and competitive industry in Britain consistent with high standards of animal welfare and care for the environment. The work of the AFRC and the agriculture departments is co-ordinated into national programmes, primarily on the recommendations of the Priorities Board for Research and Development in Agriculture and Food, which advises on the research needs of the industries and the allocation of available resources between and within areas of research.

The AFRC, a non-departmental public body, receives funds from the science budget through the Department of Education and Science, and income from work commissioned by the Ministry of Agriculture, Fisheries and Food, by industry and by other outside bodies. The Council supports research at its seven institutes, which specialise in animal health, animal physiology and genetics, grassland and the environment, arable crops, plant science, food and engineering. The Council also funds a number of groups or departments in universities and, through its research grants scheme, supports many projects in universities, polytechnics and colleges. In addition to commissioning research with the AFRC and other organisations, the Ministry carries out research and development work in the laboratories, experimental husbandry farms and horticulture stations of ADAS and in its food science laboratories.

The five Scottish Agricultural Research Institutes, funded by the Department of Agriculture and Fisheries for Scotland, cover areas of research complementary to those of the AFRC institutes, while including work relevant to the soils, crops and livestock of northern Britain. Development work in Scotland is carried out by the Scottish Agricultural College, which operates from three sites.

In Northern Ireland research is carried out by the Department of Agriculture in a number of research divisions and at the three agricultural colleges. Links with the Queen's University of Belfast and the Agricultural Research Institute of Northern Ireland include basic and applied research.

Agricultural research is also conducted or sponsored by private industry, in particular by related industries such as agrochemicals and agricultural machinery.

The food industry also funds or undertakes relevant research. The Government will continue to fund strategic research essential for the public good, for example, into food safety, human health, animal welfare and flood protection, but plans to withdraw funding from research which promises commercial application or exploitation within a reasonable timescale—for which it looks to industry to take on a greater degree of funding. Planned reductions in government expenditure on such research and development will amount to some £30 million by 1991–92.

The Government promotes extensive research relevant to the control of salmonella and listeriosis. It is contributing half the cost of a £12 million research programme, over three years, into bovine spongiform encephalopathy and has increased funding into sugar beet research. It has set up a unified organisation for horticultural research. Through the AFRC the Government sponsors studies into the consequences of global climate change, to enable agriculturists to make a planned response to possible alterations in crop production, cropping patterns, and plant and animal diseases.

Fisheries

Britain, one of the European Community's leading fishing nations, plays an active role in the implementation and development of the Community's Common Fisheries Policy (CFP), which was agreed in 1983. The CFP covers access to coastal waters, the conservation and management of fish stocks, fisheries arrangements with third countries, the allocation of catch quotas among member states, the trade in and marketing of fish and fish products, and financial aid to promote the adaptation and development of the Community's fishing fleet.

The fishing industry provides about 61 per cent of British fish supplies, and is an important source of employment and income in a number of ports. Cod, haddock, whiting, herring, plaice and sole are found in the North Sea off the east coasts of Scotland and England; mackerel, together with cod and other demersal fish, off the west coast of Scotland; sole, plaice, cod, herring and whiting in the Irish Sea; and mackerel, sole and plaice off the south-west coast of England. Nephrops, crabs, lobsters and other shellfish are found in the inshore waters all around the coast. At the end of 1988 there were nearly 17,100 fishermen in regular employment and nearly 5,400 occasionally employed. The Government aims to encourage the development of a viable, efficient and market-oriented fisheries industry within the CFP framework.

Fish Caught

In 1989 demersal fish (caught on or near the bottom of the sea) accounted for 46 per cent by weight of total British landings, pelagic fish (caught near the surface) for 41 per cent and shellfish for 13 per cent. Landings of all types of fish (excluding salmon and trout) by British fishing vessels totalled 624,425 tonnes. Cod and haddock represented 23 and 21 per cent respectively of the total value of demersal and pelagic fish landed, while anglerfish (8 per cent), whiting (7 per cent), plaice (7 per cent), mackerel (6 per cent), and sole (5 per cent) were the other most important sources of earnings to the industry. Landings of nephrops represented 11 per cent of the total value of all British landings of fish and shellfish in 1989.

Imports of fresh, frozen, cured and canned salt-water fish and shellfish in 1989 totalled 448,100 tonnes, those of freshwater fish 33,200 tonnes, those of fish meal 265,300 tonnes and those of fish oils 177,600 tonnes. Exports and re-exports of salt-water fish and fish products amounted to 369,200 tonnes and those of freshwater fish to 16,900 tonnes. The European Community has banned the import of primary whale products in order to help to conserve whale populations.

The Fishing Fleet

At the end of 1988 the British fishing fleet consisted of 7,859 inshore vessels under 24·4 m (80 ft) in length and 273 deep-sea vessels longer than 24·4 m. Among the main ports from which the fishing fleet operates are Aberdeen, Peterhead, Fraserburgh (Grampian), Lerwick (Shetland), Kinlochbervie, Ullapool (Highland), North Shields (Tyne and Wear), Grimsby (Humberside), Lowestoft (Suffolk), Brixham (Devon), Newlyn (Cornwall), and Kilkeel, Ardglass and Portavogie (Northern Ireland). Britain's distant water fleet was considerably reduced following the loss of access, for example around Iceland, caused by the extension of fishery limits to 200 miles in 1976. A much smaller fleet has, however, continued to maintain its activities in distant waters.

Fish Farming Britain's fish farming industry continues to grow quickly, with production centred on Atlantic salmon and rainbow trout, which are well suited to the climate and waters. Production of salmon and trout has grown from less than 1,000 tonnes in the early 1970s to some 29,000 tonnes of salmon and 16,000 tonnes of trout in 1989. Shellfish farming concentrates on molluscs such as oysters, mussels, clams and scallops, producing an estimated 5,000 tonnes a year.

The fish and shellfish farming industries make an important contribution to rural infrastructure, especially in the highlands and islands of Scotland. They employ more than 5,000 people. In 1989 the industries were estimated to have a combined wholesale turnover of some £150 million. Production is based on almost 1,200 businesses on some 1,800 sites.

Administration The fisheries departments are responsible for the administration of legislation concerning the fishing industry and for fisheries research. The safety and welfare of crews of fishing vessels and other matters common to shipping generally are provided for under legislation administered by the Department of Transport.

The Sea Fish Industry Authority is concerned with all aspects of the industry, including consumer interests. It undertakes research and development, provides training, and encourages quality awareness. It also administers a government grant scheme for fishing vessels, to promote a safe, efficient and modern fleet.

Fishery Limits Only British vessels may fish within 6 miles of the coast; certain other Community member states have traditional fishing rights between 6 and 12 miles, as British vessels have in other member states' coastal waters. Outside 12 miles the only non-Community countries whose vessels may fish in Community waters are those (for example, Norway) with which the Community has reciprocal fisheries agreements.

Common Fisheries Policy The CFP's system for the conservation and management of the Community's fishing resources means that total allowable catches—with these decisions based partly on independent scientific advice—are set each year in order to conserve stocks. These catch levels are then allocated between member states on a fixed percentage basis, taking account of traditional fishing patterns. Activity is also regulated by a number of technical conservation measures, including minimum mesh sizes, minimum landing sizes and closed areas designated mainly to protect young fish. Each member state is responsible for ensuring that its fishermen abide by the various fisheries regulations and their performances are monitored by the Community's inspectors.

The 1983 settlement also covered the common organisation of the market in fish and fish products, and a policy for restructuring the Community fleet during 1987–97, designed to address the current problem of over-capacity. The measures include financial assistance for the building and modernisation of fishing vessels.

Fishery relations between the European Community and other countries are extensive and are governed by different agreements. Those of most importance to Britain are with Norway, Greenland, the Faroe Islands and Sweden. Annual Community quotas have also been established in international waters in the north-west Atlantic and around Svalbard.

Fisheries Research The Ministry of Agriculture, Fisheries and Food has a research directorate comprising laboratories dealing with marine and freshwater fisheries, shellfish, marine pollution, fish farming and diseases. There are two seagoing research vessels. In Scotland the Department of Agriculture and Fisheries for Scotland provides a similar range of research and has two seagoing vessels. Work on the utilisation of fish is undertaken by a research station at Torry, Aberdeen. Department of Agriculture laboratories in Northern Ireland monitor marine and freshwater fisheries, and have a seagoing research vessel.

Salmon and Freshwater Fisheries

Salmon and sea-trout are fished commercially in inshore waters around the British coast. Eels and elvers are also taken commercially in both estuaries and freshwater. Angling for salmon and sea-trout (game fishing) and for other freshwater species (coarse fishing) is popular throughout Britain. In England and Wales fishing is licensed by the National Rivers Authority; in Scotland salmon fishing is administered by salmon district fishery boards; and in Northern Ireland there are 65 public angling waters for game and coarse fishing, and salmon rivers are accessible to Department of Agriculture permit holders.

Forestry

Woodland covers an estimated 2·38 million hectares (5·88 million acres) in Britain: about 7·3 per cent of England, 13 per cent of Scotland, 12 per cent of Wales and 5·2 per cent of Northern Ireland. The Government supports the continued expansion of forestry in order to reduce dependence on imports of timber and to provide employment in forestry and related industries.

The area of productive forest in Great Britain is 2·14 million hectares (5·27 million acres), 41 per cent of which is managed by the Forestry Commission and the rest by private owners. The rate of new planting in 1988–89 was 4,105 hectares (10,143 acres) by the Commission and 24,892 hectares (61,508 acres) by private woodland owners, mainly in Scotland. Most planting is of conifers in upland areas, though the planting of broadleaved trees is encouraged on suitable sites. An increasing proportion of new planting is by private owners. During 1988–89 the Commission grant-aided 2,643 hectares (6,531 acres) of new broadleaved planting under its various schemes, an increase of 6 per cent over the previous year. Under the Commission's Woodland Grant Scheme grants for broadleaved planting, including planting as a component of mixed woodland, are up to 50 per cent higher than those offered for planting conifers.

Total employment in state and private forests in Great Britain was estimated at 40,000 in 1988–89, including about 2,650 people engaged in processing home-grown timber.

British woodlands meet only 12 per cent of the nation's consumption of wood and wood products. At present only just over half of the Commission's woodlands are in production. The volume of timber harvested on Commission lands in 1988–89 totalled 3·64 million cubic metres (128·6 million cubic feet).

The Forestry Commission and Forestry Policy

The Forestry Commission is the national forestry authority in Great Britain. The Commissioners give advice on forestry matters and are responsible to the Secretary of State for Scotland, the Minister of Agriculture, Fisheries and Food and the Secretary of State for Wales. Timber production, landscape amenity, environmental protection and employment are all forestry policy objectives. The Commission's activities also include wildlife and flora conservation, plant health, research, and the provision of facilities for recreation. As part of a rationalisation programme to achieve greater efficiency and commercial effectiveness, the Commission has sold 76,000 hectares (188,000 acres) of plantation and plantable land since 1981 and has been asked by the Government to dispose of a further 100,000 hectares (247,000 acres) by the end of the century. The Commission is financed partly by the Government and partly by receipts from sales of timber and other produce and from rents.

The Countryside Commission and the Forestry Commission have launched an initiative to create community forests on the outskirts of major cities in England and Wales, with initial proposals for a major forest in the midlands. The Government has issued revised criteria for planting on better-quality agricultural land in Scotland.

Forestry Research

The Forestry Commission maintains two principal research stations, at Alice Holt Lodge near Farnham (Surrey) and at Bush Estate near Edinburgh, for basic and applied research into all aspects of forestry. Aid is also given for research work in universities and other institutions. Its research programme includes projects on silviculture in upland and lowland sites, and on the selection and breeding of improved growing stock.

The Forestry Commission conducts an annual forest health survey which monitors the effects of air pollution and other stress factors on a growing range of broadleaves and conifers. It has increased research into wildlife conservation and farm forestry, including an evaluation of agroforestry systems combining wide-spaced conifers and broadleaves with sheep grazing. The Government has set up an expert scientific review group on tree health in Britain.

Forestry in Northern Ireland

The Department of Agriculture may acquire land for afforestation and give financial and technical assistance for private planting. The state forest area has grown steadily since 1945. By 1990, 60,600 hectares (149,680 acres) of plantable land had been acquired, of which 59,590 hectares (147,180 acres) were planted. There were 15,000 hectares (37,000 acres) of privately owned forest. Some 500 professional and industrial staff work in state forests.

17 Transport and Communications

Major improvements in the nation's infrastructure have resulted from the construction of a network of motorways, the extension of fast inter-city rail services (such as those operated by high-speed trains), and expansion schemes at many airports. Further improvements are in progress and the Channel Tunnel will have a significant impact on travel between Britain and the continent of Europe when it starts operation in 1993. Transport policy rests on the fundamental aims of promoting economic growth and higher national prosperity, and ensuring a reasonable level of personal mobility, while improving safety, conserving and enhancing the environment, and using energy economically. Britain is taking an active part in the European Community's development of a common transport policy, in the context of the completion of the single European market by 1992.

Users' expenditure on transport (including taxation) in Britain totalled an estimated £86,600 million in 1988, of which £71,500 million represented expenditure on road transport (including buses). About 95 per cent of transport is provided by the private sector. This proportion has increased with the privatisation of the Government's shareholdings in a number of publicly owned transport undertakings, including road haulage, airline services, airports and bus operations.

Inland Transport

There has been a considerable increase in passenger travel in recent years. Travel in Great Britain rose by 30 per cent between 1978 and 1989. Travel by car and taxi rose by 42 per cent and air travel expanded rapidly. However, recently, travel by motor cycle has been declining, and travel by bus and coach and by pedal cycle has changed little. Car and taxi travel accounts for 84 per cent of passenger mileage within Great Britain, buses and coaches for about 7 per cent, rail for 7 per cent and air less than 1 per cent.

Car ownership has also risen substantially, and 66 per cent of households in Great Britain have the regular use of one or more cars, with 18 per cent having the use of two or more cars. At the end of 1989 there were 24·2 million vehicles licensed for use on the roads of Great Britain, of which 19·7 million were cars (including over 2 million cars registered with a company address); 2 million light goods vehicles; 644,000 other goods vehicles; 875,000 motor cycles, scooters and mopeds; and 122,000 public transport vehicles (including taxis).

Road haulage has a dominant position in the movement of inland freight, accounting for about 82 per cent of tonnage carried and for nearly three-fifths of tonne-km. Railways, inland waterways, coastal shipping and pipelines are important in carrying certain types of freight, particularly bulk goods.

ROADS   Motor vehicle traffic in Great Britain is continuing to grow, having risen by 6 per cent in 1989 to some 390,000 million vehicle-km. In 1989 the road network in Britain totalled some 380,400 km (236,400 miles), of which 3,000 km (1,860 miles) were trunk motorways (see Table 17.1). Although motorways and trunk roads account for less than 5 per cent of road mileage in Great Britain, they carry about one-third of road traffic, including over half of heavy goods vehicle traffic. Traffic on these roads has been growing at a much higher rate than on other roads.

Table 17.1: Road Length (as at April 1989)

km

	Public roads	Trunk roads (including motorways)	Trunk motorways[a]
England	271,615	10,830	2,536
Scotland	51,466	3,165	234
Wales	33,216	1,699	120
Northern Ireland	24,081	256	112
Britain	380,378	15,950	3,002

Sources: Department of Transport, Northern Ireland Department of the Environment, Scottish Development Department and Welsh Office.
[a]In addition, there were 68 km (42 miles) of local authority motorway in England and 24 km (15 miles) in Scotland. In April 1990, 108 km (67 miles) of trunk motorway were under construction in England.

Administration   Responsibility for trunk road motorways and other trunk roads in Great Britain rests in England with the Secretary of State for Transport, in Scotland with the Secretary of State for Scotland and in Wales with the Secretary of State for Wales. The costs of construction, improvement and maintenance are paid for by central government. The highway authorities for non-trunk roads in England are the county councils, the metropolitan district councils, the London borough councils and the Common Council of the City of London. In Wales the authorities are the county councils, and in Scotland the regional or islands councils. In Northern Ireland the Northern Ireland Department of the Environment is responsible for the construction, improvement and maintenance of public roads.

Research into road construction, traffic engineering and safety, and into problems associated with transport, is carried out by the Transport and Road Research Laboratory, the research arm of the Department of Transport.

Private Finance   The Government is keen to encourage greater private sector involvement in the financing of roads. Work on a privately financed project to provide a new bridge across the Thames between Dartford and Thurrock should be completed by 1991, while a private sector consortium is to build a second Severn Bridge, costing some £270 million and expected to be completed in 1995. The Government is holding a competition for the Birmingham northern relief road and has invited preliminary proposals for a private sector route between Birmingham and Manchester. In April 1990 it invited views on the suitability for private funding of six further potential schemes. In Scotland a competition is being held for a privately financed bridge to Skye.

Other Developments

New and improved roads have resulted in much shorter travelling times, particularly for long-distance journeys and those between cities, and have brought considerable benefits to industry, commerce and road haulage operators, and increased personal mobility. The Government has a programme to improve motorways and other trunk roads (which form a network linking major centres of population, industrial areas and ports). This is intended to assist economic growth by reducing transport costs, to remove through traffic (especially lorries) from unsuitable roads in towns and villages, and to enhance road safety.

In mid-1990, 59 national trunk road and motorway schemes were under construction in England, costing nearly £1,400 million, while over 500 schemes were in preparation. Bypasses and relief roads account for nearly one-third of the programme, which also includes projects intended to increase the traffic capacity of major through routes and to improve junctions on heavily used roads. In 1990–91 the Department of Transport is supporting 344 major local authority road schemes, the majority of which are bypasses or relief roads.

Road communications in Wales are expected to benefit from the second Severn Bridge and improvements to the M4 motorway. Other priorities in Wales are improvements to the coast road in north Wales (including the construction under the Conwy estuary of the first immersed tube road tunnel to be built in Britain) and the upgrading of roads which are important for industrial redevelopment.

The programme in Scotland includes planned extensions to the M74, M8 and M80 motorways; the improvement of strategic routes beyond central Scotland to areas such as the north east and some of the west-coast routes; and the construction of more bypasses.

In Northern Ireland the emphasis is on improving arterial routes, constructing more bypasses, and improving roads in the Belfast area, including the construction of a new cross-harbour link planned for the mid-1990s.

Licensing and Standards

Records of drivers and vehicles are maintained by the Driver and Vehicle Licensing Agency, an executive agency of the Department of Transport. It holds records on 33 million drivers and 24·2 million licensed vehicles in Great Britain. All drivers of motor vehicles, except new residents holding certain non-British licences, are required to pass the driving test before being granted a full licence to drive. The minimum ages for driving are 16 for riders of mopeds and disabled drivers of specially adapted vehicles; 17 for drivers of cars and other passenger vehicles with nine or fewer seats (including that of the driver), motor cycles and goods vehicles not over 3·5 tonnes permissible maximum weight; 18 for goods vehicles over 3·5 but not over 7·5 tonnes; and 21 for passenger vehicles with over nine seats and goods vehicles over 7·5 tonnes. In April 1990 the Agency began to issue a new harmonised European Community driving licence.

The Secretary of State for Transport has a statutory responsibility for ensuring the roadworthiness of vehicles in use on the roads. The Vehicle Inspectorate, which was the first of the Government's executive agencies, is the national testing authority. It meets this responsibility mainly through annual testing and certification of heavy goods vehicles, buses and coaches; administration of the car and motor cycle testing scheme (under which vehicles are tested at private garages authorised as test stations), and other road safety tasks, such as vehicle 'spot checks' and inspection of operators' premises. In Northern Ireland private cars five or more years old are tested at official vehicle inspection centres.

Road Safety

Although Great Britain has one of the highest densities of road traffic in the world, it has a good record on road safety, with one of the lowest road accident death rates in the European Community. In 1989 some 5,370 people were killed on the roads, about 63,200 seriously injured and 273,000 slightly injured. A number of factors, such as developments in vehicle safety standards and improvements in infrastructure (including motorways, bypasses and pedestrianisation of city centres), have contributed to the long-term decline in casualty rates.

Following a major review of road safety policy completed in 1987, the Government is seeking to reduce road casualties by one-third by the end of the century. To achieve this, resources are being concentrated initially on measures which are demonstrably cost-effective in terms of casualty reduction. Priority is given to reducing casualties among vulnerable road-users (pedestrians, cyclists and motor cyclists), particularly in urban areas, where some 70 per cent of road accidents occur. The other principal areas for achieving lower casualties are improvements in highway design and measures to combat drinking and driving; the statutory limit of breath alcohol concentration for drivers is 35 microgrammes of alcohol in 100 millilitres of breath.

In 1989 the Government announced proposals for a major reform of road traffic law to improve road safety, including changes in a wide range of driving offences and a new offence of dangerous driving. Tougher measures to deal with drinking and driving offenders are proposed, while new technology is to be utilised to improve the detection of speeding and traffic-light offences.

Traffic in Towns

Traffic management schemes are used in many urban areas to reduce congestion, create a better environment and improve road safety. These schemes include, for example, one-way streets, bus lanes, facilities for pedestrians and cyclists, and traffic calming measures (such as road humps to slow traffic in residential areas). Many towns have shopping precincts which are designed for the convenience of pedestrians and from which motor vehicles are excluded for all or part of the day. Controls over on-street parking are enforced through excess charges and fixed penalties, supported where appropriate by powers to remove vehicles. In parts of central London the use of wheel clamping to immobilise illegally parked vehicles has also been authorised.

Computerised urban traffic control systems developed by the Department of Transport and British firms have achieved international repute and are the most commonly used in the world. A recent enhancement, which continuously measures and responds to the flow of traffic, is being introduced into the majority of urban traffic control schemes.

Electronic driver information systems, which assist drivers through visual displays in their vehicles, are being developed. A pilot scheme using one such system, called 'Autoguide', is planned in the London area in 1992. Autoguide uses roadside beacons to transmit to appropriately equipped vehicles route information which can be updated continuously to take account of changing traffic conditions.

ROAD HAULAGE

Road haulage traffic by heavy goods vehicles amounted to 129,800 million tonne-km in 1989, 4 per cent more than in 1988. There has been a move towards larger and more efficient vehicles carrying heavier loads—about 77 per cent of the traffic, in terms of tonne-km, is carried in vehicles of over 25 tonnes gross laden weight. Much of the traffic is moved over short distances, with 77 per cent of the tonnage being carried on hauls of 100 km (62 miles) or less. Public haulage (private road hauliers carrying other firms' goods) accounts for 72 per cent of freight carried in Great Britain in terms of tonne-km. In 1989 the main commodities handled by heavy goods vehicles were crude minerals (392 million tonnes); food, drink and tobacco (285 million tonnes); and building materials (188 million tonnes).

The Government has introduced a number of measures to alleviate the environmental problems caused by lorries and to improve road safety. These include the provision of more relief roads and bypasses to keep lorries away from people; new standards for vehicle sideguards, noise and spray suppression; and more effective enforcement of regulations. Grants of up to 60 per cent are available towards the cost of construction or modernisation of privately owned rail or inland waterway facilities where significant environmental benefits can be obtained by keeping heavy goods vehicle traffic off unsuitable roads.

Structure of the Industry

Road haulage is predominantly an industry of small, privately owned businesses. There were some 127,000 holders of an operator's licence in 1989. About half the heavy goods vehicles are in fleets of ten or fewer vehicles. The biggest operators in Great Britain are NFC plc, Transport Development Group plc, TNT Express (UK) Ltd and United Carriers International Ltd.

Licensing and Other Controls

Those operating goods vehicles over 3·5 tonnes gross weight (with certain special exemptions) require an operator's licence. Licences are divided into restricted licences for firms carrying their own goods, and standard licences, subdivided into 'national only' and 'international', for hauliers operating for hire or reward. (In Northern Ireland operators carrying their own goods do not require a licence.) Proof of professional competence, financial standing and good repute is needed to obtain a standard licence. Regulations lay down limits on the hours worked by drivers of goods vehicles, as well as minimum rest periods. Tachographs (which automatically record speed, distance covered, driving time and stopping periods) must be fitted and used in most goods vehicles over 3·5 tonnes gross weight in Great Britain.

International Road Haulage

International road haulage has grown rapidly and about 8 million tonnes were carried in powered road vehicles to and from the continent of Europe and the Irish Republic by British registered vehicles in 1989. Over 1·3 million road goods vehicles were conveyed by ferry to the continent in 1989, of which nearly half were unaccompanied trailers. The average length of haul for British registered vehicles is some 1,160 km (720 miles) in each direction, compared with 75 km (47 miles) for internal road haulage. International road haulage is constrained by bilateral agreements with 26 other countries. Many place no restriction on the number of British lorries entering the country concerned, although some agreements specify an annual quota. The European Community (which also has two quotas of permits that allow haulage or cabotage anywhere within the Community) has agreed to full liberalisation of international road haulage within the Community, abolishing all permits from 31 December 1992.

**PASSENGER
SERVICES**

Two major measures—the Transport Act 1980 and the Transport Act 1985—have stimulated competition in long-distance express coach services and excursions, and in local bus services respectively.

Structure

Major changes in the structure of the passenger transport industry have occurred as a result of the Transport Act 1985. Privatisation of the National Bus Company (which was the largest single bus and coach operator in Britain, operating through 72 subsidiaries in England and Wales) was completed in 1988. Each subsidiary was sold separately, and encouragement was given for a buy-out by the local management or employees. Under the Transport (Scotland) Act 1989 the Scottish Bus Group, the largest operator of bus services in Scotland, is being privatised as ten separate companies. It has some 3,000 buses.

To promote competition further, the 1985 Act provided for the bus operations formerly run directly by municipal authorities and by passenger transport executives in metropolitan areas to be transferred to public transport companies. The 50 companies provide about 30 per cent of bus services. The Act allows local authorities to sell their public transport companies; by 1990 eight had been sold.

London Transport (LT) is a nationalised industry, established under the London Regional Transport Act 1984, with its board members appointed by the Secretary of State for Transport. Within LT the main wholly owned operating subsidiaries are London Underground Ltd, London Buses Ltd and Docklands Light Railway Ltd. Financial support is provided by central government. LT is required to involve the private sector in the provision of services where this is more efficient, and has been set objectives on safety, the quality of services and on its financial performance.

In Northern Ireland almost all road passenger services are provided by subsidiaries of the publicly owned Northern Ireland Transport Holding Company. Citybus Ltd operates services in the city of Belfast and Ulsterbus Ltd operates most of the services in the rest of Northern Ireland. These companies have some 300 and 1,000 vehicles respectively.

As well as the major bus operators, there are also a large number of small privately owned undertakings, often operating fewer than five vehicles. Although double-deck buses are the main type of vehicle used for urban road passenger transport in Britain, with some 23,500 in operation, there has been a substantial increase in the use of minibuses in recent years. Over 600 areas are served by more than 7,000 minibuses. In addition, there are some 49,000 other single-deck buses and coaches. Blackpool and Llandudno have Britain's only remaining tramway systems.

**Deregulation of
Bus Services**

Local bus services in Great Britain (except in London) were deregulated in 1986 by the Transport Act 1985. Bus operators are now able to run services wherever they see a commercial opportunity, and local authorities can subsidise the provision of additional socially necessary services after competitive tendering. All services, whether commercial or subsidised, have to be registered with the appropriate traffic commissioner (one for each of the nine traffic areas of Great Britain) six weeks before the commencement of the service. Similar notice is required when a service is varied or cancelled.

Deregulation led to an increase of 18 per cent in local bus mileage outside London between 1985 and 1989, with some 84 per cent of services operated without subsidy. In addition, there has been a substantial increase in the number of private operators and in the number of minibus services. The long-term decline in the number of passengers has shown signs of lessening.

In 1988–89 buses or coaches carried some 4,072 million passengers on local services outside London, a decline of 10 per cent since deregulation; the fall in patronage in 1988–89 was, however, only 1 per cent. Deregulation also had a noticeable effect during the 1980s on long-distance express coach services, bringing about reductions in fares, the provision of more services and an increase in passengers.

Taxis

There are about 49,000 licensed taxis in Great Britain, mainly in urban areas; London has some 16,000. In London and a number of other cities taxis must be purpose-built to conform to very strict requirements and drivers must have passed a test of their knowledge of the area. Private hire vehicles with drivers may be booked only through the operator and not hired on the street; in most areas outside London private hire vehicles are licensed.

The Transport Act 1985 provided arrangements for the operation of taxis and private hire vehicles which increased their role in public transport. Restrictions by local authorities on granting taxi licences were relaxed so that a licence can be refused only if a local authority is satisfied that there is no unfulfilled demand for taxis in its area. Taxi operators are able to run regular local services and can tender in competition with bus operators for services subsidised by local authorities. To do this, they may apply for a special 'restricted' bus operator's licence, allowing them to run local services without having to obtain a full bus operator's licence. Taxis and licensed private hire vehicles may also offer shared rides to passengers paying separate fares.

RAILWAYS

Railways were pioneered in Britain: the Stockton and Darlington Railway, opened in 1825, was the first public passenger railway in the world to be worked by steam power. Under the Transport Act 1947 the four large railway companies in Great Britain were brought under public ownership, and in 1962 the British Railways Board was set up to manage railway affairs and subsidiary activities. In Northern Ireland the Northern Ireland Railways Company Ltd, a subsidiary of the Northern Ireland Transport Holding Company, operates the railway service on some 320 km (200 miles) of track.

Organisation

The British Railways Board controls most of the railway network in Great Britain apart from the underground railway systems in London and Glasgow, the Tyne and Wear Metro and a few stretches of private railway. It has five business sectors responsible for the main markets: InterCity, Network SouthEast and Provincial services being responsible for the passenger services, while the other two sectors are Railfreight and Parcels. Other subsidiary businesses are British Rail Maintenance Ltd, which is responsible for maintenance and light repair of British Rail stock; and Transmark, which provides consultancy services overseas on railway and associated operations.

Private Sector Involvement

In order to concentrate its resources on running the main railway business, British Rail has sold a number of its subsidiary businesses, including its station catering business, Travellers' Fare Ltd. Its engineering subsidiary, British Rail Engineering Ltd, was sold in 1989 to a consortium of its management and employees and two private sector companies. The Government is studying the long-term options for British Rail, including the possibility of privatisation.

Operations

In 1989–90 the Board's turnover, including financial support and income from other activities but excluding internal transactions, was £3,485 million, of which £2,626 million was derived from rail passenger services and £694 million from freight services. It received grants of £501 million as compensation for the public service obligation to operate sections of the passenger network in the Provincial sector and Network SouthEast which would not otherwise cover their cost. Statistics of the Board's operations are given in Table 17.2.

Table 17.2: Railway Operations

	1984-85	1987-88	1988-89	1989-90
Passenger journeys (million)	701	727	764	746
Passenger-km (million)	29,725	33,141	34,321	33,323
Freight traffic (million tonnes)	68[a]	144	150	143
Trainload and wagonload traffic (million net tonne-km)	12,031[a]	17,466	18,103	16,742
Assets (at end of period):				
Locomotives	2,467	2,270	2,180	2,095
High Speed Train power units	197	197	197	197
Other coaching vehicles	16,433	14,648	14,258	13,833
Freight vehicles[b]	45,174	28,884	24,922	21,970
Stations (including freight and parcels)	2,524	2,554	2,596	2,610
Route open for traffic (km)	16,803	16,633	16,598	16,588

Source: British Railways Board.
[a] Affected by a considerable decline in coal traffic as the result of a major industrial dispute in coalmining.
[b] In addition, a number of privately owned wagons and locomotives are operated on the railway network for customers of British Rail. Some 13,995 freight vehicles and ten locomotives were authorised for working on the network at the end of March 1990.

In connection with the Government's wish to ensure a safe, efficient and high-quality modern railway network, new objectives for British Rail were announced in December 1989. A high priority for safety has been set, involving the implementation of the safety recommendations made by the inspector who investigated a major railway accident at Clapham Junction (south London) in December 1988. Provision for new safety expenditure of £125 million over the three years from April 1990 has been set. The objectives envisage further progress towards earning a commercial return for InterCity, Railfreight and Parcels sectors; the elimination of Network SouthEast's grant requirement by 1992–93; and a reduction of the grant to the Provincial sector.

British Rail has a substantial investment programme. Investment totalled £715 million in 1989–90 and is expected to rise to £1,421 million in 1992–93. Major areas of expenditure include completion of the electrification scheme for the east-coast main line between London and Edinburgh, new rolling stock and infrastructure improvements in Network SouthEast, and investment in new diesel multiple-unit trains in the Provincial sector.

Passenger Services

The passenger network (see map, p 359) comprises a fast inter-city network, linking the main centres of Great Britain; local stopping services; and commuter services in and around the large conurbations, especially London and south-east England. British Rail runs over 700 InterCity expresses each

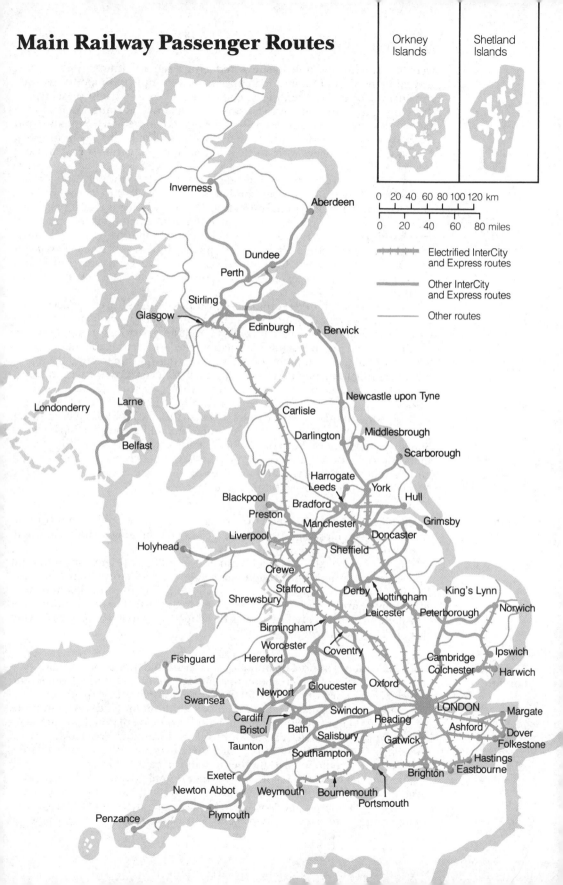

Main Railway Passenger Routes

Orkney Islands

Shetland Islands

| 0 | 20 | 40 | 60 | 80 | 100 | 120 km |

| 0 | 20 | 40 | 60 | 80 miles |

Electrified InterCity and Express routes

Other InterCity and Express routes

Other routes

Inverness

Aberdeen

Dundee

Perth

Stirling

Glasgow

Edinburgh

Berwick

Newcastle upon Tyne

Londonderry

Larne

Carlisle

Belfast

Darlington

Middlesbrough

Scarborough

Harrogate

Leeds

York

Hull

Blackpool

Bradford

Preston

Manchester

Doncaster

Grimsby

Liverpool

Holyhead

Sheffield

Crewe

Stafford

Derby

Nottingham

King's Lynn

Shrewsbury

Leicester

Peterborough

Norwich

Birmingham

Worcester

Coventry

Fishguard

Hereford

Cambridge

Ipswich

Colchester

Harwich

Gloucester

Oxford

Swansea

Newport

Swindon

LONDON

Margate

Cardiff

Reading

Ashford

Bristol

Bath

Salisbury

Gatwick

Dover

Taunton

Southampton

Folkestone

Hastings

Brighton

Eastbourne

Exeter

Weymouth

Bournemouth

Newton Abbot

Portsmouth

Penzance

Plymouth

weekday, serving about 90 business and leisure centres. InterCity 125 trains, travelling at maximum sustained speeds of 125 mph (201 km/h), provide over half of InterCity train mileage and are the world's fastest diesel trains. They operate from London to the west of England and south Wales; to the East Midlands; to Yorkshire, north-east England and eastern Scotland; and on cross-country services through the West Midlands, linking south-west England or south Wales with north-west England or north-east England and Edinburgh.

About 27 per cent of route-mileage is electrified, including British Rail's busiest InterCity route, linking London, the West Midlands, the North West and Glasgow. The most significant electrification scheme is that for the east-coast main line between London and Edinburgh (including the line from Doncaster to Leeds), involving electrification of some 644 km (400 miles) and costing £450 million at 1990–91 prices. InterCity 225 electric trains are already in operation between King's Cross and Doncaster and Leeds. Electric services will be extended to Newcastle upon Tyne and Edinburgh in 1991.

Two new types of diesel multiple-unit trains—the lightweight 'Pacer' and the medium-weight 'Sprinter'—are being introduced, while many of the older electric multiple units used for commuting services in London and south-east England are being replaced by new, more efficient rolling stock. The first of a new generation of 'Networker' trains is due to enter service in Kent in spring 1992 and there are plans to introduce the new trains in Essex. Some 400 coaches have been ordered, with a further 276 approved in principle. A diesel version has been ordered for non-electrified lines to the west of London and should enter service at the end of 1991. Three major new rail links to airports are planned: a new link under construction between Stansted airport and London, a joint venture with BAA plc for a £235 million project (to be financed largely by BAA) between Heathrow airport and Paddington (London), and a link to connect Manchester airport to the Manchester to Wilmslow (Cheshire) line.

Freight

Over 90 per cent of rail freight traffic is of bulk commodities, most of it in trainloads. The most significant bulk freight commodities handled are coal, coke, iron and steel, building materials and petroleum.

The opening of the Channel Tunnel (see p 361) presents an important opportunity for non-bulk freight movement. Freight routes in Kent and Sussex are being upgraded in preparation for the traffic, and new locomotives are being purchased. Container traffic to the continent of Europe and further afield is being developed and new container-carrying wagons have been ordered.

Railways in London

London Underground Ltd operates Underground trains on 408 km (254 miles) of railway, of which about 169 km (105 miles) are underground, and serves 273 stations, with some 460 trains operating in the peak period. Some 765 million passenger journeys were made on London Underground trains in 1989–90. Major investment in the Underground is planned, including an extension of the Jubilee Line to Stratford (east London) via Docklands and the north Greenwich peninsula, while the Government is also considering options which would involve another new line in central London.

The Docklands Light Railway, a 12-km (7·5-mile) route with 15 stations, began operating in 1987 and is now being upgraded. Extensions westward to the City of London and eastward to Beckton are under construction. Engineering studies are in progress for a new light railway network planned by London Transport and British Rail for the Croydon area of south London.

Other Urban Railways

Other urban railways in Great Britain are the Glasgow Underground and the Tyne and Wear Metro, a 56-km (35-mile) light rapid transit system with over 40 stations. The first stage of the Manchester Metrolink project, to be designed, built and operated by the GMA Group (a private sector consortium), will from 1991–92 link Manchester's main railway termini and provide improved services to Bury and Altrincham as a result of conversion of existing British Rail services to light rapid transit. In the West Midlands work is planned on another major light rail project, while light rapid transit systems are also being considered in a number of other areas, including Bristol, Edinburgh, Glasgow, Sheffield and Southampton.

Private Railways

There are over 70 small, privately owned passenger-carrying railways in Great Britain, mostly operated on a voluntary basis and providing limited services for tourists and railway enthusiasts. The main aim of most of these railways, such as the Severn Valley Railway, is the preservation of steam traction.

Channel Tunnel

Construction work is in progress on the Channel Tunnel project to provide twin single-track rail tunnels between Britain and France in the largest civil engineering project in Europe to be financed by the private sector. The project, with a total financing requirement of £8,500 million, is being undertaken by Eurotunnel, a partnership between two companies, one British and one French—the Channel Tunnel Group Ltd and France Manche SA respectively. Design and construction are being carried out for Eurotunnel by ten of the largest British and French contractors, which together have formed a single contractor, Transmanche Link. Services are due to start in 1993, and the Channel Tunnel is expected to bring substantial benefits to industry and to travellers throughout Britain from the quicker and more reliable carriage of passengers and freight.

The Treaty between the French and British governments relating to the fixed link (Channel Tunnel) contains provisions to safeguard the public interest in matters such as safety and the environment, and also deals with matters of national jurisdiction, providing arrangements for arbitration in the event of disputes over interpretation. The Channel Tunnel Act 1987 ratified the Treaty, enabling implementation of the Concession Agreement between the British and French governments and the Channel Tunnel Group and France Manche. The agreement gives the concessionaires the right to operate the tunnel for 55 years.

Eurotunnel Services

Eurotunnel will operate shuttle trains through the tunnel between the terminals at Cheriton (near Folkestone) and Coquelles (near Calais), with the journey taking about 35 minutes. Shuttle trains will provide a no-booking, drive-on, drive-off service, with separate shuttles for passengers and freight. Initially Eurotunnel is planning to run tourist shuttle services every 15 minutes and freight shuttle services every 20 minutes. As traffic grows, the frequency of services will be increased. On the opening of the tunnel a peak of some 200 movements a day in each direction is expected (including through rail services).

Through Rail Services

About 50 per cent of the capacity of the Channel Tunnel has been allocated to through rail passenger and freight services. High-speed passenger services are planned to run at least every hour between London and Paris, and London and Brussels. Through services to other European destinations and from the Midlands, northern England and Scotland to the continent are under consideration. British Rail plans to invest £1,100 million in new passenger and freight rolling stock, track and signalling improvements, and terminal facilities for the start of international services in 1993; over £600 million has already been approved by the Secretary of State for Transport.

To meet the forecast growth in demand for through rail services, additional capacity will eventually be required between London and the Channel Tunnel. This will be provided by the construction of a new high-speed rail link. British Rail is reviewing its proposals for the section of route from the North Downs to London (Waterloo and King's Cross) to maximise the benefits for commuters and to improve the financial viability of the project.

INLAND WATERWAYS

The inland waterways of Great Britain are popular for recreation, make a valuable contribution to the environment and play an important part in land drainage and water supply. They are also used to a limited extent for freight-carrying. An official survey of inland waterway freight traffic reported that in 1988, 68 million tonnes of freight were carried on inland waterways and estuaries, amounting to some 2,400 million tonne-km (1·5 per cent of freight traffic by tonne-km in Great Britain). About 50 per cent (in tonne-km) was carried in south-east England, mainly on the River Thames. The publicly owned British Waterways Board is responsible for some 3,200 km (2,000 miles) of waterways in Great Britain. The majority of waterways are maintained primarily for leisure use, but about 620 km (385 miles) are maintained as commercial waterways for private sector traffic. The Board is taking steps to develop its business more commercially with greater responsiveness to market needs. In 1989–90 the Board's turnover amounted to £24·1 million and it received a government grant of £45·6 million to maintain its waterways to statutory standards.

Ports

There are about 80 ports of commercial significance in Great Britain, but in addition there are many small harbours which handle small amounts of cargo or mainly serve fishing or recreational interests. Port authorities are of three broad types—trusts, local authorities and companies—and most operate with statutory powers under private Acts of Parliament. Major ports controlled by trusts include Clyde, Dover, Forth, London, Medway, Milford Haven, and Tees and Hartlepool. Local authorities own many small ports but also the much larger ports of Bristol and Portsmouth, and the oil ports in Orkney and Shetland.

Associated British Ports Holdings PLC (a private sector company) owns and operates 22 ports, including Southampton, Grimsby and Immingham, Hull, Newport, Cardiff and Swansea. Other major ports owned by companies include Felixstowe, Liverpool and Manchester, and a group of ferry ports, including Harwich (Parkeston Quay) and Stranraer.

The Government has suggested that ports not already owned by companies may wish to consider whether company status would be advantageous. A former local authority port, Boston (Lincolnshire), was transferred to private sector ownership at the beginning of 1990. The trust ports of Clyde and Tees and Hartlepool have brought Bills before Parliament which would provide for their conversion into companies.

In 1989 the Dock Labour Scheme, which controlled employment in the older major ports, was abolished. Since its abolition there have been indications of substantial increases in productivity in ports, more flexible working practices and higher investment.

Port Traffic In 1989 traffic through the ports of Great Britain amounted to 465 million tonnes, comprising 127 million tonnes of exports, 171 million tonnes of imports and 166 million tonnes of domestic traffic (which included offshore traffic, landings of sea-dredged aggregates and material shipped for dumping at sea). About 53 per cent of the traffic was in fuels, mainly petroleum and petroleum products. Traffic through Northern Ireland ports totalled 15 million tonnes.

Britain's main ports, in terms of total tonnage handled, are given in Table 17.3. Sullom Voe (Shetland), Milford Haven and Forth mostly handle oil, while the main ports for non-fuel traffic are London, Tees and Hartlepool, Grimsby and Immingham, Felixstowe and Dover. Ports on the south and east coasts have increasingly gained traffic at the expense of those on the west coast as the emphasis of Britain's trade has switched towards the continent of Europe, and with the changing patterns of shipping which have accompanied the worldwide switch from conventional handling methods to container and roll-on modes. Dover and Felixstowe are the main ports to have benefited, while the growth of roll-on traffic has also favoured many small ports (such as Ramsgate, Ipswich, Portsmouth and Great Yarmouth).

Table 17.3: Traffic through the Principal Ports of Great Britain[a]

million tonnes

	1975	1985	1986	1987	1988	1989
London	50·3	51·6	53·6	48·9	53·7	54·0
Sullom Voe	—	59·0	57·2	50·0	50·6	40·7
Tees and Hartlepool	20·2	30·6	30·7	33·9	37·4	39·3
Grimsby and Immingham	22·0	29·1	32·0	32·2	35·0	38·1
Milford Haven	44·9	32·4	30·0	32·7	33·3	33·0
Southampton	25·3	25·2	25·7	27·2	31·4	26·1
Forth	8·4	29·1	28·8	30·0	29·0	22·9
Liverpool	23·4	10·4	10·7	10·2	19·6	20·2
Felixstowe	4·1	10·1	10·8	13·3	15·6	16·5
Medway	21·7	10·4	10·4	11·6	12·7	14·0
Dover	3·7	9·3	9·9	10·6	10·4	13·5

Source: Department of Transport.

[a]Belfast and Larne are the main ports in Northern Ireland and handled 7·2 million tonnes and 3·9 million tonnes respectively in 1989.

Container and roll-on traffic in Great Britain has almost trebled since 1975 to 78 million tonnes in 1989 and now accounts for about 73 per cent of non-bulk traffic. The leading ports for container traffic are Felixstowe, London and Southampton. Those for roll-on traffic are Dover (Britain's leading seaport in terms of the value of trade handled), Felixstowe, Portsmouth, Grimsby and Immingham, and Harwich. Other traffics that have expanded in recent years are minerals, vehicles and forest products.

Development Most recent major port developments have been at east- and south-coast ports. For example, at Felixstowe a £42 million container terminal, completed in 1986, raised the port's container-handling capacity by about 50 per cent. A £50 million extension to the terminal was completed in January 1990. Extra capacity for ferry services has recently been provided at a number of other ports, including Dartford, Dover, Hull, Portsmouth and Ramsgate. New facilities are being developed for bulk and containerised cargoes on the Medway, and there are plans for bulk and roll-on cargoes on the Humber.

Purpose-built terminals for oil from the British sector of the North Sea have been built at Hound Point on the Forth, on the Tees, at Flotta and at Sullom Voe (one of the largest oil terminals in the world). Supply bases for offshore oil and gas installations have been built at a number of ports, notably Aberdeen, Great Yarmouth and Heysham.

Shipping

The tonnage of the British registered trading fleet has been declining in recent years. In April 1990 British companies owned 801 trading vessels of 15·5 million deadweight tonnes. These included 209 vessels totalling 9·5 million deadweight tonnes used as oil, chemical or gas carriers and 576 vessels totalling 5·9 million tonnes employed as dry bulk carriers, container ships or other types of cargo ships. The great majority of these ships are registered in Britain or British dependent territories such as Bermuda. In September 1990 a joint working party of the Government and the General Council of British Shipping produced a report on the merchant shipping industry which contained an agreed analysis and made a number of recommendations.

Services

About 93 per cent by weight (76 per cent by value) of Britain's overseas trade is carried by sea, while the proportion of passengers travelling to or from Britain by sea is only about a third, compared with about one-half in the early 1960s.

Cargo Services

In 1989 British seaborne trade amounted to 283 million tonnes (valued at £162,000 million) or 780,000 million tonne-km (484,500 million tonne miles). British registered ships carried 21 per cent by weight and 35 per cent by value. Tanker cargo accounted for 41 per cent of this trade by weight, but only 6 per cent by value, and foodstuffs and manufactured goods accounted for 84 per cent by value.

British cargo liner tonnage is dominated by a relatively small number of large private sector groups and container consortia. Many of the deep-sea liner services from Britain are operated by container ships. There are many roll-on, roll-off services accommodating passengers and their cars and commercial vehicles between Britain and the continent of Europe, and several freight-only roll-on, roll-off services to the Irish Republic, the continent of Europe, and to some more distant countries.

British shipping companies operating liner services have associated with each other and with the companies of other countries operating on the same routes in a series of 'conferences' designed to secure standardisation and stability of rates, and to maintain frequency and regularity of services. Conferences serve all the major trades to and from Britain.

Passenger Services

Almost all of the 28·8 million passengers who arrived at or departed from British ports in 1989 travelled to or from the continent of Europe or the Irish Republic. Remaining long-distance passenger ships are used for cruising and in 1989 some 67,000 passengers embarked on pleasure cruises from British ports.

Traffic from the southern and south-eastern ports accounts for a substantial proportion of traffic to the continent of Europe. The main British operators are Sealink UK Ltd and P and O. As well as roll-on, roll-off ferries passengers are able to travel by hovercraft, which are operated by Hoverspeed Ltd between Dover and Boulogne, and Dover and Calais, or hydrofoil. In August 1990 Hoverspeed inaugurated a high-speed catamaran service between Portsmouth and Cherbourg.

Passenger and freight ferry services are also operated to many of the offshore islands, such as the Isle of Wight, the Orkney and Shetland islands, and the islands off the west coast of Scotland.

Merchant Shipping Legislation

The Government's policy is one of minimum intervention and the encouragement of free and fair competition. However, under the Merchant Shipping Acts there are regulations, administered by the Department of Transport, for marine safety and welfare, and for preventing and cleaning up pollution from ships. The Acts also contain certain reserve powers for protecting shipping and trading interests from measures adopted or proposed by overseas governments.

The Merchant Shipping Act 1988 contains provisions to improve standards of marine safety, update the law on ship registration and ensure that Britain's strategic maritime requirements are met. The Government has made funds available for Merchant Navy officer training, the repatriation of crews in the deep-sea trades and a Reserve of ex-seafarers willing to serve in the Merchant Navy in an emergency. Among the measures to improve the safety of roll-on, roll-off ferries, following the sinking of the *Herald of Free Enterprise* in 1987 with the loss of 189 lives, are a new duty on shipowners to ensure the safe operation of their vessels, while other provisions have tightened the duties of masters and their crews. The majority of measures introduced by Britain have been incorporated in the relevant international maritime safety convention.

The first stage of a European Community shipping policy involved agreement in 1986 on four regulations designed to liberalise the Community's international trade, establish a competitive regime for shipping, and enable the Community to take action to combat protectionism from other countries and to counter unfair pricing practices. Under the second stage, now under consideration, a range of measures has been proposed to harmonise operating conditions and strengthen the competitiveness of Community members' merchant fleets.

Safety at Sea

The Coastguard Service, administered by the Department of Transport, is responsible for co-ordinating civil maritime search and rescue operations around the coastline of Britain. In a maritime emergency the Coastguard calls on and co-ordinates the appropriate facilities, such as lifeboats of the Royal National Lifeboat Institution (a voluntary body), and Ministry of Defence aircraft, helicopters and ships, as well as merchant shipping, commercial aircraft and ferries. The Coastguard has three long-range civil helicopters for search and rescue work. In 1989 the Coastguard Service co-ordinated action in nearly 6,800 incidents (including cliff rescues), in which 11,500 people were assisted.

The lighthouse authorities are: for England and Wales the Corporation of Trinity House, for Scotland the Northern Lighthouse Board and for Ireland the Commissioners of Irish Lights. They control about 370 lighthouses, and many minor lights and buoys. Responsibility for pilotage rests with harbour authorities under the Pilotage Act 1987.

Compliance with traffic separation schemes around the shores of Britain is mandatory for all vessels of countries party to the Convention on the

International Regulations for Preventing Collisions at Sea 1972. The most important scheme affecting British waters is in the Dover Strait, the world's busiest seaway. Britain and France jointly operate the Channel Navigation Information Service, which provides navigational information and also monitors the movement of vessels in the strait.

Civil Aviation

Britain's substantial civil air transport industry is continuing to develop to meet the increasing demand for air travel, particularly international travel. Airlines are re-equipping their fleets with the most modern aircraft, many airports are being modernised and expanded, and investment is helping to improve air traffic control capacity.

Role of the Government

The Secretary of State for Transport is responsible for international matters including negotiation of air service agreements with more than 100 other countries, the licensing and control of public transport operations into Britain by overseas operators and British participation in the activities of international aviation bodies. Other responsibilities include airports policy, amenity matters (such as aircraft noise), aviation security policy and investigation of accidents.

The Government's civil aviation policy aims to maintain high standards of safety, to encourage a sound and competitive multi-airline industry in Britain, and to promote competition in international and internal services. In its negotiations with other countries on bilateral air service agreements it is proposing the adoption of more liberal measures. New agreements with an increasing number of other countries are resulting in greater competition, leading to increased traffic and lower fares. The Government has taken the lead in encouraging airline competition within the European Community, as a first step towards meeting the Community's objective that by 1992 air transport should be part of a single internal market. As a result, airlines have greater freedom in setting fares and determining the number and capacity of services provided.

Civil Aviation Authority

The Civil Aviation Authority (CAA) is an independent statutory body responsible for the economic and safety regulation of the industry and, jointly with the Ministry of Defence, for the provision of air navigation services. Members of the CAA board are appointed by the Secretary of State for Transport.

Under the Civil Aviation Act 1982 the CAA's primary objectives are to ensure that British airlines provide air services to satisfy all substantial categories of public demand at the lowest charges consistent with a high standard of safety and to further the reasonable interests of air transport users.

Air Traffic

Total capacity offered on all services by British airlines amounted to 18,723 million available tonne-km in 1989: 13,427 million tonne-km on scheduled services and 5,296 million tonne-km on non-scheduled services. The airlines carry 35·2 million passengers a year on scheduled services and 24·4 million on charter flights. In 1989 some 75·4 million passengers travelled by air (international terminal passengers) to or from Britain, 5 per cent more than in 1988.

In 1989 the value of Britain's overseas trade carried by air was some £21,317 million and the proportions carried by air amounted to 21 per cent of the value of exports and 18 per cent of imports. Air freight is important for the carriage of goods with a high value-to-weight ratio, especially where speed of movement is essential. Precious stones, live animals, medicinal and pharmaceutical products, clothing, leather and skins, and scientific instruments are major categories in which a relatively high proportion of exports is sent by air.

Structure of the Airline Industry

Major changes in the structure of the airline industry have occurred. With the sale by the Government of its shares in British Airways in 1987, the civil airline industry is entirely in the private sector. In 1988 British Airways acquired control of British Caledonian Group Plc, the holding company for a group of which British Caledonian Airways (then the second largest British scheduled airline) was the principal subsidiary.

British Airways

British Airways Plc is one of the world's leading airlines. In terms of international scheduled services it is the largest in the world. During 1989–90 British Airways' turnover was £4,838 million (including £4,715 million from airline operations), and the British Airways group carried 25·2 million passengers on scheduled and charter flights.

The British Airways scheduled route network serves over 160 destinations in some 75 countries. Its main operating base is London's Heathrow airport, but services from Gatwick and regional centres such as Manchester and Birmingham have been expanding. Scheduled Concorde supersonic services are operated from London (Heathrow) to New York, Washington, Miami and Toronto, crossing the Atlantic in about half the time taken by subsonic aircraft. In March 1990 British Airways had a fleet of 224 aircraft, the largest fleet in Western Europe, comprising 7 Concordes, 47 Boeing 747s (including 8 of 21 747-400s ordered), 8 McDonnell-Douglas DC10s, 17 Lockheed TriStars, 36 Boeing 757s, 7 Airbus A320s, 47 Boeing 737s, 4 Boeing 767s (with a further 13 on order), 34 BAC One-Elevens, 8 British Aerospace Advanced Turboprops and 8 British Aerospace 748s. Orders for 58 aircraft have been placed and the fleet is expected to increase to 250 by March 1994.

Other Airlines

About 570 aircraft are operated by other airlines. Dan-Air Services is a major operator of both scheduled and charter services, and had a fleet of 50 aircraft at the end of 1989. British Midland and Air UK are both major domestic airlines and also operate a number of international and charter services. Air Europe has greatly expanded its scheduled services to Europe (which include some former British Caledonian routes) and is also a major charter operator. It operates 21 aircraft. Virgin Atlantic began scheduled services between Gatwick and New York (Newark) in 1984 and is also extending its services to other routes.

Britannia Airways carried over 6 million passengers in 1989 and is one of the largest charter operators in the world. It has charter flights from 16 airports to 80 destinations in Europe and elsewhere, mostly operated for its associated company Thomson Holidays. It has 40 aircraft.

Helicopters and Other Aerial Work

Helicopters are engaged on a variety of work, but are mainly employed on the large-scale operations connected with the exploitation of Britain's offshore oil and gas resources. The two main helicopter operators in Britain are Bristow Helicopters and British International Helicopters, with 57 and 26 helicopters respectively. Light aircraft and helicopters are also involved in other activities, such as charter operations, search and rescue services, crop-spraying, and aerial survey and photography.

Air Safety

The CAA is responsible for both technical and operational safety. Its Safety Regulation Group deals with the development and application of safety requirements for commercial and private aviation operations, flight crew and ground engineer licensing and training, aerodromes, and fire and rescue services.

Every company operating aircraft used for commercial purposes must possess an Air Operator's Certificate, which is granted by the CAA when it is satisfied that the operator is competent to secure the safe operation of its aircraft. The CAA's flight operations inspectors (who are experienced airline pilots) and airworthiness surveyors check that satisfactory standards are maintained.

Each member of the flight crew of a British registered aircraft and every licensed ground engineer must hold the appropriate official licence issued by the CAA. Except for those with acceptable military or other qualifying experience, all applicants for a first professional licence must have undertaken a full-time course of instruction which has been approved by the CAA.

Air Traffic Control and Navigation Services

Responsibility for civil and military air traffic control over Britain and the surrounding seas rests with the National Air Traffic Services (NATS), jointly operated by the CAA and the Ministry of Defence. At 24 civil aerodromes, including most of the major British airports, the NATS provides the navigation services necessary for aircraft taking off and landing, and integrates them into the flow of traffic within British airspace.

Britain is one of 11 members of Eurocontrol, a European air traffic control body. In recent years Britain has put forward a number of initiatives, including the Central Flow Management Unit, which will be fully operational in 1993, and an initiative agreed in April 1990 to increase airspace capacity by integrating air traffic control systems and optimising the air traffic route network. For Britain the CAA has a substantial annual investment programme of about £100 million, which will include the construction of a new air traffic control centre for England and Wales.

Airports

Of the 141 licensed civil aerodromes in Britain, about one-fifth handle more than 100,000 passengers a year each. Twelve handle over 1 million passengers a year each and these are shown in Table 17.4. In 1989 Britain's civil airports handled a total of 100·6 million passengers (98·9 million terminal passengers and nearly 1·7 million in transit), and 1·1 million tonnes of freight. Heathrow airport is the world's busiest airport for international travel and is Britain's most important airport for passengers and air freight handling 39·9 million passengers (including transit passengers) and 686,200 tonnes of freight in 1989. Gatwick is the world's second busiest international airport.

Ownership and Control

Eight airports—Heathrow, Gatwick and Stansted in south-east England, Glasgow, Edinburgh, Prestwick and Aberdeen in Scotland, and Southampton—are owned and operated by BAA plc, the private sector successor company to the British Airports Authority. Together they handle about 70 per cent of air passengers and 85 per cent of air cargo traffic in Britain. The Government's shares in BAA plc were sold in 1987.

Many of the other public airports are controlled by local authorities. In early 1990, 16 major local authority airports were operating as Companies Act companies. The Government is encouraging the introduction of private capital into the new companies and in May 1990 British Aerospace acquired a 76 per cent stake in Liverpool airport.

Table 17.4: Passenger Traffic at Britain's Main Airports

million passengers

	1979	1984	1987	1988	1989
London (Heathrow)	28·0	29·2	34·7	37·5	39·6
London (Gatwick)	8·7	14·0	19·4	20·7	21·1
Manchester	3·5	6·0	8·6	9·5	10·1
Glasgow	2·4	2·7	3·4	3·6	3·9
Birmingham	1·6	1·7	2·6	2·8	3·3
Luton	2·2	1·8	2·6	2·8	2·8
Edinburgh	1·2	1·5	1·8	2·1	2·4
Belfast (Aldergrove)	1·4	1·6	2·1	2·2	2·2
Aberdeen	1·3	1·8	1·5	1·6	1·7
Newcastle upon Tyne	0·9	1·1	1·3	1·4	1·5
East Midlands	0·6	1·1	1·3	1·3	1·5
London (Stansted)	0·3	0·5	0·7	1·0	1·3

Source: Civil Aviation Authority.
Note: Statistics relate to terminal passengers only and exclude those in transit.

Under the Airports Act 1986 the CAA has responsibility for the economic regulation of major airport companies. These powers enable the CAA to take appropriate steps to remedy practices considered to be against the public interest, in particular any abuse of an airport's monopoly position.

All airports used for public transport and training flights must be licensed by the CAA. Stringent requirements, such as the provision of adequate fire-fighting, medical and rescue services, suitable physical characteristics and visual aids, must be satisfied before a licence is granted. Strict aviation security measures are in force, and the Aviation and Maritime Security Act 1990 provides for greater powers to enforce security requirements.

Development

The Government's policy is to promote a strong and competitive British airline industry by providing airport capacity where it is needed and by making effective use of existing capacity, including regional airports.

A fourth major terminal at Heathrow was opened in 1986 and the first phase of a second major terminal at Gatwick was completed in 1988. Under major expansion plans at Stansted, a new terminal will open in March 1991, with a capacity on completion of the first phase of the project of 8 million passengers a year. Outline planning permission has been granted for further expansion to cater for 15 million passengers a year.

Under major expansion plans at Manchester, the first phase of a second terminal is under construction and is expected to open in 1993, increasing capacity by one-half to 18 million passengers a year. A second terminal is also under construction at Birmingham, for completion in 1991, increasing capacity to 6 million passengers a year. Construction of a new airport at Sheffield is planned to start in 1992. Facilities are also being improved at other regional airports.

Communications

The telecommunications services sector is one of the most rapidly growing in the economy. Major changes occurred in the 1980s with the privatisation of British Telecom (formerly a public corporation) and the abolition of its monopoly on the main telecommunications services with the entry into operation of a second major telecommunications carrier, Mercury Communications. The British Telecommunications Act 1981 and the Telecommunications Act 1984 were the main Acts implementing the Government's policy of establishing a more competitive industry which is more responsive to consumer demand. The Government intends to start a review of the 'duopoly' policy in November 1990.

Licensing

The 1984 Act instituted new arrangements requiring those running telecommunications systems (including British Telecom) to be licensed by the Secretary of State for Trade and Industry.

There has been a wide range of other liberalisation measures, the most recent being a new version of the branch systems general licence issued in 1989, which covers most private domestic and business use of telecommunications. It sets out the arrangements by which private users may connect their systems (including payphones) to the public systems, install their own wiring and take advantage of private lines leased from the public operators. The licence included further significant liberalisation and simplified regulatory procedures. For inland private circuits leased from the public telecommunications operators simple resale was permitted, while other changes allowed greater flexibility in installing, maintaining and using call routing apparatus. The licence also covers the licensing of value added and data services, previously covered by a separate class licence. Other areas in which competition has been increased include mobile communications (see p 373), specialised satellite services, the supply of telephone apparatus and the provision of public payphones.

Office of Telecommunications

The Office of Telecommunications (OFTEL), a non-ministerial government department established under the Telecommunications Act 1984, is the independent regulatory body for the telecommunications industry. It is headed by the Director General of Telecommunications, among whose functions are to ensure that licensees comply with the conditions of their licences; to promote effective competition in the telecommunications industry; to provide advice to the Secretary of State for Trade and Industry on telecommunications matters; and to investigate complaints. The Director General also has a duty to promote the interests of consumers in respect of prices, quality and variety in telecommunications services.

British Telecom

Under the Telecommunications Act 1984 British Telecom was reconstituted as a public limited company and a majority of the ordinary voting shares were sold to private investors in 1984. It has over 1·2 million registered shareholders and 95 per cent of its 230,000 eligible employees are also shareholders.

British Telecom operates around 19·3 million residential lines and 5·7 million business lines. It runs the world's sixth largest public telecommunications network, including 110,000 telex connections, 90,000 public payphones, and a wide range of specialised voice, data, text and visual services. The inland telephone and telex networks are fully automatic. International services are also highly developed, and international direct dialling is available from any telephone line in Britain to 200 countries representing 99 per cent of the world's telephones. Automatic telex service is available to 2 million customers in over 200 countries.

In 1989–90 the company made a pre-tax profit of £2,692 million on a record turnover of £12,315 million. Expenditure on capital equipment and other assets totalled £3,115 million, of which £952 million went on modernising exchanges with digital equipment. About £230 million was spent on research and development.

Network Modernisation

British Telecom is investing some £2,600 million a year in the modernisation and expansion of its network to meet the increasing demand for basic telephone services and for more specialised services. The company has about 1 million km (625,000 miles) of optical fibre laid in its network in Britain, accounting for two-thirds of its trunk network, a higher proportion than any other world operator. There are more than 3,000 digital exchanges serving a total of 10 million lines, and three-quarters of its customers are served by modern local exchanges of various types. The combination of digital exchange switching and digital transmission techniques, using optical fibre cable and microwave radio links, is substantially improving the quality of telephone services for residential and business customers, as well as making possible a wider range of services through the company's main network. An Integrated Services Digital Network for business customers became available in April 1990.

General Services

British Telecom provides numerous services, including a free facility for emergency calls to the police, fire, ambulance, coastguard, lifeboat and air-sea rescue services; a free directory inquiries service; and various chargeable operator-connected services, such as transfer charge and alarm calls. The operator-handled Freefone service and automatic 'LinkLine' facilities enable callers to contact organisations anywhere in Britain, either free or at local call rates. Timeline (formerly known as the Speaking Clock) gives callers the time. British Telecom also provides a number of Callstream services, which allow callers to obtain information by paying a premium call rate. Other premium-rate services are offered by independent service providers using the British Telecom network. In 1988 the company opened a £70 million optical fibre flexible access system, for intensive voice and data traffic, to serve the financial organisations of the City of London.

Under a public payphone service modernisation programme, costing some £160 million, all its public payphones have been equipped with push-button equipment and the majority of red kiosks replaced by more modern facilities. A number of cashless call developments are being carried out, including the Phonecard service, using prepaid encoded cards; Phonecard payphones account for 17,000 of the total of 91,000 payphones. There are about 300,000 rented payphones on premises to which the public has access and these are also being upgraded with modern push-button equipment.

Prestel, British Telecom's videotex service, and Telecom Gold (an electronic mail and information service) form part of the company's data services division, Tymnet. Prestel was the first service of its kind to enable a wide variety of computer-stored information to be called up on a special television receiver via the telephone. Some 100,000 terminals are attached to Prestel, 57 per cent in businesses and 43 per cent in homes. Through its 'Gateway' links with other databases, a wide range of other services, such as home shopping and banking services and holiday booking and reservation facilities, is available; there is also a link with a cable television network.

There has been rapid growth in British Telecom's mobile communications services, including its paging service, which, with 450,000 customers, is the largest of its kind in the world.

International Services

British Telecom International is the company's division handling international networks and services. It is the second largest shareholder in the International Telecommunications Satellite Organisation (of which

119 countries are members) and in the International Maritime Satellite Organisation, with interests in a number of other consortia.

A substantial proportion of the intercontinental telephone traffic to or from Britain is carried by satellite. British Telecom operates satellite earth stations at Goonhilly Downs (Cornwall), Madley (near Hereford), London Docklands and Aberdeen. The Docklands earth station has six 13-m (43-ft) dish aerials and five smaller aerials. Using the latest digital techniques, it handles advanced business data and videoconferencing services to the continent of Europe and North America as well as for 23 cable television channels. British Telecom's range of digital transmission services includes a number available overseas, including 'Satstream' private circuit digital links covering North America and Western Europe using small-dish aerials, and an 'International Kilostream' private circuit service available to the United States, Australia and most major business centres in Asia and the rest of Europe.

Digital transmission techniques have been introduced for services to the United States, Japan, Hong Kong and Australia via the Madley station. The London–Tokyo link, which was set up in 1986, includes the first all-digital telephone link between two continents, giving faster connections and clearer speech.

Extensive direct-dial maritime satellite services are available for vessels worldwide, and limited in-flight operator-controlled telephone call facilities are available via Portishead radio station near Bristol.

Recent improvements in submarine cable design (including the use of optical fibre technology) have helped to increase capacity and reduce pressure on satellite systems. The world's first international undersea optical fibre cable, between Britain and Belgium, began operating in 1986. The first transatlantic optical fibre cable (TAT 8) entered service in 1988, with 8,000 circuits and a capacity of 40,000 simultaneous telephone calls. A further high capacity transatlantic optical fibre cable (TAT 9), which will cost about £250 million and be able to carry about 75,000 telephone calls simultaneously, is expected to be in operation by 1991.

British Telecom's overseas consultancy service, Telconsult, is engaged on over 250 projects in more than 60 countries.

Mercury

Mercury Communications Ltd, a wholly owned subsidiary of Cable and Wireless plc, operates under licence as the competing fixed telecommunications carrier in Britain, enabling the company to offer a wide range of services, both nationally and internationally. Its wholly digital trunk network, comprising some 2,600 km (1,600 miles) of optical fibre cables and 2,000 km (1,200 miles) of digital microwave links, is centred on Birmingham and links over 75 towns and cities, including Edinburgh, Hull, Brighton and Cardiff.

National and international switched telephone services for business customers began in 1986, and services for small businesses and residential customers are now established. Mercury also provides an extensive range of enhanced services, including national and international telex and packet data services, electronic messaging and nationwide radiopaging, as well as a range of associated equipment used at customers' premises. Mercury's 'Centrex' service, the first in Europe, provides business customers with all the advanced facilities (such as inward direct dialling and call forwarding) available on a modern switchboard from equipment located at Mercury's public exchanges, so that customers do not have to purchase their own system. In 1988 Mercury introduced its first public payphone service, in London, and this is being extended.

International services are provided by two satellite communications centres in London's Docklands and Oxfordshire, serving North America, Europe, the Middle East, the Far East and Australia. Mercury has been developing new optical fibre submarine cable links, and agreements have been reached with the majority of European telecommunications authorities to provide Mercury with direct links with Europe. Mercury is the British operator involved in the first private transatlantic optical fibre cable (see p 374).

Mobile communications

The Government has taken a number of measures to encourage the expansion of mobile radio telecommunications services. It has licensed Racal-Vodafone Ltd (part of the Racal Electronics Group) and Telecom Securicor Cellular Radio Ltd (a joint venture between British Telecom and Securicor) to run competing national cellular radio telephone systems. Considerable investment has been made in establishing their networks to provide increased capacity for the growing number of cellular radio telephone users, estimated at over 1 million in mid-1990.

In 1989 the Government announced an increase in the number of channels available for cellular radio and the issue of licences for 'Telepoint' systems, which allow subscribers to make outgoing telephone calls from public places and other locations where Telepoint base stations have been established, using their own portable digital cordless handsets. Services are provided by four companies under licence: Ferranti; BYPS; Phonepoint; and Mercury Callpoint.

Britain will be the first country to offer personal communications network (PCN) services, which would allow the same telephone to be used at home, at work and in a mobile capacity. In 1989 the Government allocated licences to three operators—Mercury PCN Ltd, Microtel Communications Ltd and Unitel Ltd—to run PCNs in the frequency range 1·7 to 1·9 gigahertz. The first service is expected to start in late 1992.

Two national operators (GEC National One and Band 3 Radio Ltd) have been licensed to offer a nationwide trunked mobile radio service, while a number of licences have been awarded for London and regional services.

Other Services

The Department of Trade and Industry has licensed over 40 companies which have been awarded franchises by the Cable Authority to run local broadband cable telecommunications systems. These systems may carry television and, in conjunction with British Telecom or Mercury Communications, a range of telecommunications services. At present they mainly provide television programmes, but some are already offering interactive services, including local voice telephony.

Home banking services, accessed by multi-frequency telephone, are expanding. They are being developed by a variety of banks, for example, the TSB through its Speedlink service.

Cable and Wireless

Cable and Wireless plc provides or manages a varied range of telecommunications activities, mostly overseas in over 40 countries. Its main business is the provision and operation of public telecommunications services in 37 countries and territories under franchises granted by the governments concerned. It also provides and manages telecommunications services and facilities for public and private sector customers, and undertakes consultancy work. It owns, operates or has been a consultant on over 40 satellite earth stations, and has a fleet of nine cableships and two submersible vehicle systems for laying and maintaining submarine telecommunications cables. The company's strategic objective is the construction of a broadband digital network linking major world economic and financial centres: London, New York, Tokyo and Hong Kong. The first leg of the 'Global Digital Highway', the private transatlantic optical fibre cable linking Britain, the Irish Republic, the United States and Bermuda, entered service in 1989, and the North Pacific Cable, the first direct cable between the United States and Japan, is scheduled for completion by the end of 1990.

Postal Services
The Post Office, founded in 1635, pioneered postal services and was the first to issue adhesive postage stamps as proof of advance payment for mail. The Royal Mail provides deliveries to 24 million addresses and handles over 58 million letters and parcels each working day (over 14,000 million items a year). Mail is collected from over 100,000 posting boxes, as well as from post offices and large postal users. The Post Office has a monopoly on the conveyance of letters, but under the British Telecommunications Act 1981 the Secretary of State for Trade and Industry has the power to suspend the monopoly in certain areas or for certain categories of mail and to license others to provide competing services. The Secretary of State has suspended the monopoly on letters subject to a minimum fee of £1, and has issued general licences enabling mail to be transferred between document exchanges and allowing charitable organisations to carry Christmas and New Year cards.

All of the Royal Mail's 80 sorting offices are equipped with mechanical handling equipment and have mainly taken over the work of hundreds of sorting offices handling letters manually. Each address in Britain has a postcode and the British system is the most sophisticated in the world, allowing mechanised sorting down to part of a street on a postman's round and, in some cases, to an individual address. The Post Office has reorganised its parcels operations, and in February 1990 announced investment of £80 million in the service, which has been renamed Royal Mail Parcelforce. A programme of modernisation includes the establishment of 150 local collection and delivery depots throughout Britain.

As well as postal and Girobank services, post offices handle a wide range of transactions. In much of its counter service the Post Office acts as an agent for government departments and local authorities. The Post Office is introducing new technology into its counter services to reduce costs and raise productivity, while providing an improved range of services to customers. There are 20,900 post offices, of which some 1,300 are operated directly by the Post Office. The remainder are operated on an agency basis by sub postmasters.

Post Office Specialist Services
The Post Office provides a range of specialist services. 'Datapost', a door-to-door delivery service, has overnight links throughout Britain and provides an international service to over 160 countries. 'Datapost Sameday' provides rapid delivery within or between more than 100 cities and towns in Britain and between London and Amsterdam, Paris and Dublin. 'The Royal Mail Facsimile Service', the world's first international public facsimile transmission service sending letters and other documents electronically, provides high-speed mail links between more than 100 post offices in Britain as well as to and from some 40 other countries. The Philatelic Bureau in Edinburgh handles about one-third of the Post Office's philatelic business, much of it involving sales to overseas collectors or dealers. The British Post Consultancy Service offers advice and assistance on all aspects of postal business to overseas postal administrations, and nearly 40 countries have used its services since 1965.

Private Courier and Express Service Operators

Private sector couriers and express operators are able to handle time-sensitive door-to-door deliveries, subject to a minimum fee of £1. The courier/express service industry has grown rapidly, by about 20 per cent a year, and the revenue created by the carriage of these items handled is estimated at over £1,500 million a year. Britain is one of the main providers of monitored express deliveries in Europe, with London an important centre for air courier/express traffic.

18 Employment

Employment in Britian has risen substantially since the mid-1980s, with the workforce in employment having increased by 3·5 million between March 1983 and December 1989, when it totalled a record 27·1 million. This was a larger rise than in any other European country. It has been accompanied by a considerable decline in unemployment, which fell for nearly four years after the peak of mid-1986. This represented the longest period of falling unemployment since the second world war.

The Government has taken a number of steps to improve the operation of the labour market, with the aim of creating an economic climate in which business can flourish and create more jobs. These include increasing the flexibility of the labour market, removing burdens on employers (including regulatory barriers which hinder recruitment) and encouraging better training. However, it has expressed concern about the operation of the European Community's draft Social Charter, covering various aspects of employment. The Government has indicated its willingness to accept some of the proposed regulations, such as on health and safety, but opposes a number of other proposals which it believes would add to labour costs and discourage employment.

TRENDS IN THE LABOUR MARKET

The total workforce in June 1989 was 28·6 million, of whom over 22·7 million (nearly 12 million men and almost 10·8 million women) were classed as employees in employment (see Table 18.1). Major trends have included the growth in the proportion of the workforce accounted for by women, as more married women have sought work, especially in part-time employment; and a substantial increase in self-employment. Between 1979 and 1989 the number of self-employed people is estimated to have risen by 70 per cent to 3·2 million, representing 11·3 per cent of the workforce.

Table 18.1: Manpower in Britain 1979-89

Thousands (as at June), seasonally adjusted

	1979	1984	1985	1986	1987	1988	1989
Employees in employment[a]	23,145	21,228	21,414	21,379	21,575	22,265	22,740
Self employed	1,906	2,496	2,610	2,627	2,860	2,986	3,241
Unemployed[b]	1,215	3,083	3,213	3,318	2,992	2,425	1,813
Armed forces	314	326	326	322	319	316	308
Work-related government training programmes[c]	—	175	176	226	311	343	462
Workforce[d]	26,580	27,309	27,739	27,871	28,057	28,334	28,564

Sources: Department of Employment and Northern Ireland Department of Economic Development.
[a] Part-time workers are counted as full units.
[b] Figures are adjusted for discontinuities and exclude school-leavers.
[c] Not seasonally adjusted.
[d] Comprises employees in employment, the self-employed, the armed forces, participants in work-related government training programmes and the unemployed (including school-leavers).

Patterns of Employment

There have been substantial changes in the nature and location of employment, with a marked shift, as in other industrialised countries, from manufacturing to service industries. Between 1955 and 1989 the proportion of employees in employment engaged in service industries rose from 42 per cent to 69 per cent as higher living standards and technological developments stimulated the growth of many service industries. During the period 1980 to 1989 the number of employees in service industries rose by 2 million (14 per cent) to 15·7 million (see Table 18.2). Employment in most service industries, with some exceptions such as transport, has grown considerably. The largest rise in this period was in the banking, finance and insurance sector (by 58 per cent to 2·7 million), while there was also a substantial increase in hotels and catering (16 per cent). Manufacturing industry accounted for 43 per cent of employees in employment in 1955, but by 1989 the proportion had fallen to 23 per cent. Nearly all manufacturing industries experienced a decline in employment as markets for manufactured goods changed and as new technology brought greater efficiency.

Table 18.2: Employees in Employment

Industry or service (1980 Standard Industrial Classification)	Thousands (as at June)				Per cent 1989
	1980	1984	1988	1989	
Primary sector	1,099	956	800	771	3·4
Agriculture, forestry and fishing	373	340	313	300	1·3
Energy and water supply	727	616	487	471	2·1
Manufacturing	6,937	5,409	5,221	5,233	23·0
Construction	1,243	1,037	1,044	1,062	4·7
Services	13,712	13,836	15,206	15,679	68·9
Wholesale distribution and repairs	1,132	1,132	1,145	1,172	5·2
Retail distribution	2,177	2,054	2,162	2,256	9·9
Hotels and catering	972	1,010	1,083	1,123	4·9
Transport	1,049	908	889	910	4·0
Postal services and communications	437	432	437	451	2·0
Banking, finance and insurance	1,695	1,969	2,475	2,675	11·8
Public administration	1,667	1,602	1,677	1,650	7·3
Education	1,642	1,602	1,756	1,797	7·9
Health	1,258	1,298	1,438	1,484	6·5
Other services	1,682	1,829	2,145	2,161	9·5
Total	22,991	21,238	22,272	22,745	100·0

Sources: Department of Employment and Northern Ireland Department of Economic Development.
[a] Figures are not seasonally adjusted.
[b] In June 1989 employment in the main sectors of manufacturing industry included 797,000 in mechanical engineering; 641,000 in office machinery, electrical engineering and instruments; 572,000 in food, drink and tobacco; 557,000 in textiles, leather, footwear and clothing; 497,000 in paper products, printing and publishing; 471,000 in timber, wooden furniture, rubber and plastics; 326,000 in chemicals and man-made fibres; and 271,000 in motor vehicles and parts.
Note: Differences between totals and the sums of their component parts are due to rounding.

Unemployment Unemployment reached its peak in June 1986 when, on a seasonally adjusted basis (excluding school-leavers), it totalled over 3·1 million, 11·2 per cent of the workforce. Subsequently it declined significantly, and in the first seven months of 1990 it was about 1·6 million (5·7 per cent of the work-force), one of the lowest rates in the European Community. Unemployment fell in all regions, with reductions being greatest in some of the regions with above-average unemployment (such as the North, Scotland and Wales). There was a fall of 24 per cent in long-term unemployment (those unemployed for a year or more) to 514,000 in the year to July 1990. Unemployment remains high in some areas, particularly those with the greatest dependence on traditional manufacturing industries and in inner cities.

TRAINING A wide-ranging survey of training in Great Britain, conducted by the Training Agency, has indicated that a substantial amount of training is undertaken. It found that about 350 million days of training were undertaken by trainees and students in 1986-87, equivalent to about 7 per cent of the number of days worked by all employees in 1987. The total accounting costs of training in Great Britain, including the implicit cost to trainees of earnings foregone while in training, were about £33,000 million in 1986–87, representing 8 per cent of gross domestic product. Employers' net costs were estimated at some £18,000 million. The health sector provided most training in terms of the number of days per employee, followed by education and central government.

Government Policy In 1988 the Government set out its new framework for training and enterprise, designed to contribute more effectively to Britain's international competitiveness. Features of the new framework are a greater role for employers in the organisation and finance of training, with this responsibility being devolved as much as possible to local areas; training and vocational education designed to contribute to business success and economic growth; and recognised national standards of competence to cover all sectors and occupations, with training available so that people can secure qualifications based on these standards. In December 1989 the Government set a range of training objectives for the 1990s relating to training activity and qualifications under the new National Vocational Qualification (see p 382).

Training Agency The Training Agency operates within the Department of Employment group. Its purpose is to promote training and encourage enterprise. It develops and delivers the Government's training and vocational education programmes. It also aims to develop effective arrangements for training and vocational education which will contribute to business success and economic growth, and to reducing unemployment.

Its responsibilities are discharged through a network of ten operational offices, together with 57 area offices. The latter contract with external training managers, who arrange and deliver training.

Developments are in progress to replace the area offices by privately run local training organisations; in England and Wales there will be 82 such organisations, known as Training and Enterprise Councils (TECs).

Training and Enterprise Councils Training and Enterprise Councils are business-led community partnerships bringing together at local level people interested in training and enterprise. TECs are being set up to make training and enterprise activities more relevant to the needs of employers and individuals locally. Their introduction reflects the Government's commitment to encourage the public sector and the private sector to work together. It also reflects the Government's aim to ensure that the private sector has a leading role in training and enterprise programmes. TECs will be allowed considerable flexibility in their contracts with the Government to adapt programmes to meet local needs.

TECs are consulting widely with individuals and organisations, including representatives from education and the voluntary sector. Many are including representatives from these sectors on their boards.

TECs will have executive responsibility for annual expenditure of about £2,500 million. Individual TEC budgets will range from about £5 million to £40 million a year. Funding of TECs will be performance-related and based on their output. They will be accountable through contracts related to agreed corporate and business plans.

National Training Task Force

In 1989 the National Training Task Force was established, with 15 members appointed for four years. Members were selected for their commitment to training rather than as representatives of interest groups, although members are drawn from a wide spectrum including employers, trade unions, the voluntary sector, local authorities and education. Its most important job is to assist in the establishment and development of TECs. In addition, it is helping to promote to employers the importance of investing in the skills of their workforce.

Industry Training Organisations

Industry Training Organisations (ITOs) have a major role in developing occupational standards and reviewing future skill requirements for their sectors. The Government's preference is for them to be employer-led voluntary bodies. Accordingly, the system of statutory training boards is being phased out. In December 1989 the Government announced voluntary arrangements to replace most of the remaining seven boards, which cover about 25 per cent of the civilian workforce. There are over 100 independent ITOs, many of which supersede former statutory boards, and they cover sectors employing about 45 per cent of the civilian workforce. The National Council of Industry Training Organisations, a voluntary body set up to represent the interests of independent ITOs, aims to improve the effectiveness of these bodies, for example, by encouraging good practice.

Employment Training

Employment Training was launched in 1988 to bring together a range of training programmes. The scheme is designed to provide a flexible and individually tailored training programme of up to 12 months, especially for the longer-term unemployed. An individual's training needs are identified by training agents and an agreed action plan is drawn up. Training is delivered by training managers under contract with the Training Agency. For 1990–91 Employment Training has a budget of £1,200 million to provide training opportunities for up to 450,000 trainees.

Entry to the programme is through a variety of routes, including a Restart interview or by application at a jobcentre. The emphasis of the programme is on high-quality training. Accordingly, training agents and managers are required to gain approved status as a demonstration of the quality of the training provider. Trainees receive a training allowance of £10 a week more than their benefit entitlement, and they also receive help towards fares and some other expenses.

Business Growth Training

In 1989 the Government introduced Business Growth Training, designed to encourage companies to improve their business performance through more effective training which is closely linked to their business plans. There is a range of flexible programmes designed to help mainly small- to medium-size businesses to improve their planning, and to develop the business skills of owner-managers. In addition, the programmes are designed to develop in management teams a more strategic approach to managing change and to training the workforce in the skills required for firms to compete successfully. For example, there are one-day seminars for owner-managers in marketing, accounting and general management, and other programmes to help them to manage the growth of their businesses. Training is available for self-employed people setting up in business. The Government contributes about £55 million a year to these programmes. TECs are taking over the running and development of business and enterprise training to meet the future needs of local employers.

Enterprise Allowance Scheme

The Enterprise Allowance Scheme helps unemployed people wishing to start their own business, but who would be deterred by the prospect of losing benefit once they began. Entrants, who must have access to at least £1,000 to invest in the business, receive an allowance of £40 a week for a year when they start the business. Over 500,000 new businesses have been set up since the scheme began in 1982. Surveys have shown that 76 per cent are still trading 18 months after starting operations.

Youth Training

The Youth Training Scheme (YTS) was introduced in Great Britain in 1983 and was expanded in 1986 to offer two years of training for 16-year-old school-leavers and one year for 17-year-old school-leavers. Over 2 million young people were trained on the YTS.

Youth Training, which succeeded the YTS in 1990, is designed to give all young people the opportunity to achieve a vocational qualification or a credit towards a qualification. It puts more emphasis on raising the level of qualifications of new entrants to the workforce and concentrates on results such as acquiring vocational qualifications rather than on time spent in training. It aims to increase the relevance to work of training provided and to improve the employment prospects of young people.

The Training Credits Scheme, announced by the Government in March 1990, is a new initiative in youth training. It represents an entitlement to train to approved standards for young people who have left full-time education to join the labour market. It is expected that 11 pilot credits schemes will be in place to run from April 1991.

Education Initiatives

The Government is promoting closer links between the education system and industry and commerce. The Technical and Vocational Education Initiative, administered in Great Britain by the Department of Employment in co-operation with local education authorities, is intended to ensure that the education of 14- to 18-year-olds provides them with learning opportunities which will equip them for working life. This is implemented by requiring the school curriculum to relate to the working environment, and through improving skills and qualifications, particularly in science, technology and modern languages. The scheme also provides work experience and work shadowing placements; encourages young people to be more enterprising; and provides counselling, guidance and opportunities to progress to higher levels of achievement. The scheme aims by mid-1993 to include all students aged 14 to 18 in maintained schools and colleges. Some 3,000 schools or colleges are involved in the initiative, with over 500,000 students participating.

In January 1990 the Government announced an extension of its 'Compacts' initiative (launched in 1988) in designated inner city areas.

Compacts are local agreements between employers, local education authorities and training providers in which young people, supported by their school or college, work to achieve agreed targets, and employers undertake to provide further training or jobs for those attaining such targets. By August 1990, 38 compacts were in operation, with over 300 schools participating, covering nearly 55,000 young people. Compacts will eventually be run by the TECs.

Under the Enterprise and Education Initiative, all pupils have the opportunity to gain at least two weeks of suitable work experience before leaving school, and teachers have the opportunity to obtain business experience. The Enterprise in Higher Education Initiative is designed to ensure that students acquire the aptitudes and competence required by industry in the 1990s.

Vocational Qualifications

The National Council for Vocational Qualifications (NCVQ) was set up in 1986 to reform and rationalise the vocational qualifications system in England, Wales and Northern Ireland. It aims to make qualifications more accessible and more relevant by basing them on standards of competence set by industry, and to establish a coherent framework—the National Vocational Qualification—based on defined levels of achievement to which qualifications in all sectors can be assigned or accredited. The aim is to have the framework for levels I to IV (from the most basic level to the management supervisory level) fully operational by the end of 1992. Eventually it is expected to cover all occupational levels up to and including the professions. Scotland has not been covered by the NCVQ as it already had its own modular system, but in 1989 the Government announced that a system of Scottish Vocational Qualifications would be introduced, which would be compatible with the framework in Great Britain.

Other Training Measures

Open learning opportunities have been increased by the creation of the Open College, an independent company which promotes the acquisition of skills through the method of open learning. Over 60,000 people have taken its courses since 1987. Further funds were announced in 1989: a maximum of £12 million for its commercial activities over the three years to 1992, and a further £6 million for its broadcasting activities. The Government's aim is for the College to be self-financing by March 1992.

In 1988 the Department of Employment, in partnership with three major banks, made career development loans available nationally following a pilot initiative. The loans help individuals to pay for vocational training by offering deferred payments on loans until up to three months after the training period, with interest on loans being paid by the Department.

Scotland

Under the Enterprise and New Towns (Scotland) Act 1990 two new bodies—Scottish Enterprise for the lowlands of Scotland, and Highlands and Islands Enterprise for the highlands and islands area—will be created. They will assume responsibility for the functions of economic development and training currently exercised by the Scottish Development Agency, the Highlands and Islands Development Board and the Training Agency in Scotland. Two-thirds of the members of their boards will have a background in business or industry. The new bodies will exercise a strong strategic role. Their main duties will be to stimulate self-sustaining economic development, to maintain and safeguard employment, to enhance employment skills, and to promote industrial efficiency and international competitiveness.

Scottish Enterprise and Highlands and Islands Enterprise will contract much of their work out to a network of local enterprise companies (led by the private sector). The network is almost complete, with prospective companies throughout Scotland developing business plans upon which operating contracts will be based. The companies will be similar to the TECs, but with wider economic functions.

Northern Ireland

The Training and Employment Agency was established in April 1990 as an executive agency within the Department of Economic Development for Northern Ireland. It is responsible for the training and employment services previously administered by the Department's labour market group as well as for the functions of the majority of the industrial training boards, which are being encouraged to become non-statutory training organisations. The Agency aims to maximise the contribution of employment and training services towards strengthening the Northern Ireland economy. It works closely with industry, particularly in the identification of training needs. The Agency is responsible for helping to ensure that training needs are met, for encouraging investment in training by industry, and for stimulating the development of training within the private sector.

Northern Ireland has its own training schemes. Major changes in the Youth Training Programme (in which some 9,000 young people are participating) were implemented in April 1990 to enhance the quality of training and increase its relevance to young people and employers. Training will form an increasingly important element of the Action for Community Employment scheme, which provides temporary employment of up to a year for long-term unemployed adults. The Vocational Education Programme is designed to stimulate the development of a more vocationally based curriculum in schools.

EMPLOYMENT SERVICES

The main priorities of the Employment Service, which became an executive agency of the Department of Employment in April 1990, are to provide help for people unemployed for over six months and those with disabilities or disadvantages, and to maintain the accurate and prompt payment of benefit to unemployed people, while ensuring that payment is made only to those entitled. The Employment Service has two main ways of helping the unemployed to find work: by placing people directly into jobs or by offering guidance and counselling so that people can find the best route to return to employment, for example, by training.

The jobcentre network handles about one-third of vacancies in the economy, and 81 per cent of the 1·85 million people whom it placed in jobs in 1989–90 were unemployed.

Counselling

The counselling services of the Employment Service have been developed to tackle the loss of contact with the labour market experienced by the long-term unemployed and to regenerate their motivation to seek work. Client advisers in unemployment benefit offices interview every newly unemployed person and offer advice on the financial help and on the jobs and training opportunities available.

If a person's unemployment lasts for six months or longer, he or she is invited to an interview with a Restart counsellor every six months to discuss problems which may be hindering the search for employment, with the aim of agreeing a course of action to help in returning to work. This could include direct placement in a job, enrolment on a training programme or a Restart course (a five-day course designed to rebuild self-confidence and motivation, and including help with job-hunting techniques), a place in a Jobclub (where participants are given training sessions in job-hunting skills and then have access to a resource centre where facilities are available to help on intensive jobsearch), or help towards self-employment through the Enterprise Allowance Scheme (see p 381).

A further group of counsellors, claimant advisers, work closely with the Restart counsellors and concentrate on giving the unemployed advice on benefits, especially those which can be claimed while in employment.

Other Functions

The Employment Service also aims to help people with disabilities to find work. All Employment Service programmes make provision for people with disabilities. Disablement Resettlement Officers offer practical help and counselling, and a wide range of programmes, such as one offering sheltered employment opportunities, is available. In 1989–90 an estimated 81,000 people with disabilities were helped by these special programmes.

The Employment Service plays a full role within the Government's inner city initiative, modifying its national schemes to meet the special needs and circumstances of its inner city users.

Incentives to Work

The Government has taken action to improve incentives to work, such as raising personal tax allowances and reducing the standard rate of income tax to 25 per cent, while improving benefits for people in work. These measures, together with reforms in the social security system implemented in 1988, have helped to ensure that people are better off in work than remaining unemployed.

The Jobstart Allowance of £20 a week is available for up to six months to eligible long-term unemployed applicants who accept a full-time job with gross pay of less than £90 a week. Its purpose is to encourage long-term unemployed people, particularly those on high levels of benefit, to take jobs which they might not otherwise have considered.

Careers Service

Under the Employment and Training Act 1973 local education authorities must provide a careers service for people attending educational institutions other than universities (which normally have their own careers service) and an employment service for those leaving them. The careers services in Wales and Scotland are the responsibility of the respective Secretaries of State, while in Northern Ireland responsibility rests with the Training and Employment Agency.

INDUSTRIAL RELATIONS

The structure of industrial relations in Britain has been established mainly on a voluntary basis. The system is based chiefly on the organisation of employees and employers into trade unions and employers' associations, and on freely conducted negotiations at all levels.

Collective Bargaining and Joint Consultation

In many industries terms and conditions of employment and procedures for the conduct of industrial relations have traditionally been settled by negotiation and agreement between employers or employers' associations and trade unions. For collective bargaining and other purposes trade unions are widely recognised, especially in the public sector (including nationalised industries) and in large firms and establishments. Agreements may be industry-wide, as has generally been the case in the public sector, but they are often supplemented by local agreements in companies or factories (plant bargaining). Individual companies may have their own agreements, either for the whole company or for each plant.

In some industries, companies and factories, negotiations are conducted by meetings held when necessary, while in others joint negotiating councils or committees have been established on a permanent basis. Joint committees are fairly widespread, especially in large firms. The scope of the various bodies (from national joint industrial councils for whole industries to works councils and committees in individual workplaces) varies widely. It can cover such additional matters as production plans, training, education, welfare and safety. Day-to-day negotiations on various aspects of pay (such as bonuses or performance pay) are normally handled at plant level. Arrangements for collective bargaining normally suffice to settle all questions which are raised, but there is often provision for matters which cannot be settled in this way to be referred to independent conciliation or arbitration. The Employment Protection Act 1975, as amended by the Employment Act 1980, makes provision for information needed for collective bargaining purposes to be disclosed by employers to trade unions, subject to certain safeguards.

Developments

In recent years there have been a number of developments which have affected Britain's industrial relations system. An important labour market development has been the continuing growth in part-time, temporary and sub-contracting employment. Together with the growth of self employment, this has encouraged greater labour market flexibility. Many employers have sought greater flexibility through a closer relationship between pay and performance, particularly through performance-related pay schemes (such as merit pay). In many sectors job demarcation (for example, between manual, technical and clerical skills) has been relaxed.

Other developments have included the introduction of new technology and related organisational changes. There has been a trend away from national bargaining machinery towards bargaining at a more local level; the proportion of the workforce covered by multi-employer national agreements declined from 60 per cent in 1978 to 35 per cent in 1989. The Government has favoured moves away from national pay bargaining towards systems where pay increases are dependent primarily on performance, merit, company profitability, and demand and supply in the local labour market. Areas in which national industry-wide pay bargaining has recently been ended include merchant shipping, the printing of national newspapers, commercial broadcasting and the London clearing banks. Where industry-wide bargaining remains important, employers often seek a degree of flexibility to permit modifications to national agreements. Another recent feature has been the development of 'new style' agreements, often associated with overseas-owned (particularly Japanese) companies, although they are also found in British-owned firms. These agreements often involve the recognition of a single union for all of a company's employees (particularly for companies recognising unions for the first time), 'single status' (involving the elimination of the traditional distinction between managers, supervisors and other employees), a greater emphasis on employee participation, and flexibility in working practices.

Trade Unions

Trade unions have members in nearly all occupations. As well as negotiating pay and other terms and conditions of employment with employers, they provide benefits and services such as educational facilities, legal advice and aid in work-related cases. Trade unions vary widely in the composition of their membership, and may be organised either by occupation (for example, they may recruit clerical staff or managers wherever employed) or by industry, while some are based on a combination of both.

There has been a decline in trade union membership, and by the end of 1988 total union membership was about 10·4 million, of whom 80 per cent were in the 23 largest unions. The decline reflects the moves away from manufacturing and public services (both of which have a relatively high level of membership).

The number of unions has also fallen, reflecting an increase in merger activity and the absorption by larger unions of small unions and of long-established craft unions. For example, in 1989 the General, Municipal, Boilermakers and Allied Trades Union (the third largest union) merged with the Association of Professional, Executive, Clerical and Computer Staff and was renamed the GMB. Several other unions are discussing possible mergers. At the end of 1989 there were 342 trade unions on the list maintained by the Certification Officer. To be eligible for entry on the list a trade union must show that it consists wholly or mainly of workers and that its principal purposes include the regulation of relations between workers and employers or between workers and employers' associations.

Six unions had over 500,000 members at the end of 1988: the Transport and General Workers' Union (1·3 million), the Amalgamated Engineering Union (794,000), the General, Municipal, Boilermakers and Allied Trades Union (790,000), the National and Local Government Officers' Association (755,000), the Manufacturing, Science and Finance Union (653,000) and the National Union of Public Employees (635,000).

Trade union organisation varies widely, but the central governing body usually consists of a national executive council or committee, elected by a secret ballot of the individual members and responsible to the conference of delegates from local branches, normally held annually. Many unions also have regional and district organisations. At the level of the individual member there are local branches, covering one or more workplaces. The organising of members in individual places of work and the negotiation of local pay agreements with management at the workplace may be done by full-time district officials of the union or, in many cases, by elected workplace representatives (sometimes called 'shop stewards'). Where two or more unions have members in the same workplace, representatives' or shop stewards' committees may be formed to discuss matters of common concern.

Trades Union Congress

In Britain the national centre of the trade union movement is the Trades Union Congress (TUC), founded in 1868. Its affiliated membership comprises 77 trade unions which together represent 8·4 million people, or some 81 per cent of all trade unionists in Britain. It has more members than any other trade union centre in Western Europe. The TUC's objectives are to promote the interests of its affiliated organisations and to improve the economic and social conditions of working people. It exercises power through influence rather than through sanctions. The TUC deals with all general questions which concern trade unions, both nationally and internationally, and it provides a forum in which affiliated unions can collectively determine policy. There are eight TUC regional councils for England and a Wales Trades Union Council.

The annual Congress convenes in September to discuss matters of concern to trade unionists. A General Council represents the TUC between annual meetings by carrying out Congress decisions, watching economic and social developments, providing educational and advisory services to unions, and presenting in national debate the trade union viewpoint on economic, social and industrial issues. The TUC organises extensive education services relating to many aspects of trade unionism and other subjects, such as health and safety. In recent years several unions have extended considerably their range of services, particularly financial services. In 1988 the TUC agreed on the establishment of a major initial package of member services available to all its constituent unions. The decision on whether to provide a particular service rests with individual unions.

The TUC plays an active part in international trade union activity, through its affiliation to the International Confederation of Free Trade Unions and the European Trade Union Confederation. It also nominates the British workers' delegation to the annual International Labour Conference.

Scotland and Northern Ireland

Trade unions in Scotland also have their own national central body, the Scottish Trades Union Congress, which in many respects is similar in constitution and function to the TUC. Trade unions in Northern Ireland are represented by the Northern Ireland Committee of the Irish Congress of Trade Unions (ICTU). Most trade unionists in Northern Ireland are members of organisations affiliated to the ICTU, while the majority also belong to unions based in Great Britain which are also affiliated to the TUC. The Northern Ireland Committee of the ICTU enjoys a high degree of autonomy.

Legal Framework

Major changes to trade union legislation in Great Britain have been introduced by the Government through four main Acts—the Employment Acts 1980 and 1982, the Trade Union Act 1984 and the Employment Act 1988—with the intention of obtaining a better balance between trade unions and employers with regard to rights and responsibilities within industrial relations and increasing democracy in trade unions. Similar legislation applies or is being enacted in Northern Ireland. The Employment Bill, now before Parliament, provides for the implementation of the Government's proposals for further reform of industrial relations on the closed shop (see below), secondary industrial action and unofficial action.

Legal Immunities

For most of the twentieth century trade unions, their officials and members enjoyed immunity from legal action when they organised certain industrial activity which might otherwise have been actionable by law. However, the Employment Act 1980 removed civil law immunity from those organising certain forms of secondary action (such as 'sympathetic' strikes) and limited lawful picketing to peaceful picketing at the picket's own workplace. The 1982 Act rescinds the trade unions' almost complete immunity from all civil actions by bringing their position into line with that of their individual officials and members. Trade unions now have immunity only for organising industrial action in furtherance or contemplation of a lawful trade dispute. The Trade Union Act 1984 removed legal immunity from trade unions which call a strike without first holding a properly conducted secret ballot of members concerned and securing a majority vote for this action.

The Employment Bill includes provisions which would remove the immunity for acts in contemplation or furtherance of trade disputes when there had been secondary action (the definition of which would be modified to cover action among those working or performing services under contract) other than in the course of peaceful picketing. The Bill would also amend the 1982 Act so that when unions organise industrial action they would be liable for the actions of all their officials (including workplace representatives).

Closed Shop

The Employment Act 1988 provided for the removal of the remaining statutory support for the closed shop (where there is an agreement between an employer and one or more unions that union membership is a condition of employment). The Act made it unlawful to organise or threaten industrial action to establish or maintain any sort of closed shop practice. Dismissal of an employee for non-membership of a union is now unfair in all circumstances.

However, the Government has been particularly concerned about the operation of the pre-entry closed shop, where, in order to obtain employment, an individual must belong to, or be willing to join, a union. It believes that this can raise labour costs significantly and have adverse effects on profitability and jobs. About 1·3 million people were estimated to be in pre-entry closed shops in 1989. Accordingly, the Employment Bill would make it unlawful to refuse to employ someone on grounds of trade union membership or non-membership. Anyone refused employment on such grounds would be able to complain to an industrial tribunal.

Elections

Provisions governing trade union elections were included in the Trade Union Act 1984 and extended from 1989 under the Employment Act 1988. All trade union general secretaries, presidents and those participating in decisions taken by principal executive committees (including non-voting members), subject to certain exemptions, are required to be elected by a secret ballot of the members at least once every five years. Elections for all those covered by the statutory election requirement or for political funds must be conducted by post and ballots must be independently scrutinised. Trade unions are also required to compile and maintain a register of members' names and addresses.

Members' Rights

Trade union legislation has also given members various other statutory rights. For example, under the Employment Act 1988 a union member has the right to restrain his or her trade union from inducing the member and others to take any kind of industrial action unless the action is supported by a properly conducted secret ballot. He or she also has the right not to be disciplined unjustifiably by the union if, for example, he or she chooses to go to work or cross a picket line rather than take industrial action. Other rights include the right of members to inspect their union's accounting records and the right for 'check-off' arrangements (the automatic deduction of union subscriptions) to be stopped if members inform their employer that they are leaving the union.

To help trade union members in enforcing their statutory rights, the 1988 Act established a Commissioner for the Rights of Trade Union Members. The Commissioner is empowered to grant assistance to a union member contemplating or taking court proceedings against his or her union where such proceedings are necessary to enforce certain statutory rights.

Political Funds

A trade union is legally permitted to engage in party political activity provided that a majority of its membership has voted in favour in a ballot and that all such activity is financed by a separate contribution which any individual member can opt out of paying without prejudicing his or her ordinary benefits and rights. At the end of 1989, 56 unions maintained a political fund. The Trade Union Act 1984 requires trade unions with political funds to ballot their members at regular intervals to decide whether the funds should be retained.

Employers' Organisations

Many employers in Britain are members of employers' organisations, some of which are wholly concerned with labour matters, although others are also concerned with commercial matters or trade associations. The primary aims of such organisations are to help to establish suitable terms and conditions of employment; to promote good relations with employees and the efficient use of manpower; and to provide means of settling any disputes which may arise.

Combined employers' organisations and trade associations may also represent to the Government members' points of view as manufacturers or traders on commercial matters.

Employers' organisations are usually organised on an industry basis rather than a product basis, for example, the Engineering Employers' Federation. A few are purely local in character or deal with a section of an industry or, for example, with small businesses; most are national and are concerned with the whole of an industry. In some of the main industries there are local or regional organisations combined into national federations. In others, within which different firms are engaged in making different principal products, there is a complex structure with national and regional federations for parts of an industry as well as for the industry as a whole. At the end of 1989, 139 listed and 176 unlisted employers' associations were known to the Certification Officer. Those which are national organisations negotiate the national collective agreements for their industry with the trade unions concerned; most of these national organisations belong to the Confederation of British Industry.

Confederation of British Industry

The Confederation of British Industry (CBI) is the largest central employers' organisation in Britain, representing directly or indirectly some 250,000 businesses which together employ about half the working population. It aims primarily to ensure that Government, national and international institutions and the public understand the needs, intentions and problems of business. Membership ranges from the smallest to the largest companies, private sector and nationalised, and covers a broad spectrum which includes manufacturing, agriculture, construction, distribution, mining, finance, retailing and insurance. Most national employers' organisations, trade associations and some chambers of commerce are members. Policy is determined by a council of 400 members, and there is a permanent staff of 295; there are 13 regional offices and an office in Brussels. The CBI is the British member of the Union of Industries of the European Community.

Terms and Conditions of Employment

Basic rates of pay vary widely, and in private industry rates are frequently determined locally, with less importance attached to national agreements. Higher rates are usually paid for overtime and shift work, and weekly earnings may be further increased by incentive bonus schemes or other performance-related arrangements.

Earnings

According to the latest available information from the Department of Employment's New Earnings Survey, the average weekly earnings (including overtime payments) in April 1989 of full-time employees on adult rates were £239·70 (£269·50 for men and £182·30 for women). Earnings were higher for non-manual employees (£264·90) than for manual employees (£203·20). Some 53 per cent of manual employees and 21 per cent of non-manual employees received overtime payments. Women's earnings are markedly lower than those of men, partly because on average they work shorter hours, with less overtime paid at premium rates, and partly because they tend to be concentrated in the less well-paid jobs. In the year to June 1990 the underlying average increase in earnings was about 10 per cent.

Remuneration in commercial, technical and professional careers is normally by annual salary paid monthly, often on a scale carrying annual increments. Many of the top posts in leading commercial and industrial companies carry salaries which are performance-related, and the majority are between £100,000 and £300,000 a year before tax, reflecting increasing competition for top management. Senior management salaries are generally in the range of £40,000 to £100,000 a year, while middle management salaries typically fall between £20,000 and £40,000 a year.

There has been a move towards performance-related pay, which has been encouraged by the Government (see p 385). Since 1987 income tax relief has been available for employees receiving profit-related pay under schemes registered by the Inland Revenue. By April 1990, 1,175 schemes had been registered, covering over 232,000 employees.

Employee Share Schemes

The Government has taken a number of steps to encourage direct ownership by employees of shares in the businesses for which they work. The number of profit-sharing and savings-related share option schemes, which must be open to all eligible employees in a company, has risen from 30 in 1979 to over 1,780 in 1990, benefiting over 2 million employees.

Other Benefits

Additional benefits exist in varying degrees. About half of employees in employment are covered by pension schemes provided by their employers. Many employees are also covered by occupational sick-pay schemes which are additional or complementary to the state schemes, and by schemes to provide private medical treatment. Such benefits are more usual among clerical and professional employees than among manual workers. The provision of low-priced meals at the place of employment is usual in large undertakings and quite common in smaller ones. Many offices and shops which are unable to provide canteen facilities for their staff have adopted luncheon voucher schemes. Company cars are provided for directors and employees in a wide variety of circumstances. Other fringe benefits available include life assurance, telephone allowances and low-interest loans.

Hours of Work

The basic working week in Great Britain is in the range 37·5 to 40 hours for manual work and 35 to 38 for non-manual work; a five-day week is usually worked. While the basic working week has been gradually shortening, the general trend in actual hours worked has been rising since 1981. In April 1989 the average actual hours worked for full-time employees was 42·3 for men, compared with 37·6 for women. Men and women in non-manual occupations generally work less overtime than manual employees.

In general, there are no limits on hours worked by adults except in a few occupations (such as for drivers of goods vehicles and public service vehicles). Restrictions on working hours for women and for school-leavers aged under 18 were repealed by the Sex Discrimination Act 1986 and the Employment Act 1989.

Holidays with Pay

There are no general statutory entitlements to holidays, and holiday entitlements are frequently determined by collective agreements. These generally provide for at least four weeks' paid holiday a year, and nearly all manual employees covered by national collective agreements have entitlements of four weeks or more, with nearly 25 per cent having five weeks or more. Non-manual workers tend to have longer holidays than manual workers. Holiday entitlements may also be dependent upon length of service.

Office of Manpower Economics

The Office of Manpower Economics is an independent non-statutory organisation responsible for servicing independent review bodies which advise on the pay of various public-sector groups. These are the Top Salaries Review Body, the Armed Forces' Pay Review Body, the Doctors' and Dentists' Review Body, and the Review Body for Nurses and other National

Forestry

Millions of trees in Britain were destroyed in gales in 1987 and 1990. Scientists at Osney Laboratory at Oxford University are investigating ways of reducing the damage by experimenting with simulated forests in wind tunnels.

Mixed woodland at Glenmore Forest Park, near Inverness, Scotland. The Forestry Commission is encouraging mixed and broadleaved planting through its Woodland Grant scheme.

Computer Applications

Software developed by the Faculty of Music at Oxford University with support from the British Technology Group enables musicians to use a standard personal computer to produce a musical score ready for printing. As the music is 'played' in on the keyboard, it can be heard and it also appears on the screen in notation.

Rolls-Royce plc is using computers for the initial testing of the Trent, the world's most powerful turbofan engine. The scanning laser Doppler test shown here enables the engineer to visualise any vibration in the turbine blades.

Rheology, the study of the viscosity of materials, has become increasingly important in many industries. Carri-med has developed an advanced rheometer that combines a simple mechanical drive and highly sophisticated microprocessor techniques.

Computer sculptor William Latham has developed a new form of computer art. He creates on the screen three-dimensional forms that can be rotated and viewed from any point, and lit using multiple light sources.

Transport

The new Class 60 locomotive has just come into service with British Rail. Its main task is to haul heavy freight trains.

Plessey's 'Watchman' radars have been installed in the air traffic control room at Stansted airport, near London. The Civil Aviation Authority has embarked on an ambitious investment programme to enable London's airports to cope with the growth in forecast demand.

Health Service professions. The Office also provides services for the Pharmacists' Review Panel, the Police Negotiating Board and the Civil Service Arbitration Tribunal. It is responsible for research into pay and associated matters as requested by the Government.

Wages Councils Wages councils fix statutory minimum pay for 2·5 million workers aged 21 and over, primarily in service industries such as retailing, catering and hairdressing. There are 26 councils in Great Britain, each consisting of equal numbers of representatives of employers and employees in the relevant industry and up to five independent members. The Wages Act 1986 empowers each council to fix a minimum hourly rate, an overtime rate and a limit on the amount an employer can charge for accommodation provided. However, the Government has doubts on whether a statutory system is relevant for pay determination in the 1990s, and following a consultation exercise it announced in March 1990 that it would keep the system under review.

In Northern Ireland nine wages councils fix statutory minimum pay for some 36,000 workers.

Employment Protection Employment protection legislation provides a number of safeguards for employees. For example, most employees are entitled to receive from their employers written information on their terms and conditions of employment, while minimum periods of notice when employment is to be terminated are laid down for both employers and employees. Employees with a minimum period of service of two years are entitled to lump-sum redundancy payments if their jobs cease to exist (for example, because of technological improvements or a fall in demand) and their employers cannot offer suitable alternative work. The cost is partly met from a fund subscribed to by both sides of industry. Protection against unfair dismissal is provided by machinery under which an employee who has been in continuous employment, normally for two years or more, may complain to an industrial tribunal against an employer for unfair dismissal, and, if successful, obtain reinstatement, re-engagement or compensation. Most employed women who become pregnant and have completed two years continuous employment have the right to return to their former job, or its equivalent, after maternity absence. Legislation forbids any employment of children under 13 years of age, and employment in any industrial undertaking of children who have not reached the statutory minimum school-leaving age, with some exceptions for family undertakings.

The Government is keeping under review the legislation affecting terms and conditions of employment. Its aim is to ensure that the obligations placed on employers do not involve significant costs which discourage recruitment. The Employment Act 1989 contained a number of provisions designed to reduce burdens on employers. For example, employers with fewer than 20 employees have become exempt from the requirement to provide employees with a separate note of disciplinary rules in the written statement of their main terms and conditions of employment.

Equal Opportunities The Race Relations Act 1976 makes it unlawful to discriminate on grounds of colour, race, nationality (including citizenship) or ethnic or national origin, in employment, training and related matters. The Department of Employment operates a nationwide Race Relations Employment Advisory Service which operates from five main areas of ethnic minority settlement. Its objective is to promote the Government's policies aimed at eliminating racial discrimination in employment and promoting fair treatment and equality of opportunity in employment. Advisers provide employers with advice and practical help in developing and implementing effective equal opportunity strategies, including awareness training for senior managers and personnel staff, and the introduction of ethnic monitoring.

The Sex Discrimination Act 1975 makes it unlawful to discriminate in employment, training and related matters in Great Britain on the grounds of sex or against married people. The employment provisions were amended by the Sex Discrimination Act 1986 to bring legislation into line with a European Community directive on equal treatment. In addition, the Employment Act 1989 contains provisions to promote equality of opportunity in employment and vocational training, and to meet European Community obligations by repealing most legislation that discriminated in employment between women and men. The Equal Pay Act 1970, as amended in 1984, requires that a woman doing the same or broadly similar work to a man, or work which has an equal value, should receive equal pay and conditions of employment.

Practical advice to employers and others on the best arrangements for implementing equal opportunities policies in Great Britain is given in codes of practice from the Commission for Racial Equality and from the Equal Opportunities Commission.

Northern Ireland   Similar legislation to that in Great Britain on equal pay and sex discrimination applies in Northern Ireland, but there is no legislation on race relations. The Fair Employment (Northern Ireland) Act 1989 is designed to strengthen an earlier Act of 1976 which made unlawful discrimination in employment on grounds of religious belief or political opinion. Under the Act two new bodies have been established. A Fair Employment Commission has succeeded the Fair Employment Agency and has the task of promoting equality of opportunity and investigating employment practices, with powers to issue legally enforceable directions. A Fair Employment Tribunal adjudicates on individual complaints of religious or political discrimination and enforces the Commission's directions. The Act also requires all major employers to provide equality of opportunity by annual monitoring of workforces and periodic reviewing of employment practices to see if 'affirmative action' is required to rectify under-representation of either the Protestant or Roman Catholic community. Indirect discrimination has also been made illegal.

Advisory, Conciliation and Arbitration Service   The Advisory, Conciliation and Arbitration Service (ACAS) is an independent statutory body with the general duty of promoting the improvement of industrial relations. ACAS is directed by a council consisting of a full-time chairman and employer, trade union and independent members experienced in industrial relations. The Service conciliates in industrial disputes in both the public and private sectors. ACAS assistance was sought in nearly 1,200 disputes in 1989. In addition, there were 167 further requests for ACAS to provide arbitration. It may do this either by appointing single arbitrators or boards of arbitration or by referring cases to the Central Arbitration Committee (see below). Although ACAS has prime responsibility for helping to resolve disputes, and has also set up major committees of inquiry, the Secretary of State for Employment retains powers to appoint a court of inquiry or committee of investigation into a dispute. However, these are rarely used.

ACAS gives advice on all aspects of industrial relations and employment policies to employers, managers, trade unions, employee representatives and individuals. It handled nearly 350,000 inquiries in 1989. Specialist staff made nearly 7,300 advisory visits. ACAS also carries particular responsibility for attempting conciliation on complaints of infringement of individual employee rights. These include individual complaints of unfair dismissal; complaints under the Equal Pay Act 1970, including claims for equal pay for work of equal value; and complaints on employment matters under the Sex Discrimination Acts 1975 and 1986 and the Race Relations Act 1976. There were over 48,800 individual conciliation cases in 1989. Its Work Research Unit aims to encourage industry and commerce to adopt measures that can lead to improvements in the quality of working life and so to improvements in economic performance.

In Northern Ireland the Labour Relations Agency, an independent statutory body, provides services similar to those provided by ACAS in Great Britain.

Central Arbitration Committee

The Central Arbitration Committee is an independent standing arbitration body. It provides boards of arbitration for the settlement of trade disputes referred to it with the consent of the parties concerned. It also adjudicates on claims made under the disclosure of information provisions of the Employment Protection Act 1975.

HEALTH AND SAFETY AT WORK

Employers have a duty in civil and criminal law to take reasonable care of their employees, and others affected by their work activities, and to provide a safe system of working, while employees have a duty of care towards each other and also to take care of their own safety. The principal legislation is the Health and Safety at Work etc. Act 1974. Its purpose is to secure the health, safety and welfare of people at work and to provide for the protection of the public whose health and safety might be affected by work activities. The Act places general duties on everyone concerned with work activities, including employers, the self-employed, employees, manufacturers and suppliers.

The 1974 Act is superimposed on earlier health and safety legislation and regulations. Earlier legislation imposes specific obligations and standards on, for example, occupiers of particular types of premises or employers engaged in particular activities. It covers such matters as the fencing of machinery, precautions against the exposure of people to toxic dusts and gases, precautions against fire, the safe condition of premises, and cleanliness, lighting, temperature and ventilation.

Some of the earlier legislation was replaced immediately by the 1974 Act, but the remainder continues in force pending its progressive replacement by regulations and codes of practice. Regulations made under the Act govern the establishment of first-aid facilities, the control of work with lead and the control of major accident hazards in industry. Each set of regulations is supported by either an approved code of practice or other guidance material. Further steps were taken in 1989 with the introduction of regulations which provide a comprehensive approach to the control of exposure to virtually all substances hazardous to health in all types of work and workplace. They represent the most significant change in health and safety legislation since the 1974 Act. In 1990 regulations on electricity at work, pressure systems and noise at work came into force. The last implemented a European Community directive. Consideration is being given to the implementation of other health and safety directives by 1992.

A basic principle underlying the 1974 Act is that employers, in consultation with their employees, should have the responsibility of working out health and safety arrangements, within the broad obligations of the law, to suit their own workplaces. Employers with five or more employees must draw up a written policy for safety and health, and must inform their employees of the policy and of the arrangements for its implementation. In workplaces where negotiations take place with a trade union, the union may appoint safety representatives to be the employees' official channel for representation and consultation over safety matters.

Recent statistics indicate a reduction in the rate of major and other reported injuries to employees, although a high rate of injuries remains in certain industries, such as construction.

The Health and Safety Commission

The Health and Safety Commission, established by the 1974 Act and accountable to Parliament through the Secretary of State for Employment, has responsibility for developing policies, including guidance, codes of practice, or proposals for regulations. In the case of proposals for changes in legislation, the Commission consults those who would be affected and makes recommendations to the Secretary of State concerned. The Commission has an independent chairman, three members appointed after consultation with employers' organisations, three after consultation with the trade unions, two after consultation with local authority associations and one representing the public interest.

The Health and Safety Commission has seven subject advisory committees: on toxic substances, dangerous substances, dangerous pathogens, genetic manipulation, the safety of nuclear installations, the safe transport of radioactive materials and medical matters. There are also 11 industry advisory committees: for agriculture, ceramics, construction, education, foundries, health services, oil, paper and board, printing, railways and rubber.

The Health and Safety Executive

The 1974 Act also set up the Health and Safety Executive, which includes government inspectorates covering a range of work activities, including the Factory Inspectorate, which also deals with a large number of activities outside factories, such as hospitals and educational establishments. There are also inspectorates for mines, agriculture, quarries, nuclear installations and explosives. The Executive also includes the Health Policy Division, the Technology Division and the Research and Laboratory Services Division. The inspectors, who have powers of entry and enforcement, seek compliance with health and safety legislation in individual workplaces and give advice. The Employment Medical Advisory Service provides a nationwide service of advice on the medical aspects of employment problems to employers, employees, trade unions, doctors and others.

The Technology Division provides technical advice on industrial health and safety matters. The Research and Laboratory Services Division provides scientific and medical support and testing services. It carries out research both in its own laboratories and through universities and other institutions on a contract basis, often jointly funded by industry. Areas of study include explosion risks, fires, protective equipment, methods for monitoring airborne contaminants, occupational medicine and hygiene, and the safety of engineering systems.

In some premises, mostly offices, shops, warehouses, restaurants and hotels, health and safety legislation is enforced by inspectors appointed by local authorities, working under guidance from the Health and Safety Commission. Some other official bodies work under agency agreement with the Commission, for example, the Department of Energy (concerned with health and safety in the oil industry) and the Railway Inspectorate. The latter, which is concerned with worker safety on the railways, will be transferred from the Department of Transport to the Health and Safety Executive in late 1990.

Northern Ireland

In Northern Ireland the Health and Safety Agency, roughly corresponding to the Health and Safety Commission, and an Employment Medical Advisory Service were set up by the Health and Safety at Work (NI) Order 1978. The general requirements of the Northern Ireland health and safety legislation are broadly similar to those for Great Britain. They are enforced mainly by the Department of Economic Development through its Health and Safety Inspectorate.

19 Public Finance

Public finance is concerned with taxation, expenditure and borrowing (or debt repayment) by central and local government, management of the public sector's assets and liabilities and the financing of public corporations. Central government raises money from individuals and companies by direct and indirect taxation and from National Insurance contributions. It spends money on goods and services, such as health and defence, and in payments to people, such as social security and pensions. Local government receives substantial grants from central government and raises revenue mainly through the community charge and rates (local property taxes, which may be levied on domestic and business properties). Domestic rates were abolished in 1989 in Scotland and in 1990 in England and Wales and replaced by the community charge (see pp 406-7); they continue in Northern Ireland. Business rates apply throughout Britain. Local government provides services such as education, police and fire services, and refuse collection. The diagram (see p 404) shows the relative importance of the various items of receipts (including borrowing) and expenditure for general government.

The government department responsible for broad control of public finance and expenditure is HM Treasury. The Bank of England (the central bank) advises the Government on financial matters, executes monetary policy and acts as banker to the Government.

PUBLIC EXPENDITURE The three main definitions of public expenditure are general government expenditure, the planning total and Supply expenditure.

General government expenditure is the spending of central and local government, excluding transfers between them such as central government grants to local authorities. It is the key public spending aggregate and is used in the medium-term financial strategy (see below), where public spending is set in the context of macroeconomic policy. It is more appropriate than the other measures for making international comparisons as it is usually less affected by institutional differences.

The planning total is used by the Government for the purposes of planning and control. The Government seeks to achieve its wider medium-term objective (expressed in terms of general government expenditure) by controlling spending within this total. The planning total covers central government's own expenditure, the support it provides or approves for local authority expenditure, the financing requirements of public corporations (including nationalised industries), privatisation proceeds and a reserve to cover unanticipated expenditure.

Supply expenditure is financed out of money voted by Parliament in the Supply Estimates (see below). Supply expenditure—practically all of which appears in the planning total—covers most of central government's own spending (the main exception being expenditure financed from the National Insurance Fund) and central government support for local authority expenditure.

The background to the present Government's planning of public expenditure is the medium-term financial strategy, introduced in 1980. The Government's aim is to preserve a firm financial framework in order to maintain downward pressure on inflation with the ultimate goal of price stability, and to ensure the continuation of the conditions for sustainable growth. With commitments also to reduce taxation and curb the role of the State, the Government therefore sought to reduce public expenditure as a proportion of national output as well. By 1990 non-North Sea taxes, National Insurance contributions and the community charge amounted to around 37 per cent of non-North Sea gross domestic product. General government expenditure (excluding privatisation proceeds) as a proportion of gross domestic product fell from over 46 per cent in the early 1980s to 39 per cent by 1989–90, and the Government expects this level to continue for the following three years.

Table 19.1 gives projections for government expenditure and receipts and public sector debt repayment for the years up to 1993–94.

Table 19.1: Projected Public Expenditure, Receipts and Debt Repayment

£ thousand million

	1990–91	1991–92	1992–93	1993–94
General government expenditure	213	225	238	250
of which: public expenditure planning total	*179*	*192*	*203*	*215*
General government receipts	219	229	240	253
of which: taxes	*170*	*177*	*186*	*196*
National Insurance and other contributions	*36*	*38*	*40*	*43*
Fiscal adjustments[a]	—	1	2	3
Market and overseas debt repayment of public corporations	1	0	0	0
Public sector debt repayment (PSDR)	7	3	0	0
PSDR as percentage of gross domestic product	1·25	0·5	0	0

Source: *Financial Statement and Budget Report 1990-91.*
[a]These imply lower taxes or higher expenditure than assumed in the figures for general government expenditure and receipts.

The Planning Cycle

Each year the Government conducts a review of its expenditure plans for the forthcoming three years (the 'public expenditure survey') and publishes the resulting totals, together with any changes in National Insurance, in the Autumn Statement in November. Details of these plans are published early in the following year. In the years up to 1990 this detailed information was presented in the annual public expenditure White Paper. From 1991 it will be given in a series of departmental reports. The detailed summary analyses which were given in the White Paper will be published in a supplement to the Autumn Statement.

The Government's updating of the medium-term financial strategy and consequent plans for the public finances over the following year, including any tax changes, are set out in the Financial Statement and Budget Report, published with the Budget around the end of the financial year (31 March). Details of the tax changes are included in the Finance Bill, which is presented to Parliament shortly after the Budget and becomes law during the summer.

Public Expenditure Totals

Public expenditure totals are analysed in Table 19.2. The largest departmental programmes are those of the Department of Social Security (38 per cent of central government's own expenditure), the Department of Health and the Office of Population Censuses and Surveys (16 per cent) and the Ministry of Defence (15 per cent).

About half of local authority spending is financed by grants from central government. The rest is met from the community charge and rates, surpluses on trading, rents and borrowing. Education accounts for over one-third of local authority spending; law and order, housing and other environmental services, personal social services and transport account for most of the remainder.

Table 19.2: Planned Public Expenditure Totals

£ thousand million

	1990–91	1991–92	1992–93
Central government's own expenditure	137·8	145·3	152·3
Central government support for local authorities	41·8	43·7	44·8
Financing requirements for public corporations	1·4	2·3	2·3
Privatisation proceeds	−5·8	−5·0	−5·0
Reserve	3·0	6·0	9·0
Planning total	179·0	192·3	203·4
Local authority self-financed expenditure	13·3	14·0	15·0
Central government debt interest	17·0	15·5	15·0
Other adjustments	3·4	3·5	4·5
General government expenditure	212·7	225·0	238·0

Source: *Financial Statement and Budget Report 1990-91.*
Differences between totals and the sums of their component parts are due to rounding.

Reserve

Planned expenditure includes an unallocated reserve for each year of the plans to cover all additions to departmental spending, whether arising from policy changes, new initiatives or revisions to the estimated costs of demand-led programmes. For the current year the reserve is used as a control mechanism. The reserve has been set at higher levels for each of the next two years but some will normally be allocated to departments as spending forecasts are made firmer within the public expenditure planning total. The balance will be retained for contingencies which might arise during the current year.

Cash Limits

Some 40 per cent of general government expenditure is subject to control by cash limits (external financing limits in the case of nationalised industries). Another 40 per cent consists of demand-led services (for example, social security benefits); once policy and rates of payment have been determined, expenditure in the short run depends on the number of eligible recipients. The remaining 20 per cent is current expenditure of local authorities, which central government does not directly control; however, the major part of the contribution by central government to such expenditure, rate support or revenue support grant, is subject to cash limits.

Once fixed, cash limits are not usually revised during the year. There is, however, a limited facility for carrying forward underspending on the capital and running costs components of cash limits. If any overspending of cash limits occurs, a corresponding deduction is normally made from the limits for the following year.

The Estimates

The annual public expenditure survey conducted by HM Treasury provides the basis for the Estimates which each government department submits to HM Treasury in December, giving details of its cash requirements for the financial year beginning in the following April. After Treasury approval, these Supply Estimates are presented to Parliament in March, usually at the same time as the Budget (see p 401). Parliament approves them in July as part of the Annual Appropriation Act, expenditure between 1 April and this date being covered by Votes on Account approved before the start of the financial year.

Supplementary Estimates may also be presented to Parliament during the course of the year. If any Supply Estimate is overspent, the Public Accounts Committee (see below) may investigate fully before Parliament is asked to approve any Excess Vote to balance the account. In each parliamentary session, up to three 'Estimates days' are available for debates on the Supply Estimates, following scrutiny by select committees of the House of Commons.

Examination and Audit of Public Expenditure

Examination of public expenditure is carried out by select committees of the House of Commons, which study in detail the activities of particular government departments and require the attendance of ministers and officials for cross-examination. The audit of the Government's spending which follows up the control inherent in parliamentary approval of the Estimates is exercised through the functions of the Comptroller and Auditor General and the Public Accounts Committee.

Comptroller and Auditor General

The Comptroller and Auditor General, an officer of the House of Commons appointed by the Crown, has two distinct functions. The duty of Comptroller General is to ensure that all revenue and other public money payable to the Consolidated Fund and the National Loans Fund (see p 401) is duly paid and that all payments out of these funds are authorised by statute. The duty of Auditor General is to certify the accounts of all government departments and those of a wide range of other public sector bodies; to examine revenue accounts and inventories; and to report the results of his examinations to Parliament. The Comptroller and Auditor General also has wide statutory powers to carry out, and report to Parliament on, examinations of economy, efficiency and effectiveness in the use of resources by those bodies audited or to which the Comptroller and Auditor General has right of access.

Public Accounts Committee

The Public Accounts Committee considers the accounts of government departments and the Comptroller and Auditor General's reports on them and on departments' use of their resources. The Committee takes evidence from the official heads of departments and relevant public sector bodies and submits to Parliament reports which carry considerable weight; its recommendations are taken very seriously by the departments and organisations that it examines. The Government's formal reply to the reports is presented to Parliament by HM Treasury in the form of Treasury minutes, and the reports and minutes are usually debated annually in the Commons.

Central Government Financial Funds

The Government's sterling expenditure is largely met out of the Consolidated Fund, an account at the Bank of England into which tax receipts and other revenues are paid. This is also known as the Exchequer. Any excess of expenditure over receipts is met by the National Loans Fund, which is another official sterling account at the Bank of England and is the repository for funds borrowed by the Government. The National Insurance Fund, into which contributions are paid by employers and employed people, is used mainly to pay for social security benefits; a small proportion of National Insurance contributions is paid direct to the Consolidated Fund in order to help finance the National Health Service.

THE BUDGET

The Budget, which usually takes place in March, sets out the Government's proposals for changes in taxation and is the main occasion for an annual review of economic policy. The proposals are announced to the House of Commons by the Chancellor of the Exchequer in the Budget statement and are published in the Financial Statement and Budget Report. This report also contains a review of recent developments in the economy, together with an economic forecast, and sets out the fiscal and monetary framework within which economic policy operates. This is the medium-term financial strategy (see p 398).

The Budget statement is followed by the moving of a set of Budget resolutions in which the proposals are embodied. These resolutions are the foundation of the Finance Bill, in which the proposals are set out for detailed consideration by Parliament. Some of the resolutions give temporary effect, under the Provisional Collection of Taxes Act 1968, to certain of the tax proposals in the Budget. This enables the Government to collect certain taxes provisionally, at the levels provided by the Budget proposals, pending enactment of the Finance Bill.

The bulk of the tax proposals are concerned with changes in the level or coverage of taxes, the introduction of new taxes or the abolition of existing ones, and changes in the administrative machinery. These changes are made not only with regard to the revenue required but also with regard to their effect on the way the economy performs.

For two taxes—income tax and corporation tax—annual Ways and Means resolutions followed by Finance Bill clauses are required to maintain their existence, since they are annual rather than permanent taxes. Thus, a Budget and a Finance Bill are necessary at or about the beginning of each financial year. Following completion of its parliamentary stages, the Finance Bill becomes an Act, usually around the end of July. Tax changes can be made at other times, however, either by specific legislation or by the use of the regulator, which permits limited changes between Budgets in value added tax (by up to 25 per cent) and the main excise duties (by up to 10 per cent).

MAIN SOURCES OF REVENUE

The main sources of revenue are: taxes on income (including profits), which include personal income tax, corporation tax and petroleum revenue tax; taxes on capital, which comprise inheritance tax and capital gains tax; and taxes on expenditure, which include value added tax (VAT) and customs and excise duties. Other sources of revenue are National Insurance contributions, which give entitlement to a range of benefits, and the community charge and business rates.

Taxes on individual incomes are progressive in that larger incomes bear a proportionately greater amount of tax. Thresholds and rate bands for income tax, inheritance tax and capital gains tax are raised automatically each year in line with the rise in retail prices over the previous calendar year unless Parliament decides otherwise. The Inland Revenue assesses and collects the taxes on income, profits and capital and also stamp duty. HM Customs and Excise collects the most important taxes on expenditure (VAT, most duties and car tax). Vehicle excise duty is the responsibility of the Department of Transport and National Insurance contributions that of the Department of Social Security (although the latter are generally collected by the Inland Revenue). The community charge and business rates are collected by local authorities.

Taxes on Income

Income Tax

Income tax is imposed for the year of assessment beginning on 6 April. For 1990–91 the basic rate of 25 per cent applies to the first £20,700 of taxable income. A rate of 40 per cent applies to income above this level. These rates apply to total income, including both earned and investment income.

A number of personal allowances and reliefs reduce the amount of a person's taxable income compared with gross income. Since April 1990 there has been a system of independent taxation for husbands and wives. All taxpayers, irrespective of sex or marital status, are entitled to a personal allowance against income from all sources. Married women pay their own tax on the basis of their own income. In addition, there is a married couple's allowance, which goes to the husband in the first instance. However, if his income is not high enough to use it in full, he can transfer the unused portion to his wife, to set against her income. The current values of the main allowances are £3,005 for the personal allowance and £1,720 for the married couple's allowance.

Assuming only the basic personal allowances, a single person or married woman with an income of £12,000 in 1990–91 pays £2,249 in income tax, while a married man with the same income pays £1,819. The amount of tax payable by a single person or married woman varies from, for example, £999 on an annual income of £7,000 to £23,693 on one of £70,000. Among the most important of the reliefs is that for mortgage interest payments on borrowing for house purchase up to the statutory limit of £30,000. Relief at the basic rate is usually given 'at source' (that is, repayments which the borrower makes to the lender are reduced to take account of tax at the basic rate and the tax refund is then passed directly by the tax authorities to the building society or bank making the loan rather than to the individual taxpayer). Another relief is that under the Business Expansion Scheme, whereby certain investors in trading companies without a stock market quotation (usually small companies) are able to obtain relief on up to £40,000 invested in any one year.

Most wage and salary earners pay their income tax under a Pay-As-You-Earn (PAYE) system whereby tax is deducted (and accounted for to the Inland Revenue) by the employer, thus enabling employees to keep as up to date as possible with their tax payments.

In general, income tax is charged on all income which originates in Britain (although some forms of income—such as certain social security benefits—are exempt) and on all income arising abroad of people resident in Britain. Interest on certain British government securities belonging to people not ordinarily resident in Britain is exempt. Britain has entered into agreements with many countries to provide relief from double taxation; where such agreements are not in force unilateral relief is often allowed. British residents working abroad for the whole year benefit from 100 per cent tax relief.

Corporation Tax

The rates of company tax in Britain are lower than in most other industrialised countries. Companies pay corporation tax on their income after deduction of certain allowances and any capital gains. A company which distributes profits to its shareholders is required to make an advance payment of corporation tax to the Inland Revenue. In general, this payment is set against a company's liability to corporation tax on its income and capital gains. The recipient of the distribution (if resident in Britain) is entitled to a tax credit, which satisfies his or her liability to income tax at the basic rate.

The main rate of corporation tax is 35 per cent, with a reduced rate of 25 per cent for small companies (those with profits below £200,000 in a year). Marginal relief between the main rate and the small companies' rate is allowed for companies with profits between £200,000 and £1 million.

Expenditure on plant and machinery qualifies for annual allowances of 25 per cent. These are given on a 'reducing balance' basis, which is to say that 25 per cent of the total cost may be offset in the first year, 25 per cent of the remaining 75 per cent in the second year and so on. Special arrangements exist for plant and machinery treated as a short-life asset. There is a 100 per cent allowance for expenditure on scientific research. Annual allowances are given for capital expenditure on the construction of industrial and certain other buildings based on a 25-year life (that is, 4 per cent of the cost per year for 25 years). If taxable profits are insufficient to absorb the available allowances, the excess can be carried forward and set against future profits for an indefinite period.

Petroleum Revenue Tax

Petroleum revenue tax (deductible in computing profits for corporation tax) is charged on profits from the production, as opposed to the refining or other forms of processing, of oil and gas under licence in Britain and on its Continental Shelf. The rate of tax is 75 per cent. Each licensee of an oilfield is charged on the profits from that field after deduction of certain allowances and reliefs which, among other things, encourage exploration, appraisal and future field development. The tax is computed at half-yearly intervals and the bulk of it is collected in monthly instalments.

Taxes on Capital
Inheritance Tax

Inheritance tax applies to transfers of personal wealth made on, or up to seven years before, the donor's death. Subject to certain exemptions and reliefs, the first £128,000 of the cumulative total of chargeable transfers is not liable to tax; higher amounts are taxed at a single rate of 40 per cent. A tapered system of relief reduces the tax on transfers made between three and seven years before the donor's death. Relief ranges from 20 per cent of the tax payable on transfers made between three and four years prior to death to 80 per cent on those made between six and seven years prior to death.

There are several exemptions. All transfers to a spouse living in Britain are exempt while gifts and bequests to charities, political parties and heritage bodies are also normally exempt. Business property qualifies for relief of up to 50 per cent.

Capital Gains Tax

Capital gains realised on the disposal of assets are liable to capital gains tax or, in the case of companies, to corporation tax. Individuals are exempt from tax in respect of total net gains of up to £5,000 in any one year and most

Planned Receipts and Expenditure of General Government 1990-91

Pence in every pound

Receipts				Expenditure
			10	Defence
Income tax	26		1	Foreign and Commonwealth Office
			1	Agriculture, Fisheries and Food
			1	Trade and Industry
Corporation tax	10		2	Employment
			2	Transport
Capital gains tax	1		3	Environment – housing
Inheritance tax	1		1	Environment – other environmental services
			10	Environment – local government
Value added tax	15		3	Home Office and legal departments
			3	Education and Science
Community charge and local authority rates	11		10	Health
Duties on petrol, alcoholic drinks and tobacco	9		26	Social Security
Petroleum revenue tax and oil royalties	1			
			5	Scotland
National insurance and other contributions	17		2	Wales
			3	Northern Ireland
Interest and dividends	3		2	Chancellor of the Exchequer's departments
			1	Other departments
Gross trading surpluses and rent	1		6	Local authority self–financed expenditure
Other duties, taxes, levies and royalties	6		1	Reserve
			8	Central government debt interest
Other receipts	1		2	Accounting adjustments
General government borrowing requirement	−3	−2		Privatisation proceeds
Total	100	100		**Total**

Cash totals £212,700 million

Sources: *Financial Statement and Budget Report 1990–91* and *The Government's Expenditure Plans 1990–91 to 1992–93*.

Note: Differences between totals and the sum of their component parts are due to rounding.

trusts on gains of up to £2,500. Gains are treated as the taxpayer's top slice of income, being charged at the individual's higher income tax rate or the company's higher corporation tax rate.

Only gains arising since March 1982 are subject to tax and the effects of inflation are allowed for when measuring gains. The tax on certain types of gift and certain deemed disposals of assets may be deferred until the assets are sold. Some assets, including the principal private residence, movable possessions worth less than £6,000 (and any movable possessions with a predictable life of less than 50 years except those on which the expenditure qualifies for a capital allowance), private motor cars, and National Savings Certificates and Bonds are normally exempt. Gains on government securities and certain corporate bonds are exempt from the tax, as are gains on shares owned under the Personal Equity Plan (designed to encourage wider share ownership).

Taxes on Expenditure
Value Added Tax

Value added tax (VAT) is a broadly based tax, chargeable at 15 per cent. It is collected at each stage in the production and distribution of goods and services by taxable persons (generally those whose business has a turnover of more than £25,400 a year). The final tax is borne by the consumer. When a taxable person purchases taxable goods or services, the supplier charges VAT (the taxable person's input tax). When the taxable person supplies taxable goods or services to customers, then they in turn are charged VAT (the taxable person's output tax). The difference between the output tax and the input tax is paid to, or repaid by, HM Customs and Excise.

Certain goods and services are relieved from VAT, either by charging at a zero rate (a taxable person does not charge tax to a customer but reclaims any input tax paid to suppliers) or by exemption (a taxable person does not charge a customer any output tax and is not entitled to deduct or reclaim the input tax). Zero-rating applies to exports and to most food; books, newspapers and periodicals; fuel (except for petrol and other fuels for road use) and power for domestic users; construction of new residential buildings; certain international services; public transport fares; caravans and houseboats; young children's clothing and footwear; drugs and medicines supplied on prescription; specified aids for handicapped people; and certain supplies by or to charities. Exemption applies to land (including rents), insurance, postal services, betting, gaming (other than by gaming machines and lotteries), finance, education, health, burial and cremation, and supplies by trade unions and professional bodies to their members.

Customs Duties

Customs duties are chargeable in accordance with the Common Customs Tariff of the European Community (no such duties are chargeable on goods which qualify as Community goods). Special customs import and export procedures are operated under the Common Agricultural Policy and Community levies are chargeable on a wide range of agricultural products from non-Community countries. Under the single European market programme, all remaining barriers to the free movement within the European Community of goods, services, capital and people will be abolished by the end of 1992.

Excise Duties

Hydrocarbon oils used as road fuel bear higher rates of duty than those used for other purposes. Kerosene, most lubricating oils and other oils used for certain industrial processes are free of duty. There are duties on spirits, beer, wine, made-wine, cider and perry, based on alcoholic strength and volume. Spirits used for scientific, medical, research and industrial processes are generally free of duty. The cigarette duty is based partly on a charge per

1,000 cigarettes and partly on a percentage of retail price. Duty on other tobacco products is based on weight. Duties are charged on off-course betting, pool betting, gaming in casinos, bingo and gaming machines. The rates vary with the particular form of gambling. Duty is charged either as a percentage of gross or net stakes or, in the case of gaming machines, as a fixed amount per machine according to the cost of playing it and its prize level.

Vehicle excise duty on a private motor car or light van is £100 a year; for motor cycles it is £10, £20 or £40 a year according to engine capacity. The duty on goods vehicles is levied on the basis of gross weight and, if over 12 tonnes, according to the number of axles; the duty is designed to ensure that such vehicles cover at least their road costs through the tax paid (licence duty and fuel duty). The duty on taxis and buses varies according to seating capacity.

Car Tax

Cars, motor cycles, scooters, mopeds and some motor caravans, whether British made or imported, are chargeable with car tax at 10 per cent of the wholesale value (motor caravans are charged at 10 per cent of 60 per cent of the wholesale value). VAT is charged on the price including car tax.

Stamp Duty

Certain kinds of transfer are subject to stamp duty. These include purchases of houses (1 per cent on the total price if this exceeds £30,000) and instruments such as declarations of trust (usually 50p). Stamp duty is also charged on transfers of stocks and shares other than government stocks (broadly 0·5 per cent of the value of the transaction). However, the Government announced in 1990 that this would be abolished in late 1991–92. Transfers by gift and transfers to charities are exempt.

OTHER REVENUE
National Insurance Contributions

There are four classes of National Insurance contribution: Class 1—paid by employees and their employers; Class 2—paid by the self-employed; Class 3—paid voluntarily for pension purposes; and Class 4—paid by the self-employed on their taxable profits over a set lower limit, currently £5,450 a year, and up to a set upper limit, currently £18,200 a year (in addition to their Class 2 contribution).

Employees with earnings no higher than £46 a week do not pay Class 1 contributions. Contributions on earnings above this threshold are at the rate of 2 per cent of the first £46 of total earnings and 9 per cent of the balance, up to the upper earnings limit of £350 a week. Employers' contributions are subject to the same threshold. On earnings above the threshold, contributions rise in stages from 5 per cent of total earnings up to a maximum of 10·45 per cent when earnings are £175 or more a week; there is no upper earnings limit.

Class 2 and Class 3 contributions are at a flat rate—£4·55 and £4·45 a week respectively. The self-employed may claim exemption from payment of Class 2 contributions if their profits are expected to be below £2,600 for the 1990–91 tax year.

Class 4 contributions are payable at the rate of 6·3 per cent.

The Community Charge and National Non-domestic Rate

The system of local authority finance in Great Britain (but not Northern Ireland) has been reformed. The new system was introduced in Scotland in April 1989 and in England and Wales in April 1990. It aims to increase the responsiveness and accountability of councils to their electorates, replacing domestic rates with a community charge, reforming the system of central government grants to local authorities and (in England and Wales) establishing a national non-domestic rate. The community charge is set at a level reflecting spending decisions reached by a council, for which it has to account to its electors. It is payable by almost all resident adults. The national non-domestic rate is set by central government (although collected by local authorities). It is paid into a national pool and then redistributed to local authorities.

FINANCIAL CONTROL

Control of the public sector finances is a central part of the Government's medium-term financial strategy. Since 1987–88 the public sector has been in surplus, so that the Government has repaid debt. In 1989–90 the public sector debt repayment (PSDR) amounted to some £8,000 million, equal to around 1·5 per cent of gross domestic product (GDP). Even without privatisation proceeds these amounts represent substantial surpluses. The intention is for a return to balance by 1992–93. The Government sees balanced public finances as a firm buttress for monetary policy in the defeat of inflation. They also ensure that public debt and debt interest fall steadily in relation to GDP.

The major government debt instrument is known as gilt-edged stock as there is no risk of default. Gilt-edged stock is marketable and is widely traded. Individuals may also make transactions through post offices in stocks included on the National Savings Stock Register. Pension funds and life insurance companies have the largest holdings. The Bank of England on behalf of the Government issues both conventional and indexed stock (on which principal and interest are linked to the movement in the retail prices index).

With there being a sizeable PSDR, the Bank has in recent years been purchasing gilt-edged stock rather than making new issues. One method of doing so is by reverse auctions. The first reverse auction was held in 1989.

An important additional source of government finance is the range of National Savings products, which are non-marketable and are designed to attract personal savings. The chief products are Income Bonds, National Savings Certificates (which may be index-linked), the Investment Account and Capital Bonds.

Other central government debt instruments are Treasury bills and certificates of tax deposit. Sterling Treasury bills are sold at a weekly tender; the majority have a maturity of three months. The Government has also issued bills denominated and payable in European Currency Units (ECUs) since 1988. The proceeds have been added to the official foreign exchange reserves as opposed to being used to finance public expenditure. Certificates of tax deposit may be purchased by individuals or corporate bodies to be tendered in settlement of a range of taxes and are non-marketable.

The bulk of public corporations' borrowing is met by central government, although their temporary borrowing needs are met largely from the market, usually under Treasury guarantee. That part of local authority borrowing met by central government is supplied by authorisation of Parliament through the Public Works Loan Board from the National Loans Fund. (The Board remains an independent body even though it is merged for administrative purposes with the former National Debt Office, forming the National Investment and Loans Office.) The local authorities may also borrow directly from the market, both short-term and long-term, through a range of instruments. Some public corporations and local authorities also borrow on occasion, under special statutory power and with Treasury consent, in foreign currencies.

Net Public Sector Debt

Public sector debt repayment (or borrowing) each year represents a subtraction from (or an addition to) the net debt of the public sector. This debt is the consolidated debt of the public sector less its holdings of liquid assets. At the end of March 1989 consolidated debt amounted to nearly £201,000 million. Central government accounted for nearly 95 per cent, local authorities for almost 4 per cent and public corporations for 2 per cent. With consolidated liquid assets amounting to £42,000 million, net public sector debt was £158,000 million. Central government accounted for 74 per cent of consolidated liquid assets, local authorities for 20 per cent and public corporations for 6 per cent.

20 Banking and Financial Institutions

Britain is a major financial centre providing a wide range of specialised services. Historically the industry was located in the famous 'Square Mile' in the City of London. This remains broadly the case, even though the markets for financial and related services have grown and diversified greatly. 'The City' refers to a collection of markets and institutions in and around the Square Mile. This area has the greatest concentration of banks in the world (responsible for about a fifth of total international bank lending), the world's biggest insurance industry (with about one-fifth of the international market) and one of the world's largest stock exchanges. It is also the principal international centre for transactions in a large number of commodities.

Banking, finance, insurance, business services and leasing accounted for 14 per cent of Britain's total output in 1989, a share which has risen sharply over the past decade. Banking, finance and insurance accounted for 4·1 per cent of employment in March 1990. The net identified overseas earnings of British financial institutions in 1989 were £6,184 million.

Development of Financial Services

The increase in the rate of international movements of capital in the 1960s and 1970s mainly took the form of increased bank lending and foreign exchange trading. London became the international centre of this activity, particularly in the eurocurrency markets (see p 421), and the number of overseas banks represented in London is larger than in any other financial centre. In the last decade, with increasing international competition in financial services and with developments in technology, there has been a rapid growth in the international markets for securities. London has again played an important role, especially in the market for eurobonds, in a variety of currencies (see p 421).

Supervision

Three Acts have helped Britain's financial services industry to respond to the new competitive climate, while at the same time maintaining adequate safeguards for the investing public: the Financial Services Act 1986, the Building Societies Act 1986 (see p 414) and the Banking Act 1987 (see p 411). They have also enabled the implementation in Britain of certain European Community (EC) directives on banking and building societies, investment services and securities transactions.

Under the Financial Services Act a new supervisory framework has been built up. Investment businesses (those effecting transactions in, managing or giving advice on investments) require authorisation and have to obey rules of conduct based on principles set out in the legislation. Supervision is in the hands of the Securities and Investments Board (SIB), which is empowered to recognise self-regulating organisations (SROs) provided that they offer investors protection equivalent to that provided by the SIB. The SROs are practitioner-based bodies. Most investment businesses have opted to achieve authorisation by obtaining membership of an SRO. The SROs are the Association of Futures Brokers and Dealers (AFBD); the Financial Intermediaries, Managers and Brokers Regulatory Association (FIMBRA),

Assets of Selected Groups of Financial Institutions, 1983 and 1988

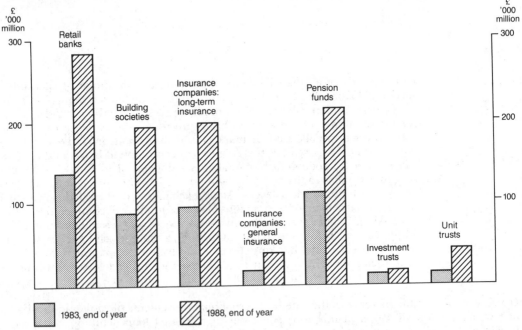

Sources: Central Statistical Office, Bank of England

which covers firms such as insurance brokers; the Investment Management Regulatory Organisation (IMRO), for concerns such as merchant banks and pension fund managers with mainly corporate clients; the Life Assurance and Unit Trust Regulatory Organisation (LAUTRO); and The Securities Association (TSA), whose members include the member firms of The International Stock Exchange.

In each Act there is provision for improved co-operation and information-sharing between supervisors in different financial sectors. The Bank of England, the Building Societies Commission (see p 415), the Department of Trade and Industry, the SIB and the SROs have statutory responsibility for financial supervision in the sectors to which these Acts apply. There are strengthened government powers to investigate insider dealing (dealing carried out on the basis of privileged access to relevant information), and a separate department, the Serious Fraud Office, to deal with cases of serious or complex fraud. The Government is helping to extend international co-operation in investigating suspected breaches of rules or requirements in the field of investment business: agreements about exchange of information are in place with the United States and Japan.

Changes within the financial services sector as a whole have been eroding traditional distinctions between financial institutions, with single firms providing a broader range of services, both in domestic and international markets.

THE BANK OF ENGLAND   The Bank of England was established in 1694 by Act of Parliament and Royal Charter as a corporate body; the entire capital stock was acquired by the Government under the Bank of England Act 1946. The Bank's main functions are to execute monetary policy, to act as banker to the Government, to act as a note-issuing authority and to exercise prudential supervision over, and to provide banking facilities for, the banking system. As agent for the Government, the Bank of England is responsible for arranging government borrowing or repayment of debt and for managing the National Debt. It also manages the Exchange Equalisation Account (see below) and maintains the register of holdings of government securities on behalf of the Treasury. More generally, the Bank has a responsibility for overseeing the soundness of the financial system as a whole.

The Bank of England has the sole right in England and Wales to issue banknotes. The note issue is no longer backed by gold but by government and other securities. The Scottish and Northern Ireland banks have limited rights to issue notes. These issues, apart from a small amount specified by legislation for each bank, must be fully covered by holdings of Bank of England notes. Responsibility for the provision of coin lies with the Royal Mint, a government trading fund which became an executive agency in April 1990.

The Bank is able to influence money-market conditions through its dealings with the discount houses (see p 416), which developed in the nineteenth century as bill brokers for industrialists. The discount houses hold mainly Treasury, local authority and commercial bills, and negotiable certificates of deposit financed by short-term loans from the banks. If on a particular day there is a shortage of cash in the banking system as a result, for example, of large tax payments, the Bank relieves the shortage either by buying bills from the discount houses or by lending directly to them. This permits the banks to replenish their cash balances at the Bank by recalling some of their short-term loans to the discount houses. The terms on which the Bank's dealings with the discount houses take place allow the authorities to set and maintain interest rates at the level they consider appropriate.

Under the Financial Services Act 1986, the Bank is responsible for the supervision of the main wholesale markets in London for money, foreign exchange and gold bullion. (The markets are wholesale in the sense that the participants are professional operators dealing in substantial amounts of money.)

Under the Banking Act 1987, deposit-taking organisations require authorisation from the Bank of England (unless they are specifically exempted) and are subject to the Bank of England's supervision. The Act created a Board of Banking Supervision and increased the Bank's powers to modify the conduct of banking institutions, to investigate cases of illegal deposit-taking, to block bank mergers and takeovers on prudential grounds and to require information from banks. The Act also enables information to be shared, in strictly controlled ways, among supervisors in different financial services, and permits auditors to make reports to the Bank of England about a bank if the circumstances justify it.

On behalf of the Treasury, the Bank manages the Exchange Equalisation Account (EEA), which holds Britain's official reserves of gold, foreign exchange, Special Drawing Rights (SDRs, which are claims on the International Monetary Fund) and European Currency Units (ECUs). Using the resources of the EEA, the Bank may intervene in the foreign exchange markets to check undue fluctuations in the exchange value of sterling.

BANKS AND BUILDING SOCIETIES

In addition to banks, which are authorised under the Banking Act 1987 and are supervised by the Bank of England, the chief institutions which offer banking services are the building societies and the National Savings Bank.

Banks and building societies are broadly covered by the definition of 'credit institutions' used in EC banking legislation. The First Banking Directive, adopted in 1977, established the principle of non-discrimination for credit institutions in one member state wishing to operate elsewhere in the Community. The Second Banking Directive, which comes into operation at the beginning of 1993, will complete the single European market in banking by establishing mutual recognition of home country authorisation for credit institutions.

A useful distinction is that between 'retail' banking and 'wholesale' banking. Retail banking is primarily for personal customers and small businesses. Its main services are cash deposit and withdrawal facilities, and systems for transferring funds, notably by cheque. Competition between the banks and the building societies in the provision of money transmission services to individuals has increased during the last two decades and is expected to increase further (see p 414). Building societies can now also offer money transmission services to companies. Wholesale business involves the taking of large deposits at higher rates of interest, the deployment of funds in money-market instruments (see p 420) and the making of large loans and investments. Nearly all the banks in Britain engage in some wholesale activities and some, such as the merchant and overseas banks, centre their business on them. Many such wholesale dealings are conducted on the inter-bank market, that is, between banks themselves.

In May 1990 there were 546 institutions authorised under the Banking Act 1987, including retail banks, merchant banks, branches of overseas banks, discount houses and banking subsidiaries of both banking and non-banking institutions from Britain and overseas. Of these, 340 were members of the British Bankers' Association.

Retail Banks

The major retail banks are those with a significant branch network, offering a full range of financial services to both individuals and companies. They provide current accounts including, generally, interest-bearing current accounts; deposit accounts; and various kinds of loan arrangements, together with a full range of money transmission facilities increasingly featuring plastic card technology.

The dominant banks in England and Wales are Barclays, Lloyds, Midland, National Westminster and the TSB Group; and in Scotland the Bank of Scotland and The Royal Bank of Scotland. Together with the Standard Chartered Bank (see p 416), these make up the Committee of London and Scottish Bankers, which represents its members to the Government. Other important retail banks are the Clydesdale Bank, the Co-operative Bank, the Yorkshire Bank and Girobank, which was previously a subsidiary of the Post Office but which was offered for sale to the private sector and in 1990 became a subsidiary of the Alliance and Leicester Building Society. Northern Ireland is served by branch networks of five banks.

With the growth of the financial services sector since the 1970s, and a relaxation of restrictions on competition among financial institutions, the major banks have diversified their services. They have lent more money for house purchases, and have established or acquired substantial interests in finance houses, leasing and factoring companies, merchant banks, securities dealers, insurance companies, unit trust companies and estate agencies.

The banks provide loan facilities to industrial companies and, since the 1970s, have provided more medium- and long-term loans than they did formerly. They have also become important providers of finance for small firms. They have supported a loan guarantee scheme under which 70 per cent of the value of loans to small companies is guaranteed by the

Government, and some banks have set up special subsidiaries to provide equity finance for companies (see p 419).

Most retail banks also conduct international operations, which account for a substantial proportion of their business. In addition to maintaining overseas subsidiaries, they are active in eurocurrency markets (see p 421).

Deposits and Assets

The total liabilities/assets of the retail banks amounted to £410,000 million at the end of March 1990. Of the liabilities, 68 per cent was sterling deposits, 16 per cent other currency deposits, and the remainder items in suspense or transmission, and capital and other funds. Of the £278,000 million of sterling deposits, sight deposits (which can be withdrawn on demand) constituted about 40 per cent and time deposits (which can be withdrawn only on some period of notice) some 60 per cent. The banks' main liquid assets consist of money at call (mainly short-term loans to discount houses), their holdings of Treasury and some other bills, short-dated British government securities and balances at the Bank of England. They also hold a proportion of their assets as portfolio investments (mainly longer-dated British government securities) or trade investments.

Branches and Accounts

At the beginning of 1990 the retail banks in Great Britain, including Abbey National (see p 415), operated through some 14,200 branches and sub-branches. National Westminster had the largest number (2,997), followed by Barclays (2,645), Lloyds (2,184), Midland (2,042), TSB (1,538), and The Royal Bank of Scotland (842). Some 85 per cent of adults in Britain have a current account and over one-third a deposit account.

Payment Systems and Services

The main inter-bank payment clearing systems are administered by three separate companies operating under an umbrella organisation, the Association for Payment Clearing Services. One company covers bulk paper clearings (cheques and credit transfers). A second covers high-value clearings for same-day settlement, comprising the electronic nationwide service CHAPS (Clearing House Automated Payment System) and the paper Town Clearing, which operates only in the City of London. A third covers the bulk electronic clearing, Bankers Automated Clearing Services (BACS), which includes standing orders and direct debits. Membership of each of these clearing companies is open to any bank or financial institution that meets the criteria for appropriate supervision and volume of transactions.

All the major retail banks have substantial networks of automated teller machines or cash dispensers with, in all, about 13,000 machines at the beginning of 1990. These give customers access to cash and other services up to 24 hours a day. Many banks and building societies offer home banking services to their customers whereby they can use telephone or screen-based access devices to obtain account information, make transfers and pay bills.

The banks and major building societies also offer their customers cheque guarantee cards which entitle holders to reciprocal encashment facilities up to, generally, £50 a day. The cards will also guarantee transactions with retailers up to the same amount. Some cards have limits of £100 or £250. Uniform eurocheques supported by a eurocheque card are available from all major banks. These standard-format, high-security cheques may be used to obtain cash or make payments in Britain, elsewhere in Europe and in a few other overseas countries. The cheques are made out in the currency of the country in which they are being used, with a guarantee limit of approximately £100 per cheque.

Credit cards associated with major retail banks are also a popular means of payment. The earliest, Barclaycard, was launched in 1966 and is part of the

Visa world system. At the beginning of 1990 Visa cards were issued by 30 financial institutions in Britain, with a total of some 16·5 million cards on issue. In addition, there were 12·1 million cards on issue affiliated to the Mastercard worldwide system, most of which carried the Access label. Each type of card has over 300,000 outlets. The major banks now all issue cards under both international systems and for some cards there is an annual fee. Some of the major retail stores issue their own cards, which operate like credit cards.

A charge card, like a credit card, enables the holder to make retail payments, but there is either no credit limit or a very high limit, and the balance must be settled in full on receipt of a monthly statement. An annual fee is generally payable. The main examples are American Express, Diners Club and bank gold cards. Charge cards are generally available only to higher-income customers.

Debit cards, which allow payments to be deducted directly from the purchaser's bank account, have been introduced by Barclays (Connect), Lloyds (Visa payment card), TSB (Bankcard), and a joint venture of Midland, National Westminster and The Royal Bank of Scotland (Switch). The Bank of Scotland and the Yorkshire Bank have joined Switch. Unlike other cards, Switch operates only through EFTPOS terminals.

'EFTPOS' (electronic funds transfer at point of sale) is a system which enables shoppers to pay for goods using a debit or credit card to transfer funds electronically via terminals in retail premises. Several major EFTPOS schemes are well established, with altogether more than 60,000 terminals, a number that is growing quickly.

Building Societies

Building societies are mutual institutions, owned by their savers and borrowers. They raise short-term deposits from savers, who are generally able to withdraw their money on demand or at short notice. The societies provide long-term loans, mostly at variable rates of interest, against the security of property—usually private dwellings purchased for owner-occupation.

Building societies are the major lenders for house purchase in Britain and are the principal repository for the personal sector's liquid assets (although banks' shares have increased in both areas since 1985). Some 60 per cent of adults have building society savings accounts. Competition among the building societies and between building societies and other financial institutions has increased in the last decade. A variety of savings schemes has been established, and a growing number of societies provide current account facilities such as cheque books and automated teller machines. In 1990 there were some 2,750 building society automated teller machines, about 20 per cent of the total. Nine building societies issue credit cards (see p 413).

At the end of 1989 there were 126 registered societies, of which 107 were members of The Building Societies Association, with assets totalling £187,000 million; about £44,000 million was advanced in new mortgages in the course of the year. The three largest societies (the Halifax, Nationwide Anglia and Woolwich) account for nearly 50 per cent of the total assets of all societies and the 20 largest for some 90 per cent.

The Building Societies Act 1986 allows the societies to provide a wider range of services. Up to 17·5 per cent of a society's commercial assets may be used for purposes other than loans on first mortgage of owner-occupied houses, including up to 7·5 per cent in other types of asset such as unsecured loans. These limits will increase to 25 per cent and 15 per cent respectively in 1993. Directly or through subsidiaries, societies may now offer services within the general areas of banking, investment, insurance, trusteeship, executorship and estate agency. Societies may also operate throughout the European Community. However, their main business will continue to be the provision of financial and housing-related services.

The 1986 Act established the Building Societies Commission to carry out the prudential supervision of building societies. It also made provision for a society to seek the approval of its members to convert into a public limited company. In this event the society becomes an authorised institution under the Banking Act 1987 (see p 411) and is then supervised by the Bank of England. The Abbey National pursued this course and no longer contributes to building society statistics.

The Council of Mortgage Lenders is a trade body established in 1989 for all mortgage lending institutions, including building societies, insurance companies, finance houses and banks.

National Savings Bank

The National Savings Bank is run by the Department for National Savings, based in Glasgow, and provides a system for depositing and withdrawing savings at 20,000 post offices around the country or by post.

There are about 20 million accounts. Ordinary Accounts earn interest at a rate which depends on the balance maintained; the first £70 of annual interest is tax free. Investment Accounts earn a higher, variable rate of interest, which is taxable. At the end of August 1990 the sum of the two accounts totalled £9,900 million. Other National Savings instruments include tax-free Savings Certificates, which either pay a fixed rate of interest alone or a (lower) fixed rate of interest combined with index-linking; Premium Bonds, where interest is paid in the form of prizes chosen by lottery; and taxable Income and Capital Bonds.

All National Savings interest is paid without deduction of tax at source and some instruments encourage savers to leave their savings untouched for five years. The National Savings Bank does not offer lending facilities. At the end of August 1990 the total amount of money invested in National Savings was £35,800 million, and this forms a part of government borrowing.

Merchant Banks

Merchant banks have traditionally been concerned primarily with the accepting (or guaranteeing) of commercial bills and with the sponsoring of capital issues on behalf of their customers. Today they have a widely diversified and complex range of activities, with important roles in international finance and the short-term capital markets; the provision of expert advice and financial services to British industrial companies, especially where mergers, takeovers and other forms of corporate reorganisation are involved; and in the management of investment holdings, including trusts, pensions and other funds. A number of merchant banks have become part of financial conglomerates, offering an even wider range of financial services than hitherto. The four largest retail banks all have merchant banking subsidiaries. The British branches of some overseas banks also engage in merchant banking.

Overseas Banks

A total of 288 overseas banks were represented in Britain in January 1990. Of these, 44 were from the United States and 29 from Japan. They provide a comprehensive banking service in many parts of the world and engage in the financing of trade not only between Britain and other countries but also between third-party countries. Citibank of the United States is expanding its activities in the retail banking market in Britain and has joined the high-value clearing system (see p 413).

British Overseas Banks

A number of banks have their head offices in Britain but operate mainly abroad, often specialising in particular regions such as Latin America or East

Asia through extensive branch networks. The major bank in this sector is Standard Chartered.

The Discount Houses

The discount houses, of which there are nine, are specialised institutions unique in their function and central position in the British monetary system. They act as financial intermediaries between the Bank of England and the rest of the banking sector, promoting an orderly flow of short-term funds between the authorities and the banks, and lending to the Government by guaranteeing to tender for the whole of the weekly offer of Treasury bills (which are instruments to raise funds over a period of up to six months). In return for acting as intermediaries, the discount houses have privileged daily access to the Bank of England, which acts as 'lender of last resort'. Assets of the discount houses consist mainly of Treasury and commercial bills, negotiable certificates of deposit and short-term loans. Their liabilities consist mainly of short-term deposits.

INSURANCE

The British insurance industry provides a comprehensive and competitive service domestically and internationally. It falls broadly into two parts: long-term life insurance, where contracts may be for periods of many years; and general insurance, including accident and short-term life insurance, where contracts are for a year or less. The London market is the world's leading centre for insurance and for the placement of international reinsurance. It has been estimated that it handles some 20 per cent of general insurance business placed on the international market.

In addition to the British companies and Lloyd's, a large number of overseas companies are represented, with which many British companies have formed close relationships. Some British companies confine their activities to domestic business but most large companies undertaking general business transact a substantial amount overseas through branches and agencies or affiliated local companies.

Insurance companies carrying on business in Britain are supervised by the Department of Trade and Industry under the Insurance Companies Act 1982. Marketing of life insurance is regulated by the Securities and Investments Board (see p 409). EC directives cover reinsurance, compulsory motor insurance, freedom of establishment for life and non-life insurers, Community co-insurance and insurance intermediaries. A directive regulating cross-frontier trade in non-life insurance services came into force in June 1990, and agreement has been reached on a directive on cross-frontier trade in life insurance services.

Some 830 companies are authorised to carry on one or more classes of insurance business in Britain, of which 7 per cent are European Community companies with their head office outside Britain, and a further 10 per cent are companies established outside the Community. The total invested assets of these companies amounted to £238,000 million at the beginning of 1990. Some 450 companies belong to the Association of British Insurers (ABI). These account for 90 per cent of British insurance business and 97 per cent of life business. Some companies are mutual institutions, owned by their policy holders. Insurance is also available from some friendly societies—mutual institutions administered by trustees.

Long-term Insurance

Long-term insurance is handled by some 270 companies. As well as providing life cover, long-term insurance is a vehicle for saving and investment by individuals, premiums being invested in securities and other assets. The net long-term insurance premium income of ABI member companies in 1989 was some £29,000 million.

General Insurance

General insurance business is undertaken by insurance companies and by Lloyd's. It covers fire, accident, general liability, short-term life, motor, marine, aviation and transport. Total ABI member company premiums in 1989 were some £25,000 million, of which £8,000 million was for motor insurance and £1,600 million for marine, aviation and transport insurance. The bulk of business in the latter categories was written through the Institute of London Underwriters (see below).

Lloyd's

Lloyd's, the origins of which go back to the seventeenth century, is an incorporated society of private insurers in London. Although its activities were originally confined to the conduct of marine insurance, a very considerable worldwide market for the transaction of other classes of insurance business (such as aviation and motor) has been built up.

Lloyd's is not a company but a market for insurance administered by the Council of Lloyd's. Business is carried out for individual elected underwriting members, or 'names', who must show sufficient available wealth and lodge a deposit. Insurance is transacted for them with unlimited liability, in competition with each other and with insurance companies. At the beginning of 1990 there were 27,800 members, grouped into 401 syndicates. Each syndicate is managed by an underwriting agent responsible for appointing a professional underwriter to accept insurance risks and settle claims on the syndicate members' behalf. Insurance may only be placed through accredited Lloyd's brokers, who negotiate with Lloyd's syndicates on behalf of the insured.

The net premium income of Lloyd's in 1989 was some £4,200 million, of which around £500 million was for motor insurance and around £1,500 million was for marine, aviation and transport insurance.

Institute of London Underwriters

The Institute of London Underwriters was formed in 1884, originally as a trade association for marine underwriters. It now provides a market where insurance companies transact marine, commercial transport and aviation business. The Institute issues combined policies in its own name which are underwritten by the companies which form its membership. The premium income processed by the Institute in 1989 was some £1,600 million. About half of its 116 member companies are branches or subsidiaries of overseas companies.

Insurance Brokers

Insurance brokers, acting on behalf of the insured, are a valuable part of the company market and an essential part of the Lloyd's market. Many brokers specialise in reinsurance business, acting as intermediaries in the exchange of contracts between companies, both British and overseas, and often acting as London representatives of the latter. The Insurance Brokers (Registration) Act 1977 provides for the voluntary registration and regulation of insurance brokers by the Insurance Brokers Registration Council. Only those so registered can use the title 'insurance broker'. In August 1990 some 17,000 individuals were registered with the Council, through 1,493 partnerships or sole traderships and 3,161 limited companies.

INVESTMENT FUNDS
Pension Funds

Virtually all occupational pension schemes are based on trust funds managed so as to protect the interests of the members. Pension contributions are invested either directly in the securities and other investment markets or through intermediaries such as insurance companies. The funds are a dominant force in securities markets. The Government has introduced legislation to allow people more choice in opting out of occupational pension schemes and setting up personal pension arrangements. Some 10·5 million people belong to occupational pension schemes and about 3·5 million to personal pension schemes. The market value of assets held directly by pension funds rose from £2,000 million in 1957 to some £215,000 million at the beginning of 1989, when 13 per cent was in British government securities and 69 per cent in company securities.

Investment and Unit Trusts

Investment and unit trusts enable investors in securities to spread their risks and obtain the benefit of skilled management. Investment trusts are companies which observe certain requirements of The International Stock Exchange and the tax authorities, and invest in securities for the benefit of their shareholders. The total assets of the 164 members of the Association of Investment Trust Companies at the beginning of 1990 amounted to some £19,400 million.

Unit trusts are constituted by trust deed between a management company and a trustee company which holds the assets. Normally, the managers sell units to the public and also repurchase them on demand. The sums held must be invested in securities. The costs of running the trust are met partly by an initial charge which forms part of the price of a unit and partly by a periodic service charge which is usually taken out of the trust's income.

Under the Financial Services Act 1986 (see p 409) unit trusts are authorised and regulated by the Department of Trade and Industry (DTI), most of whose powers are delegated to the SIB (see p 409). At present authorised unit trusts may hold their assets in a wide variety of securities and money market funds. Arrangements to allow them to invest in futures and options (see pp 420 and 421), and property have been proposed by the DTI.

Most existing authorised unit trusts qualify for certification under the terms of the EC UCITS (Undertaking for Collective Investment in Transferable Securities) directive. The SIB is responsible for issuing UCITS certificates to schemes based in Britain and for receiving notifications from UCITS schemes based in other member states.

In March 1990 there were 4·9 million unit trust holdings, with a total value of some £56,000 million.

COMPANY FINANCING INSTITUTIONS

There are many specialised financial institutions meeting the needs of specific groups of borrowers which are not adequately covered by other institutions. They are to be found in both the public and the private sectors. Some of the latter were set up with official support, but with financing from banks and other financial institutions. They may offer loan finance or equity capital.

The main private sector institutions are described below. Among public sector agencies are the British Technology Group, the Scottish and Welsh Development Agencies, the Industrial Development Board in Northern Ireland, the Co-operative Development Agency and ECGD (the Export Credits Guarantee Department), Britain's official export credit insurer.

Finance Houses

Finance houses are major providers of instalment credit facilities for the personal sector and of both loan and leasing finance (see below) to the corporate sector. Forty-six firms constitute the Finance Houses Association (FHA); at the beginning of 1990 loan and leasing credit outstanding to the members of the FHA was some £40,000 million. Many of the finance houses are owned by banks, and most are institutions authorised under the Banking Act 1987.

Leasing Companies

Leasing companies buy and own plant or equipment required and chosen by businesses and lease it at an agreed rental. This form of finance grew quickly in importance in the 1970s, partly because the leasing companies were able to take advantage of investment incentives to the benefit of customers whose tax position would otherwise have made this impossible. In 1989 the 72 members of the Equipment Leasing Association acquired assets in Britain valued at some £13,600 million, which represented 27 per cent of all investment in plant and machinery.

Factoring Companies

Factoring comprises a range of financial services which provide growing companies with a flexible source of finance in exchange for the outstanding invoices due to them. Since the early 1960s factoring has developed as a major financial service, covering international activities as well as domestic trade. In 1989 member companies of the Association of British Factors and Discounters handled business of £11,600 million (representing about 90 per cent of all factoring business in Britain) and some 7,500 companies made use of the Association's services.

Venture Capital Companies

Venture capital companies meet the need for medium- and long-term capital when such funds are not easily or directly available from traditional sources such as the stock market or the banks.

There are over 120 British venture capital companies which take equity stakes in small and medium-sized firms. Many of these companies are subsidiaries of other financial institutions, including banks, insurance companies and pension funds. The 124 full members of the British Venture Capital Association invested a total of over £1,600 million in Britain, elsewhere in Europe, and in the United States in 1989, an increase of 18 per cent on the previous year. (Approximately 25 per cent of this amount represented the venture capital element of 3i investment.)

Formerly Investors in Industry, 3i supports investment programmes over a whole range of industries. During the year ended 31 March 1990 the corporation invested £597 million. Within the last few years it has become increasingly prominent in financing management 'buy-outs', which involve the purchase of businesses from their owners by the management and other staff. The shares in 3i are owned by the Bank of England (15 per cent) and six of the major retail banks.

FINANCIAL MARKETS

The City of London has a wide range of organised financial markets. They include The International Stock Exchange, the foreign exchange market, the options and financial futures market, the eurobond and eurocurrency markets, the Lloyd's insurance market (see p 417), and the bullion and commodity markets.

The International Stock Exchange

The International Stock Exchange of the United Kingdom and the Republic of Ireland has its main administrative centre in London. There are also centres in Belfast, Birmingham, Dublin, Glasgow and Manchester.

The Exchange has changed radically in recent years. Its rules on membership were altered to allow corporate ownership of member firms; the system under which dealers charged fixed minimum scales of commission to investors was abolished in favour of negotiated commissions; dealers were permitted to trade in securities both on their own behalf, as principals, and on behalf of clients, as agents, these two roles formerly having been kept distinct; and a screen-based dealing system came into operation, which has been so successful that the trading floor has been closed (except for dealing in traded options). These changes were popularly known as 'Big Bang'.

The International Stock Exchange is one of the largest in the world in terms of the number and variety of securities listed. Its turnover of equities in 1989 accounted for some 10 per cent of equity trading worldwide. Some 7,700 securities are quoted; at the end of June 1990 these had a market value of £2,100,000 million. More than 5,000 securities of companies are quoted, including those of a growing number of leading overseas companies, with a value of some £1,800,000 million. The remainder is made up of British and overseas government and corporation stocks as well as eurobonds (see p 421).

In recent years the largest market for new issues has been that for companies' securities, including issues of shares resulting from the Government's privatisation programme. Trading in British government securities ('gilt-edged stocks') in the first three months of 1990 accounted for about 60 per cent of transactions by value (excluding traded options). New issues are made on the Government's behalf by the Bank of England when required.

The Exchange's London Traded Options Market enables investors not only to buy options to purchase or sell shares in the future at pre-fixed prices, but also to trade in the options themselves. There is trading in around 70 equity options of prominent British and overseas companies and in stock index options. The Market is due to merge with the London International Financial Futures Exchange (see p 421) before the end of 1990.

Listing Changes   The International Stock Exchange altered its rules in 1990 to conform to EC directives on listing particulars, prospectuses and mutual recognition. The major effect of the EC directive on Mutual Recognition of Listing Particulars is that, subject to certain limitations, each member state is required to recognise listing particulars accepted in another member state. In order to put British companies on an equal footing with those in other EC countries the Exchange reduced the minimum trading record requirement for full listing from five years to three. At the same time the corresponding requirement for the Unlisted Securities Market, on which the securities of smaller companies are quoted, was reduced from three years to two. The Third Market, which previously provided a structure for dealing in the securities of companies which did not qualify for the Unlisted Securities Market, is to be phased out at the end of 1990. A majority of Third Market companies are expected to join the Unlisted Securities Market.

The Money Markets   The London money markets channel wholesale funds (mainly short-term) from lenders to borrowers. They consist of a series of integrated groups of financial institutions conducting negotiations primarily by telephone, telex and automated dealing systems, there being no physical market-place. Under the Financial Services Act 1986 (see p 409), the Bank of England is responsible for regulating some market participants and has developed a code of conduct which is observed by all market participants. The discount houses (see p 416) play an important role. The main financial instruments dealt in are bills (issued by the Treasury, local authorities or companies), certificates of deposit (CDs, large-denomination transferable deposits) and short-term deposits. The bill markets and the markets in which the discount houses borrow from the rest of the banking system are often referred to as the 'traditional' markets. Newer markets, known as 'parallel' markets, emerged in the 1960s, and include the inter-bank market and the market in CDs. Since a large proportion of the latter is held by banks, the CD market is effectively an extension of the inter-bank market.

Capital markets have been undergoing continuous transformation since the 1960s (see p 409). In the 1980s a trend towards the 'securitisation of debt' developed: that is to say, major borrowers increasingly raised funds by issuing securities instead of seeking bank loans. In 1986 large companies were permitted to develop a sterling commercial paper market: this consisted initially of issues of short-term debt denominated in sterling with a maturity of up to one year. Since 1989 the sterling commercial paper and the short-term corporate bond markets have been consolidated. The range of issuers has been broadened since 1986 to include, for example, banks and building societies, certain unquoted companies and overseas public sector bodies. The market now provides a way for such bodies to issue short-term debt of up to five years' maturity and to borrow directly from the money market by issuing short-term debt of up to five years' maturity.

The Euromarkets

The eurocurrency market enables banks to deal in deposits and loans denominated in a currency other than that of the country in which the bank is situated. Transactions can thus be carried out in eurodollars, euro-deutschmarks, euroyen and so on. London and Tokyo are the main world centres for this business.

The eurobond market performs a similar service in transferring funds from lenders to borrowers but over a longer period by means of bonds issued in currencies other than that of the issuing country. Transactions in both markets tend to be in large denominations. The markets developed in the late 1950s following the restoration of convertibility between the major currencies, partly in order to avoid incurring the costs of exchange control and other regulations. The participants in the markets include multinational corporations, non-bank financial institutions, and governments, as well as the international banking community.

In the 1980s there has been considerable growth in the euro-commercial paper market. As with the establishment of the sterling commercial paper market (see above) this represents a further movement towards the securitisation of debt.

The Foreign Exchange Market

The foreign exchange market has no physical centre, but consists of telephone links between the participants, which include banks, other financial institutions and several firms of foreign exchange brokers which act as intermediaries between the banks. It provides those engaged in international trade and investment with foreign currencies for their transactions. The banks are in close contact with financial centres abroad and are able to quote buying and selling rates for both spot and forward delivery in a wide range of currencies and maturities. The forward market enables traders and dealers who, at a given date in the future, wish to receive or make a specific foreign currency payment, to contract in advance to sell or buy the foreign currency involved for sterling at a fixed exchange rate. A Bank of England survey in April 1989 showed that average daily turnover on London's foreign exchange market was about £110,000 million, making it the largest such market in the world.

Financial Futures

The London International Financial Futures Exchange (LIFFE) trades on the floor of the Royal Exchange building. About 200 banks, other financial institutions, brokers and individual traders are members of the market. Futures markets allow parties that could be affected by movements in prices, interest rates or exchange rates to reduce their vulnerability or to speculate on the possibility of making a gain. Financial futures contracts are legally binding documents for the purchase or sale of a fixed amount of a financial commodity, at a price agreed in the present, on a specified future date. They facilitate the transfer of risk from those who do not wish to bear it to those who are prepared to bear it. LIFFE has the widest range of financial futures and options products of any exchange in the world. In August 1990 the average number of futures and futures options contracts traded daily was about 150,000, with a turnover of some £32,500 million. LIFFE is due to merge with the London Traded Options Market (see p 420) before the end of 1990.

The London Bullion Market

Over 60 banks, securities and trading companies comprise the London gold and silver markets which, like the foreign exchange market, trade by telephone and telex links. Five of the members meet twice daily to establish a London fixing price for gold which provides a reference point for worldwide dealings. The silver fixing is held once a day and has three participants. Although much interest centres upon the fixings, active dealing takes place throughout the day. London and Zurich are the main world centres for gold dealings.

Commodity, Shipping and Freight Markets

Britain remains the principal international centre for transactions in a large number of commodities, although most of the sales negotiated in London relate to consignments which never pass through the ports of Britain. The need for close links with sources of finance and with shipping and insurance services often determined the location of these markets in the City of London. There are also futures markets in cocoa, coffee, grains (wheat and barley), rubber, soya bean meal, sugar, pigmeat, non-ferrous metals (aluminium, copper, lead, nickel, silver and zinc), potatoes, gas oil (heating oil) and crude petroleum oil. The markets are collaborating in the development of new arrangements to safeguard participants.

In ship brokerage, London's Baltic Exchange is responsible for a substantial proportion of the world's tramp fixtures. A freight futures market is in operation there. All Britain's agricultural futures markets are operated from the Baltic Exchange and physical commodity trading is also carried out there.

21 Overseas Trade

Overseas trade has been of vital importance to the British economy for hundreds of years, and especially since the mid-nineteenth century, when the rapid growth of industry, commerce and shipping was accompanied by Britain's development as an international trading centre. Today, although small in area and accounting for only about 1 per cent of the world's population, Britain is the fifth largest trading nation in the world, and, as a member of the European Community, part of the world's largest trading bloc, which accounts for about one-third of all trade.

Exports of goods and services in 1989 were equivalent to over one-quarter of gross domestic product (GDP). Britain is a major supplier of machinery, vehicles, aerospace products, electrical and electronic equipment and chemicals, and a significant oil exporter. It relies upon imports for about one-third of total consumption of foodstuffs, and for many of the basic materials needed for its industries. Trade in invisibles is also of great significance to the economy: in 1989 overseas earnings from services were equivalent to nearly one-third of those from total visible exports.

VISIBLE TRADE In 1989 Britain's exports of goods were valued at about £92,800 million and its imports of goods at some £116,600 million on a balance-of-payments basis (see Table 21.1). Between 1988 and 1989 exports rose by 4·9 per cent in terms of volume and by 7·8 per cent in terms of unit value, leading to an increase in the total value of exports of almost 15 per cent. Import volume rose by 7·6 per cent, unit value rose by 6·9 per cent and total value also rose by nearly 15 per cent.

Table 21.1: Exports and Imports 1986–89 (balance-of-payments basis)

	1986	1987	1988	1989
Value (£ million)				
Exports f.o.b.[a]	72,656	79,446	80,776	92,792
Imports f.o.b.[a]	82,141	90,669	101,854	116,632
Volume index (1985 = 100)				
Exports	104·2	109·7	111·8	117·3
Imports	107·4	115·3	131·0	140·9
Unit value index (1985 = 100)				
Exports	90·2	93·8	93·9	101·2
Imports	95·3	97·8	96·7	103·4
Terms of trade (1985 = 100)[b]	94·6	95·9	97·1	97·9

Source: *Monthly Review of External Trade Statistics.*
[a]f.o.b. = free on board, that is, all costs accruing up to the time of placing the goods on board the exporting vessel having been paid by the seller.
[b]Export unit value index as a percentage of import unit value index.

Commodity Composition

Britain has traditionally been an exporter of manufactured goods (both semi-manufactures and finished manufactures) and an importer of food and basic materials. In 1970 manufactures accounted for 85 per cent of exports. The proportion fell sharply in the early 1980s—to around 67 per cent by the middle of the decade—as fuels increased their share; it has since risen, to 81 per cent in 1989. The share of finished manufactures in total imports rose from 25 per cent in 1970 to 52 per cent in 1989. Machinery and transport equipment account for a little over one-third of exports and a similar proportion of imports. Export sectors that have declined in relative importance include textiles and vehicles. Textiles accounted for 5 per cent of total exports in 1970 but only 2 per cent in 1989; the corresponding figures for vehicles were 11 per cent and 6 per cent. Over the same period, the share of food, beverages and tobacco in total imports fell from 22 per cent to 9 per cent and that of basic materials from 15 per cent to 5 per cent.

Table 21.2: Commodity Composition of Trade 1989[a]

	Exports (f.o.b.)		Imports (c.i.f.)[b]	
	£ million	per cent	£ million	per cent
Non-manufactures	15,067	16·1	24,147	20·0
Food, beverages and tobacco	6,555	7·0	11,430	9·5
Basic materials	2,348	2·5	6,482	5·4
Fuels	6,164	6·6	6,235	5·2
Manufactures	76,291	81·5	95,075	78·7
Semi-manufactures	26,860	28·7	32,171	26·6
of which: Chemicals	12,350	13·2	10,441	8·6
Textiles	2,205	2·4	3,770	3·1
Iron and steel	2,894	3·1	2,795	2·3
Non-ferrous metals	1,968	2·1	3,070	2·5
Metal manufactures	1,787	1·9	2,483	2·1
Other	5,656	6·0	9,612	8·0
Finished manufactures	49,431	52·8	62,904	52·1
of which: Machinery	26,687	28·5	30,387	25·2
Road vehicles	6,071	6·5	13,003	10·8
Clothing and footwear	1,672	1·8	4,515	3·7
Scientific instruments and photographic apparatus	3,928	4·2	3,994	3·3
Other	11,073	11·8	11,005	9·1
Miscellaneous	2,287	2·4	1,565	1·3
Total	93,646	100·0	120,789	100·0

Source: *Monthly Review of External Trade Statistics.*
[a]On an overseas trade statistics basis. (This differs from a balance of payments basis because, for imports, it includes the cost of insurance and freight and, for both exports and imports, includes returned goods.)
[b]c.i.f. = cost, insurance and freight, that is, including shipping, insurance and other expenses incurred in the delivery of goods as far as their place of importation in Britain. Some of these expenses represent earnings by companies resident in Britain and are more appropriate to the invisibles account.
Note: Differences between totals and the sums of their component parts are due to rounding.

Since the mid-1970s North Sea oil has made a significant contribution to Britain's overseas trade both in terms of exports and in terms of import substitution. In 1989 exports of fuels in volume terms were over three and a half times their 1975 level; imports were about two-thirds their 1975 level. Over this period the share of fuels in exports changed from 4 per cent to 7 per cent and in imports from 18 per cent to 5 per cent. North Sea oil production has now passed its peak of the mid-1980s, when exports of fuels had accounted for over 20 per cent of total exports. The surplus on trade in oil fell sharply between 1988 and 1989, due in part to the effect of accidents on North Sea oil installations, but still amounted to nearly £1,500 million.

Since the early 1960s Britain's imports of semi-manufactures have exceeded those of basic materials; they are now almost five times as high. This reflects the increasing tendency for producing countries to carry out the processing of primary products up to the semi-finished and, on occasions, the finished stage. The fall in the share of food imports (from around 35 per cent of total imports in the 1950s to 8 per cent in 1989) is a result both of the increasing extent to which food demand has been met from domestic agriculture and the decline in the proportion of total expenditure devoted to food.

Geographical Distribution

Britain's overseas trade is mainly—and increasingly—with other developed countries. In 1970 these accounted for 73 per cent of exports and a similar proportion of imports; by 1989 the shares were 80 per cent and 86 per cent respectively. In 1970 non-oil developing countries accounted for 17 per cent of Britain's exports and for 15 per cent of Britain's imports; by 1989 both proportions had fallen to 10 per cent. In 1972 (the year before Britain joined the European Community) around one-third of Britain's trade was with the other 11 countries which now make up the Community. The proportion is now about one-half, and is expected to increase with the completion of the single European market in 1992 (see p 428). Trade with other Commonwealth countries has declined in importance.

Geographical Distribution of Trade 1989

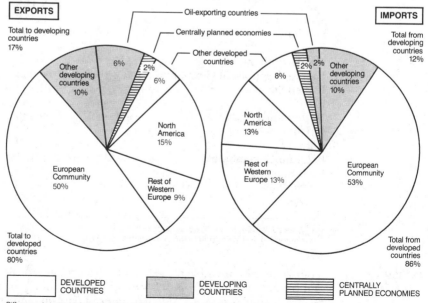

Differences between totals and the sums of their component parts are due to rounding.
Source: *Monthly Review of External Trade Statistics.*

European Community countries accounted for seven of the top ten export markets and for six of the ten leading suppliers of goods to Britain in 1989 (see Table 21.3). Since 1981 the United States has been Britain's largest single market and the Federal Republic of Germany Britain's largest single supplier. In 1989 the United States accounted for 13 per cent of Britain's exports while the Federal Republic of Germany supplied almost 17 per cent of Britain's imports. There have been a number of changes in the trends of Britain's overseas trade in recent years. The increase in wealth of the oil-exporting countries during the 1970s led to a sharp increase in their imports from all sources and by the early 1980s they were taking some 12 per cent of Britain's exports. There was then a fall in the capacity of these countries to absorb imports (partly because of a reduction in the price of oil) so that, by 1989, their share of Britain's exports had fallen to 6 per cent. In 1973 the oil-exporting countries supplied 10 per cent of Britain's imports but, with Britain achieving self-sufficiency in oil, the proportion had fallen below 2 per cent by 1989. Japan now accounts for nearly 6 per cent of Britain's imports, almost twice the proportion of ten years previously.

Table 21.3: Britain's Main Markets and Suppliers 1989[a]

	Value (£ million)	Share (per cent)
Main markets		
United States	12,099	12·9
Federal Republic of Germany	11,111	11·9
France	9,462	10·1
Netherlands	6,515	7·0
Belgium/Luxembourg	4,873	5·2
Irish Republic	4,715	5·0
Italy	4,631	4·9
Spain	3,138	3·4
Saudi Arabia	2,433	2·6
Sweden	2,350	2·5
Main suppliers		
Federal Republic of Germany	20,005	16·6
United States	12,889	10·7
France	10,785	8·9
Netherlands	9,586	7·9
Japan	7,108	5·9
Italy	6,702	5·5
Belgium/Luxembourg	5,701	4·7
Irish Republic	4,279	3·5
Switzerland	4,126	3·4
Sweden	3,748	3·1

Source: *Monthly Review of External Trade Statistics.*
[a]On an overseas trade statistics basis. Exports are f.o.b.; imports c.i.f.

INVISIBLE TRANSACTIONS   Transactions on invisible trade fall into three main groups: services (receipts and payments arising from services, as distinct from goods, supplied to and received from overseas residents); interest, profits and dividends (income arising from outward and inward investment, loans and other capital transactions); and transfers between Britain and other countries.

Invisible trade is of fundamental importance to Britain's economy; overseas earnings from invisibles amounted to £109,000 million in 1989—over one-half of Britain's total overseas earnings. Britain's share of world invisible trade is some 14 per cent and earnings are second only to those of the United States. In 1989 Britain's invisibles surplus was the largest in the world, according to figures from the Organisation for Economic Co-operation and Development (OECD). Services have been in surplus for over 20 years, while interest, profits and dividends have rarely been in deficit; transfers, however, have almost always been in deficit. For invisible trade as a whole, the deficit of general government is more than offset by the substantial surplus of the private sector (including public corporations), to give an overall surplus. General government transactions are relatively unimportant in either the services or the interest, profits and dividends accounts but they form the greater part of the transfers account. In 1989 the private sector had a surplus of over £11,000 million on invisible trade while government had a deficit of £7,000 million. The British Invisible Exports Council, which is financed almost entirely by contributions from the private sector, promotes measures to encourage invisible trade.

Table 21.4: Britain's Invisible Transactions 1989

£ million

	Credits	Debits	Balance
Private sector and public corporations	**104,057**	**92,830**	**11,227**
Services	29,655	23,197	6,458
of which: Sea transport	3,870	3,840	30
Civil aviation	3,758	4,261	−503
Travel	6,877	9,290	−2,413
Financial and other services	15,150	5,806	9,344
Interest, profits and dividends	72,652	67,583	5,069
Transfers	1,750	2,050	−300
General government	**4,540**	**11,553**	**−7,013**
Services	449	2,698	−2,249
Interest, profits and dividends	1,948	2,435	−487
Transfers	2,143	6,420	−4,277
National accounts statistical adjustment	500	—	500
Total invisible transactions	**109,098**	**104,384**	**4,714**

Source: *United Kingdom Balance of Payments 1990 Edition.*
Note: Differences between totals and the sums of their component parts are due to rounding.

Earnings from private sector services rose in value by almost 9 per cent in 1989 to £29,700 million; debits, at £23,200 million, were nearly 11 per cent higher than a year previously, but the surplus was about 2 per cent more than in 1988. The deficits on civil aviation and travel were outweighed by the surplus on financial and other services.

The surplus on private sector interest, profits and dividends was £5,100 million in 1989—somewhat lower than in 1988. Earnings on portfolio investment (investment in overseas securities) and on direct investment overseas remained high—at £7,000 million and £17,100 million respectively—reflecting in part the substantial volume of overseas investment following the abolition of exchange controls in 1979 and changes in the method of foreign currency lending by banks located in Britain.

The deficit on private sector transfers in 1989 was £300 million, while that on government transfers was £4,300 million, mainly as a result of contributions and subscriptions to the European Community and other international organisations, and bilateral aid.

COMMERCIAL POLICY

Britain remains committed to the open multilateral trading system and to the further liberalisation of world trade. To this end it has taken a leading part in the activities of such organisations as the General Agreement on Tariffs and Trade (GATT), the International Monetary Fund, the OECD and the United Nations Conference on Trade and Development, and has given full support to the new round of multilateral trade negotiations (see below). Since joining the European Community in 1973, Britain has conducted its external commercial policy through the Community. The Community's common customs tariff is, at a trade-weighted average of 2·5 per cent, at a low level, similar to the tariffs of most major non-Community industrialised countries.

Single European Market

Britain strongly supports the drive to complete the single European market by the end of 1992. The single market programme is designed to eliminate the remaining trade barriers within the Community and is expected to provide substantial opportunities for business and benefits for consumers.

The single European market programme was launched in 1985 and, by August 1990, 184 out of a proposed 282 measures had been adopted or agreed in principle. By March 1990, Britain had turned more single market measures into national legislation than any other member of the Community.

General Agreement on Tariffs and Trade

Tariffs and non-tariff barriers to trade have been considerably reduced in the seven rounds of multilateral trade negotiations completed since 1947 under the auspices of GATT, the most recent one completed being the Tokyo Round (1973–79). Britain participates in these negotiations as a member of the European Community.

The eighth round of GATT multilateral trade negotiations (the Uruguay Round) was launched in September 1986. The negotiations are expected to conclude in December 1990. The Uruguay Round is the most ambitious and wide-ranging round of trade negotiations ever, covering 15 areas. Its main concerns are to bring trade in agriculture and textiles fully within the GATT system; to achieve further reductions in tariff and non-tariff barriers; to extend GATT disciplines to the new areas of intellectual property, investment and services; and to strengthen the GATT system, so that it can deal more effectively with trade distortions and disputes.

European Community Agreements

Britain applies the common customs tariff to all countries neither belonging to, nor having any special arrangement with, the European Community. There is duty-free trade between those member states that joined before 1986. Portugal and Spain joined at the beginning of that year. Their trade with the rest of the Community is in a transitional stage: tariffs on industrial products are due to be phased out by the start of 1993, but those on certain agricultural products will be dismantled over a longer period.

The Community has reciprocal agreements with the European Free Trade Association (EFTA) countries (Austria, Finland, Iceland, Norway, Sweden and Switzerland), which allow for industrial products to be traded free of duty. Following the Luxembourg Declaration of 1984, the Community and EFTA are working towards closer economic co-operation. In 1989 Community and EFTA ministers agreed on further action to this end and to remove remaining non-tariff barriers to trade, with the aim of creating a European Economic Area encompassing the Community and EFTA.

The Community also has reciprocal preferential trading agreements with Cyprus, Israel, Malta and Turkey and non-reciprocal agreements with Algeria, Morocco, Tunisia, Egypt, Jordan, the Occupied Territories, Lebanon, Syria and Yugoslavia and, under the fourth Lomé Convention, a group of 68 African, Caribbean and Pacific developing countries. The Lomé Convention gives these countries free access (subject to certain safeguards) to the Community for industrial goods and most agricultural products.

Tariff preference is also given to developing countries (under the Generalised Scheme of Preferences), the Faroe Islands, and the overseas dependencies and territories of member states.

The Community also has economic co-operation agreements with a number of Latin American countries, with the People's Republic of China and with the six members of the Association of South East Asian Nations.

Following the establishment of diplomatic relations between the Central and Eastern European countries and the Community, the Community negotiated trade, commercial and economic co-operation agreements with Hungary, Czechoslovakia, Bulgaria, Poland and the Soviet Union. These agreements cover trade concessions and co-operation in areas such as energy, agriculture, transport and the environment. A similar agreement with Romania is expected to be concluded in late 1990. The next stage, as economic and political reform is consolidated, will be the development of closer association agreements with individual Eastern and Central European countries.

CONTROLS ON TRADE

Britain maintains few restrictions on its international trade. Most goods may be imported freely and only a narrow range of goods is subject to any sort of export control.

Import Controls

In accordance with its international obligations under GATT and to the European Community, Britain has progressively removed almost all quantitative import restrictions imposed on economic grounds. The few remaining quantitative restrictions mainly affect textile goods (in view of the rapid contraction of the domestic textile industry). They stem primarily from the Multi-Fibre Arrangement (MFA), under which there exists a series of agreements covering international trade in textiles, designed to balance the interests of both exporting and importing countries. The present MFA is due to expire in 1991 and it is intended that new arrangements should be governed by GATT.

A small number of quantitative restrictions are also maintained against non-GATT countries. Britain, in accordance with European Community directives, operates a ban on the import from North Korea and South Africa of certain iron and steel products and from South Africa of gold coins. Quantitative restrictions have been removed from imports of goods of Community origin. However, there are exceptions: Britain continues to apply internationally recognised restrictions on non-economic grounds on imports from all countries of products such as firearms, ammunition and nuclear materials. Other government departments apply similar non-economic restrictions on goods such as meat and poultry; animals, birds, bees, fish and plants and some of their derivatives; controlled drugs; explosives; fireworks; certain offensive weapons; certain citizens' band radios; indecent or obscene articles and products derived from endangered species.

Export Controls

The great majority of British exports are not subject to any government control or direction except for presentation and declaration to HM Customs and Excise on export for the purpose of collecting the overseas trade statistics. However, there are controls governing such exports as military equipment and advanced industrial goods of strategic significance as well as nuclear-related goods, steel exports to the United States, and certain chemicals and items controlled under the Middle Technology Control Regime.

Other controls include those for health certification purposes on certain animals, meat and fish exported to another member of the European Community; on endangered animal and plant species; on photographic and artistic material over a certain age and value; and on documents, manuscripts and archaeological items.

The Co-ordinating Committee for Multilateral Export Controls (COCOM),[1] of which Britain is a member, announced major changes in 1990 to the control of exports on certain goods and technologies that are enforced by its members. Many items have been removed from control, and significant relaxations have been achieved on the controls on telecommunications equipment, computers and machine tools. COCOM is continuing to seek to remove and relax its controls on other industrial goods and technologies in order that the burden placed upon exporters by these controls is reduced as much as possible. The Government wishes to assist in creating more favourable export conditions while maintaining an embargo on the most strategically sensitive equipment and technologies.

GOVERNMENT SERVICES

The Government assists exporters by creating conditions favourable to the export trade and by providing information and advice about opportunities for trade in other countries, services designed to help exporters and improve exporting practices, and credit insurance facilities.

Export Promotion Services

The British Overseas Trade Board (the export arm of the Department of Trade and Industry—DTI) guides and directs the Government's export promotion efforts, including the provision of export services. Among these services are the dissemination of export intelligence, assistance to British exporters in appointing agents and researching potential markets overseas, help at trade fairs and other promotional events overseas, and support for firms participating in trade missions. The Board comprises mainly representatives of commerce and industry with personal involvement in exporting, but also includes representatives of the DTI, the ECGD (Export Credits Guarantee Department) and the Foreign and Commonwealth Office. It operates under the general authority of the Secretary of State for Trade and Industry. In 1989–90 about £122 million was spent on support for exporters.

---

[1]COCOM is an informal body of countries of the North Atlantic Treaty Organisation except Iceland, plus Australia and Japan. It was established in 1950 to co-ordinate controls on East–West trade and on the export of strategic equipment, including atomic energy material, munitions and industrial goods of potential military use.

Following a review of the deployment of export resources in 1990, the Board identified priorities for official export promotion both in terms of geographical markets and of industrial sectors within them. The markets of Western Europe and of the Pacific Rim countries were designated as highest priority targets.

Exporters wanting assistance and advice can initially consult the export section of the regional offices of the DTI throughout Britain and, through these offices, the DTI's overseas trade divisions in London and the commercial posts of the British Diplomatic Service overseas. The Scottish Export Office (Industry Department for Scotland), the Welsh Office and the Industrial Development Board for Northern Ireland (Department of Economic Development) also act as the equivalent of the DTI's regional offices.

ECGD

ECGD is Britain's official export credit insurer. It is a government department responsible to the Secretary of State for Trade and Industry. In July 1990 the Government announced eventual executive agency status for ECGD's Project Group, which deals with capital goods exports on medium-term credit. The Insurance Services Group, which covers exports on short-term credit, will be separated and sold by tender in 1991.

ECGD provides credit insurance for about one-fifth of the country's export trade and insures exporters of both goods and services against non-payment by overseas buyers. The main risks covered include insolvency or protracted default of the buyer, governmental action which stops the British exporter receiving payment, new import restrictions, and war or civil disturbance in the buyer's country. Cover may commence from the date of shipment or from the date of contract (at higher premiums).

Under the Aid and Trade Provision, aid combined with export credits may be provided to developing countries to support projects which promise opportunities to British exporters. In April 1990 ECGD announced that its credit insurance scheme would be open to exporters seeking to invest in Eastern Europe.

BALANCE OF PAYMENTS

The balance-of-payments statistics record transactions between residents of Britain and non-residents. The transactions are classified into two groups:

Table 21.5: Britain's Balance of Payments 1985–89

£ million

	1985	1986	1987	1988	1989
Current account					
Visible trade balance	−3,345	−9,485	−11,223	−21,078	−23,840
Invisible transactions					
balance	6,095	9,462	7,042	5,927	4,714
Current balance	2,750	−24	−4,182	−15,151	−19,126
Financial account					
Transactions in assets					
and liabilities					
British external assets	−52,919	−92,888	−83,633	−56,244	−86,253
British external liabilities	45,677	84,375	84,103	63,258	90,255
Balancing item	4,491	8,536	3,713	8,136	15,124

Source: *United Kingdom Balance of Payments 1990 Edition.*
Note: Differences between totals and the sums of their component parts are due to rounding.

current account (visibles and invisibles) and transactions in assets and liabilities. The balance on current account shows whether Britain has had a surplus of income over expenditure.

Traditionally Britain has had a deficit on visible trade and a surplus on trade in invisibles. In 1988 and 1989 the deficit on visible trade exceeded £20,000 million. The increase in the degree of integration in the international economy has enhanced differences in the pattern of investment and savings opportunities. With the British economy expanding rapidly, there has been a marked increase in investment unmatched by a corresponding rise in savings; Britain has thus been importing capital. Since the balance of payments must balance, a deficit on current account has been the inevitable result. The deficit has arisen from private sector behaviour; in the same way, it is likely to fall as the gap between private sector investment and savings narrows.

The surplus on invisibles fell from £5,900 million in 1988 to £4,700 million in 1989. The surplus on services rose while that on interest, profits and dividends fell. The deficit on transfers rose.

Capital Flows

Britain has no exchange controls; residents are free to acquire foreign currency for any purpose, including direct and portfolio investment overseas. There are also no controls on the lending of sterling abroad and non-residents may freely acquire sterling for any purpose. Gold may be freely bought and sold. The abolition of exchange controls in 1979 means that Britain meets its full obligations on capital movements under the OECD code on capital movements and under European Community directives. The Government welcomes both outward and inward investment. Outward investment helps to develop markets for British exports, while providing earnings in the form of interest, profits and dividends. Inward investment creates employment directly; introduces new technology, products, management styles and attitudes; and provides an opportunity to increase exports or substitute imports. Inward investment is particularly encouraged by the DTI's Invest in Britain Bureau.

Inward direct investment almost doubled in 1989 compared with 1988, to a record £18,300 million. In 1989 direct investment overseas by British residents was £19,400 million. Outward portfolio investment was £36,800 million. The inflow of direct and portfolio investment into Britain amounted to £29,200 million. An analysis of transactions in Britain's external assets and liabilities is given in Table 21.6.

External Assets and Liabilities

At the end of 1989 Britain's identified external assets exceeded identified external liabilities by £113,000 million; only Japan had higher net external assets. Net assets of the private sector and public corporations amounted to £103,000 million and those of general government to £10,000 million.[2]

Direct investment assets overseas of British residents (investment in branches, subsidiaries and associated companies) totalled £140,000 million at the end of 1989 and portfolio investment £221,000 million. At the end of 1987 (the latest year for which data are available) over 84 per cent of direct investment was in developed countries, with over 35 per cent in the United States and nearly 28 per cent in the European Community. In terms of industries, manufacturing accounted for 35 per cent of direct investment holdings. By type of company, oil companies were responsible for 26 per cent, insurance companies for 7 per cent and banks for 4 per cent.

---

[2]The significance of any inventory of Britain's aggregate external assets and liabilities is limited because a variety of claims and obligations are included that are very dissimilar in kind, in degree of liquidity and in method of valuation.

Table 21.6: Summary of Transactions in External Assets[a] and Liabilities[b] 1987–89

£ million

	1987	1988	1989
Overseas direct investment in Britain	8,681	9,218	18,344
Overseas portfolio investment in Britain	17,710	13,220	10,860
British direct investment overseas	−19,198	−20,685	−19,365
British portfolio investment overseas	3,323	−9,870	−36,781
Borrowing from overseas	56,139	39,916	59,629
Deposits and lending overseas	−54,949	−22,037	−34,604
Official reserves[a]	−12,012	−2,761	5,439
Other external liabilities of general government	1,572	904	1,422
Other external assets of central government	−796	−891	−942
Total	469	7,015	4,002

Source: *United Kingdom Balance of Payments 1990 Edition.*
[a]Increase − / decrease +.
[b]Increase + / decrease −.
Note: Differences between totals and the sums of their component parts are due to rounding.

Direct investment in Britain by overseas residents amounted to £87,000 million at the end of 1989 and portfolio investment to £100,000 million. At the end of 1987 investment from developed countries accounted for 95 per cent of overseas direct investment in Britain: 46 per cent originated in the United States and 26 per cent in the European Community. A total of 36 per cent was in manufacturing. Oil companies were responsible for 29 per cent, insurance companies for 4 per cent and banks for 10 per cent.

Another type of overseas transaction is company cross-border acquisitions and mergers. In 1989 overseas acquisitions and mergers less disposals carried out by British companies were valued at £20,300 million, while the corresponding figure for operations in Britain by overseas companies was £8,300 million. The United States accounted for just over 80 per cent of the value of acquisitions and mergers by British companies. The United States accounted for 43 per cent of the value of acquisitions and mergers by overseas companies and the European Community for 35 per cent.

22 Promotion of Science and Technology

Britain has for centuries been in the forefront of innovation in science and technology, and its record of achievement in relation to the size of its population is in many respects unsurpassed. Recent important work includes that of Professor Michael Green on superstring theories, which may lead to an understanding of the ultimate nature of matter, and Professor Alec Jeffreys's invention in 1985 of genetic fingerprinting. The first combined heart, lungs and liver transplant was carried out at Papworth Hospital, Cambridge, in 1986. Agricultural research in Britain has produced the first environmentally benign microbial pesticides.

Nobel prizes for science have been won by 70 British citizens, a number exceeded only by the United States, and Table 22.1 lists British laureates (excluding those in economic sciences) since 1970.

Research and Development Expenditure

International comparisons of expenditure on research and development (R & D) are based on definitions agreed by the Organisation for Economic Co-operation and Development. According to these, total expenditure in Britain on scientific research and development in 1988 was about £10,300 million, 2·2 per cent of gross domestic product. Some 51 per cent of this was provided by industry and 37 per cent by government. Significant contributions were also made by overseas sources, private endowments, trusts and charities.

The pattern of research activity is as diverse as the pattern of research funding. Government finance for R & D goes to its own research establishments, to institutions of higher education and to private industry. In many cases nationalised and private-sector industries finance their own research and run their own laboratories. Industry also funds university research and spends money on contracts to government establishments. Charities may have their own laboratories in addition to offering research grants for outside work.

Expenditure in Industry

According to a sample survey, expenditure on R & D in industry in 1988 amounted to £6,861 million, of which £1,133 million came from government, £830 million from overseas and the remaining £4,898 million mainly from industry's own funds. The most important areas of expenditure were electronics (£2,064 million), chemicals (£1,574 million) and aerospace (£814 million).

Expenditure by Government

Government figures for its R & D expenditure differ somewhat from those used in international comparisons and those resulting from industrial surveys because they include expenditure on social science and the humanities, and also expenditure overseas. In addition, survey methods tend to produce an understatement of government funding of research in industry. Total government R & D expenditure in 1988–89 was some £4,900

Table 22.1: Recent British Winners of Nobel Prizes for Science

	Year of award	Category	Subject
Sir Bernard Katz	1970	Physiology or Medicine (jointly)	The role of neural transmitter substances
Professor Dennis Gabor	1971	Physics	Invention of holography
Professor Rodney Porter	1972	Physiology or Medicine (jointly)	Discoveries concerning the chemical structure of antibodies
Professor Brian Josephson	1973	Physics	Work on superconductivity
Professor Nikolaas Tinbergen	1973	Physiology or Medicine (jointly)	The organisation of individual and social behaviour patterns
Professor Sir Geoffrey Wilkinson	1973	Chemistry (jointly)	Work on organometallic compounds
Sir Martin Ryle and Professor Anthony Hewish	1974	Physics	Development of new types of radio telesocopes
Sir Nevill Mott	1977	Physics (jointly)	Theoretical investigations of the electronic structure of magnetic systems
Dr Peter Mitchell	1978	Chemistry	Contributions to the understanding of biological energy transfer
Sir Godfrey Hounsfield	1979	Physiology or Medicine (jointly)	Computer-assisted assembly of X-ray information in three dimensions
Dr Frederick Sanger	1980	Chemistry (jointly)	Determination of base sequences in nucleic acids
Sir Aaron Klug	1982	Chemistry	Work on the structure of viruses and genetic material in cells
Sir John Vane	1982	Physiology or Medicine (jointly)	Clarification of the pathways of prostaglandin metabolism in the body
Dr César Milstein	1984	Physiology or Medicine (jointly)	Production of monoclonal antibodies
Sir James Black	1988	Physiology or Medicine (jointly)	Discovery of therapeutic drugs, especially for heart disease and stomach ulcers

million, the largest departmental budget being that of the Ministry of Defence. The main civil departments involved are the Department of Education and Science, which supports the research councils and the universities (see pp 439 and 441); the Department of Trade and Industry (see p 437); the Department of Energy (see p 440); and the Ministry of Agriculture, Fisheries and Food (see p 441).

Government and Scientific Research

The main objectives of the Government's expenditure on research and development are to advance scientific knowledge and develop technology in Britain as well as to support its own activities. Generally the Government seeks to enhance the contribution of both public and private research and development expenditure to improving the efficiency and competitiveness of the British economy. Its view is that government should finance the pursuit of basic scientific knowledge, but that the commercial development of scientific principles should mainly be the task of industry.

Science and technology policy is decided by collective ministerial consideration under the leadership of the Prime Minister. The Government is advised by the Chief Scientific Adviser, Cabinet Office, and by an independent Advisory Council on Science and Technology (ACOST). ACOST is composed of industrialists and scientists covering all areas of science and technology and appointed by the Prime Minister for their personal eminence in their field. In addition, there are two ex officio members, the chairman of the Advisory Board for the Research Councils (ABRC) and the chairman of the Universities Funding Council and the Innovation Advisory Board. The remit of ACOST covers defence as well as civil research, and both academic science and industrial research and development. It advises on national priorities in science and technology, on the application of science and technology, on the co-ordination of government policy and on Britain's participation in international scientific projects.

Responsibility for basic civil science rests with the Secretary of State for Education and Science, who is advised by the ABRC; that for technology rests mainly with the Secretary of State for Trade and Industry. Other departments with a substantial involvement in science and technology have a departmental advisory body; these bodies work closely with ACOST. A committee of Departmental Chief Scientists, under the chairmanship of the Chief Scientific Adviser, is responsible for co-ordination among departments. A Science and Technology Assessment Office, responsible to the Chief Scientific Adviser, evaluates the impact of government-funded research on the efficiency and competitiveness of the economy. The Centre for Exploitation of Science and Technology (CEST) was set up in 1988. By studying the evolution of markets it aims to identify the science and technologies needed to improve competitive performance in particular industries. CEST is supported by industry and by the Government.

The Department of Trade and Industry

Although most industrial research and development is financed by industry itself, the Department of Trade and Industry (DTI) provides support where there is a sound case for doing so. Following a review in 1988, the Government decided that, in general, near-market R & D should not be supported. Instead, there should be greater emphasis on collaborative programmes of pre-competitive research between companies and on encouraging collaboration between companies and higher education institutions. Technology transfer should also be given greater emphasis. The DTI spent £316 million on R & D in 1988–89, on general industrial innovation, aeronautics, space (see p 449) and its own research establishments; and £92 million on technology transfer and related activities.

General Industrial Innovation

There are four main schemes of collaborative R & D: LINK, EUREKA (see p 448), Advanced Technology Programmes and general industrial collaborative projects. They complement the European Community R & D programmes (see p 448).

The LINK scheme aims at encouraging firms to work jointly with higher education institutions on pre-competitive research relevant to industrial needs. By July 1990, 24 LINK programmes had been approved, involving total government funding of some £155 million, and mainly falling under the general headings of biotechnology, advanced materials, advanced manufacturing and electronics.

Advanced Technology Programmes encourage pre-competitive research in new technologies. Eleven programmes had been approved by August 1990, in high-temperature superconductivity, marine exploitation and several aspects of electronics and information technology.

General industrial collaborative projects are those projects supported by the DTI which do not fall under the other collaborative schemes. They include industry-led projects undertaken by research associations, non-nuclear laboratories of the United Kingdom Atomic Energy Authority (see p 440) and other government research establishments. Particular emphasis is given to encouraging the participation of small and medium-sized enterprises in all these programmes.

Following the 1988 policy review, new single-company projects are not normally supported. However, the Small Firms Merit Award for Research and Technology (SMART), a competitive scheme designed to support innovation by small companies, is an exception. In the 1989 competition 150 awards were made.

Aeronautics

In aeronautics the DTI funds programmes of research, and also the demonstration of technology prior to its commitment to specific products. Nearly half of the work supported is in industry and in universities, and half in Ministry of Defence establishments, where DTI funding allows the maximum civil benefit to be derived. A significant proportion of DTI support is now being spent on the European Wind Tunnel. Launch Aid is a form of assistance provided under the Civil Aviation Act 1982 for specific development projects in the aerospace industry.

Research Establishments

The DTI has four research establishments, which accounted for £36 million of its R & D expenditure in 1988–89. Most of their work serves to underpin regulatory, statutory and policy work. In addition, the DTI contributes directly to programmes under the various collaborative schemes. The laboratories are also involved in a variety of international activities. They provide technological services to industry which are not available commercially, run a number of industrial 'clubs' and also undertake a limited amount of research sponsored by industry.

The Laboratory of the Government Chemist provides government with a comprehensive service in analytical chemistry and develops and maintains a capability which underpins sound chemical measurement in Britain as part of the National Measurement System (see below). The National Engineering Laboratory carries out R & D in a wide range of engineering and related disciplines and maintains the British standards of flow measurement, of especial importance in the oil and gas industries. The National Physical Laboratory is Britain's national standards laboratory and the focus of the National Measurement System; in addition to developing and disseminating standards of measurement, it undertakes research on engineering materials and information technology. The Warren Spring Laboratory is devoted to environmental research, including the impact of process technology. The laboratories support industrial innovation through sponsored research and industrial 'club' projects.

The Warren Spring Laboratory and the Laboratory of the Government Chemist are now executive agencies within the public sector. The Government plans agency status for the other two and, in the long term, to privatise the National Engineering Laboratory, where roughly three-quarters of the work is for the benefit of industry.

Technology Transfer

The DTI has introduced several programmes specifically to encourage technology transfer. They promote the use of best-practice techniques and modern technology as well as exploiting the most recent research. Examples are the 'Open Systems' information technology standards programme and the 'Materials Matter' programme, concerned with modern materials and associated manufacturing methods. Each programme comprises an integrated package of activities which may include seminars, conferences and demonstration activities, as well as the production of case study material and other practical literature.

There are also general technology transfer programmes not related to specific technology areas. For example, the foundation of Regional Technology Centres has been supported, in association with the Department of Education and Science and the Training Agency, to provide a technology transfer and training focus for small and medium-sized enterprises and to help promote the expertise of higher education institutions.

The DTI maintains close contact with the British Technology Group, a self-financing public organisation which negotiates patent protection and commercial licensing for scientific and technological inventions, especially those coming from universities and other public-sector research organisations.

The Department of Education and Science

The Department of Education and Science discharges its responsibilities for basic and applied civil science mainly through the five research councils (see p 441), to which it allocates funds from its science budget. This is £897 million in 1990–91. The councils, along with their 1988–89 R & D expenditure figures, are: the Science and Engineering Research Council (£340 million), the Medical Research Council (£145 million), the Natural Environment Research Council (£82 million), the Agricultural and Food Research Council (£55 million) and the Economic and Social Research Council (£23 million). Science budget grants are also made to the Royal Society and the Fellowship of Engineering for science policy studies commissioned by the Advisory Board for the Research Councils and to the Centre for Exploitation of Science and Technology (see p 437). The allocations provide support for research in the form of grants and contracts to universities, polytechnics, research units and other establishments of the research councils; postgraduate support; and subscriptions to international scientific organisations. In addition, the Department funds the Computer Board for Universities and Research Councils, which helps to provide centrally managed computer services for the support of research in universities.

The Department is also responsible for some aspects of international scientific relations and helps to co-ordinate government policy regarding scientific and technical information. Together with the Scottish Education Department and the departments concerned with training, it funds various schemes for training both students and those working in industry in the latest technology. For example, under the Professional, Industrial and Commercial Updating (PICKUP) initiative, a network of 13 Regional Technology Centres has been established since 1987, where scientists from higher education institutions spend some of their time training employees of private sector companies in recent developments in their fields. The Department is also encouraging, through a variety of initiatives, the teaching in schools of technical and scientific subjects, such as craft, design and technology; and computing.

The Department is also the main source of funding for the universities, whose individual allocations are determined by the Universities Funding Council (see p 445). Until 1990 each university decided on the division of its resources between teaching and research. The overall proportion committed to research was thought to be about 40 per cent. Research funding is now identified separately by the Council.

The Advisory Board for the Research Councils

The Advisory Board for the Research Councils advises the Secretary of State on civil science, particularly with regard to the research council system and its links with higher education through the support of postgraduate students; the proper balance between national and international scientific activities; the resource needs of the research councils and other bodies; and the allocation of the science budget between them.

It promotes effective collaboration between the five research councils in areas of scientific overlap, and administratively. It also promotes close liaison between the councils and industrial and other users of their research, including government departments, and between them and the higher education funding councils. The Board's membership includes the heads of the research councils and senior scientists from industry and the academic world.

The Ministry of Defence

The expenditure of the Ministry of Defence (MoD) on research and development in 1988–89 was some £2,000 million. About £390 million of this was medium- and long-term applied research relevant to known military needs, much of it carried out in the MoD's Defence Research Establishments. Some £140 million of this research was carried out under contract in industry and the academic sector. The Government is committed to achieving a gradual reduction in real terms in spending on defence research and development in future years. An increasing emphasis is placed on research funded jointly with industry, and initiatives have also been taken to encourage 'spin-off' from defence technology to the civil market.

Examples of technological innovations at research establishments include research carried out at the Royal Aerospace Establishment's Propulsion Department to reduce jet engine exhaust noise, which has led to changes in Rolls-Royce's new civil engines; the pioneering work of the Royal Signals and Radar Establishment on liquid crystal displays, now widely used in the civil sector; its current development of a new, simpler type of 'supercomputer'; and the development of infra-red detectors now widely used by fire services. The Admiralty Research Establishment has, together with Plessey (now part of GEC), developed a Multi-function Electronically Scanned Adaptive Radar (MESAR), which can perform the functions of several different radars in one system.

The Government announced in 1989 that the four principal non-nuclear research establishments were to be set up as a separate organisation, with the intention that this should become an executive agency by spring 1991.

The major part of MoD R & D expenditure (more than £1,700 million in 1988–89) is on the development of individual items of equipment. Most of this takes place in industry, and represents the bulk of government expenditure on R & D in industry.

Other Government Departments

The Department of Energy funds research in support of offshore oil and gas technology, energy efficiency and the development and exploitation of British renewable energy sources. The major part of its R & D is on nuclear energy (£159 million in 1988–89), most of which is carried out by the United Kingdom Atomic Energy Authority (UKAEA), a public corporation that performs a large amount of contract research, under the name AEA Technology, in both nuclear and non-nuclear fields, and manages a variety of research 'clubs'.

The Ministry of Agriculture, Fisheries and Food co-ordinates its research programme with the Department of Agriculture and Fisheries for Scotland, the Department of Agriculture for Northern Ireland and the Agricultural and Food Research Council (see p 444). Overall, the Ministry's research has three main objectives: to protect the consumer and the environment; to assist in the formulation and assessment of policy; and to underpin the applied R & D done by the agricultural industry.

Ministry R & D includes alternative enterprises and land use; animal welfare; enhancement and conservation of the environment; micro-organisms in food; the safety assessment of chemicals in food and objective methods of determining food quality; and assessment and conservation of fish stocks. As part of the Government's re-ordering of its research priorities, support is being withdrawn from R & D which has the primary objective of developing commercial products or processes. Expenditure in 1988–89 was £119 million, about half of which was in the Ministry's own establishments. Most of the rest was in contracts to the Agricultural and Food Research Council.

The Department of the Environment funds research in seven policy areas: environmental protection, including radioactive substances; water; countryside; planning and inner cities; local government; housing; and building and construction. The largest individual sub-programme is on the safe disposal of radioactive waste. Other environmental protection sub-programmes cover research on air quality, noise, toxic substances, con-taminated land and controlled waste management. An area of research of increasing importance is that of pollution-related climate change.

The Department of Health manages health-related R & D programmes directly and also funds non-departmental bodies which carry out research in support of their statutory duties. The National Biological Standards Board, through the National Institute for Biological Standards and Control, is responsible for preparing, holding and distributing standard preparations; the control testing of biological substances; and associated research and development.

The National Computing Centre promotes best practice in software engineering in industry and the Central Computer and Telecommunications Agency, part of HM Treasury, encourages the establishment of standards of computer compatibility and the best use of information technology in the public sector.

THE RESEARCH COUNCILS

Each of the four research councils engaged in scientific research is an autonomous body established under Royal Charter, with membership drawn from the universities, professions, industry and the Government. They conduct research through their own establishments and by supporting selected research, study and training in universities and other higher education establishments. In addition to funding from the Department of Education and Science (see p 439), they also receive income for research commissioned by departments under the customer–contractor principle and from the private sector. Income from commissioned research is particularly important for the Agricultural and Food Research Council and the Natural Environment Research Council.

The rights and responsibility for the commercial exploitation of research carried out with the support of research council grants rest with the institution receiving the grant, subject to the existence of procedures agreed with the sponsoring research council. Universities and research institutes may make use of the expertise of the British Technology Group (see p 439) to patent and license their inventions, but are not obliged to do so.

Science and Engineering Research Council

The Science and Engineering Research Council (SERC) is responsible for the support of research and postgraduate training in pure and applied science (including engineering) outside the areas of agriculture, medicine and the environment. Expenditure is divided among contributions to international organisations (£90 million in 1988–89, see p 449); research grants, chiefly to higher education institutions (£121 million); and the Council's own establishments (£96 million). The SERC also funds postgraduate training (£57 million). The Council has initiated plans for Interdisciplinary Research Centres in the fields of high-temperature superconductivity, engineering design, surface science, molecular sciences, semiconductor materials, high performance materials, polymer science and technology, process simulation integration and control, and optical and laser related science and technology. It encourages collaboration between higher education and industry, partly by sponsoring co-ordinated research programmes in areas of special industrial concern.

The SERC maintains four research establishments: the Rutherford Appleton Laboratory at Chilton (Oxfordshire), the Daresbury Laboratory at Warrington (Cheshire), the Royal Greenwich Observatory at Cambridge and the Royal Observatory, Edinburgh. They are centres of specialised research and provide experimental facilities beyond the resources of individual academic institutions, and also undertake contract research.

SERC research support is organised under four boards, covering astronomy and planetary science (£63 million in 1988–89); nuclear physics (£83 million); science (£100 million); and engineering (£96 million). In recent years the SERC's policy has been to transfer funds from the first two of these, representing largely 'big' science and basic research, to the second two, representing largely strategic research on a smaller scale.

Nuclear Physics

The Nuclear Physics Board supports particle physics and nuclear structure physics. The Rutherford Appleton Laboratory co-ordinates Britain's experimental particle physics research programme and links university researchers with overseas centres such as CERN (see p 449). The nuclear structure physics programme is concentrated largely at Daresbury, where the 20-million volt tandem accelerator is being made increasingly powerful.

Astronomy and Planetary Science

The Astronomy and Planetary Science Board supports space science including contributions to international programmes (see p 449), ground-based astronomy and geophysics. In optical astronomy the SERC is a principal partner in the international observatory on the island of La Palma in the Canary Islands. This contains four telescopes, including the 4·2-m William Herschel. Opened in 1987, it is the third largest single-mirror optical telescope in the world. On Mauna Kea, Hawaii, the SERC has a 3·8-m infra-red telescope, the largest telescope in the world designed specifically for infra-red observations, and the 15-m James Clerk Maxwell radio telescope (built in collaboration with the Netherlands and Canada).

Science

The Science Board supports academic research in chemistry, mainstream physics, mathematics, the biological sciences and science-based archaeology. Its main priority is the provision of research grants to universities and polytechnics. About 50 per cent of grants are awarded as part of co-ordinated programmes of interdisciplinary strategic research falling within the areas of materials; molecular sciences; and mathematics, computational and cognitive science. They may be part of a LINK programme (see p 437) or associated with an Interdisciplinary Research Centre. The Daresbury Laboratory operates a synchrotron radiation facility which provides high-intensity electromagnetic radiation used in a wide range of experiments in protein crystallography, surface physics, chemical structure and materials science. Other special facilities include, at the Rutherford Appleton Laboratory, the spallation neutron source (called 'ISIS'), the world's leading pulsed neutron facility; and a high-power laser facility which is used to study plasmas.

Engineering

The Engineering Board, whose funding has increased greatly in recent years, supports strategic research underpinned by work in the core sciences. It tries to identify areas of promising national strategic importance and initiates co-ordinated programmes of research which will generate knowledge of specific benefit to British industry and sustain the introduction of advanced technology. Some of the areas that have been identified for priority action are training, information technology in engineering, computer software research, materials research, biotechnology (where a special directorate funded jointly with the Science Board is in operation) and supercomputing in engineering. The Teaching Company scheme is jointly sponsored by the SERC and the DTI, with contributions from the Northern Ireland Department of Economic Development and the Economic and Social Research Council. The scheme supports some 350 collaborative ventures between academic engineering departments and industrial companies to improve their manufacturing and management methods and performance.

Medical Research Council

The Medical Research Council (MRC) is the main government agency for the support of biomedical research, both at its own centres and units, which together account for about three-quarters of its budget, and by means of grants to research workers at higher education institutions and hospitals. Its major research establishments are the National Institute for Medical Research at Mill Hill, London; the Clinical Research Centre at Northwick Park Hospital, London; and the Laboratory of Molecular Biology at Cambridge. The Council also has more than 50 other research units, located in universities and medical schools throughout Britain. Two Inter-disciplinary Research Centres are being set up, in toxicology and molecular medicine, and two more are planned, in cell biology and protein engineering.

The MRC's scientists and doctors have pioneered developments in molecular biology, therapeutic clinical trials, applied psychology, and methods of imaging the body such as magnetic resonance and ultrasound. The Council's larger research programmes include those into psychiatric and neurological (including Alzheimer's) disease, heart and respiratory ailments, infectious diseases, tropical medicine, and antenatal screening for cystic fibrosis and muscular dystrophy. Major new projects are specially funded work on all aspects of AIDS; research on vaccines against meningitis and whooping cough; and the mapping of the human genome, the complete sequence of genes in a human cell. Recent achievements include the determination, at the Virology Unit in Glasgow and the Laboratory of Molecular Biology, of the DNA sequences of three of the disease-causing herpes viruses.

The Council's policy is to foster collaboration between its establishments and industry in order to promote the transfer of industrially relevant skills and technologies, the exploitation of Council discoveries, and the development of new products in the health care field. A Centre for Collaborative Research at Mill Hill provides a consultancy service for the analysis of problems; acts as an information source for channelling advice to industrial, academic and clinical partners; and also undertakes collaborative projects with industry and the universities.

Natural Environment Research Council

The Natural Environment Research Council (NERC) aims at advancing understanding of the natural processes of the planet and of the impact of human activities through research in the physical and biological sciences at its own institutes, at grant-aided institutions and in universities and polytechnics. The NERC's three science directorates cover terrestrial and freshwater, earth, and marine and atmospheric sciences. The NERC supports 11 institutes, three grant-aided associations and four units in universities. The institutes include the British Antarctic Survey, the British Geological Survey, the Institute of Terrestrial Ecology and the Institute of Oceanographic Sciences Deacon Laboratory in Surrey. The associations include the Scottish Marine Biological Association. The NERC is taking the lead in establishing an Interdisciplinary Research Centre in population biology at Imperial College, Silwood Park, Berkshire.

About 70 per cent of the NERC's funds are provided from the science budget and about 30 per cent by research commissioned by public authorities and industry in Britain and overseas.

Examples of work include GLORIA, a unique side-scan sonar developed by geophysicists, which is being used to map areas of the ocean floor around the world; the North Sea Project to develop a prognostic water quality model; and a study to discover how carbon dioxide is absorbed by the oceans and buried in the sea-floor sediments, helping to balance the 'greenhouse effect'. British Antarctic Survey scientists were the first to identify the hole in the ozone layer above Antarctica.

Applied projects in progress overseas include those on biological pest control, regeneration of tropical hardwoods and drip irrigation techniques for tropical crops. The NERC also offers specialist data services providing information on various subjects, including biology and ecology, from satellite and aircraft surveys and its research vessels, as well as through its various centres and units in Britain.

Agricultural and Food Research Council

The Agricultural and Food Research Council (AFRC) supports research underpinning agriculture, food and the non-medical biologically based industries, having regard to social needs and environmental consequences. Work is carried out at the seven AFRC institutes (Animal Health, Animal Physiology and Genetics, Arable Crops, Engineering, Food, Grassland and Environmental Research, Plant Science), at the British Society for Horticultural Research and in universities and polytechnics. It is co-ordinated with that of the Scottish Agricultural Research Institutes, funded by the Department of Agriculture and Fisheries for Scotland. The Council plans to double its support for higher education institutions over the next five years to 30 per cent of its core science budget funding.

The AFRC at present draws approximately 55 per cent of its funding from the science budget, about a third from the Ministry of Agriculture, Fisheries and Food (MAFF) for commissioned research, and an increasing proportion from industry. In the light of a decline in commissioned research from the MAFF (see p 441), the Council aims at raising 25 per cent of its institute funding from commercial and other sources by 1994–95.

Recent achievements include identification of the molecular genetics of the production in wheat grains of the proteins which determine bread-making qualities; use of anti-sense technology to identify gene expression during plant development; exploitation of the bacterium *Streptomyces coelicolar* for the industrial production of new antibiotics; demonstration of the transmissibility of bovine spongiform encephalopathy and its link with scrapie in sheep; development of new ways of genetically engineering lactic acid bacteria, including a prototype food grade marker system based on lactose genes; design of rapid methods of detecting food poisoning organisms; and the demonstration in developmental genetics that male and female genomes are not functionally equivalent.

UNIVERSITY RESEARCH

About half the research carried out in universities is financed from resources allocated by the Universities Funding Council. These funds contribute to the cost of academic staff—who teach as well as carry out research—and provide for the research infrastructure in the form of support staff, administration, equipment and accommodation.

Scientific research in the universities and other institutions of higher education is also supported through the research councils, in two ways. First, between a quarter and a third of postgraduate students in science and technology receive maintenance awards from the research councils. Secondly, grants and contracts are given to the universities and other institutions by the research councils for specified projects, particularly in new or developing areas of research.

The other main channels of support for scientific research in the universities are various government departments, the Royal Society, industry and the independent foundations. Universities are encouraged to recover the full cost of research from these foundations. They are also encouraged to direct their resources into those areas where they have existing research strength or where they see a prospect of establishing strong groups in new and promising spheres of science and technology.

Increasingly close relationships are being fostered between the universities, industry and the Government in numerous joint projects. British universities' earnings from industry and other outside agencies are rising rapidly and amounted to some £630 million in 1988–89. The money comes from research contracts and royalties on the exploitation of university innovations. Many universities now operate industrial liaison service units, which are linked together by university directors of industrial liaison.

Technological breakthroughs in the university sector in the 1980s included optoelectronic devices for future super-fast optical computers at Heriot-Watt University, Edinburgh, and techniques for the active cancellation of sound and other vibrations (whereby unwanted noise is cancelled out by generating a noise which interferes destructively with it) pioneered at the universities of Cambridge and Essex. Important research on optical fibres is being carried out at Southampton, Exeter and Essex universities; on liquid crystal displays at Hull and Manchester; and on pharmaceutical products and biotechnology at Strathclyde.

Science Parks

Science parks provide both existing and new businesses using high technology with an environment in which they have easy access to the research expertise of higher education institutions. By January 1990 there were 38 such parks in operation at or near universities and similar organisations, with a further 20 under construction or planned. One of the first to be established (in 1972), and still the largest, is the Cambridge Science Park, where some 80 companies occupy most of a 53-hectare (130-acre) site, with room for further companies.

Britain's science parks now provide accommodation for around 900 companies, employing over 12,000 people. They range from subsidiaries of large corporations, such as the British Oxygen Company, Olivetti and British Petroleum, to a wide variety of new and recently formed businesses. A survey conducted for the United Kingdom Science Park Association showed that companies on parks tended to exhibit high growth and low failure rates. The main areas in which science park companies are involved are computing, electronics, instrumentation, robotics, electrical engineering, chemicals and biotechnology, with the emphasis on research, design, development, consultancy, testing and training activities rather than large-scale manufacturing.

OTHER RESEARCH ORGANISATIONS
Charitable Foundations

Charitable foundations sponsoring research in Britain include the Cancer Research Campaign, the Chester Beatty Institute for Cancer Research, the Ciba Foundation, the Imperial Cancer Research Fund, the Institute for Cancer Research, the Leverhulme Foundation, the Nuffield Foundation, the Wellcome Trust and the Wolfson Foundation. In 1989 the largest spenders on medical research were the Imperial Cancer Research Fund at £42 million and the Wellcome Trust at £40 million.

Industrial Research Organisations

The Association of Independent Research and Technology Organisations links 43 such institutions, which between them employ about 9,400 people and had a turnover of about £300 million in 1989. These are limited companies undertaking research contracts and providing consultancy and training services to 20,000 companies in particular branches of industry. In addition to payment for this work, many are supported by membership fees from firms in their sectors and by government grants.

The British Technology Group (see p 439) also finances new technology projects, as do a number of venture capital companies.

Professional Institutions

There are numerous technical institutions and professional associations many of which promote their own disciplines or are interested in the education and professional well-being of their members. The Council of Science and Technology Institutes has seven member institutes representing biology, chemical engineering, chemistry, food science and technology geology, hospital physics and physics.

The Engineering Council, established in 1981, promotes the study of all types of engineering in schools and other organisations, in co-operation with its 300 industrial affiliates, including large private sector companies and government departments. Together with 45 professional engineering institutions, the Council accredits courses in higher education institutions. I also maintains a register of about 285,000 engineers and technicians with varying levels of qualifications. The Engineering Council advises the Government on a range of academic, industrial and professional issues.

The national academy of engineering in Britain is the Fellowship of Engineering, set up in 1976, which promotes the discipline and advises the Government on related policy issues. Its membership consists of distinguished engineers.

The Learned Societies

More than 300 learned societies in Britain play an important part in the promotion of science and technology through meetings, publications and sponsorship.

Royal Society

The most prestigious of the learned societies is the Royal Society, or, more fully, the Royal Society of London for Improving Natural Knowledge founded in 1660, which is equivalent to national academies of science in other countries. It is the oldest such academy in the world to have enjoyed continuous existence. The Society has over 1,000 Fellows, many of whom serve on the governmental advisory councils and committees concerned with research. It administers a grant-in-aid from the Department of Education and Science (£14 million in 1990–91) which represents some 75 per cent of its annual expenditure. The remainder is derived from private funds.

The Royal Society encourages scientific research and its application through a programme of meetings and lectures, its publications, and through the award of grants, fellowships and other funding, 214 appointments being administered in 1990. It recognises scientific and technological achievements through election to the Fellowship and the award of medals and endowed lectureships. As the national academy of sciences, it promotes international scientific relations, representing Britain in a number of international non-governmental organisations and is involved in a variety of international scientific programmes. It also facilitates collaborative projects and the exchange of scientists through bilateral agreements with academies and research councils throughout the world. It provides independent advice on scientific matters, notably to government, and represents and supports the scientific community as a whole. The Society is increasingly active in promoting science understanding and awareness in the public, and also science education. It supports research into the history of science.

Other Societies

In Scotland, the Royal Society of Edinburgh, established in 1783, promotes science through scholarships, the organisation of meetings and symposia, the publication of journals and the award of prizes. The Society also administers various fellowship schemes for post-doctoral research workers.

Three other major institutions publicise scientific developments through lectures and publications for specialists and for schoolchildren. Of these, the British Association for the Advancement of Science, founded in 1831, is mainly concerned with science, while the Royal Society of Arts, dating from 1754, deals with the arts and commerce as well as science. The Royal Institution, founded in 1799, also performs these functions and in addition runs its own research laboratories.

Zoological Gardens

The Zoological Society of London, an independent scientific body, runs the world-famous London Zoo, which occupies some 15 hectares (36 acres) of Regent's Park, London. The Society also runs Whipsnade Wild Animal Park near Dunstable (Bedfordshire), and is responsible for the Institute of Zoology, which carries out research in conservation and comparative medicine. It also organises scientific meetings and symposia, publishes scientific journals and maintains one of the largest zoological libraries in the world. Other well-known zoos include those at Edinburgh, Bristol, Chester, Dudley, Chessington and Marwell (near Winchester).

Botanical Gardens

The Royal Botanic Gardens, founded in 1759, cover 121 hectares (300 acres) at Kew (west London) and a 187-hectare (462-acre) estate at Wakehurst Place, Ardingly (West Sussex). They contain the largest collections of living and dried plants in the world. Research is conducted into all aspects of plant life, including physiology, biochemistry, genetics, economic botany and the conservation of rare species.

The Royal Botanic Garden in Edinburgh, founded in 1670, is a centre for research into taxonomy, for the conservation and study of living plants and for horticultural education.

Scientific Museums

The Natural History Museum, which now includes the Geological Museum, contains the national collections of extant and fossil animals and plants, as well as rocks and meteorites. It has some 60 million specimens, ranging in size from a blue whale skeleton to minute insects. The Museum is one of the world's principal centres for the study of natural history. Its research concentrates on areas which exploit its taxonomic expertise and which relate to the advisory service it offers to institutions all over the world.

The Science Museum, with a world renowned collection of more than 200,000 objects, promotes understanding of the history of science, technology, industry and medicine. Exhibits of equipment, instruments and machinery tell the story of the history of science and industry from the first steam locomotive and the beginnings of photography to space travel and computer technology.

These two museums are in South Kensington, London. Other important collections include the Museum of Science and Industry in Birmingham, the Museum of the History of Science at Oxford, and the Royal Scottish Museum, Edinburgh.

INTERNATIONAL SCIENTIFIC RELATIONS

European Community

British researchers, companies and higher education institutions take part in European Community (EC) programmes for research and development. The Community's aim in R & D is to strengthen the scientific and technological basis of European industry and to encourage it to become more competitive at an international level. The Second Framework Programme (1987–91) has Community funding of some £3,600 million and covers eight areas: health and environment, information technology and telecommunications, industry, biological resources, energy, development, marine resources, and European science and technology co-operation. Overall, British organisations secure some 20 per cent of the total funding available. This is broadly equal to Britain's contribution to the R & D budget.

There are three major programmes related to industrial competitiveness. The European Strategic Programme for Research and Development in Information Technology (ESPRIT) has a total budget of about £1,000 million and British organisations are involved in 134 out of the 181 projects so far approved in the second phase. Basic Research in Industrial Technologies for Europe/European Research in Advanced Materials (BRITE/EURAM) has a budget of some £360 million and British organisations participate in 96 of the 163 contracts under the existing programme. Research and Development in Advanced Communications Technologies in Europe (RACE) has a budget of some £380 million and British organisations participate in 82 of the 91 contracts in the first phase.

The Third Framework Programme (1990–94), providing Community funding of £4,200 million, will overlap and interlock with the Second. Industrial research continues to be important under the new programme, which gives greater priority to the environment.

Britain participates in the Joint European Torus nuclear fusion project, JET, which is based at Culham, Oxfordshire, and which is part of the European Community's collaborative research effort.

Non-EC Activities

More than 180 British companies or organisations are involved in some 100 projects (out of a total of 390) in EUREKA, the European framework for promoting collaboration in the development of advanced technologies. (The members of EUREKA are the 12 countries of the European Community, the six countries of the European Free Trade Association, Turkey, and the European Commission.)

Britain is a member of the European Organisation for Nuclear Research

(CERN) in Geneva. Britain's contributions to CERN, to the high-flux neutron source at the Institut Laue-Langevin and to the European Synchrotron Radiation Facility, both at Grenoble, are paid through the SERC. The SERC is also a partner in the European Incoherent Scatter radar facilities in northern Scandinavia, which are used for atmospheric research. Through the NERC Britain is a member of the Ocean Drilling Program led by the United States, and through the MRC of the European Molecular Biology Organisation.

Britain is also a member of the science and technology committees of international organisations such as the Organisation for Economic Co-operation and Development and the North Atlantic Treaty Organisation, and various specialised agencies of the United Nations.

Britain has concluded a number of inter-governmental and inter-agency agreements with other countries for co-operation in science and technology. Among non-governmental organisations, the five research councils, the Royal Society and the British Academy were founder members of the European Science Foundation in 1974. The research councils also maintain a joint office in Brussels to further European co-operation in research.

Staff in British Embassies and High Commissions promote contacts in science and technology between Britain and the countries in which they are accredited. The British Council promotes better understanding and knowledge of Britain and its scientific and technological achievements by encouraging exchanges of specialists; by the provision of specialised information; by fostering co-operation in research, training and education; and—in the newly industrialising countries and developing countries—by identifying and managing developmental projects in the technological, scientific and educational sectors. Many British companies are involved in commercial co-operative research projects with overseas manufacturers.

Space Activities

Britain's involvement in civil space research is co-ordinated by the British National Space Centre. The Government spent about £150 million on all space activities in 1988–89, chiefly through the DTI and the SERC. Of this 60 per cent went towards the work of the European Space Agency (ESA). The remainder supported a programme of research and development in government establishments, universities and companies. British industry has led the consortia which have developed all the communications satellites for the ESA to date. The largest ever communications satellite, Olympus, was launched in 1989. Britain is also developing the main active microwave instrument for an earth observation satellite, ERS-1, to be launched in 1991. Another British instrument, to provide extremely accurate measurements of sea surface temperature, will also fly on ERS-1. A new £20 million Earth Observation Data Centre is being established at Farnborough (Hampshire) to process and disseminate ERS data to users.

Britain is contributing £250 million to the development and use of Columbus, Europe's contribution to the United States-led International Space Station project, which will be used mainly for earth observation. Britain is playing the leading role in constructing the Columbus polar-orbiting platform and is providing key elements of the instrument payload.

British groups have been selected to participate in almost all of the ESA's science missions, including the 1986 launch of the British-built Giotto spacecraft, which investigated Halley's Comet, and the Infrared Space Observatory. Britain will contribute £76 million to the Cluster and SOHO missions to be launched in 1995 to study the Sun, the Earth's magnetosphere and the solar wind, and also expects to have a substantial involvement in the ESA's X-ray spectroscopy mission due for launch in 1998.

Participation in ESA missions is complemented by bilateral arrangements for space research with other countries, notably the United States through its National Aeronautics and Space Administration (NASA), the Soviet Union and the People's Republic of China. British groups have participated in several NASA space science missions, and have developed instruments for NASA's Upper Atmosphere Research Satellite. Other collaborations include the development of the wide field camera for the Federal Republic of Germany's X-ray satellite ROSAT, launched in 1990 from Cape Canaveral in the United States, and the X-ray sensor for the Japanese-built Ginga satellite. British scientists will also be involved in the Soviet Union's Spectrum-X-Gamma X-ray mission due for launch in 1993 and are taking part in studies relating to the Soviet mission to Mars and one of its satellites, Phobos.

23 Promotion of the Arts

Artistic and cultural activity in Britain ranges from the highest professional standards to the enthusiastic support and participation of amateurs. London is one of the leading world centres for drama, music, opera and dance, and festivals held in towns and cities throughout the country attract much interest. Glasgow, which has developed into an important artistic centre, was chosen as European City of Culture for 1990. Many British playwrights, composers, film-makers, sculptors, painters, writers, actors, singers, choreographers and dancers enjoy international reputations. Television and radio play an important role in bringing a wide range of artistic events to a large audience. At an amateur level, innumerable choral, orchestral, operatic, dramatic and other societies for the arts make use of local talent and resources. Arts activities introduced and developed by the ethnic minorities are also flourishing.

Policies

The objectives of the Government's policies for the arts are to develop a high standard of artistic and cultural activity throughout Britain; to encourage innovation and scholarship; and to promote public access to, and appreciation of, the arts and the cultural heritage. This is achieved through the provision of funds and advice, and through the expansion of total resources by encouraging partnership with the private sector, including business sponsorship. National museums and galleries are encouraged and given an incentive to increase their resources, for example, through trading and other activities. In 1990–91 these sources will provide an estimated £39 million. An important concept in funding policy is the 'arm's length' principle, by which government funds are distributed to arts organisations indirectly, through bodies such as the Arts Councils and the British Film Institute; this helps safeguard against political interference in the arts.

Administration

Promotion and patronage of the arts are the concern of both official and unofficial bodies. The Government and local authorities play an active part, and a substantial and increasing amount of help comes from private sources, including trusts and commercial concerns.

The Minister for the Arts is responsible for general arts policy and heads the Office of Arts and Libraries, which administers government expenditure on national museums and art galleries in England, the Arts Council, the British Library and other national arts and heritage bodies. English Heritage (the Historic Buildings and Monuments Commission for England) manages 400 ancient monuments and historic buildings on behalf of the Department of the Environment. The regulation of the film industry and of broadcasting is conducted by the Department of Trade and Industry and the Home Office respectively. The Secretaries of State for Wales, Scotland and Northern Ireland are responsible for the national museums, galleries and libraries in their countries, and for other cultural matters.

Local authorities maintain more than 1,000 local museums and art galleries and some 4,000 public libraries in England. They also support many arts organisations and artistic events in their respective areas, providing grant aid for professional and voluntary organisations, including orchestras and theatre, opera and dance companies; and undertake direct promotions through local arts councils. Local authorities also contribute to the cost of new or converted buildings for the arts. Arts education in schools, colleges, polytechnics, evening institutes and community centres is the responsibility of central government education departments, in partnership with local education authorities and voluntary bodies.

Finance

Since 1988 the Government has set the arts budget for a three-year period in order to give recipient arts bodies a firm basis on which to plan future activities and to encourage greater self-reliance and diversification in their sources of funding. It considers that this strategy has proved successful in encouraging arts bodies to match their plans and priorities to a realistic view of the total resources likely to be available. The three-year settlement applies to the larger part of the central government arts programme. Planned central government expenditure through the Office of Arts and Libraries amounts to £494 million in 1990–91. About 33 per cent is spent on 11 national galleries and museums in England, with 35 per cent channelled through the Arts Council to support the performing and visual arts throughout England, Scotland and Wales; about 12 per cent goes to the British Library. Grants are also made to the British Film Institute, the Crafts Council, certain other museums and arts bodies, and to the National Heritage Memorial Fund. The Fund provides assistance to organisations wishing to acquire, for the public benefit, land, buildings, works of art and other objects associated with the national heritage. Additional central government expenditure on arts and libraries in Scotland, Wales and Northern Ireland amounts to £87 million.

Industrial and commercial concerns offer a vital and growing source of sponsorship and patronage to a wide range of arts, including exhibitions, concerts and opera seasons. The Business Sponsorship Incentive Scheme was launched by the Office of Arts and Libraries in co-operation with the Association for Business Sponsorship of the Arts in Great Britain in 1984, with the aim of raising the overall level of business sponsorship. (A similar scheme was set up in Northern Ireland in 1987.) In its first five years the scheme attracted over £31 million of new money into the arts and over 1,300 new sponsors. An estimated 70 per cent of the awards has been made to arts organisations outside London. In 1990–91 the scheme is making available £3·5 million to match new sponsorships. Further support is encouraged by tax concessions which allow companies and individuals to obtain tax relief on donations to arts charities. For example, under the Gift Aid scheme, announced in March 1990, single gifts of between £600 and £5 million in any one year qualify for tax relief. Two new arts marketing schemes were introduced in 1989–90 with funds of £150,000, aimed at helping organisations find ways of increasing their audiences, in particular those of young people, multi-cultural groups and the retired.

Arts Councils

The independent Arts Council of Great Britain, established in 1946, is the main channel for government aid to the performing and visual arts. Its principal objects are to improve the knowledge, understanding and practice of the performing and visual arts, increase their accessibility to the public, and advise and co-operate with government departments, local authorities and other organisations. The Council gives financial help and advice to organisations ranging from the major opera, dance and drama companies; orchestras and festivals; to small touring theatres and experimental groups.

It also trains arts administrators and helps arts organisations to develop other sources of income. It encourages contemporary dance, mime, jazz, literature, photography and art films, and helps professional creative writers, choreographers, composers, artists and photographers through a variety of schemes. It also promotes art exhibitions and tours by opera, dance and drama companies and contemporary music groups; and makes funds available for some specialist training courses in the arts. The Council has allocated £2 million a year from 1988–89 to 1991–92 for increased touring to help widen access to the arts throughout England, Wales and Scotland; one new initiative is the funding of a three-year touring programme by the four leading London symphony orchestras, involving some 30 concerts a year.

Under a ten-year development programme launched in 1984, the Council has been increasing its funding of the arts in the regions. In the first five years support for new activities concentrated on art, dance, drama, music and education—focusing on 13 main centres of population throughout England. Greater emphasis is being placed on obtaining funds through partnership arrangements with local authorities and other agencies, and from commercial sources.

Organisations in Scotland and Wales receive their subsidies through the Scottish and Welsh Arts Councils, which are committees of the Arts Council of Great Britain with a large measure of autonomy. Northern Ireland has an independent Arts Council with aims and functions similar to those of the Arts Council of Great Britain.

Developments

The Government has announced plans for changing the structure of arts funding in England, to take effect from April 1993. These will strengthen the policy-making role of the Arts Council and involve a major shift in direct funding responsibilities from the Council to the regional arts associations (see below). The Council will retain the funding of the four national companies—the Royal Opera House, the English National Opera, the Royal Shakespeare Company and the Royal National Theatre—and a number of other centres of excellence and will retain responsibility for touring, broadcasting, research, education and training. The regional arts associations will become regional arts boards, each with its own chairman, and will be subject to greater financial accountability through a system of forward planning and budgeting, under the direction of the Arts Council.

Local Arts Councils

Local arts councils in towns and communities throughout Britain, some of them founded and supported by local authorities, aim to develop and co-ordinate arts activities in their localities. Industrial and commercial interests also give financial help.

Regional Arts Associations

Regional development of the arts is promoted by 12 regional arts associations in England and three in Wales. They bring together all those in a region, from local authorities and private companies to local artists, with an interest in improving the artistic life of their area. Their aim is to ensure that the arts are more widely available and that artists receive support at regional as well as national level. They offer financial assistance to artists and arts organisations, and advise on, and in some cases promote, activities. The associations are financed mainly by the Arts Council, with smaller sums from the British Film Institute, the Crafts Council and local authorities, and these interests are represented on their governing bodies. Business sponsorship is also an increasingly important source of regional funds.

As a result of proposed changes for arts funding in England (see p 453), the existing 12 regional arts associations will be replaced by ten regional arts boards in April 1991.

Arts of Ethnic Minorities

A wide range of arts activities is undertaken by ethnic minorities, embracing both the traditional and new forms of artistic expression. In its support for ethnic minority arts the Arts Council has, over the last five years, devoted particular attention to black and Asian dance and drama. The Commonwealth Institute arranges a varied programme of artistic events and festivals, and the Minorities Arts Advisory Service is an independent organisation which provides advice and information on, and training in, the arts of the ethnic minority communities.

Arts Centres

More than 250 arts centres in Britain provide opportunities for the enjoyment of and participation in a range of activities in both the performing and visual arts, with educational projects becoming increasingly important. Nearly all are professionally managed and most are supported by volunteer groups. About 80 per cent of all arts centres are converted buildings, including former churches, warehouses, schools, town halls and private houses. Nearly 70 per cent arrange holiday programmes for young people. The centres are assisted mainly by regional arts associations and local authorities, with some help from the Arts Council and other organisations. Many theatres and art galleries also provide a focal point for the community by making available facilities for other arts.

British Council

The British Council promotes a knowledge of British culture overseas and maintains libraries in many of the 90 or so countries in which it is represented. The Council initiates or supports overseas tours by British theatre companies, orchestras, choirs, opera and dance companies, and jazz, rock and folk groups, as well as by individual actors, musicians and artists. It also arranges for directors, designers, choreographers and conductors to work with overseas companies, orchestras and choirs. The Council organises and supports fine arts and other exhibitions overseas as well as British participation in international exhibitions and film festivals. It also maintains film libraries in many of the countries in which it works, and encourages professional interchange between Britain and other countries in all cultural fields.

Visiting Arts Office

The Visiting Arts Office, an autonomous body administered by the British Council, promotes foreign arts in Britain. It provides a clearing house for British and overseas arts organisations, advises on touring matters and makes awards for projects.

Broadcasting Organisations

Both BBC radio and television and the independent companies broadcast a wide variety of drama (including adaptations of novels and stage plays), opera, ballet, and music; and general arts magazine programmes and documentaries. These have won many international awards at festivals such as the Prix Italia and Montreux International Television Festivals. Independent television companies also make grants for arts promotion in their regions.

The BBC has orchestras which employ many of Britain's full-time professional musicians, and each week it broadcasts nearly 100 hours of classical and other music (both live and recorded) on its Radio 3 channel. A large part of the output of Radios 1 and 2 and of many independent local radio stations is popular and light music. The BBC regularly commissions

Communications

An artificial ear on the Head and Torso Simulator enables a British Telecom technician to monitor the loudness of telephone equipment as part of a project to benefit hearing-impaired users.

Mercury Communications introduced its first public payphone system in 1988, and the service is now being extended.

Libraries

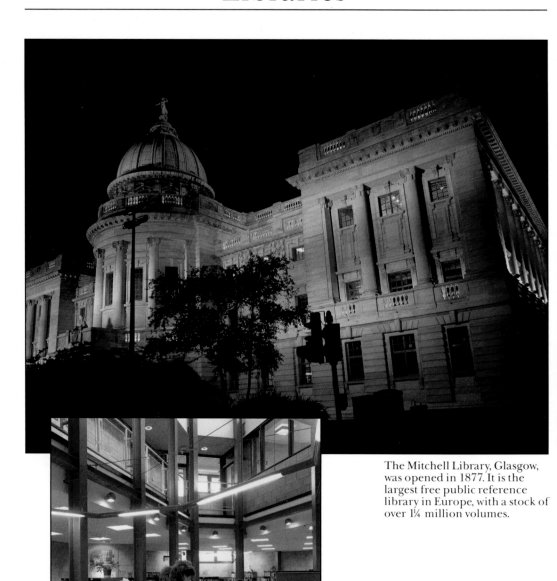

The Mitchell Library, Glasgow, was opened in 1877. It is the largest free public reference library in Europe, with a stock of over 1¼ million volumes.

The modern public library at Derringham Bank in Hull, Humberside, operates a fully computerised issue system.

The county library at Pembroke Dock in Carmarthen, Wales, is built on one level, providing easy access for disabled users. It also houses an art gallery.

The Belfast Central Library, which celebrated its centenary in 1988, offers reference and lending facilities, as well as special services to prisons, schools and hospitals.

Broadcasting

Jazz FM, Britain's first radio station devoted to jazz music, was launched in March 1990. It broadcasts a mixture of live and recorded music 24 hours a day to listeners in the London area.

The Ginger Tree, a co-production by the British Broadcasting Corporation and the Japanese television company NHK, was the first programme made in High Definition Television to be broadcast in Britain. It has been sold to 17 countries.

new music, particularly by British composers, and sponsors concerts, competitions and festivals. Each summer it presents and broadcasts the BBC Promenade Concerts at the Royal Albert Hall.

Festivals

Some 650 professional arts festivals take place in Britain each year. The Edinburgh International Festival, featuring a wide range of arts, is the largest of its kind in the world. Other annual festivals held in the Scottish capital include International Folk and Jazz Festivals and the Film and Television Festival, while the Mayfest, the second largest festival in Britain, takes place in Glasgow. Some well-known festivals concentrating on music are the Three Choirs Festival, which has taken place annually for 260 years in Gloucester, Worcester or Hereford; the Cheltenham Festival, largely devoted to contemporary British music; and the Aldeburgh and Bath festivals. Among others catering for a number of art forms are the Royal National Eisteddfod of Wales, the Llangollen International Musical Eisteddfod, the National Gaelic Mod in Scotland, and the festivals in Belfast, Brighton, Buxton, Chichester, Harrogate, Malvern, Pitlochry, Salisbury, Windsor and York.

DRAMA
Professional
Theatre

Britain is one of the world's major centres for theatre, and has a long and rich dramatic tradition. There are many companies based in London and other major cities and towns, as well as numerous touring companies which visit theatres, festivals and other venues throughout Britain, including arts and sports centres and social and working men's clubs. There are 60 companies in receipt of subsidies from the Arts Council; 26 of these are touring companies. Contemporary British playwrights who have received international recognition include Harold Pinter, Tom Stoppard, Alan Ayckbourn, Caryl Churchill, Alan Bennett, Peter Shaffer, and David Hare. The musicals of Andrew Lloyd Webber have been highly successful both in Britain and overseas. Among the best-known directors are Sir Peter Hall, Trevor Nunn, Peter Brook, Richard Eyre, Jonathan Miller, Terry Hands and Deborah Warner, while the many British performers who enjoy international reputations include Dame Peggy Ashcroft, Sir John Gielgud, Sir Alec Guinness, Vanessa Redgrave, Ian McKellen, Derek Jacobi, Jeremy Irons, Albert Finney, Dame Judi Dench, Glenda Jackson and Diana Rigg. British designers such as John Bury, Ralph Koltai and Carl Toms are internationally recognised.

Britain has about 300 theatres intended for professional use which can seat between 200 and 2,300 people. Some are privately owned, but most are owned either municipally or by non-profit-distributing organisations. Over 30 of these house resident theatre companies receiving subsidies from the Arts Council. London is the main focus, with a hundred or so West End and suburban theatres, 15 of them permanently occupied by subsidised companies. These include the Royal National Theatre, which stages a wide range of modern and classical plays in its three auditoriums in the South Bank Centre; the Royal Shakespeare Company, which presents plays mainly by Shakespeare and his contemporaries, as well as modern work, both in Stratford-upon-Avon and in its two auditoriums in the City's Barbican Centre; and the English Stage Company at the Royal Court Theatre, which stages the work of the most talented new playwrights.

In 1989 the partial remains of two Elizabethan theatres, the Rose Theatre, where most of Christopher Marlowe's plays were performed, and the Globe Theatre, where Shakespeare acted, were excavated on the south bank of the Thames in central London; the Globe has since been listed as an ancient monument. A modern reconstruction of the Globe Theatre, on its original site, is in progress. This is planned to open in 1992, at the cost of £18 million.

Regional Theatres

Outside London most cities and many large towns have at least one theatre; some, like the Theatre Royal, Newcastle upon Tyne, date from the eighteenth century and have been handsomely restored. Others, like the Crucible Theatre, Sheffield, and the Theatre Royal, Plymouth, have been built to the latest designs. Universities such as those in Aberystwyth, Manchester, Exeter and Southampton have theatres which house professional companies playing to the general public. A major new theatre, the West Yorkshire Playhouse, opened in Leeds in March 1990. Most regional repertory companies mount about eight to ten productions a year; several have studio theatres in addition to the main auditorium, where they present new or experimental drama and plays of specialist interest. Repertory theatres also often function as a social centre and meeting place by offering events such as concerts, poetry readings and exhibitions, and by providing restaurants, bars and theatre shops. Successful productions from regional theatre companies often transfer to London's West End, while the largest regional theatres receive visits from the Royal National Theatre or the Royal Shakespeare Company. The English Shakespeare Company, a recently formed classical company, tours worldwide.

Theatre for Young People

A number of companies provide theatre for young audiences. Unicorn Theatre for Children and Polka Children's Theatre, both in London, present plays specially written and directed for young people; and the Whirligig Theatre tours throughout Britain. The Young Vic Company in London and Contact Theatre Company in Manchester stage plays for young people. There are numerous Theatre-in-Education companies which perform in schools for all age ranges and abilities. Some of these companies operate independently—Theatre Centre, for example, plays in London and tours further afield. Others are attached to regional repertory theatres such as the Belgrade in Coventry and the West Yorkshire Playhouse in Leeds. Most regional repertory theatres also mount occasional productions for younger audiences, and concessionary ticket prices are generally available for those at school, college or university. There are also a number of puppet companies.

There has been a marked growth in youth theatres, which number more than 500 in England alone; both the National Youth Theatre in London and the Scottish Youth Theatre in Glasgow offer early acting opportunities to young people.

Dramatic Training

Training for actors, directors and stage managers is provided mainly in drama schools. Among the best known are the Royal Academy of Dramatic Art, the Central School of Speech and Drama, the London Academy of Music and Dramatic Art, and the Drama Centre (all in London); the Bristol Old Vic School, the Royal Scottish Academy of Music and Drama (Glasgow) and the Manchester Polytechnic School of Drama. Theatre design courses, often based in art schools, are available for people wanting to train as stage designers. A number of universities, polytechnics and other colleges offer courses in drama.

Amateur Theatre

There are several thousand amateur dramatic societies throughout Britain. Their work is encouraged by a number of organisations, such as the Central Council for Amateur Theatre, the National Drama Conference, the Scottish Community Drama Association and the Association of Ulster Drama Festivals. Amateur companies sometimes receive financial support from local government, regional arts associations and other bodies.

MUSIC, OPERA AND DANCE

A wide range of musical interests is catered for in Britain, ranging from classical music to rock and pop music. the latter being extremely popular, especially among younger people. Folk music, jazz, light music and brass band music also have substantial followings.

Music
Orchestral and Choral

Seasons of orchestral and choral concerts are promoted every year in many large towns and cities. The principal concert-halls in central London are the Royal Festival Hall in the South Bank Centre, next to which are the Queen Elizabeth Hall and the Purcell Room, which accommodate smaller-scale performances; the Barbican Hall (part of the Barbican Centre for Arts and Conferences); the Royal Albert Hall; the Wigmore Hall, a recital centre; and St John's, Smith Square.

The leading symphony orchestras are the London Philharmonic, the London Symphony, the Philharmonia, the Royal Philharmonic, the BBC Symphony, the Royal Liverpool Philharmonic, the Hallé (Manchester), the City of Birmingham Symphony, the Bournemouth Symphony, and the Ulster and the Scottish National Orchestras. The BBC's six orchestras provide broadcast concerts which are often open to the public. There are also specialised string and chamber orchestras such as the English Chamber Orchestra, the Academy of St Martin-in-the-Fields, the Academy of Ancient Music, the Bournemouth Sinfonietta, the Northern Sinfonia (Newcastle upon Tyne), the Scottish Ensemble and the Scottish Chamber Orchestra. The London Sinfonietta specialises in performing contemporary music.

British conductors such as Sir Colin Davis, Jane Glover, Sir Neville Marriner, Simon Rattle and Jeffrey Tate reach a wide audience through their recordings as well as by their performances. The works of living composers such as Sir Michael Tippett, Sir Peter Maxwell Davies and Sir Harrison Birtwistle enjoy international acclaim. Younger composers include George Benjamin, Oliver Knussen, Colin Matthews, Nigel Osborne and Robert Saxton. The Master of the Queen's Music, Malcolm Williamson, holds an office within the Royal Household with responsibility for organising and writing music for state occasions.

The principal choral societies include the Bach Choir, the Brighton Festival Chorus, the Royal Choral Society, the Huddersfield Choral Society, the Cardiff Polyphonic Choir, the Edinburgh International Festival Chorus and the Belfast Philharmonic Society. Almost all the leading orchestras maintain their own choral societies. The English tradition of church singing is represented by choirs such as those of King's College Chapel, Cambridge, and Christ Church Cathedral, Oxford. There are many male-voice choirs in Wales and in certain parts of England.

Pop and Rock Music

Among the characteristics of modern pop and rock music are the diversity of styles, the frequency with which new styles and stars emerge, and the short lifespan of many groups. Electric guitars and drums usually provide the instrumental basis, but there has been an increasing use of brass instruments, while many groups have adopted synthesisers. In the 1960s and 1970s groups such as the Beatles, the Rolling Stones, the Who, Led Zeppelin and Pink Floyd achieved international success. British groups continue to have enormous appeal to audiences throughout the world and often set new trends in music. Some of the more recent groups include Def Leppard, the Eurythmics, Fine Young Cannibals, the Pet Shop Boys and Wet Wet Wet. Well-known performers include George Michael, David Bowie, Phil Collins,

Paul McCartney and Lisa Stansfield. In recent years black musicians have made a large contribution to the development of popular music.

Jazz

Jazz has an enthusiastic following in Britain and is played in numerous clubs and public houses. British musicians such as Barbara Thompson, Stan Tracey, John Surman, Andy Sheppard and Courtney Pine have established strong reputations throughout Europe. Festivals of jazz music are held annually at Camden (London), Edinburgh, Glasgow, Crawley (West Sussex) and at a number of other places. Jazz Services provides a national touring network.

Jazz FM, Britain's first radio station devoted exclusively to jazz, was launched in March 1990. It broadcasts both live and recorded music 24 hours a day to listeners in the London area.

Opera and Dance

Regular seasons of opera and ballet are held at the Royal Opera House, Covent Garden, London. The Royal Opera and Royal Ballet, which rank among the world's finest companies, are supported by a permanent orchestra. Seasons of opera in English are given by the English National Opera at the London Coliseum. Scottish Opera has regular winter seasons at the Theatre Royal in Glasgow, and tours mainly in Scotland and northern England. Welsh National Opera presents seasons in Cardiff and other cities. Opera 80 takes opera to towns throughout England, playing in a wide range of venues. Opera North, based in Leeds, undertakes tours primarily in the north of England and Opera Factory stages experimental work in opera and music theatre. Opera in Northern Ireland is promoted by Opera, Northern Ireland.

An opera season for which international casts are specially assembled is held every summer at Glyndebourne in East Sussex. This is followed by an autumn tour by Glyndebourne Touring Opera, often using casts drawn from the chorus of the festival season.

Subsidised Dance Companies

Subsidised dance companies include: the Birmingham (formerly Sadler's Wells) Royal Ballet, which is based in the English regions; English National Ballet, which divides its performances between London and the regions; Northern Ballet Theatre, which is based in Manchester and also tours widely throughout England, and Scottish Ballet, based in Glasgow. Also included are Rambert Dance (Britain's oldest ballet company, which re-formed in 1966 as a leading contemporary dance company); London Contemporary Dance Theatre, which provides regular seasons in London besides touring extensively; Adzido (Pan African Dance Ensemble) and African People's Dance Company. The Arts Council also supports Dance Umbrella, an organisation which promotes an annual festival of contemporary dance. In addition, the three Arts Councils and the regional arts associations support individual artists and offer project grants to several small groups.

Training

Professional training in music is given mainly at colleges of music. The leading London colleges are the Royal Academy of Music, the Royal College of Music, the Guildhall School of Music and Drama and Trinity College of Music. Outside London the main centres are the Royal Scottish Academy of Music and Drama in Glasgow, the Royal Northern College of Music in Manchester, the Welsh College of Music and Drama, Cardiff, and the Birmingham Conservatoire. The National Opera Studio provides advanced training courses.

Leading dance schools include the Royal Ballet School, the Ballet Rambert

School and the London School of Contemporary Dance which, with many private schools, have helped in raising British dance to its present standard. Dance is now a subject for degree studies at the Laban Centre, the University of Surrey and Dartington College of the Arts. Courses for students intending to work with community groups are available at three institutions.

A city technology college offering studies in drama, music and dance to pupils aged from 13 to 18, with the emphasis on the application of technology to the performing arts, is due to open in Croydon, Surrey, in September 1991. The capital cost, amounting to £5·9 million, will be shared between the Government (60 per cent) and the British phonographic industry (40 per cent).

Youth and Music, an organisation affiliated to the international Jeunesses Musicales, encourages attendance by young people at opera, dance and concert performances. Special performances of orchestral music for children include the Robert Mayer Concerts, held in London on Saturday mornings. Ludus Dance in Education Company and Outreach (in the north of England) work mainly with young people. Scottish Ballet Steps Out works in schools throughout Scotland.

Many children learn to play musical instruments at school, and some take the examinations of the Associated Board of the Royal Schools of Music. Music is one of the foundation subjects in the National Curriculum in publicly maintained schools in England and Wales. The National Youth Orchestras of Great Britain, of Scotland and of Wales and other youth orchestras are noted for their high standards. Nearly a third of the players in the European Community Youth Orchestra come from Britain. There is also a National Youth Jazz Orchestra.

National Youth Music Theatre, which is based in London, gives young people between 11 and 18 the opportunity to perform music theatre under the guidance of professional directors and choreographers. All the work takes place in the school holidays.

FILMS

British films, actors, and the creative and technical services supporting them are widely acclaimed in international film festivals and other events. Besides feature films, including co-productions with other countries, the industry produces films for television as well as promotional, advertising, industrial, scientific, educational and training films.

There are approximately 1,560 cinema screens in Britain and estimated attendances in 1989 amounted to about 90 million. Cinema attendance figures declined rapidly between the mid-1950s and the early 1980s, due mainly to competition from television. However, cinema-going started to increase in 1986, partly as a result of British Film Year (1985), which was successful in promoting the cinema and British films. The present resurgence can be attributed partly to the rapid growth in the rental of video films, which has stimulated not only an interest in films generally but also a wish to see popular action films in their original medium. There has been a growth in recent years in the number of grant-aided regional film theatres and film societies offering alternative programmes to those of the commercial cinema chains.

Government Support for the Film Industry

Following a wide-ranging review of the film industry, measures were taken by the Government in 1985 to remove certain statutory controls on cinemas which had become outdated and were no longer contributing to the industry's development. British Screen Finance, a private sector company with shareholders from the film and television industries, was set up in 1986 to provide a source of finance for new film-makers with commercially viable productions who have difficulty in attracting funding. The company, investing its own money, together with contributions from the Government amounting to £7·5 million over five years, part-finances the production of low- and medium-budget films involving largely British talent. With further government funding of £2·5 million over five years, the company manages schemes to encourage the early stages of film project development and the production of short films.

An annual government grant (£12·7 million for 1990–91) is made to the British Film Institute and one of over £656,000 to the Scottish Film Council and the Scottish Film Production Fund. In June 1990 the Government agreed to provide £5 million over three years to help British film producers seeking to enter European co-production.

British Film Institute

The development of film, video and television as an art form is promoted by the British Film Institute, founded in 1933, and in Scotland by the Scottish Film Council. The Institute offers direct financial and technical help through its Film Production Board to new and experienced film-makers who cannot find support elsewhere, and helps to fund film and video workshops in liaison with the Channel Four Television Company.

It administers the National Film Theatre in London and the National Film Archive, and has a library from which films and video-cassettes may be hired. The Institute's Information Division holds extensive international collections of books, periodicals, scripts, stills and posters. Its Education Department aims to enable as many people as possible to discover new ways of producing and enjoying film, video and television.

The National Film Archive contains over 150,000 films, including newsreels and other miscellaneous items, and over 35,000 television programmes. BFI South Bank comprises the Museum of the Moving Image (see p 464), and the National Film Theatre. The latter has two cinemas showing films of historical, artistic or technical interest, and is unique in offering regular programmes unrestricted by commercial considerations or by the date or country of origin of the films. Each autumn it mounts the London Film Festival, at which some 150 new films from all over the world are screened.

The British Film Institute has promoted, and helps to fund, the development of some 40 regional film theatres, and is involved in establishing film and television centres with a range of activities and facilities in a number of major cities. It also co-operates with the regional arts associations and grant-aids their film activities. The Institute received £500,000 in incentive funding in 1989–90, which it is using to generate a further £1 million from other sources. It has raised some £15 million from private sources for capital development.

The Welsh Arts Council acts as the Institute's agent in Wales. In Scotland the Scottish Film Council supports regional film theatres, administers the Scottish Film Archive, and promotes and provides material for media education. Together with the Scottish Arts Council, it has set up the Scottish Film Production Fund, which makes grants towards film production in Scotland. Grants in Northern Ireland are made by the Arts Council of Northern Ireland. An annual festival of film and television in the Celtic countries is held in rotation in Scotland, Wales, Ireland and France.

Children's Film

The Children's Film and Television Foundation produces and distributes entertainment films specially designed for children. These are shown largely through the medium of video and television.

Training in Film Production

The National Film and Television School, which is financed jointly by the Government and the film and television industry, offers postgraduate and short course training for directors, editors, camera technicians, animators and other specialists. Training in film production is also given at the London International Film School, the Royal College of Art, and at some polytechnics and other institutions.

Cinema Licensing and Film Classification

Cinemas showing films to the public must be licensed by local authorities, which have a legal duty to prohibit the admission of children under 16 to unsuitable films, and may prevent the showing of any film. In assessing the suitability of films the authorities normally rely on the judgment of an independent non-statutory body, the British Board of Film Classification, to which films offered to the public must be submitted. The Board was set up on the initiative of the cinema industry to ensure a proper standard is maintained in films shown to the public. It does not use any written code of censorship, but can require cuts to be made before granting a certificate; very rarely, it refuses a certificate.

Films passed by the Board are put into one of six categories: U meaning universal—suitable for all; PG, meaning parental guidance, in which some scenes may be unsuitable for young children; 12, 15 and 18, for people of not less than 12, 15 and 18 years of age respectively; and Restricted 18, for restricted showing only at segregated premises to which no one under 18 is admitted—for example, licensed cinema clubs.

Videos

The British Board of Film Classification is also legally responsible for the classification of videos. The system of classification is similar to that for films. It is an offence to supply commercially a video which has not been classified or to supply it in contravention of its classification—for example, to sell or hire a video classified 18 to a person under the age of 18.

VISUAL ARTS

State support for the visual arts consists largely of maintenance and purchase grants for the national museums and galleries, purchase grants for municipal museums and galleries, and funding through local authorities, the Museums and Galleries Commission and the area museum councils (see p 462). It also includes funding for living artists channelled through the Arts Councils, the Crafts Council and the regional arts associations, and grants towards the cost of art education. The Government encourages high standards of industrial design and craftsmanship through grants to the Design Council.

All national museums and galleries are financed chiefly from government funds. They may levy entrance charges to their permanent collections, special exhibitions and outstations at their discretion. Government policy is to give priority to the conservation of the buildings and collections of the national institutions rather than to increasing purchase grants for acquisitions. All the national collections are managed by independent trustees.

Museums and art galleries maintained by local authorities, universities and private benefactions may receive help in building up their collections through annual government grants administered by the Museums and Galleries Commission (for England and Wales) and the Scottish Museums Council. Financial and practical assistance to both national and local museums and galleries is also given by the Arts Council and by trusts and voluntary bodies, including the Calouste Gulbenkian Foundation, the National Art-Collections Fund and the Contemporary Art Society.

Pre-eminent works of art accepted by the Government in place of inheritance tax are allocated to public galleries. In 1989–90, total government spending on this scheme amounted to a record level of over £11·5 million. Financial help may be available from the National Heritage Memorial Fund, which was allocated £3 million by the Government in 1990–91. In recent years, the Fund has made important contributions towards pictures bought by the Birmingham, Leeds and Manchester City Art Galleries, and by the national galleries and museums.

In co-operation with regional arts associations, the Arts Council makes grants towards the public display of the visual arts, especially contemporary and experimental works, and the publication of books and magazines. It also encourages the commissioning of works of art in public places. The South Bank Board maintains a collection of contemporary British art and organises touring exhibitions throughout the country on behalf of the Arts Council. The Council supports a number of art and photography galleries in London, including the Hayward Gallery, Serpentine Gallery, Photographers' Gallery and Whitechapel Art Gallery; and in the regions, the Arnolfini in Bristol and the Museum of Modern Art in Oxford. It also provides support for artists and photographers through purchasing and commissioning fellowships and residencies. Similar support is given by the Scottish Arts Council to galleries in Scotland such as the Fruitmarket Gallery in Edinburgh. The Welsh and Northern Ireland Arts Councils have galleries in Cardiff and Belfast respectively.

A number of modern British sculptors and painters have international reputations, and have received international prizes and commissions for major works in foreign cities. Among the best known are Francis Bacon, David Hockney, Lucian Freud, Eduardo Paolozzi and Richard Long.

Museums and Art Galleries

A major expansion in the number of museums is taking place and many are introducing new display techniques that attract increasing numbers of visitors. About 100 million people a year attend some 2,500 museums and galleries open to the public, which include the major national collections and a wide variety of municipally and independently or privately owned institutions. Government provision for museums and galleries is £174 million in 1991–92. The Museums and Galleries Improvement Fund, which is jointly financed by the Government and the Wolfson Charities, was announced in March 1990. The Fund, which will have an initial annual budget of £4 million for three years, will be available for renovating and improving galleries, focusing on priority work which museums are unable to fund fully from their own resources.

The Government takes advice on policy matters from the Museums and Galleries Commission. The Commission also promotes co-operation between national and provincial institutions. Nine area museum councils supply technical services and advice on conservation, display, documentation and publicity.

The Government encourages the loan of objects from national and provincial museums and gallery collections so that works of art can be seen by as wide a public as possible. It provides funds for promoting the touring of exhibitions and for facilitating the loan of items between institutions.

Museums Association

The independent Museums Association, to which many museums and art galleries and their staffs belong, and which has many overseas members, facilitates exchange of information and discussion of matters relating to museums and galleries, and is an examining body for professional qualifications. It provides training, seminar, research and publishing programmes. Its subsidiary, Museum Enterprises, provides consultancy services to museums and galleries in planning, trading and recruitment.

The Museum Training Institute, announced in 1989, is responsible for developing training standards and programmes.

National Collections

The national museums and art galleries, most of which are located in London, contain some of the world's most comprehensive collections of objects of artistic, archaeological, scientific, historical and general interest. They are the British Museum (including the Museum of Mankind), the Natural History Museum, the Victoria and Albert Museum (V & A), the Science Museum, the National Gallery, the Tate Gallery, the National Portrait Gallery, the Imperial War Museum, the National Army Museum, the Royal Air Force Museum, the National Maritime Museum, the Wallace Collection, the Geological Museum and a group of museums and galleries on Merseyside. Some of the museums in London have branches in the regions, examples being the National Railway Museum (York) and the National Museum of Photography, Film and Television (Bradford), which are part of the Science Museum. The V & A plans to open a branch in Bradford.

Recent developments at the Tate Gallery have included the opening in 1987 of the Clore Gallery to house the paintings bequeathed to the nation by J. M. W. Turner, and the opening of the Tate Gallery in Liverpool in 1988. An extension to the National Gallery, which is being financed by the Sainsbury family, is under construction. The Theatre Museum, a branch of the V & A, opened in Covent Garden, London, in 1987.

In Scotland the national collections are held by the National Museums of Scotland and the National Galleries of Scotland. The former includes the Royal Museum of Scotland and the Scottish United Services Museum, both in Edinburgh; the Museum of Flight, near North Berwick; the Scottish Agricultural Museum, at Ingliston; and the Shambellie House Museum of Costume, near Dumfries. The latter collection comprises the National Gallery of Scotland, the Scottish National Portrait Gallery and the Scottish National Gallery of Modern Art. The National Museum of Wales (where a major expansion scheme is in progress), in Cardiff, has a branch at St Fagan's Castle, where the Welsh Folk Museum is housed; an Industrial and Maritime Museum in Cardiff's dockland; the Museum of the Woollen Industry at Drefach Felindre; and the Slate Museum at Llanberis. Northern Ireland has two national museums: the Ulster Museum in Belfast and the Ulster Folk and Transport Museum in County Down.

Other Collections

Other important collections in London include the Royal Armouries in the Tower of London, the Museum of London, Sir John Soane's Museum, the Courtauld collection and the London Transport Museum. The Queen's Gallery in Buckingham Palace has exhibitions of pictures from the extensive royal collections.

Most cities and towns have museums devoted to art, archaeology and natural history, usually administered by the local authorities but sometimes by local learned societies or by individuals or trustees. Both Oxford and Cambridge are rich in museums. Many are associated with their universities, such as the Ashmolean Museum in Oxford (founded in 1683—the oldest in the world), and the Fitzwilliam Museum in Cambridge. Many private art collections in historic family mansions, including those owned by the National Trusts, are open to the public, while an increasing number of open air museums depict the regional life of an area or preserve early industrial remains. These include the Weald and Downland Museum in West Sussex, the North of England Open Air Museum in Durham, and the Ironbridge Gorge Museum in Shropshire. Skills of the past are revived in a number of 'living' museums like the Gladstone Pottery Museum near Stoke-on-Trent and the Quarry Bank Mill at Styal in Cheshire.

Among the newest museums are the National Horseracing Museum at Newmarket; the Jorvik Viking Centre, a reconstruction of the Viking settlement in York; a new maritime museum in Portsmouth, housing the restored wreck of the *Mary Rose*, the flagship of Henry VIII, which sank in 1545 and was raised in 1982; and Catalyst: Museum of the Chemical Industry, at Widnes, Cheshire. The Burrell Collection in Glasgow houses a world-famous series of tapestries, paintings and *objets d'art*. The Museum of the Moving Image, which opened on the South Bank of the Thames in 1988, traces the history of film and television and features displays of moving images ranging from ancient shadow theatre to future technologies.

Apart from their permanent collections, most museums and galleries stage temporary exhibitions on particular themes. There are also a number of national art exhibiting societies, the most famous being the Royal Academy of Arts at Burlington House. The Academy holds an annual Summer Exhibition, where the works of hundreds of professional and amateur artists can be seen, and important exhibitions during the rest of the year. The Royal Scottish Academy holds annual exhibitions in Edinburgh. There are also children's exhibitions, including the National Exhibition of Children's Art.

Crafts

Government aid for the crafts, amounting to just over £2·5 million in 1990–91, is administered in England and Wales by the Crafts Council. The Council supports artist craftsmen and women by promoting interest in their work, making it accessible to the public and encouraging the creation and appreciation of articles of fine craftsmanship. Grants are available to help with training, setting up workshops and acquiring equipment. The Council arranges exhibitions and seminars and circulates information. It also runs a British crafts shop at the Victoria and Albert Museum. Funding is given to the Welsh Arts Council and the regional arts associations in England for the support of crafts, and to Contemporary Applied Art, a membership organisation that holds exhibitions and sells work through its London gallery.

Scotland receives a separate government grant for support for crafts.

Training in Art and Design

Most practical education in art and design is provided in colleges of art (among the best known of which are the Slade School and the Royal College of Art, both in London), further education colleges and private art schools. The London Institute was formed in 1986 from a merger of four art colleges in London with a number of other colleges. Degrees at postgraduate level are awarded by the Royal College of Art. Art is also taught at an advanced level at the four Scottish Central (Art) Institutions.

Courses at universities and polytechnics concentrate largely on academic disciplines such as the history of art. The leading institutions include the Courtauld and Warburg Institutes of the University of London and the Department of Classical Art and Archaeology at University College, London. Art is one of the foundation subjects in the National Curriculum in publicly maintained schools in England and Wales; and the Society for Education through Art encourages, among other activities, the purchase by schools of original works of art by organising an annual Pictures for Schools exhibition.

The Open College of the Arts, launched in 1987, offers correspondence courses in art and design, painting, sculpture, textiles, photography and creative writing to people wishing to study at home.

The Art Market

London is a major centre for the international art market, and sales of works of art take place in the main auction houses (two of the longest established being Sotheby's and Christie's), and through private dealers. Certain items are covered by export control. These are: works of art and collectors' items over 50 years old and worth £20,000 or more (£5,000 or more in the case of British historical portraits); photographic material over 50 years old and valued at £500 or more an item; and documents, manuscripts and archives over 50 years old, irrespective of value. A licence from the Department of Trade and Industry is required before such items can be exported. If the Department's advisers recommend withholding a licence, the matter is referred to the Reviewing Committee on the Export of Works of Art. If the Committee considers a work to be of national importance it can advise the Government to withhold the export licence for a specified time to give a public museum or art gallery an opportunity to buy at a fair price.

LITERATURE AND LIBRARIES

A number of literary activities receive public subsidy through the Arts Council of Great Britain. In 1989, for example, the Council supported the Silver Jubilee Conference of the Association for Commonwealth Literature and Language Studies, held in Britain for the first time. The Council further developed its scheme to support the translation into English of works written in other languages, with special priority being given to books in Asian, East European and Scandinavian languages. It also established a touring network for writers. Financial assistance was given to help set up a black literary archive, partly based on recorded materials; to improve the management of multicultural publishing presses; and to provide school teachers with the opportunities to consider how best to introduce non-Western literature into the classroom.

There are free public libraries throughout Britain, private libraries and several private literary societies. Book reviews are featured in the press and on television and radio and numerous periodicals concerned with literature are published. Recognition of outstanding literary merit is provided by a number of awards, some of the most valuable being the Booker, National Cash Register and Whitbread prizes. Awards to encourage young writers include those of the Somerset Maugham Trust Fund and the E. C. Gregory Trust Fund. Many British writers are internationally recognised and in 1983 the Nobel prize for literature was awarded to the novelist Sir William Golding. Other well-known living authors include Graham Greene, Anthony Burgess, Penelope Lively and Iris Murdoch. Distinguished British poets include Ted Hughes, the Poet Laureate, who writes verse to mark royal occasions; Geoffrey Hill; Tony Harrison; James Berry; Gavin Ewart; and Elizabeth Jennings.

Authors' Copyright and Performers' Protection

Original literary, dramatic, musical or artistic works, films and sound recordings are automatically protected in Britain. This protection is given to foreign works under the terms of international conventions.[1] The copyright owner has rights against unauthorised reproduction, public performance and broadcasting of his or her work. In most cases the author is the first owner of the copyright, and the term of copyright is the life of the author and a period of 50 years after his or her death (50 years from the date of release for films and sound recordings).

The Copyright, Designs and Patents Act 1988 reformed and restated the copyright law, defining copyright as a property right capable, like any other property, of being exploited, used, bought or sold. It also introduced the concept of moral rights, whereby authors have the right to be identified on their works and to object to any unjustified modifications of them. The Act

---

[1] All countries which are members of the Berne Copyright Convention and the Universal Copyright Convention are obliged to protect the works of British nationals and works first published in Britain.

introduced a statutory framework of civil rights to protect performers against the trading in unauthorised recordings of live performance, the term of protection for these rights being 50 years from the year in which the performance is given.

Literary and Philological Societies

Societies to promote literature include the English Association and the Royal Society of Literature. The British Academy for the Promotion of Historical, Philosophical and Philological Studies (the British Academy) is the leading society for studies in the humanities.

Other specialist societies are the Early English Text Society, the Bibliographical Society and several societies devoted to particular authors, the largest of which is the Dickens Fellowship. Various societies, such as the Poetry Society, sponsor poetry readings and recitals.

Libraries
The British Library

The British Library, the national library of Britain, is one of the world's greatest libraries. Its collections comprise over 18 million items—monographs, manuscripts, maps, newspapers, patents, stamps and recorded sound. Publishers are obliged to deposit there a copy of most items published or sold in Britain.

The Science Reference and Information Service manages a comprehensive collection of material on modern science, technology and commerce. It also includes the national patents collection.

The National Bibliographic Service processes material legally deposited at the Library for inclusion in catalogues and maintains a machine-readable database of bibliographical records from which is derived the *British National Bibliography* (a list of new and forthcoming British books) and a range of automated bibliographical services.

The Research and Development Department is a major source of funding for research and development in library and information services.

The Library's Document Supply Centre at Boston Spa (West Yorkshire) is the national centre for inter-library lending within Britain and between Britain and countries overseas. It supplies 3·5 million requests a year, mostly from its own stock of 7 million documents.

The Library's new London headquarters at St Pancras is being built at a cost of £450 million, and will be open to the public from 1993. It will provide reading rooms for most of the Library's London-based collections—humanities, science, technology and industry—and also specialist reading areas. The new Library will also offer greatly improved services, including exhibition galleries, a bookshop, a lecture theatre and a conference centre.

Other Libraries

The National Libraries of Scotland and Wales, the Bodleian Library of Oxford University and the Cambridge University Library can also claim copies of all new British publications under legal deposit. The first phase of a new building for the National Library of Scotland was opened in 1989. Costing £11·5 million, it provides 49 km (30 miles) of storage shelving and accommodates a map library, lending services and the Scottish Science Library. Work on the next stage is expected to start in late 1990, for completion in 1994.

Some of the national museums and government departments have important libraries. The Public Record Office contains the records of the superior courts of law and of most government departments, as well as famous historical documents. The Scottish Record Office in Edinburgh serves the same purpose.

Besides a number of great private collections, such as that of the London Library, there are the rich resources of the learned societies and institutions.

Examples are the libraries of the Royal Institute of International Affairs, the Commonwealth Trust, the Royal Geographical Society, the Royal Academy of Music, the National Library for the Blind and the Book Trust. The Poetry Library, owned by the Arts Council, is a national collection of twentieth century poetry written in or translated into English.

University Libraries

The university libraries of Oxford and Cambridge are unmatched by those of the more recent foundations, although the combined library resources of the colleges and institutions of the University of London total 9 million volumes, the John Rylands University Library in Manchester contains 3·4 million volumes, Edinburgh 2 million, Leeds 1·8 million, and Birmingham, Glasgow, Liverpool and Aberdeen each have over one million volumes. Many universities have important research collections in special subjects; examples include the Barnes Medical Library at Birmingham and the British Library of Political and Economic Science at the London School of Economics.

Special Libraries

Numerous associations and commercial and industrial organisations run library and information services. Although most are primarily intended for use within the organisation, many special libraries can be used, by arrangement, by people interested in the area covered, and the specialist publications held are often available for inter-library lending.

Public Libraries

Local authorities have a duty to provide a free lending and reference library service in their areas, and Britain's network of libraries has a total stock of about 137 million books. Over half of the total population are members of public libraries. Some areas are served by mobile libraries, and domiciliary services cater for people unable to visit a library. Many libraries have collections of records, audio- and video-cassettes, and musical scores for loan to the public, while a number also lend from collections of works of art, which may be originals or reproductions. Most libraries hold documents on local history, and nearly all provide children's departments, while reference and information sections and art, music, commercial and technical departments meet the growing and more specific demands in these fields. The information role is one of increasing importance for many libraries, and greater use is being made of information technology, including micro-computers and reference databases.

The Government remains committed to providing a free basic library service—the borrowing and consultation of books and other printed materials—but believes there is scope for greater private sector involvement. In 1988 it made available £250,000 a year over three years for an incentive funding scheme to encourage new developments and increase efficiency in public library services in England. Priority is given to projects involving collaboration with other libraries and the private sector.

The Local Government and Housing Act 1989 protects the core of the free public library service. It enables public library authorities to charge for some services, such as research services and the lending of non-printed materials, including cassettes and records.

The Public Lending Right Scheme gives registered authors the right to receive payment from a central fund (totalling £3·5 million in 1990–91) for the use of their books borrowed from public libraries. Payment is made in proportion to the number of times the authors' books are lent out. The Government is advised on library and information matters by four library and information services councils or committees, representing England, Wales, Scotland and Northern Ireland.

The Library Association

The Library Association is the principal professional organisation for those engaged in library and information services. Founded in 1877, the Association has 24,000 members working in all kinds of libraries and information units. It maintains a Register of Chartered Librarians and publishes books, pamphlets and official journals.

Historical Manuscripts

The Royal Commission on Historical Manuscripts is the central investigatory and advisory body on manuscripts, records and archives other than the public records. It maintains a National Register of Archives and advises owners, custodians and government, assists researchers and co-ordinates the activities of bodies working in the field. The Government has announced support of £300,000 over three years from 1990–91 towards the establishment of a National Manuscripts Conservation Trust, whose purpose is to provide assistance to record offices, libraries and other owners of manuscripts and archives accessible to the public.

Books

In 1989 British publishers issued nearly 62,000 separate titles, of which about 46,000 were new titles and the remainder reprints and new editions. The British publishing industry devotes much effort to developing overseas markets, and in 1989 the value of exports of British books amounted to over £660 million. The industry is also noted for its interest in new technological developments, including electronic publishing and the development of software for educational and other purposes.

Among the leading organisations representing publishing and distribution interests are the Publishers Association, which has 200 members, and the Booksellers' Association, with 3,300 members. The Publishers Association, through its associated body the Book Development Council, promotes the export of British books worldwide.

The British Council publicises British books through its 116 libraries overseas, participation in international book fairs and a programme of travelling exhibitions. The Council also publishes a monthly periodical, *British Book News*.

The Book Trust, whose membership includes authors, publishers, booksellers, librarians and readers, encourages an interest in books and arranges exhibitions throughout Britain.

24 The Press

More daily newspapers, national and regional, are sold per person in Britain than in most other developed countries. On an average day two out of three people over the age of 15 read a national morning newspaper; about three out of four read a Sunday newspaper. Three out of four adults regularly read a paid-for regional or local newspaper as well as a free local paper. National papers have a total circulation of 15·8 million on weekdays and 17·9 million on Sundays, though the total readership is considerably greater. There are about 135 daily (Monday to Saturday) and Sunday newspapers, 2,000 weekly paid-for and free newspapers (including business, sporting and religious newspapers) and some 7,000 periodical publications.

There is no state control or censorship of the press, but it is subject to the general laws on publication (see p 479). With the aim of improving the present largely voluntary system of press regulation in Britain, both the Press Council (see p 478) and the national newpapers have published codes of conduct and new procedures for dealing with readers' complaints. In addition, a government-appointed committee has recommended the setting up by the newspaper industry of a Press Complaints Commission, in a final attempt to make self-regulation of the press work properly. It also proposes that physical intrusion into privacy by journalists should, in certain circumstances, be unlawful (see p 478). These measures were prompted by growing criticism of press standards, with allegations of unjustified invasion of privacy and inaccurate and biased reporting, among other abuses, resulting in calls for increased government regulation of the press.

The press caters for a variety of political views, interests and levels of education. Newspapers are almost always financially independent of any political party; where they express pronounced views and show obvious political leanings in their editorial comments, these derive from proprietorial and other non-party influences. Nevertheless, during general election campaigns many newspapers recommend their readers to vote for a particular political party. Even newspapers which adopt strong political views in their editorial columns include feature and other types of articles by authors of a variety of political persuasions. In order to preserve their character and traditions, a few newspapers and periodicals are governed by various trustee-type arrangements. Others have management arrangements to ensure their editors' authority and independence.

Working practices have undergone profound changes throughout the newspaper industry in response to the challenges posed by computer-based technology and the need to contain costs; using computerised technology can reduce the initial capital outlay required to produce new papers.

Newsprint, about three-quarters of which is imported, forms 24 per cent of average national newspaper costs; labour represents about 55 per cent. Revenue from sales accounts for varying proportions of income. Many newspapers and periodicals derive considerable earnings from their

Table 24.1: National Newspapers

Title and foundation date	Controlled by	Circulation[a] average January–June 1990
National dailies		
'Populars'		
Daily Express (1900)	United Newspapers	1,561,754
Daily Mail (1896)	Associated Newspapers Group	1,670,036
Daily Mirror (1903)	Mirror Group Newspapers (1986)	3,129,890
Daily Star (1978)	United Newspapers	919,133
Morning Star (1966)	Morning Star Co-operative Society	18,000
The Sun (1964)	News International	3,936,692
Today (1986)	News International	581,240
'Qualities'		
Financial Times (1888)	Pearson	291,531
The Daily Telegraph (1855)	The Daily Telegraph	1,113,033
The Guardian (1821)	The Guardian and Manchester Evening News	430,458
The Independent (1986)	Newspaper Publishing	414,357
The Times (1785)	News International	432,453
National Sundays		
'Populars'		
News of the World (1843)	News International	5,036,019
Sunday Express (1918)	United Newspapers	1,727,376
Sunday Mirror (1963)	Mirror Group Newspapers (1986)	2,910,867
Sunday Sport (1986)	Apollo	451,951
The Mail on Sunday (1982)	Associated Newspapers Group	1,889,431
The People (1881)	Mirror Group Newspapers (1986)	2,588,468
'Qualities'		
Sunday Telegraph (1961)	The Daily Telegraph	656,120
The Independent on Sunday (1990)	Newspaper Publishing	362,647
The Observer (1791)	Lonrho International	566,854
The Sunday Correspondent (1989)	The Sunday Correspondent Ltd	205,947
The Sunday Times (1822)	News International	1,186,667

[a]Circulation figures are those of the Audit Bureau of Circulations (consisting of publishers, advertisers and advertising agencies) and are certified average daily or weekly net sales for the period. The circulation figure of the *Morning Star* is otherwise audited. The circulation figures for *The Daily Telegraph* and the *Sunday Telegraph* are from January to June 1989, and for *The Independent on Sunday* from February to June 1990.

advertising; total current yearly spending of £2,900 million on newspaper advertising makes newspapers by far the largest advertising medium in Britain.

Unlike most of its European counterparts the British press receives no subsidies and relatively few tax and postal concessions. Newspaper and magazine sales (but not advertising receipts) are zero-rated for value added tax. Newspapers registered with the Post Office receive a concession on postal rates, and there are concessions on 'per-word' rates for international press telegrams and photo-telegrams. Like all postal customers, publishers can obtain reductions in charges for regular bulk postings.

In discussions on a 'new world information and communication order' Britain has opposed measures designed to increase governmental regulation of the media or to limit the free flow of information. At the same time, it has reaffirmed its willingness to support efforts to improve communications systems in the developing world.

Newspaper Ownership

Ownership of the national, London and regional daily newspapers is concentrated in the hands of a number of large press publishing groups (the groups controlling the national press are listed in Table 24.1). There are, in addition, some 350 independent regional and local newspaper publishers.

Although most enterprises are organised as limited liability companies, individual and partner proprietorship survives. The large national newspaper and periodical publishers are major corporations with interests ranging over the whole field of publishing and communications; some have shares in independent television and radio companies while others are involved in industrial and commercial activities.

The law provides safeguards against the risks inherent in undue concentration of the means of communication. For instance, if it appears that newspaper shareholdings in independent television or independent local radio companies have led or are leading to results contrary to the public interest, the Independent Broadcasting Authority (which regulates commercial television and radio) can, with the consent of the Home Secretary, notify the companies that their programmes may cease to be transmitted. There are additional controls over newspaper interests in cable television services. It is unlawful to transfer a newspaper or newspaper assets to a proprietor whose newspapers have an average daily circulation amounting, with that of the newspaper to be taken over, to 500,000 or more copies without the written consent of the Secretary of State for Trade and Industry. Except in certain limited cases, consent may be given only after the Secretary of State has referred the matter to the Monopolies and Mergers Commission and received its report.

The Government has included new proposals for preventing excessive cross-media ownership in the Broadcasting Bill currently before Parliament, and has set up an independent inquiry into cross-media promotion.

The National Press

Twelve morning daily papers and 11 Sunday papers (see Table 24.1) circulate throughout most parts of Britain, and are known as national newspapers. Formerly they were produced in or near Fleet Street in London with, in some cases, northern editions being printed in Manchester. All of the national papers have now moved their editorial and printing facilities to other parts of London (including the Docklands) or away from the capital altogether; some use contract printing. *Today*, launched in 1986, is printed at Poyle (Middlesex) and Manchester. *The Independent*, which also began publishing in 1986, uses printing presses in Bradford, Northampton and Portsmouth. Scottish editions of *The Sun*, *The Times*, *News of the World* and *The Sunday Times* are printed in Glasgow. In order to improve distribution and sales overseas, editions of the *Financial Times* are printed in Frankfurt, Roubaix (northern France), New Jersey and Tokyo, while *The Guardian* prints an international edition in Frankfurt.

Several newspapers have had very long and distinguished histories: for example, *The Observer*, first published in 1791, is the oldest national Sunday newspaper in the world, and *The Times*, one of the most influential newspapers and Britain's oldest daily national newspaper, began publication in 1785. A new quality Sunday paper, *The Sunday Correspondent*, was launched in 1989, and *The Independent* started a Sunday edition in January 1990. In May 1990 Mirror Group Newspapers began publishing *The European*, a weekly English-language international newspaper. It is printed in Britain, France, the Federal Republic of Germany and Hungary.

The leading Scottish papers, *The Scotsman* and the *Glasgow Herald*, have a considerable circulation outside Scotland.

National newspapers are often thought of as either 'quality' or 'popular' papers on the basis of differences in style and content. Quality newspapers are directed at readers who want full information on a wide range of public matters and are prepared to spend a considerable amount of time reading it. Popular newspapers appeal to people wanting news of a more entertaining character, presented in a more concise form and with ample illustrations. At present, all quality papers, apart from *The Sunday Correspondent*, are broadsheet in format and all popular papers, with the exception of the *Sunday Express*, tabloid. Five dailies and five Sundays are usually described as quality newspapers. Many newspapers are printed in colour, while a number of papers produce colour magazines as part of the Saturday or Sunday paper. Several of the Sunday newspapers (and some of the dailies on Saturday) publish sections with articles on travel, food and wine, and other leisure topics.

There is a growing market for news and information in the electronic media, and quality papers like the *Financial Times* provide material for use on databases and videotext services such as Prestel. *The Times* supplies a news service to Sky Television, a direct broadcasting by satellite (DBS) company under the same ownership.

The total circulation of national newspapers amounted to 33 million in 1989, compared with 32 million in 1982. Sales of quality papers have risen by 20 per cent since 1982, while the popular press has experienced a fall of 5 per cent.

Regional Newspapers
England

The regional newspapers of England (outside London, around 70 morning or evening dailies and Sundays and some 700 newspapers appearing once or twice a week) provide mainly regional and local news. The daily newspapers also give coverage of national and international affairs. Generally, regional evening newspapers are non-political, while the morning newspapers adopt a more positive political stance and tend to be independent or conservative in outlook.

Of the morning papers the *Yorkshire Post* (Leeds), the *Northern Echo* (Darlington) and the *Eastern Daily Press* (Norwich) each have a circulation of around 90,000, and two provincial Sunday papers—the *Sunday Sun* (Newcastle upon Tyne) and the *Sunday Mercury* (Birmingham)—sell 115,000 and 150,000 copies respectively. Circulation figures of evening papers start at about 11,000 and most are in the 20,000 to 100,000 range. Those with much larger sales include the *Manchester Evening News* (266,000), the *Birmingham Evening Mail* (217,000), Wolverhampton's *Express and Star* (239,000) and the *Liverpool Echo* (201,000). Paid weekly papers are of mainly local appeal and are a valuable medium for local advertising. Most have circulations in the 5,000 to 60,000 range.

There is one London evening newspaper, the *Evening Standard*, with a circulation of 517,000. A number of evening newspapers are published in the outer metropolitan area. The hundred or so local weeklies include papers for every district in Greater London, often in the form of local editions of an individual paper.

Wales

Wales has one daily morning newspaper, the *Western Mail*, published in Cardiff, with a circulation of 76,000 throughout Wales. In north Wales the *Daily Post*, published in Liverpool, gives wide coverage to events in the area. A new Sunday newspaper—*Wales on Sunday*—also published in Cardiff, with a circulation of 45,000, was launched in 1989. Evening papers published in Wales are the *South Wales Echo*, Cardiff; the *South Wales Argus*, Newport; the *South Wales Evening Post*, Swansea; and the *Evening Leader*, Wrexham. Their circulation range is between 27,000 and 90,000. North Wales is also served by the *Liverpool Echo*, while the *Shropshire Star* covers parts of north and mid-Wales, and there is coverage to a smaller extent by the *Manchester Evening News*.

The weekly press (some 82 publications) includes English-language papers, some of which carry articles in Welsh; bilingual papers; and Welsh-language papers. Welsh community newspapers receive an annual grant as part of the Government's wider financial support for the Welsh language.

Scotland

Scotland has six morning, six evening and four Sunday newspapers. The morning papers, with circulations of between 86,000 and 771,000, are *The Scotsman* (published in Edinburgh); the *Glasgow Herald*; the *Daily Record* (sister paper of the *Daily Mirror*); the *Dundee Courier and Advertiser*; the *Aberdeen Press and Journal*; and the *Scottish Daily Express* (printed in Manchester). The evening papers have circulations in the range of 11,000 to 167,000 and are the *Evening News* of Edinburgh, Glasgow's *Evening Times*, Dundee's *Evening Telegraph*, Aberdeen's *Evening Express*, the *Paisley Daily Express* and the *Greenock Telegraph*. The Sunday papers are the *Sunday Mail*, the *Sunday Post*, the *Scottish Sunday Express* (printed in Manchester), and a quality broadsheet paper, *Scotland on Sunday*, which was launched in 1988. The national Sunday newspapers *The Observer* and *The Sunday Times* carry Scottish supplements.

Local weekly newspapers number 113 and there are 60 free local papers.

Northern Ireland

Northern Ireland has two morning newspapers, one evening and three Sunday papers, all published in Belfast, with circulations ranging from 24,000 to 137,000. They are the *News Letter* (unionist), the *Irish News* (nationalist), the evening *Belfast Telegraph*, the *Sunday News*, *Sunday Life* and *Sunday World* (Northern Ireland edition). The *News Letter*, established in 1737, is the oldest English-language newspaper in the world. There are about 45 weeklies. Newspapers from the Irish Republic, as well as the British national press, are widely read in Northern Ireland.

Free Distribution Newspapers

Some 1,150 free distribution newspapers, mostly weekly and financed by advertising, are now published in Britain; over half of them are produced by established newspaper publishers. They have enjoyed rapid growth in recent years and now have an estimated total weekly circulation of about 43 million.

Europe's first daily free distribution paper, the *Daily News* (published four days a week), was launched in Birmingham in 1984.

Ethnic Minority Publications

Some 100 newspapers and magazines are produced by members of the ethnic minorities, about 60 of which are intended for the Asian community. Most are published weekly or monthly. They include the Asian newspapers *The Daily Jang*, *New Life*, *Indiamail* and *Asian Times*; and *The Weekly Gleaner*—a local edition of the *Jamaican Gleaner*—and *West Indian Digest*. *The Voice* and *Caribbean Times* are aimed at the black population in general, as is the magazine *Root*; *Chic* is a fashion and beauty magazine. An Arabic daily, *Al-Arab*, is also produced in Britain.

The Periodical Press

The 7,000 periodical publications are classified as 'consumer general interest', 'special interest' and 'business-to-business'. There are also several hundred 'house magazines' produced by industrial undertakings, business houses or public services for the benefit of their employees and/or clients, and some 500 free consumer magazines. Directories and similar publications number more than 2,000. The 'alternative' press comprises a large number of titles, many of them devoted to radical politics, community matters, religion, the occult, science or ecology.

Consumer general and specialist periodicals comprise magazines for a wide range of interests. These include women's magazines; publications for children; religious periodicals; fiction magazines; magazines dealing with sport, motoring, gardening, teenage interests and pop music; hobbies, humour and retirement; and computer magazines. Also included are the publications of learned societies, trade unions, regiments, universities and other organisations.

The weekly periodicals with the highest sales are *Radio Times* and *TV Times*, which alone are allowed to carry full details of the coming week's television and radio programmes. Each has a circulation of around 3 million. The *Radio Times/TV Times* listings duopoly will come to an end in March 1991, and the advent of competition is likely to reduce the circulation figures of both magazines.

Woman's Weekly, Woman's Own, Woman, Weekly News (which sells mainly in Scotland) and *My Weekly* have circulations in the 490,000 to 1 million range, and *Woman's Realm* and *Chat* 523,000 and 331,000 respectively. A new magazine aimed at young women, *Me*, has built up a circulation of over one million since 1989, when it first appeared. In recent years several women's magazines from overseas have achieved large circulations; *Prima* and *Best*, for instance, each sell around 825,000 copies, while *Bella* and *Hello!* are also widely read. *Smash Hits*, with a circulation of 661,000, is a fortnightly magazine dealing with pop music and teenage life styles.

Investors Chronicle is one of a number of periodicals for people with business and investment interests. Of monthly magazines *Reader's Digest* has the highest circulation (1·5 million).

The leading journals of opinion include *The Economist*, an independent conservative publication covering a wider range of topics than its title implies. The *New Statesman and Society* reviews social issues, politics, literature and the arts from an independent socialist point of view, while the *Spectator* covers similar subjects from an independent conservative standpoint. *Tribune* represents certain left-wing views within the Labour Party.

New Scientist reports on science and technology in terms that the non-specialist can understand. Articles and features relating largely to television and radio programmes appear in *The Listener*. *Punch*, traditionally the leading humorous periodical, and *Private Eye*, a satirical fortnightly, also cover public affairs. Weekly 'listings' magazines, including *Time Out* and *City Limits*, provide details of cultural and other events in London and other large cities.

Literary and political journals and those specialising in international and Commonwealth affairs, published monthly or quarterly, generally appeal to the more serious reader. Business, scientific and professional journals, publication of which ranges from twice weekly to quarterly, are an important aspect of British publishing and business communication, many having a considerable circulation overseas. There are about 4,000 publications covering business and industrial affairs.

Periodicals published in England circulate throughout Britain. In Wales there are also several monthly and quarterly journals published in both

Welsh and English. In Scotland there are three monthly illustrated periodicals, a weekly paper devoted to farming interests, a number of literary journals and numerous popular magazines. Northern Ireland has weekly, monthly and quarterly publications covering business, professional and leisure interests.

New Printing Technology

The heavy production costs of newspapers and periodicals continue to encourage publishers to look for ways of reducing these costs, often by using advanced computer systems to control editing and production processes. The 'front end' or 'single stroking' system, for example, allows journalists or advertising staff to input 'copy' directly into a video terminal, and then by pressing a button to transform it automatically into computer-set columns of type. Although it is possible for these columns to be assembled electronically on a page-sized screen, turned into a full page, and made automatically into a plate ready for transfer to the printing press, at present very few such systems are in operation. Most involve the production of bromides from the computer setting, which are pasted up into columns before being placed in a plate-making machine.

The most advanced systems present opportunities for reorganisation which have implications throughout a newspaper office and may give rise to disputes over staffing levels and other industrial relations problems. Generally, and most recently in the case of national newspapers, the introduction of computerised systems has led to substantial reductions in workforces, particularly, but not solely, among print workers.

All the national newspapers utilise computer technology, while its use in the provincial press, which has generally led the way in adopting new techniques, is widespread. Journalists type articles directly into, and edit them on, computer terminals; colour pictures and graphics are entered into the same system electronically. News International, publisher of three daily and two Sunday papers, has at its London Docklands headquarters more than 500 computer terminals, one of the largest systems installed at one time anywhere in the world. The *Financial Times* opened a new printing plant in the Docklands in 1988 with about 200 production workers, compared with the 650 employed at its former printing facility in the City of London.

Other national papers have moved into new computer-based printing plants outside Fleet Street. Where printing plants are some distance from editorial offices, pages for printing are sent by facsimile machine from typesetter to print plant.

Other technological developments include the use of full-colour printing, and a switch from traditional letterpress printing to the web-offset litho or plastic-plate processes. The new Docklands plant of the Associated Newspapers Group uses flexography, a rubber-plate process.

News Agencies

The principal news agencies in Britain are Reuters, an international news organisation registered in London, the Press Association and Extel Financial.

Reuters is a publicly owned company, employing some 10,000 full-time staff in 82 countries. It has 1,270 journalists, over 860 of whom work outside Britain. The company serves subscribers in 158 countries, including financial institutions; commodities houses; traders in currencies, equities and bonds; major corporations; news agencies; newspapers; and radio and television stations.

Reuters has developed the world's most extensive international private satellite and cable communications network to transmit its services. It provides the media with general and economic news, news pictures and graphics, and television news. Services for business clients comprise constantly updated price information and news, historical information, facilities for computerised trading; and the supply of communications and other equipment for financial dealing rooms. Information is distributed through video terminals and teleprinters.

Visnews, a television news agency whose service is estimated to reach 1,500 million viewers every day, is jointly owned by Reuters.

The Press Association, the British and Irish national news agency, is co-operatively owned by the principal daily newspapers of Britain outside London, and of the Irish Republic. It offers national and regional newspapers and broadcasters a comprehensive range of home news—general and parliamentary news, legal reports, and all types of financial, commercial and sports news—and includes in its services to regional papers the world news of Reuters and Associated Press.

News is teleprinted from London by the Press Association, certain items being available in Dataformat, as camera-ready copy. Its 'Newsfile' operation provides general news, sports and foreign news on screen to non-media as well as media clients by means of telephone and viewdata terminals. The photographic department offers newspapers and broadcasters a daily service of pictures from Britain and overseas; these are wired to the regional press. The NewsFeatures service supplies reports of local or special interest and provides exclusive rights to syndicated features. There is also a dial-in graphics facility as well as extensive cuttings and photograph libraries.

Extel Financial supplies information and services to financial and business communities throughout the world. Based in London, it has a network of offices in Europe and the United States and direct representation in Japan and South-East Asia. Data are collected from all the world's major stock exchanges, from companies and from the international press. The agency is a major source of reference material on companies and securities. It supplies a comprehensive range of data products on international financial matters, and undertakes investment accounting for banks, insurance companies and other institutions. Up-to-the-minute business and company news is made available by the agency's specialist financial news operation.

The British press and broadcasting organisations are also catered for by Associated Press and United Press International, which are British subsidiaries of United States news agencies.

A number of other British, Commonwealth and foreign agencies and news services have offices in London, and there are minor agencies in other cities, mostly specialising in various aspects of newspaper and periodical requirements. Syndication of features is not as common in Britain as in some countries, but a few agencies specialise in this type of work.

Training for Journalism

The National Council for the Training of Journalists (NCTJ), which represents the principal regional press organisations, sets and conducts examinations, and organises short training courses for journalists.

The two main methods of entry into newspaper journalism are selection for a one-year NCTJ pre-entry course at a college of further education or direct recruitment by a regional or local newspaper. Both categories of entrant take part in an apprenticeship scheme consisting of 'on-the-job' training, and block-release courses (preceded by a period of distance learning) are provided for those who have not attended a pre-entry course. There are similar courses for press photographers.

Postgraduate diploma courses in journalism are available at the University of Wales College of Cardiff; the City University, London; and Lancashire Polytechnic, Preston. Courses are provided by the Newspaper Society

Training Service for regional newspapers in such subjects as newspaper sales, advertising, industrial relations and management.

Specialist training courses for journalists and editorial managers from developing countries are offered by the Thomson Foundation in Cardiff. The Foundation also conducts training courses in developing countries and provides consultants to assist newspapers and magazines in advertising, management, circulation and the introduction and operation of new technology. It runs an international journalism training centre in collaboration with Xinhua News Agency in Peking.

Reuters offers assistance to overseas journalists to study and train in Britain, as well as in other parts of Europe and the United States. The Reuter Foundation awards fellowships to journalists from developing nations to spend a year at Oxford University. The company has also started to run practical training courses in London for journalists from Eastern Europe; these cover international news writing and business news skills.

The Periodicals Training Council is the official training organisation in periodical publishing. It offers a wide range of short courses covering management, editorial work, advertisement sales and circulation sales. It has special responsibility for editorial training and administers an industry-wide editorial training scheme for those already in employment. The postgraduate courses in journalism at the University of Wales College of Cardiff and the City University, London, contain periodical journalism options, and the London College of Printing provides postgraduate courses and General Certificate of Education Advanced level courses in periodical journalism. Reed Business Publishing, one of the largest publishing companies, has an in-company training course for suitable candidates from the general public on a fee-paying basis.

Press Institutions

Employers' organisations include the Newspaper Publishers Association, whose members publish national newspapers, and the Newspaper Society, which represents the regional, local and London suburban press. The Scottish Daily Newspaper Society represents the interests of daily and Sunday newspapers in Scotland; the Scottish Newspaper Publishers' Association acts on behalf of the owners of weekly newspapers in Scotland; and Associated Northern Ireland Newspapers is made up of proprietors of weekly newspapers in Northern Ireland. The membership of the Periodical Publishers' Association embraces the majority of independent publishers of business, professional and consumer journals.

Organisations representing journalists are the National Union of Journalists, with some 32,000 members, and the Institute of Journalists, with about 2,500 members. The two main printing unions are the Society of Graphical and Allied Trades (SOGAT) '82, with about 190,000 members; and the National Graphical Association 1982, with around 130,000 members.

The Guild of British Newspaper Editors is the officially recognised professional body for newspaper editors. It has approximately 400 members and aims to maintain the professional status and independence of editors, to defend the freedom of the press, and to improve the education and training of journalists. The British Association of Industrial Editors is the professional organisation to which most editors of house journals belong. The Association of British Editors represents the whole range of media, including radio, television, newspapers and magazines.

The main aim of the Foreign Press Association, formed in 1888, is to help the correspondents of overseas newspapers in their work by arranging press conferences, tours, briefings, and other services and facilities.

The Press Council

The Press Council is a voluntary and non-statutory body founded by the newspaper industry in 1953, on the recommendation of the first Royal Commission on the press, to safeguard press freedom and to ensure that the press conducts itself responsibly. It comprises equal numbers of press and non-press members with an independent chairman. Among its other duties, the Council keeps under review any developments likely to restrict the supply of information of public interest and importance; reports on developments in the press which may tend towards greater concentration or monopoly; and publishes its adjudications and periodic reports recording its work. The Council's annual reports usually include press statistics and articles on the structure of leading press groups.

Press Conduct

The Press Council's best-known function is dealing with complaints from the public about the content and conduct of the press. It has no power to impose penalties on publications which it has found guilty of malpractice, but relies on the sanction of adverse publicity. It can censure newspapers, magazines, editors and journalists, and issues adjudications which the editor of the newspaper or magazine criticised by the Council has a moral obligation to publish in full. The Council sometimes initiates inquiries into aspects of press conduct without first receiving public complaints.

In 1989 the Press Council issued a newspaper code of practice, which it drew up with the co-operation of national and regional newspapers and magazines. This covered such matters as accuracy, opportunity to reply, respect for privacy, payments for articles by criminals or their associates, intrusion into grief, references to race and colour and several other topics that have caused concern. The Council has also devised a shorter and speedier reader complaints procedure to be used alongside existing processes. Papers and magazines are encouraged to publish all Press Council adjudications concerning them; in appropriate cases the Council also makes a recommendation that an apology be made to the complainant. Newspapers' own 'in-house' complaints procedures should not, according to the Council, be considered a substitute for the overall regulatory role of the Press Council.

The national newspapers have published their own common code of practice relating to respect for privacy, opportunity for reply, corrections, conduct of journalists, references to race, colour and religion and payments to criminals. Readers' representatives have been appointed by most papers to handle complaints and breaches of the code, as well as to help guarantee standards of accuracy, fairness and good behaviour on the part of journalists.

The Government has welcomed a report on privacy and the press by an independent committee, under the chairmanship of Mr David Calcutt, QC. Published in June 1990, the report recommends the formation of a non-statutory Press Complaints Commission by the newspaper industry in place of the Press Council. It also proposes creating three new criminal offences of physical intrusion to obtain personal information for publication. Reporting restrictions on criminal cases would be extended so that the anonymity granted to rape victims would apply also to victims of other sexual offences.

The Press Complaints Commission would, under the Calcutt Committee's proposals, operate a code of practice more specific and comprehensive than those published by the national papers and the Press Council. The newspaper industry would be allowed 12 months to establish the Commission, whose performance the Government would review after 18 months of operation to see whether a statutory underpinning was required. In the event of the industry not setting up the Commission, the Government would, with regret, draw up a statutory framework.

Advertising Practice

Advertising practice in the press (and in the cinema and on posters) is regulated and controlled by the Advertising Standards Authority, an independent body. It aims to promote and enforce the highest standards of advertising in the interests of the public and the industry, in particular through the British Code of Advertising Practice. The objects of the code are to ensure that advertisements are legal, decent, honest and truthful; that they are prepared with a sense of responsibility to the consumer; that they conform to the principles of fair competition as generally accepted in business; and that no advertisement brings advertising into disrepute or reduces confidence in advertising as a service to industry and the public.

The Authority's chief activities are monitoring advertisements for their compliance with the code; initiating modifications to the code; and dealing with complaints received direct from members of the public. Its main sanction is the recommendation to media that advertisements considered to be in breach of the code should not be published. It also publishes regular reports on the results of its investigations, naming the companies involved. The Director General of Fair Trading has the power to seek a court injunction to prevent the publication of a misleading advertisement.

The Press and the Law

The press generally has the same freedom as the individual to comment on matters of public interest. There are no specific press laws, but certain statutes include sections which apply to the press. There is a legal requirement to reproduce 'the printer's imprint' (the printer's name and place of publication) on all publications, including newspapers. Publishers are legally obliged to deposit copies of newspapers and other publications at the British Library and to make annual returns to Companies House in the rare circumstances in which a newspaper is not printed and published as a joint stock company.

Other legal provisions relate to the extent of newspaper ownership in television and radio companies; the transfer of newspaper assets; restrictions on reporting certain types of court proceedings and on publishing material likely to stir up racial hatred; and the right of press representatives to be admitted to meetings of local authorities. There are also restrictions on the publication of advertisement and investment circulars, governed by Acts dealing with the publication of false or misleading descriptions of goods and services and with fraud. Advertisements for remedies for certain diseases are covered by public health legislation. Legal restrictions are imposed on certain types of prize competition; and copyrights come under various copyright laws.

Of particular relevance to the press are laws on contempt of court, official secrets, libel and defamation. A newspaper may not publish comments on the conduct of judicial proceedings which are likely to prejudice the courts' reputation for fairness before or during the actual proceedings, nor may it publish before or during a trial anything which might tend to influence the result.

The unauthorised acquisition and publication of information from state and official sources is an offence under the Official Secrets Acts 1911 and 1989. Newspapers are also liable to proceedings for seditious libel and incitement to disaffection.

Most legal proceedings against the press are libel actions brought by private individuals. In such cases, the editor, proprietor, publishers, printer and distributor of the newspaper, as well as the author, may all be held responsible.

Government officials and representatives of the media form the Defence, Press and Broadcasting Committee, which has agreed that in some circumstances the publication of certain categories of information might endanger national security. Details of these categories are contained in Defence Notices (D Notices) circulated to the media, members of which are asked to seek advice from the Secretary of the Committee, a retired senior military officer, before publishing information in these areas. Compliance with any advice offered by the Secretary is expected but there is no legal force behind it and the final decision on whether to publish rests with the editor, producer or publisher concerned.

25 Television and Radio

Broadcasting is based on the tradition that it is a public service accountable to the people through Parliament. Two public bodies—the British Broadcasting Corporation (BBC) and the Independent Broadcasting Authority (IBA)—provide television and radio services throughout Britain. Under legislation before Parliament, the IBA would be replaced by two new bodies—the Independent Television Commission (ITC) and the Radio Authority (see below). In Wales the Welsh Fourth Channel Authority is responsible for programmes on one television channel. The authorities work to broad requirements and objectives defined by Parliament, but are otherwise independent in the day-to-day conduct of business.

As well as regulating broadcasting generally, the Home Secretary is answerable to Parliament on broad policy questions, and may issue directions on a number of technical and other matters. Since 1988, for example, the BBC and the independent sector have been prohibited from broadcasting direct statements made by representatives of Northern Ireland terrorist organisations and their supporters. During election campaigns the policy is modified.

Developments in Broadcasting

Throughout the 1980s the British broadcasting system has been characterised by change: the major technical developments of satellite, cable and microwave transmissions as well as the availability of increased radio frequencies have made it possible to offer viewers and listeners a much greater range of choice and have introduced a period of greatly increased competition.

The Broadcasting Bill, introduced in Parliament in December 1989, aims to lay the foundations for a more competitive and efficient broadcasting framework in Britain. This would allow viewers and listeners much greater choice while at the same time promoting quality and diversity as well as high standards of decency and taste. A new independent national television service and as many as three new national commercial radio stations would be established, and there would be opportunities to launch hundreds of private local and community radio stations. Local delivery operators would be able to provide national and local television channels by cable or microwave. Clear and extensive rules would be laid down to ensure that ownership remained widely spread and that unhealthy concentrations and cross-media ownership would be checked.

Broadcasting Standards

The independence enjoyed by the broadcasting authorities carries with it certain obligations over programmes and programme content. Programmes must display, as far as possible, a proper balance and wide range of subject matter, impartiality in matters of controversy, accuracy in news coverage, and must not offend against good taste. Codes of guidance on violence in television programmes, particularly during hours when large numbers of children are likely to be viewing, are operated by both authorities.

A code of advertising standards and practice is operated by the IBA; the BBC does not broadcast commercial advertisements. A Broadcasting Complaints Commission deals with allegations of unfair treatment or infringement of privacy in programmes. Publicly available video recordings are classified according to their suitability for different audiences.

Broadcasting
Standards
Council

A new Broadcasting Standards Council has been set up to act as a focus for public concern about the portrayal of violence and sex, and about standards of taste and decency, in television and radio programmes and in video recordings; it has drawn up a code of practice on these matters. The Council monitors programmes, examines complaints and undertakes research.

The Broadcasting Bill provides for the Council to be given statutory powers under which the BBC and other broadcasting regulatory bodies' codes of practice would be required to reflect the Council's own code of practice. Broadcasters would be obliged to publish the Council's findings on complaints in whatever form it considered appropriate. Programmes broadcast to Britain from abroad would be monitored by the Council. The Government would have powers to ban unacceptable foreign satellite services receivable in Britain, and anyone in Britain supporting such a service could be prosecuted for a criminal offence. In addition, the broadcasters' current exemption from legislation relating to obscenity and incitement to racial hatred would be removed.

The British
Broadcasting
Corporation

The constitution and finances of the BBC are governed by Royal Charter and by a Licence and Agreement. The Corporation's board of 12 governors, including the chairman, vice-chairman and national governors for Scotland, Wales and Northern Ireland, is appointed by the Queen on the advice of the Government and has ultimate responsibility for all aspects of broadcasting on the BBC. Committees advise it on a wide range of matters, including religious broadcasting, agriculture, schools broadcasting, continuing education, science, and charitable appeals. The governors appoint the Director-General, the Corporation's chief executive officer, who heads the BBC's board of management, which is in charge of the daily running of the services.

The National Broadcasting Councils for Scotland, Wales and Northern Ireland control the policy and content of television and radio programmes intended primarily for reception in their areas. Local radio councils, representative of the local community, advise on the development and operation of the BBC's local radio stations. In 1989 the BBC issued guidelines to programme makers offering practical advice across the whole range of programming, including the presentation of news and political issues.

The domestic services of the BBC are financed principally from the sale of television licences. Households with television must buy an annual licence costing £24 for black and white or £71 for colour. Over 19·5 million licences were current in April 1990, of which about 18 million were for colour. Licence income is supplemented by profits from trading activities, including television programme exports, sale of recordings and publications connected with BBC programmes, hire and sale of educational films, film library sales, and exhibitions based on programmes. More than two-thirds of expenditure on domestic services relates to television. The BBC meets the cost of its local radio stations, while some local education authorities help to make educational programmes.

The BBC's World Service is financed by a grant-in-aid from the Foreign and Commonwealth Office.

The Broadcasting Bill left untouched the BBC's public service broadcasting role of providing high-quality programmes with wide appeal that educate, inform and entertain. For some time to come it will continue to be financed largely by the licence fee, the collection of which is to become the responsibility of the BBC from April 1991, and the government grant for the World Service.

Independent Broadcasting

The IBA's constitution and finances are governed by statute. It does not produce radio or television programmes; these are provided by independent programme companies on a regional basis and by the Channel Four Television Company (a wholly owned subsidiary of the IBA). The IBA's main functions are to appoint the companies, supervise programme arrangements, control advertising, and build, own and operate transmitting stations.

The IBA's finance comes from annual rental payments made by the television and radio programme companies for the use of its transmitters. The television programme companies are also liable to pay the IBA a levy related to their profit and net advertising revenue for transfer to government funds.

The ITV Programme Companies

Fifteen independent (ITV) companies hold contracts to provide programmes in the 14 independent television regions. Two companies share the contract for London, one providing programmes during weekdays and the other at the weekend. A contract to supply a national early morning television service, transmitted on the ITV network, is held by an additional company. The companies operate on a commercial basis, deriving most of their revenue from the sale of advertising time. The financial resources, advertising revenue and programme production of the companies vary considerably, depending largely on the size of population in the areas in which they operate. Although newspapers may acquire an interest in programme companies, there are safeguards to ensure against concentration of media ownership and thereby protect the public interest.

In consultation with the IBA, each company plans the content of the programmes to be broadcast in its area. These are produced by the company itself, or by other programme companies or bought from elsewhere. There are restrictions on the amount of time devoted to screening television programmes acquired from abroad. The five largest companies—two serving London and three serving north-west England, the Midlands and Yorkshire—provide more programmes for broadcast elsewhere on the national network than do the smaller ones. A common news service is provided 24 hours a day by Independent Television News (ITN), a non-profit-making company in which all the programme companies are shareholders. Negotiations for the supply, exchange and purchase of programmes and their co-ordinated transmission through the independent television network take place largely on the Network Programme Committee, which consists of representatives of all the programme companies and of the IBA.

Independent Local Radio

Similar principles apply to independent local radio. The programme companies are under contract to the IBA, operating under its control and financed by advertising revenue. News coverage is supplied as a common service by Independent Radio News.

Proposed Legislation

Under the Broadcasting Bill, the Independent Television Commission and the Radio Authority would succeed the Independent Broadcasting Authority and the Cable Authority (see p 486) on 1 January 1991. The ITC would be responsible for licensing and regulating all commercially funded television services originating in Britain, including British-based satellite and cable channels. It would be financed by a licence fee paid by franchise-holders. Until the end of 1992, when the present ITV franchises (see p 483) end, it would continue to fulfil the IBA's obligations in respect of the ITV contracts. From 1993, when the new Channel 3 (ITV's successor) licences would begin, the ITC would not be the broadcaster or 'publisher' of programmes. These responsibilities would be passed to the new licensees.

Although the ITC would supervise with a 'light touch', in that it would not be involved in detailed scheduling of programmes, it would have wider powers than the IBA to enforce licence conditions and rules designed to limit cross-media ownership and excessive concentration of ownership.

There is provision in the Bill for privatising the IBA's transmission system early in 1991.

The role of the new Radio Authority would be to assign frequencies, issue licences and regulate all independent radio stations (see p 487).

Television

Television viewing is by far the most popular leisure pastime in Britain: nearly everyone watches television, average viewing time per person being just over 25 hours a week. About 50 per cent of households have two or more receivers. The growth in use of video-cassette recorders and equipment (including home computers) for playing television games has for many people increased the choice of entertainment available in the home. Some 68 per cent of households rent or own a video-cassette recorder.

Britain is one of the world's foremost exporters of television productions; in 1989 the overseas earnings of the television companies amounted to £194 million. British television productions continue to win large numbers of international awards.

Four television channels are in operation. BBC 1 and BBC 2 are operated by the BBC; ITV is controlled by, and Channel 4 is owned by, the IBA. All four channels broadcast on 625 lines uhf (ultra-high frequency). More than 90 per cent of the population live within range of transmission.

Both the BBC and the commercial television companies enter into co-production agreements with overseas television corporations in order to make new programmes economically.

BBC

Apart from a break during the second world war the BBC has been making regular television broadcasts since 1936. An average of 124 hours of programmes is transmitted by BBC 1 and 114 by BBC 2 every week; all BBC 2 programmes and the majority of those on BBC 1 are broadcast on the national network. Approximately 60 per cent of the BBC's home-produced network programmes for 1988–89 were produced in London.

Through co-ordinated planning of its two services the BBC caters simultaneously for people of different interests. While both services cover the whole range of television output, BBC 1 presents more programmes of general interest, such as light entertainment, sport, current affairs, children's programmes and outside broadcasts. BBC 2 places greater emphasis on minority interests, but also provides documentaries, travel programmes, serious drama, music, programmes on pastimes and international films. On BBC 1 the daytime schedule consists of an early morning television service of news and information (from Monday to Friday), as well as documentaries, children's programmes, films and other programmes catering for many interests throughout the rest of the morning and afternoon.

ITV

The first regular ITV programmes began in London in 1955. ITV programmes are broadcast 24 hours a day in all parts of the country. About one-third of ITV's output comprises informative programmes—including news, documentaries, and programmes on current affairs, education and religion. The remainder covers sport, comedy, drama, game shows, films, and a wide range of other programmes with popular appeal. Over a half of programmes are produced by the programme companies and ITN. A national early morning television service on ITV transmits over three hours of news, information, current affairs and light entertainment daily.

Channel 4

Channel 4, which began broadcasting in 1982, provides a national television service throughout Britain, except in Wales, which has a corresponding service (Sianel 4 Cymru—S4C). It is obliged to present programmes that are complementary to those of ITV, appealing to tastes and interests not normally catered for by the original independent service. It must present a suitable proportion (about 15 per cent) of educational programmes, encourage innovation and experiment, and include a substantial proportion of programmes from independent producers. An early morning news and current affairs service was launched in 1989. Late-night programmes are transmitted until the early hours of the morning. Channel 4 broadcasts for approximately 140 hours a week, about half of which are devoted to informative programmes.

The service, both nationally and in Wales, is financed by subscriptions from the programme companies in return for advertising time in fourth channel programmes broadcast in their own regions. In Wales programmes on the fourth channel are run and controlled by the Welsh Fourth Channel Authority, appointed by the Home Secretary. The Authority is required to ensure that a significant proportion (in practice some 23 hours a week) are in the Welsh language and that those broadcast between 18·30 and 22·00 hours are mainly in Welsh. At other times the Welsh fourth channel shows national Channel 4 programmes.

Proposed Legislation

Under the Broadcasting Bill, the present independent television system (ITV) would, from January 1993, be replaced by Channel 3, made up of regionally based licensees of the Independent Television Commission (see p 483), which would decide the areas to be covered. Licences would be awarded by competitive tender to the highest bidder who had passed a quality threshold, but in exceptional cases a lower bid might be selected. Such circumstances might include those where an applicant was offering a quality of service significantly better than the quality of service offered by the highest bidder. There would be substantial safeguards for quality programming, with licensees being required to provide a diverse programme service, a proportion of good quality programmes, as well as high quality news and current affairs programmes and a reasonable amount of children's and religious programmes. There would also be, for the first time, a statutory requirement to present programmes made in and about the region.

The proposed legislation would oblige the BBC and ITV to acquire 25 per cent of their original programmes from independent producers.

Channel 4 and S4C's distinctive remit to screen diverse programmes would be strengthened and the services guaranteed by special arrangements to protect revenue levels. Channel 4 would become a public corporation, selling its own advertising time and retaining the proceeds. SC4 would be government funded.

A new national terrestrial television channel—Channel 5, covering about

70 per cent of households—would be established during 1993. Franchises would be awarded by competitive tender subject to a quality threshold and would have similar programming requirements to Channel 3. The channel would be financed by advertising, subscription or sponsorship, or a combination of all three.

The Broadcasting Bill would provide for the further development of local television services using both cable and microwave transmission systems, in some cases carrying over 30 channels.

Teletext

The BBC and independent television each operate a teletext service, offering constantly updated information on a broad variety of subjects, including news, sport, travel, local weather conditions and entertainment. The teletext system allows the television signal to carry additional information which can be selected and displayed as 'pages' of text and graphics on receivers equipped with the necessary decoders. Both Ceefax, the BBC's service, and independent television's Oracle service have a subtitling facility for certain of their programmes for people with hearing difficulties.

The Broadcasting Bill would introduce a new regulatory system for the licensing of spare capacity within the television signal. This would allow more varied use of spare capacity—data transfer, for instance—but the position of teletext on commercial television would be safeguarded. The proposed Channels 3 and 5 would be obliged to offer a subtitling service for at least 50 per cent of their programmes by 1998, with further increases after that.

Radio teletext, pioneered in Britain by the IBA and independent radio, uses spare capacity on VHF(very high frequency)/FM frequencies to provide up-to-the-moment financial information in London on hand-held receivers.

Cable Services

The vast majority of cable systems have in the past been used solely to relay broadcast television and radio services in order to improve reception quality, to avoid 'screening' by buildings or the local topography, or because external aerials are not allowed on some residential buildings.

Under the Cable and Broadcasting Act 1984 a more general expansion of non-broadcast cable television services was permitted and a national Cable Authority was established to issue licences, supervise programme services and promote cable development. Cable investment must be privately financed. Regulation is as light as possible to allow the development of a wide range of services and facilities, and flexible enough to adapt to changing technology. There are safeguards for existing broadcasting services.

By July 1990 the Cable Authority had awarded 135 new broadband (multi-channel) cable franchises covering 14·5 million homes. Some 50 broadband franchises are expected to be in operation by the end of 1990, with the remaining ones likely to be operational during 1991.

The new broadband cable systems at present carry up to 30 television channels, including the terrestrial broadcasts, satellite television, channels delivered by videotape and local services. Some also provide their own telephone services, home shopping and other interactive services. In June 1990 over 1·5 million homes were capable of receiving all available cable services. The number of homes receiving such services was more than 300,000. By 1996 two-thirds of British homes are expected to have access to cable. Cable operators are represented by the Cable Television Association.

Under the Broadcasting Bill, the Cable Authority would hand over its responsibilities to the Independent Television Commission in January 1991.

Broadcasting by Satellite

Several British-based satellite television channels have been set up to supply programmes to cable operators in Britain and, in many cases, throughout Europe. While some offer general entertainment, others concentrate on specific areas of interest, such as sport, music and children's programmes.

Since 1989 direct broadcasting by satellite (DBS), by which television pictures are transmitted directly by satellite into people's homes, has been available throughout Britain from the privately financed Astra satellite, which transmits 16 channels, including eight in English. Four are controlled by Sky Television and provide light entertainment, news, feature films and sport. W. H. Smith operates a sports and general entertainment channel as well as a children's channel and MTV, a pop video channel.

British Satellite Broadcasting, the programme contractor appointed by the IBA to run the five satellite broadcasting channels allocated to Britain by international agreement, began broadcasting in April 1990. Its five separate national programme services cover news and information, sport, feature films, popular music and general entertainment; all are commercial services funded by advertising and subscription.

The signals from satellite broadcasting are receivable on specially designed aerials and reception equipment.

Radio

Practically every home in Britain has a radio set, and car radios and portable sets have greatly increased daytime listening. BBC Radio has five national channels. Radio 1 broadcasts rock and pop music, while Radio 2 (on VHF/FM only) transmits a broad range of popular music and light entertainment 24 hours a day. Although Radio 3 broadcasts mainly classical music, it also presents drama, poetry, short stories and talks, and Test match cricket. Radio 4 is the main speech network, providing the principal news and current affairs service, as well as drama, comedy, documentaries and panel games. It also carries parliamentary coverage and live relays of major public events. In August 1990 the BBC launched Radio 5 (on medium wave only), which is devoted chiefly to sport and education.

There are 37 BBC local radio stations serving England and the Channel Islands, and regional and community radio services in Scotland, Wales and Northern Ireland, in addition to 70 independent local radio (ILR) stations throughout Britain. Further BBC and ILR stations are planned. About 90 per cent of the population is served by BBC or ILR stations. Broadcasts supply a comprehensive service of local news and information, music and other entertainment, education, consumer advice and coverage of local events, and offer listeners a chance to air their views, often by using the phone-in technique.

More than 300 hospitals and many universities have closed-circuit radio stations. The organisers of sporting events can apply for licences to transmit their own radio broadcasts supplying information and commentaries locally.

Proposed Legislation

Under the Broadcasting Bill, a new Radio Authority would take over responsibility for independent radio from the IBA on 1 January 1991. Like the Independent Television Commission (see p 483), it would supervise with a light touch. The new authority would allocate licences, by competitive tender, for up to three national commercial radio services. One of these would be required to be speech-based and another to include a large proportion of music that was not pop music. In the course of the 1990s, some 200 to 300 new stations could come on the air, including neighbourhood and community of interest stations. Local audience demands and the extent to which the service would broaden the range of local programmes would affect local licence allocation.

As a step towards the new arrangements, the Government has approved the issue of contracts for 23 new community of interest and ethnic minority radio stations under existing legislation. The first to go on the air, in October 1989, was Sunset Radio, aimed at Manchester's multi-cultural population. Jazz FM became the first of the new London music stations, starting up in March 1990.

Under the Broadcasting Bill, strict controls on the limits of ownership of local and national radio would be imposed by the Government in the interests of a competitive radio broadcasting market. Powers to deter illegal ('pirate') broadcasters would be strengthened.

Educational and Special Interest Broadcasting

Both the BBC and independent television broadcast educational programmes for children and students in schools of all kinds, as well as for pre-school children, and for adults in colleges and other institutions and in their homes. Broadcasts to schools deal with most subjects of the curriculum, while education programmes for adults cover many fields of learning, vocational training and recreation. Supporting material, in the form of books, pamphlets, filmstrips, computer software, and audio and video cassettes, is available to supplement the programmes.

The BBC broadcasts television and radio programmes made specially for students of the Open University, most of whose undergraduate courses contain video and audio components, some of them on cassette for use with correspondence texts. The BBC Open University Centre also produces educational and training audio-visual materials in collaboration with external agencies such as the Department of Trade and Industry, the Department of Education and Science, and the Engineering Industry Training Board. The Open College, an independent company set up in 1987 with government support, transmits courses on Channel 4 ranging from basic literacy and numeracy to high-level technological studies.

The BBC will continue to provide programmes for schools and to contribute to the operation of the Open University. The proposed Independent Television Commission (see p 483) would have a duty to ensure that schools programmes were presented on independent television.

Permission has been granted to the BBC to operate an overnight television subscription service which is planned to start broadcasting in spring 1991. Specialist services may include the arts, music and wildlife programmes as well as legal and farming programmes. The BBC is planning to develop other specialist television services for the professions, business and industry; a decoder or specially adapted video recorder will be needed to receive the services.

BBC World Service

The BBC World Service broadcasts by radio worldwide, using English and 35 other languages, for over 785 hours a week. The main objectives are to give unbiased news, reflect British opinion and project British life, culture and developments in science and industry. News bulletins, current affairs programmes, political commentaries and topical magazine programmes form the main part of the output, with a full sports service, music, drama and general entertainment. Regular listeners are estimated to number 120 million.

The languages in which the World Service broadcasts and the length of time each is on the air are prescribed by the Government. Apart from this the BBC has full responsibility and is completely independent in determining the content of news and other programmes. A plan to improve audibility is in progress.

There are broadcasts by radio for 24 hours a day in English, which are supplemented at peak listening times by programmes of special interest to Africa, South Asia and the Falkland Islands.

BBC World Service news bulletins and other programmes are re-broadcast by more than 250 stations in over 60 countries, which receive the programmes by satellite. Two World Service departments also specialise in supplying radio material for re-broadcast. One sells recordings to more than 100 countries, while the other sends by airmail some 260 tapes of original programmes to over 50 countries each week.

BBC English is the most extensive language-teaching undertaking in the world. English lessons are broadcast daily by radio with explanations in over 25 languages, including English, and re-broadcast by many radio stations. BBC English television programmes are also shown in more than 100 countries. A wide range of printed and audio material accompanies these programmes.

Another part of the World Service, BBC Monitoring, listens to and reports on foreign broadcasts, supplying a daily flow of significant news and comment from overseas to the BBC and the Government. This information is also sold to the press, to companies, to academic staff and public bodies.

COI Overseas Radio and Television Services

The Central Office of Information (COI), which provides publicity material and other information services on behalf of government departments and other public agencies, produces radio programmes for overseas. A wide range of recorded material is sent to radio stations in over 100 countries. COI television services provide material such as documentary and magazine programmes for distribution to overseas stations.

Advertising

The BBC does not give publicity to any firm or organised interest except when it is necessary in order to make effective and informative programmes. It must not broadcast any commercial advertisement or any sponsored programme; it may, however, cover sponsored events.

Advertisements are broadcast on independent television at the beginning and end of programmes as well as in breaks during programmes. Advertisers are not permitted directly to influence programme content or editorial control. Food manufacturers are the largest category of advertisers. Sponsorship of certain programmes shown by independent television is permitted, provided that it conforms with IBA guidelines and relevant legislation.

Advertisements must be clearly distinguishable and separate from programmes, and the time given to them must not be so great as to detract from the value of the programmes as a medium of information, education or entertainment. Advertising is limited to seven and a half minutes an hour between 18.00 and 23.00 hours, with the overall amount of advertising throughout the day normally restricted to seven minutes an hour. Independent television's Oracle teletext service (see p 486) carries paginated advertisements. Independent local radio stations are normally limited to a maximum of nine minutes of advertising each hour.

Codes of Practice

The IBA has a code governing standards and practice in advertising on television and radio, and giving guidance on the types and methods of advertisement which are prohibited; these include political and religious advertising and advertisements for cigarettes or betting. Advertisements may not be inserted in certain types of programme, such as broadcasts to schools. A comparable code was adopted by the Cable Authority, which is responsible for advertising control and policy on cable television. Both the IBA and the Cable Authority have the power to prevent transmission of advertisements which they consider misleading. The IBA has endorsed the Principles for Advertising by Direct Satellite Broadcasting, which were drawn up by the European Broadcasting Union. The Broadcasting Bill contains provisions giving the proposed Independent Television Commission and the Radio Authority powers comparable to those of the IBA and the Cable Authority. The Broadcasting Standards Council's code of practice (see p 482) will cover advertisements.

Government Publicity

The Government has no general privileged access to radio or television but government publicity material to support non-political campaigns may be broadcast on independent radio and television. This is prepared through the COI and broadcast and paid for on a normal commercial basis. Short public service items, concerning health, safety and welfare, are also produced by the COI for free transmission by the BBC and independent television and radio.

Parliamentary and Political Broadcasting

The proceedings of the Houses of Parliament are recorded round-the-clock by the BBC for its parliamentary sound archive. The proceedings of both Houses of Parliament may be broadcast on television and radio, either live, or more usually in recorded and edited form on news and current affairs programmes.

In 1989 the House of Commons voted in favour of televising its proceedings for an eight-month experimental period, and in July 1990 decided to allow televising permanently. Proceedings are recorded by an independent company appointed by the House of Commons Broadcasting Unit, which makes television pictures available to the BBC, Independent Television News and other approved broadcasters for use in news and current affairs programmes. Television reporting of the Commons proceedings is subject to strict rules about what can be shown, and coverage is overseen by a select committee of the House of Commons. Broadcasters will finance the service until at least July 1991. Proceedings of the House of Lords have been televised since 1985.

Ministerial and party political broadcasts are transmitted periodically on radio and television under rules agreed between the major political parties, the BBC and the IBA, and there are special arrangements for the period following the announcement of a general election. Under the Broadcasting Bill, independent television would be required to show party political broadcasts, and the Independent Television Commission would be responsible for drawing up appropriate rules for Channels 3, 4 and 5.

Audience Research

Both the BBC and the independent sector are required to keep themselves informed on the state of public opinion about the programmes (and, in the case of independent television and radio, the advertising) they broadcast. This is done through the continuous measurement of the size and composition of audiences and their opinions of programmes. For television, this work is undertaken through the Broadcasters' Audience Research Board, which is owned jointly by the BBC and the IBA. Information is collected from a panel of about 3,000 homes throughout Britain chosen as representative of all private households in the country with a television set. Meters attached to each television set and linked to a central computer are used to record times of viewing, numbers of viewers and programmes watched. The BBC and independent local radio use different systems of radio audience measurement.

Regular surveys are conducted by both the BBC and the independent sector to gauge audience opinion on television and radio services. Public opinion is further assessed by both bodies through the work of their many advisory committees, councils and panels (whose members are drawn from a wide cross-section of the public). In addition, there are regular public meetings to debate services, and careful consideration is given to correspondence and telephone calls from listeners and viewers.

Technical Developments

One of the most important recent developments in television has been in news coverage, where compact electronic cameras have replaced film cameras, eliminating the need for film processing and enabling pictures to be transmitted directly to a studio or recorded on video tape on location. Other advances include the adoption of digital video tape recorders, the increasing use of computer-aided equipment for picture generation and manipulation, the use of portable satellite links to transmit pictures from remote locations to studios, and the introduction of stereo sound based on the BBC's NICAM 728 digital system. The Radio Data System was developed for the British market by the BBC and is being adopted throughout Europe. It offers automatic radio tuning and station identification, and is especially useful for car radios.

The IBA is in the process of equipping its television networks for digital stereo sound. It is also engaged in the further development of digital techniques for studio applications and inter-city links. In satellite broadcasting, the MAC transmission format was developed by IBA engineers, and the European Broadcasting Union recommends use of the MAC/packet family for all direct broadcasting by satellite (DBS). In Britain the DBS service provided by British Satellite Broadcasting uses the D-MAC format, considered to produce a significant improvement in picture and sound quality over traditional methods of transmission. The IBA devised refinements for the MAC system compatible with widescreen television. As a result, the full 1,250 line high definition television (HDTV) is being developed by the EUREKA 95 group of European manufacturers.

The BBC and IBA co-operated in the development of teletext, and teletext sets in 30 countries are based on the British system. British Telecom's public viewdata service, 'Prestel', offers a broad range of information transmitted by telephone and viewed on the television screen.

The Government has authorised British Telecom, in conjunction with several British telecommunications firms, to transmit television pictures over a fibre-optic communications network in a field trial. British Telecom has also demonstrated a method of transmitting television using radio signals with extremely short wavelengths.

International Relations

The BBC and the IBA (together with the Independent Television Association) are active members of the European Broadcasting Union. This body manages Eurovision, the international network of television news and programme exchange, and is responsible for the technical and administrative arrangements for co-ordinating the exchange of programmes and news over the Eurovision network and intercontinental satellite links. It also maintains a technical monitoring station where frequency measurements and other observations on broadcasting stations are carried out. The Union provides a forum linking the major public services and national broadcasters of Western Europe and other parts of the world and co-ordinates co-operation in radio and television.

Co-operation between governments takes place within the Council of Europe (linking 23 countries) and the European Community (comprising 12 member states). Britain has signed a Council of Europe Convention on the regulation of broadcasting across frontiers. Rules have been devised covering programme standards, advertising, sponsorship and a number of other matters. Under these, programmes must not be indecent, contain pornography, give undue prominence to violence or be likely to incite racial hatred; nor should programmes unsuitable for children be broadcast at a time when they can be expected to be watching. A comparable European Community directive on cross-border broadcasting has been approved by member states.

Visnews is the largest television news agency in the world, supplying world newsfilm to over 400 broadcasters in 85 countries and running bureaux in 29 major cities throughout the world. The BBC and Reuters are shareholders in the company. Worldwide Television News, owned by Independent Television News, the American Broadcasting Company and Channel 9 in Australia, supplies news services to 1,000 broadcasters in 75 countries. Both agencies provide services through the Eurovision network and by satellite.

The BBC and the IBA are associate members of the Asian Pacific Broadcasting Union, and the BBC also belongs to the Commonwealth Broadcasting Association, whose members share such facilities as studios, recording channels and programme contributions.

The BBC provides technical aid, particularly in training the staff of other broadcasting organisations throughout the world; members of its staff are seconded for service overseas.

The Government finances a number of overseas students on broadcasting training courses at the BBC, the British Council,[1] and the Thomson Foundation Television College in Glasgow, which sends lecturers and arranges courses overseas.

The BBC and the IBA participate in the work of the International Telecommunications Union, the United Nations agency responsible for regulating and controlling all international telecommunications services, including radio and television. It also allocates and registers all radio frequencies, and promotes and co-ordinates the international study of technical problems in broadcasting. The BBC and the IBA are also represented on the United Kingdom Committee of the International Special Committee on Radio Interference.

---

[1]The British Council aims to promote a wider knowledge of Britain and the English language abroad and to develop closer cultural relations between Britain and other countries.

26 Sport and Recreation

The British invented and codified the rules of many of the sports and games now played all over the world, and there is widespread interest in most kinds of sport throughout Britain. Large crowds attend occasions such as the football and rugby league Challenge Cup Finals at Wembley Stadium, international rugby union matches at Twickenham (near London), Murrayfield (Edinburgh) and Cardiff Arms Park; the Wimbledon lawn tennis championships; the classic horse races; the Open Golf Championship; Grand Prix motor racing; and international cricket matches.

Extensive coverage on television (2,655 hours on the four terrestrial channels in 1989) has helped to generate interest in a wide variety of sports and recreations including basketball, darts, snooker, ice skating, skiing and athletics, while American football and baseball are becoming known to the British public through televised transmissions from the United States. The advent of direct broadcasting by satellite and the greater availability of cable are increasing televised coverage of sport substantially. The satellite broadcasting services Sky Television and British Satellite Broadcasting both have channels devoted to sport operating seven days a week, while Screensport, a competing satellite channel, also broadcasts sporting events daily.

Levels of participation in sport have been rising, due mainly to the increase in leisure time and facilities, greater mobility and improvements in living standards. A growing awareness of the importance of regular exercise for good health has been reflected in the upsurge of interest in jogging, keep fit and dance-related forms of exercise. It has been estimated that 25 million people over the age of 13 regularly take part in sport or exercise, with men outnumbering women. Walking, including rambling and hiking, is by far the most popular recreation, followed by swimming, football, golf, keep fit and yoga, athletics, angling, squash, badminton and cycling. Other widely practised spare-time physical activities include gardening and 'do-it-yourself' repair and improvement work.

Policies

The Government has long recognised the importance of physical recreation for the health and general welfare of the community; the social role that sport can play has become more important at a time of rapid change in work and leisure patterns. Success in sport is also thought to strengthen Britain's international status and prestige. The ten-year strategy for the development of sport in England drawn up by the Sports Council in 1982, and reviewed in 1988, is to encourage further participation, particularly among women and young people; to provide adequate facilities for the whole community, especially in the inner cities and in deprived rural areas; and to continue to encourage high standards of performance. Similar strategies are being followed by the Sports Councils for Scotland, Wales and Northern Ireland.

The Sports Council's 'Action Sport' programme, designed principally to encourage socially disadvantaged people to take up sport and recreation, has been managed in partnership with local authorities; around 60 schemes are still running with the aid of Sports Council funding. Many local authorities have gone on to provide their own schemes without Sports Council financial support. The Council has also supported initiatives aimed at strengthening links between football clubs and their local communities. 'What's Your Sport?', a campaign to increase participation in sports, was launched by the four Sports Councils in 1987.

In 1987 the Government initiated a public debate on the future direction of official sports policy. It asked whether a correct balance was being achieved between funding sporting excellence and encouraging wider participation, and whether enough was being done to promote private sector investment in sport, especially through corporate sponsorship. A major review of sport and recreation provision in inner cities was undertaken in 1988 by a government-appointed group of business people, athletes and sports administrators. The main conclusions were that there was a need for more small, local facilities and for ways of enabling inner city communities to run their own facilities.

Drug Misuse

The problem of drug-taking in sport in order to improve performance unfairly has been a cause of concern both to the Sports Councils and to the governing bodies of sport. A campaign to tackle the problem, launched by the Sports Council, led to the introduction of a new drug testing regime in 1988. This provides for random testing of competitors in and out of competition by independent sampling officers, and the publication of adverse findings. The Sports Council provides financial support for the British drug testing programme. It also funds the International Olympic Committee (IOC)-accredited laboratory at London University, which carries out analysis and research into methods of detection for new drugs that unfairly aid performance.

International Co-operation

The Government and the Sports Council have taken firm action at international level by, for example, supporting the adoption of a Council of Europe Anti-Doping Charter in 1984 and by chairing an international working party to examine ways of promoting effective anti-doping measures. In 1989 Council of Europe member countries agreed a new European Convention to tackle the problem of drug abuse in sport. This anti-doping convention was a British initiative, whose main aims are to reinforce the ban on the use of drugs and doping methods specified by the IOC and to require signatory states to adopt legal and other means to restrict the availability of prohibited drugs. The convention seeks to ensure that grants are given only to those sports bodies with anti-doping regulations. Signatory states are encouraged to set up doping-control laboratories meeting IOC standards, and sports governing bodies are urged to harmonise out-of-competition testing and other anti-doping regulations with those of the IOC. Testing at international events and out-of-competition testing by international sports bodies is also promoted under the new agreement. Britain has already implemented many provisions of this agreement.

Spectator Violence

Spectator violence associated with football both in Britain and overseas has been a subject of widespread concern, and the Government has worked closely with the football authorities and the governments of other European countries to implement measures to combat the problem. The British Government has continued to press for the closest co-operation with the football authorities and the police and their counterparts throughout Europe. Within the Council of Europe, Britain contributes to the work of the

Standing Committee on the European Convention on Spectator Violence, which it chaired until July 1990. Britain was the first country to sign and ratify the Convention. It has welcomed the Committee's recommendation urging tough action against hooliganism, including prosecution where appropriate. During the World Cup finals in Italy in mid-1990, the Government worked closely with the Italian authorities on the latter's safety and security arrangements for matches involving England and Scotland.

Recognising the link between excessive alcohol consumption and crowd disorder, the Government introduced legislation in Scotland in 1980 and in the rest of Britain in 1985 to establish firm controls on the sale and possession of alcohol at football grounds and on transport to and from grounds. The Public Order Act 1986 gives courts in England and Wales the power to prohibit convicted football hooligans from attending certain matches. It also introduced a new offence of disorderly conduct and banned possession of fireworks and smoke bombs at matches. The use of closed-circuit television at all Football League grounds has greatly assisted the police in the enforcement of crowd control, as has the setting up, in 1989, of the National Football Intelligence Unit. The Unit co-ordinates police intelligence about football hooligans and strengthens liaison with overseas police forces. An agreement exists between the Football League and the police whereby the latter may insist that fixtures are rearranged if there is a danger of crowd disorder.

Following the report of the independent inquiry into the Hillsborough football stadium disaster, the Government decided, as a further aid to crowd control and safety as well as spectator comfort, that all League grounds should become all-seated by 1999 (see p 500). Although it is not to proceed with plans to establish a compulsory national football membership scheme in the light of the recommendations of the Hillsborough inquiry, the Government retains the legislative framework for the scheme and intends to implement it if alternative strategies to contain football hooliganism should fail. Courts in England and Wales have powers to impose restriction orders on convicted football hooligans to prevent them travelling abroad to attend specified matches.

Gleneagles Agreement

In accordance with the statement on apartheid in sport, agreed by the Commonwealth heads of Government at Gleneagles in Scotland in 1977, the Government seeks to discourage sporting contacts with South Africa and withholds any form of support for such contacts. However, it is up to the individuals and organisations concerned to decide whether to heed this advice.

ORGANISATION AND PROMOTION

Government policy on sport, active recreation and children's play is co-ordinated in England by the Minister for Sport, a Parliamentary Under-Secretary of State at the Department of the Environment. The Secretaries of State for Wales, Scotland and Northern Ireland have responsibilities for sport in their countries. Responsibility for the organisation and promotion of sport is largely decentralised, and many sports and recreation facilities are provided by local authorities.

The Government gives financial and other assistance through a number of official bodies and schemes. This 'arm's length' principle of funding safeguards the long-established independence of sports organisations in Britain. Some of these bodies, such as the Sports Councils and the Countryside Commissions, have specific responsibilities for sport and/or recreation, and help other public and private bodies to make facilities available. Others, like the Forestry Commission and the Nature Conservancy Council, provide recreational amenities in addition to their main functions.

Individual sports are run by 395 independent governing bodies, whose functions usually include drawing up rules, holding events, regulating membership, selecting and training national teams and promoting international links. There are also organisations representing people who take part in more informal physical recreation, such as walking and cycling.

A National Coaching Foundation was established in 1983 to improve the knowledge and practice of coaching. There are 16 national coaching centres. The Foundation's work complements that of the four Sports Councils and the governing bodies of sports.

Sheffield is to host the World Student Games in 1991, with financial assistance worth around £3 million from the Sports Council. Over £9 million is being provided by the Government for games-related projects under various programmes designed to promote urban renewal.

Sports Councils   Government assistance for the development of sport in Britain is channelled through four independent bodies—the Sports Council (for England and for general matters affecting Britain as a whole), the Sports Council for Wales, the Scottish Sports Council and the Sports Council for Northern Ireland. In Northern Ireland the Department of Education makes direct grants towards the capital cost of facilities to local authorities and voluntary sports bodies.

The Councils are allocating government funds amounting to about £56 million in 1990–91. They make grants for sports development, coaching and administration to the governing bodies of sports and other national organisations, and administer the national sports centres. Grants and loans are also made to voluntary organisations, local authorities and, in some cases, to commercial organisations, to help them to provide sports facilities. The Sports Council assists British representatives at international sports meetings and encourages links with international and overseas organisations. All four Councils have information centres supplying data on a wide range of sports topics.

The Sports Council consults with the Central Council of Physical Recreation, comprising members of the national governing and representative bodies of sport and physical recreation in England. The equivalent bodies in Scotland, Wales and Northern Ireland are the Scottish and Welsh Sports Associations and the Northern Ireland Council of Physical Recreation.

Ten regional councils for sport and recreation in England, on each of which sporting, recreational, educational, and local authority interests are represented, advise on investment in and the planning of sporting and recreational facilities and the promotion of sport.

About 70 per cent of the Sports Council's budget is directed at increasing participation by the general public; an objective is to encourage 1·25 million more women and 750,000 more men to take part in sport over the next few years. The Sports Council is exploring ways of attracting greater private sector investment in sport, including the use of incentive funding schemes whereby public money is used to generate revenue from private sources.

The Countryside Commissions   The Countryside Commission for England and Wales and the Countryside Commission for Scotland are responsible for conserving and improving the natural beauty and amenity of the countryside, and encouraging the provision and improvement of facilities for open-air recreation.

Government support in 1990–91 amounts to £23 million for the Countryside Commission for England and Wales, of which almost one-half will be spent on recreation. The Commission has launched a series of policy initiatives aimed at increasing people's enjoyment of the countryside. These focus on the maintenance and sign-posting of public footpaths and other 'rights of way' and the development of national routes for long-distance walking and riding. Rural communities are encouraged to build up local facilities which promote public enjoyment of the countryside. These initiatives operate alongside established policies for financing local authorities and private bodies to make available country parks, picnic sites and informal recreation facilities.

In Northern Ireland the Ulster Countryside Committee advises the Department of the Environment on the preservation of amenities and the designation of 'areas of outstanding natural beauty'.

British Waterways Board

The British Waterways Board is a publicly owned body responsible for the management and development of much of Great Britain's inland waterways, which are preserved primarily for leisure use. Many leisure and recreational pursuits are practised on waterways and reservoirs and in waterside buildings; these include angling and numerous types of sailing and boating.

The British Olympic Association

The British Olympic Association, founded in 1905, is the national Olympic committee for Britain and its primary function is to organise the participation of British teams in the Olympic Games. The Association comprises representatives of the 29 governing bodies of those sports in the programme of the Olympic Games (summer and winter). It determines the size of the British teams, raises funds, makes all arrangements and provides a headquarters staff for the management of the teams. It also makes major contributions in the fields of coaching, drug testing and control, and sports medicine. The Association's British Olympic Medical Centre provides a medical back-up service for competitors before and during the Olympic Games.

In 1988 the British Olympic Association, the Sports Council and the Central Council of Physical Recreation agreed to form the British International Sports Committee to co-ordinate and promote British interests at international sporting forums.

Children's Play

The Minister for Sport is responsible for co-ordinating policy on children's play in England. The Sports Council is responsible for the National Children's Play and Recreation Unit. This advises the Government on policy and practice regarding children's play and play-providers and other bodies on such issues as playground safety.

The National Playing Fields Association

The National Playing Fields Association is a charity with a Royal Charter, whose purpose is to promote the provision of recreation and play facilities for all age groups. It aims to preserve, improve and acquire playing fields, playgrounds and playspace, and to specialise in the play and recreation needs of children and young people, in particular those with special needs. There are affiliated associations in the counties of England and Wales and branches in Scotland and Northern Ireland.

Sport for People with Disabilities

Opportunities exist for people with disabilities to take part in a wide variety of physical and sporting activities. The structure of sport for disabled people is undergoing change. There are national disability sports organisations representing the seven main disability groups, but the trend is towards sports-specific governing bodies. For example, the Riding for the Disabled Association caters for some 23,000 riders and the British Disabled Water Ski Association offers training and competition to a growing number of skiers.

The governing bodies of sport are increasingly taking responsibility for both able-bodied and disabled participants. The British Paralympic Association, which liaises closely with the British Olympic Association, looks after the preparation and training of paralympic and other international teams.

In 1989 the Government published a major report calling for a reorganisation of the structure of sport for people with disabilities. Under this, disabled sportsmen and women would be integrated into able-bodied sport and the governing bodies would assume responsibility for all participants in their sport, whether able-bodied or disabled. Disabled athletes would also be encouraged to participate in sporting events either in direct competition with able-bodied athletes or in parallel events.

The British Sports Association for the Disabled aims to encourage and provide opportunities for people with disabilities to take part in all forms of sport and physical recreation. Sports clubs for disabled people throughout Britain are affiliated to the Association, which helps to organise sporting and physical activities at all levels. As well as offering advice to local clubs and groups, the Association arranges conferences, seminars and coaching courses. The Scottish Sports Association for the Disabled, the Federation of Sports Associations for the Disabled (Wales) and the Northern Ireland Sports Association for the Disabled have similar co-ordinating roles.

In the last few years greater emphasis has been placed on making provision for people with a mental handicap, and on non-competitive activities including outdoor pursuits. Evidence of the latter is seen in the growing number of specialist centres, such as those run by the Calvert Trust. More community facilities are becoming available and disabled awareness courses are offered to professional and voluntary staff.

Britain has continued to play an active part at international level since Sir Ludwig Guttmann began sport for paraplegics and established the first sports stadium in the world designed for people with disabilities at Stoke Mandeville in Buckinghamshire in 1969. At the Paralympic Games in Seoul, Korea, held in 1988, the British team gained 62 gold, 67 silver and 53 bronze medals, finishing third in the overall medals table. More than 2,000 athletes with a mental handicap took part in the European Summer Special Olympic Games held in Glasgow in July 1990.

Private Sponsorship

Increasing numbers of sports receive financial sponsorship from commercial organisations, and its importance as a source of funding is recognised by the Government and the Sports Councils. The estimated value of commercial sponsorship was £200 million in 1989. Sponsorship may take the form of financing specific events, or of grants to individual sports organisations or sportsmen and women. The Sports Aid Foundation and Sports Aid Trust raise and distribute funds from industry, commerce and private sponsors in order to assist the training of talented individuals; grants are awarded on the recommendation of the governing bodies of sport. The Scottish and Welsh Sports Aid Foundations and the Ulster Sports and Recreation Trust fulfil similar functions. Sponsorship advisory services are run by the Sports Councils and the Central Council of Physical Recreation.

Successive governments have negotiated voluntary agreements with the tobacco industry to regulate tobacco companies' sponsorship of sport, the last one having come into force in 1987. This is designed to bring about a reduction in spending by tobacco firms on sports sponsorship and introduces a ceiling on promotional activity. It prohibits sponsorship of events where a majority of the participants are under 18 years of age or which are designed to appeal mainly to spectators under 18. The depiction of any participants in a sport in media advertising is not permitted, and strict controls are imposed on siting of signs at televised events and on the size of health warnings on these signs.

PROVISION OF FACILITIES

Local authorities are major providers of land and large-scale facilities for community recreation: their estimated annual expenditure on sport and recreation amounts to about £1,000 million in Britain. Provision of facilities was substantially increased in the 1970s to meet the growing demand and to encourage expansion of participation. The facilities include parks, lakes, playing fields, sports halls, tennis courts, golf courses, swimming pools, gymnasiums and sports centres catering for a wide range of activities. Local authorities manage over 1,700 indoor centres, largely built in the last 20 years, as well as numerous outdoor amenities for sport and recreation.

The Government is instituting competitive tendering for the management of local authority sports and leisure facilities to make them more cost-effective and responsive to consumer demand. School and college facilities are to be exempted from competition, and councils will retain controls over pricing, admission and opening hours.

Increased emphasis is being placed on the need to provide new and improved sports facilities in areas of urban deprivation. A broad range of sports and recreational projects in urban areas have been supported under the Government's Urban Programme. The Derelict Land Grant scheme offers funding towards sports and recreational facilities on reclaimed sites. Under the Water Act 1989, water companies are required to ensure that water and land under their control are put to the best use for sport and recreation.

Recreational facilities are also made available by local sports clubs. Some cater for indoor recreation, but more common are those providing sports grounds, particularly for cricket, football, rugby, hockey, tennis and golf. Many clubs linked to business firms cater for sporting activities. Commercial facilities include tenpin bowling centres, ice and roller-skating rinks, squash courts, golf courses and driving ranges, curling rinks, riding stables, marinas and, increasingly, fitness centres. The Civil Service sports club, with a membership of 250,000, has extensive facilities at its disposal for a large number of sports.

Sports in Education

Publicly maintained schools must provide for the physical education of their pupils. Physical education is one of the ten foundation subjects of the National Curriculum, which are compulsory for all schoolchildren in England and Wales between the ages of 5 and 16. It also features in the recommended curriculum for Scottish schools. All schools (except those solely for infants) are expected to have a playing field or the use of one, and most secondary schools have a gymnasium. Some have other amenities such as swimming pools, sports halls and halls designed for dance and movement. The School Sports Forum was established by the Sports Council in 1987 to consider all aspects of the provision of sport in schools.

Sports and recreation facilities are available at institutions of higher and further education, some of which have departments of physical education. There are also 'centres of sporting excellence', often at universities and other colleges, which enable selected young athletes to develop their talents and which cater, where appropriate, for their educational needs.

To achieve the maximum use of sports facilities, the Government and the Sports Councils are encouraging greater community use of sports halls and other facilities owned by schools, colleges and institutions such as football clubs. Stronger links are being developed between schools and the wider community to ensure that children have access to sports amenities which clubs and associations can make available outside school hours.

Safety at Sports Grounds

Safety at sports grounds and stadiums is governed by legislation. Following the fire at Bradford City Football Ground in 1985 in which 56 people died and the disaster at Hillsborough Football Stadium, Sheffield, in April 1989, when 95 spectators were crushed to death, safety standards are being strengthened. The Fire Safety and Safety of Places of Sport Act 1987 is designed to improve provisions for the safety of spectators at sports grounds and indoor sports premises. It empowers local authorities to restrict or ban the admission of spectators to sports grounds where there is a serious risk to safety, and requires them to arrange for the inspection of designated football, rugby and cricket grounds with stands for over 500 spectators. Indoor sporting events may only take place after the inspection of premises by local authority safety experts.

The committee of inquiry into the Hillsborough tragedy, whose final report was issued in January 1990, recommended that the number of spectators in sports grounds be reduced and that all those responsible for controlling crowds exercise greater vigilance and control in the interests of safety. It recommended the phased introduction of all-seated stadiums; dismantling of perimeter fences; improved arrangements for crowd control and better training for police and stewards; and the upgrading of stadiums and facilities by the clubs.

The Government has accepted all the recommendations relating to safety and is setting up a Football Licensing Authority to license grounds in England and Wales satisfying its conditions. The Authority will also monitor the way in which local authorities carry out their safety functions. First and Second Division grounds will be required to be all-seated by 1994 and by 1999 no standing will be allowed at any Football League ground.

Sports Centres

Five national sports centres, four in England and one in Wales, are run by the Sports Council, and offer a range of competition and training facilities. As well as running residential courses for national teams, coaches and enthusiasts from all over Britain, the centres are used extensively by local sports clubs and the local community. Combined facilities for a number of sports are available at three of the centres: Crystal Palace in south-east London, Bisham Abbey in Buckinghamshire and Lilleshall in Shropshire. Crystal Palace provides major competition venues for athletics, swimming and a variety of indoor sports; and Lilleshall houses the training school of the Football Association. The other two are specialist centres: the National Water Sports Centre at Holme Pierrepont, Nottinghamshire, which caters for rowing, canoeing and water-skiing; and the Plas-y-Brenin National Centre for Mountain Activities in north Wales.

The Sports Council for Wales runs the National Sports Centre for Wales in Cardiff and the National Outdoor Pursuits Centre at Plas Menai in north Wales. The Scottish Sports Council operates three national sports training centres: Glenmore Lodge near Aviemore for outdoor pursuits, Inverclyde at Largs for general sports, and a national water sports training centre on Great Cumbrae Isle in the Firth of Clyde. The Sports Council for Northern Ireland operates one national facility, the Northern Ireland Mountain Centre at Tollymore in County Down.

Some 1,500 swimming pools and 2,000 sports centres serve local rather than national needs; in Northern Ireland there has been a major development of multi-purpose centres. Several privately run centres cater for specialised interests, such as the British Equestrian Centre, run by the British Horse Society, and the Ludwig Guttmann Sports Centre for the Disabled at Stoke Mandeville.

POPULAR SPORTS AND RECREATIONS

Some of the major sports and recreations in Britain are described below. The increased provision of sports centres has improved opportunities for participation in indoor sports such as basketball, volleyball, fencing, judo, karate and other martial arts, gymnastics, squash, table tennis and shooting. Almost all outdoor sports have continued to gain in popularity, including 'high-risk' activities such as rock-climbing and sub-aqua diving. The number of people enjoying the recreational amenities of the countryside, rivers and coastline is also growing.

Sportsmen and women may be professionals (paid players) or amateurs. Some sports—such as hockey and rowing—are amateur, but in others the distinction between amateur status and professional status is less strictly defined, or does not exist. The Amateur Athletic Association, for example, allows payments to be made into trust funds held by many top-ranking athletes.

Angling

The most popular country sport is fishing, and there are about 4 million anglers in Britain. Many fish for salmon and trout, particularly in the rivers and lochs of Scotland and in Wales, but in England and Wales the most widely practised form of fishing is for coarse fish such as pike, perch, carp, tench and bream. There are separate organisations in England, Wales, Scotland and Northern Ireland for game (salmon and trout), coarse and sea fishing clubs, which are co-ordinated in England and Wales by the National Anglers' Council.

The National Federation of Anglers in England organises national championships for coarse fishing and enters a team in the world angling championships. England won the world team event in 1987 and 1988 and the individual title in 1989. Most coarse fishing is let to angling clubs by private owners, while those fishing for trout and salmon may rent a stretch of river, join a club, or pay for the right to fish by the day, week or month. Coastal and deep-sea fishing are free to all, apart from salmon and sea trout fishing, which is by licence only.

Association Football

The largest spectator sport and one of the most popular participation sports, association football was first developed and codified in England during the nineteenth century. It is controlled by separate football associations in England, Wales, Scotland and Northern Ireland. In England over 335 clubs are affiliated to the English Football Association (FA) and 42,000 clubs to regional or district associations. The full-time professional clubs in England and Wales belong to the Football League (92 clubs) and in Scotland to the Scottish Football League (38 clubs); the clubs play in four divisions in England and Wales and three in Scotland. In Northern Ireland, 14 semi-professional clubs play in the Irish Football League. During the season, which lasts from August until May, attendances at over 2,000 English league matches total about 19 million. The Football Association, founded in 1863, and the Football League, founded in 1888, were both the first of their kind in the world.

The annual competitions for the FA Challenge Cup, the Rumbelow's League Cup, the Tennent's Scottish Cup, the Skol Cup (formerly the Scottish League Cup), the Irish Cup and the Welsh FA Cup are organised on a knock-out basis. The finals are played at Wembley Stadium, London; at Hampden Park, Glasgow; at Windsor Park, Belfast; and at the ground of one of the finalists in Wales.

The Sports Councils have made grants to a number of clubs and local authorities to enable them to modernise or expand football facilities in areas of urban deprivation. Grants for various improvements such as all-weather pitches are also made throughout Britain by the Football Associations and the Football Trust, a body financed by the football pools (see p 512) companies. The Government has reduced pool betting duty on the understanding that the revenue foregone by the Government is given to the Football Trust to be used for ground improvements.

Athletics

Amateur athletics is governed in England by the Amateur Athletic Association (which, formed in 1880, was the first national governing body for athletics) and by the Women's Amateur Athletic Association. Scotland, Wales and Northern Ireland have their own associations. International athletics and the selection of British teams are the concern of the Amateur Athletic Association, which also administers coaching schemes. For the Olympic Games and the world and European championships one team represents Britain.

Athletics is attracting increasing numbers of participants, both men and women, in part because of the success of British competitors and the wide coverage of athletics events on television.

Many British athletes, especially middle-distance runners, have enjoyed distinguished reputations: in 1954, for example, Dr (now Sir) Roger Bannister became the first man to run a mile in under four minutes. More recently British athletes won six silver and two bronze medals at the 1988 Olympic Games in Seoul, Korea, while the British men's team finished third behind the United States and a team representing Europe at the World Cup in Barcelona in 1989. At the Commonwealth Games held in Auckland in 1990, England, Wales, Scotland and Northern Ireland competed separately and between them gained 16 gold medals for athletics. In September 1990 Britain had one world champion—Fatima Whitbread in the women's javelin, while Britons held world records in the 800 metres (Sebastian Coe), the mile (Steve Cram), the decathlon (Daley Thompson) and the men's javelin (Steve Backley).

Badminton

The sport of badminton takes its name from the Duke of Beaufort's country home, Badminton House, where badminton was first played in the nineteenth century. Badminton is organised by the Badminton Association of England and the Scottish, Welsh and Irish Badminton Unions. There are also English, Welsh and Scottish schools badminton associations. Around 4 million people are estimated to play the sport in Britain. From 1992 badminton will become a full Olympic sport.

Basketball

Basketball is played in Britain, mainly indoors, by both men and women. There are about 1,000 registered clubs and the sport is played in most secondary schools and many other institutions. In all, over 1 million people participate and its popularity has been increasing rapidly. The English Basket Ball Association is the governing body of the sport in England, and there are similar associations in Wales, Scotland and Ireland. The leading clubs play in the National Basketball Leagues and the main events of the year are the Coca-Cola National Cup Finals held at London Arena, and the Carlsberg Basketball Championships staged at the National Exhibition Centre, Birmingham.

Billiards and Snooker

The character of the present game of billiards was established in Britain at the end of the seventeenth century. Snooker, a more varied game invented by the British in India in 1875, has greatly increased in popularity and become a major spectator sport as a result of widespread television coverage of the professional tournaments. It is estimated that between 7 and 8 million people now play the game. British players have an outstanding record in snooker and have dominated the major professional championships. The main tournament is the annual Embassy World Professional Championship, held in Sheffield. British winners include Steve Davis (1981, 1983, 1984, 1987, 1988 and 1989), Joe Johnson (1986), Dennis Taylor (1985), Alex Higgins (1972 and 1982) and Stephen Hendry (1990).

The controlling body for the non-professional game is the Billiards and Snooker Control Council, which holds the copyright of the rules. The World Professional Billiards and Snooker Association is responsible for professional players, and organises professional events. An increasing number of women play billiards and snooker; their representative body is the World Ladies Billiards and Snooker Association.

Bowls

Bowls has been played in Britain since the thirteenth century. The game of lawn bowls is played on a flat green. In the Midlands, the north of England and north Wales a variation called crown green bowls is played, so named because the centre of the green is higher than its boundaries. Lawn and crown green bowls are mainly summer games; in winter indoor bowls takes place on synthetic greens and is growing in popularity. Once regarded as a pastime for the elderly, bowls is increasingly enjoyed by adults of all ages.

About 4,000 lawn bowling clubs are affiliated to the English, Scottish, Welsh and Irish (Northern Ireland Region) Bowling Associations, which, together with the Women's Bowling Associations for the four countries, play to the rules of the International Bowling Board. Other associations, including the English Bowling Federation, are not under the Board's control. The British Crown Green Bowling Association is the governing body of crown green bowls, and has 2,500 affiliated clubs.

The outstanding player is David Bryant, who has won six world championships.

Boxing

Boxing in its modern form, which has been adopted in many overseas countries, dates from 1865, when the Marquess of Queensberry drew up a set of rules eliminating much of the brutality that had characterised prize-fighting and making skill the basis of the sport. Boxing is both amateur and professional, and in both strict medical regulations are observed.

All amateur boxing in England, including schoolboy, club, association and combined services boxing (in the armed forces), is controlled by the Amateur Boxing Association. England is divided into eight associations; there are separate associations in Scotland and Wales. Northern Ireland forms part of the Irish Boxing Association. The associations organise amateur boxing championships as well as training courses for referees, coaches and others. Teams take part in international meetings including the Commonwealth and Olympic Games, and European and World championships. Richard Woodhall won a bronze medal in the light-middleweight class at the 1988 Olympic Games.

Professional boxing is controlled by the British Boxing Board of Control. The Board appoints inspectors, medical officers and representatives to ensure that regulations are observed and to guard against overmatching and exploitation. British boxing has a distinguished record and at various times British boxers have held European, Commonwealth and world championship titles. Dave McAuley is the current International Boxing Federation (IBF) world flyweight champion, Dennis Andries the World Boxing Council world light-heavyweight champion and Nigel Benn the World Boxing Organisation world middleweight champion.

Chess

Chess is growing in popularity and England now ranks second among chess-playing nations, having taken silver medals at the last three chess Olympics. Scotland, Wales and Ireland are separately represented. There are local chess clubs and leagues throughout Britain and the game is widely played in schools and colleges. Important domestic competitions include the British Championships (for all ages), the National Club Championships, the County Championships and the Leigh Grand Prix. Britain now hosts more major international chess events than ever before, recent events including the Pilkington Glass World Championships quarter- and semi-final matches in 1988 and 1989. The Hastings Chess Congress, dating from 1895, is the world's longest running annual international chess tournament.

The governing bodies of the game are the British Chess Federation (responsible for England and for co-ordinating activity among the home nations), the Scottish Chess Association and the Welsh and Ulster Chess Unions.

Cricket

Cricket is among the most popular of summer sports and is sometimes called the English national game, having been played as early as the 1550s. Among the many clubs founded in the eighteenth century is the Marylebone Cricket Club (MCC), which continues to frame the rules of the game. The Club is based at Lord's cricket ground in north London, the administrative centre of the world game. Men's cricket in Britain is governed by the Cricket Council, consisting of representatives of the Test and County Cricket Board (representing first-class cricket), the National Cricket Association (representing club and junior cricket), the Minor County Cricket Association, the Scottish Cricket Union, the Irish Cricket Union and the MCC.

Cricket is played in schools, colleges and universities, and in towns and villages amateur teams play weekly games from late April to the end of September. Throughout Britain there is a network of league cricket contested by teams of Saturday afternoon players.

The main competition in professional cricket is the Britannic Assurance County Championship of three-day and four-day games played by 17 county teams, which also take part in three one-day competitions—the Benson and Hedges Cup, the National Westminster Bank Trophy, and the Refuge Assurance League, played on Sundays. Some of the best supported games are the annual series of five-day Cornhill Insurance Test matches played between England and a touring team from Australia, India, New Zealand, Pakistan, Sri Lanka or the West Indies. A team representing England usually tours one or more of these countries in the British winter. Texaco Trophy one-day international games also attract large crowds. A World Cup competition takes place every four to five years, with some of the smaller cricketing nations as well as the major countries competing; India and Pakistan jointly staged the last one in 1987.

Cricket is also played by women and girls, the governing body being the Women's Cricket Association, founded in 1926. Women's cricket clubs have regular local fixtures, usually played at weekends, and may participate in the national league and club knock-out competitions. There are regular county matches as well as an area championship and a territorial competition. Test match series and a World Cup competition are played, with both major and minor cricketing nations taking part.

Curling

The ice sport of curling originated in Scotland, where it is played by men and women now almost exclusively indoors. The governing body of the sport in Scotland is the Royal Caledonian Curling Club, which was formed in 1838; it has over 22,000 members. Curling is played in 24 other countries, including

England and Wales. European and World championship competitions take place annually.

Cycling

Since the 1970s there has been a resurgence of interest in cycling, both as a means of transport and as a sport and recreation, and this has led central and local government to make greater provision for cycling. Activities include road and track racing, cycle speedway, time-trialling, cyclo-cross, mountain biking, touring, bicycle polo and bicycle moto-cross.

The British Cycling Federation is the governing body for cycling as a sport, with 900 affiliated clubs. The Cyclists' Touring Club, formed in 1878, is the national association for recreational cycling and represents cyclists' interests in general. The Scottish Cyclists Union controls the sport in Scotland.

The British cyclist Robert Millar won the Kellogg's Tour of Britain in 1989 and Shane Sutton was the winner of Britain's 33rd Milk Race in 1990.

Darts

Darts, an indoor game which has its origins in medieval archery, is played mainly in public houses and gained in popularity as a result of widespread television coverage of the professional game. It is estimated that around 5 million people play the game regularly. Darts is organised in Britain by the British Darts Organisation, which forms part of the World Darts Federation; its rules have become the code for the world sport. The Organisation arranges events in Britain which bring entrants from as many as 45 countries. A World Cup tournament is staged every two years; England won the 1989 competition, held in Toronto. The main individual title in the game is the Embassy World Professional Championship. British players have dominated the event and in 1990 the title was won by Phillip Taylor.

Equestrianism

Equestrian activities include recreational riding, show jumping and carriage driving. The art of riding is promoted by the British Horse Society, which is concerned with the welfare of horses, road safety, riding paths and training. It runs the British Equestrian Centre at Stoneleigh in Warwickshire. With some 51,000 members, the Society is the parent body of the Pony Club and the Riding Club movements, which hold rallies, meetings and competitions culminating in annual national championships. Leading horse trials, comprising dressage, cross-country riding and show jumping, are held every year at Badminton (Avon), Windsor (Berkshire), Bramham (West Yorkshire), Burghley House (Lincolnshire) and Blair Castle (Tayside).

Show jumping is regulated and promoted by the British Show Jumping Association, which has over 15,000 members and some 2,500 shows affiliated to it. The major show jumping events each year include the Royal International Horse Show at the National Exhibition Centre, Birmingham; the Horse of the Year Show at Wembley in London; the Olympia International Show Jumping Championships in London; and the Hickstead Nations Cup and Derby meetings at Bolney in West Sussex.

The authority responsible for equestrian competitions (other than racing) at international and Olympic level is the British Equestrian Federation, which co-ordinates the activities of the British Horse Society and the British Show Jumping Association. British equestrian teams have an outstanding record in international competitions. The British three-day event team gained a silver medal at the 1988 Olympic Games, while Ian Stark won the silver medal and Virginia Leng won the bronze medal in the three-day individual competition. At the World Equestrian Games held in Stockholm in 1990 Great Britain gained one gold, four silver and one bronze medal.

Field Sports

British field sports include hunting (on horseback and on foot), fishing, shooting, stalking, falconry and coursing. Fox hunting on horseback with a pack of hounds is the most popular British hunting sport, and there are over 350 packs of hounds of all kinds in Britain.

Game shooting as an organised sport probably originated in the early nineteenth century, and takes place in many parts of Britain. Game consists of grouse, black-game, ptarmigan, partridge and pheasant, species which are protected by law during a close season, when they are allowed to breed on numerous estates supervised by gamekeepers. It is necessary to have a licence to kill game and a certificate issued by the police to own a shot-gun.

The British Field Sports Society looks after the interests of all field sports. Public opposition to field sports is considerable and is organised through such bodies as the League Against Cruel Sports.

Golf

Golf originated in Scotland, where for centuries it has carried the title of the Royal and Ancient Game. The oldest golf club in the world is the Honourable Company of Edinburgh Golfers. The Royal and Ancient Golf Club, the ruling authority of the sport for most of the world, is situated at St Andrews on the east coast. Golf is played throughout Britain and there are golf courses near most towns, a few of them owned by local authorities.

The main event of the British golfing year is the Open Championship, one of the world's leading tournaments. Other important events include the Walker Cup and Curtis Cup matches for amateurs, played between Great Britain and Ireland and the United States, and the Ryder Cup match for professionals, played between Europe and the United States. Among the leading British professional players are Nick Faldo, Sandy Lyle, Ian Woosnam and Sam Torrance. Sandy Lyle won the United States Masters golf tournament in 1988 and Nick Faldo was the winner in 1989 and 1990. In 1987 Laura Davies became the first British woman to win the United States Open Championship for women.

Gymnastics

Gymnastics is divided into three main disciplines: artistic or Olympic gymnastics, rhythmic gymnastics and sports acrobatics. Both men and women compete in artistic gymnastics, although the apparatus used differs. Men use the floor, pommel horse, rings, vault, parallel bars and horizontal bar, while women exercise on the vault, asymmetric bars, beam and floor. Rhythmic gymnastics is for women only and consists of routines performed to music with ribbon, balls, clubs, hoop or rope. Sports acrobatics is gymnastics with people rather than apparatus.

In recent years there has been a significant rise in participation in the sport, particularly among schoolchildren, and there are now about 1,000 clubs with some 79,000 members. The British Amateur Gymnastics Association is the governing body for men and women gymnasts in Britain; the Welsh, Scottish and Northern Ireland Associations are affiliated to it. There are independent English and British Schools' Gymnastic Associations.

Highland Games

Scottish Highland Games, at which sports, dancing and piping competitions take place, attract large numbers of spectators from all over the world. The sports include tossing the caber, putting the weight and throwing the hammer. Among better-known Highland Games are the annual Braemar Gathering, the Argyllshire and Cowal Gatherings and the meeting at Aboyne.

Hockey (Field and Indoor)

Variants of hockey have been played in Britain for at least five centuries, and some, like hurling in Ireland and shinty in Scotland, are still played. The modern game was started in the nineteenth century by the Hockey Association (of England), which was founded in 1886 and acts as the governing body for men's hockey. There are parallel associations in Scotland, Wales and Ireland. Throughout England there are 820 men's hockey clubs, many of which have junior sections. Large numbers of schools also play the game (500 are affiliated to the Hockey Association). Cup competitions and leagues are played at national, divisional or district, and club levels both indoors (six-a-side) and outdoors, and there are regular international matches.

The controlling body of women's hockey in England is the All England Women's Hockey Association (founded in 1895), to which are affiliated some 950 clubs and about 2,500 schools; there are separate associations in Scotland, Wales and Ireland. League, county, club and school championships for both outdoor and indoor hockey are played annually in England. The first international women's hockey match took place in 1896. There are now regular international matches, one of which is played each year at Wembley Stadium.

Men's and women's hockey are Olympic sports, and the British men's team won a gold medal at the 1988 Olympic Games.

Ice Skating
Ice skating became popular in Britain in the late nineteenth and early twentieth centuries and takes three main forms: ice dancing, figure skating and speed-skating. The governing body for the sport is the National Skating Association of Great Britain, founded in 1879. Participation in ice skating is concentrated among the under-25s. There are over 55 ice rinks in Britain, a small number compared with many other European countries. In spite of this, British couples have won the world ice dance championship 17 times. Jayne Torvill and Christopher Dean were world ice dance champions for four successive years between 1981 and 1984, and gold medal winners at the Sarajevo winter Olympic Games in 1984.

Judo
Judo, a modern combat sport derived from the ancient Japanese arts of ju-jutsu, is growing rapidly in popularity in Britain, both as a sport and general fitness training method and as a self-defence technique. Men and women take part in judo at all levels. Dennis Stewart won a bronze medal in the under 95 kg class at the 1988 Olympics, and at the Commonwealth Games in Auckland in 1990 England won 14 gold and 2 bronze medals and Scotland one gold, three silver and four bronze medals. Recent leading British exponents of the sport include Karen Briggs, Brian Jacks, Neil Adams, Neil Eckersley, Ann Hughes and Diane Bell. More than 900 judo clubs are registered with the British Judo Association, which is the official governing body of the sport throughout Britain.

Keep Fit
Keep fit classes aim to improve stamina, strength and suppleness through a variety of fitness and creative movement activities. The Keep Fit Association, formed in 1956, receives funding from the Sports Council to promote physical fitness and a positive attitude to health in England. Its national certificated training scheme for keep fit teachers is recognised by local education authorities throughout Britain. There are autonomous associations for Scotland, Wales and Northern Ireland.

Martial Arts
A broad range of martial arts, mainly derived from Japan, the People's Republic of China, Taiwan, Hong Kong and Korea, has been introduced into Britain during the twentieth century; these include karate (the most popular of the martial arts), kung fu, aikido and kendo. Following the

increase in interest in the 1960s and 1970s, the Martial Arts Commission was established in 1977 to develop and control martial arts and maintain high standards of safety. The Commission is made up of 16 national governing bodies and has 130,000 members affiliated to it.

Motor and Motor-cycle Sports

Motor racing and rallying, and motor-cycle racing, are popular spectator sports in Britain. The governing body for four-wheeled motor sport is the RAC (Royal Automobile Club) Motor Sports Association. The Association issues licences for a variety of motoring competitions and organises the Lombard RAC Rally, an event in the contest for the World Rally Championship, and the Foster's British Grand Prix, held at the Silverstone racing circuit as part of the Formula One World Motor Racing Championship.

British car constructors including Lotus, McLaren and Williams have enjoyed outstanding successes in Grand Prix racing, and Britain has had six world champion motor racing drivers. The British driver Nigel Mansell has won a total of 16 Grand Prix races. Other popular types of motor-car sport include autocross, drag racing and karting.

Motor-cycle sport, governed by the Auto-Cycle Union in England and Wales and the Scottish Auto-Cycle Union and Motor Cycle Union of Ireland (in Northern Ireland), caters for all forms of competition on two or three wheels, from low-speed trials to Grand Prix road racing. The major events of the year are the Isle of Man TT races, the British Road Race Grand Prix and other world championship events for trials, moto-cross, speedway and track racing. The Auto-Cycle Union provides off-road training by approved instructors for riders of all ages.

Mountaineering and Rock-Climbing

The popularity of mountaineering and rock-climbing has increased steadily. Clubs in the British Mountaineering Council and the Mountaineering Council of Scotland, the representative bodies of the sport, number over 300. They range from national clubs such as the Alpine Club (founded in 1857, the oldest mountaineering club in the world) and the Scottish Mountaineering Club to small regional clubs with 20 to 30 members. The National Centres for Mountain Activities, run by the Sports Council, are at Plas-y-Brenin in north Wales, Glenmore Lodge, near Aviemore, in Scotland and Tollymore in Northern Ireland. Several local education authorities and national bodies such as the Outward Bound Trust also have mountaineering training centres. The most popular areas in Britain for climbing include the sea cliffs of Devon and Cornwall, the Peak District of Derbyshire, the Lake District, Snowdonia in north Wales and the Western Highlands of Scotland.

British mountaineers have taken a leading part in exploring mountain ranges and climbing many of the great mountains of the world, achieving, for example, the first ascent of the Matterhorn in 1865, Everest in 1953, Kangchenjunga in 1955, Everest by its south-west face in 1975, the west wall of Changabang in 1976, Kongur in 1982 and Jitchu Drake in 1988.

British rock climbers have long been recognised as among the foremost in the world; in recent decades Joe Brown, Don Whillans, Ron Fawcett, Jerry Moffatt and Johnny Dawes have all pioneered difficult routes. Britain is also at the forefront of competition climbing, where events take place on artificial walls. Simon Nadin of Britain won the first ever climbing world cup, held in 1989.

Netball

Netball derives from basketball, which was invented in the United States at the end of the nineteenth century. It is estimated that more than 60,000 adults in England play netball regularly and that a further one million participants come from schools. The sport is played almost exclusively by women and girls both indoors and outdoors.

The All England Netball Association, formed in 1926, is the governing body for the sport in England; the English Schools' Netball Association is affiliated to it. Scotland, Wales and Northern Ireland have their own governing bodies.

Racing

Horse racing takes two forms—flat racing (throughout the year) and steeplechasing and hurdle racing (normally from August to early June). The Derby, run at Epsom, is the outstanding event in the flat racing calendar. Other classic races are: the Two Thousand Guineas and the One Thousand Guineas, both run at Newmarket; the Oaks, run at Epsom; and the St Leger, run at Doncaster. The most important steeplechase and hurdle race meeting is the National Hunt Festival Meeting held at Cheltenham in March. The Grand National, run at Aintree near Liverpool, is the world's best-known steeplechase and dates from 1837.

The Jockey Club administers all horse racing in Britain. Its rules are the basis of turf procedure and it also licenses racecourses. Racing takes place on most days (excluding Sundays) throughout the year and about 14,000 horses are in training. British thoroughbreds continue to be a source of the world's best bloodstock.

The racing of greyhounds after a mechanical hare, one of Britain's most popular spectator sports, takes place at 90 tracks licensed by local authorities. Meetings are usually held two or three times a week at each track, with at least ten races a meeting. The rules for the sport are drawn up by the National Greyhound Racing Club, the sport's judiciary body. The Stewards of the Club are also responsible for overall administration and organisation. The representative body is the British Greyhound Racing Board.

Rowing

Rowing is taught in many schools, colleges and rowing clubs (including women's clubs) throughout Britain. The governing body of the sport in England is the Amateur Rowing Association; similar bodies regulate the sport in Scotland, Wales and Ireland. There are about 500 rowing clubs, and each year over 300 regattas and head races are held in England, Wales and Scotland under Association rules.

The University Boat Race, between eight-oared crews from Oxford and Cambridge, has been rowed on the Thames almost every spring since 1836. The Head of the River Race, also on the Thames, is the largest assembly of racing craft in the world, with more than 420 eights racing in procession. At the Henley Regatta in Oxfordshire, founded in 1839, crews from all over the world compete each July in various kinds of race over a straight course of 1 mile 550 yards (about 2·1 km).

The National Water Sports Centre at Holme Pierrepont, near Nottingham, has a rowing course of Olympic 2,000-metre standard, as does Strathclyde Park in west-central Scotland. Britain won the gold medal in the men's coxless pairs and a bronze in the men's coxed pairs events at the 1988 Olympic Games.

Rugby Football

Rugby football takes its name from Rugby School, in Warwickshire, where it is believed to have originated in 1823. Since 1893 the game has been played according to two different codes: rugby union (a 15-a-side game) is played by amateurs and rugby league (a 13-a-side game) by professionals as well as amateurs.

Rugby union is played under the auspices of the Rugby Football Union in England and similar bodies in Wales, Scotland and Ireland. Important domestic competitions include the divisional and county championships in England, the league and national club knock-out competitions in England

and Wales; and the National League and Inter-District Championships in Scotland. The Five Nations Tournament between England, Scotland, Wales, Ireland and France is contested each year and there are overseas tours by the national sides and by the British Lions, a team representing Great Britain and Ireland. In 1987 teams from 16 countries competed for the first time in a world cup competition held in Australia and New Zealand. The final rounds of the next one, which will involve 37 countries, will be staged in Britain and France in autumn 1991.

Rugby league, played mainly in the north of England, is enjoying unprecedented popularity as a spectator sport. The governing body of the professional game is the Rugby Football League, which sends touring teams representing Great Britain to Australia, New Zealand and Papua New Guinea; annual matches are also played against France. The Challenge Cup Final, the major club match of the season, is played at Wembley Stadium in London. The amateur game is governed by the British Amateur Rugby League Association. Matches between England and France are held each year and tours are arranged to Australia and New Zealand. A national league consisting of ten leading clubs was formed in 1986, and a second division came into existence in 1989.

Sailing

Sailing has always been popular in Britain, and the Royal Yachting Association, the governing body for the sport, has more than 70,000 members and 1,500 clubs and classes. Sailing in dinghies. motor yachts, windsurfers, powerboats and cruisers takes place at clubs throughout Britain. At the 1988 Olympics Mike McIntyre and Bryn Vaile gained a gold medal in the 'Star' class and in 1989 Britain won the offshore racing Admiral's Cup.

Skiing

When there is sufficient snow, skiing takes place in several parts of Britain. The governing body of the sport is the British Ski Federation and there are separate national councils. Skiing in Scotland has become very popular, especially at the winter sports centres established in the Cairngorms, Deeside, Glencoe and Glenshee, where ski-runs equal to those in other areas of Europe have been developed. Ski-lifts, ski-tows and professional instruction of a high quality are now available. There are also some 115 artificial ski-slopes throughout Great Britain. Interest in cross-country skiing has been increasing. There are nearly 300 ski clubs in Britain, and it is estimated that about 1·5 million people take part in the sport.

Squash Rackets

Squash rackets originated at Harrow School in the 1850s. There are separate governing bodies for England, Wales, Scotland and Ireland. The governing body in England for men's and women's squash is the Squash Rackets Association, formed in 1989. Squash enjoyed a period of very rapid growth during the 1970s and remains a popular sport. There are 9,250 squash courts in England, and the estimated number of players in Britain is 2·6 million. The main tournament held in Britain is the British Open Championship. England currently holds the world title for women's team squash, and Martine le Moignan is the present women's world champion.

Sub-Aqua

Underwater activities include wreck and reef exploration, underwater photography, marine life study and nautical archaeology. The British Sub-Aqua Club is the governing body for all underwater techniques. It promotes safe diving, training, science and sport. The Club is the largest of its kind in the world, with over 36,000 members and more than 1,250 branches in Britain and overseas.

Swimming

Swimming is enjoyed by millions of people in Britain, many of whom learn to swim at public baths, schools or swimming clubs. Instruction and coaching are provided by qualified teachers who hold certificates awarded by the Amateur Swimming Associations in England, Wales, Scotland and Northern Ireland, to which nearly 2,000 clubs are affiliated. Northern Ireland forms part of the Irish Amateur Swimming Association. The Associations control swimming, diving, synchronised swimming and water polo championships and competitions.

For major international competitions, such as the Olympic Games and the World and European Championships, England, Scotland and Wales compete together as one team under the auspices of the Amateur Swimming Federation of Great Britain. At the 1988 Olympics, Britain won a gold, a silver and a bronze medal. The British swimmer Adrian Moorhouse broke the 100-metre breaststroke world record in 1989.

Table Tennis

The origins of table tennis are uncertain, but it developed in Britain from around the middle of last century, becoming an Olympic sport in 1988. As well as being one of the most popular indoor sports for young people, it is played by a broad age range of adults, with men outnumbering women. Requiring relatively simple and inexpensive equipment, table tennis is played in schools, youth clubs and private clubs. Britain's leading professional player is Desmond Douglas.

The governing body for men's and women's table tennis in England is the English Table Tennis Association, to which some 8,000 clubs are affiliated. There are separate governing bodies in Scotland, Wales and Northern Ireland.

Tennis

The modern game of tennis originated in England in 1872 and the first championships were played at Wimbledon in 1877. The controlling body in Great Britain, the Lawn Tennis Association, was founded in 1888; Northern Ireland forms part of the Irish Lawn Tennis Association. The main event of the season is the annual Wimbledon fortnight, widely regarded as the most important tennis event in the world. This draws large crowds, with the ground at the All England Club accommodating around 30,000 spectators. There are also national and county championships and national competitions for boys' and girls' schools.

Tenpin Bowling

Tenpin bowling is played at some 1,500 indoor bowling centres throughout Britain. More than 25,000 people belong to the sport's governing body, the British Tenpin Bowling Association.

Volleyball

Volleyball was established in Britain in the 1950s, having first been played in the United States at the end of the nineteenth century. The number of registered players in Britain grew substantially in the 1980s, with men at first far outnumbering women; today, of the total of 25,000 registered players, about 11,000 are women. Volleyball is popular among schoolchildren and university and college students. Mini-volley is a version of the game adapted to the abilities of children under 13. Although volleyball can be played outdoors, it is normally played in indoor sports halls.

The English Volleyball Association (formed in 1971), the Scottish Volleyball Association (formed in 1964), the Welsh Volleyball Association (re-established in 1981) and the Northern Ireland Volleyball Association (formed in 1970) act as the sport's governing bodies for both men and women.

GAMBLING

Various forms of commercial betting and gaming are permitted in Britain under strict regulations. In 1989–90 the total money staked, excluding gaming machines, was estimated at £9,600 million.

Betting takes place mainly on horse or greyhound racing, and on football matches (usually through football pools). Racing bets may be made at racecourses and greyhound tracks, or through some 10,000 licensed off-course betting offices which take some 90 per cent of the money staked. A form of pool betting—totalisator betting—is organised on course by the Horserace Totalisator Board (HTB). Bookmakers and the HTB contribute a levy to the Horserace Betting Levy Board, which promotes the improvement of horse racing and breeding and the advancement of veterinary science.

Gaming includes the playing of casino and card games, gaming machines and bingo. There are 119 licensed casinos operating in Britain, 21 of them in London. An estimated 3 million people, mainly women, play bingo in commercial bingo halls.

In addition, legislation allows local authorities and certain other bodies to hold lotteries.

Appendix 1

Currency
The unit of currency is the pound sterling divided into 100 new pence (p). There are seven coins: £1; 50p; 20p; 10p; 5p; 2p and 1p.

Bank of England notes are issued for sums of £5, £10, £20 and £50.

Metric Conversions for British Weights and Measures

Length

1 inch	=	2·54 centimetres
12 inches = 1 foot	=	30·48 centimetres
3 feet = 1 yard	=	0·914 metre
1,760 yards = 1 mile	=	1·609 kilometres

Area

	1 square inch =	6·452 square centimetres
144 square inches	= 1 square foot =	929·03 square centimetres
9 square feet	= 1 square yard =	0·836 square metre
4,840 square yards	= 1 acre =	0·405 hectare
640 acres	= 1 square mile =	2·59 square kilometres

Capacity

	1 pint	= 0·568 litre
2 pints	= 1 quart	= 1·136 litres
4 quarts	= 1 gallon	= 4·546 litres
8 gallons	= 1 bushel	= 36·37 litres
8 bushels	= 1 quarter	= 2·909 hectolitres

Weight (Avoirdupois)

	1 ounce (oz)	= 28·35 grammes
16 oz	= 1 pound (lb)	= 0·454 kilogramme
14 lb	= 1 stone (st)	= 6·35 kilogrammes
112 lb	= 1 hundredweight (cwt)	= 50·8 kilogrammes
20 cwt (2,240 lb)	= 1 long ton	= 1·016 tonnes
2,000 lb	= 1 short ton	= 0·907 tonne

Double Conversion Tables for Measures and Weights

(Use the figures in the central column with those to the left or right, depending on which conversion is required. For example, 1 centimetre = 0·394 inch, and 1 inch = 2·540 centimetres.)

Centi-metres	Inches	Metres	Yards	kilo-metres	Miles	Hec-tares	Acres
2·540	1 0·394	0·914	1 1·094	1·609	1 0·621	0·405	1 2·471
5·080	2 0·787	1·829	2 2·187	3·219	2 1·243	0·809	2 4·942
7·620	3 1·181	2·743	3 3·281	4·828	3 1·864	1·214	3 7·413
10·160	4 1·575	3·658	4 4·374	6·437	4 2·485	1·619	4 9·884
12·700	5 1·969	4·572	5 5·468	8·047	5 3·107	2·023	5 12·355
15·240	6 2·362	5·486	6 6·562	9·656	6 3·728	2·428	6 14·826
17·780	7 2·756	6·401	7 7·655	11·265	7 4·350	2·833	7 17·298
20·320	8 3·150	7·315	8 8·749	12·875	8 4·971	3·237	8 19·768
22·860	9 3·543	8·230	9 9·843	14·484	9 5·592	3·642	9 22·239
25·400	10 3·937	9·144	10 10·936	16·093	10 6·214	4·047	10 24·711

Kilo-grammes		Av. Pounds	Litres		Pints	Litres		Gallons
0·454	1	2·205	0·568	1	1·760	4·546	1	0·220
0·907	2	4·409	1·136	2	3·520	9·092	2	0·440
1·361	3	6·614	1·705	3	5·279	13·638	3	0·660
1·814	4	8·818	2·273	4	7·039	18·184	4	0·880
2·268	5	11·023	2·841	5	8·799	22·730	5	1·100
2·722	6	13·228	3·409	6	10·559	27·276	6	1·320
3·175	7	15·432	3·978	7	12·319	31·822	7	1·540
3·629	8	17·637	4·546	8	14·078	36·368	8	1·760
4·082	9	19·842	5·114	9	15·838	40·914	9	1·980
4·536	10	20·046	5·682	10	17·598	45·460	10	2·200

Thermometrical Table

$0° C = 32° F$

$100° C = 212° F$

To convert degrees Fahrenheit into degrees Celsius: subtract 32, then multiply by 5/9; degrees Celsius into degrees Fahrenheit: multiply by 9/5, then add 32.

Bank and Public Holidays in Britain, 1991

Tuesday 1 January	New Year's Day
Wednesday 2 January	Bank Holiday (Scotland only)
Monday 18 March	Bank Holiday (Northern Ireland only)
Friday 29 March	Good Friday
Monday 1 April	Easter Monday (England, Wales and Northern Ireland only)
Monday 6 May	Early May Bank Holiday
Monday 27 May	Spring Bank Holiday
Friday 12 July	Orangeman's Day (Northern Ireland only)
Monday 5 August	Bank Holiday (Scotland only)
Monday 26 August	Summer Bank Holiday (England, Wales and Northern Ireland only)
Wednesday 25 December	Christmas Day
Thursday 26 December	Boxing Day

Appendix 2

Guide to Sources
The principal official periodical sources used in the preparation of this edition are given below:

Chapter 1 Land and People
Social Trends, Population Trends, Regional Trends, General Household Survey, Family Expenditure Survey

Chapter 3 Overseas Relations
British Aid Statistics, British Overseas Aid, Arms Control and Disarmament Quarterly Review, Developments in the European Community

Chapter 4 Defence
Statement on the Defence Estimates

Chapter 5 Justice and the Law
Criminal Statistics, England and Wales; Criminal Statistics, Scotland

Chapter 7 Education
Education Statistics for the United Kingdom

Chapter 8 Planning, Housing and Urban Regeneration
General Household Survey, Housing and Construction Statistics

Chapter 9 Environmental Protection
Digest of Environmental Protection and Water Statistics

Chapter 11 National Economy
United Kingdom National Accounts (the 'Blue Book'), Employment Gazette

Chapter 12 Framework of Industry
United Kingdom National Accounts (the 'Blue Book'), Monthly Digest of Statistics

Chapter 13 Manufacturing Industry
Size Analyses of United Kingdom Businesses, Business Monitors, United Kingdom National Accounts (the 'Blue Book'), Monthly Digest of Statistics, Employment Gazette

Chapter 14 Construction and Service Industries
Size Analyses of United Kingdom Businesses, Employment Gazette, Business Monitors

Chapter 15 Energy and Natural Resources
Digest of United Kingdom Energy Statistics, Development of the Oil and Gas Resources of the United Kingdom (the 'Brown Book'), United Kingdom Minerals Yearbook

Chaper 16   Agriculture, Fisheries and Forestry
Agriculture in the United Kingdom

Chapter 17   Transport and Communications
Transport Statistics, Great Britain

Chapter 18   Employment
Employment Gazette, New Earnings Survey

Chapter 19   Public Finance
Financial Statement and Budget Report, The Government's Expenditure Plans (the public expenditure White Paper)

Chapter 21   Overseas Trade
Monthly Review of External Trade Statistics, United Kingdom Balance of Payments (the 'Pink Book'), Business Bulletins

Chapter 25   Television and Radio
BBC's *Annual Report and Accounts,* IBA's *Annual Report and Accounts*

Full purchasing details of British Government publications can be obtained from the annual list *Government Publications* issued by Her Majesty's Stationery Office (HMSO), which has agents overseas. The list includes all Bills and Acts of Parliament and the official parliamentary report *Hansard,* White Papers, annual reports, reports of official committees and most publications of government departments including the Central Statistical Office, which publishes a *Guide to Official Statistics.* HMSO also sells in Britain many titles published by international organisations such as the United Nations, the European Community and the Organisation for Economic Co-operation and Development.

A Catalogue of British Official Publications not Published by HMSO, published by Chadwyck-Healey, lists the more specialised departmental publications. Details of this and other commercial publications are available from bookshops or, overseas, from the British Council.

Index

Items are indexed under England, Northern Ireland, Scotland or Wales only where they are matters peculiar to these countries; otherwise they are indexed under the relevant subject headings.

Bold type in a sequence of figures indicates main references.

F

N

Acknowledgments for photographs
Press Association (facing p 70). Overseas Development Administration (facing p 134). Ministry of Defence Public Relations (between pp 134 and 135). Scottish Tourist Board (between pp 230 and 231). *Country Life* and Syndication International (between pp 326 and 327). Dave Wilson (facing p 327). Line-up/Jazz FM and British Broadcasting Corporation (facing p 455).

Cover illustration by John Clementson.

Printed in the United Kingdom for HMSO
Dd 291968 C100 1/91